IN THE DAYS OF McKINLEY

IN THE DAYS OF McKINLEY

IN THE DAYS OF McKINLEY

· · ·

by Margaret Leech

Publishers HARPER & BROTHERS New York

*The author takes this opportunity
of paying tribute to Vassar College
on the occasion of its Centennial.*

To those whose childhood knew the three-dimensional stereopticon and the colorful velocity of the magic lantern; who remember the wonder of the known voice pulsating over the telephone wire, and the exhilaration of the privileged pioneers of automotive power, speeding at twenty miles an hour through a distracted countryside.

That's all a man can hope for during his lifetime—to set an example—and when he is dead, to be an inspiration for history.

McKinley in conversation with Cortelyou, Cortelyou diary, December 29, 1899.

CONTENTS

CONTENTS

Thirty-two pages of photographs have been
inserted in two sections, following pages
246 and 438.

viii

IN THE DAYS OF McKINLEY

THE MAJOR AND HIS WIFE

THE NOTICE in *The Evening Reposi-*
tory that the Governor was coming home had brought a crowd to the depot
to meet the train from Columbus. The January dusk was thickening when
McKinley shook the last welcoming hand, and was free to escort his wife,
attended by her maid and Mrs. Heistand, to the carriage.

Through the pale gloom of North Market Street, the horses clopped to
the goal of months of planning and anticipation, a white frame house
set in a neatly fenced lawn. It had once belonged to the McKinleys. They
had sold it twenty years before; and then, as the Governor's second term
began to draw to a close and they were looking for a place in Canton, they
had found that their old property was available for rent and had gone to see
it again. McKinley had written that repairs were needed; and, after some
dickering over the lease, that they had concluded to take the house.
His terse phrases had not disclosed the emotion that attended the transaction. For twenty years, spent in hotels and on visits to other people's
houses, McKinley had longed for a home of his own, and he wanted this
particular house above all others. As he had stood with Ida in the vacant,
neglected rooms, memories had flooded back of the first five years of their
marriage. More than a dwelling place, this was the shrine of their early
joys and sorrows.

The single shadow on a radiant prospect had been the question of the
furnishings. The Governor of Ohio, experienced in many domestic problems, was baffled by this one. In the room he had used as an office in the
Saxton house in Canton, there was a shabby old lounge, which he prized
very much; and he had set his heart on owning an elaborately carved table

1

of Ohio woods that he had seen exhibited at the Chicago World's Fair in 1893. He had no trouble in ordering linens and blankets—specifying seven double blankets, "good and wide"—through Mrs. McKinley's cousin, Mary Goodman McWilliams, whose husband was an official of Marshall Field's and could get things at wholesale prices. Colonel John N. Taylor of the East Liverpool potteries was sending some handsome sets of china, and Mrs. McKinley herself chose the silver knives and forks. But, except for a few treasured personal possessions, the McKinleys had nothing else. They would have been in serious perplexity, if Mrs. Herrick had not come to the rescue.

Myron T. Herrick, a good-looking Cleveland banker who was active in the Ohio Republican party, had been appointed a colonel on the Governor's staff, and the two couples had become great friends. During a week-end visit, the McKinleys had begun by asking Mrs. Herrick's guidance on carpets and curtains, and ended by leaving all the purchases to her taste. She had shown a generous interest, and she must have been touched by the Governor's eagerness for a fine home and his gratitude for a woman's help in arranging it. On concluding to have the old lounge covered in leather for his library room, he wrote Mrs. Herrick, "it will be necessary for you to select a couch for our bed-room and some sort of a sofa or whatever is best for our parlor. You can do this," he explained, "knowing the color of the carpets, etc., better than we can." It was an innocent letter, trustful and elated. "We are looking forward with the greatest zest," McKinley said, "to our new experience in housekeeping."

Fulfillment was at hand in the January dusk, as the carriage turned into a modest semicircle of driveway. Trees and vines and flowerbeds were stark with winter, the iron urns were ghostly, and the porch was bare, but the glowing windows promised comfort and coziness inside. Captain Heistand was there to receive them, rather dubious that the training of West Point and the duty of instructing the Ohio National Guard had qualified him as an interior decorator. Though he had faithfully carried out Mrs. Herrick's instructions, placing the furniture as she had suggested, he wished that she might have made another trip from Cleveland to "approve or alter," and it worried him that there was no plush cover for the dining-room table. But Heistand's doubts were quickly dispelled. The Governor and his wife were as delighted as a bridal couple with their shining little house and its tasteful furnishings. There in the library was the comfortable lounge, with its new leather covering. In the bow window of the sitting room, the table of Ohio woods stood impressively on its great claw feet. The silver knives and forks were laid on the supper table, and the good, wide blankets were tucked in place on the brass beds in the first-floor bedroom. Soon the personal belongings would be unpacked: the Governor's files and letterbooks and reports; Mrs. McKinley's silver toilet articles and the wools for her crocheting; the two small rocking chairs; all the souvenirs and presents; the framed photographs of family and friends and the Governor's black horse Midnight; and the oil painting of little Katie, who had died when she was four and a half.

It was January of 1896, and William McKinley did not plan to make a long stay in Canton, but he would never forget the wonder of this homecoming. One day he would buy the house again, planning to end his life there. In all America there was no mansion so fine and costly that it was to be compared in McKinley's mind with the snug cottage on North Market Street.

Two nights after the Governor's return, there was a grand public welcome. Stormy weather did not dampen the enthusiasm of the townsfolk and the big delegations that had come streaming in from all parts of Stark County. Red and blue fire flashed and sizzled in the rain, and the parade was a bright snake of Roman candles. Only McKinley's "mascot," the Grand Army Band, was missing from its accustomed place at the head of the line of march. For years Canton's famous band had been serenading and escorting Canton's famous citizen, but the members had no dress overcoats and the rain would have ruined their uniforms. In the shelter of the courthouse, they struck up "Home, Sweet Home" as the Governor stepped out on the balcony. A big bouquet of red carnations was thrust into his arms; and, with a smile on his lips and in his luminous grey eyes, he listened to the brassy strains and to that other music of the crowd's applause.

McKinley's mind could reach back to the days when Canton was a country town, set in a rich farming region. He had seen its pleasant rural atmosphere yield to the invasion of industry a willing and prideful submission. It had grown to a thriving city of nearly thirty thousand inhabitants, vying with Akron and Youngstown. Only the severe depression of business had placed a check on its further expansion. In 1896, there were idle men and smokeless stacks in Canton, as everywhere else in America. The Democrats were in power at Washington, and their blundering tariff act furnished a text that McKinley was ready in expounding, but this hour of nonpartisan concord did not offer a seemly occasion for a political speech. The Governor raised his resonant voice to tell of his love for Canton and the county of "old Molly Stark," and to speak, in the vein of sentiment into which he easily fell, of the alterations made by time and

3

the familiar faces that now were missing.

Many circles had been broken in a quarter of a century: friends and neighbors, associates at the bar, comrades of the Grand Army. McKinley, in the last seven years, had mourned the loss of his father, his sister Anna, and his brothers James and David. The past rose before the Governor as he stood on the courthouse balcony, an authoritative man of nearly fifty-three, with the hair thinning on his temples and an ample girth stretching his coat. To the older people in the crowd, he was still the slender, handsome Major who had brought his hopes to Canton, marking it as a thriving town where he might make his way.

William McKinley, Junior, born in 1843 at Niles, Ohio, was the seventh of the nine children of William and Nancy Allison McKinley. The father's Scotch-Irish and English Puritan forebears had early settled in Pennsylvania, and both of his grandfathers had fought in the Revolution. The son of one of them, James McKinley, had joined the westward tide, becoming manager of a charcoal furnace in Ohio; and his son, in turn, followed the trade of mining and manufacturing pig iron. At various times, William McKinley, Senior, bought or rented two or three small furnaces in the Mahoning Valley, and another, in partnership with his younger brother Benjamin, in Pennsylvania. He was a stubborn, vigorous, industrious man, but his labors provided little more than the necessities for his large family, and his means were severely straitened in the hard times of the Buchanan administration.

To share a life of struggle and austerity, the iron founder had been fortunate in choosing a capable girl of Scottish descent, thrifty, pious, and strong-minded. In his later years, old Mr. McKinley liked to remember that their bridal tour had been a trip from New Lisbon to a spring, where they took a draught of cool water from a gourd dipper. Since they were married in January, this must have been a frosty, as well as an abstemious excursion. Nancy Allison had come to marriage without expectation of material ease, content to do her duty and rear her children in the love and fear of God, according to the principles of the Methodist Church. The strict discipline of her rule was tempered by motherly affection; and it was a sign of tender and sensible care that in this pioneer home only one child, the girl born after William, died in infancy.

The father's management of a furnace at Niles led him to settle in the hamlet where William was born and spent the first nine years of his life. The little boy used to drive the cows to and from pasture. He remembered as an elderly man how cold his bare feet got, and that he used to warm them by pressing them into the earth where the cows had lain. It had

4

been "pure *luxury*," McKinley said, never equaled in his experience.

Niles afforded only the primitive schooling that the parents themselves had received. They were ambitious for their children, and the education of the three eldest was probably arranged by sending them to relatives or friends in larger communities. David, James, and Anna were old enough to make their way in the world when in 1852 the family moved to the village of Poland, where there was a high school. Advantages for the younger children were obtained at the sacrifice of the father's convenience. Poland, near Youngstown, was distant from his work, and he was obliged to spend much of his time away from home. Nancy Allison assumed the main responsibility of rearing Mary, Sarah Elizabeth, Helen, William, and Abner, and seeing that they applied themselves to their lessons at the Poland Academy. William, an earnest student, was destined for college. He was diligent, rather than clever, but he enjoyed reciting; and, as he grew older, he excelled at public speaking and in the lively contests of the debating societies. He was serious and rather delicate, and he seems never to have taken much interest in sports or games. He was extremely fond of the company of his mother and three older sisters. His environment was narrow and plain, but William grew up with the sunny optimism of temperament and the capacity for warm affection that come from a secure and happy childhood.

Between the mother and this serious boy, there was a close bond of sympathy. His was the gentler nature, in its submissiveness to the attachment and its dutiful acceptance of Nancy Allison's precepts of a righteous life, the sanctity of the home, and the veneration due to womanhood. Like David and Anna, William inherited his mother's deeply religious nature. At the age of ten he made a public profession of faith, marching to the mourners' bench at a revival meeting, and at sixteen he became a devout communicant of the Methodist Church. Nancy Allison's ambition was to rear a son for the ministry. William already showed every qualification for a pastor and preacher when he was graduated from the Poland Academy at the age of seventeen. That autumn, he entered Allegheny College at Meadville, Pennsylvania.

William fell ill at the end of his first term, and in midwinter returned home to recuperate. Financial disaster overtook the family before he was well enough to go back to college. Years later, McKinley received a letter from a man who had mined coal and ore at his father's Pennsylvania furnace before the Rebellion. It told a sorry tale of angry creditors and unpaid hands. The sheriff had locked the doors of the store; Ben McKinley had bought a lot of horses "on time," and left for California; his older brother had promised to pay—when he could. In 1861, young William

5

went to work, teaching school and then clerking in the post office to scrape together the money to continue his studies. That spring Fort Sumter fell. Loyalty to the Union flamed in the Western Reserve, and in June William was stirred by the excitement of a patriotic mass meeting, at which many volunteers stepped forward to enlist for three months' service. His cousin and close friend, William McKinley Osborne of Youngstown, was visiting the family at Poland. The two boys did not act on impulse, but talked the matter over, and concluded "in cold blood" that it was their duty to enlist. McKinley's mother accepted his decision, and Will Osborne knew that Aunt Nancy's attitude would carry weight with his father, even though he was a Democrat. The cousins went together to the big camp near Columbus. On learning that the quota of three months' men had been filled, they were mustered in for three years or the duration. McKinley served in the Union army for four years. Osborne soon fell ill, and was discharged.

When the Twenty-third Ohio was dispatched to western Virginia, McKinley exchanged a sheltered home for the rigors and perils of camp and field without qualm or apprehension. In the summer, he wrote a lively letter to another cousin, William K. Miller. There was a hint of the tourist in the description of the very nice camp site "on one of Virginia's delightful hills" above the Monongahela, where the soldiers bathed and had "some fine times." There was a humorous account of a night patrol on which an ambitious lieutenant prodded the bushes for "seceshers" and stuck a skunk, and McKinley himself stood guard in a cornfield, with his old musket cocked for a hog or a calf. He had at once adapted himself to army life, loving the fun and the comradeship. When the Twenty-third Ohio saw rugged action against rebel irregulars in the Valley, McKinley proved to be a good soldier, who cheerfully accepted discipline and hardship. A more surprising trait was his indifference to danger. He was not reckless, but serenely confident. Many years later, he told a group of men in Boston that he had taken leave of his weeping mother with the firm assurance that he would return to her alive and well. He never went into battle, he said, with any fear of being injured —he did not seem to think it possible that any harm could come to him.

McKinley's exemplary conduct was noted by the benign, square-bearded Cincinnati lawyer Rutherford B. Hayes, who became lieutenant colonel of the regiment. Hayes was particularly impressed by the lad's unusual executive ability. The next summer, when the outfit was ordered to Washington and attached to the Army of the Potomac, McKinley was made commissary sergeant. He was in charge of his brigade's supplies when the army advanced in the Maryland campaign. Between two hard marches, McKinley had caught his first glimpse of the national capital, a city menaced by the Confederate movement to the north, looking for deliverance to the tramping host in blue.

On the bloody field of Antietam, McKinley performed a minor exploit —he drove a mule team into the thick of the battle, carrying hot meat and coffee to the troops. This service in the front line was a novelty, so widely commended that McKinley was emboldened to think that he might get a commission. Hayes, as a reward for gallantry at South Mountain, had been placed in command of the regiment. In his eagerness for promotion, McKinley appealed to the regimental surgeon, who was the new colonel's brother-in-law, to pass on the word that he would not object to a recommendation. This bit of wire-pulling was entirely in character. McKinley was and would remain exceedingly modest, devoid of egotism or boastfulness, but he did not undervalue himself, and he never saw any harm in asking a favor in a nice, indirect way. Hayes, who had been impressed by the performance at Antietam, was glad to praise the sergeant to the governor of Ohio. When McKinley went home in the autumn of 1862—on the only leave he received during the war—he was proud of the bars on his shoulder straps, and bubbled over with enthusiasm in recounting his experiences to his family.

As an officer, McKinley was closely associated with Hayes. Presently, promoted to first lieutenant, he was serving on the colonel's staff. In his letters home, Hayes described McKinley as "a handsome bright, gallant boy," and "one of the bravest and finest officers in the army." McKinley found his proper place in the capacity of aide-de-camp. He was not by nature combative or aggressive. He was cool, courteous, and methodical, and he had become an expert horseman, useful to a commander in battle. In 1864, when he obtained a captaincy, he saw hot fighting in the Valley, and had more than one horse shot under him. He distinguished himself at the Union repulse at Kernstown by a daring gallop under fire to give an unsupported regiment the signal to retreat. Hayes commented on his gallantry at Winchester. His conduct at Opequan was officially mentioned. After service on the staffs of various generals, McKinley was mustered out in 1865, with the brevet commission of major, signed "A. Lincoln," for gallant and meritorious service in the Shenandoah Valley.

William's homecoming joyfully ended the long ordeal of his anxious parents. As he had expected, he had escaped without a scratch. It was scarcely less remarkable that he had been untouched by the infections of the unsanitary camps. At twenty-two, McKinley had matured into vigorous manhood. The stern education of war had hardened his body and disciplined his character, and he had gained in poise and presence, and in

7

the force and tenacity of his political convictions. Even as a boy, he had closely followed the news—the papers had been the one request he had made of Cousin William Miller, in response to an offer to get him anything he needed. McKinley was dedicated to the party of his wartime idol, Lincoln, for whom he had cast his first vote in 1864 on the march to Martinsburg, with an ambulance serving as an election booth and an empty candle container as a ballot box. He was an ardent advocate of the party's moral aim of civil rights for the Negro, but he had no desire for vengeance on the defeated South. His sympathies lay with the generous program of Reconstruction that Lincoln had proposed, rather than with the vindictive policies of the Republican radicals. To McKinley's mind, the crowning culmination of Grant's masterful campaign was the magnanimity that the Union commander had shown at Appomattox. By 1865, McKinley had had his fill of the bitterness of conflict. On going through a hospital, he had remarked a Union surgeon's friendliness with some of the Confederate wounded. When he learned that they were brother Masons, he made haste to join an order whose bonds transcended the differences of war, and was inducted into Masonry, at the hands of a Confederate master, in a lodge at Winchester. Apart from memorial or patriotic addresses he was from time to time called upon to make, McKinley never alluded publicly to the battlefield. The rattle of musketry and the thunder of cannon were notably absent from his speeches, even in his frequent appearances at Grand Army encampments, where such references were expected. Memories of the sacred Cause, of duty, and of comradeship were all that he cared to evoke. The rest was a chapter that was closed when he put off his uniform.

Like many another brave and faithful soldier, McKinley left the army with an abiding hatred of war, and a strong belief that arbitration was a civilized principle, which should prevail in the settlement of all disputes. It was not inconsistent with this conviction that he at first thought of accepting a second lieutenancy that was offered him in the regular Army. North and South, the country was drained and sickened by civil strife, and determined never to be involved in a foreign war; and it was carnage and destruction, not military life, that McKinley detested. As an elderly man, he sent a letter of advice to his nephew, James, who had become a lieutenant in the regular establishment. "I am very deeply interested in your success," McKinley wrote, "and I want you to make a good soldier. Be attentive to all your duties. Do everything the best you know how and if you are in doubt ask some superior officer the best way to do it. Be careful about your writing. See that your words are spelled correctly. Better have a little pocket dictionary with you. It mars an official paper or letter to have a word misspelled." Nearly thirty-four years had passed since McKinley wore the Union blue, but his admonitions conjure up the correct young officer he had been.

McKinley's family frowned on a military career, and the opposition was probably not unwelcome. The veteran might well have felt obliged to support himself by the only profession he had learned. He felt no vocation for the church, in spite of his mother's influence; but he was greatly attracted by the idea of going into politics. The training of a lawyer was nearly an indispensable preparation, and it was soon arranged that William should read law in the office of a rising young attorney in the vicinity. A year later, with the financial help of his eldest sister Anna, he completed his studies at the law school at Albany, New York.

In the autumn of 1866, McKinley wrote to tell Rutherford Hayes about his choice of a profession. He regarded this mild, kindly man, with his fine moral character and whole-souled devotion to the Republican party, as a paragon of virtue and wisdom. Hayes, moreover, was by far the most prominent person McKinley knew. He had risen to the rank of brigadier, brevetted major general for his services; and, on the strength of his gallant record, he had been elected to Congress in 1864. When McKinley solicited Hayes's interest in his future, the older man was campaigning, with every prospect of success, for a second term.

Hayes replied in a cordial way, but his comment on McKinley's adoption of the legal profession was scarcely encouraging. "With your business capacity and experience," he wrote, "I would have preferred Rail Roading or some commercial business. A man in any of our Western towns with half your wit ought to be independent at forty in business. As a lawyer, a man sacrifices independence to ambition which is a bad bargain at the best." McKinley carefully preserved this letter, putting it away in a little tin box where he kept valuable papers; but he did not heed its advice. It was surprising advice from a lawyer and politician, and it showed a faulty understanding of McKinley's abilities. His neat paper work as a staff officer had demonstrated the aptitude of a first-rate clerk, but McKinley had none of the shrewd and imaginative drive for profit that makes for business success. He wanted to earn a good living, and enjoy comfort and financial security. The accumulation of wealth held no interest for him at all. The greatest flight of pecuniary fancy that McKinley would ever know was the poor man's dream of finding oil on his land. While he was cautious in his investments and usually meticulous in his transactions, he risked his early savings to assist a friend, who fleeced him. The incident was evidence of McKinley's generosity and trustfulness, but not of his business acumen.

9

America, building its railroads, its industries, and its fortunes, was already absorbed in the worship of material gain. Yet, even in a money-mad nation, there were other avenues to success than business. McKinley had shown a singular gift for inspiring confidence and affection; he liked public speaking; and of the ambition that Hayes seemed to disparage he had a bountiful endowment. As he plugged away at his law books, he intended to follow his former colonel's example, rather than his counsel. It was a family tradition that the McKinleys were stubborn. A year later, William was making political speeches, stumping in Hayes's campaign for governor of Ohio.

Meanwhile, McKinley had spent a term at the Albany Law School, passed his bar examinations, and set himself up in Canton. Miss Anna McKinley, twelve years older than her brother, had become the principal of a grammar school there, and her rare character and gracious ways had made her much beloved. She was eager to have William settle in Canton, and in the early spring of 1867 he paid Anna a visit, meeting the young people of the community, and looking over the situation. He found a friendly, flourishing, progressive town, the seat of Stark County, with a bar of good reputation. William promptly decided on Canton as the place where he would build his practice and make his home.

The fledgling lawyer's capital comprised good looks, a pleasing personality, and a spotless character. He was rather short, but he carried his slim, well-muscled body with military erectness, and moved with a quick step and an easy swing of the shoulders. His shining gray eyes were intent. His warm smile exhaled a buoyant confidence, and his voice, a low tenor verging on a baritone, was musical and strong. McKinley's moral rectitude was written, like a certificate of character, on his pale, handsome face. He wrote his nephew, James, in later years, "look after your diet and living, take no intoxicants, indulge in no immoral practices. Keep your life and your speech both clean, and be brave." In four years of army life, McKinley had not learned to drink or smoke or swear. His mind was prudish, and he was undoubtedly chaste. His roommate at Albany testified to the decorum of his conduct at law school. McKinley knew so little of the pleasures of the flesh that, when he went to Albany, he had never tasted ice cream. He was handed a plate of it by Judge Amasa J. Parker's lovely daughter Grace at the annual reception for the new law students. "Poor Mrs. Parker," he said, after sampling the delicacy—"do not tell her the custard got frozen." McKinley never forgot how sweetly Miss Grace explained about ice cream. "You know, I was a simple country boy," he said in recounting the incident.

A lack of worldly sophistication was not a drawback, but a positive advantage to the newcomer in Canton. This was a simple country town, this was America in 1867, and Major William McKinley, Junior, was esteemed as a Christian gentleman. There was no sham in his virtue, and only one touch of subtlety—he precisely understood its usefulness to the advancement on which he was determined.

Even in Canton, the Major might have appeared exceptionally circumspect for his years. He was a dashing horseman, but he took no interest in competitive sports, or in any other exercise except walking. Dancing, cards, and theatrical entertainment had been as rigidly forbidden in his strict Methodist home as those other snares of Satan, wine and tobacco. McKinley had a natural love of fun. He liked to play with children, and his chuckle was hearty and infectious. He was easygoing, sweet-tempered, and gregarious, susceptible to the charms of a pretty face and feminine refinement, but he did not feel entirely at ease in idle pleasure-seeking. He once confided to a friend that he had always had to struggle with self-consciousness, instancing the fact that a church social made him want to run away. On his single attempt at taking part in comedy, an impromptu minstrel show on a camping trip, he was so shamed by his blacked-up face that he rushed off the stage. McKinley was not a lively or obtrusive figure in any gathering, unless he was on the speaker's platform; and the only fancy costumes that he could wear without embarrassment were the oilcloth cape and cap of a Republican torchlight parade and the uniforms of the fraternal orders.

If McKinley was not precisely a good fellow, he was a great joiner, with a keen sense of group loyalty. He had made a fraternity, Sigma Alpha Epsilon, during his brief stay at Allegheny College. He was active in the veterans' organizations, and wore the bronze badge of the G.A.R. and the red, white, and blue ribbon of the Loyal Legion. He hastened to affiliate with the Masonic lodge in Canton, taking a number of higher degrees and eventually becoming a Knight Templar. He joined the Knights of Pythias. He was greatly interested in the Y.M.C.A., progressing from its literary club, in which he took the affirmative in a debate on woman suffrage, to the presidency of the Canton branch. He immediately offered his services to the county Republican committee, and in time assumed its chairmanship. He was a faithful member of the First Methodist Church, and was made superintendent of the Sunday school.

In these associations, the young McKinley enjoyed a participation and performance of function that he did not find in purely social gatherings, but he was never exclusive, or hostile to the affiliations of other people. Though Stark County was a Democratic stronghold, McKinley remained on good terms with all his neighbors, even when the passions of Reconstruction were burning. His devout Methodism did not lead him to concern himself with dogma or denominational differences. The loving-kindness of God was McKinley's religion, and the source of his inner serenity. His favorite hymns—"Nearer, My God, to Thee," "Lead, Kindly Light," "Jesus, Lover of my Soul," "There's A Wideness in God's Mercy"—were expressions of a sustaining spiritual communion. As president of the Y.M.C.A., he stressed the devotional aspect of the organization, gathering the young men of every denomination at street meetings of song and prayer. He made many friends among Canton's large Roman Catholic population, of German and Irish extraction. In a day of sharp sectarian prejudice, McKinley was devoid of bigotry, possessing as a grace of his nature the tolerance that is unconscious of its own virtue. Before he had been in Canton for a year, he had gained a remarkably wide popularity. He had also established himself in his profession, and attained standing in the county as a political orator.

On his arrival, McKinley had been armed with a letter of introduction to an elderly judge, and he presented it with the suggestion that he should be taken into partnership. The old man was thinking of retirement and wanted a young partner, but he was somewhat flustered by this sudden proposition from a stranger. He made hurried inquiries, and tested McKinley out by entrusting him with a case; and, as all went well, he assented to the arrangement. This association launched the Major at the Canton bar. He was already assured of a comfortable practice when the judge died the next year. McKinley did not evidence any legal brilliance or profundity, but he was hard-working and thorough, and he made an excellent impression in court, where his fair-mindedness and courtesy were combined with a talent for presenting a complicated case in plain language that a jury could understand. In his nine years of active practice, he prospered modestly, investing his savings in local real estate and Ohio industries. The most interesting of his cases was his defense of a group of Massillon miners, imprisoned for riot in 1876 during one of the periodic violent strikes in the coal-mining industry. McKinley was in sympathy with the workers' grievances, and undertook a case that had aroused much prejudice in the community. He succeeded in getting all the offenders released except one, who served a term in prison. When their friends made up a purse for the attorney's fee, McKinley refused to accept payment from the impoverished strikers. His good offices redounded to his political advantage by winning him the loyal friendship of labor in Stark County.

McKinley's appearances on political platforms had begun in the autumn

12

of 1867, when he lauded that soldier and statesman Rutherford B. Hayes for governor of Ohio. The campaign issue was Negro suffrage. An amendment to the Ohio constitution was defeated, but Hayes was narrowly elected. He carried Stark County, and the Major's reputation was made as a speaker. It did not count against him that he was a personal friend of the Governor, and could recommend a man for an appointment. In the following year of the national elections, with General Grant as the Republican standard-bearer, McKinley formed Grant clubs, organized the townships, staged big demonstrations, and fervently addressed rallies for the peerless leader of the Union armies. On the county ticket, McKinley's name appeared as candidate for prosecuting attorney, a nomination perhaps intended as an empty compliment, since the office was habitually held by a Democrat. But the Major managed a campaign so energetic that he was elected in the swing to the Republican party.

McKinley was at this time identified with the temperance movement, and for a number of years was the leading speaker in Stark County on behalf of total abstinence. The most notable activity of his single term as prosecuting attorney was his war on the illicit sale of liquor. The town of Alliance was an especial offender, and its saloons offered a temptation to the boys at the nearby college of Mount Union. McKinley secured indictments against all the proprietors, calling a number of college students as witnesses. One of them, Philander C. Knox, told such a straight story of his own misdeeds that McKinley was able to convict the saloonkeepers largely on his testimony. The lad's honesty and manliness made an impression on McKinley, and he did not lose sight of Phil Knox when he went on to become one of the biggest lawyers in Pittsburgh.

While the Major was occupied with the new experience of officeholding, his parents yielded to the persuasion that he and Anna had exerted to unite the family in Canton. David and James, like their Uncle Ben, had gone to California. Sarah Elizabeth was living in Cleveland with her husband Andrew J. Duncan. Mary had married a Poland man, and her death in 1868 may have severed the parents' ties with the village. The next year William bought a small frame house on the corner of Shorb and Tuscarawas streets, humbler than his future home on North Market, but of the same architectural lineage; and, when Anna had fitted it up, the old people moved to town with Abner, another prospective lawyer, and Helen, a gentle spinster who had given up schoolteaching to stay with her mother. The senior William had been expected to retire, but he invested in a furnace in Michigan, and acted as its manager for the next seven years. William was proud of his father's obstinate industry and upright, independent character. His mother was, as she had always been, the light of

the home. In Canton, she was soon known to everyone as Mother Mc-
Kinley. Her son's devotion became a byword, as people saw the respect
and solicitude with which the Major treated her, and the courtly manner
in which he escorted her to church.

McKinley's love for his mother and his adherence to her early teachings
would never alter; but, though he was a good man and doing the Lord's
work in cleaning up the saloons, she could not be entirely reconciled to the
political career for which he was so plainly destined. It is probable that by
this time William had begun the use of tobacco, the politicians' vice, to
which many young party workers were first tempted by the package of
three cigars, tied with red, white, and blue ribbon, which was laid at every
place on Republican banquet tables. Before Mother McKinley had been
many months in Canton, she must have seen that still another influence
was drawing William into a worldly environment, and inducing him to
take part in the frivolous diversions that had not hitherto attracted him.

Late in the year of 1869, the Saxton sisters swept back to Canton from
Europe, as glorious as conquerors with their loot—lace and coral and
cameos, gloves and false hair and ermine muffs, and a Swiss music box, with
eight tunes, which they had bought for Ma. The younger, christened Mary,
but always called Pina—Piney, as it was pronounced—was a pleasant, sensi-
ble-looking girl. Ida was the pretty one, with delicate, piquant features,
masses of auburn hair, and languorous blue eyes under a marble brow.

The Canton banker and businessman, James A. Saxton, was a man of
substance. He and his wife could afford to indulge their daughters and
their only boy George. But, beyond the externals of a fortunate environment, no trace remains of Ida's childhood years, and only a few pictures
record her development from a plump, round-faced adolescent to a slim
and fashionable beauty. One group photograph, taken when she was nineteen, suggests that vanity dictated the elegance of her formal poses. Ida
looks indolent and untidy, as she slouches forward to lean on the knee
of her cousin, Mary Goodman, fondly holding her hand, while Pina stands
gazing moodily into space in the background. At about this time, Ida and
Pina were sent to finish their education at a well-known school for girls,
Brooke Hall seminary at Media, Pennsylvania. Ida was rather old for
boarding school, but she evidently enjoyed it, for she kept sentimental
memories of Brooke Hall and its head mistress "the beloved Miss Eastman." More than thirty years later, Ida was still on affectionate terms
with one of her teachers, Miss Harriet Gault, and was so interested in
holding a reunion with her former schoolmates that she gave a luncheon
for the Brooke Hall alumnae association.

14

Only two events are chronicled for the year after Ida was "finished." On a picnic in the summer, she was introduced to Major McKinley, who was then visiting his sister—a meeting that seems to have made no particular impression on either side. The following spring, Ida won a prize for her performance in the amateur show—tableaux, pantomime, singing, and dancing—given at the Canton Opera House to raise money to build a new Presbyterian church. A year later, Ida and Pina set out to acquire the polish of a European tour.

To Miss Jeannette Alexander, the Canton schoolteacher who conducted the trip, the charge and company of Ida Saxton constituted an eight months' ordeal. Miss Alexander had been thwarted in her desire to take her brother along as business manager, and she became convinced that Ida had instigated the opposition because the brother was not one of her admirers. "She set her head he should not come," Miss Alexander wrote home, "and that earned the day for there is no let up when she does set her head." Pina was kind, and once lent Miss Alexander fifteen dollars. Ida was inconsiderate and unmanageable. She went her own way to shops and places of amusement; and, to the chaperone's indignation, conspired with another young lady to attend the theater "with some gentlemen" in Paris. Miss Alexander herself was not an ideal traveling companion. She was hypersensitive and homesick. She found palaces tiresome, and was disgruntled because her "class" was too small to make the enterprise profitable. Nevertheless, her letters and her diary of the tour convey a convincing impression that the "head strong" Ida was an extreme example of the type of personality that is euphemistically described as "spoiled."

If Ida Saxton had a childhood history of nervous illness, it had left no mark on the face and form of the woman of twenty-two. Little Harry Frease, one of her pupils at the Presbyterian Sunday school, would always remember the healthy bloom of his pretty teacher. But Ida appears to have been restless and dissatisfied when she came back to Canton. An eager suitor was waiting for Pina—Marshall Barber, a young man who liked amateur theatricals, and was good at clog dancing and cutting capers. Marshall did not have much push, but Pina loved him. Ida could not give her heart to any of the suitors she attracted. Perhaps she was brooding over the memory of an unidentified Mr. Wright. Pina had found her shocked and weeping on the veranda of their hotel in Geneva, when the news of his death came. Mr. Saxton, in any case, decided that Ida needed an occupation. He was a broad-minded man, with advanced ideas of the capacities of women. On hearing of the friction with Miss Alexander, he had actually expressed willingness to have his daughters continue their travels without a chaperone. He now made the still more extraordinary proposal that Ida should go to work in his bank, and acquire the training of a businesswoman. Brooke Hall had offered more "finish" than substantial education, but Ida was clever enough to justify her father's expectations. It is a surprising twist in a love story of the early Grant era that, when Ida's path again crossed that of Major McKinley, she was a cashier in the First National Bank of Canton.

If Ida "set her head" to capture the good-looking Major, he was a willing victim. He fell madly, devotedly in love, with all the repressed passion of his deeply emotional nature. He was entranced by Ida's beauty, by her imperious ways, by her willfulness and feminine caprices. Canton was soon buzzing with gossip, as every week these two met between their respective Sunday schools, and tarried in conversation in full view of the town. Ida developed a chilly aversion for a pleasant girl whom McKinley had sometimes squired. At a social at the house of her uncle, Joseph Saxton, Ida showed great anxiety because McKinley was late. Until the suspense was broken by his arrival, she pestered every guest with questions. "Have you seen the Major?" "Do you imagine the Major is sick?" "Has the Major been called from the city?" McKinley was probably the only person in Canton who remained uncertain of Ida's sentiments. One day, while taking her for a drive, he conquered his diffidence and proposed. Ida accepted him without hesitation. She might have been expected to look higher in the way of fortune, but she could not have made a better choice in terms of worth and character. Mr. Saxton gave the couple his blessing and the house on North Market Street. The wedding, celebrated in January of 1871 in the brand new Presbyterian church, was a social milestone in Canton. Ida, radiant in ivory white satin and point lace, was attended by Pina in pink silk and Amelia Bockius in corn color. Abner McKinley and Will Osborne stood up with the bridegroom. There was a large reception at the Saxton homestead, and Miss Alexander, who was among the guests, admired the many beautiful presents, and pronounced the wedding a grand affair.

After a honeymoon in New York, the bridal pair came home to set up housekeeping, and make merry at informal gatherings with the other young couples of Canton and nearby towns. A little girl was born on the next Christmas Day. They named her Katherine for Ida's mother. McKinley was the fondest of husbands, with a strong sentiment for home and family, and a deep tenderness for children. He was working for his beautiful wife and blonde baby when he argued his causes in court and campaigned for a second presidential term for Grant. McKinley's marriage brought him the greatest happiness of his life. The happiness lasted a little over two years.

Six months after Katie's birth, Ida again became pregnant. Just when her time was at hand, in the early spring of 1873, her own mother died. Ida was shocked and distracted beyond the usual experience of a daughter's grief when she underwent a hard labor. She was seriously ill, and the frail infant, her namesake, lived less than five months. It was mentioned that Mrs. McKinley suffered from phlebitis, but no explanation was offered for the fact that nerve specialists were called in consultation. The fact was that she had developed convulsions that seemed to point to some damage to the brain; and, after the baby's death, it was whispered in Canton that Ida McKinley had fits. She was in a severe depression, leaving Katie's care largely to Pina, yet hysterically apprehensive about the child. Thomas Beer, whose father knew Canton well, heard that Mrs. McKinley would scarcely let Katie out of her sight, except to take a drive with her father, and would hold the little girl on her lap for hours, weeping in a darkened room. Abner McKinley, according to Thomas Beer, once found Katie swinging on the gate, and asked her to take a walk with him. "No, I mustn't go out of the yard," Katie said, "or God'll punish mamma some more."

Ida did not remain bedridden. She dressed. She began to see her friends. But the pretty, pleasure-seeking young woman McKinley had married had changed to a feeble, self-centered nervous invalid. The phlebitis left her a cripple who stood and walked with difficulty and pain. For the rest of her life, Ida was an epileptic, subject to frequent attacks of *petit mal*, a brief loss of consciousness, and at irregular intervals to prolonged and violent seizures.

In this ruined home, there was left the brightness of little Katie, a solid, fair-haired child, with a handsome, serious face like her father's. Katie died in 1876. That was the year that McKinley was elected to Congress.

Sorrow and anxiety did not swerve McKinley's course. He was energetic in 1875 in Hayes's third campaign for the governorship, stumping Ohio in opposition to the greenback craze, and preaching the Republican policy of the resumption of specie payments. He came to the decision that the time was ripe for his election to Congress; and, in spite of the heavy expense of Ida's illness and the high cost of living in Washington, deliberately chose to exchange an annual income of $10,000 from his law practice for the congressman's salary of half that amount. The next year, when Hayes was running for President, McKinley announced his own candidacy for Congress, and readily secured the nomination. In the heartbreaking months after Katie's death, he waged the vigorous campaign that resulted in

17

My precious Corpe:
I received your
dear good letter this morning
and it has given me new
inspiration. I suppose from the
tone of your letter you are
either *unwell* or *expecting* to
be. I hope you are safe though.
If not take three doses of
Bromide. during that period.
I am very well. So is James
I will get Maps Poor to get
the thread you want. It is
awful lonesome without you.
I am anxious for the next two
weeks to roll around. when
I will find you ... you here
with me. Your friends all
send much love.
Yours faithfully
W. McKinley Jr.

A solicitous letter from McKinley to his wife in 1880 illustrates his anxiety for her when they were parted.

his election. But, though domestic tragedy did not weaken McKinley, it altered him. His buoyant youthfulness was gone. He showed the fortitude and quick compassion that are the grace of those who have greatly suffered, but he also grew guarded and reticent. In the first shock of his trouble, he was sometimes abstracted. There were stories that he forgot important testimony that had been given in court; that his intense gaze became a fixed stare, as though he were mustering all his faculties in an effort at concentration. A part of his mind seemed always to be listening. He was absorbed in the practice of his secondary career of psychiatric nurse.

Over the years, the chart of Ida's health showed a zigzag line consistent only in its irregularity. The routine of minor convulsions and the predictable nervous disturbances of her menstrual cycle were varied by blinding headaches and formidable epileptic attacks, and also by the heavy colds and digestive upsets to which she was subject. Although she was never well, she was sometimes better, and McKinley clung to a belief that she would eventually recover. As though his love could work the miracle of her cure, he was tireless in ministering to her mental and physical comfort. He grew soft-voiced and cautious, and developed resources of tact in appeasing and diverting Ida. He spent his free hours sitting in stuffy rooms and driving in closed carriages because she avoided fresh air. Her headaches often required him to pass the evening in the dark. McKinley learned how to support his wife's weight on his arm, timing his quick step to her faltering pace; and how to hold her head, when her temples throbbed with the pressure of an oncoming attack. He became skilled in judging the severity of her seizures, and professionally adept at handling them. McKinley's own healthy nervous system enabled him to endure the constant strain. He remained calm, patient, and even-tempered. When Ida was cheerful, his spirits mounted. He did not worry or borrow trouble, as long as he was near her. He slept soundly. He hoped.

On the subject of his wife's illness, McKinley's lips were sealed. To inquiries about her health, he politely responded that Mrs. McKinley was not so well, or that she was feeling better. He turned an imperturbable face to the pitying eyes of Canton, and his reserve forbade impertinent questioning. In the presence of other people, McKinley's attitude toward Ida's repellent symptoms was so casual as to appear indifferent. He always sat beside her in the dining room or parlor. At the first sign of rigidity, he was alert. He threw his handkerchief or a napkin over her convulsed face, removing it when she relaxed. Ida usually resumed a conversation where she had left off, without seeming to realize that there had been an interruption. McKinley's matter-of-fact manner forbade a whisper of comment, exacted from the company obliviousness that anything out of the ordinary had occurred.

On Ida's lovely face, the skin tautened to a strained mask. Her eyes were sharp with pain and fear, or dulled by sedatives. Her hair was cropped short because she could not bear the weight of braids and hairpins. This was the wife with whom an ambitious young congressman set out to conquer Washington. This was the woman McKinley proudly escorted on his arm to functions at the Executive Mansion.

Ida suffered so much that it seems unkind to say that she could exert herself when she pleased. Yet, while it was generally understood that Mrs. McKinley's health did not permit her to attend dinners or receptions or to return calls, she made a number of social appearances during her first four years in Washington. An electoral commission had decided the disputed presidential contest of 1876 in favor of the Republicans, and President Hayes and his wife were the McKinleys' closest friends at the capital. The Major's loyal campaign services had cemented the wartime relationship. The sweet-faced temperance crusader, Lucy Hayes, and the children of the family had grown fond of the Stark County orator and his afflicted wife. Webb and young Rutherford were McKinley's friends, in their own right. Little Fanny, unused to hotels, thought it "quite thrilling" to call on Mrs. McKinley at the Ebbitt House. In later years, Ida liked to tell that she had once spent two weeks as the substitute mistress of the Executive Mansion, while she and her husband kept the Hayes children company in their parents' absence. Ida also made friends with Mrs. Hayes's attractive niece, Emily Platt. During the second winter in Washington, Russell Hastings, a one-legged veteran of the war and the dearest of McKinley's comrades, paid a visit to the capital, and spent much time at the Ebbitt House. A romance between Hastings and Miss Platt flourished in Mrs. McKinley's sitting room, and led to a wedding at the Executive Mansion.

In view of all these close associations, it was perhaps not surprising that Ida made the effort of calling at the mansion and dining privately with the Hayes family. But Ida's ill health did not deter her from attending the formal state dinners to which the McKinleys were invited. Once she promenaded around the East Room on the President's arm. It is equally remarkable that she twice went, without McKinley, to lunch with Lucy Hayes.

"We wish you were here again," the Congressman wrote his friend, when Hayes's single term was over. The recreation had been pleasurable to McKinley, as well as beneficial to Ida's spirits. James Garfield's presidency might have renewed the connection with the mansion, for this other Ohio congressman was also McKinley's friend, and had often brought his boys to call at the Ebbitt House; but Garfield was shot only four months after taking office, and McKinley had no ties with the elegant New Yorker, Chester Arthur. Grover Cleveland's administration was a bleak time for Republicans, and they returned to power with the election of Benjamin Harrison, with whom McKinley's relations were coldly political. When Mrs. McKinley ceased to be an intimate of the mansion, her social activities came to an end.

For the rest of McKinley's laborious years in Congress, his leisure was largely spent alone with his wife, acting as her companion and secretary, and taking her for the drives that were the only outings she enjoyed. On entering Congress, McKinley had decided to specialize on the tariff, and the mastery of the complicated subject necessitated many hours of study. He frequently worked until late at night, poring over trade reports and schedules, and holding conferences with the representatives of the protected industries. At the Ebbitt House, he was the first guest down in the morning, collecting his mail and newspapers at seven, in order to put in two hours' work before breakfasting with Mrs. McKinley. He had become a heavy smoker; and, as tobacco was disagreeable to his wife, he took his after-supper cigar in the open air, pacing up and down the sidewalk in front of the hotel. A newspaper correspondent thought that McKinley seemed restless, always walking when he was not busy at his desk, but this restricted evening promenade was the only outdoor exercise that a vigorous and still youthful man was free to take.

Though the suite at the Ebbitt House was modest, a congressman's salary did not go far in Washington, even in the eighties. McKinley's savings—$10,000 when he entered Congress—had been partly invested in erecting an office building, the McKinley Block, in Canton. He must have derived some income from the rentals, and possibly in the first few years from his law office, which he maintained for a time with his brother Abner as his active partner. But there was evidence that McKinley was strapped for money in the sale of the North Market Street house, and also in the fact that he was repeatedly forced to borrow the funds to finance his early campaigns for re-election. Congressmen were at that time obliged to pay their own office expenses, and McKinley engaged an extra room across the hall from his living quarters at the hotel. Besides the bills for doctors and medicines, Ida's illness made it necessary to engage a personal maid, trained in her care, who was always with her in her husband's absence. Mrs. McKinley's tastes were luxurious, and the inheritance she received on her father's death in 1887 must have given McKinley some relief from ten years of strain to make ends meet. He was once offered a position as attorney for a large western railroad at a salary of $25,000 or more, and took a day or two to consider it. In the end, he said he thought it would be better to stay in Congress—"that he was familiar with his work there and had an idea he was serving the country a little."

Ida fades into a dim figure in the congressional years. The recollections of Canton are all dreary, or worse. On a jolly camping party on a stream near Waynesburg, Mrs. McKinley was prostrate in her tent with a bad headache, unable to endure the racket of the small boys. Thomas Beer heard that McKinley's mention of a good-looking woman he had seen at President Garfield's funeral threw his wife into a fit of hysterics, culminating in a severe epileptic attack. On a visit to Pina while Congress was in session in 1888, Ida fell into a seizure so violent and prolonged that the family doctor despaired of saving her life. McKinley, hastily summoned, sat all night by her bed, caressing her, calling her name, imploring her to answer him. Ida recovered in the morning, coming back to consciousness with the words, "I knew you would come." Canton talked about McKinley's martyrdom, but his private life went nearly unobserved in Washington. For a time, the McKinleys ate at the table with Mr. and Mrs. Harvey Watterson, dyed-in-the-wool Democrats, whose son Henry owned the Louisville *Courier-Journal*. Ida endeared herself to the elderly couple, and was like a daughter to Mr. Watterson after his wife's death. Two or three women friends sometimes came to keep Mrs. McKinley company. Congressmen brought their families to call, and people from Ohio dropped in to pay their respects and tell the news from home. Ida was always eager to see children, made much of them, and gave them little presents. She was greatly preoccupied with her clothes, constantly demanding her husband's advice on problems of samples and trimmings. The most vivid impression is that of a plaintive voice, summoning McKinley on trivial pretexts from his conferences across the hall, while his visitors shrugged their irritation at the interruption of important business.

Ida liked to sit in a small, ornately carved rocking chair, which had been hers as a child. Fancywork, embroidering in wools or crocheting bedroom slippers, was her only occupation. Leaving everything else to her husband and her maid, she sank into a sedentary invalidism. But she still liked to travel, and twice in the congressional years McKinley took her to California.

If a man is to spend his life under the checkrein of anxiety and in obedience to a sick woman's whims, he must have work to keep him sane. McKinley found his release in his political career. He escaped from his personal tragedy on the floor of the House, sparring adroitly in debate, and on campaign platforms, preaching Republican doctrine. He learned to put aside his worry and heartache, and absorb himself in the world of public affairs, the exercise of diplomacy, the plotting of policy, the chess game of strategy. In committee rooms, he was attentive and vigilant, a rather noncommittal man in a tightly buttoned frock coat, with a cigar between his fingers or a quid bulging his cheek. Possibly because of his wife's dislike of cigars, McKinley had formed the habit of chewing or, more accurately, mouthing tobacco. He did not use a plug, but the broken half of one of his favorite imported Garcías. Young James Garfield noticed that his aim was remarkably good, as he sat after lunch in the House restaurant, listening more than he talked.

McKinley enjoyed to the full the social hours of this masculine world: the anecdote, the laughter, the company drawing on their cigars and turning to the next man who was "reminded." He was not much of a hand at telling a story himself, but he relished the savor of a joke, if there was nothing vulgar about it. He had a quiet irony and a graceful lightness of touch that made him an agreeable companion, smiling and responsive in the blue haze of smoke. McKinley was more than popular—he was beloved. Scores of his associates were his friends, and many of them held him in worshipful admiration. Even his political opponents were attracted by the peculiar sweetness of his personality. He was never effusive. His reserved manner restrained but did not conceal the sentimentalism of his heart. It glowed in words and acts of friendliness, in the light that kindled his eyes, in the way he had of throwing his arm across another man's shoulders.

As McKinley's reputation grew, he became a figure of great public interest, and thousands of Americans flocked to meet him and hear him speak. His short, dignified stature and pale, resolute face earned him the newspaper sobriquet of "the young Napoleon." He became a practiced orator, learning to cast over his audiences the spell of his vibrant voice, which, like his ideas, had a harmonious monotony. He was an indefatigable handshaker, using the technique that Hayes had taught him, a quick grasp that anticipated a crippling squeeze on his own hand. But the cordiality of his greeting was not studied or perfunctory. He communicated a warmth as positive as sunlight. A word from him at a reception could win a stranger's loyalty.

In his public appearances, McKinley was happy and fulfilled. Demands and encroachments did not fatigue him, but endued him with fresh strength. Brought up in a large family, he was used to having people around him, and seemed scarcely to feel the need of privacy. Politics had become his hobby, as well as his profession. He had no opportunity for riding, or for the long walks he had once liked to take. He had few intellectual resources. If he had ever possessed a germ of taste, it had died of inanition. In literature and music, he looked for an obvious sentimental, patriotic, or religious content. The old hymns were the noblest poetry McKinley knew. He liked Father Ryan's "Song of the Mystic," and sometimes quoted a favorite commonplace stanza. He was deeply moved by a little poem, "Recompense," which Myron Herrick sent him at the time of his father's death. The concluding lines were,

> . . . When we shall wake,
> I am quite sure we will be very glad
> That for a little while we were so sad.

McKinley caused this poem to be read at his father's funeral, and in a grateful letter to Herrick pronounced it one of the most beautiful things he ever remembered to have seen.

As a student of economics, McKinley was interested in facts that were serviceable in the House debates and in his public addresses. He applied himself to the tariff question to implement his convictions, not to enlarge or correct them. In any broad discussion of political economy, his opinions were impoverished and ingenuous. McKinley vastly admired men of culture, sought their acquaintance, and bespoke their recognition in public office. He felt the disadvantage of his own interrupted schooling, and expressed regret that he had never found time to continue his studies; but, like most successful men of limited education, he increasingly tended to emphasize the superiority of practical experience over theoretical knowledge. He was also alienated from the modern system of higher education by the discovery that "free trade" ideas had become "a fashion" in American colleges. "I would rather have my political economy founded upon the every-day experience of the puddler or the potter than the learning of the professor," he caustically remarked in 1888. "Do not permit college ideals to warp you," he warned the students of Mount Union in 1896. With the passing years, McKinley's desire to improve his mind became scarcely more than lip service to a recollected aspiration. After he was elected governor of Ohio, he read two books that Herrick sent him as a Christmas present. There is no other mention of his reading, apart from the newspapers. McKinley had formed the politician's habit of learning by ear. He told his stenographer, Opha Moore, that he learned more from people than from books, and settled the matter to his own satisfaction by adding that the people wrote the books.

The thin young clerk who took the Governor's dictation observed him with a rather acid reticence. With his agile pencil racing, Moore privately noted that McKinley's vocabulary was small, but he could not withhold admiration of the golden quality of the big voice. Its even flow was not hypnotic—it made you feel pleasant. Only a stenographer, Moore remarked, would notice that it never wearied. Though McKinley was orderly and methodical, Moore thought that Governor Foraker had shown superior executive talent. McKinley's great advantage was his ability to work calmly and evenly, without flurries of irritability or impatience. In his four years at Columbus, the only occasion on which Moore ever saw him "peeved" was one time when an Ohio politician told him a dirty story. "I wish that fellow would stay away from here," McKinley disgustedly remarked, after the caller was gone.

At forty-nine, when McKinley became governor of his beloved Buckeye State, he had settled into a decorous, dignified, and sedentary middle age. He did not speak as vehemently or work as tirelessly as he had done in Congress. With greater leisure at his disposal, he found that a walk of half a mile satisfied his need for exercise; and, though he was fond of his black horse Midnight, he was growing too heavy to take much pleasure in riding. Yet he was in perfect health, with glowing skin and bright eyes, and a springing step that belied his age and weight. His whole and tranquil mind was a wellspring of quiet energy. A kind of careless optimism infused his most ordinary gestures. He had a startling way of shaving, rapidly plying a straight-blade razor without troubling to look in the mirror. So Opha Moore would find McKinley in the morning when he carried the Governor's mail over to the hotel: a poised and vigorous man, refreshed by a sound night's sleep, lightly pacing the room as he scraped his lathered face. His undershirt showed his powerfully muscled shoulders, and the mark of the initiation to a secret order on his breast. Years later, William Allen White granted McKinley "a matinée idol's virility."

The Executive Chamber at the State House was a spacious, wood-paneled room, lined with portraits of Ohio dignitaries. A large electric chandelier hung from the high, blue-tinted ceiling. There were soft, deep sofas and easy chairs. When the weather was chilly, a fire crackled beneath the marble mantel. The plain people of Ohio were often awed by this grandeur, as they straggled, in small groups or jostling delegations, to Governor McKinley's massive desk in the middle of the chamber. He was accessible to all who cared to call. Public prominence had increased his dignity, without altering his country-bred simplicity. He showed no sign of self-importance or affectation. In conversation, he drawled a homely, colloquial phrase. He had the good manners of the provinces, ceremonious and hearty. He looked the part of a rural statesman. Though he wore his frock coat like a uniform, his everyday appearance was not impeccably neat. Tobacco stains sometimes lingered on his satin lapels, and shadowed the corners of his mouth. A cuspidor was planted within convenient range of his chair. A farmer or a laboringman did not feel ill at ease when he sat down to talk with the Governor, but he carried away from the interview a sense of McKinley's prestige, and a strong conviction of his good will and moral earnestness. This middle-aged, reticent, experienced politician communicated a curiously potent impression of selfless nobility of character. Like the vanished grace of a ballet dancer, it can be described but not evoked. It moved the high-minded Bellamy Storer to call McKinley an anachronism—"a mediaeval knight in the dusty arena of Ohio politics."

As governor of Ohio, McKinley emerges in the ripeness of his maturity. He was still the Christian gentleman of his youth, educated only in the acquirement of superb political skills. His driving ambition was masked by his imperturbable serenity. As he moved confidently toward his goal, his life had become fuller and more enjoyable. The dreariness of the congressional period of drudgery and domestic seclusion did not rest on the years at Columbus.

McKinley had obtained the services of a full-time "secretary" during his last term in Congress by giving the appointment of assistant clerk of the Ways and Means Committee to one of the House stenographers, a former page boy named Charles Bawsel. This young man was brought to Columbus as chief executive clerk. Besides Opha Moore, who was well known at the State House as a shorthand expert, McKinley also acquired a full-dress private secretary in the person of a former newspaperman, James Boyle, a Canadian who had gained a knowledge of Ohio politics by working on the Cincinnati Commercial-Gazette. Joseph P. Smith, another newspaperman and one of McKinley's most loyal and loving friends, was made state librarian. He was a native of Ohio and a diligent student of local history, and McKinley relied on him to supply information for his speeches. Joe slaved for McKinley, borrowed money from him, scolded him, worshiped him. Another member of the Governor's official family was Captain H. O. S. Heistand of the Eleventh U.S. Infantry, assigned as instructor to the Ohio National Guard. He and his wife lived at the same hotel as the McKinleys, and were soon much in their company. Heistand was so active in the Governor's affairs that it was supposed that he occupied some vague secretarial position. Mrs. Heistand, an executive little person, was devoted to Mrs. McKinley.

At Columbus, McKinley found himself in enjoyment of the easiest financial circumstances he had known since entering politics. He received a salary of $8,000 a year, and his living expenses were lower than in Washington. During most of his two terms, the Governor and his wife occupied a pleasant suite of rooms at the Chittenden, across from the State Capitol. When the hotel burned down, they moved to the nearby Neil House, where a commodious apartment—office, parlor, bedroom, dining room, storeroom, and maid's room—was especially fitted for their use. McKinley could at this time have had a large income, if he had not scrupled to augment his means by practices that were common enough in public life. Among the offers he rejected were a lucrative proposal from a lecture bureau and the highly paid sinecure of the directorship of a life insurance company. McKinley preferred a clear conscience. His position was dignified, and even modestly luxurious. The great joy of these years was the fact that Ida was "better."

Middle age was kinder to Ida than her ruined youth had been. The violent attacks and wild hysteria subsided. She settled into the routine of her illness, living in her husband's career and appeased by the constant assurance of his devotion. The New York physician, Dr. J. N. Bishop, remarked Mrs. McKinley's "great composure and control of her surroundings." Still more surprisingly, the Canton family doctor and friend, Dr. T. H. Phillips, gave the opinion that she had a good deal of the Major's temperament, and did not worry. The improvement in Ida's spirits was so marked that McKinley was radiantly hopeful that she was at last on the road to complete recovery. In laying his ambitious plans for his future, McKinley never spoke of his wife. He was incapable of regarding her as a handicap to his career. Ida's illness was the greatest cross he had to bear, but only because she suffered. He thought of her as a woman fitted to adorn the highest position, and bent every effort toward seeking the cure that would enable her to enjoy it without strain. He drew encouragement from every new doctor and remedy. He placed faith for a time in osteopathy. He was heartened by the prayers of many friends, both Protestants and Catholics. In 1893, McKinley sent Ida to New York for a course of intensive medical treatment. It was probably during this stay that she came under the charge of Dr. Bishop, with whose potions she was liberally dosed for years. He continued to follow the case largely by correspondence, but McKinley willingly paid his large bills, because his medicine "agreed with" Ida. Bromides were the usual prescription for epilepsy, and sedatives increased the rather remote calm that became characteristic of Mrs. McKinley. To McKinley's grievous disappointment, she still had her attacks. It was established in Columbus that she was an invalid, who could not discharge the duties of the Governor's wife, but Ida was by no means secluded. She had her little coterie, and basked in the reflected light of McKinley's growing prominence. For the first time since his marriage, he had the happiness of a normal social life, as Ida welcomed his friends to the hotel parlor, and accompanied him on week-end visits to the fine mansions of the Mark Hannas and the Myron Herricks in Cleveland and the Bellamy Storers in Cincinnati. At these house parties, McKinley overflowed with good spirits from breakfast until the last goodnights were said. He joined with his whole soul in the informal Sunday evening concerts of sacred music, calling for "Nearer, My God, to Thee," and "Lead, Kindly Light," and singing with radiance on his face. The visits gave him the companionship and the taste of home life for which he had long been starved.

Mrs. McKinley comes into clear focus during the years at Columbus: a frail, dressy, aging woman, resigned to her illness and pleased with her position; tart and irritable when put out, but gracious to those who won her favor; and always rhapsodizing over children. Her crocheting had become an absorbing hobby. She turned out bedroom slippers with mechanical rapidity. Her total output was said to have numbered several thousand. When her maid had mounted them on cork soles and laced them with satin ribbon—blue for the blue wool and lavender for the drab—the slippers were repetitiously distributed to friends of both sexes and every age. Ida also made black satin neckties, which McKinley wore knotted in big, old-fashioned bows. Another of her hobbies was jewelry cleaning. After burnishing her own trinkets, Ida had energy to spare for other people's, and snatched a tarnished watch chain in disgust from the lean stomach of Opha Moore. In this picture of a busy, cheerful invalid, the final touch of sentiment was Mrs. McKinley's clinging dependence on her husband. She leaned fondly on his arm. Her sweetest smile was for him. She plied him with endearments, never using his given name, but calling him "my dearest," "my precious," or "my precious love." Yet these affecting manifestations often failed to move the beholder. In Ida's feeble clinging, there was a jealous possessiveness that, even to sympathetic eyes, made McKinley's patience and tenderness seem superhuman.

Those who refuse to credit the possibility of a lifelong romance can find an element of anxiety in McKinley's attentiveness to Ida. He was apprehensive about her whenever they were parted. Strangers were startled by the alacrity with which he sprang to his feet at her summons. In an established ritual at Columbus, the Governor turned each morning as he entered the Capitol grounds to salute Mrs. McKinley's window; and punctually at three every afternoon he suspended the business of Ohio for a ceremony of handkerchief-waving between his office and the hotel. But to elaborate the factor of compunction is to obscure the basic truth that McKinley idolized his wife. After twenty years of this marriage, he ardently signed a letter, "Your faithful Husband and always your lover." Ida's most trivial concerns

Dec 11 1896

My darling wife —

I received your message this morning announcing your safe arrival at Chicago which gave me great comfort. I wired you this morning and have no doubt you received my despatch. This day has been very much like all the days since the Election many — many visitors. I guess they are done for the day. Everything is going on pleasantly here, but you are greatly missed I assure you. I hope you will keep well & come back greatly benefitted and have that part of your wardrobe provided which was your special mission. Please give Mary & Sofie & the boys my love & believe me

Your faithful Husband
and always your lover

W. McKinley

McKinley's ardent letter to his wife was written while she was on a shopping trip to Chicago. He joined her there a few days later.

engaged his interest. To her dresses and her jewelry and even to the problems of her fancy-work, he brought an enthusiasm too glowing to be feigned. There was keen anticipation in his appeal to Mrs. Herrick for a half yard of cambric and a steel needle for making tidies, and "a little piece of a stripe" of a crochet pattern, which Ida had "not yet mastered." When Mr. and Mrs. Storer first met the faded cripple, McKinley eagerly told them, "Ida was the most beautiful girl you ever saw," adding, "She is beautiful to me now." McKinley's friends naturally resented the tyranny of his marriage, but Ida was the center of his emotional life. With all its disadvantages, this was a union of deep intimacy and tenderness.

Paradoxically, Ida had broadened McKinley's capacity for enjoyment and made him socially more adaptable. Her taste for luxury softened the austerity of his early training. He learned to admire laces and to select pretty pieces of jewelry. He grew extravagantly fond of flowers, preferring a brilliant pink carnation to Ida's favorite, the rose. McKinley lost his early rigorous insistence on total abstinence. He cared nothing for drinking, but he permitted wine to be served at his table, and occasionally took a glass on festive occasions. Ida's lessons in cribbage and euchre led him into many lively contests with the Herricks and other friends. Ida introduced her husband to musicales and also to the drama. She was fond of the theater, and did not suffer there from the crowds and confinement that prevented her from attending church. As governor, McKinley frequently took his wife to the Cleveland Opera House, where a box was always placed at their disposal by the owner, Mark Hanna. They met many famous stars of the touring stock companies, and became especially friendly with Joseph Jefferson. According to Hanna, McKinley enjoyed Shakespeare, and conscientiously "read up" before attending the performances. But his favorite plays were *Rip Van Winkle* and *The Cricket on the Hearth*, which he saw again and again with Jefferson in the lead. McKinley also greatly enjoyed Roland Reed's "hits" in *The Politician*, which was given in Cleveland during his second campaign for governor.

In their private life, the McKinleys had developed a comfortable identity of habit. Both were sound sleepers, liking long nights of rest, and hearty eaters of plain food, putting away army breakfasts of fruit, coffee, eggs, hot breads, potatoes, steak or chops, and sometimes fish. Their solitary evenings were often spent at cribbage. Ida was a petulant and bad-tempered loser, but McKinley reveled in her skill. Pleasure trips always found Ida packed and ready. She was a good traveler and a willing guest, at home anywhere. McKinley grew increasingly dependent on the daily outing of Ida's drives, as age and weight disinclined him to ride. Their love of children was a great bond. A gesture of affection was all that Ida had to give. She dissolved in tears when she held a sleeping infant in her arms, or grew overexcited, emptying the contents of her bag of jewels on the carpet for Opha Moore's baby to play with. But Ida longed for the sight and touch of her "little friends," and was always urging people to bring them to call. The prattle and racket in the parlor were a delight to McKinley, who had a charming way with children and was happy and at ease in their company.

Ida was incapable of selfless devotion, but she gave her husband all the love she had. His career came first, and she accepted its demands on his time, even when they entailed his absence from home. She expatiated tirelessly on the theme of McKinley's goodness and greatness. With fierce loyalty, she took offense at the slightest hint of detraction, lashing out at a good friend, Will Kuhns, because he happened to speak of McKinley as a "politician," instead of a "statesman." Ida was a caustic critic of those in whom she suspected self-interest or insincerity, and Opha Moore thought her a better judge of men than McKinley. She showed an affectionate wifely solicitude in times of illness or anxiety. When McKinley lost his savings, she was insistent on placing her fortune at the disposal of his creditors. When he wanted their old home in Canton, Ida's memories mingled tenderly with his in joy and sorrow. They were like a bridal couple as they settled down again in the frame house on North Market Street.

Before leaving Columbus, McKinley told a reporter that he was looking forward to his return to private life "with the pleasure of a schoolboy preparing for a vacation." The Republican National Convention was looming up in June, and McKinley was busy with conferences and correspondence; but he found leisure hours for the pleasures of this homecoming. Its greatest satisfaction was the opportunity of seeing his mother every day. His father had died during his first term as governor, but Nancy Allison, born in 1809, the year of Lincoln's birth, was still an active woman in 1896. She had not resigned her household duties to her daughter Helen, but kept a light hand for pastry and a brisk way with the broom on her front porch. Neat and erect in her black cloak and bonnet, Mother McKinley walked to church with her arm resting lightly on William's; and, with the small, inscrutable smile of the very old, shared her son with Ida at the family gatherings. Time had not altered the mother's indomitable character, nor weakened the support that William found in her affection. She did not fuss over children; but, when James's death left two orphans in William's charge, it was his mother, not his wife, who gave them a home. McKinley was enormously fond of his wards, young James and Grace. They were often at the North Market Street house, and Pina and Marshall Barber's seven lively youngsters added to the merrymaking of the return to Canton.

The town rang with greetings to the Major, as he stopped in the street to shake hands, and dropped in to call at offices and banks and stores. Except for a handful of relatives and old friends who called McKinley "Will," the military title was the most familiar nickname that he had ever received, and it was used in Canton as the privilege and proof of long association. He was the same Major, simple and hearty, and yet there was something about him that made his cordiality a compliment. When a man's name is on the front page of a nation's newspapers, he is changed, however natural his manners. He has the gloss of authority and importance—the look of having been polished by the public gaze. McKinley's attire had become immaculate. He gave up the habit of chewing tobacco. His dignity was awe-inspiring. His noble brow evoked comparison with Daniel Webster's. To Canton, he looked every inch the presidential candidate.

Those who knew McKinley best were those who most revered him. His eminence was no more than his townsfolk had expected. Ever since his first election to Congress, people in Canton had prophesied that some day he would be President. There was only one whispered reservation—what would he do with Ida Saxton, that millstone around his neck? She was sitting in the bow window on North Market Street, as she had sat for twenty years in hotels, surrounded by comfort and supplied with service. Besides her personal maid and the good plain cook the Major had engaged, there was a colored waiter, Floyd, who took charge of running the house, and busy little Mrs. Heistand was always at her beck and call. Ida never stirred a foot except to walk to a carriage, or raised a hand for anything more useful than crocheting. She was entirely incapable of assuming the social obligations of the White House. If the McKinleys went to Washington, Canton concluded, they would have to take someone along to act as official hostess—perhaps Pina's eldest daughter Mary, who was a sweet, pretty girl, and a great favorite of both her aunt and uncle.

But the gossips had left out of account the most potent factor in the McKinleys' social arrangements—the will and pride of Ida Saxton. She had lived in semi-retirement at Columbus, putting in merely a perfunctory appearance at the Governor's official receptions, but in the last year she had given a large formal party, with dancing; and now, as she sat crocheting, she was planning to dazzle her home town with one of the most brilliant functions it had ever seen. Formal cards of invitation to a silver wedding celebration were soon scattered broadcast over Canton, Columbus, Massillon, Alliance, Akron, Youngstown, Cleveland, and even farther afield. McKinley signed a contract to pay $400 for refreshments for six hundred persons, and the caterer held himself ready to serve a hundred more. Two separate suppers were stipulated, since the limited capacity of the house necessitated dividing the reception and prolonging it until late in the evening.

All through a mild day of early February, trains disgorged the well-dressed ladies and gentlemen who formed the vanguard of the crowds that were destined for North Market Street that year. The McKinleys' walk was carpeted from the gate to the front stoop, and two locomotive head-lights were set on the lawn to illuminate the way for the evening arrivals. Under a canvas erected on the back porch, the caterer's assistants prepared the double services of a collation of chicken and lobster salads, sweets, lemonade, coffee, and claret. From three until five and again from seven until eleven, the guests passed through rooms banked in roses, carnations, and hyacinths, while an eight-piece orchestra discoursed music in the hall. At her husband's side in the bow window of the parlor, Mrs. McKinley received in her wedding gown of ivory satin and point lace, holding a great bouquet of white roses. Her face was drawn and withered, her close-cropped hair was faded; but, ghastly in the bridal finery, she smiled a gracious welcome for six hours.

Ida had made a heroic effort, and it was dictated by a heroic purpose. As must have been evident to all but the most obtuse, she had "set her head" that, if her husband became President, she was prepared to take her rightful place as First Lady at the White House.

· 2 ·
CHAMPION OF PROTECTION

MCKINLEY had entered elective office
in a spirit of dedication to the principles of the party of Lincoln. Twelve
years after the war, the basis of a Union soldier's political allegiance was already open to challenge. The doom of civil rights for the Negro was foretold in the necessity for conciliating the South. The voice of Lincoln
was drowned in the unrest of financial depression, the demand for currency inflation, the uproar against the monopolies, and the strife between
capital and labor. But McKinley's loyalty was not confused by changing
issues. He stood on the Republican platform, satisfied that its declarations
embodied the noblest expression of American patriotism and promised
the highest fulfillment of the national welfare.

During McKinley's service in Congress, scattered protests arose and
swelled that representative government had become the rule of plutocracy,
that both major parties fattened on the subsidies of business, and that
courts and legislatures bowed to the will of the corporations. These were
still the protests of the few. The danger of the relationship between government and big business was not generally apprehended, and such strictures
seemed to McKinley a passing phase of minority opinion, subversive or
misguided. As the foremost exponent of the high protective tariff, he played
a major role in leading the Republican party to its eventual identification
with the moneyed interests. He acted in the belief that he was serving all
the people by promoting American prosperity.

The national veneration for private enterprise was not proof against the
flagrant abuses of the railroads and the trusts. Appeals for their regulation
became a demand on which the Republicans felt obliged to act. McKinley

34

voted with his party to pass the first timid, though precedent-breaking measures of federal control, the Interstate Commerce and Sherman Anti-trust Acts; but his primary concern was always the encouragement, not the curtailment of business. He said very little on the question of the trusts, and obviously had not yet recognized its importance. The postwar revolution in American industry was too cataclysmic for the ready comprehension of men who had grown to maturity in a simple economy and formed their political ideas in the service of the Union. The march of the new issues left them in the rear, clinging devoutly to the standards of a bygone day. Yet Congressman McKinley was not classed with the Old Guard of reaction. Young Robert La Follette of Wisconsin, who saw much of him on the Ways and Means Committee, thought that he "represented the newer view." Within the framework of his basic, fixed beliefs, McKinley was exceedingly flexible in his opinions. His critics called him changeable and lacking in convictions, but McKinley's adaptability was a political advantage. It denoted a ready sympathy with contemporary trends which counterbalanced his rigid position on the tariff. "Of course, McKinley was a high protectionist," La Follette wrote, "but on the great new questions as they arose he was generally on the side of the public against private interests."

McKinley's supreme political talent was his identification with the people. In a time of ferment and transition, Americans longed for a voice of resolute affirmation which would appease their qualms of conscience and assure them that they were the noblest, as they were fast becoming the richest people in the world. This was the voice with which McKinley spoke, not only to the wealthy and privileged few, but to the rank and file of Republicans, small manufacturers and merchants, farmers and workingmen. In brain and heart, he was himself the average middle-class American, abounding in optimism, proud of the national efficiency and enterprise; respectful of self-made success, and pious in devotion to the past. It was the faith of the fathers that McKinley invoked in every crisis; and in nothing was he more typical of his countrymen than in his willingness to turn that faith to the cause of material betterment.

Congress was the school of McKinley's education. It made him a pre-eminently "practical" politician, always ready to concede and take as much as it was possible to get. "We cannot always do what is best," he once told a gathering of his comrades at Canton, "but we can do what is practical at the time." A deliberate man with infinite resources of patience, he was content to progress by easy stages toward the millennium. Some private legerdemain must have reconciled him to the "practical" methods that were employed. The struggles in the "dusty arena" of Ohio were notorious. Medieval knight or not, McKinley fought shoulder to shoulder with highly irregular partisans. He scrupulously shunned the bribe and the bargain, but his purity must have involved an intricate self-deception, a timely looking away and convenient forgetfulness.

Political life confirmed McKinley in an excessive cautiousness. The inner minds of few public men have been so well concealed. He left almost no personal papers. He rarely wrote a private letter. Apart from his public utterances, the record of the spoken word is small. He sometimes obscured his views by a fog of phraseology, conventional or oracular. Often in private conversation, it seems that he merely listened sympathetically. People, convinced that he agreed with them, were at a loss to remember what he had said. Even his intimates frequently had to guess what he was thinking. Yet McKinley did not seem an enigma to the men who knew him. Everyone found it easy to describe his simple character. Many people called him pliant and amiable. Close associates were surprised to learn that he always contrived to have his way. A very few saw stubborn, secret strength.

All the circumstances of McKinley's youth had favored his adherence to the Republican principle of the protective tariff. The very village of his birth had been named for Hezekiah Niles, an early protectionist. The duty on foreign iron had not been an abstract idea to an ironfounder's son, but the source of bread and butter, and memories of want rang in McKinley's phrases when he spoke of the low-tariff years of his boyhood. His early opinions had been confirmed by the miners and farmers and workingmen with whom he dealt as a lawyer. Stark County was rich in both iron ore and coal. It had many flocks of sheep, and more than half a million pounds of wool came annually to the Canton market. Canton had also become a center for the manufacture of agricultural machinery, producing more reapers and mowers than any other town in the United States. Protection blessed these industries with high prices and good wages, brisk trade and plentiful employment. On a rural and small-town scale, McKinley had seen at first hand that the enrichment of the few trickled down to shower welfare on the mass. He carried to Congress an emotional conviction that the solution for all the country's economic ills was to make the already high tariff rates still higher.

The object of the radical wing of the Republican protectionists was to prevent all competition of foreign goods with native products. Their doctrine held that the United States should live entirely within itself, aloof economically as well as politically from foreign entanglements. The "American nationalism" that McKinley was eager to preach was an extreme expression of isolationism. In the years that followed the Civil War, the slogan of "America for Americans" rang with the overtones of sacred traditions and inherited prejudices. Absorbed in the final settlement of its frontiers and the colossal expansion of its business, the country retained the isolationist sentiments of a small agricultural republic, remote, self-sufficient, and distrustful of the nations of the Old World. In the oratory of the high protectionists, Great Britain was still the arch-enemy, with her policy of free trade, her cheap labor and low-priced commodities, and her big American market for iron and steel, wool, china, glass, and a long list of other items. Though McKinley was too reasonable and temperate to become a demagogue, his diatribes against foreign importations, and against the products of British industry in particular, were appeals to popular prejudice.

The combination of a narrow patriotism and zeal for the home market strongly commended itself to conservative businessmen, but in McKinley's first years in Congress the prevailing tendency of the Republican party was toward a downward revision of the tariff. There was a general weariness of the high wartime rates, and the popular resurgence of the Democratic party had led many Republicans to adopt a moderate stand on the issue. The Treasury was disturbed by revenues vastly in excess of the national expenditures. Some forward-looking businessmen were saying that American products needed outlets overseas. The hard times of the seventies and eighties discredited the panacea of protection, and the sleepy public conscience was stirred by the propaganda against the trusts. McKinley's biennial campaigns in Ohio were arduous and often uncertain of outcome. A Democratic legislature twice gerrymandered the state, forcing McKinley to fight against heavy odds in a new district. On home ground in 1882, he faced such effective opposition that he was returned by a perilously narrow margin, and was eventually, by a party vote, unseated. McKinley's fourteen years in the House suffered a break of a little more than the short session of one Congress, but the interruption did not impede his steady rise to prominence.

When McKinley entered the House, as for the greater part of his time there, the Democrats were in the majority in the lower chamber. The obscure Republican congressman had had to work for recognition. After being overlooked for more than a year for important committee assignments, McKinley attracted attention by his first set speech on the tariff, so closely reasoned and studded with statistics that it served as a reference for Republican speakers in future. His friendship with Hayes was of no help in his apprenticeship, for the President did not command the support of the leaders of the Congress. On the currency issue, moreover, McKinley openly differed from the administration. He was constant to the gold standard, as implied in the resumption of specie payment for greenbacks, a Republican policy which was put in operation under the aegis of Hayes and his Secretary of the Treasury, John Sherman. But McKinley followed a strong inflationary drift on silver, voting for free coinage and then for the limited issues of the Bland-Allison Bill; and, when Hayes vetoed the measure, McKinley cast his vote with the majority that passed the act over the veto. No party irregularity was involved. The Republicans were divided and uncertain on the money controversy, and for many years to come would seek to reconcile it by keeping one foot on the gold standard and the other in the silver camp.

Beyond his votes for inflation, McKinley took small interest in the involved financial subject. He plugged industriously at the tariff, and after three years his concentration was rewarded by a place on the Ways and Means Committee, for which Garfield recommended him on his own nomination for the Presidency. The appointment introduced McKinley to the practice of his specialty. The hasty tariff legislation that the Republicans enacted in 1883 was a disappointing compromise, but the experience enriched McKinley's education. He became expert in adjusting the minute details of schedules that closed loopholes for foreign intrusion. He learned the subtle art of preparing a bill that raised the rates while giving a conciliatory appearance of reducing them. McKinley's days were spent among the lobbyists who fell like locusts on Washington, thronging the Capitol, and sitting in committee rooms and offices; and by evening he entertained the persistent supplicants who came to catch his private ear. Every industry was arrayed against the others, and each was divided by its own internecine feuds—flock masters against woolen manufacturers, planters of cane and beets against sugar refiners. The party duels in committee were rehearsals for the performance on the floor, and McKinley developed a lively skill in debate. His aptness in retort and exact illustration gave him something of a boxer's speed in sparring, and his sallies of irony at the expense of Democratic policies often caused hearty merriment on the Republican side. Apart from the coterie of his greatest admirers, McKinley was not generally regarded as a man of quite the first rank, either in brains or leadership. Cynical politicians smiled at his ingenuous belief in patriotic and party platitudes. He had the reputation of being diplomatic rather than forceful, anxious to avoid giving offense, and careful to keep a weather eye on the trend of public opinion. Yet McKinley had authority and a curious emotional power. "McKinley was a magnetic speaker," La Follette wrote; "he had a clear, bell-like quality of voice, with a thrill in it. He spoke with dignity, but with freedom of action. The pupils of his eyes would

38

dilate until they were almost black, and his face, naturally without much color, would become almost like marble—a strong face and a noble head. When interrupted either in a speech or debate, instead of seeking to put his man at a disadvantage . . . he sought to win him. He never had a harsh word for a harsh word, but rather a kindly appeal: 'Come now, let us put the personal element aside and consider the principle involved.'"

As a hard-working Republican regular, McKinley had won favor in the party's national councils, and at the convention of 1884 he was a member of the resolutions committee, reporting the platform and briefly occupying the chair. But he was still little known to the country, when in 1888 his advancement was fortuitously accelerated by the action of President Cleveland. Alarmed by the swollen surplus in the Treasury, Cleveland had devoted his third annual message exclusively to an assault on the protective tariff. This unprecedented emphasis centralized the issue, uniting the Republicans and making support of the high tariff the touchstone of party loyalty. In obedience to the President's instructions, the Ways and Means Committee prepared a moderate tariff measure, which was assailed in the minority report as "a radical reversal of the tariff policy of our government." The indignant protest of the Republican members had been largely written by McKinley, and in the ensuing debate he rose to national reputation as the champion of protection.

McKinley was ready to answer the knock of opportunity. The authority of factual information reinforced the earnestness of the long address in which he besought the maintenance of the policy that had brought the country a marvelous prosperity; and, in the name of every category of citizens, pled that America should not be made the dumping ground of foreign products. A close scrutiny of the bill had acquainted McKinley with every chink of weakness and inconsistency. His speech was hot with spirited, demolishing attack and the taunts of sarcasm and ridicule. He even made use of a theatrical trick, which was entirely out of character, and which accomplished nothing but to rock the Republicans and the galleries with laughter and applause. In making the point that the tariff on woolen goods did not raise the price of clothing, he seized and tore open a bundle on his desk; and, snatching out a coat, vest, and pair of trousers, he waved them, with the bill of ten dollars for their purchase, at Leopold Morse of Massachusetts, the Democratic congressman and clothier at whose shop the suit had been sold. This unique departure from a correct forensic demeanor was evidence of the excited feeling to which McKinley had been stirred by the President's indictment, and especially by the connection between the tariff and the trusts that was a ringing challenge in both the message and the debate. These "vicious assaults" were new to McKinley. He urged that the "unnatural associations" should be crushed, but his comments on the question were feeble and naïve. He vehemently denied the responsibility of the tariff, instancing the oil and whisky trusts, and accused the President and his party of seeking to array class against class. He finished off the trusts by denouncing them in the worst terms in his vocabulary—they were foreign, originating in free-trade countries.

Although McKinley's reputation as a fair and pleasant adversary survived the great debate on the Mills Bill, he did not make his mark by sweet reasonableness alone. He was a partisan in 1888. He privately admired Cleveland's stubborn and courageous character, and esteemed the honesty of many of his Democratic colleagues, but he did not hesitate to impugn the motives of their "British policy," nor to accuse the President of dispensing official favors on its behalf. McKinley declared on the floor of the House that the Democratic measure had been inspired by importers and foreign producers, most of them aliens. The next month, in reporting the Republican platform at the national convention in Chicago, he voiced still more vehement accusations, stating that the proposal to destroy the American system of protection had been made "at the joint behest of the whiskey trust and the agents of foreign manufacturers."

McKinley was chairman of the Resolutions Committee at Chicago. The Republican platform contained an uncompromising declaration for protection, favoring the entire repeal of the internal revenue taxes, if necessary, rather than the surrender of any part of the tariff system. The party of Lincoln was not bound to the chariot of the corporations without dissenting murmurs. Mr. Joseph Medill, the proprietor of the low-tariff Chicago *Tribune*, represented a large section of Republican opinion when he grumbled to Senator Cullom of Illinois that, if the party lost the election, McKinley would be the cause. "About two thousand millionaires run the policies of the Rep. party and make its tariffs," Medill wrote. "Whatever duties protect the two thousand plutocrats is protection to American industries. Whatever don't is free trade."

In spite of the murmurs, the high-tariff trend had swept the Republican convention of 1888. Freshly crowned with the laurels of the great debate, the "young Napoleon" of protection was a marked man, greeted with cheers. Four years before, he had worked for the presidential nomination of James G. Blaine, the plumed knight, whose lance had been broken by Grover Cleveland. This year, McKinley was pledged by state instructions and personal commitment to support Senator John Sherman, the brother of the Union general, the leader of the Ohio Republicans, and the party's elder statesman. It was truly said of Sherman that his record was the record of the Republican party. He had been active in its first organization in his state, entering the House of Representatives six years before the Civil War, and elected to the Senate before the fall of Sumter. As chairman of the Committee on Finance and as Hayes's Secretary of the Treasury, he had become the foremost Republican authority on financial questions. He was a figure of immense and cold prestige, admired but not beloved, and at the two preceding conventions he had failed to receive the nomination he coveted as the reward for his long service. But in 1888 he was the favorite contender in a somewhat dull collection of aspirants, and his supporters were confident of success, if a movement to Blaine could be forestalled. Blaine had positively refused to run again, but his name hung over the convention like a magnet that pulled attention from the field of the actual candidates. Although his earlier leadership had alienated many Republicans, he had kept a vociferously loyal following. The strategy of his backers was to scatter their strength in opposition to Sherman on the early ballots, and then stampede the convention. It was widely conjectured that a dark horse might win the race.

In this uncertain situation, a particularly intense scrutiny was directed on the Ohio delegation. It was simmering with disaffection under its instructions for Sherman, with a strong Blaine sentiment ready to blow off the lid; and, by way of complication, Ohio was eager for representation on the national ticket, and two of her younger men, McKinley and Foraker, had been mentioned for either first or second place. In glitter of personality, the Congressman was outshone by the impetuous Cincinnati lawyer who headed the Ohio delegation. Joseph B. Foraker—"Fire Alarm Joe"—was serving his second term as governor of the state. He was a stirring orator, scoffing and sarcastic, with a hair-trigger temper that vibrated to the tips of his mustache; and he was an aggressive partisan and waver of the bloody shirt, who had gained country-wide publicity by his defiance of President Cleveland's request for the return of captured Confederate battle flags. Incidentally, Foraker was a shrewd politician. As governor, he had built a strong personal machine. Though he had given Sherman a solemn promise of support, he was not entirely trusted by Sherman's friends.

The Senator's campaign manager and financial backer was a Cleveland millionaire named Marcus Alonzo Hanna, who had become influential in the Ohio Republican party as a donor and solicitor of funds. He had an itch for political power exercised behind the scenes through association with prominent public men. Foraker had attracted him. Hanna had sought Foraker's friendship, showered him with attentions, and aided him with money in his second campaign. For various reasons, including fric-

41

tion over the patronage, Hanna's feeling had somewhat cooled before the convention. The Governor, for his part, felt slighted because he had not been fully consulted on the convention strategy, and had been asked merely to second Sherman's nomination. He had been quick to suspect that, in case of an upset, the Sherman people would throw their weight to McKinley as their second presidential choice.

Whether Foraker's adherence to Sherman had been perfidious all along, or whether he was merely an impulsive opportunist, he soon came to feel that the state endorsement was a burden. The early balloting disclosed that Sherman was fatally weak. Signs of backing for McKinley verified Foraker's jealous suspicions. A rumor swept the convention that Blaine had consented to run. Foraker at once gave out a statement that he and most of the Ohio delegation would vote for Blaine, since Sherman's case was hopeless and they were honorably absolved from further obligation. The convention was shocked into accusations of treachery, which were echoed in Ohio; and, on the arrival of another refusal from Blaine, Foraker backtracked to Sherman. He rejected offers of support from the Blaine faction for his own presidential candidacy, but he could not undo the damage of his temporary bolt, nor erase the impression that he had acted from a double motive of self-interest and a desire to hurt McKinley's chances.

Meanwhile, McKinley had pursued a different course. With an earnestness that could not be questioned, he denied to all comers that he would permit his name to be placed in nomination. He detested the intrigues by which the state bosses tried to control conventions. A witness asserted that McKinley dismissed emissaries from the New York boss, Tom Platt, with "violent profanity." Though the statement was surely exaggerated, it indicates outspoken indignation at the overtures of the machine. In spite of his denials, McKinley still received a few ballots. As they persisted, he interrupted the roll call to address the convention. In the name of his loyalty to the state he loved, his fidelity to John Sherman, and his personal integrity, he asked—he demanded—that no delegate should cast a further ballot for him. He had climbed on a chair to speak. His manner was agitated, and deep feeling accentuated the pallor of his face. In the sincerity of his words and bearing, there was something of old-fashioned honor, which moved the seasoned politicians and newspaper correspondents in the convention hall. An upsurge of sentiment for McKinley, stronger than the evidence of a continued scattering of votes, was remarked among the delegations before the convention settled down, amid rumors of a deal with Tom Platt, to the prosaic but respectable choice of General Benjamin Harrison of Indiana.

McKinley was not as clever as Foraker, but he emerged from the convention of 1888 with a vastly higher reputation. Not the least important result of his conduct was its effect on Hanna. He had dedicated himself, heart and pocketbook, to the aging Sherman's interests, but now he needed a new star to which to hitch his wagon. In the words of his brother-in-law, James Ford Rhodes, Hanna "decided no longer to put his money on the wrong horse." The events of the convention had permanently estranged him from the mettlesome Foraker, and drawn him into intimate relations with McKinley. Hanna liked a man who stuck to a bargain, and he admired the high-minded way in which McKinley had done it. Under a hard-boiled exterior, Hanna had a sentimental heart, with a big capacity for hero worship.

The Democrats renominated Cleveland, and the tariff was the foremost issue in the election of 1888. With Harrison and high protection on their banners, the Republicans won a victory that was effective, if not overwhelming. When the Fifty-first Congress assembled in December of 1889, the party controlled the national government, the Executive office and both branches of the legislature, for the first time in sixteen years. McKinley was a candidate for the Speakership of the House. It was his good fortune to lose. He once admitted in later years that he had never been so anxious for success as in that campaign—and added that, if he had been elected Speaker, he would probably have remained a member of Congress from Ohio.

In the contest, McKinley faced a powerful opponent, Thomas Brackett Reed of Maine, the recognized leader of the House Republicans and the greatest parliamentarian of his day. To a formidable partisanship, Reed brought the wealth of an original and well-furnished mind. He was widely read and traveled, and kept a diary in French; and the force and range of his intelligence won the admiration of his colleagues, and made him the idol of such highbrows as the cultured, fox-hunting congressman from Massachusetts, Henry Cabot Lodge. But Reed, like many intellectuals, had a vein of sadism that provoked fear and sullen enmity. He was unsparing in his caustic sneers, and he was endowed with wit, a gift as dangerous as it is rare in American politics. "Everybody enjoys Reed's sarcastic comments and keen wit," McKinley once remarked, "except the fellow who is the subject of his satire."

McKinley would have made an admirably fair and diplomatic moderating officer; but in 1890 the House Republicans stood in need of a Speaker who was bold and uncompromising. Under the outworn rules by which the body was governed, a minority had the power to block the public business—an advantage to the Republicans in their lean years, but a restraint that now consigned their narrow majority to impotence. These rules had been a target for Reed's attack. He had the aggressiveness and the parliamentary resource to modify them. Popularity was pitted against these qualifications, and in the end popularity lost. Though McKinley had made no direct effort on his own behalf, Mark Hanna had come to Washington to lend his aid in the last week of the canvass. McKinley concealed his sore disappointment, and made light of his defeat. As the leading contestant, he received from Reed the chairmanship of the Ways and Means Committee, and became the majority leader on the floor of the House. Joseph G. Cannon of Illinois, another aspirant to the Speakership, was made chairman of the Appropriations Committee. McKinley and Cannon were also appointed members of the powerful Committee on Rules, and with Reed formed a triumvirate that controlled the House in the Fifty-first Congress.

McKinley was Reed's faithful ally, supporting him at every point of peremptory innovation. Reed shut off filibustering with a high hand that earned him the epithet of "Czar." The Republicans rallied to support his controversial rulings and push through their big program. The session was the longest but one that had ever been held in the history of national legislation. McKinley would proudly remember that this was a Congress with convictions, a Congress that "did things," but the public regarded its unusual activity with more apprehension than approval. The compromise legislation of the Sherman Silver Purchase Act antagonized both free-coinage and sound-money men. There was general disgust at the plunder of the Treasury for Grand Army pensions. The provisions of a new tariff act alarmed the country with the threat of rising prices. The tariff had become a hazardous issue for both parties, a third rail that it had proved politically fatal to touch. The radical schedules of the McKinley Bill were primarily responsible for a widespread revulsion against Republican ascendancy in "the Billion Dollar Congress."

The chairmanship of the Ways and Means Committee was McKinley's opportunity to direct the preparation of a bill that embodied the doctrine of protection in its purest form. The McKinley Bill, as the tariff legislation of 1890 was known to the country, was entitled "an act to reduce the revenue." The tariffs on raw sugar and molasses were entirely remitted for the purpose of cutting off between $50,000,000 and $60,000,000 of the Treasury's annual income at one clip, while a bounty for the compensation of the American sugar planters provided for the yearly expenditure of six or seven millions more. The internal revenue tax on tobacco was reduced. Duties were slightly lowered on products that had ceased to be

44

of central importance to the protective system; and, with the admitted intention of further shearing the revenue through tariffs prohibitive to importations, high rates were maintained, raised, or initiated on all manufactured commodities that were subject to foreign competition. The lobbies, in effect, wrote their own schedules. In the extreme view on which the Republicans of the House had become united, the old rationale of fostering infant industries was lost in the assumption that the government of the United States should be the nurse of giants, and, by a still more radical extension of the protective principle, of infants conceived but still unborn. McKinley had lent a willing ear to the propagandists for the American manufacture of tin plate, which was imported in large quantities from Great Britain, and a heavy impost was levied on behalf of a nonexistent industry.

When McKinley presented the bill in the spring of 1890, he was acutely conscious of its vulnerability to the opposition's criticism, but he gave no evidence of having considered its effect on the general public. In spite of the many duties on hitherto untaxed articles of everyday use, the bill had one tremendous claim to popular approval. The tariff on sugar had long been a heavy grievance to the American consumer, and its removal could have been advertised as a blessing to every household in the land. McKinley did not avail himself of his best talking point. In the course of a dry and rather extenuatory argument, he merely read off "sugar up to and including No. 16 Dutch standard in color," toward the end of the alphabetical roster of articles placed on the free list, which included acorns, beeswax, dandelion roots, and olive oil unfit for eating.

McKinley threw away an advantage that could never be regained. The sugar schedule was extremely vulnerable to attack. It retained a sufficiently high tariff on refined sugar to safeguard the enormous profits of the sugar trust, and the provision of a bounty for the domestic producers was an unprecedented handout to a special industry. In the debate, McKinley and his supporters were forced on the defensive, and the boon of free sugar was lost in the uproar.

McKinley had adhered to this schedule in the face of internal party division. It was disliked by many protectionists, and especially opposed by the Republican trade expansionists, who were acutely concerned over the deterioration of American commerce with the Latin American countries, which had enacted high retaliatory duties on American products. The farmers were crying for new markets for their superabundant wheat and other crops, and industrialists were beginning to anticipate the same need for the surplus output of mills and factories. The situation had stimulated interest in the policy of commercial reciprocity, fitfully tried by the government, but at this time in operation only in the case of Hawaii. The plan of agreements for the exchange of tariff concessions in the Western Hemisphere was hampered by the tendency of Republican legislation to remove the duties on the raw materials which furnished the main American bargaining points. Coffee, hides, and other imports had already been placed on the free list before the McKinley Bill capped the climax by abolishing the duty on sugar.

The most prominent advocate of reciprocity was Blaine, whom Harrison had appointed Secretary of State. The sessions of the first Pan-American Conference had been in progress at Washington, with Blaine in the chair, during the months when the McKinley Bill was being framed. Blaine had insistently but vainly pressed his objections to the sugar clause on the Republican members of the Ways and Means Committee. He finally turned to the expedient of an amendment that would leave a loophole for concessions, and sent two emissaries to the House committee to explore the possibility of compromise. One of them, John W. Foster, held a number of conferences with McKinley, discussing at length the whole question of reciprocity, to which he remarked that the Congressman had given very little consideration. Foster said that "it was understood" that McKinley favored Blaine's plan, but McKinley's presentation of his tariff bill left no doubt that he did not mean to have it cluttered with arrangements for lowering the rates, and resented the pressure that the Secretary of State had attempted to exert.

McKinley in 1890 could no longer ignore the question of American commerce overseas. Only two years earlier, he had dismissed foreign markets for agricultural products as "one of the delusions of free trade." His speech now abounded in elaborate references to the subject. McKinley treated foreign trade as politely as though it had been a cantankerous member of the opposition. He said that we were proud of it, and that it was of great value and must be sacredly guarded, and that it had always flourished under the protective tariff. But he also spoke with some acerbity of "the croaking about foreign trade" and its "peculiar sanctity," and alluded with suspect courtesy to "the illustrious man who presides over the State Department." McKinley said that America had always been the loser whenever reciprocity had been tried. He was not going to discuss the question. He would leave it to the illustrious man. "This is a domestic bill," McKinley asserted; "it is not a foreign bill." This was the only address in which McKinley ever referred sarcastically to a Republican.

McKinley did not know in early May, as he learned in the weary months ahead, that provisions for reciprocity were to form a part of the tariff act. Blaine, backed by President Harrison, urged the question on the Finance Committee of the Senate, and at length made public a letter that glowingly described the advantage of trade concessions to the farmer. The idea caught on, and in the resultant chorus of approval the Finance Committee wrote in the proviso for which Blaine asked, along with more than 460 other amendments. As finally accepted in conference, the McKinley Bill contained the larger part of the Senate's alterations.

Since the American government lacked the basis for negotiation by concession, the reciprocity arrangements took a negative form, comprising a threat rather than an offer. The President was empowered to impose retaliatory duties on the products of any country that, in his opinion, levied unjust tariffs on the exports of the United States. Some Republicans argued on constitutional grounds against awarding the Executive such large discretion, but protests soon withered in the sunshine of the farmers' enthusiasm. The reciprocity principle became sound party doctrine, a new embellishment of the protective system.

McKinley never again scoffed at trade agreements. The people wanted them. The party had gone on record for them. But his natural soreness over the successful raid on the tariff must have been aggravated at first by the great popularity of the agreements and the boastful claims of the Blaine adherents. More than a year after the bill passed, the assertion of a Republican senator that it had been put through only with Blaine's help brought McKinley a letter from Tom Reed. "Your bill floated by the buoyancy of the support of Blaine!" Reed wrote. "Well this is rather delightful. As I remember it Blaine supported you on that part of his knife which was in your back!" McKinley must have been grateful for Reed's sympathy. Though they later became estranged, he always kept a copy of that letter.

The Senate had taken all summer to pass the McKinley Bill. It was long delayed by the recalcitrance of the Republican senators from six newly created states of the Far West, who made silver-purchase legislation the price of their support of the tariff. The bill went to conference in September, and was signed by the President in October. Just one month before the congressional elections, the act was immediately put in operation, except for the sugar and tin-plate sections.

The bare threat of the new rates had been sufficient excuse for sharp traders to mark up their goods. Prices continued to mount long before the effect of the tariff could be felt, and regardless of whether or not it would increase the cost of the merchandise. Fair weather for Democratic candidates was the promise of the polls, while the Republicans fumbled with the slogan "Bill McKinley and the McKinley Bill." The name of the champion of protection had become a household word, but it did not yet appear that he had been lucky to lose the Speakership contest and rise to prominence as the author of the tariff.

McKinley's only respite from the Washington summer had been two hurried trips to Ohio, to attend the funeral of his sister, Anna, and to sound the issues in a speech at Massillon. With ten months of killing work behind him, he went back to begin a belated campaign for re-election. The Democrats for a third time had gerrymandered the state, confronting McKinley with such a large adverse majority that the handicap was widely and harshly rebuked. He set out with dogged determination to conquer his hostile district, slogging day and night over muddy wagon roads, snatching a few hours' sleep in the cabooses of freight trains. The Democrats countered with energetic opposition and some use of unfair tactics. Peddlers were hired to frighten the farmers with tin cups at twenty-five cents and coffee pots at a dollar and a half. McKinley made converts among his country audiences, but not enough to save him from going down in the Republican debacle in November.

On election night, in the dim and deserted campaign headquarters in Canton, the candidate sat with George Frease, the editor of the *Repository*. "In the time of darkest defeat," McKinley told his friend, "victory may be nearest." Adversity moved him to a more exalted confidence and, in the editorial he penned that night for the newspaper, to a more eloquent expression than he usually commanded. "Protection was never stronger than it is at this hour," McKinley wrote. ". . . Passion and prejudice, ignorance and willful misrepresentation are masterful for the hour against any great public law. . . . Increased prosperity, which is sure to come, will outrun the maligner and the vilifier."

The injustice of the gerrymander and McKinley's gallant fight were the theme of the Republican newspapers of Ohio. They declared that his campaign had made him the next governor, and their praise and prophecy were echoed by the party press outside the state. Amid acclaim for his moral victory, McKinley took his wife to Chicago on vacation. One day at the Grand Pacific Hotel, he met two fellow victims of the Democratic landslide, Joe Cannon of Missouri and Thomas H. Carter of Montana. Cannon listened while the others made light of their defeat. McKinley said that "upon the whole he was really glad that it happened that way." "That is what I am saying to everyone," Cannon retorted, "but, boys, don't let's lie to one another."

Cannon's quip was widely repeated—Carter dined out on it for years—but it does not appear that in McKinley's case he was altogether right. Defeat by fraud, it was stated, had made McKinley a far greater power than election would have done. The losing candidate and his friend, Mr. Hanna, were satisfied with the outcome. "I agree with you," McKinley wrote to Hanna from Chicago, "that defeat under the circumstances was for the best." A postscript added, "There is no occasion for alarm. We must take no backward step."

Cannon belonged to the coterie of congressmen who liked McKinley in rather a condescending way. He once said that McKinley kept his ear to the ground so close that he got it full of grasshoppers. Like a lot of other smart politicians, Joe Cannon did not guess how carefully this transparently simple congressman was laying his plans to capture the highest office of all.

• 3 •

REPUBLICAN SUCCESS STORY

THE roll of the drums of public opinion was reverberant on the tariff. It told McKinley that, for the time being, the protectionist leader was better away from Washington. At the end of the short session of the Fifty-first Congress, McKinley would be out of office. The governorship of Ohio offered an ideal waiting post, but he was not immediately responsive to the movement for his nomination. He did not want to risk a second defeat in his home state.

Although Ohio was dependably Republican in the presidential elections, it was given to Democratic tantrums in off years, and the convention of 1888 had laid open a deep factional split in the Republican party. Foraker, practicing law in Cincinnati, was only technically out of politics. His furious grudge at Hanna and others of the Sherman group made him bad-tempered and perverse. McKinley had kept out of the quarrel, but the winter passed before he was assured of united support for his candidacy. In the spring, he called on Foraker and asked him to make the nominating speech. McKinley was honored at banquets at Cincinnati and Cleveland. He then returned to the East to address a number of other large banquets, and did not definitively return to Ohio for two months after the adjournment of Congress. At the Ohio Republican Convention in June, Foraker outdid himself in rousing oratory, and Major William McKinley, Junior, was nominated by acclamation.

Behind the scenes of the campaign moved the Cleveland millionaire who wanted vicarious power. Hanna's natural aptitudes had been whetted in 1888 by his experience as a member of the Republican National Committee, under the chairmanship of Senator Matthew S. Quay, the boss of Pennsylvania. Harrison's campaign had been financed by "frying the fat" out of the manufacturers who benefited from the tariff, and Hanna had acquitted himself well in securing contributions in Ohio. Three years later, he collected a fund for McKinley on the same principle, and did not hesitate to go outside Ohio, soliciting subscriptions in Chicago and Pittsburgh to serve the long-range interests of protection. Apart from collecting money, Hanna had not much time to devote to McKinley's campaign. The ostensible unity of the Ohio Republicans was shattered by the discovery that Foraker was gunning for John Sherman's seat in the Senate, and Hanna made Foraker's discomfiture his primary concern. It was a hard battle, not conclusively won until Hanna fought out the last skirmishes in Columbus the next winter.

McKinley, meanwhile, had got himself comfortably elected in a year of continued Republican reverses. His campaign, made solely on national issues, was closely watched by the country as a contest of more than local significance. In relation to McKinley's future, its chief interest lies in the publicity it afforded to his expressions on the question of the currency.

McKinley's flirtation with the radical inflationists had ended in his first term in Congress, but he was removed from the position of the Eastern "goldbugs" by his inland background and lack of interest in foreign trade, and by his concern for silver as an American product that was entitled to "protection." He had found a congenial middle ground in the double standard of the bimetallist system. The use of both gold and silver had been recommended in recent Republican platforms. The hope was to establish a ratio between the two metals by international agreement, but attempts to do so had failed of success. With the progressive decline in the intrinsic value of silver, Europe was drifting toward gold as the single monetary standard.

As silver sentiment swept the West, Congress had enacted a makeshift measure, the Sherman Silver Purchase Act of 1890. Though it was regarded with misgivings by most Republican leaders, including Sherman himself, McKinley had cordially commended it. The desirability of silver circulation figured so largely in his utterances at this time that a deft shift of emphasis, only a year later, had nearly the effect of a conversion. The currency was a leading issue in the Ohio campaign, and McKinley met it aggressively. In his opening speech at his birthplace, Niles, he solemnly declared, "We cannot gamble with anything so sacred as money." In a widely publicized debate with the Democratic candidate, he forcibly argued for a dollar worth one hundred cents. He did not minimize the subject of the tariff—there was no "backward step"—but he hailed the victory of the Republican ticket as the vindication of "a sound and uncorrupted currency," as well as of the protective policy.

Thus, in 1891, McKinley had improved his standing with the goldbugs; but the rapport was not to endure. Two years later, during his second gubernatorial campaign, he again sought to conciliate the silver elements. The country was in the throes of financial panic. President Cleveland blamed the Silver Purchase Act for the dwindling gold reserve in the Treasury, and called Congress in special session to repeal it. He was supported by Sherman and other leading Republicans, but McKinley's voice was raised in protest, and in dogmatic assertion that the important product, silver, "should not be discriminated against."

McKinley's utterances on the currency did not add to his reputation. Conscious that he was speaking for the record, he chose his words with care, but he always undervalued the importance of the money agitation, and showed a tendency to brush it aside, as though it were a red herring drawn across the national path to distract attention from that great clue to prosperity, the tariff. Like most Republican politicians, McKinley was trying to straddle an issue on which an increasing cleavage of opinion made compromise untenable. Though he adhered to a belief in "honest money," according to the bimetallist definition, his frequent shifts of emphasis made his statements seem inconsistent and evasive, and fully deserved the criticism that they were dictated by expediency.

During his two terms as governor, McKinley did not mention the national issues in his official papers. His inaugural address in January of 1892 was a practical and well-informed discussion of state problems, which stressed the public welfare and convenience, and struck the political gong only in condemning the gerrymander. He made no attempt to build up a personal machine, as Foraker had done, but devoted himself to his executive duties. Only during the labor outbreaks of 1894 was McKinley's work exacting. There was no friction with the legislature. The large Republican majority was in harmony with McKinley's purposes. The governor of Ohio, in any event, lacked the veto power. McKinley's administration was not especially notable, but it was competent and conscientious, and from first to last it was eminently satisfactory to the Republicans of Ohio.

The financial difficulties of the state caused McKinley, on assuming office, to enjoin economy on the legislature, and also to request authority for a study of the question of tax revision. He appointed a bipartisan commission to ascertain constitutional means for increasing the revenues without laying heavier burdens on real estate and other property that already bore its full share. The commission's report included the proposal of a franchise tax on corporations, which was embodied in a bill passed in the face of considerable opposition from the business interests. Foraker expressed indignation at the idea of assessing the property of telegraph, telephone, and express companies. Hanna worked actively to defeat the measure. The only reliable evidence of McKinley's attitude is to be found in his subsequent messages, which consistently urged further remedies for the problem. Though in the depression year of 1894 he advised a short session and little legislation, he promised a more equitable system of taxation, and a number of additional corporation taxes were imposed during his second term. In McKinley's final address to the legislature in 1896, he commended the provisions made for fairer taxation and increased revenues, and emphasized the need for still further action. The taxes levied on business organizations were extremely small, and McKinley evidently believed them to be supported by public opinion and justified by the needs of the Ohio treasury. As far as possible, he maintained a neutral position. He confined himself to generalizations, and left the rest to the tax commission and the legislature. Far from opposing the corporations, he never referred to them, except by implication.

The labor laws enacted by the legislature bore unmistakable signs of McKinley's direct influence. The acts for the protection of railroad and streetcar employees from accident and exposure responded to the suggestions of his inaugural. A bill was also passed to fine employers for preventing their workers from joining unions. McKinley took an especially keen interest in a new industrial arbitration bill, which was founded on the pioneering act of Massachusetts and closely followed recommendations that he himself had made in Congress. These early laws were chiefly important because of their recognition of the right of labor to be heard before an impartial tribunal. Compulsory arbitration was not contemplated, and there was no provision for enforcement. The Ohio act was, nevertheless, responsible for settling numerous disputes, notably in railroad and coal-mining strikes in 1894. McKinley frequently supported his efficient arbitration board by exerting his personal influence to win concessions from both sides. At his own wish, the fact of his participation was suppressed, and remained generally unknown. He had, as he wrote a Massillon newspaperman, "no desire to indulge in any pyrotechnics."

McKinley had for many years enjoyed great popularity among the workingmen of Ohio. Among the delegations that came to pledge their loyalty in his second campaign for the governorship was a group of Massillon miners, who had not forgotten his voluntary and successful defense of the strikers seventeen years before. His sympathy with the workers'

grievances was shown in his efforts for arbitration, but in the fierce industrial strife of the depression, McKinley was obliged to antagonize the
labor elements by suppressing demonstrations of riot and mob violence.
The first occasion, in the spring of 1894, was the disorder created by his
old friends, the Stark County miners, whose long and bitter strike ante-
dated and also outlasted the general strike called by the United Mine
Workers in the bituminous coal regions. Infuriated by the transit through
Ohio of coal from West Virginia, the Massillon men seized and sidetracked
trains, stoned their crews, tore up rails, and burned bridges. McKinley
was bombarded by frantic telegrams from county sheriffs, appealing to the
Governor for assistance.

The preservation of the public peace was a cardinal principle in Mc-
Kinley's code of executive responsibility, and it overbore his political
cautiousness and aversion to the use of force. He summoned John McBride,
the president of the United Mine Workers, who was directing the strike
from headquarters across from the State Capitol. "John, you have gone
too far," McKinley said. "If you don't stop it before evening, I will call
out the entire National Guard of the State to keep the railroad running."
The first detachments were ordered out that night. As the violence spread,
McKinley dispatched regiment after regiment to the disturbed areas. He
had noticed in war, he told Opha Moore, that there was no fight if a
brigade met a division. Peace was restored without bloodshed. McKinley
strictly enjoined the officers of the Guard to avoid conflict with the miners,
and there was no difficulty in controlling the militiamen, many of whom
came from workers' families. The Governor's action was applauded as
prompt and courageous. The opposition's main point of attack was his
extravagance in recklessly spending the public money to support so large
a body of troops. Like many other state executives that year, McKinley
had been forced to act in the absence of the legislature. Pending an appropriation in the next session, the banks of Ohio evidenced their confidence in the Governor by uniting to supply the funds for the payment of
the militia.

McKinley's temperate disposition toward the rioters was in some
quarters condemned. *The Chicago Herald* classed him with Altgeld, the
Populist governor of Illinois, complaining that they were both on their
knees, asking favors of "desperadoes and outlaws." The *Cleveland Plain
Dealer* remarked, "Bridge burners, train wreckers and highwaymen are
usually shot on sight." But *The Canton Repository* commented that it was
only humane to keep them from anarchy by milder means, if possible.
McKinley's home-town newspaper faithfully reflected his opinions on all
other subjects, and presumably on this one. "If some coal operators in

the craze of competition did not forget that coal miners are human beings," the *Repository* said on June 18, "the expensive coal strike might have been averted."

Ohio's labor troubles were overshadowed by the disturbances in other states, notably by the fierce outbreaks that attended the great Pullman strike in Illinois, but McKinley's administration had vivid evidence of the working-class revolt that was alarming the nation. John McBride stated in a speech at Columbus that the lawlessness of the coal strike in Ohio had been but a fraction of what might have occurred, and instanced the fact that in one region the strikers had had fourteen cannon trained on a mine. The industrial centers shivered at the furious clashes between street-car strikers and police, and the demonstrations of hungry mobs of radical-minded immigrants, Italians, Hungarians, and Poles. The most famous of the marching bands of the unemployed was the ragged column that Jacob Silica Coxey led from Massillon to Washington. Respectable citizens ridiculed Coxey's "army," once it was safely out of Ohio, but its leader did not seem quite so absurd in the autumn, when he ran for Congress on the Populist ticket and cut sharply into the Democratic vote in his district.

Coxey wanted to create projects for the unemployed and set them to work at building roads, financed by a bond issue, but this was considered a crackpot scheme by serious people. The function of government in economic crises was confined to preserving order. McKinley followed the accepted course, repeatedly sending the militia to centers of disturbance. "I do not care if my political career is not twenty-four hours long," he told one threatening group of strikers, "these outrages must stop if it takes every soldier in Ohio." His firm action was successful in keeping the peace, and in the long run it did not seriously impair his standing with labor. McKinley's continued exertions for arbitration brought him in touch with union representatives, who were convinced of his good will. He privately contributed to relief funds for both unemployed and strikers, and officially sent carloads of provisions to the destitute miners of the Hocking Valley. The industrial warfare that followed the panic of 1893 earned most men in public life the hatred of either conservative citizens or labor groups. McKinley, to a remarkable degree, succeeded in retaining the respect of both sides.

While McKinley was on display as a dutiful executive, his prominence was steady increasing outside his home state. The Republican convention of 1892 marked his ascent to the topmost level of national politics. He was a figure of central importance, elected permanent chairman, received with tremendous ovations, besieged by crowds of admirers. In the minds of the party leaders, McKinley was established as the strongly probable presidential candidate in 1896.

Among the delegates who assembled in June at Minneapolis, there was small enthusiasm for the Republican President. Honest, independent, grouchy old Harrison had chilled his party's loyalty with his brusque manners, and frozen it by his ingratitude. Matt Quay of Pennsylvania had met personal antagonism after his invaluable services in the national campaign. Tom Platt of New York was infuriated by what he considered the betrayal of a positive pledge to make him Secretary of the Treasury. Almost every prominent member of the party had been snubbed in seeking political favors at the Executive Mansion. Harrison had used the patronage in a highly irregular way—as it suited him to do—and there was considerable disaffection to his renomination.

The party machinery and the weight of precedent were on Harrison's side, but Mark Hanna was prepared for the off-chance of a well-developed opposition. A few days before the convention met, he went to Minneapolis and opened unofficial headquarters for McKinley at the West House. Simultaneously, an event occurred that somewhat disturbed the confidence of the compact Harrison forces. Blaine abruptly resigned. As Secretary of State, he had given the administration its greatest prestige, and rumors of his coolness toward Harrison had been discredited by his continued presence in the Cabinet. His timely resignation provided a rallying point for the anti-Harrison elements, and improved the prospect that a compromise candidate might be selected.

Mr. H. H. Kohlsaat, a Chicago newspaper proprietor who was privy to Hanna's plans, said that there was no actual intention of trying to nominate McKinley in a year that promised further Republican adversity. But the badges were ready, McKinley's name was printed on tally sheets, and Hanna spent the early days of the convention in organizing his strategy, and bargaining with the Blaine men. For the first time in four years, he brought himself to speak to Foraker, holding out the olive branch in return for a solid Ohio delegation for McKinley. It soon proved that the Blaine sentiment was not strong enough to block the drive for Harrison, and the McKinley headquarters were closed as quietly as they had been opened.

Hanna thought that, if McKinley had spoken, he would have won the support of the Blaine adherents and made inroads on the Harrison column. McKinley, however, appeared to ignore the activities on his behalf. He repeatedly affirmed his strong allegiance to Harrison, and emphatically refused to permit his own name to be used. He did not show the emotional loyalty he had given to John Sherman—McKinley, too, had been repulsed at the White House. The mention of his candidacy evoked smiling denial, not expostulation; but his attitude was irreproachably correct in maintaining the President's right to a second nomination. During the roll call, McKinley challenged Ohio's votes for himself from the chair, and insisted that his alternate's vote be changed. Harrison was nominated on the first ballot, with McKinley all but tying with Blaine for second place.

Hoarse and exhausted, McKinley drove back to the West House in the scorching heat. Outside the hotel, a crowd surrounded his carriage, and bore him into the lobby on their shoulders. The portly and circumspect Governor of Ohio was carried in dreadful embarrassment to the elevators, with one bare, gartered leg exposed. "What voice I have left is for Harrison," McKinley said, "and my heart goes with my voice." In the privacy of Mr. Kohlsaat's room, he took refuge from further demonstrations. The two men stripped to their underwear, and threw themselves on the bed. They were presently joined by another, with a fleshy, mobile, clever face and shining red-brown eyes. Kohlsaat draped the plush sofa with the top sheet from the bed, and Mark Hanna undressed and stretched himself out. For a while, the hot stillness was broken only by the tinkle of ice water and the sound of heavy breathing. "My God, William," Hanna said at last, "that was a damned close squeak." The three men lay thinking of the auguries that pointed to 1896.

No time was lost in forming long-range plans for McKinley's nomination at the next Republican convention. A reliable adherent, Charles Dick, was urged by the Governor and Hanna to accept the chairmanship of the Ohio committee, with the express purpose of ensuring the favorable trend of every local campaign in the next four years. Hanna's influence also appeared in the arrangements of the Republican National Committee for an extensive speaking tour, which made McKinley prominent on the stump from Iowa and Minnesota to Maine in the national campaign of 1892. While he said nothing publicly that hinted at his ambition, McKinley did not hesitate to declare it in sympathetic circles. During the summer, he paid a visit to his cousin, William McKinley Osborne, who had moved to Boston, where he served for a time as police commissioner, and dabbled rather ineffectually in Massachusetts politics. Osborne invited a number of prominent Republicans to a series of luncheons in McKinley's honor. Samuel L. Powers, a Boston attorney and later a member of Congress, was deeply impressed by the fatalistic confidence with which McKinley predicted his own nomination and election in 1896.

Cleveland, for the third time the Democratic candidate, had the advantage in 1892. The tariff was again the issue; and the Republicans, handicapped by a dull candidate, were fighting without much enthusiasm on the defensive. A spate of strikes damaged the protectionist appeal to the interest of the workers. At the Homestead steel mills, Henry Frick displayed capitalist management in its ugliest and most relentless light, and the bloody war was costly to the party that had written the steel schedules. Meanwhile, the mortgaged farmers of the Northwest were marching in droves from their traditional Republican allegiance, and the crusading Populist party entered the national field with free silver on their standards. Silver hung in the air with the pale light of an approaching hurricane. The Democrats were as ambiguous as the Republicans on the issue, and Cleveland was a gold man; but the balance was somewhat redressed by his running mate, Adlai E. Stevenson, a silverite from Illinois. In November, with the assistance in many states of the third-party movement, the Democrats carried the country, commanding for the first time since the Civil War a majority of both houses of Congress.

The rebuke to the Republicans was more severe than the conservatives had expected or intended. Radical notions of inflation and free trade were flaming through the Democratic party. The southern delegations in Congress were infiltrated with men whose hearts and aims were with the agrarian revolt, whose constituents were blood brothers of the western farmers. The currency problem became acute in the winter. As the gold reserve in the Treasury shrank, the flickering shadow of financial uncertainty began to fall across the country. A comparatively small business failure in Youngstown, Ohio, again brought McKinley into national prominence. There was no prestige in the publicity. The Governor of Ohio was bankrupt.

Robert L. Walker, a resident of Poland and a respected banker and manufacturer, had been McKinley's friend since boyhood. He had financed several of the early congressional campaigns, advancing cash loans which McKinley repaid from his salary. In recent years, Walker had engaged in the manufacture of goods stamped out of tin plate, and he had applied to McKinley to tide him over a temporary embarrassment by endorsing his paper for $17,000. McKinley was glad to oblige his friend. Though he was something of an easy mark, a sharper and meaner man might have found it hard to refuse. In subsequent transactions, however, McKinley was trusting to a fault. Without scrutiny or investigation, he signed the purported renewals that Walker continued to present. According to Kohlsaat, these were actually "notes in blank." Walker raised them in a desperate effort to forestall his financial collapse.

When Walker's crash came, McKinley was on his way to New York to join Mrs. McKinley, who had been undergoing a course of medical treatment. He was to speak at a banquet, and then bring his wife home.

A telegram from his Columbus office reached him as his train entered New York State. He got off, and took the first train back to Ohio. On reaching Youngstown, he learned that he was involved for sums greater than he possessed. He gave out a statement that he would pay every dollar of the paper he had signed. He had a thrifty, middle-class horror of debt, and his first thought was that he would be forced to abandon politics. He went to Cleveland, and for most of the next week remained in seclusion at Myron Herrick's house. It was an index of his mental anguish that he left it to his brother, Abner, to fetch Mrs. McKinley from New York. Hanna was away, but Mr. Kohlsaat soon arrived to offer financial help and arrange, in consultation with Herrick and other friends, to meet the immediate obligations. A telegram from Bellamy Storer, offering $10,000, was a ray of hope in McKinley's misery. Mrs. Storer was told that he cried out, "Myron, this is salvation." But the liabilities were fast proving far greater than McKinley had expected. They eventually mounted to a total of $130,000.

On Hanna's return, McKinley turned over his property for the benefit of his creditors. His wife, on her own insistence, did the same. McKinley's early investments had been well advised, and his assets at this time amounted to more than $20,000. Mrs. McKinley's fortune was estimated as worth some $70,000 at auction. Herrick, Kohlsaat, and Judge William R. Day of Canton were the Governor's trustees, while Hanna acted for Mrs. McKinley. All talk of retirement from politics was promptly silenced after Hanna came home. When Kohlsaat issued a story that the Governor would resign, McKinley gave out a statement denying it. Meanwhile, Hanna had set to work to raise a fund, obtaining most of the money in Cleveland, Chicago, and Pittsburgh. The successful lawyer Philander C. Knox was among the friends who came to McKinley's assistance, but many large donations were secured on the basis of the Governor's importance to the Republican party. The list included John Hay, Charles P. Taft, Andrew Carnegie, and Henry C. Frick. A few weeks later, the debt was paid off, and the McKinleys' property was returned to them intact.

McKinley quickly regained his poise. He had deeply felt the embarrassment of his position, but Hanna's fund was "salvation" to his career, and he was persuaded to view it in the impersonal light of political subscriptions. On the other hand, McKinley's pride was outraged by the voluntary offerings, large and small, which rained on Cleveland and Columbus. Opha Moore said that the amounts received at the Governor's office were large enough to have taken care of his entire indebtedness. McKinley returned them all. His humiliation at appearing as "a beggar" in need of public

59

charity at first induced his trustees to follow the same course, but they presently gave up the effort to stem the flood of spontaneous generosity. Five thousand donations, many of them from Democrats, were said to have been made for the payment of McKinley's debts. His trouble had awakened strong sympathy, not only for a kindly man whose trust had been betrayed, but for an honest politician who had not used public office for personal gain. The whole circumstance of McKinley's bankruptcy and the liberality of his friends became, as the Democratic *Brooklyn Eagle* later commented, "a matter of hearthstone pleasure around the land."

Bankruptcy was a commonplace in the black year of 1893, as panic spread its blight over the banks and industries, and the reiterated tale of failures on a grand scale became a monotonous din of financial collapse. The search for political omens turned an unusual interest on the Ohio elections. The storm of antipathy to "McKinleyism" had largely subsided, as the scare of rocketing prices wore off, and the advantage of cheap sugar was felt. At various Republican gatherings, notably at the banquet of the Home Market Club of Boston, McKinley had been named for the presidency. Campaigning on the national issues for his second term as governor, he confidently hammered the theme of protection while demanding justice for silver. He spoke of the tariff of 1890 as a great public measure, which had been traduced before it had had time to prove its merits, and blamed the condition of business on the "free trade" promises of the Democrats. The answer of Ohio was a thumping plurality for McKinley of 81,000 votes—the greatest Republican victory in the state since the Civil War.

Congratulatory telegrams and letters snowed the Governor's desk, hailing him as the next President. The awaited reaction had begun. McKinley's program for the next two years was to fix protection in the minds of the mass of the Republicans as the cure-all for the economic disturbances. His most serious handicap at the outset—a necessarily defensive position on the existing tariff rates—was removed when the Democrats produced a tariff of their own, amid an odorous scandal of sugar speculation on the part of senators of both parties.

The Wilson-Gorman tariff was a botch that pleased no one. Democratic insurgents in the Senate had insisted on high rates, which obliterated the principle of revision, and on duties on sugar, which caused a universal grievance. Cancellation of the reciprocity provisions disappointed the farmers; and, indeed, to many other Americans the abrogation of the existing agreements seemed to savor of partisan reprisal at home and bad faith abroad. Capitalists resented a timid levy of an income tax—a flat 2 per cent on incomes over $4,000—and Populists were outraged when the

Supreme Court declared that the tax was unconstitutional. Finally, in operation, the Wilson-Gorman Act proved ineffectual in raising revenue for the depleted Treasury.

To attain a controversial and fruitless end, the country had been harassed by uncertainty over the tariff schedules for nine months of the dreary depression year of 1894. Closed mills and factories mocked the memory of a teeming production that had seemed too vigorous to flag. Hard times traveled from the East to carry destitution to agricultural regions already impoverished by debt and drought. The whole nation was infected with distrust of the national administration. The President incurred the enduring hostility of labor by sending federal troops to quell the Pullman strike, and exasperated his estrangement from the silverites by selling government bonds for gold to a banking syndicate formed by the house of Morgan; but all classes of Americans were touched with disaffection to a regime of want, fear, and despair.

In the South and West, converts flocked to the silver advocates of both the major parties, or to the Populists, who promised both inflation and government reform. The industrial centers were hotbeds of radical agitation, as idle workmen, laid off or striking against drastic wage cuts, threatened revolt against the exploitation of the plutocrats. But hard times and Cleveland's massive unpopularity also moved men's thoughts toward the high protective tariff, which promised work and wages and a full dinner pail.

The demands for McKinley's services in the campaign of 1894 were more numerous than he could fulfill. Republican state committees vied to secure the assistance of the champion of protection. Though he lacked the gift of literary composition and the gestures of dramatic delivery, McKinley had gained an unrivaled reputation as a compelling orator. He gave a plain, commonsense talk, easily understood by anyone. He spoke positively and directly, sawing the air with his arm, or punching his clenched right fist against the open fingers of his left hand. It was his method to speak softly at first, gradually increasing the strength and resonance of his tone until he achieved a thundering climax. He often ended his sentences on a rising inflection, in the style of an inspirational preacher. McKinley's fervor was irresistible to his audiences. He was better than a spellbinder. He was a vote-getter.

The whirlwind campaign of the Governor of Ohio was a sensation of the autumn. He flashed through sixteen states, making 371 speeches. He stirred meetings of farmers who were hostile to the tariff. He electrified labor groups. In response to appeals from New Orleans, he invaded the deep South to address a huge and enthusiastic audience. The industrial cities of the East roared with applause for McKinley. In Iowa, he was obliged to speak twenty-three times in a single day. In the Populist strongholds of Nebraska and Kansas, he was received with affectionate acclaim, and children, let out of school to meet his train, brought so many offerings that the Governor's car looked like a county fair, spilling over with fruit and flowers.

McKinley's lance was ready for the Wilson-Gorman tariff. Notwithstanding its protective features, he did not hesitate to assail the "free-trade" policy of the Democrats. He presented a list of the products that had been left untaxed. He protested against the neglect of the sheep raisers. He thrust at Democratic subservience to the sugar trust. He described the Democratic slogan of open world markets as "a great free-trade shadow-dance," and at the same time condemned the destruction of the splendid trade that had been opened up with the Latin American countries under the operation of Republican reciprocity. Low-tariff men had said that the issue of protection was dead, mortally wounded by the McKinley Act, finished off by the Democrats, but their hopeful predictions were silenced in the roar of the people's cheers for "Protection, Patriotism, and Prosperity."

When the voters spoke in November, the majority in the House of Representatives was overwhelmingly reversed. Republican governors and legislatures, elected in nearly every northern state, foretold a drastic reduction of Democratic ascendancy in the Senate. Two years in advance the presidential election was plainly starred for Republican victory. Mark Hanna resigned from his coal and iron concern to make politics his business.

Early in 1895, Hanna rented a house in Thomasville, Georgia, and went to spend the winter there. The organization for McKinley's nomination had been quietly but actively at work. Charles Dick and Joe Smith had recently made a number of trips in the interest of promoting his candidacy, especially in the South. Though the states below the Mason and Dixon line could not deliver an electoral vote for the Republicans, they were fully represented at the party's national conventions on the basis of a population which included the disenfranchised Negroes. In every case, the state conventions were controlled by a small coterie. It was Hanna's idea that if he could line up these coteries for McKinley and give them a little instruction in strategy, he could be sure of securing a backlog of southern delegations well in advance of the national convention. His method of approach was novel because it was entirely social. It was arranged that the

McKinleys should pay the Hannas a three weeks' visit in March. Hanna then invited prominent Republicans from all parts of the South to meet the distinguished Governor of Ohio during his stay at Thomasville.

The social approach was not only ingratiating to the Southerners, but adapted to the wishes of the candidate. While lending himself to private mention of his presidential aspirations, McKinley refused to avow them publicly. After the campaign of 1894, he strictly limited his engagements outside Ohio. He had been greatly disturbed because newspaper correspondents had placed a "ridiculous" construction on one of his week ends with Hanna in Cleveland. He described his trip South as "a little rest and outing," and declined all invitations to make speeches during his stay in Georgia. "I cannot get the consent of my mind," McKinley wrote Colonel J. F. Hanson of Macon, "to do anything that places me in the position of seeming to seek an office and anything I might say or do would at once be interpreted as an effort in that direction. Everything looks very comfortable and anything like seeking to promote my personal interests is very distasteful to me." The visit developed in a highly satisfactory manner. Hanna's large house was suited to dispensing a freehanded hospitality, and there was a pleasant sun parlor in which the guests could relax and smoke while they talked over the political situation. The prominent Southerners were delighted with their reception, and so were the crowds of callers, black and white, who came to pay their respects. When the Governor went back to Columbus, he left behind him a host of new admirers, who had been captivated by his famous charm and cordiality, and by his earnest desire for complete reconciliation between North and South. Outside Georgia, the circumstances of McKinley's "little rest and outing" attracted remarkably little notice in the press or in political circles.

Later in the spring, McKinley's cautiousness was overborne by the manifest advantages of an invitation to speak in Hartford, Connecticut, where Mr. J. Addison Porter, a wealthy and politically ambitious young newspaper proprietor, had recently formed a "McKinley-for-President" club. This was a desirable example for other communities to follow, and it also represented a break in New England's loyalty to Tom Reed, who was looming as a rival candidate, enthusiastically supported by Cabot Lodge, Theodore Roosevelt, and other influential Republicans. McKinley's speech at the banquet of the Hartford club was productive of good results. As he wrote Colonel John Hay, he had found "the sentiment in every way most favorable." Nevertheless, his appearance under such auspices had been a bold step. It was construed as a tacit bid for the Republican nomination, and McKinley took care not to call attention to his candidacy again. He was soon fully preoccupied by a political upset in Ohio. Hanna had a dread of overconfidence, but he must have become unduly complacent about the situation at home. Under his very nose, Foraker seized control of the Ohio Republican Convention in June, and dictated the ticket and the platform. An unusual feature was the unqualified endorsement of Foraker for United States senator in 1896.

The McKinley-Hanna men were out. The Foraker crowd was in. The convention had endorsed McKinley for the presidential nomination, but the opposing faction held the power to threaten divided support from Ohio at the national convention. The Governor's influential friends went quietly to work to promote the semblance of party harmony. McKinley's principal task was to exhibit his hold on the affections of the electorate. Inconspicuous on the national stage, he was indefatigable at home in 1895, energetically supporting the gubernatorial candidacy of Foraker's friend and financial backer, Asa S. Bushnell. Huge crowds greeted McKinley everywhere with roaring applause. The estrangement of the labor groups proved to be a myth, as the coal towns cheered the Governor to the echo and factory workers shouted their allegiance. Bushnell was elected by a slightly greater plurality than McKinley had received in 1893. The legislature gained such a large Republican majority that Foraker was assured of his election to the Senate. But the demonstration of McKinley's personal popularity had bound the triumphant opposing faction to an active support of his presidential candidacy.

After McKinley had made his last address to the legislature and handed Bushnell his commission with a warm and graceful speech, he went into seclusion at Canton. The North Market Street house was like a dynamo from which issued a voiceless hum of activity. Mark Hanna, on returning from Georgia the year before, had assumed personal direction of the preliminary canvass. A telephone apparatus on the wall of McKinley's library communicated directly with the wall of Hanna's office. Joe Smith divided his time between Canton and Cleveland. Boyle and Heistand were at the Canton end, assisted by Mrs. McKinley's cousin, Sam Saxton, and a "female typewriter." Telegraph messengers ran in and out. Republican dignitaries came to confer—the Negro factotum, Floyd, was said to set the table for twelve at every meal—and correspondents from the press services and the big city newspapers lurked hopefully on the front porch. Mrs. McKinley held court in the bow window of the parlor. She smilingly touched her gold-headed cane as she spoke of her lameness, and gave out little interviews on the gaiety of her girlhood, her romance with the Major, and her love for little children. Miss Harry-Dele Hallmark of the Philadephia *Press* found Mrs. McKinley vital, saw in her eyes "the steel badge of courage," and recorded the impression that White House entertaining would not be too much for her.

Across the hall, the Major sat in silence, refusing comment on all political questions; but Canton heard the beating wings of great events as the sunshine warmed and the roses bloomed, and the last struggle was joined between the Republican professionals and the Cleveland business-man who had undertaken to guide the destinies of Ohio's favorite son.

· 4 ·

FRONT PORCH

IN THE later years of the nineteenth century, the American scene was diversified by three celebrated friendships. The letters of John and Henry attest that the "hearts" of the exclusive Washington salon were joined in a rare intellectual communion. The correspondence of Cabot and Theodore, concerned though it was with their grosser political ambitions, reveals an affinity scarcely less elevated in refinement and sympathetic exchange. The love of William and Mark has not left a comparable record. Their few surviving letters are confidential rather than intimate. There are formal missives from William, most of them dictated and faintly odorous of the letterpress or carbon copy; and some scribbled notes from Mark on minor political questions, usually matters of patronage. Perhaps not much has been concealed or destroyed. When parted, these two communicated over the long-distance telephone, or through that more ancient medium, the private emissary. They were practical men, without a trace of the scholar or dilettante. The basis of their alliance was the commitment of the Republican party to the business interests.

Mark's first overtures to William had disclosed the harmony of their minds, both in political purpose and in the choice of the human instrument for its fulfillment. Hanna had shrewdly appraised the America of his day. He saw that the problems of government had become problems of money. He wanted to place the corporations in the saddle, and make them pay in advance for the ride. McKinley looked upon the great industrialists as the leaders in the march of national progress, the source of high wages and full employment for all the people; and he thought of their financial backing of his presidential candidacy as a contribution to the patriotic cause of protection. Hanna put the situation in balder terms, but both arrived at the same conclusion.

The partnership had naturally involved a close personal association. Hanna was an expansive man, bluff, hearty, and dynamic. Though his speech was rough and his manner aggressive, he made warm friends, as well as hot enemies; and his advanced opinions on the relations of management and labor, and his just and cordial dealings with his own employees had brought him the esteem of the workingmen of Ohio. In choosing McKinley as the object on which to lavish his energies, Hanna had not made a purely rational decision. He had been magnetized by a polar attraction. Cynical in his acceptance of contemporary political practices, Hanna was drawn to McKinley's scruples and idealistic standards, like a hardened man of the world who becomes infatuated with virgin innocence. That his influence ruled McKinley was the invention of the political opposition, of young Mr. Hearst's newspapers in particular. Hanna, on the contrary, treated McKinley with conspicuous deference. The Kansas City reporter, Mr. Will A. White, who thought Hanna the better man of the two, was obliged to admit that he was "just a shade obsequious in McKinley's presence." McKinley gave the orders, Charles G. Dawes noticed in his close association with both men, and Hanna obeyed them without question. Kohlsaat wrote that Hanna's attitude toward McKinley was "always that of a big, bashful boy toward the girl he loves." Hanna told the story himself. He said that somehow he felt for McKinley an affection that could not be explained; but he explained it very well.

It made Hanna feel twenty years younger to spend a social evening with McKinley. On a house party, the Governor was like a big boy. When he laughed, he laughed heartily all over, enjoying a joke on himself and loving to get a joke on Hanna, and ring all the changes on it. At their Sunday evening concerts, he would urge Hanna to raise his tuneless voice, insisting that it was a sweet tenor. He was "a pleasant tease." He was fond of the theater, and delighted in meeting the actors who came to Hanna's house. Once, in 1894, he went with Hanna to a football game, Yale-Princeton. It was their first game, and "all Greek" to them both, but McKinley was keenly interested. Hanna noticed how much attention he attracted from the college boys, and overheard the question, "Who is that distinguished-looking man—the one that looks like Napoleon?"

The best times of all for Hanna were the hours late at night in the den at his house in Cleveland, when the other members of the house party had gone to bed, and just the two of them had their "heart-to-heart" talks, puffing their cigars and looking into each other's faces. Hanna had a revelation then of a man of noble ideals, who loved mankind much more than he did himself. Years later, he could still see the kindly, quizzical look in McKinley's eyes when he said, "Mark, this seems to be right and fair and just. I think so, don't you?" Hanna remembered, too, how McKinley's eyes would sparkle at the suggestion that his tariff bill had brought Republican defeat, and how he would admit it might be so, "but wait and see, Mark—wait and see." Hanna remembered that McKinley said, "A good soldier must *always* be ready for duty," and, another time, "There are some things, Mark, I would not do and *cannot* do, even to become President of the United States."

To those who knew McKinley, there was nothing remarkable in Hanna's hero worship. McKinley inspired that kind of devotion in many men—in his cousin, Will Osborne, in Charles Dick, Joe Smith, and a hundred others. And what was McKinley's response to Hanna's outpouring of ardor and respect? He was prodigal of friendship in all his close political associations. Hanna signally possessed the qualities McKinley most highly valued —loyalty, modesty, fortitude, unselfishness. McKinley repaid loyalty in kind. He relied on Hanna. He was grateful.

McKinley, however, was naturally attracted to men of mental refinement, moral rectitude, and deep religious feeling. Colonel John Hay and Senator Hoar of Massachusetts commanded his highest esteem, as well as affection. There were Rutherford Hayes and Russell Hastings from the war years, William R. Day of the Canton bar, John D. Long in Congress, Myron Herrick at Columbus. In middle age, McKinley remained as eager as a boy in forming new attachments. He and Garret Hobart were devoted friends almost as soon as they met. He became intimate with two much younger men, Charles G. Dawes and George B. Cortelyou. McKinley expressed his regard without constraint. "I seem to feel lost if I do not hear from you daily," he wrote Herrick from Columbus; and again, "I have been sick to see you and hear from you." "You have won exceptional honor—you had long ago won my heart," he wrote Dawes in 1896. When Senator Hoar opposed him politically, McKinley grasped the old man's hand, and said with tears in his eyes, "I shall always love you, whatever you do." The record is rich in evidence of McKinley's warm feeling for the friends who shared his conceptions of duty, patriotism, and public service, and with whom he spoke "heart-to-heart" of the sorrows of man's lot on earth and his aspirations for immortality in the hereafter.

Hanna was outside this circle of intimacy. He belonged in the category of politicians who respected McKinley's idealism, but were perpetually amazed at the revelation, finding it strange as well as admirable. These men did not possess the key to McKinley's inmost sentiments. In love and confidence, he gave them less than he received. Because Hanna gave so much, McKinley appears the colder and poorer man in his personal relationship with the frank, profane, cheerfully ignoble realist who was so useful to his fortunes.

Together these two made one perfect politician. In the foreground was the zealous protagonist of his party's causes, the speaker who could inspire faith in well-worn platitudes, the moralist who spurned commitments, the diplomat who avoided unpleasantness. Behind him moved the practical businessman, whose brain was unclouded by muzzy ideals; the clever organizer, who could push and publicize, make deals and raise money; the blunt and bad-tempered fighter. McKinley's indirection of mind and method combined with his cautiousness and diffidence to unfit him for openly promoting his own advancement. His reticence was always his great flaw as a leader. With the growth of his importance, he had become increasingly formal and guarded, wary of committing himself on all points except the tariff. McKinley's political skills were instinctive. He did not comprehend or cultivate the art of public relations. His excessive modesty was a curious defect in a man of such resolute ambition. McKinley could freely ask favors for others; he could work boldly for the party; but he shrank from seeming to put his own interests forward, and preferred neglect even to favorable personal notice in the newspapers.

On the candidate's behalf, Mark Hanna pulled the powerful strings of money and organization and publicity. "He has advertised McKinley," Theodore Roosevelt would exclaim, "as if he were a patent medicine." McKinley was like a talented artist who needed an impresario, a press agent, and an angel. In Mark Hanna, he found all three.

Hanna once told a gathering in Cleveland that, when he had first broached to McKinley the subject of the presidential nomination, the Governor had said that he would not accept it on condition of any pledges of office or remuneration. This conversation, Hanna declared, had "made of him a better man and changed the current of his thought," but it did not entirely change the current of his activities. In the late autumn of 1895, when the Republican professionals belatedly awoke to the effectiveness of McKinley's canvass, Hanna went to New York to confer with the most powerful of the state bosses, Senator Matt Quay and ex-Senator Tom Platt. They were a curious pair of dictators, disreputable and absolute. Quay was up to his elbows in the treasury of Pennsylvania, but he was not a boodler of the ordinary stamp. He was the Indian's friend, adopted by certain tribes, and initiated into their rites. He was an accomplished linguist, and a student of military and religious history; and he carried an Elzevir Horace, along with Pennsylvania, in his pocket. Platt, the "Easy Boss," was a more commonplace representative of political corruption. His chief singularity was that he was personally honest. The vast sums he handled for the New York corporations were used to purchase other men. For the rest, Platt was an expert and vengeful intriguer, whose organization—which he always reverently spelled with a capital O—gripped the Republican party in every rural county and city ward of New York. These were the two with whom Hanna sat down to bargain for the votes of their states at the national convention. Quay, with his dark, weary, cynical face, and scrawny, secretive old Platt, who looked like a cartoon of a village deacon, announced their terms to the amateur from Ohio.

Kohlsaat and Herrick were present in Hanna's den, when he reported to McKinley that he could get New York and Pennsylvania—under certain conditions. The terms were high. They probably included more than one Cabinet seat. Platt wanted to be Secretary of the Treasury, and he wanted the promise in writing, so that there would be no mistake this time, as there had been in the Harrison campaign. McKinley listened in silence. He pulled on his cigar, and then got up to pace the floor. "There are some things in this world that come too high," Kohlsaat remembered that he said. "If I cannot be President without promising to make Tom Platt Secretary of the Treasury, I will never be President."

Hanna made haste to agree. In urging the bosses' propositions, he had evidently been swept away by the temptation of the big block of votes that would have clinched the nomination. He could not, on serious consideration, have expected McKinley's acquiescence. McKinley was quite prepared, if he were elected President, to accord the state machines their usual bountiful helping of the federal patronage. No inducement would move him to bargain for support, far less to place on sale the highest and most responsible places in the national government. McKinley had one qualification that was lacking in the machine politicians—a deep respect for public opinion. His instinct, merely on the grounds of expediency, was surer and more farsighted than Hanna's.

McKinley's refusal to come to an agreement touched off a fierce struggle for the control of the Republican convention. The intentions of the bosses were not immediately apparent. When Foraker, at McKinley's request, talked with Platt in January, he could report only an inconclusive conversation; but Platt's ill will was soon manifest. Quay suavely professed friendship, which was at first accepted at its dubious face value. In the middle of January, Will Osborne wrote McKinley that he had thought for some time that "Quay was stringing us," and suspicions were soon confirmed by the report of a distinguished investigator, Colonel John Hay, who was exerting himself on McKinley's behalf. The Pennsylvania politicians were playing false, Hay wrote Hanna. Quay was absolutely pledged to Reed. The Reed men were also counting on Platt, though there was some evidence that the New York boss actually believed that his avowed first choice, Governor Levi P. Morton, could be nominated. Hay thought that Morton was supplying money to buy up the southern "floaters." Platt was dispensing offices with a liberal hand, and had allured General Alger, the former governor of Michigan, with the suggestion of the vice-presidency. In conclusion, Hay stated that he was afraid that they must count on the hostility of the bosses. It seemed highly probable that Quay and Platt had an understanding to act together eventually in the interest of the man they could most absolutely control, and were under no illusions about Reed or McKinley or Harrison.

The fact was that Quay had already met privately with Platt and three other state bosses to formulate plans for McKinley's defeat. The accepted strategy was to stimulate the candidacy of a host of "favorite sons." Tom Reed was depended on to hold the loyalty of New England. Ex-President Harrison was considered a "waiting candidate" in Indiana. Illinois preferred the claims of Shelby Cullom, an elderly senator of rather negative personality, chiefly noted for his work on behalf of the Interstate Commerce Commission and for a fancied resemblance to Abraham Lincoln. Senator William B. Allison, a mild, conciliatory old man of strong corporation sympathies, was the choice of Iowa. Platt's protégé, Morton, a rich Wall Street banker who had been Harrison's Vice-President and was currently serving a term as governor of New York, was a candidate of still more advanced years. Quay, remaining ostensibly neutral, at length himself became the favorite son of Pennsylvania.

The field was far from formidable. On Harrison's withdrawal in February, Reed was the only serious rival that McKinley faced, and Congressman Charles H. Grosvenor of Ohio, who was in charge of the McKinley headquarters in Washington, reported that the Reed men were discouraged. The New Englander had the disadvantage of being a sectional candidate, whose chief support came from firmly Republican states. Beyond the Mississippi, he was heartily disliked as an advocate of the gold standard. Equivocating on money and all other questions, in his mastering desire to secure the presidential nomination, Reed had weakened the enthusiasm of his admirers. Nevertheless, his claims could not be disregarded. He possessed an influential following which included Cabot Lodge and Theodore Roosevelt and other outstanding young Republicans. Reed was too high-principled to suit the machine politicians; but, if the genuine move-

71

ment for his nomination gathered sufficient impetus, it might be the last-ditch resort of the elements that were out to beat McKinley.

Hanna prepared to meet this situation with tactics that were simple in conception, though involved in execution. In appeal to the American electorate, ever distrustful of brillance in its politicians, Reed made a poor second to the genial "advance agent of prosperity," McKinley. Hanna's basic strategy was to utilize McKinley's popularity to create the impression of an irresistible demand for his nomination from Republicans of all classes, sections, and shades of opinion. Through connections already formed with leaders in various states, a stimulus was given to demonstrations in the candidate's favor. McKinley-for-President clubs, formed on the Hartford model, mushroomed in the East and Middle West. Hanna played on the disaffection to machine rule in New York and Pennsylvania, and succeeded in wresting a number of delegates from the grip of Platt and Quay. The preconvention contest affords a good example of the duality of the candidate and his manager. The one took the correct moral attitude. The other made clever use of it. McKinley's candidacy was advertised as the campaign of the people against the bosses. It was an effective slogan. McKinley would never have thought of it.

McKinley had treated silver with sufficient regard to assure the loyalty of the Rocky Mountain states, but there was no certainty about the delegations from the Middle West. They had become indispensable to success, and much of the labor of the canvass was expended on them. To quash rumors of divided support for McKinley at home, it was desirable to hold the Ohio convention at an early date. Before leaving Columbus in January, 1896, McKinley had called on Foraker, who was in the state capital for his election to the Senate. After offering his congratulations, McKinley had opened up the subject of his presidential candidacy, requesting Foraker to go to the national convention as the leader of the Ohio delegation. Foraker hung back, still mindful of the criticisms of his good faith in 1888; but at length he consented to stand for delegate at large. The Ohio convention gave McKinley a rousing send-off in March, endorsing his nomination on the usual high-tariff, bimetallist platform. Foraker's speech, though it expressed a rather excessive admiration for all the other candidates in the field, left nothing to be desired in praise of McKinley. The delegates at large were evenly apportioned between the two factions, Hanna and Grosvenor balancing Foraker and Bushnell. Endorsements of McKinley followed at the Republican conventions in Wisconsin, Nebraska, and South Dakota, as well as Oregon, while Harrison's withdrawal had left Indiana free for the McKinley workers. The progress of the early spring was heartening, but it did not completely satisfy Hanna. To clinch McKinley's nomination as inevitable, he needed the endorsement of a large state that was giving support to another candidate. Illinois was a test case that Hanna watched with intense concern. The canvass there was in charge of a young man of very limited political experience, a former lawyer in Lincoln, Nebraska, who had moved to Chicago to engage in the gas business. He was tall and lanky, with a big nose and mouth, a pale complexion, and red handlebar mustaches. "He doesn't *look* much, does he?" Hanna had remarked to Mr. Kohlsaat after one interview with Charles G. Dawes; but he had sufficient confidence in the young man's ability to leave the important canvass in Illinois in his hands.

Dawes had more than unusual ability. He had a burning conviction that McKinley should and could be President. His emotion was rooted in a boy's hero worship. He was a native of Marietta, Ohio. His father, General Rufus Dawes, had served in Congress with McKinley. Charlie had once been introduced to the Major from Stark County, and had never forgotten the meeting. He had met McKinley again at Columbus in 1894, and started at once to work for his presidential nomination in the Middle West. He was soon in close touch with Hanna on the problem of Illinois, where the entrenched Republican organization was backing the candidacy of Senator Shelby Cullom. The gas business was neglected while Dawes conducted negotiations and participated in district campaigns; consulted with Will Osborne and Joe Smith, who were giving full time to the preconvention campaign; and traveled to Ohio for conferences with the candidate and his manager. Dawes had to fight under the handicap of a hostile Chicago press. Kohlsaat's *Times-Herald* was the only newspaper in the city that favored McKinley's nomination; and, though Kohlsaat desired the eventual object, he proved cautious in antagonizing local political leaders.

McKinley had stated that he would not enter the canvass in any state that had a candidate of its own; but he went to Chicago to address the Lincoln's Birthday dinner at the Marquette Club, and was more aggressive than Hanna in urging interference with the plans of Senator Cullom. The favorite son of Illinois was "furious" at the invasion, and efforts were made to avoid a showdown by persuading him to withdraw. Although he declared that he refused to listen to the extravagant inducements offered by McKinley's friends, Cullom actually tried to drive a bargain, which was rejected. Dawes heard McKinley say that "he proposed to take the place, if it came to him, unmortgaged."

Dawes had a high conception of public service. He detested the system of boss control, and waged his fight in Illinois with the determination

73

to "make the machine sick before we get through with them." McKinley's refusal to trade confirmed the respect he had inspired years before. As a grown man of thirty, Dawes was still susceptible to hero worship. He was shrewd, cool, and ironic, but his heart was ruled by the sentiments and the strict and simple principles of his boyhood in Marietta. His emotions were touched by every tie of home and early association. He adored his beautiful, dark-eyed wife, Caro, and their two children. His personal life was exemplary. He had not yet learned to smoke, though he would soon be tempted by the beribboned cigars on the banquet tables. He did not use coarse language, though one expletive he had heard from the farm-hands, "Hell and Maria," stuck rather tantalizingly in his head. The factional politics of Illinois formed the entering wedge of a great affection between two men congenial in their moral outlook and in their family piety, notable graveyard visitors and headshakers over vacant chairs. The disparity of age increased the tenderness of the bond. In love and reverence, Charlie placed McKinley next to his father, and McKinley warmly returned the younger man's devotion. "It was with difficulty that I restrained my emotion as he spoke of his regard for me," Dawes wrote in his diary after one visit to Canton. "I have come to think so much of the man that what he said went to my heart."

A month before the Illinois State Convention, Mrs. McKinley was at work on bedroom slippers for little Rufus Fearing and Carolyn Dawes. The new friendship was well established before it was blessed in late April by the successful culmination of Dawes's efforts. The endorsement of McKinley by the Republican party of Illinois was a decisive victory. It marked the time when it was generally conceded that the Republican nomination was a foregone conclusion. Vermont joined the procession, a small but significant voice in denial of Reed's claims to the united support of his section. "He may die before the convention meets," *The Brooklyn Eagle* said of McKinley on May 1, "or be incapacitated by paralysis, but hardly any other event can deprive him of his present advantage."

As the spring days passed, Senator Quay bestirred himself to make a trip to Canton. He lunched with Governor McKinley, who accompanied him to the train on his departure. Their separation at the station seemed to indicate the most cordial relations, but Quay failed to accomplish one object of his mission, that McKinley should invite Tom Platt to visit him after the convention. Platt would be welcome, McKinley wrote Quay, but he did not feel he could send for the ex-Senator, for reasons that must be manifest. The Easy Boss, enraged by the miscarriage of his plans, was openly sneering at McKinley. Quay, with one foot on the band wagon, was still ready to join in a last-minute conspiracy to kick the candidate off, but Hanna could afford to laugh at the maneuvers of desperation. In spite of assaults by other managers he knew that he had the main part of the southern delegations. His strategy had been to force the supporters of rival candidates to bolt their conventions; and a large majority of the Republican National Committee had long since agreed to seat only the "regular" delegations. A week before the convention opened, the Committee's decisions led Joseph H. Manley, the boss of Maine, to throw in the sponge, and state that McKinley would be nominated on the first ballot.

Manley was an experienced politician who knew when he was beaten, but he was Tom Reed's manager, and the candidate called him a quitter. Surprised and outraged by McKinley's success, Reed subsequently charged that the nomination had been won by the purchase of votes, in which he himself had been too honorable to participate. Hanna, however, had been disappointed in his efforts to raise money in Chicago for the canvass. He spent $100,000 out of his own pocket, Will Osborne collected $25,000 more, and Philander Knox raised $6,000 in Pittsburgh. This was a small fund for the extensive organization that had been made in the doubtful states. Apart from McKinley's objections to buying support, Hanna had not been able to supply cash to combat the raids of Manley and Platt and other bosses on the McKinley delegations in the South. The deciding factors in the nomination were Hanna's talent for management and manipulation, the belief that McKinley was a winner, and the failure of the opposition to unite on Reed. But Reed was a rancorous and ambitious man, and he drank the gall of defeat with sour grace.

McKinley had not passed the spring in untroubled contemplation of the progress of his canvass. His emergence as a formidable contender for the Republican nomination had started the yellow press snapping at his heels, with the New York *Journal* leading the pack. McKinley's record was bare of hidden scandals. He had worked hard. He had not accumulated money. His public career had been as honest as his private life was upright. He had few enemies, and his Canton neighbors had nothing but good to tell of him. His bankruptcy was the only incident on which the *Journal* could fasten scurrilous assertion and innuendo. The Hearst correspondent Alfred Henry Lewis raked over the story, and produced tales of McKinley's reckless extravagance and his bondage to the men who had aided him. Some of the mud splashed. McKinley's financial failure became a favorite sneer, vigorously exploited for a time by the respectable *Nation*. Lewis caught public attention when he wrote, "Hanna and the others will shuffle him and deal him like a pack of cards," but he went beyond the bounds of partisan credulity in his aspersions on McKinley's former trustees as a syndicate "gambling for a White House." It was hard to connect the charming and reputable banker Myron Herrick, or fussy little Mr. Kohlsaat, who had gone from the bakery business into newspaper ownership, with a deep-laid plot to exploit the national government; while the charge became still more absurd in the case of the mild, red-whiskered country lawyer, Judge Day. The *Journal* did far better when it concentrated its venom on the alleged chief of the syndicate, the wicked millionaire, Mark Hanna. To strike at McKinley through his manager became the established policy of the Democratic opposition. Before the campaign ended, Hanna had been made the scapegoat for all the sins of money and corruption. The *Journal* did not scruple to brand him as a union-smasher, the warmest enemy of the workingman, who for thirty years had "torn at the flanks of labor like a wolf." Hanna, stung and outraged, had a hundred grounds for libel action against Alfred Henry Lewis. He contemplated bringing suit, but eventually abandoned a fight with the Hearst press.

Still more effective in influence than Lewis was the *Journal's* talented cartoonist, Homer Davenport. In the spring of 1896, he made an unknown Ohio businessman the most infamously caricatured figure in America. Hanna was depicted as a brutal, obese plutocrat, the symbol of sly malice and bloated greed, covered with moneybags and dollar signs. Behind this monster the little candidate cowered in his big Napoleonic hat. Hanna was the puppetmaster who pulled McKinley's strings; the ventriloquist who spoke through the dummy, McKinley; the organ-grinder for whom the monkey, McKinley, danced. Davenport, at this time, had never seen Hanna. It was considered a clever political stroke that the cartoonist had been taken to call on McKinley, and thus inclined to treat him sympathetically. Nevertheless, the representation of McKinley as pitiable and victimized was a poor service to his reputation. The graphic impression of his spineless subservience to Hanna would long outlast the lies of Alfred Henry Lewis.

Insidious attacks on McKinley's candidacy came from quite a different source—the American Protective Association, an oath-bound secret society for the dissemination of anti-Catholic propaganda, which had assimilated a number of patriotic orders, and had a considerable influence in Republican politics in some sections of the country. McKinley had run afoul of this hate group as Governor, because he had not discriminated on religious grounds in making appointments, and had earned its vindictive enmity by his refusal to accede to pressure. Misrepresentation was powerless to hurt him in his home state, where his religious affiliations were as well known as his tolerant opinions; but in 1896, when the A.P.A. went gunning for McKinley on a national scale, flooding the country with letters and pamphlets, many people were convinced that he was unfit for the presidency because he was a member of the Roman Catholic Church. A whispering campaign spread rumors that McKinley did not favor nonsectarian public schools, that his appointments in Ohio had been dictated by the Catholic bishop of Columbus, that his father was buried in a Catholic cemetery, that he had two children in a convent. McKinley's secretary, James Boyle, was declared to be a Jesuit. Hanna was also admitted to the Church of Rome, and dryly alluded to the A.P.A. organ, the *United American*, as "the paper that made papists of us."

Hanna did not bear the brunt of this attack. McKinley was deluged by a heavy mail of spiteful condemnation and anxious inquiry. Though he felt that there was little use in answering falsehoods, a number of formal denials were sent out by Jim Boyle from the Canton office. McKinley privately expressed a rather weary confidence that the truth must in the end prevail. It was extraordinary in American politics, he sadly wrote his cousin, Will Osborne, that the leaders of a secret order, sitting in secret judgment on a public man, should seek to dictate a presidential nomination.

McKinley was at pains to deny the persistent rumors that linked the name of Foraker with the adverse movement. He was still being warned against Foraker in April, when he asked the Senator-elect to present his name to the Republican National Convention. There was an evident partisan motive in playing up the split in local Republican politics; but if proof had been offered that Foraker was the chief blackguard of the A.P.A.'s supreme council, it is extremely improbable that McKinley would have permitted it to interfere with his sedulous cultivation of harmony in Ohio.

The A.P.A. difficulties reveal McKinley in a characteristic political attitude. He made no real effort to counter the attacks, but quietly sat out the storm until it abated with the approaching certainty of his nomination. He was disturbed, not aroused to action. He endured, but did not fight. Although McKinley was correct in refusing to dignify misrepresentations by a public denial, a forthright condemnation of the A.P.A. and all its works would have won him the applause of Catholics and decent Protestants alike. McKinley said nothing, even when it was reported that he had unequivocally endorsed the A.P.A.'s principles. Except for conventional indictments of the Democrats, he never placed himself in overt opposition to any group of Americans; and, instead of asserting leadership, he had developed a stubborn preference for "standing on" his record.

For the duration of the canvass, McKinley's manager followed the example of reticence. Naturally free and easy in his comments on current events, especially on his own successes, Hanna resisted the reporters who "bulldozed and pleaded" for comments on the results in Vermont and Illinois. He penciled a furious scribbled complaint to McKinley about Joe Smith, who had insinuated that Hanna was not doing justice to McKinley's cause. "If I am making *that mistake*," Hanna wrote, "I will correct it if your judgment says so." But McKinley was averse to encouraging any discussion of his preliminary campaign. Declining to give out interviews, the candidate preserved an impenetrable reserve on the issues.

McKinley's silence on the currency question was the cause of the most valid and effective attacks on his candidacy. Anxious to avoid any commitment that might damage his popularity in the western mining states, he maintained that his position was perfectly understood from his public utterances. But, when McKinley stood on his record on the financial question, his footing appeared perilously insecure both to his political opponents and to the goldbugs of his own party. His refusal to speak, in the face of his endorsement by western silverite conventions in 1896, antagonized and frightened businessmen, and a vociferous demand came from the Republicans of the East that the candidate should explicitly avow his opinions and intentions.

Hanna had originally favored plumping for the gold standard, but McKinley had declined to listen. He was determined to bid for the nomination on the tariff issue alone. He still regarded the furor over the currency as a passing flurry, which might be calmed by the bimetallist program. The search for an international agreement on a ratio between gold and silver had been generally consigned to the trash heap of optimistic theorizing. McKinley belonged to the diehard band of hope. He did not believe that the United States should take independent action by legislating for the unlimited coinage of silver at the old ratio of sixteen to one, but he did not intend to alienate support by discussing the question during his preliminary canvass.

The compromise of bimetallism had raveled out in the furious strain of dissension. McKinley had nothing to offer but threadbare arguments that satisfied neither side, but silence was of extreme disservice to his reputation. The candidate's denial of the legitimate public demand for enlightenment on his views lent justification to the onslaughts of the opposition. Its press rummaged through McKinley's record for plunder of inconsistency, including his early vote in the House for free silver.

He was cartooned as a sphinx, ridiculed as tongue-tied and dumb, taunted as a sly timeserver with no convictions at all. McKinley's mute effacement in Canton was interpreted as unanswerable proof that he was muzzled by Mark Hanna.

The approach of the convention made it necessary for McKinley to submit his opinions, and, in conference with Hanna and other advisers, he drafted a statement on the currency. It contained the usual pledge for sound money, with silver used to the fullest extent consistent with the maintenance of its parity with gold. While extending a welcome to international bimetallism, McKinley's proposal declared that it was meanwhile "the plain duty of the United States to maintain our present standard," and that the Republican party was therefore opposed to the free and unlimited coinage of silver. This draft was sent to Foraker, who was slated to be chairman of the Resolutions Committee. He had, however, slight influence on the currency plank, which was substantially settled before he reached St. Louis.

Hanna had come to approve McKinley's evasiveness because of its favorable effect in the Far West; but, arriving early at St. Louis for the meetings of the National Committee, he discovered a strong sentiment for the gold standard among the other delegations. While he was busy with committee affairs, a number of friends met in his room to consider the question of stiffening McKinley's statement. Myron Herrick was the moving spirit. At various times, the conferences included Will Osborne, Governor Merriam of Minnesota, Senator Proctor of Vermont, Melville Stone of the Associated Press, Charles Dawes, and Henry C. Payne, the national committeeman from Wisconsin. Payne was a rather curious member of the circle. Like other Wisconsin machine politicians, he had worked for Reed before popular demand had swept the state convention to McKinley.

Over the discussions, as menacing as an explosive, hung the bright syllable, "gold." Tacitly accepted as the money standard of the United States, it had been mentioned in previous Republican platforms only in relation to silver and paper. The little group at St. Louis at last ventured to insert the word alone. For McKinley's phrase, "to maintain our present standard," was substituted the statement that "the existing gold standard should be preserved." The change did not alter the meaning. Everyone perfectly understood what "our present standard" was, and the silverite leader, Senator Henry M. Teller of Colorado, told newspaper correspondents that the original version would have been equally unacceptable to the silver-mining states; but to sound-money Republicans, the quibble was portentous. Crisis had forced them, with trepidation and high resolve, to dare to speak of gold.

Hanna expressed his approval, and McKinley was convinced by the united recommendation. But Hanna artfully concealed his hand from the anti-McKinley delegates. He intended that the candidate and his manager should appear to yield to the overwhelming sentiment of the convention. By conveying to eastern leaders like Tom Platt and Cabot Lodge—now the junior senator from Massachusetts—the impression that he was still reluctant to call the money standard by name, Hanna incited them to consolidate the delegations for the explicit definition. When the Resolutions Committee finally produced the platform, the currency plank was essentially the statement that McKinley had approved. There was a rush to claim credit for the fateful monosyllable "gold." Mr. Kohlsaat, a latecomer at the conferences, insisted that he alone was responsible. Platt and Lodge, who had never been present at all, were leading contenders for the honor. Hanna did not disillusion them. The McKinley delegations from the South had been comfortably seated. St. Louis was plastered with McKinley posters, and waving with McKinley banners. Men with McKinley badges, canes, and hatbands rested in the McKinley lounges of the hotels, and refreshed themselves with McKinley drinks of bourbon, lemon juice, and sugar. Hanna had done his work well. He was satisfied to remain in the background.

A break with the Far West was a foregone conclusion. Anticipation marred the drama of the scene that followed the adoption of the money plank. "Silver is, we think," *The Nation* commented, "the first raw metal that has ever been wept over." Senator Teller in pathetic periods took farewell of the party to which he had given his lifelong devotion, and led the sad procession of delegates from the convention hall. As the silver men filed out, a tall Nebraska reporter and ex-congressman came striding down over the desks from his place in the back of the press stand. William Jennings Bryan looked after the Republican bolters with a gleam in his eye and a faint, satisfied smile; but the loss of the mining states did not jar the enthusiasm of the convention's proceedings, nor dim Republican confidence in the future. Glittering refulgently in the platform, gold seemed a word of magic power to purge the party of inflationists and make it with a new consistency the organization of the business interests.

The last link had been constructed in the leased wire of the Associated Press between St. Louis and Canton. Since the assemblage of the convention, McKinley's home town had suffered all the unnatural torments of the repression of strong excitement. Enjoined by the *Repository* to avoid the indignity of a premature celebration and proudly conscious that their community was the cynosure of the nation's attention, Cantonians had made their preparations with outward calm. Electric connections had been installed between the *Repository* office and the big fire gong in the City Hall tower, and between the Postal Telegraph Company and the brass cannon, borrowed from Alliance, which was mounted back of the watch factory on Dueber Heights. The parade was to form on the public square, with a band and the Grand Army veterans in the lead, followed by the population, irrespective of political loyalties. The shops did a land-office business in ammunition for shotguns and rifles, and in fireworks, bunting, flags, and McKinley portraits and souvenirs. The candidate's features appeared on gaudy badges. His bust, in tin, surmounted walking sticks. In suitable, if unintentional tribute to his bimetallist leanings, McKinley's face gleamed in sterling silver from the handles of four varieties of spoons—five o'clock tea, regular tea, orange, and ice cream—at $1.25 apiece.

On Thursday, June 18, when the nominations for the presidency were scheduled to follow the adoption of the Republican platform, Canton was undecorated and noiseless. Bicyclists, pedaling along North Market Street, cast curious glances across a shaven, dewy lawn, brightened by two white urns spilling over with flowers, and by circular beds of blazing red geraniums. The candidate's house was looped like a Christmas package with important coils of wire, which directly connected it by telegraph and long-distance telephone with the convention hall at St. Louis. Reporters had taken over the front porch, occupying the wicker armchairs and splint rockers, sprawling on the floor and steps, and perching on the railing. Privileged friends arrived, and passed inside. A group of nervously vivacious ladies clustered around the Major's wife and mother in the parlor. McKinley was seated in the library, near the telephone apparatus, in the company of his old comrade General Hastings and a few other men. The instruments of the Postal Telegraph and Western Union companies clicked competitively in the upstairs hall, and Sam Saxton read off the bulletins that came over the telephone.

Now and then McKinley crossed to the parlor to speak a cheerful word to his wife or ask her twittering entourage, "Are you young ladies getting anxious about this affair?" To the veteran Cincinnati editor, Murat Halstead, the Major's calm, grave face looked "marvelously like Daniel Webster," as he sat in the revolving chair beside his desk, with pad and pencil in hand. The news arrived almost simultaneously over the three wires that Ohio had been reached in the roster of the states, and Joseph B. Foraker was making his way to the platform. He was about to speak.

His pronouncement of McKinley's name had thrown the convention into an uproar. The telephone was silent for half an hour. Stepping over to pick up the receiver, McKinley was amazed to hear a distant confusion of cheers. Others followed his example, and shared his astonishment. The circuit on the door of the booth in the convention hall had been left open, and McKinley had actually had the extraordinary experience of hearing himself acclaimed six hundred miles away. The sound, Halstead said, was "like a storm at sea with wild, fitful shrieks of wind."

It was hard on a speaker, the Major remarked, to be held up that way —"like stopping a race horse in full career." The St. Louis operator came back to the telephone. Foraker was trying to resume his speech. "You seem to have heard the name of my candidate before," Sam Saxton read out. "Ah," McKinley said, "that is like him. He knows what he is doing, and is all right." Mark Hanna and Bushnell were embracing, Sam reported, and Grosvenor was wildly fanning Hanna's head. The tension in the parlor relaxed in smiles of amusement.

Suddenly, the bulletin came, "Alabama, 18 for McKinley." The gentlemen in the library grabbed their tally sheets. The Major sat quietly keeping score at his desk. The roster of the states rushed on. The figures mounted fast. Quick calculation soon showed that Ohio's forty-six certain votes would settle the nomination on the first ballot. Before they were reported, a man at the Major's side threw down his pencil, and offered his congratulations. McKinley went to the parlor, and kissed his wife and then his mother, as he told them that Ohio had given him the presidential nomination.

While he bent above them in a tender tableau that moved some ladies to tears, a clang reverberated from the City Hall tower and hell broke loose in Canton. Gongs and bells, cannon and guns and firecrackers, tin horns and whistles, the music of the bands, and the citizens' roars of triumph were blended in a single deafening, discordant din. Flags were thrown to the breeze, bunting smothered the buildings. Carriages, horsemen, and bicyclists whirled up North Market Street, followed by a racing crowd on foot. Sam Saxton was calling for "Central," but the announcements could not be heard in the din of victory. The crowd made a rush to the front door. McKinley's companions fled. "You have my sympathy," General Hastings dryly remarked, as he hobbled out the back way. Thousands of people flung themselves into the house, with shrieks of congratulations and "God bless you," and the ladies of the community, carried away by excitement, formed in circles to dance around the Major.

Long before the arrival of the band and the veterans, who had formed in the public square according to the program, McKinley was obliged to mount a chair on the front porch and respond to the calls of the multitude on the lawn and street. He made another speech when the parade arrived. He passed through the kitchen to address a deputation from Alliance, which stormed the back door. A special train brought a monster delegation from Massillon. As twilight fell, four thousand arrived from Akron. Villagers poured in from Carrollton, Osnaburg, and Minerva, and at ten o'clock the proud citizens of Niles paid their respects. Between five o'clock and midnight more than fifty thousand people heard McKinley speak, and it was claimed that he shook hands with most of them.

When the Major at last retired to rest, the pandemonium in Canton was unabated. An arc light on McKinley's lawn illuminated a scene of devastation. The grass was trampled. The iron fence was broken. Shrubbery, geranium beds, and rosebushes lay in ruins. Strewn across the wreckage, a dozen rifled purses bore witness that pickpockets as well as honest citizens had found cause for rejoicing in Canton's rise to national importance.

McKinley had received 661½ votes in the final ballot, while Reed, his nearest competitor, had 84½. A motion to nominate by acclamation was quickly carried, and the delegates wound up their proceedings by nominating Garret A. Hobart of New Jersey for the vice-presidency. He was a rich corporation lawyer and businessman, scarcely known to the country, but influential in the Republican party in his state; and he had been Mark Hanna's choice for the nomination. Hanna had carried everything before him. He had managed a political canvass as though it were a business enterprise. His astounding success was saluted by the cheers of the convention, and by his selection as chairman of the National Committee. Hanna was a new wonder in the political firmament—the boss of the Republican bosses.

When Hanna presently ran down from Cleveland to Canton, he had a glimpse of the turmoil with which McKinley was surrounded. The candidate was making speeches every day. He greeted parading workers from the protected industries of Ohio and adjacent states. He beamed on the big contingent from the new tin-plate mill at his birthplace, with its banner "From Niles to the White House." Crowds soon descended from Cleveland for the ratification meeting arranged by the Tippecanoe Club. Senator John M. Thurston of Nebraska arrived with his committee to make formal notification of the presidential nomination. To all and sundry, in speeches and friendly greetings, McKinley appeared as a tariff candidate, standing on a tariff platform. His references to "good money" and "full dollars" were as secondary and indefinite as though the admission of the gold standard had never been written into the Republican platform.

The declaration had produced an unfavorable reaction in many parts of the Middle West, and Hanna's reports led him to conclude that he was going to have a fight on his hands in the Mississippi Valley. He intended to get his work of education on the money question started before his summer holiday; but he did not look forward to a difficult campaign. The Republican nomination was tantamount to election in June of 1896. Appeased by the currency plank, the goldbugs looked approvingly on their candidate. Their satisfaction was unclouded for a little more than two weeks after the jubilation at St. Louis.

As the Democratic convention gathered in Chicago in July, it did not seem a formidable assemblage. The division on the money question had cut deep. As the party had disintegrated, it had been infiltrated with Populist sentiment. The inflationists were expected to wrest control of the convention from the conservative elements; but, though they were numerically dominant, they had no outstanding leaders. In the headlines of the city press and in the confabulations of political sages, no importance was attached to the youthful ex-congressman, recently engaged as a lecturer and newspaper writer, who was a member of the contesting delegation from Nebraska. William Jennings Bryan was scarcely known to the East. His fame lay in the small communities and scattered farms of the West and South. He had traveled about, preaching free silver; and he had also taken an active part in an organization of silver Democrats, who planned to capture the party's national convention. Their political ideas were strongly tinctured with Populist tenets. Bryan was their natural leader.

As soon as the Nebraska contestants were seated at Chicago, Bryan claimed and obtained a place on the Resolutions Committee, for which his delegation had favored him. The Democratic platform of 1896 sounded a new note in the pronouncements of the major parties of the United States. It was a declaration made on behalf of the masses of the people. The money plank stood first. It uncompromisingly demanded the free and unlimited coinage of both silver and gold at the ratio of sixteen to one, without waiting for the consent of any other nation. The platform condemned trafficking with banking syndicates, to their enormous profit. It denounced the protective tariff as a prolific breeder of trusts. It demanded stricter federal control of trusts and railroads, specifying the enlargement of the powers of the Interstate Commerce Commission to protect the people from robbery and oppression. Its denunciation of arbitrary federal interference in local affairs was an attack on President Cleveland's action in the Pullman strike. Its censure of "government by injunction" in labor disputes and the recommendation of an income tax defied the Supreme Court and impugned its judgment, with a plain hint that the problem might be solved by packing the Court in future.

After the platform was reported, Bryan arose to address the Democratic convention. He said nothing new, nothing that he had not said hundreds of times before. He had twice employed in public speeches the very rhetorical figure with which he concluded at Chicago: "You shall not press down upon the brow of labor this crown of thorns; you shall not crucify mankind upon a cross of gold." The Republican press took what comfort it could from the fact that the Democrats were stampeded by "a chestnut." Bryan's impassioned periods had electrified the convention, and made him its presidential candidate.

The inflationists had found their leader. The dissension over the currency flamed into open conflict in the campaign of 1896. To Bryan's standard flocked Populists and Silver Republicans, who soon held conventions to endorse the Democratic nominee. He enlisted farmers and workingmen, and all the radicals, chronic objectors, bankrupts, and visionaries to whom he was an inspired prophet. But his clarion voice reached a far wider audience. It rang across a country weary of hard times with the confident promise of plentiful money, and, when Bryan called on Americans to renew their allegiance to the rights of the common man, he awakened an ancient faith and a desire for social justice. Like the old slavery issue, the moral cause of Bryan's campaign shattered the bonds of party loyalty.

Bryan was of service to his country in laying bare the abuses of concentrated wealth and its control of government. He touched the laggard conscience of America and disturbed its complacent absorption in material success; but over his crusade, belittling its purpose and confusing its significance, floated the banner of fiat money. Bryan knew nothing of economics. He preached free silver as he might have preached Christ crucified, the hope of man's salvation. His conservative contemporaries were shocked by his folly. They were also appalled by the strength of his cause. In July, the masses seemed spellbound. Had the election been held in the first weeks after Bryan's Chicago speech, the Democrats would have carried the country. In retrospect, it does not now appear that the United States was in imminent jeopardy, or that the wildest measures of inflation could have long availed to arrest its progress and stamp out its production. In 1896, Republicans and Gold Democrats believed that they faced a crisis more serious than that of the Civil War. This was the rise of bankruptcy, nihilism, anarchy. This was red revolution.

The Republican leaders rallied to meet the challenge and man the barricades. Hanna gave up his holiday, and began a summer of hard work, directing campaign headquarters established in New York and Chicago. Cornelius N. Bliss was treasurer of the National Committee. Will Osborne was made secretary. The fight in the Mississippi Valley loomed as a grim struggle, and Hanna persuaded Henry C. Payne to head the Chicago head-quarters. Young Dawes, appointed a member of Hanna's executive com-mittee, was one of Payne's first assistants. Quay and Manley also went on the executive committee. Tom Platt fell in step to round up the vote of New York. The old lines would hold in the East, but Republican morale sank dangerously low in midsummer. The firm ground of the tariff had been swept from under McKinley's feet. The champion of protection appeared a feeble defender of the gold standard—a candidate as illogical, *The Nation* had observed, "as a Methodist preacher would be in an elec-tion for Pope of Rome." Bryan began a tremendous campaign, taking the Middle West by storm.

The collapse of Republican confidence was evident in Ohio. Party workers were lukewarm. Foraker left on a trip to Europe. The Democrats were active and jubilant. McKinley was tranquil. He benignly received his many visitors, and with his "buoyant spirit" sustained Hanna and the other campaign managers. McKinley's attitude was like that of a parson who sees his congregation carried away by the excitement of a camp meeting. He deplored the hysteria, but felt sure that his flock would soon be back in the old pews. The common people, he told his friends, would solve the question right. It was only necessary to make them understand the prin-ciples. Hanna was preparing an educational program of unexampled extent and thoroughness.

While Bryan's eloquence was the greatest single asset of the Demo-crats, he was not conducting a one-man campaign. In challenging "the interests," the transformed party had not antagonized the mining mag-nates, and it was supplied with funds to spread the gospel of silver. Hanna's plans for counterpropaganda would be costly beyond the re-sources on which he could ordinarily rely; and, while his organization was forming, he undertook to shake down the New York financiers, who had most at stake in the election. Wall Street was apathetic, cold to McKinley, and unacquainted with his manager. Hanna's first efforts met with rebuff and discouragement. Bryan had succeeded, John Hay wrote Henry Adams in September, "in scaring the gold-bugs out of their five wits;—if he had scared them a little, they would have come down handsome to Hanna. But he has scared them so blue that they think they had better keep what they have got left in their pockets against the evil day." In the end, Hanna's salesmanship prevailed. The financiers paid up, and lent Hanna their assistance in organizing a systematic collection. Banks were regularly assessed for subscriptions, and corporations and life insurance companies were induced to make liberal contributions. A campaign fund of more than three and a half million dollars—unprecedented at that time—was disbursed by the Republican National Committee. The greater part of the money came from New York and its vicinity, and it was largely expended in the doubtful states of the West.

The problem far exceeded the usual stimulus to the voters of posters, badges, rallies, political addresses, and parades. Hanna undertook to counteract the emotional fascination of "free silver" and "cheap money" by instructing hundreds of thousands of plain people in the meaning of the terms. The Committee reached out to work with rural newspapers and schoolhouse meetings. The country was invaded by an army of paid speakers, and deluged with tons of literature, printed in a dozen languages. More than a million copies were distributed of a single pamphlet, William Allen White's mocking anti-Populist tract, *What's the Matter with Kansas?* Simple economic lessons stressed the disadvantage of inflation to people of limited means—to those dependent on pensions, to holders of insurance policies and depositors in savings banks, to all who owned a bit of property, or were trying to save something for their old age or for their children. In persuasive presentation and efficient organization, the educational campaign was proof of Hanna's genius for political management.

Hanna was not a boastful man. He fully acknowledged the contribution of "McKinley's strong and noble personality" to the campaign. On the Sunday that followed his nomination, McKinley had gone with his mother to hear prayer and preaching on his behalf at the First Methodist Church, while a special telephonic connection enabled his wife to listen in at home. The text of the sermon (II Peter 1:10) was: "Wherefore the rather, brethren, give diligence to make your calling and election sure: for if ye do these things, ye shall never fall." The diligence given by the Republican candidate resulted in a campaign of extraordinary effectiveness.

McKinley's conception of his candidacy was so passive that he at first gave the impression of intending to make no campaign at all. He had decided to stay at home and address only the people who cared to visit him there. Before his nomination, he had made two speaking engagements, both nonpolitical, requiring his presence in July at the Cleveland Centennial celebration and at Mount Union College. Except for three days' absence to keep these appointments and one week end of rest in August, McKinley remained in Canton from the date of his nomination until the election, available at all hours to the public on every day but Sunday.

McKinley was no match for his younger opponent in dramatic presence and oratorical power, and he refused, as he told Dawes, to enter the com-

87

petition. He may have been influenced by the example set by Benjamin Harrison in 1892, but the idea of the "front-porch campaign" seems to have been a natural outgrowth of the many groups that visited Canton. McKinley preferred the attitude of responding to the demands of his friends, of desiring election without going to seek it. He was so reluctant to stimulate interest in his campaign that he expressed himself as "averse to anything like an effort being made to bring crowds here." The Republican National Committee was active, nevertheless, in drumming up delegations, and the railroads were glad to co-operate. Low excursion rates from all parts of the country made the trip to Canton, as the *Cleveland Plain Dealer* disgustedly remarked, "cheaper than staying at home." For the eager Republican pilgrims, the journey combined the excitement of a political demonstration with the pleasure of an outing. Decked in campaign badges, caps, and neckties, they tumbled off the trains into the welcoming arms of Canton. Committees of greeters were on hand at the depot, with the well-mounted and nattily uniformed squads of the Canton troop which had been organized for escort duty. The parades formed around their bands and banners, and, guided by the clattering horsemen, wound through a town ablaze with red, white, and blue, and noisy with the cheers of the citizens on the curbstones. At the foot of North Market Street the delegations passed beneath the ornate plaster structure of the McKinley Arch, surmounted by the candidate's portrait, and at last broke ranks to crowd onto the McKinley lawn.

There was a breathless moment when the handle of the door turned, and a blast of cheers when McKinley appeared on the front porch. The spokesman stepped forward to deliver an address in which expressions of allegiance to the candidate and to Republican principles were blended with complimentary allusions to the community or organization or industry represented by the group. McKinley listened with rapt attention. He would stand, said Captain Harry Frease of the Canton troop, "like a child looking at Santa Claus," until the speech was finished. Then, mounting a chair, McKinley talked to the people. He bade them welcome to his home, and thanked them for the honor of their call. He said a few words on the campaign issues, adapting the discussion to suit the special interests of his audience. In conclusion, he expressed a desire to shake the hand of each and every one, and held an informal reception on the porch steps.

Warmed by McKinley's cordiality and impressed by his sincerity, the excursionists carried to all parts of the country enthusiastic reports of the Republican candidate. They had been right close to him, they had shaken his hand. They had seen him in his setting, and it was all exactly right— the friendly town; the neat, unpretentious house and the porch hung with trumpet vines; and the First Methodist Church where McKinley worshiped with his mother every Sunday. Many of the visitors saw the dear old mother, sitting beside her son or rocking on her own front porch. Many saw and stared at the invalid wife. The curiosity about Mrs. McKinley was so intense that she was sometimes sent to stay on a nearby farm, but it does not appear that these absences were frequent. Canton talked, in any case, regaling the trippers with tales of Mrs. McKinley's queer ways and her husband's selfless devotion.

Throngs of women went to Canton that summer. They found in McKinley the candidate of their choice. The impression made by his "matinée idol's virility" and his courtly tributes to the weaker sex was crowned by the information of his domestic virtues. "In honoring your mother and your wife, you have honored womankind," said the leader of a female delegation, with an all-female band, from northern Ohio. The sentiment of American women was not to be despised in 1896. They had become a powerful moral force in politics, and the notion was insidiously spreading that they were entitled to the suffrage. Few as yet could boast the privilege of one of McKinley's callers, Mrs. Robert Pier Fuller of Cheyenne, who under the recent Wyoming law would vote the Republican ticket in November, but many heartily endorsed the statement she made to the newspapers, "I think Major McKinley is just lovely." McKinley's name was venerated in a nation's homes, and his married life became a fireside ideal that sanctified the solemn statesman's face on the big posters in five colors with which Mark Hanna had flooded the country.

In his campaign speeches, McKinley made no mistakes. He could ill have afforded to do so. A careless word or misplaced allusion would not only have alienated the prideful deputation on the lawn, but would have been spread before the newspaper readers of the country. Though McKinley's addresses seemed unstudied and spontaneous, they had been carefully prepared with the assistance of Joe Smith, who worked up the material on the background of each group. Precautions were also taken to avoid extempore indiscretions on the part of the spokesmen. They were required to send in advance a copy of their intended remarks, which McKinley approved and occasionally edited. As the delegations piled up in the autumn, however, there were unexpected arrivals. Captain Frease said that McKinley sometimes had only half an hour's warning before a crowd of strangers stood expectantly on the lawn. He never failed to produce an appropriate little speech. If Joe Smith had not written a dull *History of the Republican Party in Ohio*, it would be tempting to believe that he was responsible for more than the research. In simplicity, variety, and genial informality of tone, the front-porch speeches were the most felicitous that McKinley ever made.

McKinley was obliged to discuss the financial question every day, but he dexterously kept the tariff to the fore by means of lightning transitions, which at first were seriously disquieting to his critics. He slipped smoothly from sound money to high wages, from good dollars to good times, from free silver to free trade, from open mints to open mills. At the end of July, in addressing the McKinley and Hobart Club of Knoxville, Pennsylvania, the candidate made some remarks that excited great attention. "That which we call money, my fellow citizens, and with which values are measured and settlements made, must be as true as the bushel which measures the grain of the farmer, and as honest as the hours of labor which the man who toils is required to give." This was merely a good sample of the kind of oratory with which McKinley charmed rural and labor audiences; but he had more to say. "Our currency today is good—all of it as good as gold—and it is the unfaltering determination of the Republican Party to so keep and maintain it forever." At last, the friends of the honest dollar had cause for relief and rejoicing. For the first time, the candidate had uttered the word "gold." He pronounced it, *The Nation* said, "in a somewhat furtive way . . . hastening to take a good pull at the tariff to steady his nerves."

As August passed, *The Nation* and the big Democratic dailies, which were supporting McKinley only because of a still stronger antipathy to Bryan, began to look with increasing favor on the Republican candidate. They had confidently expected a fumbling and mediocre campaign. They were astonished by the versatility and political sagacity of the front-porch speeches. McKinley's remarks on the currency grew progressively pointed and emphatic, and, with the appearance of his letter of acceptance, all doubts were set at rest. The money question was placed foremost, and presented in a lucid and incisive discussion that silenced the criticisms of McKinley's "wobbliness" and mental incapacity.

A clear and direct issue had been presented to the American people, McKinley wrote, and upon its right settlement largely rested the financial honor and prosperity of the country. The mere declaration for the free coinage of silver, as made by one wing of the Democratic party and its Populist and silver allies, involved such grave peril to the nation's business and credit that conservative men everywhere were breaking away from their old party associations and uniting with other patriotic citizens in protest. McKinley cautioned his countrymen against misleading phrases and false theories. Free silver would not mean that silver dollars would be freer to the many. It would mean the free use of the United States mints for the few who were owners of silver bullion. They would receive a dollar for fifty-three cents' worth of bullion, and other people would be required to receive it as a full dollar in payment for their labor and products. The silver dollars already in use had been coined by the government—not for private account or gain—and the government had agreed to maintain their value at a parity with gold. This had at times been accomplished with peril to the public credit. The Sherman Law had failed to realize the expectation that it would advance the bullion value of silver. Under coinage at sixteen to one, the government would have neither the obligation nor the power to maintain the parity. The nation would be driven to a silver basis, with resultant reduction of property values, financial loss and damage to commerce, impairment of contractual obligations, further impoverishment of laborers and producers, and business panic of unparalleled severity. Isolated action by the United States would defer, if not defeat the hope of an international agreement, which it would be McKinley's duty, if elected, to promote. Until the ratio between the two metals was fixed by such agreement, it was "the plain duty of the United States to maintain the gold standard."

McKinley's extensive dissertation on the currency question was marked throughout by composure and moderation of tone. He said that money should be free from speculation and fluctuation, and ought never to be made the subject of partisan contention. He also observed that it was a cause for painful regret that an effort was being made by the allied parties to divide the country into classes and create distinctions which did not exist and were repugnant to the American form of government. These appeals to passion and prejudice were in the highest degree reprehensible. They were opposed to the national instinct and interest, and should be resisted by every citizen. Having administered a dignified rebuke to the Bryanites, McKinley passed on to a long discussion of "another issue of supreme importance," the tariff. He examined the defects of the unpopular Wilson-Gorman Law, and charged to its operation all the miseries of the depression. It was mere pretense, he said, to attribute the hard times to the gold standard. "Good money never made times hard." It was not an increase in the volume of money that was needed, but an increase in the volume of business. Employment, which would bring back to the people the necessities and comforts of life, was sure to follow the re-establishment of a wise protection policy. This had lost none of its virtue and importance. It should embrace the provisions for reciprocity, which had been beneficial in increasing foreign trade, but the underlying principle of the legislation must be strictly enforced. The enactment of a tariff law would be the "first duty" of the Republican party, if restored to power in the autumn.

The concluding paragraphs of the document quieted the fear of sectional legislation by dwelling on the blessings of the era of reconciliation, and pledging the promotion of a spirit of fraternal regard between the North and South. The fervor of McKinley's expressions attracted attention to these passages, but the predominant interest of the letter lay in its treatment of the currency, and it was scarcely noticed that the writer had repeatedly implied that the issue was transient and subsidiary. In the hours he had snatched for composing the paper in his beleaguered house, McKinley had accomplished a considerable political feat. He had eminently satisfied the sound-money men, from goldbugs to bimetallists, while firmly retaining his status as a tariff candidate.

McKinley's prestige steadily mounted after the publication of his letter of acceptance. The Republican National Committee distributed hundreds of thousands of copies. "Good money never made times hard" became a popular campaign slogan. It was October before Hanna's organization proved its effectiveness, but Canton was engulfed weeks earlier by the tide that rolled toward McKinley. A delegation of happy omen was that which came from Vermont, the first state to hold its fall election, crowned with results triumphantly Republican. Each lapel bore the legend "Vermont for McKinley, 39,000." Senator Redfield Proctor led the proud procession, with gold-colored neckties and cedar-decked hatbands, which marched through Canton to warble at the candidate's doorstep, "We want Yer, McKinley, Yes, We Do."

The correspondent of the free-silver *Cleveland Plain Dealer*, accustomed to scoff at the cut-rate excursions, capitulated on September 19. The opening of the floodgates, he telegraphed his newspaper, had swept Canton off its feet. That day, McKinley gave a continuous performance, making nine addresses, shaking hands with thousands. The delegations formed a solid, slowly moving procession—western railroad men, laborers from the Carnegie furnaces at Pittsburgh, Hungarian-Americans from Cleveland, hardware men, commercial travelers, farmers' associations. The Republican National Committee had organized the railroad contingent, which arrived in ten special trains from Chicago, but the *Plain Dealer* man admitted that the enthusiasm was genuine. No one who saw these crowds of sturdy citizens, he said, could fail to be impressed with the "blind faith" that the wage earners had been taught to place in McKinley. Every week that followed the formal opening of the Ohio campaign saw a greater invasion. On the last Saturday in September, special trains steamed in from morning until night, bringing over 20,000 people, who represented thirty-odd cities and towns in half a dozen states. McKinley addressed eleven gatherings, some of which comprised two, three, and even six delegations. A week later, he made sixteen speeches in a day to crowds that were estimated to number 30,000.

For eight weeks, every day but Sunday was circus day in Canton. The quiet Buckeye community had never dreamed of such delirious excitement. Past the dazzled eyes of the citizens flashed flags and banners, McKinley and Hobart umbrellas, tin canes and horns, tin plumes and streamers, glass canes, glass lilies with McKinley's portrait, badges of raw wool, gold badges, gold neckties, gold hatbands, sprigs of goldenrod, gold-trimmed bicycles. The downtown streets were glutted with parades waiting their turn, and the neighborhood of the McKinley house was black with crowds "as thick as flies around a railroad pie stand." The staid Stark County teams reared in alarm at the deafening medley of the bands, but the hearts of the Cantonians beat in time to the music of "The Honest Little Dollar's Come to Stay." Abandoning all pretense of normal existence, the townsfolk reveled in an atmosphere of carnival. The Canton troop, formed as a show escort, served as a full-time volunteer police force, shepherding and dispersing the multitudes on North Market Street. Hotels and restaurants and saloons did a land-office business. Hospitable housewives, stocking their larders with extra supplies of ham and spaghetti, kept open house for friends from out of town. Boys left sullenly for school and college, like children dragged away before the end of the party. Judge Day's son Luther, in a new cutaway coat, regretfully took leave of the McKinleys, and was consoled by the gift of the candidate's photograph. Young Mary Harter, hanging rapturously on the fence across the way, kept herself in full view of the Major when he came out to speak. "Where were you today, Mary?" he would ask, if he missed her. "I was looking for your pink dress."

McKinley was as genial and relaxed as though he were on holiday. He was ready for all comers, including a large free-silver contingent who paid him a courtesy call when Bryan spoke in Canton, and a column of Confederate veterans who shook the McKinley arch with the rebel yell. The frenzy of his admirers neither excited him nor frayed his nerves. He had felt sure all along that the American people would take the right view in the long run, and in early August he had concluded that the silver craze had reached its height. He was calmly satisfied to see his predictions verified, and bore with smiling equanimity the ruinous invasion. Like an army that does not advance to meet the enemy, McKinley had brought destruction to his own borders. The front porch was in a state of dilapidation. The slender posts had been so weakened by the grasp and pressure of the crowds that the roof was in imminent danger of tumbling on the Major's head. The demolished fence and grape arbor had been picked clean by souvenir hunters. The once green lawn had been trampled to a brown plain of earth, on which farmers' families picnicked while they waited for the speeches. In the rains of early autumn, it became a lake of mud, and North Market Street had a brief interval of respite, while the meetings adjourned to Canton's gloomy public hall, the Tabernacle.

The McKinleys' house was filled with a monstrous clutter of gifts and the debris that the retiring delegations left in their wake. The bunches of flowers faded. Cheese and butter and watermelons could be eaten. Badges and glass canes made acceptable presents to children. A place was undoubtedly found for a marble bust of McKinley, a bouquet of artificial flowers made by a bedridden Cleveland lady, a cane of weldless cold-drawn steel tubing, a miniature gold reproduction of a one-hundred-pound steel rail, and a gavel formed from a log of the cabin occupied by Lincoln at Salem, Illinois. But it is difficult to imagine where the McKinleys put the finely polished stump of a tree from Tennessee, the largest plate of galvanized iron ever rolled in the United States, the equally record-breaking sheet of bright tin, or the strip of jointed tin, sixty feet long, embellished with the names of the candidates. Live American eagles were the most inconvenient remembrances of all, and McKinley made haste to present them to the city of Canton as they were received. Five fine specimens, christened Major, McKinley, President, Hobart, and Hanna, were lodged near the wolves in the pavilion in Nimisilla Park.

In search of a semblance of privacy, the McKinleys had taken up their living quarters on the second floor of the house. There, in the perpetual din that arose from the yard, the Major did his writing and held his conferences. Governors, senators, congressmen, and other celebrities were as thick as blackberries in Canton. Foraker came home from Europe to make an intensive speaking tour, and wind up the campaign at McKinley's side on the front porch. The Republican bosses did not put in an appearance, but Matt Quay was represented by a delegation of 2,500 of his Beaver County neighbors, to whom McKinley praised the Senator as "that distinguished leader and unrivaled Republican organizer." Toward the end of October, the response came in the form of an intimate little letter. "You are doubtless glad the agony is nearly over," Quay scrawled in his all but illegible hand. He rather cautiously prophesied McKinley's overwhelming victory, issued a confidential warning against the trouble-making Pennsylvania clique to whom he ascribed his estrangement from Harrison, and concluded with the assurance that the Pennyslvania Railroad would offer McKinley a private train to Washington the following March. As success came in sight, all was well between the Republican candidate and the Senator who carried Pennsylvania in his pocket.

Other opponents of McKinley's nomination hurried to present themselves in person, to affirm their loyalty and pave the way for patronage. The railroad president, Mr. Chauncey Depew, who had been addressing audiences of farmers at the candidate's request, filled a still odder assignment by duplicating Bryan's whirlwind tour of Ohio. Two prominent penitential pilgrims were Tom Reed's friends, Henry Cabot Lodge and the New York police commissioner, Theodore Roosevelt. "Cabot and Teddy," as John Hay put it, "have been to Canton to offer their heads to the axe and their tummies to the harikari knife." Colonel Hay himself was a latecomer, though he had been doing political errands for a year on McKinley's behalf, and made a generous contribution to the candidate's personal expenses. He had dreaded the trip to Canton, "thinking it would be like talking in a boiler factory."

Colonel Hay was no longer the bright young Westerner who had gone to Washington as Lincoln's assistant secretary. He was a trained diplomat and man of letters, elderly, rich, and hypochondriacal. His intimacy with Henry Adams had sharpened and soured a natural gift for satire. He scoffed at the hullabaloo of the campaign, and always mockingly alluded to McKinley as "the Majah." Yet Hay was not content to subside into the exquisite impotence of Adams. He was uneasy to see that the sands of his importance were running out—that he had become a Republican dignitary in whose recognition there was, as Harrison had said, "no politics." In the end, Hay went to Canton and took the stump for McKinley. His interviews with "the Majah" proved more interesting than he had expected. Hay was impressed by the serenity with which McKinley sat talking in the upstairs room, leaving "his shouting worshippers" at the door. "I was more struck than ever with his mask," Hay wrote. "It is a genuine Italian ecclesiastical face of the fifteenth Century. And there are idiots who think Mark Hanna will run him!"

The national excitement mounted as election day drew near. The Democrats had the Solid South. They had a nearly solid Far West. Labor organizations and labor journals were all vociferous for free silver. Bryan's fiery and aggressive campaign seemed to have infused his cause with "a sinister vitality." In tones sharp with alarm, great Democratic and independent newspapers defied the forces of insolvency and ruin. Preachers fulminated against Bryan from their pulpits. A trainload of Union officers aroused the old soldiers of the West with bands, cannon, rockets, and speeches for Comrade McKinley. Monster torchlight parades wound through the streets of the cities, with captains of finance and industry marching in line. For a few days, business almost came to a standstill. Banks refused to make loans. Orders to factories were subject to cancellation. Workers were warned that their wages and even their jobs were contingent on the outcome of the election. With fear in their hearts, sound-money men cast their votes on November 5, and waited in suspense for the returns.

The time for suspense had ended weeks before. The great American middle class had awakened from a summer's dream of the glories of free silver. Some men had been persuaded by argument, some by the coercion of their employers. Others had been estranged by the increasingly radical tone of Bryan's speeches, and disillusioned by the knowledge that this demagogue was backed by the magnates of the silver mines. The price of wheat soared, nullifying Bryan's arguments to the farmers. The Gold Democrats, who had nominated their own candidates, concluded in large numbers to gag at the tariff and vote for McKinley. Late on election day, the newspaper bulletins began to flaunt the tidings of Republican success. Middle western and border states of the South tumbled into the gold column. At midnight it was known that, by a goodly majority in the electoral college and a popular vote larger than that received by any candidate since Grant, William McKinley had been elected President of the United States.

Late that night, Mr. Kohlsaat made a telephone call to Canton from his office at *The Chicago Times-Herald*, which had given valuable support to the Republican candidate. He was finally connected with Mother McKinley's house, and spoke with her grandson, James. After some delay, James came back to report that the newly elected President was in his mother's room. She was kneeling beside her bed, James shouted over the long-distance wire, with one arm around Uncle Will and the other around Aunt Ida. All that James could hear was, "Oh, God, keep him humble," and that, apparently, was all that Mr. Kohlsaat got for his telephone call.

· 5 ·

PRELUDE TO HIGH OFFICE

IN THE four months that followed
the election, McKinley was largely occupied with the selection of a Cabinet
that would have the confidence of the business interests. A single shadow
deflected his attention from the program of reviving prosperity. A renewed outbreak of insurrection in Cuba in 1895 had involved the Cleveland administration in serious diplomatic difficulties with Spain, and there
was a diminishing prospect that they would reach either a crisis or an adjustment before McKinley took office in March.

The foreign policy of the United States was based on the negative principle of isolation from the powers of Europe, but it was not lacking in
strong positive assertions in both the Western Hemisphere and the Far
East. While these questions had for many years been politically subordinate
to the great domestic issues, Americans were by no means indifferent to
their foreign policy. On the contrary, they were substantially united in
regarding its inherited precepts as sacrosanct. As firmly entrenched in their
minds as the conviction of their strategic security was the belief that they
were a peace-loving people, but there had never been a time when the
country had not been ready to call for war at any invasion of the Monroe
Doctrine or threat to their commercial rights in the Pacific.

A refreshed interest in national expansion, which had appeared in the
rehabilitation of the Navy and the increasing concern for foreign trade,
had been further stimulated by the hardships of the depression years. The
loss of financial confidence and the check to financial adventure had
combined with the occupation of the last frontier to turn men's thoughts
abroad. The annexation of Hawaii had become a party issue, which had

97

touched off a vehement debate in Congress on the whole subject of expansion. The most popular act of Cleveland's troubled second term had been his aggressive message to Congress on the Venezuela boundary dispute. The United States, which then possessed one completed battleship of the first class, had crowed defiance to Great Britain, and taken inordinate pride in her assent to Cleveland's demand for arbitration. The war spirit was rampant in the attempts to bully the decaying empire of Spain into abandoning her rich colony of Cuba. Congress had passed resolutions for the recognition of the belligerency of the insurrectionists. The platforms of both major political parties had expressed sympathy for Cuban independence, and the Republicans had declared the opinion that Spain had already lost control of the island.

Military insignificance enabled Americans to criticize other nations with impunity, but disapproval had gone beyond verbal interference in the colonial affairs of Spain. A Cuban junta, with headquarters in New York, was operating with great success. Americans were intriguing with the revolutionary agents, and supplying them with funds and arms. In spite of Cleveland's firm stand for neutrality, filibustering expeditions still slipped to Cuban ports. The Spanish government, pouring men and money into an inconclusive contest, had been provoked to repeated notes of protest.

By geographical and commercial, if not political right, the United States had long maintained a protective attitude toward the nearby island. For more than seventy-five years, Washington had declared that the only alternatives to Spanish control were the independence of Cuba or its annexation by purchase to the United States. The strategic aspect of Cuba had been stressed by the extended interpretation of the Monroe Doctrine and the national enthusiasm for an isthmian canal. Against this background, the insurrection had highlighted a vivid concern for loss of trade and a strong sentimental sympathy with a struggle for liberty. An old American hostility to the misrule and cruelty of Spain was fanned by the harsh methods of Governer General Valeriano Weyler, who had concentrated the rural population of Cuba in towns, where women and children were ravaged by disease and starvation. The Spanish authorities, moreover, had arrested and imprisoned a number of insurrectionists who had taken the precaution of becoming American citizens. Cleveland had been convinced that the situation in Cuba could not be indefinitely tolerated. In spite of his broad interpretation of the Monroe Doctrine in the Venezuela dispute, the Democratic President was a stubborn enemy of an expansionist foreign policy; and yet, in his last message to Congress, he sounded the warning that there might be a limit to American patience. "The United States," Cleveland wrote, "is not a country to which peace is necessary."

Though McKinley had been led along the path of expansion by the general interest in the Navy and an isthmian canal, and by the Republican projects of reciprocity and Hawaiian annexation, he would have been incapable of framing the ominous sentence contained in Cleveland's message. McKinley believed that the United States was a nation to which peace was supremely necessary. He was aware of the aroused state of public opinion, and shared his countrymen's pity for the Cubans and desire to alleviate their sufferings. He did not make light of the international difficulties, and thought it likely that Cleveland would dump them all on the new administration, in spite of Republican efforts to bring on a diplomatic crisis during the winter. The incoming President also knew that these efforts were not inspired solely by partisan motives, and that the embattled Republican expansionists would be resolute in resisting his own policy of neutrality. Nevertheless, McKinley faced the future without dread. In forming his Cabinet, his mind was primarily bent on reassuring the business community, and his first choice for Secretary of State was Senator Allison of Iowa.

On political grounds, Allison was an impeccable choice. His presidential candidacy had attracted support in the Middle West, and Iowa had given the Republicans an unexpectedly large majority in the election. Moreover, as the gray-bearded veteran of a long and conservative service in Congress and the able chairman of the Senate Committee on Finance, Allison had achieved a reputation for wisdom and skill in compromise. In omitting to consider that the tactful financial expert was inexperienced in foreign affairs, McKinley reflected the national disposition to discount the need of special training for the conduct of international relations. Iowa boasted that Allison could walk on eggs from Des Moines to Washington without breaking one of them. That was the American idea of a diplomat.

Allison had been tempted by the presidential nomination, but McKinley presently learned that he was unwilling to consider exchanging the Senate for a Cabinet seat. Meanwhile, an interview with Hanna had led to a further revision of McKinley's original plans. He had offered his manager the suitable position of the Postmaster Generalship, with its large control of patronage. But Hanna did not want to be Postmaster General. Like Allison, he preferred the Senate.

Hanna's aspirations had outgrown the exercise of indirect political power. He wanted an office in which he would not be merely the tail of McKinley's kite. It was said that Hanna would have liked to be Secretary of the Treasury, but McKinley had not made and did not make the offer. As he explained to Dawes, neither he nor Hanna considered the department "congenial" to his campaign manager. The fact was that Hanna had unfolded the suggestion that a suitable vacancy would be created in the Senate if John Sherman were to become Secretary of State.

There was much to attract McKinley to the appointment of this other financial expert, whom he had reverentially admired ever since entering politics. Sherman was now nearly seventy-four years old, and no longer in his vigorous prime. For the past ten years, he had served without particular distinction on the Foreign Relations Committee of the Senate. He had never been noted for his talents as a diplomat—none of his family had that reputation—and he had recently been excitable and intemperate in his public references to Spain. All of these things were obvious enough, but they did not weigh very heavily with McKinley. He was persuaded that the elder statesman would provide the State Department with an impressive figure-head, and inspire confidence in the new administration, at home and abroad. McKinley had an extremely light foot himself, when it came to walking on eggs. He was confident of being able to manage, with capable assistant secretaries to carry the burden of routine duties at the State Department. Nevertheless, he hesitated to accede to Hanna's suggestion. Its weakness was the assumption that Governor Bushnell would appoint Hanna to Sherman's seat in the Senate. The antagonism of the Ohio machine was openly declared by Senator-elect Foraker. After calling on Hanna and obtaining a frank statement of his hopes, Foraker went posthaste to Canton to protest that Sherman was unfit to head the State Department. He also told McKinley that the friction between Bushnell and Hanna was a likely deterrent to Hanna's appointment. McKinley was still hoping in December that his manager would take the Postmaster Generalship, and that Allison might change his mind about the State Department.

Hanna, however, was keen and confident, ready to bring pressure to bear at Columbus and Cincinnati. His first move was a trip to Washington to sound out Sherman. Soon after he returned to Cleveland, he received a letter from Sherman, stating that he would accept the portfolio of State, and mentioning that, in view of the Ohio senatorial election the next winter, he would like to be confidentially informed of the decision about "this high office" as soon as practicable. Allison had remained immovable, and in early January, McKinley sent Will Osborne to Sherman with a formal tender of the portfolio of State. Osborne could see that Sherman was delighted to receive it. The letter of acceptance was prompt and cordial. A week later, in spite of severe winter weather, Sherman went to Canton for a conference. On returning to Washington, he resigned his seat in the Senate. He would have preferred to postpone this action until Governor

Bushnell had declared himself, but Hanna persuaded him to act at once. In writing to Bushnell, Sherman claimed the right to a voice in naming his successor, and respectfully requested Hanna's appointment. He also enlisted the active interest of General Russell A. Alger of Michigan, a candidate for the War Department, who was close to Foraker.

The case had attracted wide publicity. As the weeks passed, the contest became excessively embittered. Hanna was infuriated to discover that "they" did not intend to let him into the Senate. The Foraker crowd rebelled against having to "take care of" their enemy, and their outrage was increased by newspaper statements that Bushnell did not dare to refuse. Yet the bleak fact remained that if Foraker and his faction grabbed both Senate seats for themselves, they would strongly antagonize the administration and the Republican National Committee.

The stalemate lasted for six weeks after Sherman had consented to become Secretary of State. McKinley was at last impelled to exert his influence. William R. Day carried to Columbus the personal request of the President-elect, and ten days before his inauguration McKinley was informed that Bushnell had agreed to comply.

In accepting defeat, the Foraker machine had the satisfaction of partial revenge. The impression of "a deal" had been conveyed, and rumors were winging that Sherman was unequal to the duties of Secretary of State. The indirect procedure gave wide scope to suggestions of intrigue, and encouraged an indecent exposure of Sherman's failing powers. It was asserted that McKinley had cynically connived with Hanna to force Sherman into the Cabinet. The evidence, however, seems to indicate that Sherman willingly lent himself to the arrangement, before he was humiliated by the publicity given to his infirmities. He had yielded to pressure in hastening his resignation, but his conduct had not been that of a man who was making a painful sacrifice for the sake of his party. His term in the Senate was due to expire in two years, and he did not mean to stand again for election. At a later date, Sherman came to take a resentful view of his appointment, and its circumstances were distorted by conspiratorial friends and family connections. Not the least curious aspect of their propaganda was the assumption that there was something shabby about the position of Secretary of State. McKinley supposed that he was honoring Sherman in offering him the first place in the Cabinet.

Many Republicans were indignant over the partisan and factional aspersions on Sherman's fitness for office. In the early winter, McKinley received excellent firsthand reports of the Senator's condition from Osborne and Joseph Medill of Chicago. After himself talking to Sherman at Canton,

McKinley "was convinced of both his perfect health, physically and mentally, and that his prospects of life were remarkably good." So the President-elect wrote Medill in a letter expressing his indignant conclusion that "the stories regarding Senator Sherman's 'mental decay' are without foundation and the cheap inventions of sensational writers or other evil-disposed or mistaken people."

McKinley had made a bad mistake in appointing Sherman, and its consequences were aggravated by the furor of the opposition. The attack had cast a cloud on the State Department, and subjected Sherman's every word and act to critical scrutiny; but McKinley stood by his decision. If his judgment had been affected by his desire to gratify Hanna, he had also been misled by an exaggerated respect for Sherman's capacity and an undue optimism about the adjustment with Spain. While preparing his inaugural address, McKinley wrote Sherman to ask for suggestions for a reference to Cuba, and received a rather inconsistently worded memorandum, stating that intervention was, in Sherman's belief, inevitable. McKinley mulled over this advice, editing it and cutting out the conclusion. In the end he discarded the whole memorandum. The New Year had brought a brighter prospect for the Cuban crisis and a lull in the interventionist agitation in Congress. McKinley's omission to mention Cuba in his inaugural address was a sufficient indication that he did not expect the problem to impose a strain on his aging Secretary of State.

McKinley's second bad mistake was the selection of Russell A. Alger for Secretary of War. Alger was a lumber king, whose companies operated mills and owned large tracts of timber in northern Michigan and Canada. He was self-made, but not crude. He was as smooth as butter, handsome and affable, with a narrow white beard and a charming smile; and, at ease in the enjoyment of his large fortune, he had gone in for politics. After serving as governor of Michigan, Alger had twice been the favorite son of his state at Republican National Conventions. He had also, with large G.A.R. backing, persistently applied for the War Department, and McKinley had been showered with requests to assign the office to Alger.

Alger was a suitable kind of man for McKinley's kind of Cabinet, and yet he was not exactly a strong and unimpeachable choice. He was a lightweight, pleasant and rather evasive. Though popular, he had made a number of enemies, and some of them were in the War Department. He was on terms of intimacy with Platt, Quay, and Foraker, and his own political practices had been criticized. At the Republican convention of 1888, the purchase of the "seats" of Negro delegates on Alger's behalf had been so notorious that it was loudly noised in the press. Incidentally,

Foraker always virtuously claimed that he had quarreled with Hanna at that convention because he found him paying out cash to a crowd of Negro delegates. If Hanna was so engaged—and there seems no reason to doubt that part of the story—he was buying back the votes that Foraker's crony, Alger, had bought away from Sherman. In his recently published *Recollections*, Sherman had taken a sharp dig at the past activities of "the friends of General Alger," but the insult had been overlooked, and Alger was pleased to count Sherman among his backers for the Cabinet.

McKinley had made careful inquiries about Alger's financial reputation. The result was entirely reassuring. A somewhat more equivocal matter was Alger's war record. For many years, it had seemed above reproach, for Alger had been a gallant cavalry leader, subsequently elected commander in chief of the G.A.R. But in 1892, when he was making his second bid for the presidential nomination, Charles A. Dana had spread in the columns of the New York *Sun* evidence he had been given by officers of the War Department that in 1864 Alger had been recommended for dismissal from the Army for absence from his command during action in the Shenandoah Valley. At this same time, he had sent in his resignation. He was given an honorable discharge, and later was successively promoted to the brevet ranks of brigadier and major general. In the light of these developments, the confused story did not appear to be damaging to Alger's military reputation, but the rather curious fact remained that he had never wholly cleared his name. He had talked around the charges, without frankly answering them. McKinley sent his confidential clerk, Joe Smith, to Washington for a private investigation. After researches at the War Department library, Smith made a report vindicating Alger. McKinley's old friend, Senator Julius Caesar Burrows of Michigan, confirmed Smith's conclusions. McKinley was convinced, but still wished to make sure that there would be no repetition of the charges. Burrows spoke to Tom Platt, and Platt spoke to Dana. Assurances were conveyed that *The Sun* would take "no unfriendly action" on Alger's appointment, and McKinley felt secure in going ahead with it.

The choice caused general surprise. Alger had grown quite frail. Many people thought that the scandal over his military record had aged and shaken him. (Undoubtedly, he was already suffering from the chronic heart disease which impaired his health during the McKinley administration.) It seemed, moreover, illogical to single Alger out for reward. Though he had been an original McKinley man and had ended up on the campaign junket of the Union officers, it was well known that he had strayed off with the Platt-Quay combine in the interval. As the G.A.R. was immensely gratified by Alger's selection, McKinley had probably intended it as a compliment to his old comrades. Alger was actually not a bad choice for a somnolent government department, which was stirred from its cumbersome routine only by engineering jobs in American rivers and harbors. As Mark Hanna had suggested to Alger, the War Department was the only Cabinet seat for which a busy man could spare the time from his own affairs.

The precarious state of the gold reserve made the selection of the Secretary of the Treasury of such primary importance in soothing the frayed nerves of business that it had been foremost in McKinley's mind. His first definite decision on the Cabinet had been the choice for this position of Congressman Nelson Dingley, Jr., of Maine. Dingley was a rather quaint mathematical wizard, bald and stoop-shouldered, with a rasping voice that was rendered more nasal by catarrh. He had long been a Republican mainstay of the Ways and Means Committee, credited with a large part in the preparation of the McKinley Bill, and his mastery of problems of government finance and revenue had made him one of the principal ornaments of the House. To McKinley's regret, Dingley did not want to enter the Cabinet. With the Republicans in control of the House, the New Englander would be chairman of the Ways and Means Committee, and he was already ciphering out the new tariff bill that would enrich the Treasury and bear the name of Dingley.

While McKinley was pondering his second choice, he received many endorsements of Senator Shelby Cullom. This appointment, however, would have been especially obnoxious to the original McKinley men in Illinois. Hanna and Kohlsaat had brought forward the counterproposal of Mr. Lyman J. Gage, the president of the First National Bank of Chicago, and a Gold Democrat. Though he had not previously held public office —four years earlier, he had refused Cleveland's offer of the Treasury Department—Gage was highly esteemed in Chicago, and well known to the banking world as an able and cautious financier. His designation would be a guaranty that the incoming administration would support the gold standard.

McKinley was barely acquainted with Gage, and identified him only by the recollection of his remarkably fine white whiskers, but he became fully persuaded of the desirability of naming him. He was still reluctant to issue the invitation on account of young Charlie Dawes. Many months earlier, when pressed to specify the government position he preferred, Dawes had made the astounding reply that he wanted to be the Cabinet member from Illinois. McKinley temporized. In an emotional interview with Dawes in December, he anxiously asked if the failure to give him a Cabinet seat would alter their intimate friendship—"he would not have these relations altered for three Cabinet positions." McKinley had also said that he would not put anyone else from Illinois in the Cabinet, and he still felt bound by this promise even after Dawes had warmly agreed to accept the "crowning honor" of an alternative appointment as Comptroller of the Currency.

McKinley was rescued from the dilemma over the Treasury by the fears of his Illinois friends that the place would go to Cullom. Dawes himself became sufficiently worried to plead for Mr. Gage. McKinley's relief was unbounded. On meeting Gage, he took an immediate liking to this imposing, unhurried gentleman, with a head like Sophocles. Gage would prove to be a satisfactory choice, not a great Secretary of the Treasury, but a responsible public servant, and an exceptionally congenial member of McKinley's official family.

The office of Postmaster General was one of the last to be filled. McKinley kept it open for Hanna until after the middle of February. In the interval, with the backing of Hanna and a host of other influential Republicans, the Wisconsin machine was demanding the place for the national committeeman, Henry C. Payne. While McKinley was indebted to Payne for his campaign services at the Chicago headquarters, the connection had not been entirely advantageous. Payne was an anti-union employer, and during the summer had been widely criticized for breaking a strike of street-railway workers in Milwaukee. As a politician, Payne represented in its finest flower the machine tie-up with the corporations. He was not disreputable. On the contrary, he gave an impression of devotion to the public interest. He was respected in the party for his redoubtable management and beloved for his frank and sweet-tempered personality. But, in Congress, McKinley had known Payne as a prominent lobbyist for railroads and for the beef trust, and he was reluctant to put him in his Cabinet.

As the pressure for Payne increased, McKinley turned for advice to his former colleague on the Ways and Means Committee, and ardent supporter for the presidency, Robert La Follette of Wisconsin. The youthful crusader against privilege was not a dispassionate consultant. Since his defeat for Congress in 1890, he had returned home to begin his long and ultimately successful war on the Wisconsin machine, and during the day he spent at Canton he filled McKinley's ears with stories that put an end to Payne's chances for the Cabinet. Hanna persisted in his efforts. As La Follette heard from McKinley, Hanna said to him, "You may wipe out every obligation that you feel toward me, and I'll ask no further favors of you, if you'll only put Henry Payne in the Cabinet." McKinley replied—again according to La Follette's report—"Mark, I would do anything in the world I could for you, but I cannot put a man in my Cabinet who is known as a lobbyist." Eventually, the Postmaster General-ship was bestowed on Mr. James A. Gary of Baltimore, a courtly old textile manufacturer, who had been instrumental in swinging Maryland into the Republican column in November.

Three of McKinley's old-time Congressional colleagues were readily persuaded to enter his administration. His dear friend John D. Long of Massachusetts was a Harvard-educated lawyer, a gentle and scrupulous man of limited means and scholarly tastes. His political assets were a musical voice, a pure use of English, and a lovable personality. He had three times been elected governor of Massachusetts before his service in Congress; and, on returning to private life, had remained a popular favorite whose recognition was gratifying to his home state. In making Long his Secretary of the Navy, McKinley was following an American tradition that no special aptitude or training was needed for the position. There was little to be said against this personal appointment, except that Long was in poor health. He had recently retired from law practice and had taken no part in the presidential campaign because of nervous prostra-tion, as severe emotional maladjustments were then called.

The Iowa Republicans, proud of their showing in the election, were clamoring for representation in the Cabinet. On Allison's advice, rival claims had been compromised in favor of James Wilson of Tama County for Secretary of Agriculture. "Tama Jim" had been honored in the House as a shrewd parliamentarian and a rural sage and oracle. He was a plain, sturdy, gray-bearded Scot, who plowed his own fields and sheared his own sheep, and, as professor of agriculture at Iowa State College, conducted an experiment station for modern, scientific methods of farming. McKinley was not intimate with Wilson—their service in Congress had coincided by only one term—but he knew that this was a good appointment, and he was happy to make it. In Wilson, he found a wise counselor and a steady and companionable friend.

For Secretary of the Interior, McKinley's thoughts turned to Judge Joseph McKenna of California, a bland Irishman with whom he had been associated on the Ways and Means Committee. He had forgotten, if he had ever known, that McKenna was a Roman Catholic. The Judge mentioned the fact during an interview at Canton, and added that his control of the Indian missions would be particularly objectionable to Protestants. Visions of the A.P.A. must have rushed with the speed of light through McKinley's mind, but he did not blink, as he composedly remarked that the position of which he was thinking had nothing to do with the Indian missions. It was the Attorney Generalship. McKenna thought that he would prefer it to any other Cabinet seat, and shortly after he was formally invited to accept it.

McKinley had extricated himself from the dilemma caused by his ignorance of McKenna's religious faith, but his hasty switch had opened up fresh difficulties with the New York machine. Tom Platt's lean shadow had lengthened across the federal patronage when the Albany legislature obediently elected him to the United States Senate. Platt was confidently counting on naming a Cabinet member, but the allotment of a seat to the Empire State was beset with political pitfalls. Three separate groups had to be considered: the McKinley League, the Union League Club, and the regular Republican organization. The first had earned the gratitude of the President-elect as original McKinley men, who had defied the machine on the nomination. The Union League, which for years had led the fight for good government in New York, included most of the Republicans who were fitted for the highest positions. The Platt organization, furiously hostile to both the other groups, would demand the lion's share of the federal patronage as reward for its services in the campaign. It had at first seemed fortunate that one public-spirited New Yorker, Mr. Cornelius N. Bliss, was acceptable to the machine. Platt had formerly loathed this estimable gentleman, not merely as a member of "that aristocratic and semi-disloyal body," the Union League Club, but as a potent influence in defeating his expectation of becoming Harrison's Secretary of the Treasury. Bliss, however, had made peace with the boss. McKinley had offered him the Department of the Interior with high hopes of harmony in New York, and was grievously disappointed that the ill health of Mrs. Bliss caused the offer to be declined.

Weeks passed in a tug of war between incoming President and incoming Senator from New York. For a time, Platt backed General Stewart L. Woodford, an elderly New York lawyer who was a candidate for the Navy Department. On discovering that McKinley did not think Woodford "quite sized up," Platt was moved to compromise. Since he could not get an ally, he settled for one of his least flagrant enemies. He settled for Colonel John J. McCook, another New York lawyer, who was interested in the Attorney Generalship, and to whom McKinley was warmly inclined. Tentative overtures had been made to McCook when the interview with McKenna abruptly bestowed the Attorney Generalship on California.

McCook did not want the Department of the Interior. The place was not filled until March. Just before the inauguration, Mr. Bliss, merchant prince, treasurer of the Republican National Committee, and president of the American Protective Tariff League, bowed to the interest of party and consented to enter the Cabinet.

McKinley's worries over New York had been inordinately increased by the persistence of an ambitious gentleman who suffered from asthma and was temporarily resident in Phoenix, Arizona. There were few friends to whom the President-elect was more deeply indebted; few better suited to adorn high office; none more importunate. Whitelaw Reid was the proprietor of the *New York Tribune,* historical organ of the Republicans and recent crusader against the corruption of the state machine. He had served as American minister to France before being chosen as Harrison's running mate in the losing campaign of 1892. He was seeking fresh honors, and had earned them. The *Tribune* had so effectively supported the New York sentiment for McKinley's nomination that Platt chiefly blamed Reid for the division in his delegation at the St. Louis convention. After the election, Platt's emissary to Canton had carried a warning, as well as an olive branch. Reid was the one New Yorker to whose recognition the boss would not consent. The supreme impudence of the ultimatum was its demand that Reid should be scalped for loyalty to McKinley.

Reid had also paid an early visit to Canton, and carefully tutored McKinley in the technique of resisting Platt's demands. Reports of McKinley's inclination toward Bliss soon hinted that this advice had not been taken, and Reid repeated it in a perturbed letter from Phoenix. Why should Platt be considered? he asked. The boss was engaged in utterly reckless slander of the incoming administration, and his friends were still saying that McKinley was wobbly and had no backbone. From the desert, Reid was directing a campaign for his own preferment. He wanted the Navy Department or, alternatively, the most important of the diplomatic posts, the ambassadorship to Great Britain. He obtained several endorsements for the latter position, and as his leading advocate impressed Colonel John Hay, his close friend and former associate on the *Tribune.*

McKinley was seeking to elevate the London appointment above the clamor for reward. The American ambassador would have an especially delicate assignment of allaying irritations and composing disputes; and McKinley was anxious to secure British co-operation in calling another international conference on bimetallism. After several conversations with Colonel Hay, it occurred to McKinley that this devoted Anglophile would himself be an excellent emissary. The appointment, incidentally, would bypass New York, where three other deserving gentlemen were competing for the place. While Hay was recommending Reid, McKinley was in effect asking, "Why don't you speak for yourself, John?"

Hay scarcely dared to trust the intimations of his own selection, but he was not left in doubt about Reid's fate. As McKinley's agent in letting Reid down, he enlisted the aid of Mr. Darius Ogden Mills, the candidate's father-in-law and intimate friend. In February, Reid was persuaded to give up the idea of the ambassadorship. "Get England if you can," he contritely wrote Hay; "and don't in any case be beaten by Morton or Depew." Reid spoke wistfully of the Cabinet seat, but he had grown discouraged. If it could not be arranged, he suggested that McKinley should write that he wanted him for the Cabinet or for England, but feared to impose on him either the drudgery of office or a harsh climate. Hay promptly drafted an appropriate letter. The struggle, however, was not over. Two telegrams from Reid announced a fresh assault on the Cabinet. In disgust, Hay dashed off an alternative letter, offering Reid the embassy. "In all this, I am thinking only of you," Hay wrote McKinley in forwarding the two drafts to Canton. "I have ceased thinking about Reid; he thinks enough about himself for two."

Hay plainly expected the face-saving draft to be chosen, but he was perhaps surprised by McKinley's editing of its phrases. The result was a masterpiece that Hay greatly admired. It gracefully expressed apprehension about the severe duties of a laborious administrative department and the dangers of exposure in a harsh climate. It assured Reid that if McKinley was oversolicitous, it was because of his sincere affection. It lightly tossed in the information that McKinley had Colonel Hay "in mind" for England. He hoped in future to avail himself . . . an important place would have been cheerfully tendered . . . Reid would still always "hold the post of friendship" with the President.

Between the lines of the letter, there ran a different message. In believing that the New York objections were not insuperable, after Platt had been elected senator, Reid little understood the position of Chief Magistrate under the party system. McKinley would be at pains to compensate Reid, but it was improbable that he would receive an office that required the confirmation of the Senate.

Above all other honors, Hay desired the ambassadorship. Though he forbore to solicit it, he had confided his wish to McKinley's cousin, Will Osborne. He had also assiduously cultivated McKinley's esteem. In December, he had sent the President-elect a gold ring, containing a few hairs from the head of George Washington, the authenticity of which Hay was at pains to establish. On one side of the setting were engraved the initials, "G.W.," and on the other, "W.M." Hay asked McKinley to wear this doubly monogrammed token on the day of his inauguration. "It is my confident hope and belief," Hay wrote, "that your administration may be not less glorious and the memory of it as spotless, as that of Washington." What would Henry Adams have said to that? Perhaps Hay felt that his tribute was a trifle overexuberant, for he added a request that his name should not be mentioned in connection with the gift.

A gold ring had been added to Hay's campaign contributions and errands, and his lessons in foreign relations. The wise and weary littérateur knew how little they weighed in the scales of political debt, how disproportionate to their value was the reward of the ambassadorship. The preliminaries to the conferring of high office were as elaborate as the courtship dance of the African crested crane. They did not always lead to consummation. Hay remained in suspense until shortly before the inauguration.

On the capitulation of Mr. Bliss, the slate of the Cabinet was made public. The announcement was received with general approbation. McKinley's personality was mirrored in the advisers he had chosen: reputable and dignified gentlemen, who were devoted to their families and honored in their communities; industrious, God-fearing, practical-minded gentlemen, who had made good by their own unaided efforts. Except for Long and Gary, none of them had had the advantage of college education. Gary alone had been born to even a modest prosperity. The career of Russell Alger might have furnished the theme for one of Horatio Alger's success stories, and Gage and Bliss were also examples to American youth of the rise from poverty to riches. The yellow press could excite small interest in the fact that Alger had at one time been associated with a trust, the Diamond Match Company; or that Judge McKenna had evinced sympathy for the corporations on the federal bench; or that Bliss and Gary, as textile magnates, represented the protected industries. The arrows of criticism were blunted against McKinley's faith in the American way. But one shaft struck through—that McKinley seemed to be trying to start an infirmary or an old men's home. Solid respectability appeared not quite enough for the heirs to the economic stress and troubled foreign relations of Cleveland's administration. The tottering Sherman was balanced by Judge McKenna, the baby of the lot at fifty-four. Long was an ailing fifty-nine. The others were all over sixty. McKinley had performed the feat of satisfying the business interests and the machine politicians, without yielding to their dictates; but he had not made a strong Cabinet. Only Gage, Long, and Wilson would outlast in office the strain of the next two years.

On March 1, McKinley took his departure from Canton with a party of more than fifty relatives and friends. He had been ill with the grippe, an epidemic only recently known in the United States; but, as he was drawn by four white horses down a lane of colored fire to the depot, his look of health contrasted with the frailty of the woman at his side. Mrs. McKinley had not passed a good winter, and her strength had been taxed by the exertions of getting her White House wardrobe in Chicago. She had twice been parted from her husband. He had joined her on the first trip in December, but had been unable to get away for a second time in January. On both occasions, Mrs. McKinley had stayed with her cousin, the former Mary Goodman, whose husband Lafayette McWilliams was an official of Marshall Field and Company.

In the privacy of the McWilliams residence, Mrs. McKinley held consultations with Marshall Field's head designer, and endured the ordeal of standing for the fittings. The details of her new costumes were a jealously guarded secret. She particularly wished to withhold knowledge of the gown which had been designed for the inaugural ball, and which had somewhat eclipsed the Cabinet as a subject of popular interest. Letters from all parts of the country begged Marshall Field's for information and samples. Exigent reporters beset both the store and the house. Mary McWilliams indignantly refused to satisfy their curiosity. The manager of the dressmaking department was equally reticent, but the correspondent of the New York *World* found a weak spot in the security program. His newspaper confidently published a sketch and description of a gray-blue satin brocaded in silver, with point lace forming panels on the trained skirt and draping the high-necked yoke of silver and pearl passementerie. Just such a ballgown was packed in Mrs. McKinley's trunk when she set out for Washington.

From the platform of the luxurious private train provided by the Pennsylvania Railroad, McKinley bade farewell to Canton. "I reluctantly take leave of my friends and neighbors," he said, "cherishing in my heart the sweetest memories and the tenderest thoughts of my old home—my home now, and, I trust, my home hereafter, so long as I live." His voice faltered as he spoke, and men and women wept as they shouted godspeed to the Major.

As the seven flag-draped Pullman cars rolled slowly under the shed at the Washington depot next morning, a select and dapper group stood waiting on the platform. The gentlemen of the Washington reception committee were spring fashion plates in short, light overcoats or tight-fitting Prince Alberts, with boutonnieres of violets. Governor Bushnell, on hand to represent Ohio, was surrounded by a resplendent staff. The tall, thickset dude, with pince-nez on a black cord, was Mr. J. Addison Porter of Hartford, recently appointed Secretary to the President. McKinley had expressed a wish for an informal reception. At his request, the Washington committee had abandoned plans for a parade to escort the President-elect to his temporary residence, the Ebbitt House. Compliments were quickly exchanged, and the procession of travelers formed behind the McKinleys for the march through the station. The sweaty, coal-grimed engineer grinned proudly at the spray of white carnations which the incoming President handed up to the cab as he passed the head of the train.

Mrs. McKinley's hat was trimmed with violets, and under a heavily furred cloak she wore a traveling costume of green cloth with a violet velvet front. A wheelchair was in waiting. She refused it, and made her entrance to Washington on her husband's arm. But she had passed a sleepless night, and, laden with a huge bouquet, she found the walk through the station more fatiguing than she had expected. Her face was pale when at last she stumbled out on Sixth Street in the din of the welcoming crowds and the clanging electric cars. At the head of a line of waiting carriages stood an open landau, with a team of restive grays. Mrs. McKinley was hoisted in. McKinley seated himself at her side. Mr. Porter and the chairman of the reception committee took the places opposite, and the grays dashed off toward Pennsylvania Avenue.

It is a great moment when a private citizen enters Washington to assume the highest office in the gift of his country, and feels within his grasp the glittering prize, untarnished yet by opposition and compromise, by self-doubt, weariness, and routine. As McKinley surveyed Pennsylvania Avenue and remarked on the familiarity of the scene, he must have remembered the years of struggle, of drudgery and straitened means, which had culminated in this momentous arrival. The wide street, in the sunny forenoon, blazed with bunting and flags for his inauguration. The sightseers crowded the pavement, which spilled pedestrians into the traffic of speeding herdics and bicycles from the Peace Monument to the Treasury. Blind musicians and vendors of sweet violets and yellow roses vied on the curbstones with the fakirs who hawked badges, goldbugs, shoestrings, crawling mice, and the *New York Journal's* "Yellow Kid" in plaster and fancy soap. A man with a little machine like an electric fan offered to polish gentlemen's silk hats for the inauguration. A souvenir model of McKinley's head in a Napoleonic hat was on sale for twenty-five cents, but in the confusion the occupant of the speeding landau was at first not generally recognized. Then a shout was raised, and traveled up the avenue. Men stopped and stared and removed their hats. Bicycles reeled in pursuit. An Ohio bumpkin, festooned in strings of buckeyes, tore jubilantly around the corner of Fourteenth Street. When the landau drew up in front of the Ebbitt House on F Street, two little Negroes were hanging on the dashers, and it was surrounded by an agile convoy of urchins, district messengers, and telegraph boys. So the incoming President had an escort, after all.

While McKinley received Governor Bushnell in a downstairs parlor and then retired for private conferences, the members of his party swarmed over the Ebbitt House, and were inadequately accommodated and lost their luggage, and protested and were consoled. All McKinley's nearest surviving relatives had made the trip to Washington: his mother, his sister Helen, and his wards James and Grace; his sister Sarah and her husband Andrew Duncan of Cleveland, with four children and one son-in-law; his brother Abner, who lived in New York and had joined the inaugural train with his wife and daughter at Baltimore; and four relatives from California: David's daughter Ida and her husband George Morse, and Uncle Ben McKinley and his son. The Saxtons were represented by Ida's brother George, her Aunt Maria, and Pina and Marshall Barber and their seven children, while Mary McWilliams had come on from Chicago with her family. On the whole, it was not a colorful gathering. The Washington correspondents did not find it a mine of feature stories, but Mother McKinley was a treasure-trove in herself. Since Lincoln's time, a background of pioneer simplicity had been an asset in public life. Nancy Allison, with her homespun ways and prayer-worn knees, was tailored to fit the popular ideal. The perils of the American female parent had not yet been recognized, and McKinley was lauded as another "mother's boy" in the White House.

With her arms filled with roses she had thriftily gathered from the train, Mother McKinley walked out of the Washington station into the hearts of the press and public. She was a spry and independent eighty-seven. She was "cute." While her daughter-in-law remained in retirement, Mother McKinley became the belle of the Ebbitt House, waving cheerily to the bystanders as she went in and out, or settling down for a neighborly chat in the lobby. Her eyes glinted sociably behind her spectacles, but she was not impressed by all the fuss. She had the dignity of the very old, who find it unnecessary to pretend or adapt; and perhaps, in this hour of her darling William's triumph, she still had reservations and regrets. On the morning before the inauguration, Abner was overheard pleading for her approval, "Mother, this is better than a bishopric."

The McKinleys' nieces were to play a large social role in the new administration, and the press gave them all polite notice. Ida McKinley

Morse, a statuesque and self-willed blonde, was a wife and mother, and hence less interesting than the four unmarried young ladies in the party. Pina's eldest, Mary Barber, a student at Smith College, was rapturously admired for her petite and graceful figure, her dark, curly hair, and her large, sympathetic brown eyes. Sarah Duncan was a rosy, athletic girl who was taking kindergarten training in Chicago. Grace McKinley, who was at Mount Holyoke, was said to be tall and fair, with "a commanding presence." Abner's brunette daughter, Mabel, was a cripple with a strong mezzo-soprano voice. In coming years, Mabel McKinley would be a popular artist on the big-time vaudeville circuits, singing "Nona from Arizona" and "Yankee Rose" and "Honey, You Stay in Your Own Backyard"; but in 1897 the reporters called her vivacious and talented, and let it go at that.

Two far more lively subjects for the scandal sheets were the respective only brothers of the President-elect and his wife. George Saxton, an expert wheelman, still dashing in his bicycle cap, was known in Canton as a middle-aged Lothario. The most notorious of his affairs had been his illicit connection with Mrs. Anna George, a personable dressmaker whom he had induced to leave her husband and two children. After financing Anna's divorce, Saxton had wearied of his mistress. A complex of sordid lawsuits had begun during McKinley's first term as governor; and, as recently as the past November, the Canton police had been called in to eject Anna from the Saxton Block, where she was making forcible entry in an attempt to recover alleged possessions of her own. In the inaugural party, George Saxton was noticed merely as a bachelor who made his home with the Barbers.

Abner McKinley's domestic life was above reproach. It was not possible to say, with absolute certainty, as much for his business transactions. He had prospered in New York as a promoter of various enterprises, and lived in style at the Windsor Hotel on Fifth Avenue and at the summer place he maintained at Somerset, Pennsylvania. Though Abner had neither handsome features nor a statesmanlike presence, he strongly resembled his older brother in looks and genial manner; and, like William, he had a host of friends. He was the shrewder of the two, the more venturesome and speculative, and he did not share William's fidelity to the precepts he had learned at his mother's knee. There was nothing that the newspapers cared to notice very much, just little stories of printing telegraph stock and selling worthless railroad bonds. Abner once consulted Dawes about a scheme for making artificial rubber by a process that required a period of total darkness. "That was when they put the rubber in," Dawes concluded; but he liked Abner so much that he preferred to believe he was gullible.

The President's opinion was not expressed. He never gave Abner public office, or permitted him to touch a dollar of the public funds. But Abner was often in Washington in the next four years, making useful connections with important people, and wangling private cars and other favors from the White House staff. The New York *Evening Post* once burst out with indignant charges that Abner McKinley was acting as a promoter and patronage dispenser at the government departments. He undoubtedly endeavored to profit by his name and family relationship, but there was remarkably little criticism, and no exposure of specific wrongdoing. The President must have had his private troubles with the imaginative entrepreneur who was his younger brother.

In the private parlor of the inaugural suite at the Ebbitt House, Pina Barber capably handled the reporters and other callers. Mrs. McKinley, resting behind closed doors in a pink-canopied brass bed, sent her regrets for an engagement on the evening of her arrival. In accordance with recent custom, the incoming President and his wife had been invited to dine informally at the White House, the one to discuss matters of state and the other to inspect the living quarters of the mansion and receive pointers on the domestic arrangements. Mrs. McKinley always left household cares to her husband, and her fatigue may have been increased by the thought of disclosing her incompetence to pretty young Mrs. Cleveland.

President Cleveland had been confined to his room by a severe attack of gout, but he dragged his bandaged foot downstairs to welcome McKinley. The meeting was cordial on both sides. McKinley greatly admired the Democratic President—he had called on him more than once in the last four years—and at this time Cleveland warmly reciprocated McKinley's regard. The Republican success at the polls had vindicated Cleveland's financial policy, and saved the country from Bryanism, and he was in unusual accord with the leader of the opposing party. The two men shared the aim of international arbitration. McKinley had inserted in his inaugural address a commendation of the compact with Great Britain which Cleveland had recently sent to the Senate, and he intended to follow Cleveland's course of amity toward Spain and scrupulous observance of her sovereignty. In large part, their discussion was concerned with the Cuban question. McKinley carefully went over with Cleveland the steps that had been taken to keep the peace, and voiced the fervent hope that his own efforts would meet with equal success. Cleveland would recall the "settled sadness and sincerity" of their interview.

Cleveland was convinced that war had become all but inevitable because of the strength of the interventionists in both houses of Congress, and the explosive situation at Havana, where the United States consul, General

Fitzhugh Lee, was reputedly involved in conspiracies against the Spanish authorities. Cleveland had only a faint hope that, before an inflammatory incident occurred, Spain might be induced to sell Cuba to the United States. These were the opinions of the President who was about to shed the cares of office, and escape the deluge; but, though McKinley spoke heavily of the horrors of war, he was not infected by the pessimism of the tired man with the painful, bandaged foot. Cleveland was estranged from his party, and baited by opposition and calumny. McKinley was the leader of the triumphant Republicans, and to his dealings with Congress he would bring a skill and subtlety that were not at Cleveland's command. In the springtime of his power, McKinley was confident that he could keep the nation at peace.

The next day passed in the exchange of formal calls between the Executive Mansion and the Ebbitt House, and in preparation for the ceremonies of the morrow. After attending a stag dinner given in his honor by Colonel Hay, McKinley retired early to bed. On March 4, he arose betimes. He donned a new frock coat of domestic worsted, and shoes made by a Canton cobbler, who had been a drummerboy at Gettysburg. He had a word with Secretary Porter; thanked the detectives who had guarded the door all night; admitted the waiters with the laden breakfast trays; and, greeting his mother with a kiss, affectionately drew her into the private parlor. Before the barber entered with his shining basin and towels, McKinley also had a session with Dr. T. H. Phillips of Canton. The family physician, initially provoked by Mrs. McKinley's imprudent walk through the station, had been exasperated to learn that the Major had partaken of salmon salad at Colonel Hay's dinner, and read McKinley a lecture on the necessity for a strict diet after an attack of the grippe. The devastated trays should have silenced these reproaches. The McKinleys had done full justice to porterhouse steak, broiled chicken, quail, Spanish omelet, toast, hot rolls, wheat muffins, tea, and coffee.

Shortly before ten o'clock, a crack troop of Ohio cavalry reined in their black chargers before the Ebbitt House. Senators Sherman of Ohio and Mitchell of Wisconsin presented themselves. The President entered his carriage with this congressional committee and Secretary Porter, and, preceded by the troopers, drove to the Executive Mansion to wait on President Cleveland and make the progress to the Capitol.

On the clear, windy morning, the flags swung and snapped above the sightseers who surged against the police lines on Pennsylvania Avenue. To the east of the Capitol, where a platform had been erected at the foot of the Senate steps, a multitude was solidly massed in the park. The broad plaza was a scene of animated confusion. Press photographers pivoted and focused their cameras on top of the shed that sheltered the Greenough statue of George Washington from rough weather. On a jutting stand at one side of the steps, operators were busily testing Edison's invention, the kinetoscope, which was to attempt the experiment of securing a continuous record of the proceedings for motion picture production. The sunshine glittered on the movement of military accouterments and the helmets and white sashes of the marshals and their aides. Marching clubs jostled their banners through the throng. Bands blasted out patriotic airs. Specta· tors, swarming up the trees to secure vantage points on the bare branches, applauded the diversions. The large decorated platform, with its two red leather armchairs and long rows of reserved seats, was prepared for the solemn quadrennial ceremonies of the republic, but inauguration day was celebrated in Washington as a holiday rout of the people.

In the Senate chamber, the closing proceedings were witnessed by the members of the House, the Supreme Court justices, the foreign diplomats, and the other personages who were entitled to places of honor on the inaugural platform. Garret Hobart, self-possessed and spruce, with a knot of violets in his buttonhole, was sworn in as Vice-President. The Senate was declared adjourned, and immediately reconvened in the extra session that Cleveland had proclaimed at McKinley's request. While the two Presidents, escorted by detachments of the regular Army, drove through the cheers of Pennsylvania Avenue, Hobart took up his gold-decorated gavel, delivered a sensible little speech, and administered the oath to the newly elected senators. The assemblage arose as Cleveland and McKinley entered, arm in arm. McKinley's medium stature was dwarfed by the massive form of his companion, who wore a huge woolen shoe and leaned heavily on an umbrella, and by the attenuated figure of Senator Sherman, stalking beside them with an old fur collar hooked around his neck, and carrying a badly battered silk hat.

The incoming President's party left the Senate gallery for the eastern front of the Capitol in advance of the procession of dignitaries. Mrs. McKinley wore a royal-blue velvet gown, with a plastron of Renaissance lace, a black toque bonnet edged in white, and a short sealskin cape; but onlookers were less impressed by the modish elegance of her costume than by her appearance of extreme ill health, as she tottered down the steps with the inexpert assistance of Secretary Porter. Some color came back to her chalky face when she was seated in the open air, and pride and excitement lent an unusual vivacity to her manner. A camera caught her lovely profile as she turned away from Porter, who sat staring ahead with vacuous dignity, perhaps trying to ignore the fact that his feet were muffled in the voluminous folds of Mrs. McKinley's velvet skirt. Some minutes passed before the procession of officials began to straggle out. Joyous shouts thundered back to the new Library of Congress, as McKinley came into full view of the crowd. While the dignitaries wandered about in search of their seats, he stood bowing at the front of the platform. He glanced at his family, and gave a furtive nod of recognition. Only one face was missing from the adoring clan in the reserved seats. Abner, always forward-looking in his enterprises, was rushing about the platform, directing the operators of the kinetoscope.

Order was at last restored. The stage was cleared. Chief Justice Melville Fuller moved forward. The clerk held up the big gilt-edged Bible, and in a clear, solemn voice William McKinley repeated the oath by which he was inaugurated the twenty-fifth President of the United States.

McKinley drew a roll of manuscript from his pocket, and put on his glasses. The first part of his address was concerned with the prevailing industrial disturbances, and the means of speedy relief for willing labor and useful enterprise. It was acknowledged that the financial system needed some revision. When the government was assured of adequate revenue— but not until then—changes could be made in the fiscal laws; and McKinley suggested that Congress should create a commission to study the question. The subject of international bimetallism would have the President's early and earnest attention. He declared that silver must be kept at a par with gold, and moved on to the need of increasing the revenue. By its latest popular utterance, the country was committed to a system of tariff taxation. It was the President's hope and belief that the extra session of Congress would enact that protective legislation which had always been "the firmest prop of the Treasury."

Next in importance to the subject of business conditions were the President's statements on the foreign policy of the new administration. It would be firm and dignified, watchful of the national honor, and insistent on the lawful rights of American citizens everywhere; but it would follow Washington's wise rule of noninterference in the affairs of foreign governments. "We want no wars of conquest," McKinley said; "we must avoid the temptation of territorial aggression. War should never be entered upon until every agency of peace has failed; peace is preferable to war in almost every contingency." The President commended arbitration as the true method of settling international differences, and urged on the Senate, as a duty to mankind, the early ratification of the treaty that had been concluded between the United States and Great Britain.

There were a number of other points, notably a favorable mention of the reciprocity principle, strong endorsements of civil service reform and the restoration of the American merchant marine, a severe condemnation of lynching, and a rather more perfunctory word of disapproval of trusts and unjust railroad rates. The President congratulated the country on its evidence of fraternal spirit, and pledged himself to promote the reconcilia- tion between North and South. In conclusion, he solemnly repeated the pledge he had "reverently taken before the Lord Most High."

The significant information conveyed by the inaugural address was that the question of the currency would be indefinitely postponed, and that the President would resist the efforts of the interventionists to bring on war with Spain. Old-line Democrats who had voted for McKinley were nettled at getting the tariff instead of the gold standard, and warmongers of both parties were displeased by the omission of any mention of Cuba; but the speech met with general approval. The new administration was pledged to stimulate business and fill the dinner pail, uphold American honor, and keep the nation at peace. McKinley had voiced the aspirations of the vast majority of his countrymen.

The inaugural parade, reviewed by the President from a stand in front of the Executive Mansion, was the traditional feature of the afternoon. The detachments of the small, scattered Army and Navy were usually out- numbered by the militia and civic organizations; but this year a sizable body of regular troops had been assembled. The Republicans swept back full-panoplied to power, with their eyes turned on the military glories of the past. The grand marshal, General Horace Porter, had been Grant's aide. His staff included the sons of Grant, Hayes, Garfield, and Harrison. General Grenville Dodge of Civil War fame led the division of regulars, infantry, cavalry, and artillery, which recalled to old-timers in the crowd the Grand Review of 1865.

In the chill of evening, when the last marching club had passed, the President went back to the White House to prepare for the inaugural ball. This public function, held in the huge, barnlike Pension Office on Judiciary Square, was too largely attended to permit dancing, or even a general reception, but it satisfied popular curiosity to watch the President and his party on display in their best clothes. The President was expected to show himself on a balcony, to survey the gathering for a time, and to make a promenade of the ballroom before supper, with his wife on his arm. Mrs. McKinley's ill health caused fears that she might not put in an appearance, but she did not disappoint the public. She wore her beautiful blue-and-silver dress. Diamonds sparkled in her ears, and on her bosom. There was a bouquet of violets on her shoulder, and a lace fan in her hand; and, despite the Audubon Society's rising protests against cruelty to mother birds, an aigrette was perched in her short hair. Her wadded evening wrap was of Persian-patterned lavender silk, profusely bordered with white Alaskan fox. After toiling up to the balcony of the Pension Office in all this splendor, Mrs. McKinley was unable to take part in the small reception arranged by the members of the committee in charge of the ball. But she presently took her place on the balcony, and at last nerved herself to descend for the promenade. Leaning heavily on the President's arm, she managed to get halfway around the ballroom. The procession came to a sudden halt, which was correctly interpreted by Ohioans in the company. Mrs. McKinley was gently hustled into the supper room, and seen no more that evening.

When Ida had recovered, the President took her home to bed; and, while rockets still flared across the sky, himself lay down to rest. From the darkened White House, the aura of a prudent and cautious policy seemed to bathe the country in a tranquil expectation of four years of peace. But on the palm-fringed plains of Havana province, a minor military engagement saluted McKinley's inauguration. The camp of the Fifth Corps of the Second Division of the Army of Liberty did not contain enough *licores* to celebrate the accession of the leader of the friendly Republicans. Its commander, General A. del Castillo, was moved by the reflection that the wealthy town of Güines must be well supplied with beer. He gave the order to attack. Güines fell, and that night del Castillo's ragged brigades drank deep to the health of the American President and his people, and their own dream of Cuban freedom.

· 6 ·

HONEYMOON PERIOD

Behind the Tiffany glass screen in the White House vestibule lay a fine old residence chiefly remarkable for the extreme inconvenience of its arrangements. The federal mansion, designed to accommodate the home and office of the President of a small republic, had by Lincoln's time become inadequate for both executive business and entertainment. Since then, it had acquired electric lighting, a steam-heating system, bathtubs with running water, an elevator, and a telephone. The dignified austerity of the interior was defaced by an incongruous litter of decorations which successive waves of tenants had left in their wake. But no attempt had been made to adapt the mansion to the requirements of the vastly expanded country, or even to correct the dangerous dilapidation into which it had gradually fallen. Though the Army Engineers, who were in charge of the building's maintenance, were alarmed by the hazards of fire and collapsing floors at the large receptions, the niggardly appropriations of Congress barely served to finance patchwork repairs and sporadic forays on the carpets, upholstery, and curtains.

The tradition still prevailed that both the house and the President should be accessible to the people. The grounds were, in effect, a public park. The north driveway, on which the private dining room faced, was a thoroughfare for pedestrians, and Cleveland had incurred severe criticism for closing it off. The dining room was called "private" because it was the only room on the first floor that was not open to visitors. Until two o'clock every day, sightseers were at liberty to prowl through the East Room, and admire the weighty crystal chandeliers and gloomy yellow plush ottomans. The other parlors and the state dining room were on view to all who took the trouble of obtaining cards. Public receptions were held in the afternoon, almost daily for the first two weeks after an inauguration, and three times a week thereafter. When the East Room filled up with greeters, the President went downstairs, stationed himself at the door, and shook their hands as they filed out.

On the left of the front entrance, a stairway led to the six rooms that comprised the executive offices. This eastern wing of the second floor was in the last stage of decay. The tramp of generations of place seekers had weakened the floor beams until they were as shaky as those in the great parlor underneath; and Colonel William Henry Crook, the disbursing agent of the White House, remarked that there was not a government bureau of any importance that was not better furnished than the offices of the President of the United States. The German doorkeeper, Carl Loeffler, presided over the institutional corridor, lined with wooden chairs for the waiting petitioners. One corner was reserved for the use of the news correspondents. The clerks were installed in two rooms on the north side. The larger was equipped with desks, typewriters, and copying press. The long, narrow room to the east contained the telephone. A partition across one corner concealed a toilet which served the needs of staff and callers. The President answered the calls of nature at the other end of the house.

The President's commodious office was across the hall. It communicated on the east with that of his Secretary, and on the west with the Cabinet Room. The latter was usually filled with callers. The overflow was admitted directly to the President's office. Like a number of his predecessors, McKinley soon abandoned the attempt to conduct the executive business in the hearing of a restless and attentive audience. He made the big office a waiting room, and established himself in a swivel armchair at the head of the Cabinet table, which was fitted with pens and inkstands, a blotter, and a holder for stationery. The chamber had a cheerless look, at once official and neglected. It might have been the directors' room in an old-fashioned and not very flourishing bank. But it was well lighted for evening work by the electric chandelier that writhed above the President's head in an agony of brass; and traditions lingered in the dim oil portraits on the walls, and two shabby pieces of furniture, a roll-top rosewood desk and a marble-slabbed table, which dated from Lincoln's time. McKinley was well content with his office; and there throughout his administration he received his callers, dispatched his correspondence, and prepared his papers and addresses. The adjoining oval library was used for informal receptions, and for confidential interviews when the Cabinet Room was occupied.

The west wing of the second floor, approached by the main staircase and by the elevator, contained the five bedrooms and two dressing rooms that comprised the private living quarters. Since the library had lost its original character of a family parlor, the purpose was served by the end of the corridor, closed off by a partition from the view, if not from the racket of the offices. The McKinleys slept in the spacious northwest chamber, which had the grandeur of a lofty painted ceiling and a carved marble mantel, surmounted by a handsome looking glass. It was furnished with twin brass beds, a pair of bulky mirror-paneled wardrobes, a sofa, and two tufted easy chairs. In the center, a pedestal table held an electric lamp, connected by a dangling wire with a socket of the spidery chandelier. On either side stood a spindle-backed wooden rocker, similar to those currently advertised at $1.95 apiece. The effect was that of a lodging in a rundown palace, but the McKinleys were accustomed to making themselves at home in strange surroundings. When their trunks had been unpacked, the bedroom became their own familiar place, personal and cozy with souvenirs, knickknacks, fringed scarves, ruffled pillows, all the photographs, and little Katie's portrait. The bags of yarn were produced, and Mrs. McKinley sat down to crochet beside the draped and cluttered mantelpiece.

The inconveniences of the White House did not disturb Mrs. McKinley. In the secure ring of her invalid's habits, she was indifferent to the drawbacks of the larger environment, and this new home suited her in many ways. It had stables and conservatories, which ministered to her particular pleasures. She enjoyed the prestige of her position, and the consequence of a big establishment. Above all else, she was deeply satisfied with the aspect of the mansion that was generally condemned—its public character. In the *Ladies' Home Journal* that spring, ex-President Harrison inveighed against the limitations of the White House, declaring the juxtaposition of the Chief Magistrate's office and his home "an evil combination." Mrs. McKinley was delighted to have her husband always within call. For the President, as well, it was a fortunate arrangement. With only a brief interruption of his work, he was able to go to Ida, hastening to obey the summons from the sitting room in the corridor, or the bedroom where, high above the bleak brass beds, Katie gazed down from her frame with eyes as serious as her father's.

Besides its many visitors, the mansion teemed with clerks, doorkeepers, messengers, policemen, houseworkers, and gardeners. These last, a force of twelve under the direction of the veteran horticulturist, Henry Pfister, took full possession of the parlors only when functions were impending; but they were at all times in evidence, bearing potted plants from the labyrinthine glasshouses that were connected with the mansion on the west, and disposing the bouquets they prepared in a room set apart for the purpose on the lower floor. The "basement" was otherwise the domain of the domestic staff—a steward, an electrician, a watchman, a fireman, and more than a dozen servants. The President was required to provide food for their table, and to pay the wages of the cook and of any personal servants he wished to employ. Since numerous courses of "party food" were expected at the state dinners, it was customary in the winter season to bring down a French chef from New York. For his family table, McKinley hired a good plain cook—forty dollars a month—who satisfied the demands of what *Town Topics* called "a cuisine à la Canton." Mrs. McKinley's Swiss maid, Clara Tharin, was retained at her usual monthly wage of thirty dollars. This neat and nimble little woman, an expert seamstress and invalid's attendant, was the wife of a butler with inferior qualifications and a limited command of English. To keep Clara happy in the White House, Charles Tharin was made a messenger, on the Secret Service pay roll, and they were installed in a bedroom near the McKinleys'.

The President also paid the head coachman, who supervised the stables behind the house at sixty dollars a month. Though all the other employees were paid by the government, the responsibility for managing the establishment and making decisions on its personnel rested on the President. The most important position on the domestic staff was that of the steward, a bonded officer of the government. He received a salary of $1,800 a year, and was charged with the purchase of supplies and the care of the plate, furniture, and other public property. In both of Cleveland's administrations, this post had been held by his mulatto manservant, William Sinclair, who had also continued to act as the President's valet and personal factotum. Sinclair was not remarkably efficient in the discharge of his official duties, and he was in disfavor with the dealers of the Center Market because of the premiums he exacted in return for the White House patronage. But Cleveland wanted to find a place for his valet, and his strong recommendation induced McKinley to reappoint Sinclair.

Next in importance in the household was the electrician, Ike Hoover, who received seventy-five dollars a month. Ike dated from the Harrison administration, when electricity had been installed in the old building, and possessed a unique understanding of the complicated and dangerous wiring. The other domestic employees were of various terms of service and degrees of competence. McKinley had been indirectly informed that Cleveland considered the housekeeper "too frivolous and flirty," and she was replaced. Wishing to make as few changes as possible, McKinley kept on all the servants who did their work adequately, and at least one who did not—Jerry Smith, an aged Negro of disreputable appearance and untidy habits, who was a holdover from the Grant administration. (He was sometimes listed as Simpson, doubtless because of a natural confusion with Sockless Jerry Simpson, the Kansas Populist.) Jerry, whose job it was to clean the executive wing and the front vestibule, was a constant source of vexation and complaint. He left piles of dust and trash in obscure corners, to the irritation of Colonel Bingham, the Commissioner of Public Buildings and Grounds, and annoyed Mr. Dubois, the head doorkeeper, by sweeping wastepaper, remains of lunches, and cigar butts behind the vestibule radiators; while the gardeners and police were discommoded by Jerry's custom of emptying the office water cooler and cuspidors out of the window. A climax was reached when Private Andrews, detailed for duty outside the mansion, reported to Colonel Bingham that his uniform had been wet all over by Jerry's slops. The case at length was laid before the President.

Jerry purloined a piece of Executive Mansion stationery, and composed a letter to McKinley. It was not true, he wrote, that he had "through water." He had only "squze a rag out the window," after cleaning the rug in front of the President's desk, where the spit would make it "very disagreeable for you to sit their." Jerry was a worthless servant, but he was old, engaging, and artful. "I guarantee this on the squar as a free Mason," his letter concluded. In spite of the stern faces of Colonel Bingham and Mr. Dubois, Jerry stayed on the payroll.

The Civil Service regulations protected the doorkeepers and messengers, the fireman, and the watchman; and, except for the President's Secretary and his assistant, the members of the clerical force. But transfers could be easily arranged by an incoming President who might wish to bring in familiar associates, and Colonel Crook was relieved to learn that McKinley intended to make no changes, unless they were for the good of the service. Crook could scarcely have feared for his own berth as disbursing agent, for he was a White House fixture and celebrity, who had originally been assigned to the mansion to act as Lincoln's bodyguard. The length of his employment and the volume of his reminiscences could be matched only by the old doorkeeper, Thomas Pendel, another of Lincoln's bodyguards. Pendel, who had opened the door for Lincoln when he left for Ford's Theatre, had the additional distinction of having opened the door for Garfield on his fatal departure for the railroad station. He was inordinately proud of his ill-starred connection with the two martyred Presidents, and frequently offered sightseers a curl, snipped from his mop of black hair, as a White House souvenir.

McKinley augmented the unusually small force with which Cleveland had transacted business—six in all, including the two secretaries—but the tempo was leisurely in the first months. One new clerk—Ira Smith, the nephew of McKinley's friend Colonel Taylor of the East Liverpool potteries—was occupied with Mrs. McKinley's fan mail, acknowledging letters and gifts, arranging appointments for her callers, and politely refusing the many requests for her autograph. Toward the end of 1897, the pace accelerated. The staff often worked until midnight, and sometimes on Sundays. It was eventually increased to the unprecedented strength of eighteen. But, even in the ascending graph of executive business, the White House offices kept an informal atmosphere. The youngsters played ball in the grounds, after bolting their lunchtime sandwiches; laughed behind their hands at Pendel's locks of hair and the lifts that the bantam executive clerk Benjamin F. Montgomery wore in his shoes; and wangled advances on their salaries from Colonel Crook by regaling him with smoking-room stories.

The crowded east wing enfolded McKinley in its homely cheerfulness and rich sense of the past. He liked the associates he found there, particularly noting that they never talked about his predecessors, and approving the "fine 'form'" of their loyalty. His was a friendly regime. After an absence from Washington, the President always stepped into the clerks' room with a wave and a hearty greeting—"Gentlemen, I am glad to see you all again!" McKinley was much beloved in the White House.

The Secretary to the President was by no means equally popular. Mr. J. Addison Porter bore the stigmata of wealth and culture, and had not sufficient gifts to live them down. His dressy clothes, pompous manners, and the vertical fall of his eyeglass ribbon along one stout cheek made him an object of ridicule to the reporters, and vastly increased the secret merriment in the clerks' room.

Porter had long aspired to a political career. From his grandfather Joseph Earl Sheffield, whose benefactions to Yale had founded the Sheffield Scientific School, he had inherited the means to finance *The Hartford Post* and forward his ambition for elective office. This had been gratified only by one term in the Connecticut legislature. He had sought the Republican nomination for governor of his state, and had not relinquished the hope of getting it sometime; but he had been diverted by the prospect of reward for his services as an "original McKinley man." Besides organizing the first McKinley-for-President club, Porter had been active in securing favorable support in the Connecticut delegation to the St. Louis convention. He had gone confidently to Canton, armed with a bundle of endorsements for the ambassadorship to Italy. His interview with McKinley had persuaded him to switch from Rome to a confidential post at the White House. Porter was regarded by his friends as a power behind the throne—a kind of second-string Hanna in the new administration.

McKinley was not sharply critical of his fellow men, but he had small use for effete Easterners. Porter was the oddest of his choices. The misleading factor was undoubtedly McKinley's preoccupation with making a good initial impression on the country. Porter's effective work before the National Convention had made him seem more substantial than he actually was. McKinley wanted to enhance the importance of the President's Secretary—at his instance, the title assumed new dignity by being denuded of the adjective "Private" which had hitherto been attached to it—and evidently thought that a correct and well-connected Yale graduate would make a dignified front for the executive offices. A brief experience with J. Addison Porter taught him that he had made a mistake, and one that was costly in terms of his own official convenience. The Secretary was ignorant of Washington and its public men. He had no comprehension of office management, punctuating a lax routine with bursts of temper when he found that the work was in arrears. Except for writing letters, which were couched in an effusive and patronizing style, he knew nothing of secretarial duties, and was wanting in the judgment, humility, and discipline that might have enabled him to learn them.

At the White House, McKinley was separated from all the men on whom his convenience had previously depended. Will Osborne's campaign services were repaid by the consul generalship at London, coveted for its rich perquisites. Jim Boyle was given the Liverpool consulate, another desirable post. Joe Smith received the directorship of the Bureau of American Republics, a clearinghouse for commercial information, which was the precursor of the Pan-American Union. Charles Bawsel went to Maine in the customs service. Opha Moore stayed in Columbus. The only assistant whom McKinley had brought to Washington was Captain Heistand, who was assigned to the Adjutant General's office. The newspapers spoke of him as the President's aide, but he was not on regular duty at the White House. McKinley was left with a minor Republican dude, who was as light as thistledown and nearly as incapable of useful work. He soon began to depend for help on the clerk who had acted as Cleveland's stenographer. This dark, eyeglassed, sternly handsome young man quickly disposed of a volume of correspondence, taking down McKinley's directions in fluent pothooks, and composing lucid and sensible letters. He arranged for the prompt admittance of important visitors, and got the time wasters out. He had an intelligent comprehension of the executive business, and showed alacrity and discretion in handling its details. It was quickly understood that, although J. Addison Porter had the title of Secretary, it was George B. Cortelyou who held the job.

Porter did not see that the President was temporizing with an embarrassing situation. He misinterpreted McKinley's habitual courtesy, and his great kindness when one of Porter's little girls fell ill during the summer. Confiding loyalty was added to blind self-satisfaction. McKinley could not bring himself to speak frankly to Porter. He supplanted him in all important duties, and hoped that he would resign. Cortelyou, promoted Assistant Secretary, became the President's right hand, and the "influence" courted for appointments and favors. Porter remained in evidence, but was mainly occupied with trivial business and social matters, and with a revived interest in the nomination for governor of Connecticut. McKinley cheerfully granted the supernumerary Secretary many leaves of absence for political and personal reasons, and later for failing health. The illness that finally caused his resignation in 1900 was diagnosed by the famous Dr. William Osler of Baltimore as "over mental strain." Porter died a few months later.

It is improbable that Porter ever knew what had happened to him at the White House. His imperviousness was fatuous, rather than calculating. He was accustomed to a privileged position, and undoubtedly found it quite natural that an assistant should perform the drudgery of his office. Moreover, Porter had from the first regarded the social arrangements as a major responsibility. Before going to Washington, he had interested himself in the selection of the Commissioner of Public Buildings and Grounds, an officer of the Army Engineer Corps who also acted as major-domo of the White House. It was on Porter's recommendation that McKinley had given this post to Captain Theodore A. Bingham, a paragon of military efficiency, a vigilant inspector of cracked rafters, and the terror of Jerry Smith. Bingham was slender and stiffly erect, with haughty features and a delicately waxed blond mustache. Five years' experience as attaché of the United States legations at Berlin and Rome had perfected his knowledge of protocol. He could expatiate for pages on the etiquette of the carriage—getting in, sitting, and getting out. He took a serious view of his duties as court chamberlain, and he and Porter were at once joined in alliance. They often disagreed, enlivening the east wing with furious arguments, but they always made up, and went off arm in arm to lunch.

The main project on which Porter and Bingham engaged could not be put into effect until 1898. It was nothing less than a sweeping reform of the state receptions. These occasions, currently the subject of ex-President Harrison's caustic comment in the *Ladies' Home Journal*, had become notorious for the discomfort suffered by those who desired or felt compelled to attend them. A gathering of a thousand people taxed the capacity of the mansion, which had cloakroom facilities for only a small party, and the Army engineers were agreed that a larger attendance was dangerous to the structure. But three and four thousand guests customarily passed the receiving line in the Blue Room on the appointed evenings. While it was necessary for the President to entertain more officials than the house could well accommodate, the overcrowding was increased by two other factors. The invitation lists were poorly organized, with many duplications, and a host of uninvited persons were in the habit of attending. Colonel Bingham—he had been promoted on receiving his appointment—heard horrifying stories from his brother officers. They had been unable to raise their arms at the receptions; or, if they did so, could not put them down again. One had had his arm over a lady's shoulder the better part of an hour without being able to remove it. Another had been "so irresistibly pressed" against a lady that she nearly fainted, and he was powerless to relieve her. Fainting, indeed, as Bingham was told, was the most common thing in the world. His ears rang with tales of torn shoulder knots, swords broken loose from the scabbards, crushed helmets, lost jewelry, and ruined dresses. He was shocked to hear the President's receptions described as "vulgar mobs," and particularly humiliated by the exposure of the diplomatic corps to the gatecrashers. With Porter's assistance, Bingham laid plans to end these disgraceful scenes by arranging a series of exclusive card receptions for the coming season.

The prospect sustained Bingham in the arid routine of his first months in office. One of his duties was to attend the President at his public receptions, while McKinley moved the line along with practiced dexterity, reaching to the right, swinging to the left, and reaching back for the next comer with the regularity of a pendulum. There were few other gatherings at the White House in 1897. The Washington season ended in February, and the change from a Democratic to a Republican administration had disrupted official society. The Cabinet members and their wives were offered a dinner, followed by a musicale. Mrs. McKinley, gowned in robin's-egg-blue velvet or mauve-pink satin, received her callers in the oval library, and held one formal reception for the ladies of the diplomatic corps in the Blue Parlor, where she remained seated in an armchair throughout the presentations. The only occasion that merited Colonel Bingham's attention was a reception given in May in honor of the delegates to the Universal Postal Congress, which was currently in session at the old Corcoran Art Gallery. Bingham seized the opportunity to give a practical demonstration of a proper White House function. A limited number of guests was invited, and a buffet was provided for their delectation. The affair passed off very pleasantly, with only a few gatecrashers, and Bingham was gratified by the compliments on his arrangements, notably by the expressions of the German ambassador, who had been voluble in his criticisms of White House hospitality. The next day, Bingham launched his campaign. In a memorandum to the President, he offered his congratulations on the success of the party, proposing it as a model for the formal receptions of the coming season. He urged a limit of one thousand invitations, suggesting admittance by card at the door; but he was hoping for half as many, with the innovation of a buffet. As he pompously informed McKinley, "a little something to eat and drink adds wonderfully to the enjoyment of such an occasion owing to the peculiar constitution of human nature."

The President consented to reduce the invitations to one thousand per function, and authorized Bingham and Porter to divide up the lists. Though the company at the state receptions would, as usual, be refreshed only by iced water, Bingham had carried his main point, and he threw himself enthusiastically into his preparations for the winter's program. He had developed an extensive plan for supporting the mansion's entire first floor by increasing the number of posts that were erected in the basement when crowds were expected. This improvement was effected during the President's absence in the summer. Bingham also was at pains to augment the meager supply of hat and cloak boxes, which were set up in the corridor on grand occasions.

By autumn, the labor of revising the lists had been accomplished. All was in readiness for seemly entertainment, with one important exception. The President, though informed about the intruders at the receptions, had omitted to sanction the suggestion of turning them away at the door. Bingham evidently ascribed this neglect to an obtuse understanding, for in November he drew up a lengthy memorandum, diagraming for McKinley the havoc wrought by the gatecrashers and deploring their scandalous abuse of the President's hospitality. The horrible crushes had become injurious to limb, and Bingham suggested that they might prove fatal to life itself. Scarcely less solemn was his warning of the open disgust of the diplomatic corps. He advised the President that the administration and the nation must suffer in dignity and perhaps even in foreign influence as a result of admitting "vulgar mobs" to the White House. For McKinley's enlightenment, Bingham analyzed the character of the interlopers. Some congressmen brought along their boarding house associates, hiring the carriage and telling the landlady to furnish the crowd. Others (who should have been ashamed to call themselves representatives) had escorted women of the town to the receptions. Ladies had been preceded down the line by their own house servants. "The greater part of these people," Bingham wrote, "have been such as butchers, cabmen, market and grocery clerks, and the scum of the city."

The memorandum was designed to jar the President into a decision on the question of admittance by invitation card. It did so. McKinley promptly vetoed the proposal. He had been ready enough to agree to limiting the receptions. Bingham's vindictive sentences opened his eyes to the spirit that animated the reform. For all his brass efficiency, Bingham was as myopic as Porter. He was incapable of imagining that a reputation for giving fashionable and exclusive parties might not redound to the popularity of the President of the United States. Of McKinley's democratic principles, Bingham had no conception at all. Never, in all his hours of supercilious attendance at the public receptions, did he see the joy with which the President greeted the people, or guess that, like Antaeus, McKinley was strengthened for the struggle by contact with the earth.

In appearance and deportment, the President recalled to Washington an earlier federal period. His clean-shaven face, in a day of prevalent whiskers and mustaches, was an anachronism that matched the demeanor of an old-fashioned statesman. McKinley was gracious but not informal, colloquial without familiarity; and, so far as was compatible with the dignity of his office, he dispensed with ostentation and parade. Avoiding the lax and desultory protection afforded by the Secret Service Bureau, he walked freely through the streets without a guard. Washington, recently unaccustomed to the sight of a President on foot, applauded the advent of a plain citizen to the White House.

McKinley's personal habits were lightly touched by the transition to the Presidency. He did not smoke in public, or permit himself to be photographed with a cigar. He altered his signature, which had been "Wm. McKinley" since his father's death, and wrote his Christian name in full. Though McKinley never changed his conventional style of dress, he had a larger and more expensive wardrobe than before. He ordered a number of snowy piqué waistcoats, often sported a vivid pink carnation in his buttonhole, and took to wearing his reading glasses suspended on a neat black cord around his neck. He shone with Sinclair's expert valeting and the ministrations of the barber who periodically visited the mansion to cut and treat his hair, and sometimes to shave him. The gloss of grooming befitted McKinley's position, and also reflected the new ease of his circumstances. His financial worries were over. A salary of $50,000 a year was opulence which gave scope to his naturally openhanded disposition. The President was generous to his family dependents, and to charitable and patriotic causes. He lavished finery and jewels on his wife, celebrating her

131

first birthday in the White House with the gift of a diamond brooch; and indulged in the purchase of a fine team of bays and a handsome carriage for their drives. The "cuisine à la Canton" was by no means frugal, and many guests were gathered around the bountifully laden table. Benjamin Harrison lamented that the expense of White House entertainment did not permit the President to save money; but, without stinting the official hospitality or his own liberal inclinations, McKinley was able every year to lay aside a comfortable sum, which was invested for him by Myron Herrick or Garret Hobart.

An exceptional confinement was required of the President, and McKinley started out with a resolution to keep himself fit by taking outdoor exercise. For a while, he had a saddle horse in the stable; but after a few attempts to renew his pleasure in riding, he gave it up for good. A schedule of constitutionals, though more persistently followed, was gradually curtailed in length and frequency. McKinley was finally reduced to snatching odd moments for a stroll in the grounds. On fine afternoons, he usually took a drive with his wife. He went to church on Sundays. McKinley had come to Washington with a Bible text shining in his mind: ". . . what does the Lord require of thee, but to do justly, and to love mercy, and to walk humbly with thy God?" He kept his faith alight by public worship. He attended the Metropolitan Methodist Church, joining unostentatiously in the service like any other devout parishioner.

The President spent most of his time within the four walls of the Executive Mansion, breathing the close air of rooms that were stifling in the summer, overheated in the cold. It was an existence of trying and unhealthful restriction, even for an elderly man of sedentary habit, but a strong constitution and a placid mind enabled McKinley to bear the imprisonment with equanimity. The isthmus of the second-floor corridor joined the twin continents of his world. Their atmosphere differed as the heavy redolence of cigar smoke differs from the sickroom staleness of eau de Cologne and flowers. In the east wing, the President entered the domain of public affairs and the exclusive society of men. He revived a hundred associations, and delighted in good friendships, old and new. He met the members of his Cabinet in genial sessions, lively with the chaff in which this "pleasant tease" delighted. McKinley had a constant affection for John D. Long and he soon saw much of Gage and Wilson. His Canton neighbor, Judge Day, was drawn into daily consultations as Assistant Secretary of State. McKinley brought his sympathetic Vice-President into an integral relation with the administration, depending on Garret Hobart's sound advice on many questions of government policy.

Happily, the cleavage of McKinley's interests was no longer as wide as

132

in the congressional years. His two worlds met and mingled in Mrs. McKinley's feebly smiling sociability and her partiality for Jennie Hobart, Cornelia Gage, and Caro Dawes. The transit of the corridor was symbolically short; and, though it led to the invalid's armchair, it led away from it, too. McKinley's long hours of work were justified by his proximity to his wife. His day usually ended at his desk, with Cortelyou and a privileged visitor or two. Dawes was often there, leaving Caro with Mrs. McKinley after a family dinner and a hand of euchre, or stopping in for a good-night talk on his way home from another engagement.

Dawes was welcome to drop in at all hours. Every doorkeeper knew his lanky figure, red handlebar mustaches, and wry, squinting grin. Sometimes he walked with the President in the White House grounds, known to Dawes in the accent of rural Ohio as "the yard." He always wafted to the mansion the breeze of a larger and freer world than McKinley inhabited. Dawes loved music, and played the flute and the piano. He took a zestful pleasure in the theater, parties, books, and foreign travel; and, though his heart was full of earnest sentiment, he was shrewd and smart, with a tang of Yankee humor. The President unbent a little with this lively young fellow. Once he actually confided to Dawes a mildly scatological joke, concerned with the abuse by an intoxicated American tourist of a holy-water font in Rome, and involving a severe distortion of the word "Unitarian." It made a great impression on Dawes that the decorous President told him a smoking-room story.

McKinley's moments of relaxation with Dawes and other friends were a needed antidote to a rigorous program. He worked overtime to clear the correspondence from his desk, prepare his addresses, and catch up on the newspapers. Like his predecessors, McKinley found that in his first months in office the daylight hours were consumed by the distribution of the patronage.

Theoretically, the extension of the civil service rules should have corrected this notorious abuse of an incoming President's time. Some 80,000 federal offices, more than half the total number, had been placed on the classified list; but 30,000 of them had been added as Cleveland's parting contribution to reform, and the sudden contraction of the prizes severely intensified the rapacity of the competition. Hungry job seekers and their sponsors on Capitol Hill daily descended on the White House to solicit post offices and consulates, which remained at the President's disposal.

From the first, it was evident that some changes would have to be made in Cleveland's order. Indignation in Congress foreshadowed a revolt the next winter, and the inability to choose even their own secretaries grated on every member of the Cabinet. But McKinley was unwilling to take any immediate action that would appear to challenge the sincerity of his pledges on the civil service. His spokesmen in Congress, Hanna and Grosvenor, were among the open enemies of the merit system. McKinley chose to start out by winning the commendation of the reformers. He issued an order that tightened the regulations, and deferred all modifications until a later date.

A high standard of honesty and efficiency in office was McKinley's ideal, but he set a realistic value on the presidential patronage, using it astutely to strengthen his hold on the local Republican organizations throughout the country, and to bind the support of Congress. The reconciliation of public interest and party solidarity was a task of intricate, repetitious difficulties, and these were multiplied, as in the formation of the Cabinet, by McKinley's nagging sense of gratitude. The roster of his personal obligations was inordinately lengthened by the circumstances of his nomination. He had to find means of rewarding the men who had defied the bosses on his behalf, and who were consequently passed over in state after state for regular machine politicians. In the early months in Washington, the President spent himself on a monstrous chess game, which drained the energies he needed for the business of the nation.

As all day, every day, the procession of claimants clacked past his desk, McKinley grew visibly weary. He was not altogether lacking in the salt of criticism, and was especially irked, as he once admitted to Cortelyou, by men who magnified their own importance. He had a bland resistance to pressure, but did not like to be pushed hard. The only time that Dawes ever saw the President lose his temper was after an interview with a machine politician. McKinley pounded his desk and used strong language— when his visitor had gone. Whatever reservations he felt, he entertained his voluble petitioners with patient cordiality, letting them make the most of their moment at his desk. His gray eyes were so intent and sympathetic that his callers went away convinced that they had enlisted the President's interest, and sometimes sure that they had influenced his action.

McKinley's tact—"that *never failing remedy* of yours," as Mark Hanna described it—was often sorely needed. With fewer offices to bestow than any recent President, he was often forced to the painful necessity of outright refusal. To a rare degree, he avoided giving offense. Turning a man down made him look so unhappy that, according to Senator William Mason of Illinois, the applicant felt sorry for him. Senator Edward O. Wolcott of Colorado, asked to stay for luncheon after a rebuff, later told Mrs. Hobart: "The President was such a gracious host and I enjoyed myself so much at his table, I almost forgot I had been turned down." Mr.

Kohlsaat saw an angry labor leader melted by the President's gift of a carnation for his wife. It became a byword in Washington that while Harrison had made an enemy in awarding an office, McKinley made a friend in refusing one.

Since the Civil War, the growing assertiveness of the Senate had crossed the will of every Chief Magistrate with blocked policies and defeated treaties. McKinley consistently employed the patronage to cultivate the gratitude and good will of the Republican members of the upper chamber. Yet a large number of offices eluded their recommendations and flowed to McKinley's particular friends. The President was resourceful in disarming opposition and obtaining approval of his own selections. He was punctilious in his regard for senatorial prerogatives, and observed the courtesy of consultation, even in cases in which it was not customary. A single occasion is recorded on which McKinley failed to treat a senator with appropriate respect. The veteran William P. Frye of Maine had obtained the disposition of a small consulate in Nova Scotia. When he appeared with a more important request, the President quizzically inquired, "Did I not give you the appointment of consul at Pictou?" But this levity was ill timed. Frye did not consider his share of the patronage a laughing matter, and McKinley wrote the affronted old gentleman a letter of apology.

The President's methods were well illustrated by his dealings with two senators from states where the professional politicians and the original McKinley men had been at sharpest variance. Shelby Cullom and Tom Platt were at first uncertain of their standing at the White House, and felt some awkwardness in approaching the President for favors. Both were obliged to make large concessions on the patronage, and both ended up as warm supporters of McKinley's administration. There were subtle variations in the treatment by which this result was obtained.

Cullom's relationship with the President was in one respect highly unusual. It began in an atmosphere of constraint, which terminated in a showdown. In the allotment of the Illinois patronage, Cullom had found himself caught in a squeeze between Dawes and Senator Mason, who was also McKinley's good friend. Cullom was much put out by repeated requests to yield on appointments. His ill humor was aggravated by the formal courtesy of the President's manner. It was true that McKinley was treating Cullom coldly. He had been sent a letter, or a copy of a letter, which Cullom had written, stating that certain consular appointments were the fulfillment of promises made before McKinley's nomination. The President was so indignant over this charge that he was finally goaded into showing his feeling. Cullom, in the course of a sulky consultation over

135

some office, called the President's candidate "a jackass." McKinley's suavity cracked. He pulled the offensive letter from the papers on his table, and challenged Cullom to admit its authorship. There was "a general overhauling." Cullom burst out with his grievance over being held at arm's length. The President asked what he wanted, and Cullom told him, and the President did it. The quarrel ended in a love feast.

Thereafter, Cullom reveled in exaggerating his discomfiture at the President's hands. The cream of his enjoyment was the absorbed interest with which McKinley entertained his advice, while remaining fully determined to have his own way in the end. "I always yielded," Cullom complacently wrote; "in fact, it was impossible to resist him." A striking instance was the case of General William H. Powell, a Union officer under whom McKinley had served. Cullom objected to the proposal that Powell should be made the collector of internal revenue for the southern district of Illinois. The President heard him out in distress. If Cullom had come to him in the first place, he said, he could have followed the Senator's wishes. As it was, everything was filled, and he must either give this place to Powell or "turn him out to grass." When he was a boy in the army, the President went on, Powell had taken him under his wing and looked after him. McKinley had been standing only a little way off when Powell was shot through. The pain of the old memory overcame the President. He shed tears as he spoke of Powell's wounds. Although the General had evidently made a good recovery, although a generation later he was in condition to collect the internal revenue, Cullom threw up his hands. "I am through," he said; "I have nothing more to say." Powell got the appointment.

Sentiment played no part in obtaining senatorial approval of the appointments that were displeasing to the New York organization. Senator Tom Platt had fought McKinley's nomination, and by all the rules of the game he was due for humiliation on the patronage. He was surprised by the warmth with which the President praised the campaign services of the New York machine. But though McKinley's gloves were soft, Platt felt the impact of the blows they landed. General Horace Porter, a detested enemy, was made ambassador to France. Andrew D. White, the president of Cornell University, was given the German embassy, after refusing McKinley's request to "speak to" Platt on the subject. Offices fell to the original McKinley men of New York, rebels all from Platt's jurisdiction. Whitelaw Reid was designated special ambassador to Queen Victoria's Jubilee, a mission that did not require the confirmation of the Senate. The President politely discussed his arrangements with Platt, and then carried them out. There was nothing that Platt could do but take his medicine.

The delicate balance of the New York adjustments was severely tested by the interference of Cabot Lodge. Lodge had set his heart on making Theodore Roosevelt the Assistant Secretary of the Navy. The New York City police commissioner was a faithful Republican, biting in his scorn for mugwumps, parlor socialists, and reformers, but he was aggressively critical of the practices of the machine. In settling the books of the patronage, Platt did not want to have Roosevelt charged against his already depleted side of the ledger. He was also hopeful that the civil service might have left some pickings of spoils at the Brooklyn Navy Yard.

On a visit to Canton soon after the election, Senator Lodge had forcibly presented his request as the single favor he would ask. Young Roosevelt, on his own account, had much to recommend him. He was especially qualified for the proposed position by his knowledge of naval affairs. His appointment, moreover, would have the grateful political aspect of conciliating the former supporters of Tom Reed's presidential candidacy. Yet McKinley took several months to make up his mind, and his delay was not wholly attributable to the dissidence of Senator Platt. Roosevelt, like his sponsor, was a militant-minded expansionist and hankered for war with Spain. Lodge was asking the President to plant a firebrand in an administration dedicated to the diplomatic adjustment of the Cuban crisis. "I hope he has no preconceived plans which he would wish to drive through the moment he got in," McKinley had hinted to Lodge, when the subject was broached. Lodge elicited from Roosevelt eager promises of docility to the administration and to Senator Platt. He stirred up a host of peace-loving sponsors, even including Mark Hanna. Secretary Long was persuaded to agree that he would welcome Roosevelt to the Navy Department.

Though the uncertainty long troubled the New York arrangements, Senator Platt gave in with a good grace when the President requested him to withdraw his opposition. Roosevelt, after all, would be less annoying to the machine in Washington than in New York. Secretary Bliss was one of the sponsors who carried weight. The value of his friendship was rising as signs appeared that the Secretary of the Interior was on extremely pleasant terms with Hanna. Things were working out more favorably than Platt could have dreamed of expecting. He got the New York City postmastership. More wonderful still, he got the collectorship of the port, the historic token of presidential favor. Though its perquisites had been largely shorn by the civil service, Platt basked in the prestige of its disposal. By summer, when Whitelaw Reid went off to London to sun himself in the smiles of royalty, Platt's ruffled feathers had been smoothed, and he had settled down for good in the administration's nest. Under the circumstances, he had been treated with amazing generosity; and whatever faults the boss had, ingratitude was not among them.

Ohio presented a special problem, partly because McKinley's personal obligations were heavier there than in any other state, but chiefly because of the hostility between the two Republican senators and the President's close connection with one of them. Foraker jealously resented Hanna's influence at the White House, and was on the lookout for slights. The political situation in Ohio lent some color to his suspicions. The autumn elections would determine the complexion of the legislature on which the future occupancy of Hanna's seat in the Senate depended. The indignation over the appointment had not subsided, and Hanna badly needed to mend his fences at home. Yet the President showed no tendency to discriminate against the anti-Hanna faction. He made one of his greatest concessions in deference to Foraker's wishes, withdrawing an offer to his dear friend Bellamy Storer of the post of First Assistant Secretary of State. But Foraker did not govern the President's eventual decision. The State Department position went to Judge Day, another personal appointment, but one to which Foraker could not take exception. Storer was made minister to Belgium, with Foraker's acquiescence.

Foraker described one pleasant little interview at the White House. He had asked the President to bear a friend in mind for a consular post, but the greedy applicants had swept the board nearly clean when the Senator arrived with Professor O. F. Williams in tow. McKinley confessed that he hesitated to mention the only available opening, as he had been informed that it was not desirable. It was a place called Manila, "somewhere away around on the other side of the world," Foraker recalled that McKinley said; "he did not know exactly where, for he had not had time to look it up." Foraker himself had not previously heard of the Philippine Islands in such a way as to remember them, but Professor Williams was better informed. He wanted the consulate at Manila, undesirable though it might be called. The President had scraped the bottom of the barrel for Foraker, and it was an agreeable surprise that the residue gave satisfaction.

Even with administration backing, Hanna had a strenuous fight for a favorable legislature, and was returned to the Senate by a narrow majority the next winter, but his hard-earned success was effective in discomfiting the Foraker crowd and regaining political control of Ohio. It was no small tribute to the President's diplomacy that, even under these conditions, he retained the affections of Foraker's adherents, and held the Senator himself in an erratic but outwardly cordial alliance.

Though a display of Presidential favoritism was carefully avoided, Hanna occupied a unique position in the Senate as chairman of the National Committee. He was empowered to dispose of many federal offices, particularly in the South. The pork of the Post Office Department was dispensed as usual. It should not be concluded that Hanna had a preponderant influence on the decisions made by the President himself. These, in their defects and virtues alike, bore the imprint of McKinley's code of enlightened expediency. The hodgepodge of adjustments with the Senate leaders could not result in a uniform standard of merit in the appointments. Even the consular service, whose efficiency McKinley had especially desired to improve, was largely ravaged by the spoilsmen. On the other hand, the level of the President's major appointments was extremely high; and one lustrous and politically disinterested choice, like that of Ambassador John Hay, outshone a host of petty consuls, collectors, postmasters, and department employees. McKinley was praised, even by his opponents, for his discernment and sense of public duty. Hanna had not inspired the selections that reflected great honor on the administration. No one thought of crediting them to his strictly utilitarian conception of the patronage. Yet the legend of his dominance persisted. To the anger of McKinley's admirers, it was encouraged by Hanna himself.

Hanna was a modest man, capable of selfless devotion, but he was not quite so modest and selfless in Washington as he had been in Ohio. For years he had identified himself with McKinley's fortunes, and felt an intense emotional pleasure in the association. The fulfillment of his efforts had deprived Hanna of his function. Though he voluntarily relinquished his place as chief adviser and did not seek to be a habitué of the White House, it was natural that he should jealously cling to reminders of his old priority. Moreover, as senator, Hanna's own consequence was greatly enlarged. Soon after he took his seat, he was admitted to the coterie of conservative Republicans who controlled the policies of the upper chamber. He was courted and flattered, and he did not diminish his prestige by rebuking allusions to his influence over the President. He listened indulgently to compliments on his power, and appeared to accept them as his due.

McKinley's conduct in the White House was a tacit refutation of the charge that he was Hanna's man. The label was an injustice to his reputation and a disparagement of his leadership. When the whispering gallery of Washington acquainted the President with the facts, he made no comment; but he could not have expected that Hanna would perpetuate the campaign slurs of their common enemies, and he would not have been human if he had been indifferent to the change in the quality of Hanna's loyalty. One evening Dawes dropped in at the White House after attending a dinner of Republican grandees at which Hanna had been present. "How did Hanna handle himself?" the President casually inquired. Dawes answered with a parable. He told the story of the cock who thought his crowing made the sun rise. McKinley smiled. That thoughtful smile was his only criticism of Hanna. It was inevitable that, in the years ahead, other causes of friction should arise between them. At times, the President's political standards proved grievously embarrassing to Hanna, and he would complain to Dawes of "McKinley's lack of co-operation." But, except for a period of coolness in 1900, Hanna was quick to yield to the President's tact, to the easy intimacy and teasing affection that had always claimed him. He remained innocently unaware that, at some deep level of trust, he had disappointed McKinley.

McKinley's courtship of the Senate was a stark political necessity. The narrow Republican majority was precariously divided on many important questions. The block of silver senators held the balance of power. The aggressive expansionists were obstreperous on all questions of foreign policy. In the extra session, the arbitration treaty with Great Britain was summarily defeated, and a resolution for Cuban independence flouted the peaceful pronouncements of the inaugural address. But McKinley's influence prevailed to win the Senate's compromise in a stalemate in conference on the tariff. He had staked the success of his administration on the prompt passage of protective legislation, and by midsummer the new law was written on the statute books.

In the months before the inauguration, the Republicans of the Ways and Means Committee had mapped out a moderate policy, designed to supply the desperate need for enlarged revenues, and repair the rents that the Wilson-Gorman Act had made in the fabric of protection. Since the opening of the extra session in March was the first meeting of the Fifty-fifth Congress and it was theoretically still to be organized, there had been no authority for an advance preparation of legislation, but constitutional niceties had been overlooked by Tom Reed, predestined for re-election as Speaker, and Nelson Dingley, foreordained for reappointment as chairman of Ways and Means. Dingley's conservative bill was ready when Congress assembled. It was reported three days later; and, under the crack of Reed's whip, the House passed it in less than two weeks. Reed shut off discussion of Cuba, the currency, and all other issues extraneous to the business for which the session had been expressly called. The majority sustained his refusal to appoint committees, and the House sat in idleness while the Senate thrashed out the tariff.

A comparable exhibition of Republican efficiency and restraint could not be given in the undisciplined upper chamber, with its confused alignments on the question. In reporting the amended bill, Senator Nelson Aldrich of Rhode Island copiously disclaimed the necessity for a radically high tariff, but Dingley's handiwork had already been roughly treated by the Finance Committee, and the mangling was completed in open Senate. There was scarcely a semblance of resistance to the instructions of the lobbyists. The leading members of the opposition had no wish to obstruct the plans of the corporations, while the compliance of the silver block was purchased by piling on special concessions to the western states. As finally passed by the Senate in July, the bill was amended beyond recognition; and, even after the President persuaded Allison and Aldrich to recessions on the sugar schedule, the final law imposed a somewhat higher average of duties than the McKinley Act.

But from the country there came no echo of the outcry of 1890, not so much as a murmur of protest against the threat of rising prices. Public opinion had become submissive, apathetic, and cynical. This was the third revision of the tariff in seven years. The Wilson-Gorman Act had demonstrated that rational and disinterested legislation could not be expected from either party. Would the law increase the revenue and end the Treasury deficits? Would it revive industry and put men back to work? These were the only questions asked in 1897.

Americans, bored with the subject of the tariff and tired of uncertainty, were chiefly relieved to have the policy settled. With small change, the Dingley Act would remain in force for a decade.

The only sop that Congress had thrown to public opinion was the provision for reciprocity, enshrined in Republican doctrine as protection's twin. The Dingley Act empowered the President to enter into limited agreements with foreign nations for an exchange of tariff concessions, and also to undertake, for a period of two years, the negotiation of formal treaties to the same end. The reciprocity arrangements of the McKinley Act had succeeded beyond the most sanguine expectations in enlarging American markets abroad. The Dingley Act, by laying heavy duties on raw sugar, wool, and hides, supplied the government with valuable trading points, and the expectation of a fresh stimulus to foreign commerce gave wide satisfaction to agriculture and to the business community.

The protectionist diehards of the Senate were professed converts to the reciprocity principle, but distrusted it in their hearts. Their attitude was compounded of aversion to any reduction of the excessive rates that favored the privileged corporations, and jealous antipathy to Executive encroachment on the legislative power of taxation. The commercial treaties, should any be made, would require Senate ratification, and could safely be forgotten. McKinley's record in Congress had not forewarned the Senate that he would show especial zeal in promoting them, but since 1890 McKinley had changed his mind on the subject of foreign trade. It was manifest that the end of the depression would bring a mounting surplus of manufactured as well as agricultural products. The home market was no longer central in McKinley's thoughts of prosperity. He had come to a decision that logically invalidated the exclusive doctrine of high protection, and conceded that the United States had outgrown the defensive confines of the tariff wall; but neither he nor any other faithful Republican made the admission, or acknowledged a compromise with the odious theories of free trade. Reciprocity was the resolution of the intellectual predicament, the reconciliation of the protective principle with the practical necessities of a superabundant production.

McKinley never took any course without deliberation. His conclusion had been slowly maturing in the years of the governorship. He improved his knowledge of the subject by discussions with John W. Foster, with whom he had conferred during the preparation of the tariff bill of 1890. He appointed John A. Kasson special commissioner in charge of negotiating the treaties and agreements, and took an enthusiastic interest in his progress. In his first year in office, McKinley confided to La Follette that his greatest ambition was to round out his career by gaining American supremacy in world markets. The President's horizons had stretched far beyond the continental limits that had absorbed the Congressman, and implicit in his new vision was the concept of commerce as an agency of international accord. "Good trade insures good will," he told the Commercial Club of Cincinnati. "It should be our settled purpose to open trade wherever we can, making our ships and our commerce messengers of peace and amity."

The President had gone to Cincinnati in October because Mark Hanna had suggested that it would be "well" for him to appear in Ohio before the election. Since the passage of the Dingley Act, McKinley's popularity had soared with the nation's rebounding confidence. A bumper crop of wheat and a marked rise in its price had put the farmers in good humor. The Middle West was looking up. The Ohio woolgrowers were happy. Capital was coming timidly out of hiding. Businessmen began to estimate and plan. Wherever the President went, he was hailed by cheering crowds. Even on holiday—summer visits to Bluff Point in upper New York, to Ohio, and to Pennsylvania, and an autumn excursion to the Berkshires—there had been no respite from the demands of the people, eager to hear the President speak, to draw strength from his serenity, and to feed on his strong optimism their hunger for faith in the future.

Dawes had seen him at a moment of unusual privacy in October. The President had gone from Cincinnati to Canton, where he waited over to vote, conferring at his mother's little house with the many politicians who had gathered to aid Mark Hanna in the campaign. Old Mrs. McKinley's health had failed during the summer; but, when Dawes came in at ten one evening, she was sitting up with the President, brisk, attentive, and in maternal command. "William, I am going to bed now," she said, as she kissed her son good night. "You will find some pie in the dining room on the table under a cloth, which I have put there for you." The President and Dawes obediently went in and "tried the pie."

A month later, when McKinley was completing his annual message, word came that his mother had had a stroke of paralysis. He hurried to Canton, briefly returned to Washington to transmit the message to Congress, and then went home again to wait for the end. After the funeral, he spoke to Dawes of the days he had spent at his mother's bedside. With his usual composure, he mentioned that she had been able to recognize him; but, as he said that she had put up her hands to stroke his cheeks, McKinley's control failed, and he burst into tears.

The nation's affectionate sympathy mingled with the approval that had greeted the President's message. "There is not a prime minister living today who could have written such a paper to save his neck," Ambassador Hay wrote to McKinley from London. "Every American abroad will hold his head higher after reading it." Americans at home were inclined to respectful admiration, especially for the recommendations on the currency and on Cuba. Amid the distractions of his office, the President had found time to improve his education on a number of questions. He had grasped every opportunity to pick the brains of experts. He had sounded the gamut of opinion on controversial issues, and debated them at length with his Cabinet. Learning, as he preferred, by ear, McKinley had taken an intensive course in finance and foreign relations in 1897.

The value of the dollar in world markets was of supreme importance to the President's plans for trade, and the settlement of the currency problem engaged his mind far more deeply than was evidenced by his public utterances. Legislative action was forcibly deferred. Since the Republican silver senators were allied with the opposition on the issue, no measure short of free and unlimited coinage could pass the upper chamber. Committed to an interim maintenance of the gold standard, the President at first continued to hope for some eventual inclusion of silver in the monetary system. One of his first acts was to send three commissioners to Europe to reopen the subject of international bimetallism.

In the autumn, however, a private letter from Ambassador Hay brought the information that Great Britain was immovably committed to the single gold standard. The final realization of the trend away from silver was a serious disappointment to McKinley. An unforeseen answer to his difficulties was already heralded in the news. The director of the Mint had prepared figures that showed a startling rise in the current year's gold output in South Africa, Australia, and Canada. The Klondike rush was beginning to fill American ears with stories of sudden wealth, mingled with barren hardship and gaudy adventure; and to awaken a new solicitude, evidenced in the creation of the office of surveyor general of Alaska, for defining the boundaries of the neglected American territory in the Northwest. Soon, gold would come rolling in a glittering dust storm from the Yukon, while the far-off Rand poured out the precious metal in quantities that allayed fears of its scarcity, and at last disembarrassed American politics of the frenzied cult of silver.

The triumph of the goldbugs was written in the stars, but in 1897 the purport of the new discoveries was a field for perilous imaginative speculation. The currency question, in its opposed bearings on politics and foreign trade, was one of the most perplexing of McKinley's early administration. He gave much time to the study of financial principles, conferring frequently with Secretary Gage, with Dawes, and with the leaders in the movement for a monetary commission of nonpartisan experts. The President pressed Congress, in a special message, to authorize this commission, which he had already advised in his inaugural address. He gave the leading place in his first annual message to currency reform, confining his specific suggestions to action that it might be practicable to secure—certain changes in the national banking law, and the recommendation that the Treasury, after redeeming its notes in gold, should set them aside and pay them out only in exchange for gold.

McKinley was fast moving toward the conviction that an unconditional declaration for the gold standard was indispensable to his aspirations for American prosperity. The alternative was the acceptance of the nation's status as a second-rate commercial power; but, in the political climate of the next two years, the President's definition of this policy would have been a premature and impotent gesture, damaging to the Republican party and to his own leadership.

Foreign affairs, from the first, predominated in the Cabinet discussions. Cuba was the engrossing topic, and the strained American relations with Spain stood first on the Cabinet's agenda, but in the Pacific there were also problems, old and new, which required attention and decision.

The regulation of seal fishery in the Bering Sea had long been the most irritating matter in dispute between the United States and her northern neighbor. The depredations of the Canadian fur hunters threatened the extermination of the herds; and, in writing Ambassador Hay in the summer, the President bracketed the settlement of the controversy with bimetallism as "two of the administration's greatest efforts." Negotiations were hampered by the lack of direct diplomatic channels between Washington and Ottawa. The British government, in deference to colonial interests, was cold to reopening the subject, denying the United States assertion of a supralegal international duty to regulate the fisheries by arbitration, and taking the unjustified position that the danger of extermination was nonexistent. No progress was made toward an adjustment, in spite of Hay's notes and conversations, and the exertions of John W. Foster, who had engaged in the private practice of international law, and was retained by the State Department as a special adviser. Experts of the interested nations, which included Russia and Japan, were invited to meet in Washington in the autumn. Their conference resulted in a convention whereby sealing was to be prohibited for a year, but Great Britain unexpectedly declined to participate, and the agreement was nullified by her refusal to adhere to it. All pending questions between the United States and Canada were eventually referred to a Joint High Commission, which included Canadian representatives.

Alaska and the Aleutians were not the only outlying territorial possessions that had brought the United States into involvement with foreign powers. The acquisition of the harbor of Pago Pago twenty years before had led to friction with Great Britain and Germany, both of which had soon acquired interests in the Samoan group. German aggression and intrigue in the islands had aroused the American public to talk of war in 1889. In hopes of a peaceable settlement, the United States had consented to enter into a three-power protectorate over Samoa; but this extraordinary departure from the advice of the founding fathers had only made a bad matter worse, and the imbroglio was another disturbing legacy to the McKinley administration.

Two other dots of American dominion had not given rise to international controversy. The tiny islands of Midway, casually picked up in 1867, were too insignificant to be contested, or indeed remembered. The lease of Pearl Harbor for a naval station had been a logical development of the peculiar and exclusive interest in Hawaii which the United States government had asserted for more than forty years. In the early century, American missionaries had flocked to the islands, in the wake of American traders. The strategic value of the group had been realized when the United States gained a Pacific coastline, and it had been greatly heightened by the purchase of Alaska. Since then, reciprocity treaties had made Hawaii a commercial dependency of the United States, and the ambitious American sugar planters laid plans for political union. The sons of missionaries, to give them no more opprobrious designation, had led a bloodless revolution which deposed Queen Liliuokalani in 1893; and, with the aid of the minister and the naval forces of the United States, they had set up a provisional republican government in avowed anticipation of American annexation. Their negotiations with Washington had resulted in a treaty, which was hastily concluded at the close of the Harrison administration. Cleveland withdrew it at the beginning of his second term. As a result, the national policy of predominant interest had crystallized into the Republican issue of outright possession.

McKinley believed that annexation would be commercially advantageous to the United States. Hawaii was a natural gateway to the markets of the Orient. Its sugar, moreover, had become increasingly necessary to America since Cuban importations had been cut off by the rebellion. The insular government, if somewhat dubiously established, had proved to be representative and stable. The President was assured that the union would be no less beneficial to the submissive and dwindling native population than to his own people. On taking office, he immediately reopened negotiations for a treaty, but the outlook for ratification was unpropitious. The Senate had co-operated with the Hawaiian policy of former Executives, approving the reciprocity treaties, and even initiating the provision for the lease of Pearl Harbor in the first flush of enlarging the Navy; but the small Republican majority could not hope to muster the requisite two-thirds' vote for annexation in 1897. The Cuban insurrection at once overshadowed the Hawaiian question, and, by exciting expansionist sentiment, gave it a highly controversial twist. Prominent Republicans, some of them in the Senate, were beginning to speak of Hawaii as a step toward territorial gains in the Far East. The embroilment of the issue in a program of colonial empire tended to tighten the opposition, and even to shake the support of some Republican senators who had previously favored the treaty.

The quasi-protectorate of the United States had so long been internationally recognized that Americans had come to regard any action on Hawaii as their own domestic concern. They were outraged to discover in the spring of 1897 that Japan took a lively interest in the islands. The newly westernized empire had entered on a period of soaring imperial ambition. There had been a marked enlargement of Japanese trade with Hawaii, and a massive influx of Japanese coolie labor suggested an intention to rival the time-honored American infiltration. Efforts at restricting immigration were indignantly resisted by the Tokyo government. The situation was inflamed, in the month that McKinley took office, by the action of the Honolulu authorities in excluding and returning to Japan more than a thousand immigrants. Japan sent a cruiser to Honolulu to back up her protests and claims for indemnity.

The signing of the annexation treaty in June brought a formal protest from Tokyo to Washington. The note not only expressed concern for the rights of Japanese residents and the settlement of pending claims. It also, while denying the "mischievous suggestion" of imperial designs, made the broad statement that the maintenance of the *status quo* in Hawaii was essential to the good understanding of the powers having interests in the Pacific. Three American warships had been dispatched to Honolulu, where the Japanese cruiser remained at anchor all summer. The tension of the Hawaiian officials was shared by McKinley's minister, Harold M. Sewall of Maine, who was in thorough sympathy with the imperialist sugar planters to whom he was accredited. He was so fearful that Japan might resort to force that he asked for authority, in an emergency, to land a counterforce and announce a provisional protectorate. Washington showed some reluctance to grant these extensive powers; but in July, after Senator Frye had worked on the State Department, the instructions were forthcoming. Sewall thought that an incident was avoided because, "as generally with us," the secret instructions were in the hands of "the enemy," as soon as they were sent.

The State Department had declined to admit the validity of Japan's sweeping protest, and in the course of the summer took an extremely firm tone in reminding the imperial government of the historic American interest in Hawaii. But there were repeated assurances of amity and confidence, and at length a pacifying offer to assume the Japanese claims. In December, Japan withdrew her objections to the treaty of annexation.

Beyond the islands of the Pacific, there sounded the ominous rumble of European aggression, which had at once spurred Japan to competition and checked her from estranging the friendly United States. Russia was grasping Japan's former gains in Manchuria. Germany, Great Britain, and France had moved in to feast on the crumbling empire of China. These were disturbing portents for the revival of American trade in the Far East. But in the Cabinet Room they sounded like distant thunder through the racket of Spain's struggle to hold the spoils of an ancient aggression. Cuba was on the threshold. The insurrection had lost millions of dollars to American traders and investors, and the preservation of the neutrality of the United States was costing the government millions more. The country had been provoked to an unreasoning anger by the events within a hundred miles of the Florida coast. The factor of popular sentiment was intangible, but compelling. The greatest danger to peace lay in the tinderbox of the peace-loving and inflammable American people.

Throughout the summer, the agitation had intensified, as Spain's promises of reform failed to materialize, and as Governor General Weyler's drastic measures proved effective in curbing the rebellion. Cuba, devastated and starving in a vain fight for liberty, was a reproach to the national conscience, a wound on the national spirit. Americans did not reflect that all war entails misery, or that the insurgents themselves were responsible for much of the wanton destruction. They saw only the figure of "Butcher" Weyler bestriding the prostrate island. Skeleton mothers and babies shamed the comfort of American homes, and the morning headlines made the coffee bitter on the breakfast table. The syllables "Cubansufferer" lingered mournfully on the lips of children who did not know what Cuba was, and scarcely understood suffering. The sensational Democratic press whipped up excitement in a cynical campaign for increased circulation; but it is doubtful that the horror stories of the *Journal* and the *World* in New York and their counterparts in other cities exerted as deep an influence on opinion as the sober indictment of their conservative contemporaries, Republican as well as Democratic. These newspapers did not estrange the thoughtful public by exaggeration and falsehood, or alarm it by frenzied cries for war. By declaring that conditions in Cuba were intolerable and must be stopped, they solidified the belief that intervention was the duty of Americans.

McKinley fully shared the outrage and pity of his countrymen. The official protests to Spain were not solely based on the legitimate grounds of financial loss, the imprisonment of United States citizens in Cuba, and the burden and expense of maintaining neutrality. They were eloquent in condemnation of the conduct of the war, and the violation of "human rights" by the concentration of the Cuban noncombatants. Diplomatic exchanges were at cross-purposes between the moralistic Washington administration, naïvely convinced of the legally binding provisions of "the civilized code of war," and the reactionary ministry at Madrid, which resented the appeal to sentiment as an impudent and hypocritical interference in its desperate colonial difficulties. McKinley was also hampered by delay in finding an emissary willing to undertake the post of minister to Spain. It was at last accepted by General Stewart L. Woodford, the New York lawyer who had not "quite sized up" to the Navy Department. He was given emphatic instructions that the war in Cuba must stop. It was suggested that Spain might take the initiative, but there were warnings that the inactivity of the United States could not be safely prolonged, and that some incident might at any time precipitate an emergency. The most serious doubts were expressed that Spain could ever hope to regain the allegiance of her rebellious colony.

Woodford set out in midsummer, charged with impressing Spain with the friendly purpose of the United States, while proposing the virtual relinquishment of one of Spain's richest possessions. Before he reached Madrid, a tragic occurrence brightened the prospect of his most unlikely mission. The absolutist premier, Cánovas del Castillo, was assassinated by an anarchist. When Woodford presented his credentials in the autumn, a new ministry had been formed under the premiership of the liberal leader Práxedes Mateo Sagasta, who had been an outspoken critic of the Cuban war. The United States was assured that its friendly purposes were appreciated and its grounds of interest admitted, and that the present Spanish government was bound to a change of policy that should lead to pacification. The long-promised political reforms were to be granted Cuba with the view of eventual home rule. The good faith of the ministry was soon attested by its decrees. All prisoners who were citizens of the United States were released. American sentiment was recognized by the recall of Governor General Weyler. His successor, General Ramón Blanco y Arenas, was directed to conduct the war according to humane and Christian methods, and to take immediate steps for the relief of the rural population.

Insurrection was also blazing in Spain's great Pacific colony, the Philippines. Her power was weakened and her treasury almost exhausted, but political necessity dictated that the government should not acquiesce in the dismemberment of the empire. The Madrid authorities had given no encouragement to Whitelaw Reid, who had sounded out the purchase of Cuba at McKinley's request; and, in resolution to continue the war, Sagasta and his ministers proved as obdurate as their predecessors. Nevertheless, the President had been vastly encouraged by both the promise and the performance of Spain. The largest part of his annual message was reserved for the discussion of Cuba. With an unusual severity, McKinley censured the previous Spanish policy, alluding to the "brutal" governor general, and describing the concentration of the noncombatants as "extermination" and an "abuse of the rights of the war." But he pointed out that the Sagasta government had put an end to this cruel and horrible policy, and had made promises of political reform from which it could not recede with honor. The President asked Congress to suspend action and judgment. The forcible annexation of Cuba to the United States was not to be thought of—by the American code of morality, it would be "criminal aggression." Spain should be given every reasonable chance to realize her expectations of reform. If hereafter it became a duty to intervene with force, it should be because the necessity was so clear as to command the support and approval of the civilized world.

The President pleaded for patience, and the reasonableness and wisdom of his counsel tranquilized the fever of the people. Waiting was rendered more bearable by McKinley's decision to institute a humane intervention. He had obtained permission from Spain to send food and medicines and other supplies to Cuba. On the day before Christmas, the State Department published a circular inviting public contributions to a relief fund, to be distributed through the American consul at Havana. Americans responded generously to the opportunity to express their sympathy. The depth of McKinley's own feeling may be measured by his anonymous personal subscription of $5,000 to the fund.

· 7 ·

CUBA

Every Tuesday and Friday forenoon, the President was joined at his improvised desk by the eight elderly gentlemen who were his chosen advisers. They ranged themselves around the mahogany in the order of their precedence, sitting in upholstered side chairs, mounted on casters. On the President's right was the gaunt old Secretary of State in his loose black suit and elastic-sided Romeos. His shabby white head was stiffly erect. He looked baffled and insulted, like a workman asked to perform a delicate task with a blunt and damaged tool.

John Sherman was the only man at the Cabinet table who had had experience in the field of foreign relations. What was the sum of the wisdom he had gained in the past ten years in the Senate? He had advised that the government's attitude on Cuba must be controlled by commercial interests, rather than sympathy with the struggle for liberty, and he had also advised that intervention in the name of humanity would be unavoidable. He expected war with Spain, and had urged that the United States should drive the Spanish soldiers out of Cuba. He was opposed to bringing on war, and had recently voted against appropriations for enlarging the Navy. Once an extreme expansionist, desiring the acquisition of Canada by the United States, Sherman had become adverse to any extension of the national borders. In the twilight of his statesmanship, it was not possible to discern the outlines of a policy. He did not offer to clarify his inconsistencies. Now and then, Secretary Long noted, there was "a flash of his old strength." Sherman, for the most part, was silent in council, and his silence was sullen with the resentment that burns more fiercely as other

151

passions fail. His mind was often confused, but he did not miss the point that the Acting Secretary of State was absent from the Cabinet table.

The responsibilities of the State Department had fallen heavily on the stooping shoulders of the First Assistant Secretary, Judge William R. Day of Canton. This quiet lawyer, thin and pale, with melancholy red mustaches, had no taste for Washington life or public importance. His disposition was retiring, and his health was delicate, with nerves stretched tight as fiddlestrings. But because McKinley needed him, Day had sacrificed his inclinations and his practice, and whittled down his income to a salary of $4,500 a year. In an arrangement between two Ohioans to protect and supplement a third, Day took direct charge of all important matters, except the Bering Sea dispute, which had been farmed out to John W. Foster. Ambassadors and ministers made their bows to the Secretary, and passed quickly on to the First Assistant. Members of Congress, reporters, and office seekers went straight to Day's room, without prior formalities. Day was approachable, but reticent. A stranger to the personalities of the capital, he had no special knowledge of international law, and was entirely untrained in diplomacy. He was an enigma to most of his callers.

It was a mark of McKinley's naïveté in the conduct of foreign relations that he patched up the State Department with a totally inexperienced assistant; but the President was not mistaken in his estimate of Day's wise and scholarly mind and utter devotion to himself. McKinley often took a hand in the preparation of diplomatic instructions and correspondence, and was at all times closely in touch with the situation at Madrid and in Cuba. He could rely on Day's intelligent collaboration, and the Second Assistant Secretary of State acted as mentor on the details of unfamiliar procedure. Alvey A. Adee belonged to a species of whose existence Americans were scarcely aware. He was a career diplomat. After ten years at his post, he had become ensconced by tacit consent as a permanent undersecretary, the ever-helpful expert on department routine and protocol, and the benign and humorous tutor of the innocent American representatives abroad. The indispensable Adee drafted the instructions, coded and deciphered the secret messages, analyzed the notes from foreign governments, and guided official behavior and speech on occasions of ceremony. This sweet and whimsical soul, extremely deaf, with a quacking falsetto voice, was unknown to the public, but the signature, three A's with a squiggle, was respected in Washington and in the foreign service.

Adee's personal oddity added to the vexation of the diplomatic corps, more than ordinarily puzzled by the irregularities at the State Department in the McKinley administration. "The head of the Department knows nothing," one diplomat remarked; "the First Assistant says nothing; the Second Assistant hears nothing."

To supersede Sherman was an insult to a man who had grown old in the service of his country. His weakened memory and irascible temper made it an imperative necessity. Under the cold stare of the diplomats, Sherman had suddenly crumbled, like a scrap of ancient parchment exposed to the air. Charles Dawes spoke feelingly of Day's troubles in watching the venerable Secretary and guarding the country from his mistakes. Either uninformed or forgetful of the negotiations with Hawaii, Sherman assured the Japanese minister that a treaty of annexation was not contemplated. Its ensuing announcement seemed to reflect on the good faith of the American government, and it was thought that the suspicion of duplicity had aggravated the objections of Japan. Sherman refused to acknowledge his lapses. He scented conspiracy and bad faith in his appointment—a base scheme concocted by the President and Hanna to offer him humiliation in exchange for his seat in the Senate. Annoyed by tactful references to his "impaired health," Sherman made fumbling attempts to assert himself which increased the embarrassment of Day's anomalous position. In Dawes's opinion, Day proved as great a diplomat within the Department as in foreign affairs. The unreliability of the Secretary of State was too flagrant to be concealed from his subordinates. John Foster remarked that it was pitiable in the extreme that the lowest servant knew and talked about Mr. Sherman's failing memory. The apprehensions in the Department were acute when the Secretary unexpectedly cut short his summer holiday, and returned to Washington in the absence of both the President and Day.

If Sherman had intended to take advantage of a clear field, he had made poor preparation for ensuring respect for his authority. On his vacation at Amagansett, Long Island, he had granted an interview to a representative of one of the most enterprising of the anti-administration newspapers. The New York World, desirous of embellishing a rumor that Whitelaw Reid would supplant Sherman in the Cabinet, was able to string disagreeable innuendoes on very slight material. Sherman's hostility to the Tribune proprietor was suggested by his purported reminiscences of Reid as "a little ragged boy in Cincinnati," and the story was flavored with disingenuous comments that the Secretary did not actually seem to be in such poor health as was generally supposed. Here was plain warning, but Sherman did not heed it. Soon after, on his way to Washington, he held forth to a group of reporters, which included the same World man, and this time was so imprudent as to discuss a number of diplomatic questions.

In a "meaty talk," which The World printed at length, the Secretary of State was quoted as saying that Japan had become a power to be reckoned with, but that her attitude would not affect the American position on Hawaiian annexation; that "England quarrels oftener than she fights"; and that, though the United States had been blind to the distress of Cuba, Spain would certainly lose the island. The World clothed its sneers at these indiscretions with pretended admiration of Sherman's vigor and frankness.

This publication created nationwide alarm over the conduct of the State Department. Sherman's garrulity was severely criticized, and he hastened to inform the President that the interview had been "manufactured." But the folly of having talked at all had become evident even to Sherman. The President kindly agreed with his suggestion that it was better to be silent. "As to my getting old I will not deny," Sherman persisted; "whenever you think I am too old I will retire with thanks to the Ruler of the Universe for extending my life beyond the allotted three score and ten years." There the matter rested. Sherman's pitiable situation touched the President at his most vulnerable point; and indeed the circumstances of his appointment would have deterred a more ruthless man than McKinley from requesting Sherman's resignation. The glaring fact was that, while Mark Hanna had profited by the arrangement, Sherman had lost public respect along with his Senate seat.

A dignified withdrawal from the Cabinet would have saved the last rags of Sherman's reputation, but he chose to remain in office, treating the President with deference, and bitterly criticizing him behind his back. Certain members of the Sherman clan were eager to discredit McKinley for political reasons. They zealously spread the story of the President's coarse motives, and Sherman's unwilling sacrifice for Hanna. Either unwisdom or vindictiveness blinded this small but influential faction to the danger of assisting the common political enemy. Although returning prosperity had muted hostility to the administration, the period of good feeling was drawing to an inevitable close. Democratic newspapers, sharpening their knives for attack, were at a loss to find means of exploiting Mark Hanna's influence on the President—until the Washington parlors began to buzz with Sherman's version of his appointment. The stale story was gleefully raked up, and bundled with a demand for Sherman's immediate removal from office. The hunt was in full cry in the early weeks of 1898. The country rang with the perils of Sherman's incompetence. Respectable newspapers emulated the yellow press in tasteless vituperation. The nonpartisan and reputedly judicial New York Times daily assailed the Secretary of State as decayed, palsied, doddering, and imbecile. The failings of age were indecently flaunted in proof of the President's abject obedience to Hanna and cynical indifference to the national welfare. The whispering campaign of the Sherman faction was injurious to McKinley's reputation; but its worst casualty was Sherman himself.

This was the atmosphere in which the agitation over Cuba heightened, and the government's negotiations with Spain entered anew on a critical phase. It became necessary to ask Judge Day to attend the Cabinet meetings, an added grievance to the old man who sat brooding on the President's right, wrapped in his proud delusion of persecution, comforting his self-esteem with derision of McKinley. "The general bearing of the President to his Cabinet," Sherman later wrote, "was quite different from what was generally the rule, for he assumed the powers and duties of each of them —his Cabinet councils were not a free exchange of opinions but rather the mandates of a paramount ruler."

The Secretary of the Navy kept a different recollection of McKinley at the Cabinet meetings. "There he was untrammeled," John D. Long remembered; "there his happy humor ran free; there we saw the simple goodness of his heart, the unaffected, eager desire to discharge his duty and to do right." It was a delight to Long to serve with McKinley, but he had private reservations about the Cabinet. He had soon come to the conclusion that Alger and Gary, as well as Sherman, were too old and lacking in vigor. Four cripples, Long thought, had been taken into the Cabinet, and the fourth one was himself. This stout, sweet-tempered gentleman in spats, recently emerged from the retirement of a nervous breakdown, had the habit of self-disparagement. Two men warred in Long for supremacy: the dreamer who yearned for the quiet of his farm at Buckfield, Maine, and the ambitious aspirant for position and power. The second man had never left the first at peace. Even in his reveries of Buckfield, Long thought of being "some punkins" in the village. He had taken office at a time of unusual stress at the Navy Department and his duties were heavy from the first, but Long's health improved wonderfully in Washington.

The Navy was more closely involved in the Cuban difficulties than any other government department, except that of State. The necessity for enforcing American neutrality had transformed the ships of the Atlantic Squadron into a police force, vigilant to prevent aid from reaching the insurgents. The Navy was charged with the protection of American lives and property abroad, and must stand ready to act in Cuba; and over all projects of the Department hovered the cloud of possible war. Since the administrative system did not provide for a professional head—the rank of admiral had been allowed to lapse—authority was vested solely in the civilian Secretary, who worked through six subordinate and co-equal bureau chiefs, selected from the line and the several corps of the service, and appointed for a term of four years. The head of the Bureau of Navigation, Captain Arent Schuyler Crowninshield, was in charge of naval personnel and the administration and operation of the fleet; and the other chiefs were similarly entrusted with large responsibilities in their separate fields. Long did not attempt to master the technical problems of design, armor plate, guns, ammunition, and drydocks. "What is the need of my making a dropsical tub of any lobe of my brain," he wrote in his diary, "when I have right at hand a man possessed with more knowledge than I could acquire?" Nevertheless, the experts often differed. The Secretary, as the court of last resort, was ill-equipped to judge the merits of disputes inside the Department, or between the bureaucrats and their natural antagonists, the captains of the ships. Within his own limitations and those of the system, Long functioned as a capable executive, who held his subordinates to strict account and kept the Department clean of his particular abomination, "this carrion of patronage."

The Secretary's civilian assistant had a respectable smattering of information on most of the affairs of the Department, and forcible convictions on them all. Young Mr. Roosevelt had made a hobby of naval matters, from gun turrets to strategy. He was an enthusiast for target practice and squadron maneuvers, an amateur of docks and steel, rapid-fire guns and smokeless powder. He had a plan for reducing paperwork, and was immersed in the preparation of a personnel bill that would end the friction between the line and the engineers. The focus of Roosevelt's extraordinary energies was a strong American navy. He quickly became the idol of the ambitious officers of the service, and a source of some disquiet to his superior.

Long was just and generous, as well as self-critical, and he acknowledged that Roosevelt's "push" was a useful balance to his own cautious habit, and an inspiration to the Department and the service. But the dynamo at his elbow sparked imprudence, as well as efficiency. Regardless of the administration's policy, Roosevelt started out as a propagandist for a large increase in the Navy. Though he was devoted to Long and eager to prove his docility, he could not conceal an impatient longing to interfere in the conduct of the Department. Long lectured Roosevelt like a gentle schoolmaster determined to discipline a recalcitrant youngster. He deplored his assistant's lack of cool judgment and a level head; and, besides, Long was by no means so self-disparaging as to resign himself to the fate of John Sherman.

The prevailing official opinion in 1897 was cool to a drastic extension of the shipbuilding program. The United States possessed an effective force of four battleships of the first class, two of the second, and forty-eight other vessels ranging from armored cruisers to torpedo boats; while five additional battleships of the first class, sixteen torpedo boats, and one submarine boat were under construction. The new battleships, to be sure, were far from completion. Work was at a standstill on three of them because it was impossible to obtain armor plate at the price that had been fixed by Congress. It still appeared to the administration and to conservative members of Congress that a potentially formidable force had been authorized; and that, pending an improvement of the government finances, naval appropriations should be primarily directed toward enlarging personnel, providing drydocks capable of accommodating the biggest ships, and repairing deficiencies of armament and munitions.

This was the kind of thinking against which Roosevelt butted his head when he entered an administration concerned with peace and prosperity. It was undeniable that the American Navy was adequate for the "national defense," but the phrase set Roosevelt's teeth on edge. He wanted six more battleships, six more large cruisers, and seventy-five more torpedo boats—a navy superior to Germany's, a Pacific fleet stronger than Japan's. Roosevelt wanted to fight; and, as Cuba presented the likeliest prospect of immediate dispute, he wanted to fight with Spain.

Roosevelt's head was buzzing with copious draughts of the doctrines of Captain Alfred T. Mahan, with whom he was in earnest confidential correspondence. The prophet of the American expansionists had been more widely honored abroad than in his own country, but Roosevelt had seen the vision that dazzled a chosen few—the United States as a great and aggressive power in two oceans, dominating an isthmian canal that joined them. To turn Spain out of Cuba was necessary to the control of the Caribbean, on which the mastery of the canal would depend. Roosevelt did not think that war with a second-rate naval power would cause much strain on the country, or interruption to the revival of prosperity; and it would serve the useful purpose of giving the armed forces "actual practice" in combat and logistics. This was militarism so bald that Roosevelt supplied a toupee of moral justification. War would ennoble the American nation by purging the people of their preoccupation with material gain. It would unseat the timid ideal of peace, whose flabby sentimentalism Roosevelt despised, and enthrone the soldierly virtues, which he never tired of praising. Roosevelt's mentality at this time lay somewhere between that of a boy scout and the young Kaiser Wilhelm of Germany, but he was quite aware that the American public would shrink from the glorification of war.

He fully developed his theme only to mettlesome patriots like Lodge and Mahan. In pleading with Secretary Long to recommend additional ships, Roosevelt argued that a powerful navy was a guarantee of peace and "the cheapest kind of insurance." "Make the plea that this is a measure of peace and not of war," he cautioned Mahan in enlisting his influence with Long.

Roosevelt's artfulness was unconvincing because his real feelings were irrepressible. A few months after taking office, he burst out to the Naval War College with a flag-waving appeal for a strong navy, applauding the martial spirit and the supreme triumphs of war. Long did not like this speech; and he liked still less Roosevelt's address in early August to the Naval Reserve of Ohio, which supplemented John Sherman's indiscretions by hurling defiance at Japan from the Navy Department. The newspaper headlines and comments "nearly threw the Secretary into a fit," Roosevelt wrote Cabot Lodge, "and he gave me as severe a wigging as his invariable courtesy and kindness would permit." Roosevelt meekly promised to subside. He made no more rousing speeches, and submitted his publications to Long's blue pencil. He called himself "an Assistant Secretary of chastened spirit." He backed down on the shipbuilding program, and begged for a mere minimal increase, which would maintain the continuity of the principle. The President was favorable to this, but Long at first refused to listen to even a single Pacific battleship and a few torpedo boats. The Secretary had developed a streak of mild obstinacy during a summer's rest on his farm in Maine. Roosevelt was on tenterhooks until November, when Long was obliged to admit that he was recommending the battleship and the torpedo boats in his annual report. The Secretary carefully explained that he had intended to do this all along. He did not want it thought that he had been "converted," and warned Roosevelt against giving that impression.

Long's sensitiveness about his authority had not induced him to curtail his extended holiday; and, during the weeks of his absence, his professedly chastened assistant had "a bully time" as Acting Secretary, getting ahead with his pet projects and interfering to his heart's content. The occasion of his most highhanded meddling was an impending vacancy in the command of the Asiatic Squadron. Roosevelt, though the avowed enemy of political pull, had tried to influence some appointments. Secretary Long had rebuffed his efforts; but, with Secretary Long in Maine, Roosevelt could indulge his desire to ensure that there would be a prompt attack on the Philippines in case of war with Spain.

There was nothing singular in the direction of Roosevelt's thoughts. It was far more remarkable that, in a country seething with hostility to Spain, most people had remained indifferent to the existence of her exposed possessions in the Pacific. A new outbreak of insurrection against Spanish rule had kept the Philippines in the news for more than a year. But the islands were distant and little known. They were not connected with the United States by important commercial exchanges, and did not offer a field for the Protestant missionary societies. Even the warmakers were largely oblivious of the pertinent facts that Spain occupied a vulnerable position in the Pacific and that her resources were being drained by a second rebellion. Foraker, grooming himself to join the jingoes in the Senate, had scarcely heard of the Philippines. To Americans, war with Spain meant war over Cuba. Except for the naval strategists and their disciples, a naïve and parochial nation did not look beyond the theater of the Caribbean.

The most striking exception to the general indifference was an elderly commodore, whose dreams of fame were centered on the Philippines. George Dewey, the president of the Board of Inspection and Survey, was a fit, ruddy little Vermonter of nearly sixty, with frosty hair and mustaches and an authoritarian manner. He had had his only experience of combat as a young lieutenant in the Civil War, but his ambition had not been extinguished by thirty-four years of routine duty. His service under Farragut still burned gloriously in Dewey's memory. Farragut was the hero on whom he had modeled his career; and Farragut had been sixty-one when his first chance came for distinction. Dewey believed that war with Spain was inevitable. He was entitled to a squadron, and had set his heart on obtaining the Pacific command because it was remote from the red tape of the Washington bureaucrats and the bogey of the national defense. Roosevelt was the warm champion of this self-reliant officer who longed for resolute action.

A vacancy was in prospect in the European as well as the Asiatic Squadron, and another eligible commodore was an eager applicant for assignment. John A. Howell, a plump old officer with spaniel's eyes and splendid burnsides, was the commandant of the League Island Navy Yard at Philadelphia. He was an authority on steel and ordnance, and the author of several inventions, including a torpedo directed by a gyroscopic device. Howell ranked Dewey, but had previously been passed over for squadron command, and was fearful of another disappointment. He had been involved in altercations which had made him enemies in the service, and was not in favor with the officers of the Department bureaus. Moreover, at the meetings of the armor board, Howell had been a cause of irritation to Roosevelt, whom he impressed as indecisive and afraid of responsibility. But the much-criticized Commodore had the sympathy of an influential

159

Republican member of the Senate Committee on Naval Affairs. Senator William E. Chandler of New Hampshire had been Secretary of the Navy in the Arthur administration, and knew the prejudices of "the mutual admiration clique" at the Department. He was familiar with Howell's case, thought that injustice had been done a capable officer, and wanted to set it right. Incidentally, Chandler was expecting to obtain a staff position for his son if Howell's orders materialized.

Just before Long returned from his holiday, Roosevelt was dismayed to find in the Secretary's mail a letter from Senator Chandler, urging that nothing should interfere with giving Howell a squadron as soon as his turn arrived. Since there were openings in two commands, it is not apparent that this request necessarily jeopardized Dewey's chances for the Pacific. For some reason, however, the Bureau of Navigation preferred even Howell to Dewey for this command. Captain Crowninshield made the recommendations on personnel, and Roosevelt was aghast at the danger that Howell would get the Asiatic Squadron, and muff the attack on the Philippines. He felt that the situation warranted extreme measures, and proposed that Dewey should exert political pull on his own behalf. This advice imposed slight strain on Roosevelt's conscience. He argued that, while it was unpardonable for an officer to bring pressure for a soft place, leniency should be observed toward a man who used his influence to get near "the flashing of the guns."

Dewey made the correct demurrals, when asked if he knew any senators; but, under Roosevelt's prodding, he was soon able to recall that Redfield Proctor was an old family friend. A better connection could scarcely have been found. Senator Proctor, the marble king of Vermont and a former Secretary of War, was a solid and highly respected Republican who was close to the President. When Dewey called to present his case, Proctor expressed delight that the matter had been mentioned. He went the same day to the White House and obtained McKinley's promise that the Vermonter should have the command of the Asiatic Squadron. In due course, the chief of the Bureau of Navigation prepared Dewey's orders, and also those assigning Howell to the European Squadron.

Secretary Long stiffly informed Chandler of the arrangements. He was grateful for the Senator's response, praising Long's wisdom and justice. He was trying, Long wrote, to do the best he could; but he sounded rather weary, in spite of his recent vacation. He never spoke of his discovery that "this carrion of patronage" was odorous in the Navy Department, and indeed explicitly stated that Dewey's selection had been his own decision. Roosevelt said that both he and Proctor urged Dewey on Long, and that the Secretary finally followed their advice, though Dewey was not apparently his first choice. Dewey believed that Long disliked his assignment, and was indignant over the way in which it had been brought about; but the little Commodore cherished a greater resentment toward Long's principal adviser, the chief of the Bureau of Navigation. Dewey was not given the customary acting rank of rear admiral when he received his orders. No one could have known better than Crowninshield, Dewey bitterly remarked, how subordinate this slight would make the squadron commander's position in his intercourse abroad.

The President's attitude toward Dewey's appointment rests under as thick obscurity as the controversy in the Department. He may unthinkingly have regarded Proctor's recommendation as a normal political request, or he may have been predisposed to Dewey by information of his peculiar fitness for command in the Pacific. Thoughts of that potential theater of war had recently been implanted in McKinley's mind. Among the more legitimate activities of the "hot-weather Secretary" of the Navy had been the education of the President in strategy. Roosevelt's great opportunity for extensive private conversations with McKinley had come in the middle of September, when the President returned to Washington while Long was still away. McKinley could scarcely have found a consultant whose personality was in stronger contrast with his own. Roosevelt's cultured speech was studded with adjectives like "bully" and "infernal," with epithets like "trumps" and "bounders." His face, with its beribboned pince-nez, bore a startling resemblance to the haughty countenance of Addison Porter, whom Roosevelt incidentally thought "a trump." The New Yorker was a dude, but a vigorous mutation from the type—voluble and violently opinionated, with a rasping voice and exaggerated grimaces. Though he had scorned McKinley as a peace-loving servant of the business interests, Roosevelt had recently been moved to admiration of the President. The meetings between the two oddly assorted companions were amazingly congenial. Roosevelt was invited to dine at the White House, and was twice sent for to accompany the President on his afternoon drives. McKinley paid the Acting Secretary the kindest compliments on his work at the Navy Department. He laughed heartily at Roosevelt's stories, and smiled when the younger man talked of his intention to go to war himself. What would Mrs. Roosevelt think of it? the President asked. But he added that he thought he could guarantee that Roosevelt would have his opportunity, if war by any chance arose. Roosevelt was bursting with technical details of ships and armament, the importance of preparedness, and the necessity for grasping the initiative in attack on Cuba, on the coast of Spain, and in the Pacific. When he had finished his exposition, he was well satisfied with the firmness of the President's purpose. McKinley was "a bit of a jollier," and of course he wanted to avoid trouble, but still Roosevelt thought that he could be depended on to deal thoroughly and well with any international difficulty.

The President had been emphatically advised that, on the outbreak of hostilities with Spain, the Asiatic Squadron should blockade and, if possible, take Manila. Did he wonder where he had heard of that place before? Perhaps the name had lingered in his memory since Foraker's friend, Professor Williams, had eagerly accepted the consulate there. It would crop up again in the plans of the naval strategists. When Commodore Dewey sailed from San Francisco in December, he had been instructed to strike at the Spanish force at Manila, in the event of war. But the President remained vague about the precise location of the Philippines. As he said to Mr. Kohlsaat, "he could not have told where those darned islands were within two thousand miles." McKinley's thoughts, like those of the American people, were concerned with Spain's rebellious colony in the Western Hemisphere. He was anxiously looking to the Sagasta ministry and its new governor general in Cuba to work out an acceptable adjustment in 1898.

The expectations of the President's message were not fulfilled by the news from Cuba in midwinter. Americans were disillusioned by the uninterrupted tale of suffering and mortality among the *reconcentrados*, and by the failure of popular support for the autonomy program, which Blanco had at once initiated, though it had not yet been ratified by the Spanish Cortes. A humane and moderate policy stood between two fires. The insurgents, fighting for total independence, rejected both political reforms and relief of the misery that had won them American support. The Spanish army and the loyalist residents vindictively opposed assistance to their enemies, and agitated against giving them a voice in the insular government. With the new year, trouble thickened at Havana, a hotbed of loyalist sentiment, where anti-American feeling was fanned by the suspicion that the United States consul general, Fitzhugh Lee, was intriguing with the insurrectionists. This spirited old Virginia politician, a former commander of Confederate cavalry, was in hearty sympathy with rebellion, and had urged the Cleveland administration to intervene on behalf of Cuban independence.

McKinley, though "abundantly warned" by Cleveland against Fitz Lee, did not share his predecessor's disapproval of the Democratic consul. He had kept Lee in office, commending his devotion to American interests; and, when criticism came from Madrid, the President warmly defended the courage and dignity with which Lee had borne himself in frequently unfriendly surroundings. The Republican administration had also been responsive to Lee's desire that, in case of necessity, he could call for naval assistance. Cleveland's State Department had vaguely assented to this request, but it ran counter to the policy which then prevailed at Washington. Cleveland had been so determined to avoid a show of force in the neighborhood of Cuba that he had intermitted not only the Navy's winter drills in southern waters, but even the usual visits of courtesy to Havana. The McKinley administration had from the first intended to resume these visits as an evidence of normal friendly intercourse and a polite reminder that the United States stood ready to protect its nationals at times of disturbance abroad. But the interruption had at once created an additional awkwardness in American relations with Spain and laid the renewal of the program open to a hostile interpretation; and no conclusion had been reached until October, when favorable omens at Madrid had decided the President to hold a vessel in readiness. The second-class battleship *Maine* was selected, and in early December was ordered to Key West. Actually an armored cruiser, trim and menacing, with high twin smokestacks and lean sides shining with white paint, the *Maine* was a potent representative of the might of the new American Navy. Her commander, Captain Charles D. Sigsbee, was an officer in whose judgment and diplomacy the Navy Department reposed confidence. The government emphasized the precautionary nature of Sigsbee's assignment by instructing him to place himself in communication with General Lee, and on notice of an emergency to proceed to Havana and offer asylum to the American citizens who still remained in Cuba.

In the second week of January, the unrest at Havana moved Washington to alert the Navy, and to order the North Atlantic Squadron and a flotilla of torpedo boats to drill off the coast of Florida. The day after these orders were given, mobs led by Spanish officers attacked the offices of the Havana newspapers that had supported the program of home rule. Fearful that rioting would spread beyond General Blanco's control, Fitz Lee telegraphed Washington that ships should be prepared to move promptly. This advice was superfluous, since for more than a month a vessel had been directly subject to Lee's call. He had not used his authority, and did not at this time desire the presence of an American warship, except as a last resort.

The disturbances at the Cuban capital and the responsive flare of excitement in the United States soon persuaded the Washington government that the time had come for a reversal of Cleveland's policy. On January 24, after a long and extremely cordial conversation with Dupuy de Lôme, the Spanish minister, Judge Day broached the President's decision to send the *Maine* to Havana, solely as a mark of friendship and international courtesy, and with no other intention. On receiving the minister's assent, Day went with Long to the President; and orders were at once dispatched to the *Maine*, and also to the cruiser *Montgomery*, which was directed to touch at the Cuban ports of Santiago and Matanzas. Fitz Lee received the news with dismay. Outward quiet had been restored at Havana. He hastened to advise a week's delay, and was still more insistent after an interview with the local officials. They professed, Lee telegraphed, to find an ulterior motive in sending the battleship, and feared that its presence might obstruct the autonomy program and possibly touch off a popular demonstration. Madrid also received the notification with sharp disquiet. McKinley's earnest will for peace had not allayed Spanish distrust of the intentions of the Republican administration. The Sagasta government, offended by the severe censure of the preceding ministry in the President's annual message, had been nervously watching the movements of the American fleet in southern waters, and was worried by reports of the adverse reaction of the administration and the American people to the Havana disorders. Apprehension was felt that some mischance might occur if United States warships made a protracted stay in Cuban ports. Nevertheless, Madrid expressed cordial agreement, and proposed to reciprocate by sending Spanish vessels to call at American ports.

The announcement of the visits, with emphasis on their friendly character, flurried the American public with skepticism and alarm. The government could not advertise its dread of an anti-American demonstration at Havana, and did not at any time admit the motive. Secretary Long, who particularly disliked the policy of barring the Cuban capital to the ships of the United States, wrote in his private diary that the given explanation was the sole reason for the orders to the *Maine* and *Montgomery*. This was true only in the deep and limited sense that the Washington government desired peace with Spain, and was striving to reduce the danger of the gravest threat to peace—injury to American lives and property at the hands of Spanish subjects. The keen anxiety of McKinley and his advisers had been disclosed by the instructions to Captain Sigsbee, and was attested by the speed with which they had acted on Dupuy de Lôme's acquiescence, without heeding General Lee's objections or awaiting the response of Madrid.

The administration had taken a calculated risk, but suspense was of short duration. Reassuring news quickly came of the warm official reception accorded the *Maine* at Havana; and General Lee, delighted by the happy outcome of the government's decision, enthusiastically welcomed the presence of the battleship. The President must have felt a great relief. On the evening after the arrival of the *Maine*, he spoke expansively to the Spanish minister, whom he singled out for unusual attention at the diplomatic dinner at the White House.

McKinley's criticism of the Cánovas ministry had been peculiarly exasperating to the reactionary diplomat whom Cánovas had appointed to represent Spain at Washington. Señor Enrique Dupuy de Lôme was respected for his dignified reserve and the patriotic energy with which he had labored to hunt down filibustering expeditions and combat the propaganda of the Cuban junta; but his soft, proud face was seared with the irritations of nearly three years' service in a country hostile to his own. Recently it had been his uncongenial duty to support the autonomous government in Cuba, and advocate to the State Department its proposals for commercial reciprocity with the United States. Dupuy de Lôme was not in sympathy with a liberal colonial policy. He despised the President of the United States and the concessions he had won from the Sagasta ministry.

The first diplomatic dinner of the McKinley administration was, like all large White House banquets, served in the corridor. A number of small tables had been set out in the state dining room; and when the gentlemen retired there for coffee and cigars, the President invited the Spanish minister to sit at his table. There were nine envoys who took precedence; but, in his uniform glittering with gold braid and decorations, Señor Dupuy was seated in the company of the ambassadors of Britain, Germany, and France. He was approached, when they arose, by the President. "I see that we have only good news," McKinley said; and, with a complimentary allusion to the Spaniard's understanding of the political situation, he spoke of Republican discipline in Congress and the improvement in the strength of "our position," and concluded with the assurance, "you have no occasion to be other than satisfied and confident." All the foreign diplomats were witnesses of this scene. Dupuy's haughty enmity was softened by the distinguished attention and the President's manifest sincerity. There was gratified vanity in the Minister's report to his government; but his mind might have been uneasy, for the month before he had done a foolish thing. He had written a Spanish friend in Havana a letter which abused McKinley as a cheap, vacillating politician, and sneered at the autonomous government of Cuba and its reciprocity program. This letter had not been delivered.

Havana was swarming with agents who were vigilant to serve the propagandists of the insurgent cause. Early in February, a telephone call informed Dupuy de Lôme that his letter had fallen into the hands of the Cuban junta in New York, and would be published the next day in the *Journal*. Judge Day, on hearing the report, wasted no time on diplomatic circumlocutions. He was perhaps uninformed that time should be so wasted. Calling at the Spanish legation, Day simply asked Señor Dupuy if he had written the letter; and was, with equal directness, told that he had.

The President, examining the translation of the missive which Judge Day placed on his desk, saw that Señor Dupuy had indeed reason to be other than satisfied and confident. His usefulness to Spain at Washington was ended. Before General Woodford could make representations at Madrid for his recall, the Minister had cabled his resignation and made his preparations to depart.

When the "de Lome" letter appeared on the front page of every newspaper in the country, the *Maine* had been at Havana for two weeks. So long a stay had not been intended, but Washington had yielded to General Lee's persuasions. The good effect of the visit had changed his mind. He was so well satisfied that he wanted a warship permanently assigned to the Cuban capital. The doubts of the American public had been lulled by reports of the hospitality of the Spanish authorities to Captain Sigsbee and his officers. The stories conjured up a gay and peaceful scene: the slim white battleship riding in the pretty harbor, with the Stars and Stripes flying, while launches chuffed to and fro with white-uniformed loads of Americans and Spaniards. The picture was slashed by Dupuy de Lôme's pen, with its disclosure of coarse contempt for the President, and cynical ill faith toward Cuba. The country raged against the perfidy of Spain, but the unfortunate publication caused no interruption of the exchange of courtesies at Havana. For still another week, the *Maine* lay at the buoy designated by the captain of the port, and the American officers continued to enjoy a round of dinners, balls, receptions, and bullfights.

In the early hours of February 16, lights flashed in the windows of the Navy Department on Seventeenth Street, and messengers posted through the darkness of the sleeping city. The Washington social season was at its height. Young people were driving home from a great ball; and Helen Long, finding a courier at her father's door, carried up the dispatch to his bed. In the first pallor of dawn, a naval officer aroused the President. He was not on time for breakfast that morning, and his house guest, Myron Herrick, teased him for being late and asked him why he looked so stern. McKinley's face did not light with an answering smile. The night before, the *Maine* had been split by an explosion, and with more than 250 of her men had sunk in flames beneath the waters of Havana harbor.

The sense of black calamity had not been matched in Washington since the midsummer day of 1881 when President Garfield had fallen sorely wounded in the Pennsylvania Station. Flags drooped from their mastheads. Official functions were canceled. Crowds gathered quietly before the White House, and surged through the State, War and Navy Building across the way. Outside Secretary Long's office, people massed around a little model of the *Maine*. They watched workmen open the glass case, take down the tiny ensign from the peak, and place one raised at half-mast on the stern. Catastrophe held the country, from coast to coast, in a hush of mourning and suspense. The silence of America was heavy with the question: Was this hostile attack?

The extras of the yellow press, crying treachery and vengeance, gave back the only answer. Captain Sigsbee could offer no information, and asked that public opinion be suspended. The Navy Department issued a statement that the cause of the disaster was unknown, and promptly appointed a naval board of inquiry, whose expert qualifications were beyond dispute. The presiding officer was Captain William T. Sampson, the commander of the battleship *Iowa*, and an authority on ordnance, while the judge advocate, Lieutenant Commander Adolph Marix, had previously served as executive officer of the *Maine*, and possessed a thorough knowledge of her construction. Responsible newspapers and public men, rallying to the administration's support, counseled calm and self-restraint. The Madrid government, the Queen Regent, and Governor General Blanco expressed their regret and sympathy. Word came of official mourning at Havana, of honors paid the American dead and care given the wounded. The Spanish cruiser *Vizcaya* innocently glided into New York harbor, returning the courtesy of the visit of the *Maine*. The protestations of Spain that the disaster must have been caused by an accident were echoed by many men who dreaded war. The modern steel ships, propelled by steam and laden with tons of explosives, were still widely regarded as dangerous experiments. Senator Eugene Hale of Maine, the chairman of the Committee on Naval Affairs, told reporters that a battleship was little less than a volcano.

The President refrained from a message or statement that bore directly on the tumultuous question; but, in an address at the University of Pennsylvania on February 22, he spoke with solemn significance of Washington's reliance on God, and his belief in a sober public judgment and good faith toward all nations. The instruction was understood and implicitly obeyed. The unanimity of the President's support in the ordeal of suspense had never, Senator Lodge said, been equaled or approached at any crisis in American history. Lodge spoke from a full heart. The warmakers were compelled for five weeks to accede to an attitude of wise deliberation, while divers and wrecking crews worked in Havana harbor and the board of inquiry sat behind closed doors.

The President privately confided his views to a new and younger friend, Senator Charles W. Fairbanks of Indiana. "I don't propose to be swept off my feet by the catastrophe," McKinley said. "My duty is plain. We must learn the truth and endeavor, if possible, to fix the responsibility. The country can afford to withhold its judgment and not strike an avenging blow until the truth is known. The Administration will go on preparing for war, but still hoping to avert it. It will not be plunged into war until it is ready for it." But the President's mood was deeply serious. He expressed fear that the effect of the tragedy might embarrass his negotiations for intervention in Cuba.

Public judgment was restrained, but it was not suspended. The conviction spread that evidence favorable to Spain would have been promptly discovered and disclosed. Enemy attack was a more acceptable idea to most Americans than the slur at their technical skills and the humiliation of their proud new power at sea. The theory of accident was gradually rejected by all but the pacifist element. The "war feeling," as it was called, insidiously possessed the minds of men who did not own a conscious desire for aggression or revenge. It was the feeling that war was coming, the feeling that makes wars come. Offers of enlistment flooded into Washington. Americans trusted the President, not only for guidance in conduct befitting the nation, but for preparedness to meet the issue that lay ahead.

Overnight, John D. Long had stepped into the limelight. His desk was piled with mail. Reporters besieged his office door. The jogtrot of the Navy Department had accelerated to a gallop. The mobilizing of the squadrons and the spurt of overtime production at yards and arsenals and factories consoled the people for the news columns in which they fearfully read of the armored might of Spain. The loss of one battleship had brought a startled realization that the United States was not a match for a second-rate naval power. Since the night of February 15, the American Navy could boast only seven modern armor-clads, and the great battleship *Oregon* was in the Pacific, separated by a journey of many weeks from the eastern seaboard.

The emergency preparations jolted the Secretary of the Navy into a thousand immediate decisions on the movements of the fleet, on the mobilization of the naval militia, on recruiting, equipment, fuel, supplies, construction, and repairs. The grave risk was taken of ordering the *Oregon* to make the long and perilous voyage around the Horn. Plans were hastily laid to ransack the yards and chandleries of Europe for additional ships and stores, and to supplement a makeshift auxiliary force of revenue cutters and lighthouse tenders with merchant steamers, yachts, and tugboats, which could be converted to the Navy's use. The purchase of these vessels—frequently at exorbitant prices demanded by American owners in the government's necessity—was initiated as soon as funds were provided by Congress. On March 8, a bill was introduced in the House appropriating $50,000,000 to be expended by the President for the national defense. General Joe Wheeler, representative from Alabama, greeted its report with a rebel yell. Party and sectional differences were forgotten. The bill was at once unanimously passed. The Senate followed suit the next day. The unprecedented grant of power to the Executive was received with universal approbation. There were not a half dozen sane persons in the country, said *The New York Times* on March 9, who doubted that the great sum would be expended with judgment and absolute integrity. The action of Congress was a dizzying stimulus to patriotic emotion, stirring sober citizens to a conviction that the United States was threatened from without, and elating them with a sense of unity and high resolution at a time of crisis.

The onus of the Navy Department's purchases fell on Assistant Secretary Roosevelt. He was working like a demon, but he had little faith in tardy improvisations. He was burning to atone by aggression for the shortcomings of American sea power, and rush off the entire Atlantic fleet to Havana to avenge "an act of dirty treachery." The judicial inquiry into the *Maine* disaster had snapped Roosevelt's allegiance to the administration. With war within his grasp, the President had held back; and Roosevelt disgustedly concluded that McKinley had "no more backbone than a chocolate éclair." In wild frustration at the government's slow pace, Roosevelt had privately discussed with Senator Lodge the measures he might take to speed things up at the Navy Department. His chance had come in late February, when his weary chief decided to take a short leave of absence and temporarily empowered Roosevelt with his authority. Roosevelt spent one strenuous afternoon, firing off telegrams and cables and even messages to Congress, and issuing peremptory orders to move ships and guns and ammunition. But most of these gestures were wasted. The famous dispatch alerting Dewey to mobilize his squadron at Hong Kong and prepare for offensive operations in the Philippines was at once repetitive and premature, and had no actual bearing on subsequent events. The main effect of Roosevelt's rampage was to bring Long back posthaste to the Department the next morning, persuaded that his assistant was too nervous to be entrusted with serious responsibility.

The appropriation for the "national defense" had been made in response to the President's request. The military stalemate in Cuba and the fiasco of the measures of relief and reform had convinced McKinley that the time had come for a showdown with Spain. For three years, the American government had ineffectually protested that conditions in Cuba were intolerable and uttered hollow warnings that the United States would be compelled to intervene. McKinley had arrived at the decision that the war must stop, not at some future indefinite date, but with the onset of the spring rains, and that the summer should see the end of the misery of Cuba. He intended to ask Congress for a special fund of half a million dollars, and feed the starving Cubans, whether Spain objected or not.

The objections of Spain had been vividly foreshadowed in February. The sinking of the *Maine* had occurred at a time of critical diplomatic disagreement. The Madrid government, angered by the President's message and fearful of the political consequences of further yielding to the United States, had frigidly declined to reopen discussions on Cuba. A sharply hostile note had advised Washington that a self-respecting nation must repel by force intervention in its exclusively domestic concerns. General Woodford had informed the Spanish authorities that he considered this note a serious mistake. He had proved to be an emissary of unusual ability, forthright and vigorous in his presentment of the American case, yet sympathetic in his understanding of the susceptibilities and the political dilemma of the government to which he was accredited. From the first, Woodford had not been optimistic of reaching a peaceful solution. By February, he had become assured that Spain had reached the limit of concessions, and that the Sagasta ministry preferred war with the United States to its own overthrow and the possible fall of the dynasty. The answer of the American government was to back with military preparations its new proposals for an immediate armistice in Cuba, the full revocation of the *reconcentrado* order, and an assurance of co-operation in the distribution of provisions and supplies.

The President had faced and was making ready for the possible eventuality of armed intervention. Sobered by his grave decision, he was certain of his duty to the Cuban people, and satisfied that an ultimate resort to force, should diplomatic methods fail, would be justified by world opinion; but McKinley did not expect that diplomacy would fail. He expected that the firm intention of the American government and the unified purpose of the American people would bring Spain to terms. An armistice in Cuba was the first step toward a peace conference with the insurgents, toward a tender of the good offices of the United States and eventual arbitration for the independence of the island. The military preparations were primarily designed to jolt the Spanish government out of its proud and unrealistic refusal to negotiate. Long spoke of the appropriation as a "peace measure," and looked forward to its "mollifying influence" on the excitement of the

Spanish public. Dawes, after calling to congratulate McKinley on the compliment of the immense sum that Congress had placed in his hands, remarked with satisfaction that it added to the President's "power to control the situation in the interests of honorable peace."

The subject of the *Maine* was properly excluded from the pending negotiations. The President was resolved to dissociate his Cuban policy from the taint of retaliation. It is probable that for a time he was satisfied that the report would give Spain the benefit of the doubt. Though there is no direct evidence of the President's opinion, a record exists of the thoughts of Secretary Long, McKinley's closest friend in the Cabinet and in daily consultation at the White House at this period. Long was at first apprehensive of the official involvement of Spain, and he was much relieved by the assurances of Fitzhugh Lee that General Blanco and his associates should be entirely exonerated from complicity. Laying the blame on some unknown and totally unauthorized conspirators, Lee presented a suggestion that a mine might have been secretly planted at a point where the hull of the *Maine* would hit it as she swung at her buoy, and that the resultant explosion had set off the magazine in which the saluting powder was kept. At the end of February, the President called Long into a conference with Judge Day on this communication, and Long in his turn summoned the chief of the Navy's Ordnance Bureau. As a result of the four-cornered discussion, Long concluded that Lee's explanation was "probable," and that Spain could be charged only with negligence in failing to protect the American battleship. "I believe that war will be averted," Long wrote in his diary, "for I am satisfied that the Spanish Government is not responsible for the disaster."

Should the board of inquiry sustain the charge of negligence, the President intended to make a demand for reparations from Spain as a separate proposition, unrelated to the negotiations on Cuba. In spite of the country's agitation, McKinley had strong reasons to believe that the massive sentiment of the people repudiated a war of vengeance. His attitude of judicial delay had been received with overwhelming approval. The business community, adverse to dislocation of the new prosperity, had rallied behind the President. He read the desire for peace in the enormous mail that showered on the White House and in the beseeching faces of the men and women who thronged to clasp his hand three afternoons a week. Congress had crowned the President's leadership with the compliment of $50,000,000. It was the means of arming the United States, but in that hour of felicitation and applause McKinley could not doubt his "power to control the situation" at home. Rumors that he favored the adjournment of Congress had no basis in fact. He told Dawes that if a movement for adjournment were made, he would send an immediate message, asking Congress to remain.

Nor is it apparent that McKinley recognized the danger of stimulating the "war feeling" by preparations for war. The appropriation for the national defense, three weeks after the sinking of the *Maine*, had perhaps been the fatal step; but not in its effect on Spain. The display of mighty resources and unanimous purpose proved to be a cogent "peace measure." The news, as General Woodford wrote the President, "has not excited the Spaniards—it has stunned them." For the first time, Woodford was encouraged to hope that war might be avoided. He observed a new realism in the attitude of the Spanish government and people, and foresaw that an exhausted and impoverished nation might be relieved to part with her irreconcilable colony in the Caribbean.

On March 17, when Woodford composed a letter dilating on the auspicious auguries in Spain, Senator Redfield Proctor made a speech in the Senate.

A number of members of Congress had recently visited Cuba on a tour of investigation. Proctor was the first to speak. He had a reputation for steady judgment. He was said to have been in conference at the White House since his return. The keenest interest attached to his opinions, but Proctor had declined to be interviewed before delivering his formal report to the Senate. He arose in a packed, attentive chamber, with news correspondents eagerly hanging on a speech that would make headlines throughout the country.

Proctor had evidently been fully acquainted with McKinley's policy. He made only a passing reference to the sinking of the *Maine*. He refrained from suggesting a plan for intervention in Cuba. Without striving for sensation or even for eloquence, he gave a "dry, passionless, statistical recital" of the agony of Cuba under Spanish misrule. The solemn and terrible testimony was more moving than hysterical oratory. "It is just as if Proctor had held up his right hand and sworn to it," said old Senator Frye. Proctor had adhered to the letter of the President's policy, but his speech was a powerful plea for immediate armed intervention. The warmakers of the Senate embraced a new ally, and Speaker Reed sneered at the marble king of Vermont, "A war will make a large market for gravestones."

Proctor's speech was the signal for an outburst of rabid hostility toward Spain. Feeling was aggravated by news that a flotilla of her torpedo boats had sailed for the other remnant of Spanish empire in the Western Hemisphere, the island of Porto Rico. The emboldened jingoes of Congress muttered their impatience with inaction. Roosevelt rushed to the State Department to urge Judge Day to treat the movement of Spanish vessels as a provocation to war. The sensational press played on the fear of attack, and raved for the national defense. The *Maine* returned to the headlines in a rumble of rumors that positive evidence had been found of an "external explosion." On the evening of March 18, Cortelyou observed an unusual nervousness in the President's manner. Mrs. McKinley had gone with Judge and Mrs. Day to the theater to see *The Old Homestead*. Her strength and good spirits had notably improved, but her absence worried the President, and he hurried abstractedly through the papers on his desk.

Two days later, though the President was "very gentle and considerate, as he always is," Cortelyou remarked a subtle change in his face. "He appeared to me careworn," Cortelyou wrote in his diary, "did not look well, and his eyes had a far-away, deep-set expression in them." In the Sunday quiet of March 20, the Navy Department had received a confidential message from Havana. The board of inquiry had reached the unanimous verdict that the *Maine* had been blown up by a submarine mine. The conclusion had been expected, but it could no longer be hoped that Congress and the country would accept it in a calm and reasonable spirit. It was common knowledge that the private possession of explosives was forbidden at Havana, that the harbor was under strict military control and surveillance, and that the *Maine* had been destroyed as she lay at the buoy that had been designated by the captain of the port. An "external explosion" had become synonymous with the guilt of Spain, and its rumor stirred the banked fires of retaliation into instant flame.

The President acted at once to accelerate the progress of the negotiations with Madrid. Judge Day sent a secret dispatch informing Woodford that the loss of the battleship might be peacefully settled, if full reparation were promptly made; but that, unless Spain took immediate steps to end the unendurable conditions in Cuba, the President would lay the question before Congress.

McKinley spent the next four days in conference with members of Senate and House. Anxious Republican leaders pressed the political danger of the administration's evident desire for peace. In an effort to rally nonpartisan support in the crisis, the President sent for influential Democrats and Populists, and frankly discussed the situation. The Capitol rang with the emotional speeches of the recent visitors to Cuba. The atmosphere was charged with expectation of the *Maine* report, and excitement rose to fever pitch on Thursday with the news that it would reach Washington that evening. Thurston of Nebraska shook the Senate with a tearful tribute to his wife, who had died on their trip to Cuba with a plea for the suffering population on her lips. A party of men lunched quietly at the White House. Mrs. McKinley had gone to Baltimore to attend a benefit for a monument to the sailors lost on the *Maine*. The President appeared calm and earnest, but he was so uneasy over his wife's excursion that, as the rainy evening fell, he rushed to meet her at the depot. It was a sudden, impulsive decision. The carriage had already left. A passing one-horse hack was hailed; and, accompanied by the manservant Tharin, the President was whirled through the dusk by a startled Negro driver, straightening his shoulders and giving a flourish to his high hat.

The White House party had safely returned when an immense crowd gathered at the Pennsylvania Station to await the evening train from the south. Shortly after half-past nine, four tired naval officers stumbled to the dim platform. Since leaving Key West, they had been on guard, watch and watch, over a ship's mail pouch, and Lieutenant Commander Marix had been asleep in the corner of the seat when the train pulled in. They were unceremoniously greeted by a cadet from the Navy Department. Through some curious oversight, a carriage had not been provided. Lieutenant John Hood, a survivor of the *Maine*, carried the canvas pouch slung under his arm as the officers plunged across the tracks in the wake of the cadet, and ran through the baggage room toward the hackstand on Sixth Street. The crowd raised a shout. People surged to the hackstand. In the press someone jostled Lieutenant Hood. His hand went to his hip. Space was respectfully cleared, and the officers made their escape. Five cabloads of reporters pursued them to the Ebbitt House. The press was eager for official confirmation of the verdict; but the blue uniforms and the bulky bag quickly vanished from the lobby, and the only information to be had was that the report would not be delivered that night.

Next morning, Friday, March 25, the Navy Department brougham drew up before the White House, bringing Secretary Long, Lieutenant Commander Marix, and the mail pouch. Its contents were formally turned over to the President in the library. Judge Day was called in, and remained for the Cabinet meeting which followed the preliminary conference. There had been another newcomer to the Cabinet in January, when the President had appointed Judge McKenna to a vacancy on the bench of the Supreme Court. John W. Griggs of New Jersey, a smart and sagacious lawyer who was close to Vice-President Hobart, had resigned as governor of his state to accept the position of Attorney General. Tall and athletic, with sharp features and thick, gray-streaked hair, Griggs was in fit and youthful contrast to the ablest of his colleagues: the gentle, cautious Long; the Olympian banker, Gage; sober, businesslike Mr. Bliss; and the sage agriculturist, James Wilson. Sherman was impotent. Mr. Gary, in poor health, slouched wearily in his chair. Alger was vivacious, but unstable. Cortelyou, anxiously taking the measure of the President's advisers in the emergency, thought that Griggs added great strength to the Cabinet.

The session began at ten-thirty and lasted all day, with an interval for lunch. The gentlemen gravely considered the conclusions drawn from an examination of the wreck of the *Maine* and from the testimony of survivors and other witnesses. The battleship had been blown up on the port side, and the shock had caused the explosion of two magazines. The naval board did not fix the responsibility, merely exonerating Captain Sigsbee and his officers from fault or negligence. There was no evidence of a conspiracy on the part of Spain or her subjects, no proof that a mine had ever been laid for any purpose in Havana harbor. A Spanish commission had also examined the wreck, and found that the explosion was of internal origin, but the American government did not concede the possibility of accident. The President had made up his mind to let the week end pass before sending the report to Congress, with a brief accompanying message, omitting any reference to Cuba. This was to be promptly followed by the request for an appropriation for relief, and by a third message which would set forth the outcome of a diplomatic conference to be held at Madrid on Tuesday, March 29. The Cabinet was in unanimous agreement with the President's course; but Alger, disturbed by the signs of political unrest, was beginning to hint at the possible necessity for war. "Peace is the desired end," Judge Day cabled Woodford late that night.

The cause of peace did not appear hopeless, if the *Maine* report could be quietly passed over. The optimistic tone of Woodford's dispatches encouraged the belief that Spain was about to grant concessions on Cuba. Day cabled again on Sunday, explicitly stating the American stipulations on the armistice and reconcentration orders. He expected that these terms would be met, and he was hoping for agreement to a further proposal, that the President should act as final arbiter between Spain and the insurgents, should peace terms not be determined by the autumn.

The crucial question was the immediate reaction to the *Maine* report. It was not doubted that the Republican majority of the House would sustain the President, or that Speaker Reed would effectively block attempts at opposition. The division of the Republicans in the Senate was the serious matter. The warmakers had redoubtable captains in Lodge, Frye, Foraker, Chandler, Cushman Davis of Minnesota, and their new recruit, Proctor. On the other hand, the conservatives were anti-war, as anxious as the business interests for the climate of prosperity; and the men with whom Mark Hanna was allied—Allison, Aldrich, Hale, Spooner of Wisconsin, and Orville Platt of Connecticut were experienced strategists. Their influence had already prevailed to adjourn the Senate for a long week end. Yet the President was far from confident of the outcome. He spoke privately of his fears of the effect of the *Maine* report on Congress and the people. War must be averted—or, at worst, deferred. "We are not prepared for war," the President said.

The message on the *Maine* was awaited with an extraordinary anticipation. Except for the Washington's Birthday speech, McKinley had not spoken, and in the spring of 1898 the silence of the President was nearly as profound as though the White House were untenanted. His channels of public communication were limited to his messages and addresses. Presidential press conferences were unheard of, and would have been considered a shockingly undignified innovation. When important decisions were impending, the Washington correspondents descended on the mansion like a force of competitive detectives, grabbing and interrogating the visitors, and reporting their remarks and facial expressions. The President himself was accorded a comparative immunity; and, in McKinley's case, comment was reduced to a minimum. It was customary to infer the trend of Executive opinion from the utterances of the President's close political associates, especially those regarded as his spokesmen in Congress; but there had been no intimation of McKinley's guarded views on the *Maine*. The war spirit had flowered in a void of Executive guidance.

By the last week in March, the failure of evasion should have been manifest to the President and his advisers. Americans had confounded the *Maine* with Cuba, and the issues could not be dissociated by their mere formal separation into different messages. The crisis demanded that the President speak in the accents of authority, sternly disown the unworthy impulse to revenge, and declare his resolute intention to act on behalf of Cuba. There were grave objections to the mention of his policy before it could be fully disclosed. The President could not publicly discuss the American stipulations to Spain without disaster to the impending negotiations; and, in the aroused temper of Congress, a premature reference to Cuba might be equally perilous to his diplomacy. It was perhaps already too late to arrest the mounting spiral of hostility to Spain; but the time had come for the President to abandon his noncommittal attitude, and risk everything on a bold assertion of leadership.

Late on the Sunday afternoon that followed the receipt of the *Maine* report, the President called Cortelyou to his desk, and very rapidly dictated the message that would be transmitted to Congress on the morrow. It recapitulated the facts of the sending of the *Maine* and her destruction;

outlined the findings of the board of inquiry, and stated that they had been communicated to Spain. The President said that he expected Spain to do what justice and honor required, and invoked, in conclusion, the "deliberate consideration" of Congress. There was no statement of the government's firm purpose, no instruction to await the message on Cuba, no standard to which conservative sentiment could rally. McKinley had remained the captive of caution and indirection, of his great political defect of silence.

Cortelyou worked through dinnertime transcribing the message. At ten o'clock, when he returned from getting a bite of supper, the President was downstairs with Hanna, Grosvenor, and other callers, and Abner McKinley, who was staying at the White House. About an hour later, the President went up to the Cabinet Room with his brother, and read the message aloud in a voice that seemed unusually deep and full. Addison Porter came in during the reading. Both he and Abner made suggestions about the concluding paragraphs, and they were frequently altered. At midnight, McKinley was still working at the end of the long table under the naked bulbs of the brass chandelier. In the end, he retained nearly his original dictation. He appeared tired, and exceedingly earnest. He repeatedly spoke of his anxiety to do the right thing, what the world and the country would consider just and honorable.

The Washington correspondents lived by their wits and their confidential relationships with men in public life. The scramble for news was a free-for-all. The opposition journals were supple in conjecture and attack, with no holds barred to the yellow press; while the Republican organs and the big syndicates had superior opportunities for access to official information. Some of the leakages had been so scandalous that unusual precautions had been taken to guard the *Maine* report. The original document, in the handwriting of Lieutenant Commander Marix, had been placed in a small safe in the executive offices immediately after the Friday Cabinet meeting. It was handed to Cortelyou on Saturday afternoon to be copied, and was removed by him for five hours to the seclusion of his own house. In the evening, he brought back the original with ten copies he had made, and saw the papers seamed and tied up and replaced in the safe. There was no occasion to examine the report on Sunday. Its restriction seemed assured until its delivery to Congress at noon on Monday, March 28; but that morning the early editions of the nation's newspapers carried an Associated Press dispatch which revealed the findings of the naval board in full and accurate detail. On hearing that the AP claimed to have had access to the report for a day, Secretary Porter summoned Colonel Charles A. Boynton, the veteran chief of the Washington bureau, who stood by while

Colonel Crook opened the safe, and found the parcel with seams and string intact. Boynton signed a "cast iron statement" that the AP's information had not been obtained from the White House. Its source was a minor mystery of the *Maine* affair.

The effect of the publication was as sensational as though the news had not been forecast. The country read the verdict as plain proof that Spain had been guilty of premeditated massacre and destruction. That Monday morning, the American people were transformed into a nation at war, humiliated by an initial defeat, burning to retaliate. "There is no stopping place short of the absolute independence of Cuba," said *The New York Times.* ". . . It would have been as easy to end the War of the Revolution at Bunker Hill or the Civil War at Bull Run as to turn back now."

Congress, gathered for the anti-climax of the report's legitimate delivery, was infuriated by the judicial phrases of the President's message. The request for "deliberate consideration" was like a reasonable word to a man in frenzy. The ranks of the belligerents swelled in an hour. The wrath of the opposition was matched by harsh, outspoken criticism from Republicans. Hitherto reliable party members talked of wresting the direction of foreign affairs from the hands of the Executive, and plunging at once into hostilities. All conservative predictions were overturned, and leaders of Senate and House rushed to the White House to tell their fears that it might be impossible to stop "a Cuban outbreak."

The President withheld his request for a relief appropriation, lest it furnish a peg for warlike resolutions, but they thundered on Tuesday from Capitol Hill without the pretext of a message on Cuba. The strategy of the Democrats was to insist on the immediate recognition of the insurgent republic. Populists and Silver Republicans met to endorse this line and present a solid front of opposition. In the Senate, Foraker and Frye announced Republican division by introducing resolutions intended to force the President's hand. Vice-President Hobart had difficulty in restoring order when the President's friend, Mason of Illinois, declared himself for war. Speaker Reed rigidly suppressed demonstrations in the House, but some fifty Republican representatives gathered in caucus to protest his interference with the will of the majority and defiantly assert the exclusive function of Congress to declare war.

In the roar of legislative revolt, the Cabinet learned that the diplomatic conference at Madrid had been adjourned until Thursday, March 31. Woodford begged that the President would withhold all action. Judge Day's answer sounded the alarm of the administration: there was the gravest apprehension that no possible effort could stop a resolution for intervention; proposals for peace in Cuba must come at once from Spain. The President fought for two days' delay, promising leaders of the Senate and House that, if his negotiations should fail, he would promptly submit all the facts to Congress. The Senate Foreign Relations Committee postponed the report of Tuesday's resolutions. It was said that the President made a direct appeal to the Republican members, Cushman Davis, Frye, Lodge, and Foraker, all of them rabid for armed intervention, two of them sponsors of resolutions they consented to defer. The rebellious Republican congressmen agreed to wait, after their delegates had called at the White House. "I pray God," the President told them, "that we may be able to keep the peace." But his hearers did not receive the impression that he was hopeful. The extremists of the opposition, flouting McKinley's efforts for patriotic unity, had cast off all restraint. They gloated over the caucus of Republican *reconcentrados*," and taunted the faithful party members with shameful subservience to the business interests. In the jargon of the demagogues of the House, the President was frightened by the wheeling vultures of Wall Street, enticed by ghouls to mortgage prostrate Cuba for the benefit of the investors in Spanish bonds. A member of one congressional delegation to the White House had accused the President to his face of doing the bidding of Wall Street. "My whole life is an answer to that statement," McKinley had quietly replied. Grosvenor, rising in the House on Thursday, pointed to the mighty preparations for war, and pleaded for trust in the administration's purpose, not to make a "shilly-shally" declaration, but to ensure that Cuba should remain forever free. The President's spokesman did not venture to speak of peace. It had become a symbol of obedience to avarice. Speaker Reed's reprimands were powerless to prevent the hisses that sounded from the galleries when the soiled and despicable word was mentioned.

Arrangements had been made to transmit General Woodford's cable directly to the White House, where a telegraph had recently been installed in charge of the executive clerk Montgomery. Secretaries Alger and Bliss, Judge Day, and Senator Hanna dined with the President on Thursday evening, and accompanied him to the Cabinet Room to wait. A few other friends were admitted. Alvey A. Adee arrived with the cipher code. A mob of reporters fumed in the corridor, straining their ears for the click of the telegraph. It began at half-past ten. By eleven, as the sound went steadily on, the tension in the corridor slackened to a gloomy certainty that the translation could not be finished in time for the morning editions. Judge Day sent word that no statement would be given out that night. Good news does not take long to tell, the reporters reasoned. The telegraph was still softly chattering when they withdrew.

The night dragged on, while the President waited. He had built strong expectancy on the favorable response of Spain; but, in the red glare of the *Maine* report, it was no longer certain that an armistice in Cuba would afford a cogent argument for peace. Its possible proposal had already been derided in Congress and the press as a perfidious trick whereby Spain might seek to gain time. At this juncture, only the independence of Cuba would appease the United States. Yet a narrow chance remained that the President could stave off war by an announcement of the complete success of his negotiations, and that militaristic fervor might abate with the cessation of fighting and the unhampered distribution of American supplies. This hope was quenched when at a late hour Adee laid the translation of Woodford's dispatch on the Cabinet table. At the last minute the Spanish government had drawn back, equivocating on the question of an armistice. The answer had been received in sorrow of heart by General Woodford, who had worked hard for peace.

Spain proposed to confide the pacification of Cuba to the new insular parliament, which would assemble in May. Meanwhile, Madrid would not "find it inconvenient to accept at once a suspension of hostilities asked for by the insurgents. . . ." The refusal to take the initiative was a mockery of the President's terms. The embattled insurgents had never been so disinclined to ask for a truce as at this time of confident expectation of American recognition and assistance. For the rest, Spain bowed to the terms of the United States. The differences over the *Maine* would be submitted to arbitration. A large appropriation had been made for Cuban relief, and aid from the United States would also be accepted. The revocation of the *reconcentrado* order, the main object of the President's long-term diplomacy, had been proclaimed. The concessions on Cuba were far greater than Madrid had ever previously dared to make, but they had come too late. Spanish reforms in Cuba were irrelevant to the American political crisis.

Spain lagged behind the timetable of the United States, but there were no reasonable grounds for breaking off negotiations with a government that had consented to every requirement but one. It was the duty of deliberate and enlightened statesmanship to renew the pressures of diplomacy, and permit Sagasta and his ministers time to work out the old and complex colonial problem which they had inherited. Time was a license that Congress denied. To explore the whole long road to the peaceable liberation of Cuba, McKinley needed months, perhaps a year or more. He had with difficulty won the respite of a few days. The President had consummately failed, not in the conduct of his diplomacy, but in restraining the belligerence of Congress and the American people.

This was the bitter draught McKinley drank, as he turned his mind to his message of intervention.

The warmakers of Congress were in the saddle. "Remember the *Maine!*" was the national slogan. It rang in martial strains, resounded from pulpits, thundered at mass meetings. American bosoms flaunted the words on gaudy badges. Music halls glorified the theme in patriotic programs. Shop-windows and family sitting rooms enshrined pictures and models of the lost battleship. Newsstands did a rushing business in chemically treated flimsies, depicting the *Maine* and a matador with a torch, which ignited to explode the paper vessel at the touch of a lighted match. The command to vengeance, printed in red on hard, white peppermint lozenges, was sticky on the lips of children. Most Americans did not speak of vengeance. They called it atonement, reparation, or justice. The old cry of *"Cuba Libre!"* mingled potently in the excitement, at once the objective and the altruistic justification of the impulse to punish Spain.

The President had become so estranged from the masses of his party that many Republicans could find no answer to the charge that he was weak and vacillating, trembling before the bond interests, apathetic to the murder of American sailors. The yellow press circulated false rumors that, in desperation, he had appealed to the Pope to mediate between the United States and Spain. McKinley's name, as odious as that of peace itself, had been hissed in hysterical demonstrations at the music halls. Republican leaders frantically besought the President to resume command, speak with a trumpet blast, brandish the flag. McKinley's political dilemma was painful. Dedicated to the interests of his party, he could not bring to its service an exultation in war, or violate the obligations of his high office by assenting to a war of revenge. Since hostilities were inevitable, the President conceived that his duty was to resist the chauvinists of Congress, and ensure that the momentous commitment should be soberly undertaken, on grounds that comported with the honor and the future welfare of the United States.

By day and by night, the President's thoughts had been darkened by the reversal of the aims with which he had entered office, the betrayal of the substantial minority of the people who still trusted him to keep the peace. McKinley had been unable to sleep. In desperate need of rest, he had vainly taken narcotics. His face had grown seamed and haggard, with sunken, darkly circled eyes. He jumped at every sound. His manner was exceedingly quiet. To a few visitors, he talked of his dread of the suffering that war entailed. Both Dawes and Cortelyou marveled at his stoicism. At the end of March, while a musicale was taking place in the East Room,

McKinley withdrew for a short time into the Red Parlor with Mr. Kohl-saat. He sat, as Kohlsaat remembered, on a large, crimson-brocade lounge, rested his head on his hands, and poured out his distress, protesting that Congress was trying to drive the country into war, that the armed services were not prepared; talking, too, of his sleepless nights and his worries about Mrs. McKinley's health. He had burst into tears, as he spoke; and perhaps this warning of shaken control prohibited other confidences. McKinley could not afford the luxury of breaking down. He whipped a tired brain and jerking nerves to the preparation of his message to Congress.

The message embodied the policy of neutral intervention which the President had intended to recommend if Spain had forced hostilities by an obdurate refusal to negotiate. It asked Congress for authority to use the military and naval forces as might be necessary to secure peace and a stable government in Cuba. The grounds of forcible intervention were stated to be the duty of humanity, the injury inflicted on American investments and trade, and the danger and expense to which the insurrection subjected the American government. The only reference to the *Maine* appeared as a pendant to the last point, in illustration of the intolerable conditions which the Spanish government was unable to control.

Neutral intervention, without recognition of Cuban independence, was of cardinal importance to McKinley's policy. In terminating the colonial rule of Spain, the United States was necessarily assuming a temporary responsibility for the island's political destiny. The self-styled republic of the insurgents could not legally claim to represent the Cuban people; and to place its leaders in power in Havana might embarrass the United States by obligations toward a government which did not possess the attributes of sovereignty. In treating this subject, McKinley had called on the able assistance of Attorney General Griggs. The entire message showed thoughtful and intelligent preparation; and yet it was not a forceful or persuasive paper. Its dry, dispassionate tone belied the request for a resort to arms. General Alger wished for "a little of that *ring*" at the end. The statement that diplomacy had been exhausted lacked logical conviction. Secretary Long thought that the narrative of the concessions of Spain seemed to lead to quite a different conclusion. He supposed that the defect was due to the great nervous strain under which the President was laboring; but the fault of the message lay in its omission of the true reason for armed intervention. There would have been no want of logic if McKinley could have permitted himself to speak of vengeance for the *Maine*.

Wednesday, April 6, was appointed for the delivery of the message. Though Congress had impatiently expected it on Monday, the lengthy paper was not laid before a special meeting of the Cabinet until that evening. Some changes were subsequently made, and the executive staff worked late on Tuesday night and early Wednesday to prepare the final copies. At noon on Wednesday, when Congress had assembled and a crowd of more than 10,000 spectators jammed the galleries and corridors of the Capitol, the President made a last-minute decision to defer the message for five days to permit the evacuation of American citizens from Cuba. An urgent telegram from General Lee occasioned the postponement, but there were other cogent reasons for the delay. The vast machinery of military preparation had scarcely been set in motion. Time was needed to augment the makeshift improvements in coast defense. To invite immediate hostilities, moreover, was to disregard the representations for peace that were being made by the nations of Europe and the Vatican.

The continental powers were motivated by jealous hostility to the United States, and fear that its aggression might result in American expansion and the spread of republican institutions. Germany, whose colonial program included the purchase of the Philippines and other Spanish islands in the Pacific, had secretly taken the lead in diplomatic efforts to persuade Spain to avoid a war she could not hope to win. It was known in Washington that Madrid was under heavy pressure to grant independence to Cuba, and that the Pope's intense anxiety for peace—earlier communicated to the White House by Archbishop John Ireland of St. Paul—had culminated in a proffer of mediation between Spain and the insurgents. The influence of Rome was paramount with the devout Queen Regent, and General Woodford had cabled a prophecy of peace; but the President no longer looked for a diplomatic settlement. Nevertheless, he wished to absolve the nation from the reproach of rushing headlong into war in insolent indifference to the efforts for conciliation. He had agreed to receive the representatives of the powers on April 7; and, though he did not acknowledge the bearing of this appointment on the delay of his message, it cannot be doubted that it influenced the desire for postponement which was opportunely served by Lee's request for time.

Long, Alger, Griggs, and Day were in the Cabinet Room on Wednesday when the President made up his mind. All of them were acquainted with McKinley's motives, tacit and admitted, but there was general consternation at the thought of the intransigent assemblage on the Hill. Congress had assumed toward the Executive an attitude scarcely less menacing and peremptory than its defiance of Spain. At this moment, moreover, legislative wrath was inflamed by the circulation at the Capitol of a recent editorial in Addison Porter's *Hartford Post*, stigmatizing the radical Cuban sympathizers as vile traitors of Benedict Arnold's stamp. This intemperate publication was accepted and furiously resented as a reflection of prevailing opinion at the White House. The President courted political disaster by provoking Congress further. Alger privately complained, "Congress will declare war in spite of him. He'll get run over and the party with him." Secretary Long, in entire sympathy with McKinley's aims, quailed at the risk involved. He advised that probably the message should go in at once; but the President, raising his hand, emphatically refused. "I will not do it," he said; "I will not send in that message today; I will not do such a thing if it will endanger the life of an American citizen in Cuba."

To convince Congress that the President's explanation was veracious, it was judged necessary to produce the evidence of Lee's telegram. Long suggested that Judge Day should go in person to the Capitol and show the dispatch to the committee chairmen; but this proposal met with objections, and it was finally decided to summon a congressional delegation to the White House. The choice fell on Cushman Davis, Lodge, and Frye of the Senate Foreign Relations Committee, and Nelson Dingley and two other leaders of the House. They came posthaste. A reporter, who saw Judge Day emerge from the conference, thought that he seemed to have aged several years since going in.

The reliable standing of the intermediaries induced Congress to receive the delay without official protest, but rage and suspicion seethed in the cloakrooms and corridors. Though it was known that the message was ready, the President's intentions were as profoundly distrusted as his great political skills. Republican solidarity had melted in the fear that McKinley might somehow contrive to postpone action indefinitely, and let the Democrats reap the rewards of the war party. The ranks of the peace Republicans were thinned by deserters who dreaded defeat in the mid-term elections, the wreckage of the Republican organization, the revival of the silver issue. Bryan had taken up the cause of Cuban independence. Tom Platt shuddered to think of the combined slogan "Free Cuba!" and "Free Silver!" in 1900. Thursday, Friday, and Saturday passed in taut suspense. A resolution for war would readily pass both houses.

The Senate was overwhelmingly lost to control. Hobart knew that he could not hold it back much longer, and had so advised the President. A united opposition of forty-six members was joined on the war issue by the greater part of the forty-three Republicans, including some representatives of big business. The jingoes were rampant to act. One influential Republican senator stormed into the State Department, shaking his fists. "Day, by——, don't your President know where the war-declaring power is lodged? Tell him by——, that if he doesn't do something Congress will exercise the power." The debacle of the Senate was so complete that administration leaders were counting the votes they could muster for a veto, should war be declared without waiting for the message. There was a dismal prospect that the requisite one-third of the Senate plus one would sustain the President.

The administration had depended on the solid party majority in the House—204 out of a total of 357 members—but the Republican "*reconcentrados*" were running wild, as boisterous for war as the opposition. Speaker Reed, a czar no longer, mocked his impotence to the reporters who clustered around his breakfast table at the Shoreham. Ex-Governor Morton of New York had written to urge the Speaker to exert his influence; if necessary, to step down from the dais and dissuade the members from war. "Dissuade them!" Reed commented, with his sarcastic smile. "Dissuade them! The Governor is too good. He might as well ask me to stand out in the middle of a Kansas waste and dissuade a cyclone." The opposition in the House required a switch of twenty-six Republican votes to pass a declaration of war. The Democratic leaders were assured of twice that number.

The ultimate humiliation was not visited on the Executive. Congress waited out the week end. Further delay was futile, and McKinley did not seek it. A more aggressive President might have broken with Congress outright, condemned the rabid warmakers, and declined to advise intervention. It would have been a lofty and courageous gesture, applauded by the pacifist minority. It would not have prevented war. The President rightly refused to abdicate his function as Commander in Chief, and leave nation, as well as party, divided and rudderless in a time of crisis.

Though Congress had the overwhelming support of the people on the war issue, the imperious and hostile treatment of the President had caused alarm. There were protests that Congress was holding a pistol to the President's head and threatening to usurp Executive authority in the conduct of foreign affairs. A reaction in McKinley's favor was manifest when he stepped at last into plain public view at the reception of the diplomatic agents of the concert of Europe. It had not promised to be an auspicious occasion for the President's reappearance. European intervention had been resentfully bruited in the press, and the President was reproved for setting an embarrassing and dangerous precedent by countenancing it. Only a delegation of scarlet-clad cardinals, bearing orders from Rome to the Executive Mansion, could have offered a greater affront to the American spirit than the formal visitation of the representatives of Great Britain, France, Germany, Italy, Russia, and Austria-Hungary. Yet the nation's proud isolation had been lightly penetrated by the knowledge that, among the hostile powers, the United States could claim one friend, and that friend the ancient enemy and eternally suspected commercial rival. The utterances of England's press and public men had been warmly sympathetic to the United States. On the eve of war, Americans did not disdain the unexpected support. Newspaper editorials were beginning to speak of hands across the sea, and recall the adage that blood is thicker than water.

England, in fact, had consented to join in representations to Washington only after her ambassador, Sir Julian Pauncefote, had consulted the American government. The President had been fully assured that the powers, discouraged by the attitude of England and embroiled in dissensions in China, would not venture to antagonize the United States by a vigorous protest. The ceremonies in the Blue Room were polite and inconclusive. Sir Julian, as the dean of the diplomatic corps, presented the joint note expressing the amiable hopes of the powers for peace. These disinterested hopes the President stated that he shared, but his short address closed with a reference to the necessity for ending a situation "the indefinite prolongation of which has become insufferable." The exchange of courtesies was summarized by the New York *World*. The six diplomats said, "We hope for humanity's sake you will not go to war." The President replied, "We hope, if we do, you will understand it is for humanity's sake." The American people read the report of these proceedings with relief, and some gratification. They liked the way the President had spoken. They liked the idea of a man from Ohio standing up to gold-braided diplomats and telling them that the situation in Cuba was insufferable.

On Saturday night, April 9, the President was informed of the results of the efforts of the powers and the Pope. The Queen Regent had instructed General Blanco to proclaim a suspension of hostilities in Cuba. It was the news for which McKinley had prayed on the night of March 31, knowing that even then it might come too late. Nine days later, the armistice was an anachronism, the ironic reminder of a bygone hope of peace, a postscript that did nothing to improve the logic of the President's message of intervention. The Cabinet met twice on Easter Sunday, but its deliberations were fruitless. The message must be sent.

After the evening Cabinet meeting, the President lingered at his desk, trying to evolve a final sentence that would take appropriate account of the capitulation of Spain to the last of the American proposals. President Hayes's son Webb was staying at the White House, and sat with McKinley while he worked. "Let us hope," the President wrote at midnight, "that under the Providence of God some way may yet be found to bring about peace without the resort to arms." He handed the paper to his companion.

"I am something of an autograph fiend," remarked Webb, who was never diffident in asking favors. "May I keep it? Will you sign your name to it?" McKinley merely jotted down the date, and gave the scrap of paper back to Webb with a smile. The reference to peace under the Providence of God was not included in the message that Mr. O. L. Pruden of the White House staff carried to the Capitol next morning.

Congress received the recommendation of neutral intervention at the President's discretion with a disaffection that flared into violent protest when the committees reported two days later. The Foreign Affairs Committee of the House brought in a joint resolution in substantial conformity with the message; and, despite the harangues of the partisans and rowdy disputes on the floor, it was promptly passed by a large majority. This action, however, did not indicate full compliance with the President's wishes, for it was understood that the war issue would be forced in the Senate. Cushman K. Davis, the chairman of the Foreign Relations Committee, presented three resolutions which were tantamount to a declaration of war. They declared the independence of the Cuban people; demanded that Spain at once relinquish authority over Cuba and withdraw her land and naval forces; and directed the President to use the forces of the United States to carry these resolutions into effect. These dictatorial instructions curtailed the exercise of Executive discretion but still fell short of the prevailing expectations in the upper chamber. Though the report was said to have been "unanimously" adopted in committee, four members, one of them a Republican, vehemently dissented from the vague declaration of Cuban independence. "Fire Alarm Joe" Foraker led Republican support for the minority report which was offered by the Democratic member, David Turpie of Indiana, with an amendment explicitly recognizing the insurgent republic. In a furious controversy that raged for four days, the President's conduct and motives were defamed in terms so reckless and slanderous that a number of conservative Republicans and a few Democrats rose to speak in his defense. The tide of resistance to his policy was too strong to check. All McKinley's political alliances, all the power of the federal patronage could not prevent the adoption of Turpie's amendment by the Senate. The final vote of 67 to 21, by which the amended resolutions were passed in the early hours of Sunday, April 17, was a blatant exhibition of the President's shattered influence over his party. Twenty-four Republican senators joined the opposition to antagonize the administration and assert the right of Congress to recognize a foreign state. Five Democrats voted with the minority of the Republicans. Among them, Senators George Gray of Delaware and Donelson

Caffery of Louisiana were outstanding in their courageous advocacy of the President's recommendations.

The President was prepared to accept the original resolutions as the utmost concessions he could wring from the Senate. The Turpie amendment was an infringement on his constitutional prerogatives to which he could not consent. So strongly did McKinley feel that it opposed the national interest that, during the debate in the Senate, he had drafted the form of a message vetoing any joint resolution of Congress that should provide for recognition of the so-called Cuban government. On Sunday he definitely decided to send it in, should the House, as then seemed likely, concur in the action of the Senate. But Republican discipline was firmly restored in the lower chamber, and its conferees made the sacrifice of the Turpie amendment the price of their acceptance of the Senate resolutions. The Senate conferees, daunted by a deadlock with the President and the House, proved unexpectedly ready to compromise. The Senate resolutions, denuded of the Turpie amendment, were adopted by both houses early on the morning of April 19.

In the heat of the preceding week, the resolutions had been expanded by a restriction on the future relation of the United States to Cuba. Senator Teller of Colorado, the leader of the western silverites who had bolted the St. Louis convention, had offered an amendment disclaiming the intention of the United States to exercise sovereignty over Cuba, except for its pacification. It had been unanimously adopted as a fourth resolution of the Senate, and was cordially accepted by the House. The pressure of the sugar interests, which were antipathetic to Cuban annexation, is a totally inadequate explanation of the enthusiasm that the Teller resolution generated in Congress, or the veneration in which it was held by the country. At this time, only a small minority of extreme expansionists were ambitious for the acquisition of Cuba. There was general repugnance to the idea of admitting to the Union an alien and insubordinate people, Roman Catholic in faith, with a large admixture of Negro blood. The advocacy of recognition of the insurgent republic had been partly motivated, in all sincerity, by the apprehension that neutral intervention savored of a desire for conquest. The Teller Amendment effaced the reproach of selfish ulterior aims, and dignified the cause of the warmakers with a moral purpose that substantially united public sentiment. *The New York Times* had dryly observed on March 3 that land-grabbing and knight-errantry were attitudes equally to be deplored; but Americans, swelling with pride in the altruistic sentiments of Congress, put on the armor of chivalry and made ready for a crusade.

The high-sounding declaration accorded with the President's earnest intentions toward the people of Cuba, and his consuming desire that the conduct of the United States should be worthy of its honorable traditions. Shouts of vengeance for the *Maine* had thundered so loudly in the intemperate debates of Congress that McKinley must have been thankful for the redress of a magnanimous assertion. The premature limitation of Executive action was fertile in legalistic difficulties for the eventual settlement with Spain, but the President always devoutly adhered to the Teller Amendment as a solemn and binding commitment of the government of the United States.

McKinley had salvaged all he could from the wreckage of his plans. Though he was forced to make war, the action of the government was based on grounds which he had recommended and which he could wholeheartedly endorse. His great relief was evident in his face and manner. The week of decision on Capitol Hill had been the grueling climax of more than a month of mental torment for the President. He had borne the final ordeal in silence and seclusion. With the submission of his message, the delegations from Congress had ceased to throng the Cabinet Room. The newspaper correspondents had moved in force to the Capitol. The President worked in unaccustomed quiet, often remaining at his desk until long after midnight, though Cortelyou, in the wish to spare him, disposed of a quantity of business on his own responsibility. McKinley carefully examined reports of the comment of the press, and the analysis of his heavy mail, with samplings favorable and adverse, which Cortelyou prepared for him each day. Except for "the blatherskite sheets," the leading newspapers of the country mainly commended the message of intervention. Cortelyou made a conservative estimate that 90 per cent of the letters endorsed the President's course; but these devoted correspondents did not represent the excitable mass of the American people. In the terrible solitude of his high office, McKinley was parched for sympathy and approval. He anxiously inquired for news that had a token of peace. His face was eagerly raised when Cortelyou brought in the mail. Many loyalties had wavered, many debts of gratitude were repudiated. Handing the President a letter from an old personal friend, Cortelyou flinched at the look of sorrow that spread over the tired face, as McKinley asked, "Is he for us?"

Cortelyou had come to revere the President. In this time of trial, he learned to love the man for his patient endurance of calumny and desertion. On the first afternoon of uproarious dispute in Congress, as Cortelyou left some messages in the Cabinet Room, he was so touched by McKinley's pale, careworn appearance that he stood hesitating outside the door, unable to bring himself to go away in silence. Correct and frozen in reserve,

Cortelyou went back, searching his heart for some word of comfort. What he found was, "Mr. President, I want to say to you that in these busy days we hope you will feel no hesitation in calling upon any of us outside at any hour of the day or night for anything we can do." For months, the overworked staff had been drudging until after midnight. The formal words were meaningless; but a pledge of love and loyalty had been given, and was gratefully accepted, as McKinley looked up to say, "Mr. Cortelyou, I know you will, I know you will, and I appreciate it."

When the decision at last was taken on terms that the President approved, he climbed from the valley of his defeat with unshaken faith, reconciled to adversity by the strong fatalism of his nature and his singular lack of egoism. McKinley had dreaded war as a man dreads a tidal wave that may engulf his house, a force too vast for indignant remonstrance or thought of personal humiliation. "The country should understand that we are striving to make our course consistent not alone for today, but for all time; the people must not be unreasonable," he said to Cortelyou during the days of waiting. If there was a hint of weary disenchantment in McKinley's words, there was no bitterness. He was spared the lash of pride and the poison of rancor. His cordial dealings with Congress were promptly restored. He had no reproaches to utter, and no grudges to pay. He dedicated himself without factiousness to the unity of the Republican party, and without partisanship to the unity of the nation. But, though McKinley's spirit showed no trace of his ordeal, his flesh was not so resilient. He was greatly aged. His smooth statesman's mask was scarred with lines of care, and his luminous eyes were clouded by the "far-away, deep-set expression" that Cortelyou had remarked. For the rest of his life, McKinley's face would wear the stern and somber record of his struggle to keep the peace.

On April 20, the President signed the resolutions of Congress, and an ultimatum to Spain, which had been prepared at the State Department. The mansion hummed with the traffic of visitors, and once more the correspondents stormed the office staircase and corridors. A number of members of Congress were in the Cabinet Room when the ultimatum was brought in. Senator Frye looked on with interest. He was a vehement old fellow, who delighted his grandchildren by stamping around his house in Maine, shouting "Fe-Fi-Fo-Fum! I smell the blood of an Englishman!" How long did the ultimatum allow? Frye eagerly inquired. Three days, the President told him. "Until Saturday; why, Judge, I suppose you would like to give them only fifteen minutes." Frye nodded assent to the President's little joke, gratified by war, happy in Republican harmony.

Judge Day's messenger carried the ultimatum to Señor Polo de Bernabé, who had succeeded Dupuy de Lôme, and returned in half an hour with a request for his passports. A cable dispatch conveyed the final terms to Minister Woodford at Madrid; but he had already been notified that diplomatic relations between Spain and the United States were at an end. The receipt of this information at the State Department on April 21 signalized the outbreak of war. The next day the President proclaimed a blockade of the principal ports of Cuba. On April 23, after receiving authorization from Congress, he published a call for 125,000 volunteers.

Late on the Friday that the blockade was proclaimed, the President walked with Secretary Long for an hour through the streets. An unusual circumstance permitted the little outing. Mrs. McKinley was away. She had gone with Pina and Mary Barber to spend the week end in New York. The walk was the longest that McKinley had taken since coming to Washington, and he said to Long that he felt the better for it. He had opened his heart to his friend on the inward struggle through which he had gone. Doubtless the President had also talked of old Mr. Gary's resignation, and the painful interview which lay before him on the morrow, when he must ask John Sherman to follow Gary's example. Judge Day was to be made Secretary of State. He did not want the place, and accepted it only as a wartime duty. As John Hay heard, "the Major had other views." But Sherman's replacement had suddenly become an imperative duty. According to Hay, "the crisis was precipitated by a lapse of memory in a conversation with the Austrian Minister of so serious a nature that the President had to put in Day without an instant's delay . . ." McKinley saw Sherman on Saturday. However gently the President explained, his point was clearly conveyed. Sherman offered his resignation two days later.

As the week drew to a close, the Navy Department was pressing for immediate action in the Philippines. Commodore Dewey had been repeatedly forewarned of the imminence of hostilities; and Washington was in receipt of the welcome news that the cruiser *Baltimore*, transferred to the Asiatic Squadron with a heavy cargo of powder and projectiles, had arrived safely at Hong Kong. Dewey's orders were sanctioned by the President on Sunday, the same day that the British proclamation of neutrality obliged the American warships to prepare to leave Hong Kong.

Since Dewey's orders later became a matter of consuming public interest, it is singular that their authorship and the circumstances of their dispatch were questionable. According to Secretary Long, they were sent before news of the British proclamation was received. He remembered going to the White House on the Sunday forenoon, and sitting beside the President on a sofa, while he read the cable that had been prepared at the Navy Department. "Mr. President, I think this ought to go," Long said. "All right, sign it," McKinley replied. Long kept a vivid memory of the President's thoughtfulness, and the deep responsibility that was written on his face; and of his own sense of the contrast between the lovely spring morning and the grim business in hand. The actual drafting of the cable, Long supposed, was the work of some clerk. He was positive that he had had no hand in it, because it used the word "commenced," whereas Long would have said "begun." He was equally sure that Crowninshield was not the author. Crowninshield, however, did not agree. A little more than three years later, when Long gave his version, the chief of the Bureau of Navigation had a distinct recollection of having written the cable himself, and he embellished his story with a wealth of explicit detail.

Crowninshield, on that Sunday forenoon, was out at the Arlington golf links. While watching a match, he caught sight of the Secretary's carriage, and went to exchange a few words with Long, who was driving out to the country with his daughter to spend the day. Soon after, Crowninshield returned to the Navy Department, and found a dispatch from Dewey, advising that he had been notified to leave Hong Kong. No orders, according to this account, had yet been prepared; and, in the Secretary's absence, Crowninshield hurried to the White House to urge an immediate answer to Dewey. He was shown up to Mrs. McKinley's sitting room in the corridor, where the President was talking with Day, Griggs, and one or two others. After some consultation on Crowninshield's news, the President asked the Attorney General to write a dispatch ordering Dewey to proceed to Manila and attack the Spanish naval forces there. "Captain, you know how to write that better than I do," Griggs said to Crowninshield; "you go and write it. You will find some blanks in the Cabinet Room." Webb Hayes was in the Cabinet Room, and got the blanks and a pencil. Crowninshield's wording was approved, with one alteration, after the President read it aloud to the company. The cable was immediately put into cipher at the Navy Department; but, at the President's request, it was not sent until Long approved it, when he came back from his day in the country.

There was, in any event, no question that on April 24 orders went to Dewey informing him that war had "commenced" and directing him to proceed to the Philippines and "commence" operations, particularly against the Spanish fleet. "You must capture vessels or destroy. Use utmost endeavors," the message ended.

The legal formality of a declaration of war was fulfilled on Monday, April 25. At a special meeting of the Cabinet—the last that John Sherman attended—the President submitted a message to Congress, recommending the declaration and reporting his proclamations of the previous week. His action was approved, and the Cabinet dispersed. Mr. Pruden started for the Capitol. The correspondents seized the releases of the message and departed. In the afternoon, the mansion was again deserted, a quiet backwater of the patriotic tumult of the nation.

The President went to his bedroom to lie down. To relieve the queer loneliness of Mrs. McKinley's absence, he had asked Webb Hayes to sleep in the empty brass twin bed. But McKinley was alone while he undressed. Webb had gone to the state bedchamber to chat with the other house guest, General Hastings. The big empty room was so quiet that the President should have been able to rest, so quiet that he could not. He padded down the hall in his dressing gown, in search of companionship and the sound of human voices. As he stretched out on a sofa near his friends, he told them to keep up their conversation or he might not be able to sleep.

At about four o'clock, the doorkeeper Loeffler appeared with the joint resolution, which Congress had quickly passed. McKinley arose and received the document, asking Webb to request the presence of Attorney General Griggs and to arrange a table. Vice-President Hobart had sent a pen for the signature. Webb fetched a second pen and the left-hand glass inkwell from the desk at the end of the Cabinet table. Griggs came upstairs, and sat down with McKinley to examine the wording of the resolution, which declared that a state of war existed, and had existed since April 21, between the United States and Spain. Everything was in order. The President signed.

The noisy road to war terminated in a bedroom, with the President clad in his dressing gown for the historic occasion. He used Hobart's pen to write "William," and the other for "McKinley" and the date. Webb Hayes got the White House pen and the inkstand as souvenirs.

· 8 ·

MANILA BAY

T HE President's proclamations sounded the trumpets of war. The country blazed with patriotic emotion. Pacifists and doubters were silenced, partisanship and sectional hostility were laid aside. The East matched the ardor of the South and West. Millionaires sold their yachts for naval auxiliaries, and Miss Helen Gould contributed $100,000 to the United States Treasury. The money, man power, and production of the whole nation were at the disposal of Washington. The Republican administration had everything necessary for a mighty prosecution of the war, excepting military preparations.

The Navy was as ready as high morale and last-minute improvisations could make it. Since the sinking of the *Maine*, the service had been geared for action. The Department had received the lion's share—thirty millions —of the appropriation that Congress had made in March, but had encountered many obstacles in spending it. The foreign market for armored ships had proved to be tight. Transformed yachts and revenue cutters and tugs were dubious substitutes for torpedo-boat destroyers and guard boats, and not enough auxiliaries could be procured to run the errands of the squadrons. Only a small quantity of smokeless powder was available; for, though it was an American invention, Congress had not provided facilities for its manufacture. The United States Navy was not a match for a second-class military power, and the Spanish ships were formidable on paper. Since a reliable intelligence system was one of several points at which the Navy Department was deficient, the captains of the ships expected a hard test in this first trial of American armor-clads in a foreign war.

194

The greatest weakness of the Department was the lack of a general staff. The need of co-ordinating the bureaus and the fleet had long been bruited, and progressive officers urged the importance of broad supervision over strategic and technical questions in time of war. Secretary Long, however, had frowned on a "comprehensive change" because of a natural conservatism, strongly tinged with regard for the prerogatives of the civilian Secretary. He had compromised on appointing an advisory group, the Naval War Board. It was at first composed of Assistant Secretary Roosevelt, Captain Crowninshield, and two other officers on shore duty. Soon after hostilities began, all but Crowninshield went on active service. They were replaced by two officers on the retired list, Rear Admiral Montgomery Sicard, recently commanding the North Atlantic Squadron, and Captain Mahan, who returned from Europe to lend his counsel in the emergency. Mahan's doctrines were beginning to attract public attention at home, and Long held him in respect; but he privately doubted that the specialist would be of much practical value. Mahan believed that wartime powers should be vested in a single chief of staff. He had little taste for conference, and none at all for having his opinion overruled. The dictatorial expert proved to be the stormy petrel of the War Board.

The original board had recommended in March that the American attack should be primarily directed on Spain's outlying and inadequately defended colonies. The control of the Atlantic was to be assured by victory in the Caribbean, before striking at the coast of peninsular Spain. The enemy would thus be subjected to the burden of long-distance transportation of reinforcements and supplies, while the plan had the additional advantage of permitting time for the organization of an American expeditionary force. Secretary Long was readily converted to this elementary strategy, and to the principle of concentration which his advisers preached. The initial action of the war was to be a close blockade of Cuba, which was selected as the main theater, with Porto Rico as a secondary and incidental objective. The simultaneous attack on the Spanish squadron in the Philippines was primarily designed to provide the Asiatic Squadron with a base in the Far East, and to avert the danger of a raid on American shipping in the Pacific.

The far more vivid fears of the Atlantic coast threatened the principle of concentration in the Caribbean. In the late winter the detention of the North Atlantic Squadron at Key West was the cause of acute uneasiness. Congress, in the years of peace, had shown only a token interest in coast defense. Four ironclads had been expressly provided for the purpose, and small appropriations had also been made for the fortifications; but the armament on shore was hopelessly outmoded, while the ships were clumsy, slow-moving monitors, entirely unadapted for pursuit. With the approach of war, the fabled speed and power of the Spanish cruisers struck terror to the Eastern seaboard. If Secretary Long had listened to all the frantic appeals from ports and resort towns, the armored strength of the Navy would have been impotently dispersed on guard duty. The compromise on which the Department settled was the creation of the Flying Squadron. Three armor-clads—the battleship *Massachusetts*, the second-class battleship *Texas*, and the cruiser *Brooklyn*—were based at Hampton Roads, subject to emergency orders. The European Squadron was recalled to home waters, and became the nucleus of a patrol force of auxiliaries, which was in operation a few weeks after the war began, under command of Commodore Howell. The alarms of the coast were also allayed by the assignment of several obsolete Civil War monitors to the principal ports, while the War Department mined the harbors, rummaged out old guns, and attempted last-minute improvements in the fortifications.

The division of the fleet was a temporary expedient to which the naval strategists were obliged to submit at the outset. The Flying Squadron was to be eventually united with the two battleships *Iowa* and *Indiana* and the cruiser *New York*, which formed the main strength of the North Atlantic Squadron; and it was the devout hope of the government that the *Oregon*, lost to communication on her voyage around the Horn, might safely return in time to make victory secure. As the nation rushed headlong toward a breach with Spain, the armor-clads were its only tangible military asset. The proof of American supremacy hung, in the anxious days of spring, on the coming naval concentration in the Caribbean.

Since the chief officer of the North Atlantic Squadron would command the united fleet, an unusual importance attached to Rear Admiral Sicard's replacement, when he was retired for ill health in late March. In the opinion of the Navy Department, the most efficient officer in the service was Captain William T. Sampson of the *Iowa*, who had recently presided over the court of inquiry on the *Maine*. He combined the attainments of a proficient scientist and a cool and decisive executive; and, as senior captain of the squadron, in acting command during Sicard's illness, he had won the confidence of officers and men. Though several commodores were eligible for assignment, the prize fell to Captain Sampson.

Secretary Long was gratified to make an appointment based on merit. Unlike Dewey, Sampson also commended himself by his modesty. He had given no intimation of a desire to succeed Sicard; and, as Long pointedly remarked, he had no friends in Congress to speak for him. Sampson, in fact, had few friends at all outside the service. He was an intellectual, without cordiality or even lively responsiveness of manner, and age and frail health had confirmed the austerity of his dedication to duty. In his prime, Sampson had possessed an imposing physical beauty, but at fifty-eight his tall form was beginning to stoop, and his handsome face, withering under its white beard and mustaches, had stiffened into impassivity. Captain French Ensor Chadwick of the flagship *New York* esteemed the new commander as a hero by nature—simple, brave, and selfless. These virtues were not apparent on a casual meeting with Sampson. He gave an impression of detachment and indifference, which was sometimes interpreted as apathy. Captain Mahan rather understated the case when he said that Sampson "lacked the tricks of the popularity hunter."

The command of the Flying Squadron was bestowed on a recently promoted commodore of vastly different characteristics. Winfield Scott Schley was a hearty old sea dog, erect, expansive, and brimming with vitality. Though his family had been settled for generations in Maryland, Schley looked like a romantic German, long-nosed, whimsical, and shrewd, with a curly little imperial and mustache. His thinning hair was foppishly dressed in tendrils over his bald spot, and there was vanity in his twinkling eyes and mobile, self-satisfied mouth. Schley had an aptitude for personal distinction and a talent for publicity. His expedition to the Arctic to rescue the Greely expedition and his firm action in the Valparaiso affair, an attack by a Chilean mob on American seamen, had gained him a national reputation and a host of prominent friends. In the peacetime Navy, Schley was better known to the public than any officer except "Fighting Bob" Evans, the picturesque and badly crippled hero of the Civil War who succeeded Sampson in command of the *Iowa*. Among his fellow officers, however, Schley was not accorded the highest rating for ability and judgment. The Bureau of Navigation fought for his assignment to the Flying Squadron because he was a commodore. Seniority had been disregarded in the case of one of the main Atlantic squadrons; the bureaucrats were insistent that a commodore should get the other; and Secretary Long was persuaded that Schley had the requisite skill and resource.

On April 21, Sampson was promoted acting Rear Admiral, and ordered to carry into effect the proclamation of blockade. This action was to be mainly directed against Havana and three other ports of northwest Cuba. The southern port of Cienfuegos, which had a railway connection with the capital, was also nominally included, for it was intended to station the Flying Squadron there as soon as it could be released from defensive duty in the Atlantic. Sampson was intensely disappointed by his orders. He was keen to reduce Havana by bombardment, but the Navy Department was solidly opposed to risking the armor-clads, and the new Rear Admiral and his captains were forced to resign themselves to the static duty of the blockade.

Schley's command would at first be independent, and his orders omitted to define his future relation to the head of the Atlantic fleet. Secretary Long anticipated a possible awkwardness, and thought that he clarified it by verbally informing Schley that he would be subordinate to Sampson after the squadrons were merged. But Schley was piqued by Sampson's advancement, and on his mind the conversation left no subsequently acknowledged impression.

The naval strategy had originally been founded on a belief that the army would promptly co-operate. Secretary Alger had frequently promised that on ten days' notice he would be ready to put an army of 40,000 in the field. His radiant assurances that everything was "mapped out" had satisfied his colleagues in the Cabinet, the warmakers of Congress, and the representatives of the press. The appropriation of March 8, however, had not produced a conspicuous stir at the War Department. The Army's share had been earmarked entirely for coast defense. The Ordnance and Engineer Corps made a hasty effort to repair the long indifference of Congress, but there had been no other signs of military activity until the middle of April, when the regular Army was mobilized.

The standing Army of the United States was limited by law to 25,000, and exceeded this number, with officers included, by about 3,000 in 1898. It was a highly efficient little army for its designated duties of detached garrison and guard service. It had gained from the sharp fighting of the Indian wars an experience in combat denied the Navy since 1865, and a decade of peace on the plains had not impaired morale or discipline. But, though the regulars were well fitted to fight a foreign war, most of their officers were not equally well qualified for command. The discouraging system of promotion had caused the retirement of many keen and active young men. Those who remained had never seen mobilization or maneuvers on an extensive scale, while the aging senior officers had only dim Civil War memories of the divisions and corps of their youth. On April 15, when orders were issued for the main body of regulars to rendezvous at New Orleans, Tampa, Mobile, and Chickamauga Park, the movement was directed by commanders who were inexpert in transporting and encamping large forces of troops.

By the time-honored tradition of the republic, the regulars were to form the nucleus of the force of citizen soldiers who would spring to arms at their country's call. The reorganization of the Army had been the subject of a hot dispute in Congress for some weeks before the war. The War Department had sponsored a bill increasing the regular Army to 104,000, establishing the three-battalion system of 1,200 men to a regiment, and providing that the units should be skeletonized to permit the temporary incorporation of volunteers. Drastic amendments were forced by the opposition of the National Guard and the historic American dread of a large standing Army. As finally passed, the law was a compromise which granted the three-battalion formation, but enlarged the regular Army to only 61,000 for a period of only two years. Meanwhile, the crisis with Spain had induced Congress to rush through a separate bill authorizing the enlistment of volunteers for a two-year term. The influence of the National Guard lobbies was again apparent in concessions to the state militia outfits. The spotty and ill-defined legislation invited confusion and conflicting interpretation, but its greatest immediate fault was the delay imposed on military organization. The basic Army bill was not enacted until April 26, five days after hostilities began. The War Department, under the most efficient management, could not have emulated the Navy's quasi-readiness for action; and, in the decades since the Civil War, it had developed into a dilatory Circumlocution Office, paralyzed by routine.

Congress was responsible for the condition of the War Department. It had been perpetually scrimped for funds, and restrictive regulations had stifled it with estimates and choked it with vouchers and records. The thirteen staff officers were exclusively preoccupied with the details of their respective bureaus, frequently overlapping, but entirely uncorrelated. Unlike their opposite numbers at the Navy Department, the military bureau chiefs were appointed for life. There was intense competition for these permanent positions, which carried an increase of rank and pay, and a measure of political influence. Political pull usually governed the selections. High-ranking assistants and civilian employees had been allowed to multiply. The War Department in 1897 required a clerical force of 1,366, twice as large as that engaged under Secretary Stanton at the height of the Civil War.

The cumbrous system had fostered an entrenched and timid bureaucracy, estranged from the needs of the active service, and independent of superior military authority. The War Department was not staffed by dunderheads, but by fixtures, immobilized and unenterprising. Even the principal luminaries, the brilliantly able Adjutant General Henry C. Corbin and the distinguished scientist, Surgeon General George M. Sternberg, were resistant to any innovation, and especially hostile to reforms that would tend to diminish their prerogatives and compel their subordination. The threat had never taken a serious form. Intelligent Army officers deplored the lack of a modern staff system, but Congress was apathetic on the question, and indeed averse to centralizing authority in a chief of staff.

Secretary Alger had an easygoing obliquity to red tape and political intrigue, and he was well satisfied to head a Department that ran itself, without much effort on his part. He had promptly disembarrassed himself of administrative details by turning them over to his assistant, George D. Meiklejohn, a Nebraska politician whose appointment had been promoted by Mark Hanna. The bureau chiefs managed the Department, with Meiklejohn's energetic help. Though Alger was in delicate health, informed observers had expected more self-assertion. The aspersions made on his Civil War record had originated at the War Department, and his abdication of authority was interpreted as an evidence of weakness. Alger apparently supposed it good policy to curry favor with the functionaries. He professed a glowing admiration for their work, and was always ready to endorse their methods, rubber-stamp their recommendations, and abet their antagonism to the Major General Commanding the Army.

During the Grant administration, an honorary sinecure had been created for the senior general of the Army of the United States by kicking him upstairs to an imposing office at the War Department. He did not, as his title implied, exercise command, and he had no clearly defined place in the structure of the bureaus; but he was entitled to pass on all Army orders, conjointly with the Secretary, and claimed an independent jurisdiction over the Adjutant General's Office and the Bureau of Inspection. This division of authority had been productive of friction from the first; and, for purposes of discord, no personality could have been better devised than that of the incumbent since 1895, Major General Nelson Appleton Miles. This "brave peacock," as Roosevelt called him, was the product of military success and public prominence in operation on a naturally vain and overbearing nature. As a youthful volunteer in the Civil War, Miles had risen meteorically to the command of an army corps. He had been nicknamed "the Indian fighter" for his prowess on the western plains. At fifty-nine, he was the *beau idéal* of an elderly soldier, with gleaming silver mustaches and a broad chest loaded with medals and citations. The handsome Major General was so much admired that he dreamed of becoming President. A born troublemaker and a tireless promoter of his own interests, he had become intensely exasperated by the frustrations of his position at the War Department; and, as the husband of one of John Sherman's nieces, he was deep in the intrigues of the anti-administration faction.

The reciprocal distrust between General Miles and Secretary Alger was an evidence of percipience on both sides. It was less creditable that, during the war with Spain, each was obsessed by a desire to thwart and discomfit the other. Alger had a streak of petty vindictiveness, but he was too soft to be ruthless. The honors of spite, in the long run, went to Miles.

In concurring with the Navy Department's plan for a joint operation at Havana, Alger had neglected to mention that Miles did not agree. The General was opposed to a land invasion of Cuba during the rainy season, and to sending a small force against entrenched positions at any time. He recommended that the first military objective should be the capture of Porto Rico, and that Havana should be invested in the autumn, after a large expeditionary force had been trained and equipped. Surgeon General Sternberg, a specialist in tropical diseases who had long resided in Cuba, advised that a summer campaign would entail a staggering mortality from yellow fever alone. It was generally taken for granted at the War Department that the invasion would be deferred. There had been no thought of securing transports, or special camp equipment or uniforms for the tropics. The supply services had not even begun to explore these requirements. Nor had they begun to provide for the prospective force of volunteers. Their energies, in the weeks before the war, were directed toward obtaining arms and supplies for the expected additions to the regular establishment. Alger, in promising to put an army of 40,000 in "the field," was double-crossing his friends the bureau chiefs, as well as General Miles.

The first joint conference of the services took place at the White House on April 20. Alger was unusually subdued. His militancy had never burned with a steady flame—"I do remember that you had your war days and your anti-war days," the President later wrote him—and he was handicapped by the presence of General Miles. When the President asked for the War Department's proposals, Alger lamely suggested that it might be a couple of months before the army would be ready to act. Miles, for his part, summarily rejected the idea of an early land attack on Havana.

Secretary Long was startled and indignant. He was not warranted in maintaining that the army should make a weak and hasty invasion in an operational season which was fast drawing to a close; but his disgust was fully justified by the manner and timing of the War Department's refusal. On the day before the blockade was proclaimed, the Navy Department was informed that the burden of the campaign would fall for an indefinite period on the North Atlantic Squadron. Long consoled himself with the reflection that popular demand would force the army to do something. True to his prophecy, the War Department soon came up with a rather footling but concrete little plan for a reconnaissance expedition of 5,000 regulars from Tampa. They were to land briefly on the south coast of Cuba and, if possible, on the northwest as well, for the purpose of forming a junction with the insurgents, and delivering munitions and supplies. The command was assigned to Brigadier General William Rufus Shafter, a fat and gouty veteran of sixty-three.

Shafter looked like a comic cartoon of a sedentary general. His figure convulsed the White House staff when he lumbered in to pay his respects to the President. A cherished memory in the east wing was the sight of the unwieldy soldier in conversation with the little clerk Montgomery, who stood on tiptoe in his built-up shoes, like a terrier sniffing a Newfoundland. Shafter was physically unsuited for reconnaissance in Cuba or any other tropical service, but there was no dark ulterior motive for his selection. He was a gruff, blunt, honest old soldier, devoid of political ambitions, and recommended by both Miles and Corbin as a vigorous and aggressive officer. *The Nation* once remarked that the generals in the war with Spain were largely selected "upon the principle which governs kissing." One reason why Shafter was singled out was that he came from Michigan, and Alger knew and liked him.

The flurry at the War Department was short-lived. Since the Navy was responsible for convoying troops and protecting their landings, the expedition was partly contingent on the possible appearance of Spanish ships in Cuban waters. On April 29, the day that Shafter was given his orders, the squadron of armored cruisers commanded by Admiral Pascual Cervera y Topete sailed from the Cape Verde Islands in a westward direction. On receipt of this formation, the whole project was cautiously postponed.

The first week of war had proved a maddening anti-climax to the impetuous temper of a people eager to prove their military valor after a generation of absorption in commercial pursuits. The trumpet blasts of the President's proclamations died away in inactivity and confusion. Citizens sprang to arms in numbers that far exceeded the call. The conflict with Spain was temporarily overshadowed at the War Department by quarrels with the militia organizations. Ornamental officers insisted on recognition. Their political backers stormed the War Department. Adjutant General Corbin was the most efficient of the bureau chiefs, but he could not work the miracle of quickly raising an army.

The blockade of Cuba was nearly as disappointing as the lag in the muster. Patriotic emotion had been stirred by the news of the departure from Key West of the North Atlantic Squadron, cleared for action and painted "an uncanny lead color," from the mighty *Iowa* to the last slim yacht and tossing little torpedo boat. Every day a flock of press boats hovered around the armor-clads. The censorship at Key West scarcely interfered with the early reports, but there was a dearth of exciting events and colorful personalities. Sampson had a dull press from the first. The correspondents did not warm to this bleak, unsociable sailor. Interest in the "blockading squadron" dwindled, once the ships took up their stations at a prudent distance from Morro Castle and the little palm-fringed forts of the northern coast of Cuba.

Americans, thwarted in their pursuit of glory, fell into the brambles of self-doubt, and gloomily questioned the worth of their modern steel ships. The great boilers and complex machinery seemed precarious substitutes for the motive power of wind and sails. At the first hostile shot, these floating volcanoes might explode and sink to the bottom, like the *Maine*, or they might turn into helpless derelicts, cut off from the colliers and coaling stations that had become the lifeline of the fleet. As fearful speculations multiplied, the Republican press took a firmly admonitory tone, rebuking the agitation for immediate results. There were reminders of the dangerous intricacy of the regulation Krag-Jörgensen rifles, and the necessity for hardening raw recruits for service in a difficult terrain and climate. There were grave warnings of the tropical rains with their fatal train of fevers, above all yellow fever, the terror of the Gulf ports. The country was adjured to place its faith in the valor of the Cuban patriots. With the assistance of the American blockade and American matériel, the insurgents might well win a decisive victory in the summer, and spare the manhood of the United States the necessity of exposure to wounds and sickness.

No argument could have been more grotesquely unsuited to the mood of the American people than the suggestion that they would prefer to sit back and let the Cubans win their battles. They were on fire for news that Sampson had demolished Morro Castle, that an invading host of volunteers had met and conquered the tyrant armies of Spain. But, as April gave place to May, no single citizen soldier had yet been sworn into the federal service. Sampson's fleet lay basking in the southern sun. The Flying Squadron was anchored at Hampton Roads. The national morale sank at the thought of the swift and powerful cruisers of Admiral Cervera, flashing across the Atlantic to lay American ports in ruin.

It was at this moment of abysmal depression that tidings came of a smashing naval victory in the Pacific. Seven thousand miles from the California coast, Commodore Dewey had defeated the Spanish squadron in Manila Bay.

The news from the Philippines had been by no means unheralded. The press had successively announced that the Asiatic Squadron had been forced to leave Hong Kong by the British proclamation of neutrality, that it had sailed from some point on the China coast to attack the Spanish fleet, and that it had been sighted off the Philippines. The public was informed that Commodore Dewey would probably be forced to capture Manila and establish a base there, since the ports of the Far East were closed to his ships and his nearest source of supplies was the coaling station at Pearl Harbor. But the distant operation was not of consuming interest to Americans until they learned that, on May 1, it had culminated in a successful engagement at sea. The extent of Dewey's achievement was not clearly disclosed in the first accounts that reached the United States on Monday, May 2, from Madrid by way of London; but the next day it was certain that the victory, though perhaps costly, had been complete. The humiliation of Spanish sea power justified American brag and banished American doubts, and set the nation reeling with pride and astonishment.

The rejoicing at Washington was subdued by anxiety for the safety of the Asiatic Squadron. Its only modern vessel was the sleek little revenue cutter *McCulloch*, which served as a dispatch boat. The fighting ships were four light "protected" cruisers, one of them an outmoded antique, and three gunboats. The Spanish fleet, though numerically larger, was believed to be inferior; but the Navy Department had had information of mines and high-powered guns at Manila Bay, and the strength of the land defenses was greatly feared. Dewey had advised the Department that he was confident of reducing them. It was not doubted that he had attempted the prohibitively dangerous venture of attacking the enemy squadron under the protection of its shore batteries. The Madrid dispatches had stated that the American ships had sustained severe damage, and had been twice forced to retire; and there was no refuge for repairs nearer than San Francisco.

The desire for a reassuring report could not immediately be satisfied. The United States had no Pacific cable, and received all news from the Far East by way of Europe. The only telegraphic connection between the Philippines and the mainland was at Hong Kong, and on Monday Washington learned that the cable had been cut near Manila. A single message had been sent to the United States before the interruption occurred. It was not addressed to the Navy Department, but to the New York *Herald*, which transmitted to the government its correspondent's report that the Spanish squadron had been completely destroyed and that the American ships were apparently uninjured. The official confirmation, for which the authorities prayed, must await the arrival of the *McCulloch* at Hong Kong.

In two days the speedy revenue cutter could streak across the six hundred miles of the China Sea, and the difference in time favored an early reception of the report. As Wednesday passed in silence, and then Thursday, and then Friday, the suspense of the authorities became increasingly acute, and the country's jubilation was threaded with alarm. Rumors winged from the west coast that the Navy Department had heard from Dewey and was suppressing his report because of the serious losses suffered by his command. Relatives and friends of men attached to the squadron telegraphed anxious inquiries. Secretary Long gave out a statement denying the receipt of the report, and promising that the facts, including all casualties, would be published as soon as they were known. The State Department had unavailingly cabled requests for information to Edwin Wildman, the acting consul general at Hong Kong, and to other American representatives in the Far East. Cots had been moved into both the State and Navy Departments. The cipher experts of the Bureau of Navigation were kept on twenty-four hour watch, and Alvey Adee divided the vigils with the Third Assistant Secretary of State, Thomas Cridler.

At daybreak on Saturday, May 7, six days after the battle, Cridler was aroused from his rest in an anteroom by a message of three words, "Hong Kong McCulloch Wildman." It was the word "McCulloch" that sent Cridler running down the corridor to alert the Bureau of Navigation. In half an hour, members of the government had been called from bed by word that Dewey's report was coming. Officials and correspondents streamed to Seventeenth Street to pack the Navy Department's corridors and reception room to suffocation. John D. Long, waiting at his desk in the sad light of a rainy morning, was handed a sheet of paper by the manager of the Western Union office. The Secretary could not forbear to glance at the four lines of writing, but he might as well have scanned the Rosetta stone. The paper was given to the translators, and Long sent a message to the reception room that, as soon as the dispatch was deciphered, he would announce the contents from the door of his office.

The minutes dragged, though the experts made short work of turning the jargon into groups of figures and then into English words. While Long pretended to busy himself at his desk and fifty agitated correspondents pressed against his closed door, Assistant Secretary Roosevelt appeared in the reception room. He was winding up his affairs at the Department, for he had resigned to become lieutenant-colonel of a volunteer cavalry regiment. As his farewell release to the press, he brought the glad tidings he had just gleaned by leaning over the shoulders of the translators. Roosevelt was too highly elated to entertain thoughts of discretion or the courtesy due to the head of the Department. He repeated Dewey's brief dispatch in detail, naming the Spanish ships that had been destroyed, and announcing the amazing fact that this overwhelmingly successful engagement had not entailed injury to any American vessel or the loss of a single American life.

Secretary Long had meanwhile examined the translation, and telephoned the President. He requested and received authorization to make the dispatch public, after censoring some purely military information. When these preliminaries had been arranged, Long opened his door and stepped into the tumult of the reception room. Apparently unaware that his thunder had been stolen, he smilingly moved to a corner window for light, and read out his amended version in his pleasant, musical voice. The correspondents had already passed out scribbled sheets to their messengers, and bicycles were scorching through the rain to the telegraph offices. Roosevelt's uncensored account appeared alongside the Department's bulletin on the front pages of the newspapers. The press, in any case, had more details of the battle than the government. The New York *World* and the Chicago *Tribune* had received stories from Manila some hours before the first official report reached Washington.

A second report, shortly delivered at the Navy Department, illuminated the scale and import of the achievement. Dewey had seized the naval station at Cavite, across the bay from Manila, and destroyed its fortifications, as well as those at the entrance to the harbor. "I control bay completely," he stated, "and can take city at any time, but I have not sufficient men to hold." Secretary Long, taking his young son with him, went at once to the President to make a formal announcement of the victory. Washington was already in an uproar of delirious celebration. Cheering crowds were massed around the White House, and Long was given an ovation as he entered. A congratulatory cable to Dewey had been substantially composed, and was immediately sent. The President thanked the Commodore and his command in the name of the American people. Dewey was informed that the President had promoted him acting Rear Admiral, and would recommend the thanks of Congress.

The eager throng still waited in the reception room of the Navy Department, but Long did not attempt another personal appearance on his return from the White House. He asked his private secretary to give out Dewey's second dispatch. Official decorum vanished at the tremendous news that Manila lay at the mercy of the American squadron. The dignitaries and correspondents broke into shouts of exultation. Among those who joined lustily in the demonstration were Senator Marcus Alonzo Hanna, the peace-loving ally of the plutocrats, and Senator Benjamin Ryan Tillman, the rabble-rousing Democratic boss of South Carolina. Each to the other, Mark and Pitchfork Ben represented the most dangerous and detestable elements in American political life. In the fraternization of patriotic rejoicing, they entered Senator Hanna's carriage and drove companionably off to the Capitol.

The President's special message on the victory was the occasion for enthusiastic expressions from Congress. Both houses passed the resolution of thanks, and authorized the appointment of another full rear admiral; and voted an appropriation of $10,000 to purchase a handsome sword for Dewey and bronze medals for his officers and men. Yet these honors seemed scarcely commensurate with the emotions of the nation, dizzy and drunk with glory, and prostrate in admiration. It would have been treason to suggest that the Spanish fleet had not been a very powerful force, or question the remarkable immunity of the Asiatic Squadron from damage. Americans vaunted the superior marksmanship of the squadron's gunners and the genius of its commander, and acclaimed Manila Bay as the greatest naval victory in written history. A previously unknown officer had become an object of idolatry to his countrymen. Dewey was revered as the quintessence of "Anglo-Saxon valor"; and his terse report of his achievement crowned his fame with the virtue of modesty—the attribute of the true hero, consecrated to duty, without thought of personal distinction.

There was a kernel of truth in the extravagant estimate of Dewey's skill and courage. His enterprise had been carefully planned and boldly executed; and, though the odds had greatly favored his success, he had risked a heavy penalty in case of failure. But Dewey's modesty existed only in the national mythology. His reticent reports reflected an egoism no less arrogant because it was ingenuous. He desired to operate with a minimum of interference from Washington, and had avoided opening communications at all until he had consolidated his victory and could present the government with a *fait accompli*. He had himself cut the Manila cable. He did not start off the *McCulloch* for Hong Kong until noon of the fourth day after the battle. For the rest of the war, Dewey kept the authorities on a meager ration of information; but he was always accessible to the press. Though he was too correct to speak vaingloriously of his exploits, he was by no means averse to having them chronicled by others. The legend of the simple, selfless hero was the creation of the three newspapermen who accompanied the Asiatic Squadron to Manila Bay.

Dewey had been especially gratified by the presence of Joseph L. Stickney of *The New York Herald*, a staff correspondent and a former naval officer. During the battle, Dewey had pressed Stickney into service as his volunteer aide on the flagship *Olympia*, and one of the Commodore's first dispatches was a cable congratulating the *Herald* on its foresight in assigning a correspondent to the squadron. The other two members of the press had been available by accident. Edward W. Harden, representing the New York *World* and the Chicago *Tribune*, was a brother-in-law of Frank Vanderlip, the Assistant Secretary of the Treasury. He had gone on a cruise to the Far East on the revenue cutter *McCulloch*, taking along John McCutcheon, the cartoonist of the Chicago *Record*. When their vessel was attached to the Asiatic Squadron, the tourists became war correspondents. On the return to Hong Kong, after the battle, Harden scored a beat by winning the rickshaw race to the cable office, but Stickney's story created the greatest sensation because it came straight from the bridge of the *Olympia*. In this firsthand report of Dewey's self-possession in the face of danger, Stickney recorded for immortality the calm order, given as the flagship moved on the roaring guns of the Spanish fleet and land batteries, "You may fire when ready, Gridley." Harden and McCutcheon, with less opportunity for observation, were imbued with an equal admiration for Dewey's heroic nonchalance. A subject of consuming public interest in all three stories was the temporary midmorning retirement of the squadron, which had given rise to anxious forebodings at home. The war correspondents lightly explained this order as a stop for breakfast. The idea of interrupting a battle at mealtime occasioned some ridicule from frivolous people, but it bespoke a godlike composure and sense of order that contributed to the Dewey legend.

Correspondents were soon sailing in droves for Manila Bay. Dapper and chatty, Admiral Dewey held court in his gleaming whites on the deck of the *Olympia*, and captivated all comers by his fortitude, as he stroked the snowy cascades of his mustache, fingered his lucky rabbit's foot, or caressed his Chinese chow dog. The press sedulously garnished the distant altar. In a harbor half the world away, Dewey remained the focus of popular adoration. His fame was celebrated in hundreds of songs and rhymes. His portrait sternly gazed from badges, banners, lithographs, and transparencies, repeating the national colors in red face, white mustache, blue eyes and uniform. The American scene was bathed in "Dewey blue," which covered the entire azure range, but was "true blue" always. Hundreds of babies were named for Dewey, and so were yachts and race horses, dogs, cats, streets, hotels, recipes, milk shakes, phosphates, cocktails, and cigars. Dewey's likeness adorned paperweights, pitchers, cups, plates, butter dishes, shaving mugs, teething rings, and rattles. Girls wore the stylish Dewey shirtwaist and the jaunty Dewey sailor hat, transfixed by Dewey hatpins, while their escorts sported Dewey neckties, scarfpins, cuff buttons, and watch charms with the Dewey rabbit's foot. A new

brand of gum was called "Dewey chewies." A pharmaceutical firm advertised a laxative with Dewey's picture and the slogan "the 'Salt' of Salts."

The cult of hero worship raged for eighteen months, surviving by some
few weeks the Admiral's return to his native soil. It was a phenomenon of
popular hysteria, profitably exploited by newspapers and manufacturers;
but it was not lacking in profound significance. The Dewey craze was the
effervescence of the ferment that the victory of Manila Bay had worked in
the minds of the American people.

The victory, from the very outset, had carried a far more spacious con-
notation than the annihilation of the Spanish squadron. Americans had
at once assumed that Dewey had "taken" the Philippines. Before news
came that his squadron controlled so much as Manila Bay, the press had
begun to discuss American responsibility for civil order in the rebellious
islands, and weigh the pros and cons of their eventual sale to Germany
or Japan. The planting of the Stars and Stripes at Cavite only confirmed
the confident belief that, by right of conquest, the United States had
acquired possession of the Philippines for the duration of the war, and
was entitled to determine their disposition afterward.

In his message on the victory, the President declared that "the great
heart of our Nation throbs, not with boasting or with greed of conquest,
but with deep gratitude." As an admonition, the statement was well
advised. As a report, it was inaccurate. The national heart was throbbing
with a conviction of American invincibility. It was bursting with the
satisfaction of having remembered the *Maine*, and leaping with the excitement of having astounded the world. All over the country, people were
talking expansion. Republican newspapers vaunted the advent of the
United States as a Pacific power. Business awoke to the advantages of a
foothold in the Far East. Churches of every denomination hailed new
fields for missionary endeavor. For the first time in the history of the
republic, there was a spontaneous popular enthusiasm for colonial dependencies.

The immediate effect was a wild acceleration of the tempo of the war
with Spain. Some people were under the impression that it was already
over, and had to be reminded that, by express declaration of Congress,
its object was the liberation of Cuba, toward which no significant step
had yet been taken. Ten days after hostilities began, a reverse might have
steeled Americans to endurance. Spectacular triumph induced a frenzied
demand to mop up the Spanish forces in Cuba and the Philippines, and
end the war at once. A delaying policy was never contemplated by the
President and his advisers. The first news from the Philippines had over-

turned all previous conceptions of the scale and timing of the army's participation. At a joint conference of the services on May 2, the decision was made to fight a land war in both hemispheres during the summer.

The little Asiatic Squadron, however sweeping its success, would be exposed to the hazards of renewed attack as long as it remained in Manila Bay. The ignominious alternative of recalling it to the Pacific coast was far from the thoughts of the Washington authorities. It was taken for granted that Dewey would hold his position and must be reinforced by troops, as well as ships. At the conference of May 2, about 5,000 troops were judged sufficient for the task, but the size of the force was soon considerably increased at the instigation of Major General Wesley Merritt, who was selected to lead the expedition.

General Merritt, commanding the Department of the East, was nearing the age of retirement, but his decisive character strongly recommended him for a remote and difficult assignment. The American troops were to sail for a *terra incognita*. The War Department was ignorant of the topography of the Philippines, and had only scanty and dated information of the numbers and distribution of the Spanish forces there. Merritt could not even learn whether he would be able to procure horses in the islands, or whether it would be possible for him to make use of field artillery. The political situation was nearly as obscure as the military. The latest native revolt had theoretically been settled in December, when the insurrectionist leaders had accepted exile in return for a large sum of money and promises of administrative reform; but letters from Consul General O. F. Williams, who had made a brief stay at Manila, testified to continued violent unrest in and around the capital.

The President was impressed by General Merritt, and encouraged a confidential expression of his opinions. Merritt privately submitted an urgent request for more than 14,000 troops, including 6,000 regulars. He was hoping for a vastly more important operation than the relief of the Asiatic Squadron—the territorial conquest of the entire Philippine archipelago. The President, however, was noncommittal about the intentions of the government. Merritt was still on tenterhooks when, on May 15, a cable was received from Dewey, who had been pressed to state the number of troops he wanted. Regarding the reduction of Manila as substantially accomplished by his victory and blockade, Dewey stated that 5,000 soldiers would be needed to "retain possession." He incidentally mentioned the assistance of Filipino rebels, who were "hemming in" Manila, and also spoke of a Spanish army of 10,000. This last information gave pause to General Miles. He voluntarily tripled Dewey's figure, recommending a force of more than 15,000. Since few regulars were left in the West, this force was to be preponderantly made up of western volunteers.

Miles, for once, was innocent of making trouble—he knew nothing of Merritt's communications to the President—but his advice nearly blew up the Philippine program. Merritt curtly rejected the recommendations, and hinted that he might resign his command. Like a victim of persecution, he gabbled his indignation to the newspaper reporters, criticizing the unreadiness of the volunteers and insisting that regulars must be withdrawn from Florida for his expedition. He was hastily summoned to Washington. A few more regulars were scraped up for him, and he was given a reputedly crack regiment of eastern militia, the Tenth Pennsylvania. Abashed by the commotion he had created, Merritt denied the reports of his insubordinate utterances, and cast no more aspersions on the volunteers. The assignment of a number of additional western recruits presently increased the Philippine force to 20,000.

Merritt's outburst did not prejudice his standing with the President. On his farewell visit to Washington, their intercourse was not only confidential, but candid. Before he left for San Francisco on May 22, Merritt saw the paper of instructions that McKinley had prepared for the army that was to effect the conquest and occupation of the Philippines.

The stated purpose of the expedition was to complete the reduction of Spanish power in the Philippines, but the paper was mainly concerned with the question of giving order and security to the islands during their possession by the United States. The administration of a conquered territory that would not become part of the Union was unprecedented in American history. In formulating his opinions, the President had the benefit of advice from John Bassett Moore, the new First Assistant Secretary of State. The appointment of this bearded, thickset young professor—a Democrat and a former official of the State Department—had been stipulated by Judge Day as a condition of his own wartime acceptance of the portfolio of State. Moore, on leave from the chair of international law at Columbia University, was regarded as the foremost American authority in his field.

While military rule in the Philippines was to be absolute, it was to bear on the native inhabitants with as little severity as possible, and detailed regulations were laid down for their protection in their personal and property rights. The commander of the expedition was enjoined, immediately on his arrival, to publish a proclamation declaring the political obligations assumed by the United States, and disowning the intention to make war upon the people, or upon any party or faction. The President was averse to an alliance with any insurgent element in the Spanish colonies; and the involvement would be doubly disadvantageous in the Philippines, where American military authority was to be supreme and undivided.

The principles set forth in the official paper were supplemented by private instructions from the President. Merritt's task was all that he had desired. He was entrusted with the greatest administrative responsibilities that had ever fallen to an American soldier. As military governor of the archipelago, he would probably have to smooth out some complications with the natives. Dewey, in his random way, spoke of their co-operation with the United States. The exiled Tagalog chieftain, Aguinaldo, had been brought out from Hong Kong on an American warship. He was organizing his forces at the American base at Cavite, and Dewey expected that he might render valuable assistance. The Navy Department emphatically reminded Dewey about avoiding an alliance with any native faction, but the authorities were not altogether easy. Merritt, who knew the President's mind, was granted large discretionary powers in dealing with the political situation in the Philippines.

The protected cruiser *Charleston*, sent to reinforce the Asiatic Squadron, was ordered to capture Guam, in the Spanish group of the Ladrones (sometimes called the Marianas). Guam was a stopping place in the ocean lanes that led from Honolulu to Manila. Hawaii was not yet a United States possession, but the President was determined that Congress should make it so, before adjournment. The patriotic climate of wartime was favorable to his purpose. Moreover, the State Department had been informed by Ambassador Hay that it was advisable to conclude annexation before peace was made, lest Germany "seek to complicate the question" with Samoa or the Philippines.

In March, the Senate annexationists had changed their strategy, abandoning the hopeless attempt to obtain ratification of the treaty in favor of direct legislation, which would require a simple majority of both houses; but the subject had not been vigorously pressed until the victory of Manila Bay dressed the Pacific acquisition in the garb of a war measure. By this time, the War Revenue Bill was before the Senate. In deference to the emergency taxes, the initiative was transferred to the lower chamber, where an appropriate resolution was introduced on May 4. The House had a large majority for annexation, with the few Republican dissidents more than balanced by expansionists of the opposition. Speaker Reed was the stubborn obstacle to consideration. He did not give in until early June. He was not in the chair when the vote was taken after a short debate. It was suspected that his slight illness was diplomatic, but his conduct did not warrant that description. A message that he would have voted nay, had he been present, was read to the House at his request by the Speaker pro tem, Congressman John Dalzell of Pennsylvania. The announcement was not only superfluous—it was, since the Speaker did not vote, absurd. Reed's rigid party discipline had changed to sullen mutiny, and the opinion was freely voiced in the House that he was animated by a desire to antagonize the President. His biographer has attempted to supply him with a moral motive by alluding to the powerful interests that wanted a guarantee that Hawaiian sugar would remain duty-free; but the sugar magnates were divided on the question, with the American Refining Company brazenly lobbying to prevent annexation. There was no moral issue. There was a wave of national ambition against which Reed dashed himself, while the President rode the crest.

Although McKinley had repeatedly recommended annexation, his determination to push it through the current session of Congress was not apparent until the bill reached the Senate. The long delay in the House had emboldened the opposition to hope that a vote might be postponed by the bell of adjournment. The minority was supported by some influential Republican conservatives who, since Manila Bay, had grown increasingly wary of Hawaii as a straw that signaled the gusts of an imperial trend. McKinley, with an unusual candor, exerted himself to persuade them. He talked "frankly and freely" to his callers, and showed "no hesitation" in expressing his concern for prompt action. There were holes in the argument of military necessity, for the friendly Republic of Hawaii was already offering every facility to American warships. The argument of Japanese aggression no longer had the impact of a looming emergency, but McKinley used it effectively. His greatest achievement was to convince Lodge's conservative colleague, old Senator Hoar. Though Hoar remained averse to American expansion overseas, he delivered an eloquent speech on behalf of acquiring Hawaii. In July, an obstinate filibuster collapsed. The hot and weary minority subsided in dread that the President might call an extra session or even, as Lodge believed was his intention if action failed, proclaim the annexation of Hawaii as a war measure. The Senate cordially embraced the resolution, and the flag of the United States was soon hoisted at Honolulu, as well as Cavite.

"We need Hawaii just as much and a good deal more than we did California," McKinley had said to Cortelyou. "It is manifest destiny." There was a chime of power in the old resounding phrase. Senator Lodge was jubilant over the changes wrought by "the irresistible pressure of events." His sharp little eyes had seen that the President's imagination was touched. Before Lodge left for his summer holiday at Nahant, he heard

McKinley speak of Hawaiian annexation as a step in a policy.

McKinley had shrewdly appraised the political portents, but he was not consciously infected by the "greed of conquest" he had reproved. He was averse to acquiring extensive territory remote from the traditional sphere of American influence. When he formulated his first draft of the peace terms, he intended that the Philippines should be left under Spanish dominion, with the exception of Manila. A single port did not seem an excessive exaction for the conquest of an archipelago; but, outside the Cavite naval station, territorial conquest existed only in the paper of instructions for General Merritt. Green western recruits had straggled into the federal camps at San Francisco, to overwhelm a handful of regular staff officers with the responsibility of providing them with subsistence and equipment for a month-long voyage and a campaign of indefinite duration in a tropical wilderness. Means of transporting a sizable body of troops were lacking. The War Department had no ships, and was not empowered to impress them; and the Pacific owners balked at accepting the government's charter terms in a season profitable for cruises. Only by dint of great exertions was the first detachment of 2,500 embarked on May 25. General Merritt, postponing his dreams of military governorship, did not leave San Francisco until the end of June.

For three months after the battle of Manila Bay, the government was forced to rely on the discretion of the uncommunicative little Admiral at the end of a severed cable ten thousand miles from Washington.

Military operations in the Caribbean also failed to keep pace with the projected terms of peace. Plans for showing military gains in Cuba and Porto Rico, which had been impetuously laid on the first news from Manila, soon became enmeshed in a complex of frustrations.

Cuba, in the accelerated program, had been tenaciously given priority by the naval strategists. At the joint conference of May 2, their view had prevailed. It was decided to enlarge Shafter's command at Tampa, and order it to seize and fortify the little port of Mariel as a base for the army of invasion. Co-operation with the Cuban insurgents did not figure in this project. Liaisons, established with their leaders, had made it certain that their military strength had been as grossly exaggerated as their faith in the disinterested motives of the United States. Unable to defeat the Spaniards by themselves, the revolutionaries wanted only munitions, food, blockade, and moral support from their powerful neighbor. In spite of the professions of the Teller Amendment, the patriot generalissimo, Máximo Gómez, was suspiciously opposed to the landing of American soldiers on Cuban soil. The alternative to a wasted summer in the main theater of the war was an expedition strong enough for independent action.

The Navy Department, however, was bent on more than a base. "On to Havana!" was the war cry of Congress and the press. In their zeal for the reduction of the Cuban capital, the naval bureaucrats forgot their recent concern with the westward movement of Cervera's squadron. Admiral Sampson was about to sail with his strongest armor-clads in search of the Spanish ships; but, though the Havana blockade would be weakened and a decisive battle might be imminent at sea, Secretary Long was eager to furnish convoys for an expedition of volunteers, as well as the advance of regulars. He was convinced that an invasion of 50,000 would at once bring about the fall of Havana, and the rest of Cuba with it. Highly indignant at hearing that there would be a delay of two weeks before a large force could move, Long sent a letter to Alger, urging him to take active steps and stressing the readiness of the Navy to bear its part.

Long was expecting miracles of the War Department. It was utterly impossible that a large volunteer expedition could be outfitted overnight. It was absurd to expect that adequate transportation could be provided, since the Navy had pre-empted all the best available vessels on the Atlantic seaboard. But the fundamental objection to the sudden change of plan was the fact that the volunteer army was not yet in existence. In the first week of May, the muster-in of the state militia regiments had barely begun, and their organization in federal encampments had not even reached the planning stage. Long, for some unexplained reason, was blind to this obvious deterrent; and so, more strangely still, was the President.

McKinley's attitude toward the grand attack on Havana is puzzling in the extreme. He was loath to send American soldiers to Cuba in the rainy season, and greatly desired a summer campaign in Porto Rico, where the climate was healthful. Porto Rico flickered on and off in the discussions of early May, but the President acquiesced in its postponement. Under the spell of Manila Bay, he seems to have been as confident as the Navy Department that Spanish resistance in Cuba would break like a rotten twig at the touch of American aggression. McKinley was also conscious of the political disadvantages of opposing an assault on Havana, and wary of involving himself in another contest with the jingoes of Congress. It still remains incomprehensible that he shared Long's belief that the volunteer army could be created merely by goading Alger to produce it. When Alger went to the White House to complain that Long was meddling in military affairs, he was coldly received. McKinley unburdened himself to Charles Dawes, immediately after the interview. "Am afraid Alger is endangering his position in the Cabinet by his actions and unwise talk," Dawes wrote in his diary. "He maintains that his prerogatives are being encroached upon. Fortunately for our cause at war, he tells the truth."

The next day, May 6, Long took the extreme measure of presenting his letter to Alger at the Cabinet meeting. Very naturally, as Long thought, Alger took some offense, and intimated that the War Department would take care of itself without any interference from the Navy. Nevertheless, Long's tactics produced the intended effect. The military bureaus were aroused by directions to secure more transports and expedite shipments of quartermaster's and subsistence supplies to Tampa. Two days after the Cabinet meeting, General Miles received orders placing him in command of an army of 70,000, and instructing him to proceed to reduce Havana.

Alger appeared to be giving a normal reaction to stimulus. He was actually performing an elaborate shadow dance. He could not, and knew that he could not produce an army of volunteers. The admission could not be dodged much longer, but he sought to put off the inevitable day of reckoning. Physically, Alger was flagging under the strain. Cortelyou noticed the next week that he had difficulty in keeping up, that he seemed tired out and unequal to the task; and perhaps exorbitant pressure had brought on a temporary mental collapse. Alger may have vaguely hoped to saddle General Miles with the blame for the unreadiness of the army. In fact, he precipitated the exposure he sought to avoid.

Miles was astounded and incensed by his orders. He was unalterably opposed to an immediate invasion of Cuba, and he was apparently the only official, except the Secretary of War himself, who fully understood the phantom character of the proposed expedition. He hurried on May 8 to the White House, righteously convinced that it was his duty to acquaint the President with the facts. One insuperable objection to his orders, Miles told McKinley, was the shortage of ammunition. Aside from the supply earmarked for the Philippines and a small amount reserved for home defense, there was not enough ammunition in the country, and not enough could be manufactured in eight weeks' time for an army of 70,000 to fight one battle.

The President's interview with Miles resulted in the suspension of the orders for the grand attack on Havana. It did not forestall the fulfillment of the tremendous efforts which the supply services had made to meet the emergency. Modern guns and specialized equipment, as well as ammunition, were lacking, and even uniforms could not be immediately provided. But huge consignments of quartermaster's stores converged on Tampa, and enormous quantities of food, including sufficient bacon for ninety days' rations for 70,000 men. There were no government depots to receive them, and nearly a thousand loaded cars presently jammed the railroad sidings from Tampa to Columbia, South Carolina.

The War Department was doomed to egregious blunders, and its short-comings were magnified by the speed-up of the military program; but neither defective organization nor unexpected requirements could account for the failure to prepare for the volunteers in the home camps. Many weeks before the war, their call had been anticipated in drafting the Army Organization Bill. It had been obvious that, like the new regiments of regulars, they would need munitions and equipment and clothing that could not be quickly manufactured. The arrangements had not been inefficiently handled—they had been entirely omitted. The dither in the press about the intricate Krag-Jörgensen rifles had been lost energy. The only arms available for the citizen soldiers were old-fashioned Springfields with black powder. The Quartermaster's Department, the great supply bureau of the Army, had awaited hostilities with warehouses empty of nearly everything but blankets, and "a pretty good stock of mess pans" left over from the Civil War.

The statements of Quartermaster General Ludington reveal the vague insouciance with which Alger had brushed off the growing uneasiness of the bureau chiefs. In talking with Alger, Ludington had repeatedly tried to find out the numbers of militiamen for which he should make arrangements. Alger at one time said about 30,000; later, about 80,000. Ludington's first official information of the government's intentions was the publication of the President's call for 125,000 volunteers. There had been no response to his timid suggestions that "possibly I ought to be doing something," and Ludington had not taken it on himself to do anything at all.

Alger's mental processes were an enigma to his contemporaries. It is hard to find a clue to the bright paralysis of will with which he had drifted into war. He eventually excused himself by casting the blame on the President. In 1901, Alger published the statement that, in allocating the emergency appropriation, McKinley had restricted the War Department's expenditures to coastal fortifications, and prohibited all other military preparations because of a meticulous construction of the term "national defense." But this unsupported explanation is utterly inconsistent with McKinley's latitude in the case of naval preparations. The evidence points rather to slackness in Executive direction, and ignorance of Alger's omissions. After the talk with Miles, the President gave the War Department his close and constant supervision. A better solution would have been to ask for Alger's resignation, but McKinley was unwilling to hurt a man so enthusiastic, so ardent in his patriotism, and, as he then believed, so loyal to himself.

For the rest of May, Alger was chiefly occupied in detaining General Miles, who was magnetically attracted to Shafter's enlarged command of 12,000 regulars at Tampa. The appearance of Admiral Cervera's squadron had caused an indefinite postponement, on the Navy's responsibility, of the Mariel operation, and also the capture of Porto Rico, which had briefly come to the fore with Admiral Sampson's approach to the island.

The enigma of Cervera's whereabouts was solved at midnight of May 12. While Sampson was seeking the Spanish cruisers at Porto Rico, they had arrived off Martinique. The news, thirty-six hours late when it reached Washington, caught the Navy badly off balance. The Flying Squadron was hastily sent from Hampton Roads to Key West, and Sampson was ordered to return with utmost dispatch. The authorities awaited the concentration of the squadrons in helpless anxiety. On May 14 it was known that Cervera had touched at Curaçao, near Venezuela. Since Sampson's movement to Porto Rico had been given wide publicity, Cuba was the overwhelmingly probable destination of the Spanish ships, and it was presumed that their next objective would be Cienfuegos, the only southern port that had a rail connection with Havana, and a port at which an adequate blockade had not yet been established. For six days, Cervera was free to enter and leave the harbor—to slip up the Yucatan Channel and penetrate the feeble array of ships that Sampson had left at Havana. Fears for the safety of the naval base at Key West were not relieved until the arrival of the Flying Squadron on May 18. But the greatest apprehension was that the enemy might elude an eventual encounter with the American armor-clads. The failure to engage or blockade the Spanish ships might indefinitely postpone the invasion of Cuba, and prolong the war in a wearisome and costly stalemate.

The Navy Department prepared to meet the emergency. In the spacious naval library on Seventeenth Street, the War Board sat until late at night, correlating messages, marking charts, and evolving strategy. The cable had given the naval expert the advantage with which the telegraph had long endowed the military commander. This was the first war in which it was possible for government to direct operations at sea. (There seemed no end, in the expanding horizons of that day, to the marvels of electricity. A young Italian named Marconi was making experiments with electromagnetic waves, and believed that they might prove practical for long-distance communication.) Americans, thrilled by the excitement of scientific progress, were proud of their new use of the cable, but still refused to place their faith in government experts. Sicard, Crowninshield, and Mahan were credited with dictatorial powers and condemned for bungling interference with the ships, and it was moodily prophesied that the triumvirate would be no match for the wily sea fox, Cervera.

Public prejudice was not altogether misguided. As an English naval commentator remarked, the telegraph was an enemy, as well as a friend. The control of Washington was bound to result in contradictory orders, misunderstandings, and delays, and its inherent defects were aggravated by the impossibility of getting accurate and timely reports. Lacking enough fast vessels to use as scouts, the Navy Department was usually obliged to depend on the advices of the American consuls in the neutral islands of the West Indies. The warships were kept dangling near the cable offices to await information that was sometimes misleading and nearly always out of date. The shortage of dispatch boats was an additional cause of inconvenience. The Associated Press carried many of Sampson's communications to and from shore. Otherwise, he was forced to batter his little torpedo boats on these unsuitable errands.

In its exposure of the naval movements, the effect of the cable was appalling. Vast sums were being expended by the great dailies and syndicates on covering the war. The hovering dispatch boats, a nuisance to the commanders by day and a worry by night, ran to shore with many imprudent disclosures. A few representatives of the American press were as keen as enemy agents in reporting the location of American ships. A strict promise of secrecy, exacted from the correspondents who accompanied Sampson to Porto Rico, had been broken by only one of them; but one was enough to verify the rumors of the squadron's whereabouts to the country and to Cervera at Martinique. The government hastily concluded an agreement with the six cable companies that had lines entering the United States. An embargo was placed on the delivery of messages detrimental to the national security, and all private cipher and code dispatches were barred. Other leakages were also stopped up. Both the War and Navy Departments posted orders forbidding their employees to hold conversation with the reporters who haunted the Seventeenth Street building. Military censorship was presently established at Tampa. In the last two weeks of May, a certain mystery shrouded what the press called the maritime chessboard in the West Indies.

The country, suspicious of official secrecy, hated the censorship. The lack of information increased a nervous sense that the war was not going well. The appearance of Cervera's cruisers in West Indian waters had coincided with the publication of the first American casualties. A torpedo boat on the Cuban blockade had been damaged by gunfire from shore;

and Sampson, before withdrawing from Porto Rico, had made an ineffectual attack on the San Juan fortifications. The American people had not bargained for a long war, and showed no sign of possessing the steady fortitude to support even slight reverses. As the squadrons converged on Key West, the government faced a heavy penalty if the Navy failed to capture or destroy the ships of Spain.

Sampson's voyage to Porto Rico had been retarded by the clumsy battleship *Indiana* and the crippled monitors of his squadron. The Navy Department had decided to reinforce the mobile Flying Squadron, and speed it to Cienfuegos. The belief that Cervera would visit that port had been confirmed by a report that he was carrying munitions for the defense of Havana. The government's strongest hopes rested on the chance that he might still be there, but the anxiety for Havana was so acute that Schley was ordered to move there temporarily, on his arrival at Key West on May 18. This necessity was obviated by the return of the North Atlantic Squadron. With his ships trailing behind him, Sampson had sped ahead on the fast cruiser *New York*, and reached Key West a few hours later than Schley.

The preceding day, a torpedo boat had met the *New York* with Washington dispatches advising Sampson of the plans for Cienfuegos, and giving him the option of commanding the operation. Sampson had been eager to return to San Juan and justify his impulsive bombardment by taking the city. Cervera's movement across the Atlantic had set the final stamp of failure on his futile and overpublicized expedition. After this smarting disappointment, the pursuit of the Spanish ships must have seemed a tempting opportunity, but, in a generous and seemingly propitiatory desire to let Schley have his chance, Sampson resolved to add his own best ship, the *Iowa*, to the Flying Squadron, and himself resume the static duty of the Havana blockade. On the arrival of the *New York*, Schley at once came on board and was informed of these decisions in a private consultation in the Admiral's cabin. This was the first meeting between the two officers since Sampson had been promoted.

It is beyond the bounds of credulity that Schley was in ignorance of his position in the united fleet. There is only Long's word for the definite verbal arrangement, and Long's memory was sometimes at fault; but, on reporting to Commodore George C. Remey, the commandant at Key West, Schley must have seen the Navy Department's dispatches, which established Sampson's supreme command. The omission of formal orders gave Schley an excuse for misunderstanding. Sampson, in their interview, had apparently sensed misconception and constraint. Long soon telegraphed Schley instructions that his command was subordinate in the Caribbean, and twice sent messages reassuring Sampson that the matter was being clarified. Whatever was guessed of Schley's attitude, it was not for a moment suspected that he would permit arrogance and pique to interfere with the performance of his duty. It came as a scandalizing shock to Sampson and the Navy Department that Schley took no initiative in finding the enemy, but wasted more than a week in vacillating and dilatory movements.

On the day that Schley sailed, May 19, the Navy Department was perplexed by information that Cervera was at Santiago, the isolated capital of the easternmost province of Cuba, where the insurgents were in force. The report, though nearly incredible, was too reliable to be disregarded, but this was not explained in forwarding it to Sampson. Under the impression that Washington was agitated by a rumor, he at first instructed Schley to send a ship to Santiago to investigate, adhering meanwhile to the adopted plan. Sampson's misapprehension was soon corrected by the Army Signal Corps at Key West. On May 23, Schley received directions to blockade Santiago with all dispatch, if he were satisfied that the enemy was not at Cienfuegos. Schley replied that he was not satisfied, and would remain where he was. He had made no effort to discover whether the Spanish ships were in port, but his negligence was soon repaired by Commander Bowman McCalla of the protected cruiser *New Orleans*. Definitely informed that Cervera's squadron was not there, Schley began to move at a snail's pace to the east. He telegraphed Washington that, while he would go to Santiago, he would not be able to blockade because of a shortage of coal and the impossibility of loading his ships from colliers in the heavy sea. Two days later, on nearing Santiago, he reversed his course, and headed back for Key West.

On the night of May 26, while the Flying Squadron was drifting aimlessly in the Caribbean, the receipt of Schley's first dispatches produced consternation in Washington. Cervera's presence at Santiago had been confirmed beyond all question. In the belief that Schley had been blockading the harbor for two days, it had been decided to send a military expedition to aid the fleet, and Sampson had been ordered to accompany it in command of a strong convoy. To the overwhelming relief of the authorities, Captain Charles E. Clark had brought the *Oregon* into Jupiter Inlet, Florida. The safe arrival of the battleship, after her perilous voyage of more than two months, contributed to an elated sense that the naval problems of the war were ended. The need of large armies for Porto Rico and Cuba, as well as for the Philippines, appeared so pressing that the President had published a call for 75,000 additional volunteers.

Schley's negative response to Sampson's orders was the first intimation that the government's program might be wrecked by Cervera's escape. Scouts and dispatch boats hunted the wandering squadron with messages that this was a crucial time, that the Navy Department relied on Schley. He was implored to surmount the coaling difficulty. He was urged to report, and peremptorily ordered to blockade. On May 28, the Department received a dispatch which Long described as "one of the most infelicitous in history." Schley stated that it was impossible for him to remain off Santiago. He was forced to return to Key West for coal, and expressed formal regrets that the Navy Department's orders could not be obeyed.

It was the darkest day of the war, Long wrote, both for the President and himself. The Navy Department held a long telegraphic conversation with Sampson, who had hastened to Key West, determined to go at once to Santiago. Late the next afternoon he was given permission to proceed. Ordering the *Oregon* to accompany the *New York*, Sampson left to assume command of the fleet. A more encouraging message had meanwhile come from Schley. A few hours after sending his infelicitous dispatch, he had experienced a sudden change of heart. His coaling troubles ceased to be insurmountable. The Flying Squadron turned again for Santiago, and established a blockade, and Schley was rewarded beyond his deserts by the discovery that he had acted in time. Cervera had been ten days in port. He had not realized the open road to escape. Two Spanish cruisers and two torpedo boats were lying in plain view near the entrance of the long land-locked harbor.

In relief at deliverance from shameful failure, Washington shirked a court-martial. There was obvious reluctance to displace a prominent and popular naval officer in the midst of war. Long vaguely left it to Sampson to ascertain the facts. The result, during the many weeks that the squadrons were merged at Santiago, was unresolved strain and hostility between the two commanders. Sampson, treating Schley with icy courtesy, did not take it upon himself to inquire into the mysterious coal shortages. He believed that Schley had not told the truth, and despised him for incompetence and misconduct. The Commodore never acknowledged Sampson's authority to the officers of his command or his cronies among the correspondents. On the flagship *Brooklyn* the impression continued to prevail that Schley was in independent command, and Sampson was regarded nearly as an interloper in the direction of the Flying Squadron.

Schley's delinquency remained for some time the best-kept secret of the war. The Associated Press correspondent assigned to his squadron was the Commodore's sycophantic admirer, and Americans delighted in stories of Schley's energy in scouring the Caribbean, and the clever maneuvers by which he had trapped the ships of Spain and bottled them up in Santiago harbor.

The "bottle" of Santiago had an extremely narrow neck. The channel was mined and flanked by fortified heights, and Sampson fully concurred with the Navy Department that the risks of forcing an entrance were prohibitive. The purpose of the Army expedition, as the Navy saw it, was to capture the fortifications at the mouth of the harbor, so that small vessels could go in to remove the mines and clear the way for the armor-clads. While waiting for the troops, Sampson established a strict blockade, disposing the squadrons in a semicircle, alerted day and night. Repeated bombardments of the land batteries made the gunners expert, and taught them discipline under fire. Battle orders were issued to the captains to ensure instant action, should the enemy attempt to escape; but, for a time, Sampson believed that he had obstructed Cervera's exit. On arrival, he had carried out a plan for sinking the collier *Merrimac* in the narrowest part of the channel, an operation designed and executed by Richmond Pearson Hobson, an ardent young lieutenant of the Naval Construction Corps. With seven men, Hobson took the doomed collier into the channel before dawn on June 3; and, under a hail of fire from the heights, exploded the electric torpedoes that had been attached to the hull. The *Merrimac* sank in flames. Hobson and his companions, floundering in the moonlit water, were rescued and taken prisoner.

This story, with Sampson's commendation of Hobson's gallantry, provided the second sensation of the war, and made the handsome lieutenant the new hero of the nation. Hobson had corked the bottle that contained the Spanish ships, and with boastful laughter Americans reconciled themselves to another blockade, and looked forward to a victory on land. The army at last was free to move. Volunteers, since the middle of May, had been moving into federal encampments. Shafter's command at Tampa, organized as the Fifth Army Corps, had swelled to 25,000 men. It was the logical choice for the Santiago operation, and rumors of its imminent departure echoed insistently from Tampa. But, when word came in mid-June of a landing, it was part of the naval program. To secure a base for the fleet and sheltered waters for coaling, Sampson had seized the outer harbor of Guantánamo Bay, and a battalion of marines had established a camp near the entrance. They were attacked by squads of Spanish soldiers, and tropical warfare suddenly was a vivid reality in the news dispatches. The Spaniards fought in Indian fashion, ambushed in the thick chaparral. By night, the scene was as romantic as a stage setting, the wild slopes flashing with points of flame and swept by the searchlights of the American cruisers in the tranquil waters below. The repeaters racketed "like fire-crackers in a barrel," and the long roll of a machine gun sounded from a launch of the *Marblehead*. The leathernecks were young recruits who had been enlisted in April for service in Cuba. They were exhausted by four days and nights of combat before the enemy was beaten back. The American people got their first sharp taste of war in the tale of this hard skirmishing.

The marines had landed. But where were the army volunteers? Where were the regulars who had been ready to leave for Mariel more than a month before? They had just, after many postponements, set out for Santiago.

The joyful news that Schley had caught the Spanish ships had incited the government to get the army expedition off at once. Thirty-two steamers were in readiness at Tampa, with a contracted capacity of 25,000 men and their animals, matériel, and stores. Shafter had already been warned to be prepared to load his whole force, including four batteries of light artillery and eight siege guns. He had been, since the suspension of the plans for Mariel, singularly out of touch with Washington, and apparently oblivious to the news. This was his first intimation, according to his aide, Lieutenant John D. Miley, that Washington intended to use his troops in action against the Spanish army. Shafter was still uninformed of his destination when, on May 29, he was ordered to leave. The next day, he received confidential instructions that he was to sail for Santiago to capture the Spanish garrison and assist the Navy in capturing the harbor and fleet. Washington, impatient for a smart little joint operation, sat out four days of waiting until a convoy, headed by the lumbering *Indiana*, could be assembled. A dejected telegram from Shafter advised that more time was needed for loading. His difficulties were elaborated in a message from General Miles, who had at last made good his escape, and reached Tampa.

The government officials were in despair at further delay. Sampson was daily asking for haste. It was becoming doubtful that the hulk of the *Merrimac* actually obstructed the channel. In the approaching season of hurricanes, the American ships might be driven from their stations, and the rains would soon impede the movement of troops. The fleet, on June 6, heavily bombarded the Santiago forts, but the great shells of the battleships and the blasts of the dynamite cruiser *Vesuvius* did not permanently silence the rude batteries. On June 7, with renewed urgency, Sampson telegraphed the Navy Department that if 10,000 men were there, the city and the Spanish fleet would fall in forty-eight hours.

This dispatch made a strong impression on the President. Orders for the instant departure of the Fifth Army Corps snapped from Washington in a telegraphic conversation between McKinley and Alger at one end of the through connection, and Miles and Shafter at the other. McKinley was so much incensed by complaints and excuses that Shafter was at length instructed, by order of the President, to sail at once with what force he had ready.

The breakdown in embarkation seemed senseless to the authorities. Even Alger sent his favorite general a sarcastic comment on the fuss over loading the ships. The Secretary of War had a personal reason for vexation with Shafter's loitering—the presence of General Miles at Tampa. Miles had shown a good deal of interest in an operation in eastern Cuba. He had been active for many weeks in forming a liaison with General Calixto García, the insurgent leader in Oriente Province. If Miles were sufficiently interested, he could assert his right to command the Fifth Army Corps. Miles, however, was vacillating, drawn to the splendid force of regulars at Tampa, but still hopeful that he might lead them to Porto Rico. His recommendation, at this juncture, that Santiago might be put off provoked the President to an emphatic No. Miles was soon flurried into advising that all plans for invasion should be abandoned; and, by the time that he suggested he might go to Santiago, Alger felt perfectly safe in ignoring the proposal.

Shafter was a rough-and-ready kind of soldier, a doer, not a worrier. He had small aptitude for logistics, and no experience in transporting and supplying an army, but his worst mistake was the failure to foresee the inevitable fiasco of an embarkation from Tampa. The jerry-built and undeveloped terminus of a railroad built by the Plant Steamship Company had been promoted at random, like Shafter himself, to a position of the first importance in the war. As a place for military concentration, Tampa's sole recommendation was its proximity to Cuba. The town, outside which the camp was miserably situated in a blistering waste of sand and pines, lay nine miles distant from the port, and the only connection with the solitary pier was a single-track railroad. These facilities were taxed by the regular passenger and express traffic between Tampa and Key West, and the naval shipments to the vessels on the Cuban blockade. The railroad was further congested by excursion trains, which the Plant system was running for trippers from all parts of the country.

When his orders came to sail and his staff officers tackled the loading, Shafter awoke to these drawbacks, and to the difficulties of transferring his supplies. Along the railroad to the north, freight cars had multiplied on sidings already cluttered with the provisions for the suspended grand invasion of early May. Since there were no invoices, and the cars were unmarked, it took days to assort their promiscuous contents. The siege guns were laboriously assembled. The wagons, on the other hand, had to be taken apart. As army impedimenta slowly moved to Port Tampa and were stowed on board, it developed that the capacity of the transports had been overstated in the contracts. Much of the matériel would have to be left behind, as well as many animals and several thousand men. The siege guns shared the fate of hospital stores and Signal Corps equipment. Mules were indispensable for pack and wagon trains, so horses were cut to a minimum, and the cavalry was dismounted, with the exception of one troop. Shafter clung to most of his regulars, but he was obliged to relinquish, besides a brigade of artillery, one cavalry outfit and three regiments of infantry. Some volunteers had to be taken along. The Seventy-first New York and the Second Massachusetts were selected as the likeliest of the poorly armed and equipped militia. The tally of citizen soldiers was completed by eight troops of the First Volunteer Cavalry, mainly recruited from western cowboys, and commanded by Colonel Leonard Wood, an Army surgeon who had distinguished himself in the Indian wars, and who had recently acted as the White House physician. Since the lieutenant colonel was the prominent young Republican, Theodore Roosevelt, the "Rough Riders" had had much publicity. In contrast to the state regiments, they had good guns and smokeless powder, and they were clad in thin khaki uniforms that made them the envy of the beflanneled, sweating regulars.

On the morning of June 7, as the first trainloads of soldiers neared the pier at Port Tampa, they were stopped by a solid mass of boxcars and flatcars, spilling out crates, bales, baggage, vehicles, and struggling mules. The track was blocked. Embarkation had come to a standstill when Shafter received the President's orders to sail. It would have been farcical to issue them to the waiting soldiers in camp. With implicit faith in the resourcefulness and spirit of his men, Shafter merely let it be known that the transports would leave at dawn. The night passed in a mad free-for-all to seize cars by sneak attack or forcible capture. The track, by some miracle of energy, was cleared. The trains began to move, and on the morning of June 8 the regiments marched down the pier, and swarmed on board the ships.

The President's orders had been obeyed; but, as Shafter wearily prepared to embark, he was handed an urgent dispatch from the War Department. The great labor of the night had been wasted. The Navy Department had been frightened by a report of lurking Spanish cruisers. Shafter was to wait for further orders before he sailed. A number of transports had already started for Key West. They were recalled to Tampa Bay, where their passengers languished for a week in their stifling holds. Though the Navy's report was quickly exposed as a false alarm, it was not a simple matter to get the fleet under way for a second time. It was necessary to replenish the water supply, and there were only four pilots to take out the ships. A last-minute rush repaired some vital omissions in the cargo. On June 14, when the fleet finally cleared for Cuba, the scenes on the pier duplicated the chaos of the first embarkation.

The expedition, as eventually constituted, comprised a military force of a little less than 17,000 officers and men, accompanied by a civilian contingent of clerks, stenographers, servants, waiters, packers, teamsters, and stevedores, and also by eighty-nine newspaper correspondents, several Cuban generals, and eleven European army officers who desired to observe the war. They were packed on a variety of wretched coastal steamers, so divested of conveniences by their owners that the doughboys called them "prison hulks." Since the civilian masters were independent of the Navy's authority and refused to keep close formation, the large convoy could offer little protection. Straggling vessels were lost to sight for many hours, while torpedo boats and gunboats scurried to round them up. Noisy with the tunes of the military bands and blazing at night like Brooklyn Bridge, the expedition resembled an unfashionable excursion in southern waters, taken at the wrong season, and escorted by a force of frantic warships.

The good fortune that attended the voyage, said Richard Harding Davis, inspired the foreign officers with the grudging envy of one who watches a novice winning at roulette. Six days after leaving Tampa, the largest invading army that had ever sailed from the United States arrived, without incident of weather or attack, off the dark green headlands that guarded Santiago.

• 9 •

THE PRESIDENT AND THE WAR

Cortelyou rejoiced that spring at the accumulating proofs of the President's popularity. With the coming of war, sober second thought replaced the rash emotionalism of the *Maine* excitement, and endorsed a levelheaded statesmanship which had preserved the national honor and gained time for military preparations. American vanity was subtly gratified by the approbation expressed in England for the conduct of the negotiations with Spain. McKinley had his own private reports from the consul general at London of extreme friendliness for the United States and esteem for himself. The esteem, like the friendliness, was new. As the exponent of a narrowly nationalistic tariff policy, especially hostile to Great Britain, McKinley had not been so popular abroad. One November, only a few years before, some Midland manufacturing towns had fed their bonfires with effigies of the Ohio congressman as well as Guy Fawkes. Now William McKinley Osborne was glowing over the manifestations of the President's "great hold upon the people over here." He heard his cousin's praises sung by Englishmen who did not know of the relationship, and their compliments made his ears "prick up with pride."

The early events of the war had largely contributed to the President's prestige at home. As the press performed a *volte-face* on the subject of the Cuban insurgents and their assistance to the American troops, McKinley was lauded for preventing recognition of a dubious republic. Manila Bay shed on the White House the reflected luster of success, soon brightened by the decision to send an army of occupation to the Philippines. There were outbursts of approval for the choice of General Merritt, and for the large powers of military government which the President was said to have

228

granted him. Signs that McKinley was in harmony with the spirit of expansion charmed the masses of the Republican party, and many Democrats, too, especially in the South; but there was a broader basis for the affection that flowed to the White House from all parts of the country. Millions of citizens who did not endorse McKinley's policies and would never cast a vote for him had come to trust his intention to shape the government's course for the benefit of all the people, without partisan bias or sectional prejudice. His desire for national unity had been demonstrated by the appointment of two former commanders of Confederate cavalry as major generals in the volunteer army. Fitzhugh Lee, ex-consul at Havana, and Joseph Wheeler, congressman from Alabama, had outlived their pristine fitness for military service. Their appointment was, in the best sense of the word, political. It cemented the loyalty of the South in wartime, and created an attachment, unprecedented in that region, to a Republican President. The effect on northern sympathies was scarcely less profound. The scars of civil strife were so lately healed that Americans saw a deeply moving symbol in the conferring of army commissions on the two rebel generals, proud to resume the Union blue and fight under the old flag.

Republican newspapers, hymning McKinley to the skies, were beginning to suggest a comparison with Lincoln. The Democratic press stiffly acknowledged the duty of "standing behind the President." The mysterious rhythm of leadership had been restored between the President and the people. Partisan attack on McKinley was suspended for the emergency.

An unexpected disclosure of the President's mind was made toward the end of May, in the midst of the hubbub which the War Revenue Bill created in the Senate. This bill was designed to raise between $95,000,000 and $100,000,000 by internal taxation. It had reanimated the advocates of silver coinage, and started a radical outcry for the elimination of the section providing for a popular loan. The "Populistic" temper of the Senate was causing uneasiness in business circles, when the President proclaimed the first reciprocity agreement concluded under the Dingley Act, an important exchange of tariff concessions with France. There was general surprise that, at a time of anxiety over the revenue, the President should take steps to reduce it; but the form in which emergency taxation was finally passed, after a delay more costly than several battleships, seemed to justify the President's confidence in the financial future of the country. Though the Senate inflationists had exacted an issue of silver certificates as the price of their agreement to pay for the war, the concession did not appear significant, once the smoke of the congressional battle had cleared.

The bond section had survived attack, and a loan of $200,000,000 at 3 per cent was an immediate success, firmly supported by the commercial interests and many times oversubscribed. Business had become converted to the war and the extension of American markets abroad, and the country could boast of the achievement of floating a United States loan without the necessity of borrowing from foreign syndicates.

The declaration of the President's sustained interest in expanding foreign trade had been doubly emphatic because of its timing and its incongruity with the country's preoccupation with the war. His action indicated a cool consistency of purpose that vastly impressed the country. On the absorbing topic, McKinley had little to say, and none of it bore on the retarded military movements and the mounting complaints of the War Department. His utterances were mainly confined to orders and proclamations. In war as in peace, he remained an impersonal figure in the newspapers—an item of "human interest" was a rarity—but it should not be assumed that he was a stranger to the Washington correspondents. His relations with the veterans among them went back twenty years; and some who had Ohio connections—Walter Wellman and W. E. Curtis, for example—were more than casual acquaintances. McKinley's keen distaste for publicity did not extend to newspapermen. A great newspaper reader, he had always enjoyed his contacts with them. George Frease of *The Canton Repository* was but one of many Ohio journalists whom McKinley numbered among his good friends. Two of them, Jim Boyle and Joe Smith, had been his confidential secretaries during the governorship. From this period, too, dated his friendship with Whitelaw Reid and the Chicago newspaper proprietor, Kohlsaat; and also one of Kohlsaat's former young men, Robert P. Porter, whom McKinley later entrusted with missions in Cuba and Porto Rico.

When he came to Washington as President, McKinley had let it be known that he would facilitate access to news on public affairs. The reporters were always welcome on the second floor of the east wing. A table, furnished with writing materials and surrounded by chairs, was reserved for their use in one corner of the corridor. Here they could prepare their stories, while keeping watch on the President's callers and other potential sources of information. The rule was one of strict impartiality. Whether the news gatherers represented faithful Republican organs or scurrilous mouthpieces of the opposition, they received precisely the same treatment. The President was cordial to all, confidentially accessible to none. His freedom from prejudice was strikingly exemplified shortly after the end of the war. Sylvester Scovel, an obstreperous reporter for the New York *World*, had been officially barred from the military forces because of insolent conduct toward General Shafter at Santiago. McKinley went out of his way to oblige the employee of a newspaper which was hotly inimical to him. The fact was not generally known, but Scovel's clearance and his fervent gratitude to the President could not have been a secret from his colleagues.

The President's attitude toward the press was one reason for the gradual development of the Executive Mansion into a news source of primary importance. Cortelyou supplied the other reason. He was the first of the presidential press secretaries. The system had taken shape in the weeks before the war, when Cortelyou began sending for the correspondents and distributing statements which he himself had written and copied off on the typewriter. The only discrimination practiced at the White House was in handing the releases first to the men from the three big press associations. The result was an accurate presentation, throughout McKinley's administration, of his policies and official conduct. Cortelyou's talent for public relations did much to regulate the hit-or-miss method of news gathering at the White House.

Cortelyou performed the same function when McKinley went away from Washington. On all extended absences—with a single exception in the summer of 1899—a carload of correspondents was attached to the President's train. Wherever he went, of course, the local reporters hovered around his party in eager search for a story. Cortelyou became known to the newspaper profession as the man to whom to apply, and from whom to expect intelligent and courteous assistance. It was a rather singular paradox that, under a President who shunned publicity, there began the first glimmering of the idea that the Executive himself was an important news source, to which the press had the right of access.

Cortelyou had begun to worry about the President's physical safety in the weeks before the war. Crank letters had multiplied in the disturbed state of public feeling. There had been threats and warnings, and perhaps worse. It was rumored that infernal machines had been delivered at the mansion. The big, run-down, accessible house invited unlawful entry. The McKinleys' living quarters were unguarded at night, for the solitary watchman did not patrol the second floor. Cortelyou was nervous about the conservatory, where he had discovered several insecurely fastened windows.

The Secret Service or Intelligence Bureau of the Treasury was charged with the protection of the President's person; but it was preoccupied with its main business of detecting counterfeiters, and had never regarded the secondary duty very seriously, except at inauguration time. Garfield's assassination had followed Lincoln's without suggesting the need of devising a systematic and continuing means of guarding the Executive. The newly appointed chief of the bureau, John E. Wilkie, was a Chicago newspaperman who had written special articles on criminal investigation, and whose first interest in wartime was in rounding up suspected Spanish spies. The emergency, however, brought the mansion a detail of Secret Service men, including a night watchman for the bedroom corridor. Cortelyou still thought that the domestic wing was inadequately protected. Although he had had the windows in the conservatory repaired, he was still uneasy about the scramble of outbuildings directly adjoining the house. There were good opportunities, Cortelyou noticed, for hiding infernal machines there.

It was useless to speak to the President of precautions. The subject did not interest him. He daily received a succession of strangers in the Cabinet Room, and three times a week greeted thousands at his public receptions. Colonel Bingham tried to keep a space cleared between the President and the crowd in the East Room, but his remonstrances were futile. Attorney General Griggs was laughed at when he asked McKinley to have a bodyguard on his outings. The President strolled around "the yard" as carelessly as ever, but he did not stay away from his desk for long. After taking a breath of air, he would hurry back to the east wing.

McKinley steered stubbornly through the gales of governmental disorder, a captain who stayed on duty at the helm, without a message to the frightened and indignant passengers. The Executive Mansion had been transformed into the military information center of the nation. Twenty-five telegraph wires and fifteen special telephone wires had been installed in Secretary Porter's corner office, which was fitted up as a "War Room," with maps papering one long wall. By day and by night, the east wing resounded with the click of the Morse code, the rattle of typewriters, and the jangle of telephone bells. The mansion had no switchboard. Its original line had a single extension, also situated in Porter's office, in a "private" booth made by stretching green flannel over a wooden frame. The new installations were separate wires leading to the departments and the Senate, and to Tampa and other cities. Montgomery, promoted a lieutenant colonel of volunteers, presided over the battery of telephones and the movable board of telegraph instruments. His desk was fitted with signal bells connected with all parts of the mansion, and a graphophone into which he could dictate messages.

The President liked to linger in the War Room, reading the telegrams or studying the maps that hung a series of puzzles on the wall. There, in the anxious days of May, he scanned the red pinflags that dubiously traced the movements of Cervera's squadron, and the white pinflags that guessed

232

the course of Schley. When, red and white, the flags were at last thickly clustered at Santiago, the Navy Department was still doubtful of the intentions of the Spanish reserve squadron at Cadiz. As it moved to the Suez Canal in June, McKinley's eyes must often have turned to the big map of the Pacific and the lonely white dots that represented the little American squadron in Manila Bay. Long, Alger, and Corbin were frequently with the President when he came to smoke his last cigar in the War Room, before he went to bed. Ingling, one of three young telegraphers who had been brought in to assist Montgomery, often had the evening shift. He would hand over the latest messages from the military commanders, and the bulletins transmitted by newspapers and agencies. If there were answers to send, Ingling had to take them down, though he had little shorthand.

While the war lasted, the President was absorbed in its conduct, in detail and in over-all direction. A litter of army business washed up every day on his desk, and Dawes asserted that he "saved Alger from many blunders" by "his constant watchfulness and supervision of the War Department." Though the Navy Department did not require a similar scrutiny, it was by no means free of vexing internal problems. Long wavered when the experts disagreed, and frequently had to be rescued from a bog of nervous uncertainty. Between the Army and Navy, the President was at all times the liaison and mediator. As Commander in Chief, he alone possessed the authority to compose the disputes that led to a stalemate in every program of united action. He presided at the joint conferences, arbitrated the contentions, and took the responsibility of ultimate decision. Cortelyou thought that the President seemed "to grow more masterful day by day"; and he watched with admiration the persuasive operation of McKinley's "infinite tact" and his "gentleness and graciousness in dealing with men."

McKinley's actual contribution is impossible to evaluate. He was obviously unable to give his full time to army management; and, in the event, the blunders from which he saved the War Department were less conspicuous than those which he did not or could not prevent. His interposition in the plans of campaign was, with a few exceptions, the secret of the joint conferences, never mentioned by the dissentient parties or by the President himself. McKinley learned about combined operations from the naval experts. He was inevitably influenced and at times perhaps overpersuaded by their opinions. Mahan, Crowninshield, and Sicard had no Army counterparts on whom the President could rely for advice on strategy. Even the capricious counsels of General Miles were not regularly available after the end of May. General Merritt was removed by his assignment to the Philippines. The President's right hand was Adjutant General Corbin, who was primarily an administrator. In so far as the military campaign in Cuba was directed from Washington, it was directed by the President. He was as resolved and indefatigable in discharging this duty as he was untrained for its performance. Alger's praise of his dictum "we must not scatter our forces" is all that remains of McKinley's guidance of the joint conferences, except a tenacious insistence on "unconditional surrender," words that echoed sternly back from Grant's demand at Donelson. The phrases conjure up a rather quaint picture of the peaceable President, earnestly airing to the conclaves of braid and brass the military platitudes of his boyhood. Yet, in the mirrors of Dawes and Cortelyou, McKinley takes on the stature of a forceful Executive, cutting through a muddle of inefficiency and divided counsels, and driving on with the war. "His strong hand was always on the helm of the War Department," Dawes wrote. "If it had not been, the result would have been demoralization." Cortelyou saw that same hand in all the movements of the armed forces, and believed that the President's determination and firm control were indispensable in the crisis. "He is the strong man of the Cabinet, the dominating force," Cortelyou concluded in June. He added that the President's "wise counsel has saved the government money and lives to an incalculable degree." Cortelyou was not prone to extravagant assertions, but he did not amplify or illustrate his statement.

A worried letter from Myron Herrick suggests an example of McKinley's vigilance over the public funds. Herrick had become interested in a new type of projectile, the Gathmann torpedo, which Hanna was promoting with great energy and had persistently recommended to the President. One evening in late July, when McKinley was entertaining these two intimate friends at dinner, he made an ambiguous comment on their interest in the invention. Though Herrick referred to this remark as a "jest," it had been sufficiently barbed to upset him. He stayed late at the White House, in hopes of a confidential word with the President. Failing an opportunity for this, Herrick returned to his hotel; and, before he went to bed, wrote to assure McKinley that the "moneymaking feature was the least of the considerations" that animated his interest in the weapon.

In summing up the President's trials in the middle of May, Cortelyou bracketed "the struggle for place" with military unpreparedness and bickering between the services. The White House was overrun with candidates for commissions. The President's German doorkeeper, Loeffler, claimed the rank of captain, and blossomed out in a gaudy and unidentified uniform to admit the place seekers of wartime. The expansion of the Navy, which somewhat more than doubled its personnel of about 12,000 officers and men, was on a far smaller scale than that of the Army, enlarged from a force of 28,000 to more than a quarter of a million; but there was not a parallel discrepancy in the commissions that lay in the President's gift. While the 856 additional naval officers were all federal appointments, the line officers of the volunteer regiments were chosen by the governors of their respective states. The President's responsibility was limited to the major generals and brigadiers and the officers of the general staff, except in the case of certain special organizations which were recruited from the country at large: a brigade of engineers, and a force of 10,000 infantry "immune" to tropical diseases. In all, McKinley disposed of 1,032 appointments in the volunteer army, and 71 second lieutenancies in the regular establishment. The competition for these places repeated the contest over the political patronage. There were 25,000 applications for the volunteer commissions, and some 2,000 for the regular lieutenancies.

The decisions on the high command of the volunteer army were made on Corbin's advice. As a young soldier, McKinley had watched a sorry parade of "political generals." Nineteen of the twenty-six major generals he commissioned, and sixty-six of the 102 brigadiers were regular Army officers. The others were graduates of West Point, or veterans of active military service. A still heavier draft was made on the standing Army—then being expanded to more than twice its former size—for the chiefs of the staff departments in the field. Four hundred regular officers were assigned to these positions, on the basis of the Adjutant General's efficiency records. This action, subsequently criticized as having impaired the regular organization, showed the intense concern of a former staff officer for the administrative branch. McKinley had earned his own shoulder straps, and he had not forgotten the complexities of the paper work at which he had become adept. He had seen the helplessness of inexperienced officers in the toils of military red tape. He also knew the opportunities that the supply departments afforded for dishonest exploitation of the government. When the President depleted the Army to secure professional staff direction, he was surely influenced by the memory of the peculating quartermasters and swindling commissaries who had disfigured the record of the Union army in the Civil War.

The decisions on the junior commissions were less methodically made. A host of applicants and their political sponsors clamored for a hearing. Alger complained that they were at his house before breakfast and after midnight. The President also gave much time to interviewing these candidates, rejecting the poorly qualified and sending off the fortunate ones with little cards to the War Department. There was no time for a searching investigation of credentials. McKinley and Alger both relied heavily on the endorsements of men in public life. These were not all Republicans. The commissions were divided among the states on the basis of population, and the Democrats of Congress received their proportionate allotment.

The young men chosen were of generally good type—the ruinous factor was the lack of any training period or program—but the appointments provoked a fearful outcry from Democratic newspapers. Reporters prowled through the camps, and scored the errors made by boggling tyros in shoulder straps. Republican names stuck out like sore thumbs from the coveted commissions: Blaine, Harrison, Allison, Foraker, Elkins, Quay, even Alger. Democratic names were conveniently overlooked. To the anti-administration press, all volunteers were noble patriots, except for the staff officers. They were incompetent civilians, foisted on the army by ignoble deals at the War Department.

Alger was berated for playing politics in wartime, but the correspondents might have been blind to the throng of applicants in the east wing. The President's attention to the staff commissions was not explained to the public. His preferment of regular Army officers, however, was reported and understood. The country approved the manifest intention to remove as large a number of military positions as possible from the area of political pressure. A further cause for satisfaction was the assignment of the troops enlisted under the second call for volunteers. The majority of the 75,000 new recruits went to reinforce already existing state regiments that had been inadequately filled under the badly drawn Volunteer Act. The consequent reduction of the crop of additional commissions was a severe disappointment to a legion of would-be officers and their sponsors in Congress. To the country at large, it was evidence of the President's sincerity, and even the opposition press applauded his refusal to use the war for party ends.

Yet the applicants continued to stream past the President's desk. "All hands," Cortelyou remarked on June 17, "are still interested in the Army appointments." Eight weeks after the war began, McKinley was still being buffeted by a furious demand for the little cards to the War Department. "Under it all, the President bears up wonderfully," Cortelyou wrote. "Only once in a great while does he show any temper. Probably it would be better for him if he gave vent to his feelings now and then."

Soon after the war began, McKinley had given vent to his feelings by administering a sharp rebuke to the admirable but politically minded Adjutant General. On the President's deciding to bestow the major generalships on Fitzhugh Lee and Joseph Wheeler, Corbin had dashed off congratulatory telegrams to the prominent Southerners, and the appointments were published in the newspapers before they were sent to the Senate. Corbin was sick with mortification, but his distress did not avert the President's wrath. "It's a good plan to call some people down now and then," McKinley remarked in relating the incident to Russell Hastings, "we all need to be called down once in a while." This was strange language from an easygoing executive, prone to overindulgence to lame dogs. Corbin, however, was not the kind of man who needed indulgence. Aggressive, honest, and superbly able, he was ready to handle the affairs of his own bureau, and any others that might come his way. His office, for many months, was open day and night. Corbin sat directly in front of the door, interviewing his crowds of callers, making instant decisions, and dispatching an enormous volume of army business. Under the peculiar organization of the War Department, the Adjutant General was vested with large powers in wartime, and Corbin was favored in extending them by Miles's eccentric character and itch for active service. He became, in all but name, the army Chief of Staff. The President, for some reason, treated him with military strictness. Mrs. Hobart reported a reprimand that Corbin received on arriving late for a White House dinner, with the excuse that his watch was slow. "Lincoln once had an adjutant general who gave this same excuse," the President remarked. " 'Well,' said Mr. Lincoln, 'either you must get a new watch or I must get a new adjutant general.' "

There was an amusingly human ring in the satisfaction with his own severity that McKinley expressed to Hastings. For the most part, in the grinding weeks of war, the President seems nearly depersonalized, scarcely more than the Executive fixed in the formal pose of duty. Only a few flashes light up the vulnerable, tired man. Cortelyou saw that he was again careworn under the "terrible strain" of May; and John D. Long marked how his face fell when, at a military review in Virginia, he was handed Schley's "infelicitous" dispatch. McKinley was much affected by the letters he received from parents of boys who had enlisted, and on a Sunday evening in late May read aloud to Colonel Herrick several touching entreaties that the troops should not be sent to Cuba during the rains. The clerk Ira Smith recalled that the President complained of one irksome task—the drudgery of having to affix his signature to every military commission. Smith would carry in a stack of documents, and deposit them before the President, removing each one as it was signed. Since the sheepskin could not be blotted, the commissions were spread out to dry on the desks and tables and finally the floor of the Cabinet Room, leaving the President stranded in a sea of parchment. "Something ought to be done about this," McKinley would grumble while he scribbled his name. "Somebody else ought to be able to sign these."

McKinley's pleasant manner was not altered by the pinpricks of annoyance or the rowel of worry; but, though he was never irritable, he often found release in irony. "Impatience is not patriotism," he caustically observed to Dawes in June. "So far as heard from, those who were so impatient at the first have not yet gone to the front." The sour little jokes with which the President regaled the White House staff convinced Cortelyou that people were mistaken in thinking that he had no sense of humor. "His ready wit and dry sayings," Cortelyou wrote, "are common occurrences to those of us who are near him." One night, when Cortelyou showed the President a begging letter from a Canton church, McKinley handed it back with the instruction, "Call that to my attention when I feel richer than now." Cortelyou was so much tickled by this sally that he set it down in his diary. It scarcely seems to bear out his assertion that the President was "very ready at repartee" and "adroit in conversation." But only the great witticisms bear transportation to the page. Cortelyou could relish the full humor of drawling inflection and satirical glance. The tensions of the day were sometimes eased while McKinley cleared his desk before he went to bed; and, in the surcease of a quiet Sunday in June, he discussed the political situation in Ohio, talking to Cortelyou about the coming Republican convention, and dictating a memorandum of suggestions which emphasized "Reciprocity and Protection" for the platform.

The President's mind was somber with larger decisions. He was debating the agenda for the peace table. "While we are conducting war and until its conclusion, we must keep all we get," he jotted on a scrap of paper; "when the war is over we must keep what we want." A strictly confidential cable from the State Department informed Ambassador Hay that the President would be inclined to grant terms of peace on the following basis: that Spain should evacuate Cuba and cede Porto Rico to the United States; and also cede a port in the Philippines and an island in the Ladrones, with a harbor for a coaling station. Beyond the end of the war, McKinley was looking ahead to the future course of his diplomacy. He became convinced of the desirability of the closer *rapprochement* with Great Britain which Ambassador Hay was earnest to promote. American relations with Russia were also much in his thoughts. The month of June witnessed the arrival at Washington of the first Russian diplomatic representative of ambassadorial rank. The State Department had drafted an address for the President to deliver on the occasion of Count Cassini's presentation, but it did not suit McKinley. Late one evening in the Cabinet Room, he "slashed it pretty vigorously," observing to Cortelyou that the coming of the Russian ambassador just at this time was a matter of much consequence, and the reply to his remarks should be drawn with great care.

"You have always been a marvel to me," Will Osborne had written his cousin, "as to the amount of work you could do and stand without showing it, but I feel some times as if that was on account of the confidence the people have in you, and how they stand under and apparently bolster you up." Some supernatural explanation seems necessary for the good health and high morale with which the President survived a spring and summer of almost unmitigated strain and drudgery. A couple of intimate friends would sometimes come for dinner, and there were two larger gatherings, one of them in honor of Mrs. McKinley's birthday. Otherwise, McKinley's recreation was restricted to a leisurely hour or so in the early evening, except on Saturday when he stayed down for the concert of the Marine Band. The little breathers in "the yard" were his only exercise, and nearly his only exposure to fresh air. Yet even when the east wing was torrid with summer heat, he could write his sister Helen that he was "standing the hard work better than I ought to have any right to expect."

Mrs. McKinley hovered vaguely at the other end of the corridor, an unwontedly neglected but not unquiet ghost. Wonderfully improved in strength, she made her patriotic contribution by tolerating her husband's long hours of work. There were no tales of interruptions or scenes in wartime, and the marriage, like happy nations, has no history at this period. As a man of intense family feeling, the President is seen only in his relation with his nephew James, eighteen years old and wishful to enlist.

Jim arrived at the White House, in response to a telegram from his uncle, and one June evening the two sat down after dinner to talk the matter over. The boy could not feel the years roll back to 1861, or guess the deep emotion with which the older man was longing that this other eighteen-year-old would show a patriotism as selfless as his own had been. McKinley was not disappointed. Jim did not hint at a commission or a safe assignment. The only favor he asked was that he and his cousin, John Barber, might join a Canton company of the Eighth Ohio Volunteers. McKinley had heard good things of this regiment and its commander, Colonel C. V. Hard, and he was glad to request that places should be found for both youngsters.

When McKinley went into his office after the talk with Jim, Cortelyou noticed that he was in unusually cheerful spirits. He seemed much interested in his nephew's determination to enlist; and, running on about it, made a mistake in signing his name. For the first time since the inauguration, he started to write the abbreviation "Wm.," as he had been used to do in Ohio. "He is a fine boy and bound to go," McKinley said. In preparing the request to Colonel Hard, he avoided an effusive recommendation. "He is a good boy," he wrote of Jim. "I am very fond of him and have the deepest interest in him. He is only 18 years old, possibly rather young for a soldier, still I can but admire his patriotism. . . ." McKinley's restrained language did not conceal his pride. "I hope he will make a good soldier," he could not resist adding. Jim, in time, earned his shoulder straps and found his career in the Army, frequently plied with admonitions from an "Uncle who loves you as dearly as though you were his own child." But the President's affection for the lad and fatherly identification with his conduct were never more touchingly betrayed than at the time of Jim's enlistment.

The episode also illuminates the stoicism of McKinley's character and his exalted standard of patriotic duty. In June, when criticisms of the federal camps were being noised in Congress and in the press of every state, the President listened rather wearily to the clamor of the people who had willed the rush into war. He was working with all his might to improve the flow of supplies and correct the defects of their distribution. Initial shortages were inevitable, and must be borne. McKinley's intense solicitude for the volunteers was always tempered by the mental habit of a soldier. He believed in military discipline, and did not think young men were harmed by undergoing a few hardships. Camp Alger, on the site of the old Bull Run battlefield and easily accessible to the Washington correspondents, was particularly notorious for its deficiencies. McKinley had seen Camp Alger. Worse camps, a generation earlier, had built the great armies of the Union. He sent his dearly loved nephew over the river without a qualm, and approvingly noticed a week later that army life had "straightened him up."

The President's stern devotion to country had not been tested by the discomforts in store for Jim. Its proof had been the assignment to which he had heartily consented. The best-trained volunteer regiments were fast being ordered into action; and, on the day that Jim crossed the Potomac with the letter to Colonel Hard, McKinley knew that the Eighth Ohio would be shortly bound for the fever hole of Santiago.

· 10 ·

SANTIAGO BAY

THE Major General Commanding the
Army came back to the War Department in a bellicose humor. Out-
maneuvered by Alger, he had let the main body of regulars escape. To be
sure, Alger had agreed that Miles might follow the Cuban expedition,
but on condition of first organizing a force for Porto Rico, and, apart from
the few regular units that Shafter had not taken, the only troops left were
militia, with obsolete arms and ammunition. Miles did not harbor a grudge
against Shafter. He deplored the difficulties of his brother officer and his
present precarious situation, and urged that troops and matériel should be
sent at once to Santiago. This zeal for Shafter's success was not altogether
disinterested. Miles was hoping that Santiago would fall before he got
there, so that he could pick off the regulars for the attack on Porto Rico.

Miles's vacillations at Tampa had undoubtedly lowered his standing
in administrative circles, but a gravely attentive audience listened to his
report at the formal conference which the President called on June 18.
The account of the breakdown at Tampa exceeded the worst fears of the
authorities. It was the breakdown of staff work, a cruel disappointment to
the President. In view of the stiff Spanish resistance at Guantánamo, there
was no disposition to make light of Miles's warnings. Arrangements were
made to organize and send on a division of volunteers, to dispatch the
mountainous stores that were lying at Tampa, and to expedite a quantity
of additional supplies, including tons of rations for the soldiers of General
García.

There was no dearth of men or provisions. The problem was to find
ships to carry them. The recent charter of twelve steamers had exhausted

241

the available shipping on the eastern seaboard, and the authorities had at long last recognized that the War Department must purchase ships. Negotiations were under way for eight transoceanic liners, but they could not be made ready for many weeks. The Navy Department was compelled to fill the immediate need by the loan of two fast auxiliary cruisers. The demand came at a particularly bad time, when the Spanish reserve fleet was reportedly bound for the Far East and Sampson was being alerted for a possible expedition to support Dewey. The President obtained a signed statement from Alger—evidence of his loss of faith in the Secretary's word-of-mouth agreements—that the cruisers were on loan for a limited period. No doubt was felt that the desperate shipping crisis would soon be somewhat eased by the return of the thirty-two transports that were then on their way to Santiago.

The first intimation of delay was contained in the reports of Shafter's disembarkation. He was unable to carry out the operation. The troops were landed by the Navy. Alger's lack of boats, as well as ships, led to another contest between the departments, with Long trying to hang on to his small craft and Alger seeking to wangle them away. On the last Saturday in June, Alger went to the Navy Department to request a convoy for a lighter and a tug that he was going to send to Shafter. When Long agreed, Alger suavely inquired, "By the way, can't you lend me a lighter and a tug?" Long could not help laughing at this devious approach. He was sorry, too, for his "unthrifty neighbor." The War Department was in sore straits on Saturday, June 25. Alger's rest had been disturbed by early morning press bulletins announcing that, before the American landing had been completed, there had been a bloody little fight at Las Guásimas in the heavily wooded hills to the east of Santiago.

Shafter's precipitate advance spurred the government to increase his reinforcements, but his fleet of old tramps, still heavy with unloaded cargo, remained in Cuban waters. Alger's pledge to return the borrowed cruisers was only a scrap of paper in the President's private file. To the distress and inconvenience of the Navy, two more of its swiftest cruisers and many lighters, tugs, barges, and launches were turned over to the War Department.

The blunder of the unloading rivaled that of the Tampa embarkation. The President had saved Alger from neither. He was as uninformed on the subject of shipping as the Quartermaster's Department of the Army. Long, however, had foreseen that the Navy would probably be called on for assistance in landing the troops. Had the President canvassed the subject in conference, he could not have missed the obvious deduction that

Shafter would also have trouble in landing his guns and other impedimenta. There were serious lapses in McKinley's liaison between the services in the preparations for Santiago. The sole reason for sending an army expedition there was to enable Admiral Sampson to enter the harbor and capture or destroy the Spanish fleet. The Navy Department and Sampson interpreted this to mean that the troops would make a direct assault on the fortifications at the harbor entrance, and the plans to reinforce Dewey were made in the belief that this attack would shortly permit a drastic reduction of Sampson's fleet. The War Department, however, ignored the Navy's assumptions, and inclined to favor Shafter's preference for an attack on the city of Santiago, four miles distant from the mouth of the harbor. These basic differences were never reconciled, and seem never to have been discussed until a later date. Shafter's orders empowered him to determine his plan of campaign. He was to confer closely with Sampson, and co-operation was enjoined on both of them. The President wisely declined to hamper the decisions of the commanders by specific instructions, but to place reliance on their agreement was negligent in the extreme. McKinley's experience should have warned him of the need for superior authority and diplomatic adjustment in the intercourse between the services.

Shafter was incapable of interpreting "co-operation" in the sense of co-ordinated action with the fleet. By his own admission, he gave no consideration to the Navy's plans. A number of powerful armor-clads were lying off Santiago, waiting for the army to do their work. Shafter could see no good reason why they should not capture the Spanish squadron for themselves. A view of the precipitous heights that guarded the harbor entrance clinched his aversion to ordering his men to assault them, within range of Cervera's guns. He fully decided to advance rapidly inland, and surround and capture the city. But Shafter said nothing of all this to Captain Chadwick of the *New York* or to Admiral Sampson, who successively boarded his steamer for consultation. He was so noncommittal that both officers believed that he agreed with the Navy's proposals, and would land at the point they recommended, a bay near the works on the west of the harbor mouth. A rude surprise was in store for Sampson at the close of the conference to which he accompanied Shafter at the insurgent camp at Aserraderos, some miles farther west. After a general discussion of a landing point, Shafter brusquely outlined his plans. His disembarkation would begin next morning at Daiquiri, sixteen miles east of the harbor; and, as soon as possible, would also be conducted at Siboney, about halfway between the two points. He would make a feint of landing at the bay near the fortifications, and requested the Navy to assist him in practicing this deception, and also to shell the coastline before the real disembarkation took place. General García, who attended the conference with some of his officers, was invited to send forces to intercept the Spanish troops as they retreated from the bombardment.

Shafter was not consulting Sampson. He was telling him. His announcement "committed" Shafter, to use his own expression, to approach Santiago by the narrow road that ran along the coast from Daiquirí to Siboney and then passed inland to the village of Sevilla, five or six miles east of the outskirts of the capital. By plain implication, the wishes of the Navy were to be ignored, yet the affronted and incredulous Sampson had not abandoned hope of some concession. Troops could still have been moved to the mouth of the harbor by marching them from Siboney along the coastal railway, under the protection of the guns of the fleet. Captain Chadwick thought that a detachment of two thousand soldiers, with the assistance of the insurgents and the marines from Guantánamo, could have carried the feebly defended batteries on the heights. But the possibility of compromise was not mentioned. Sampson did not ask for an explanation of Shafter's "change." He received the rebuff in brooding silence, punctiliously fulfilling the requests that Shafter had made, and offering to assume the disembarkation of the army.

Shafter, rejecting the only two small bays in the vicinity, had chosen to land in heavy surf on a sharp coral shore. Daiquirí had an immense pier that stood too high to use, and an awkward little wooden wharf that was unsafe in rough weather. There were no docking facilities at the somewhat smoother beach at Siboney. Very few able seamen could be obtained from the crews of the transports; while, apart from the rowboats carried by the steamers, Shafter had but one lighter, one barge, and two light-draft vessels of unspecified type. The masters of the transports refused to venture near the dangerous coast because the government had not assumed the marine insurance. It was impracticable to row the soldiers in. The boats were towed in strings by the Navy's steam launches. The animals were jumped overboard, and at first left to swim; but, after a number of them had been lost, they also were towed by the cutters to Daiquirí, where there was ground for corrals. Two of the three divisions of the Army, the batteries of artillery, and quantities of impedimenta were landed at the rickety wharf. The other division and more than three thousand Cubans waded ashore at Siboney. Shafter's preference quickly settled on Siboney because it saved eight miles of "beastly road," and much heavy cargo was carried ashore there, pending the construction of a temporary dock by the Engineers.

At considerable inconvenience to the fleet, which had left most of its boats at Key West, Sampson detached fifty cutters and other small craft for five days to disembark the army, and two hundred picked seamen performed the troublesome task with alacrity and skill. Shafter had no objection to co-operation, if it did not work both ways, and telegraphed the War Department his hearty appreciation, declaring that without the Navy he could not have landed in ten days, and perhaps not at all. Washington, for a short time, rejoiced in the illusion of harmony in the combined action at Santiago.

The two infantry divisions of the Fifth Army Corps were commanded by Brigadier Generals J. Ford Kent and Henry W. Lawton, Army colonels who had received wartime promotion. The division of dismounted cavalry was commanded by Major General Joseph Wheeler. His force and Lawton's had landed at Daiquirí, and were ordered to march to Siboney, where Kent's troops were still coming off the transports. Before reaching Cuba, Shafter had made up his mind that whatever they did at that season had to be done very quickly, but his impetuosity had been modified by the necessity of reorganizing his army and unloading his supplies. He assigned Lawton, a keen and energetic soldier, to the advance, with orders to take a strong defensive position on the Santiago road beyond Siboney. In placing the cavalry in the rear, Shafter had not reckoned with the mettle of that element, or the spunk of the little old Confederate who was the senior officer on shore. "General Wheeler, a regular game-cock," Lieutenant Colonel Roosevelt noted, "was as anxious as Lawton to get first blood. . . ." After privately reconnoitering the country back of Siboney, Wheeler contrived to push one of his brigades, under General S. B. M. Young, in front of Lawton's men for a reconnaissance in force. Determined to circumvent the infantry, two squadrons of regulars and two of volunteers set forth at dawn on June 24. The regulars, with Wheeler and Young, went by the road. The volunteers, with Colonel Leonard Wood and Roosevelt, followed a steep hillside trail. The parties crept through the dense underbrush to an entrenched enemy outpost; drew and returned fire; and, after a sharp contest, drove the Spaniards back. This rash little action, in which the small force of cavalry suffered proportionately heavy casualties, was the first engagement of the American army in the war.

The fight at Las Guásimas was a reminder of the cost of attacking entrenched positions. It showed the disadvantages of a terrain of tangled thickets, where it was impossible to deploy troops. It disclosed that the Spaniards were well supplied with modern guns and smokeless powder, and could put them to effective use. But these lessons were wasted. The routing of the Spaniards was the significant fact that elated the soldiers on the beaches, and confirmed their belief that the campaign would be a cinch. The tough veterans of the plains, trained in irregular warfare and contemptuous of "dago" courage, were champing to follow their comrades. They had, incidentally, acquired respect for one outfit of volunteers. Under machine-gun fire, the Rough Riders had borne themselves well, and the eyeglassed dude, Lieutenant Colonel Roosevelt, had proved himself a soldier.

The most important result of Las Guásimas was to accelerate the army's advance. Shafter had gained an open and well-watered area near the village of Sevilla. The forward movement was ordered, and the troops gleefully scrambled up the road in heat so oppressive that the militia regiments and many of the regulars discarded heavy equipment. Their little dogtents soon filled the space around the village, and small encampments multiplied in openings in the jungle beyond, until the vanguard of the army was close to the outer defenses of Santiago. Shafter's desire for a rapid movement had been fulfilled; and, though the cavalry had been more impulsive than he had intended, he approved the premature and unnecessary encounter. He was, nevertheless, extremely anxious that it should not be repeated, and admonished his officers to take no action, lest it bring on a general engagement before he had received his reinforcements and solved the problem of his supplies.

With his headquarters still on shipboard, Shafter spent the next few days plying between Siboney and Daiquirí, and once riding up to the front. The beaches were littered with confused heaps of ammunition boxes, bales of forage, and cases of commissary stores. The ragged village on the cliffs at Siboney was taking on the aspect of a squalid military base, with its huts housing quartermaster's laborers and affording offices for telegraph, postal, and other services; while some larger wooden sheds, erected by an American mining company, were allotted to the Medical Corps for a hospital. But, by sea and by land, the army's communications were precarious. In spite of frantic efforts by the Quartermaster's Corps, only the essentials had been unloaded, and the transports were hovering on the horizon, ready to take their departure at the first hurricane warning. The precipitate advance had made it necessary to forward all supplies over the rough and sunken track of the so-called road. It was suitable only for mule trains, which were at first used to carry the daily ration; but their capacity was inadequate, and the harried quartermasters, in two days, managed to land and assemble sixty six-mule wagons at Daiquirí. As the batteries were laboriously dragged to the front, the requirements of heavy traffic overbore Shafter's rooted objection to wasting time on road mending. On the arrival of his first reinforcements, he set the volunteers to work at repairs.

William McKinley,
the Republican candidate,
1896

Mother McKinley
at 87, brisk and
strong-minded

William McKinley, Sr.

Abner McKinley

The President's nephew,
young James, after he made
the Army his career

The lieutenant, proud of the bars
on his shoulder-straps

As a student at the Poland Academy,
McKinley enjoyed reciting and debates.

Young Major McKinley   *The lovely Miss Saxton*

The young Congressman—
listening more than he talked

Congressman and Mrs. McKinley
during a visit to San Francisco
in 1881

The McKinleys with the Hanna family
during a visit to the house
at Thomasville, Georgia

Governor and Mrs. McKinley
at a dinner at the Hannas'
in Cleveland

The presidential candidate surrounded by admiring

Every day was circus day in Canton.

pilgrims in the summer of 1896

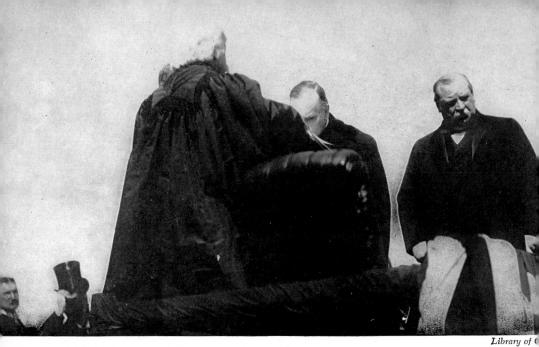

McKinley kissing the Bible at his first inauguration. The outgoing President's expression is that of a man with gout.

Mrs. McKinley waits for her husband to appear on the inaugural platform. J. Addison Porter is on her right. Mother McKinley is the second on her left.

The McKinleys' bedroom at the White House

Sightseers standing before the Tiffany glass doors in the vestibule

Charles G. Dawes at his desk
at the Treasury Department

George B. Cortelyou,
whom Mr. Dawes called
"the most efficient secretary
a public man ever had"

The desk at the end of the Cabinet table

The War Room, with Colonel B. F. Montgomery at his desk

Admiral Dewey

Rear Admiral Sampson

Secretary Alger and General Corbin at the War Department

Commodore Schley

General Nelson A. Miles,
whom Roosevelt called "a brave peacock"

General Henry W. Lawton,
who miscalculated at El Caney, met
a hero's death in the Philippines.

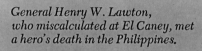

Generals Wheeler, Shafter, and Miles in conference during the negotiations for the surrender of Santiago

On June 29, when Shafter transferred his headquarters to Sevilla, the problem of his supplies was far from a solution, and most of his reinforcements had not yet arrived. He had concluded that he could wait no longer for either. His delay had already robbed his movement of the advantage of surprise, but this knowledge did not worry Shafter. He had other urgent reasons for his bulldog determination "to do it quick." Heavy showers of rain presaged the downpours of the summer, and the difficulties of his communications might soon become insuperable. He had been in tropical country before, and knew that his men would get sick if they stayed there. As he rode to join his army, a fat old man exhausted by his labors in the heat, Shafter himself felt the first tremors of fever. Two of his cavalry commanders, Wheeler and Young, had fallen seriously ill, and malaria was beginning to spread through the dogtents around Sevilla and in the scattered clearings along the road to Santiago.

The city of Santiago, fronting the landlocked harbor on the west, was guarded on the east by a chain of high, barren ridges, crowned by a complicated system of earthworks and protected by barbed-wire entanglements. The road from Sevilla wound through the jungle of an intervening valley, flanked on the north by the isolated spur of El Caney, and debouched on open ground to pass between the outer defenses, about a mile from the city itself. This was nearly the sum of the information in Shafter's possession when he went to the front. Wheeler had been ordered to make a reconnaissance, and engineers had scouted the thickets in an attempt to provide topographical maps; but neither his own officers nor General García had been able to give Shafter accurate reports of the strength of the Spaniards' positions and the distribution of their forces. The Americans offered optimistic conjectures, rather than facts. The Cubans, on the other hand, overestimated the enemy concentration at Santiago. Shafter was persuaded that there was a garrison of 12,000 men—about half the Spanish forces in the province—and that they were mainly posted at San Juan Hill, as the outer ridges were collectively known, though the name was properly applied to the highest elevation, on the left of the road, with a large blockhouse on the summit. To penetrate these defenses—to "get the enemy in my front and the city at my back," as Shafter had written Sampson—was the primary object of the attack. If the American charge swept past San Juan Hill, Shafter felt sure that he could soon make the Spaniards surrender, or drive them toward the guns of the American fleet. The reduction of El Caney was considered essential to the protection of the advance. Lawton and his brigade commander, Adna R. Chaffee, after reconnoitering this point and finding Spanish troops there, had hastened back to Siboney to urge its capture as an incident of the principal assault.

On the day after his arrival at the front, Shafter's decisions crystallized with their usual rapidity in a brain cloudy with fever. After riding dizzily out for a glance at the terrain, he called in his divisional commanders, and announced his plans for taking Santiago the next morning. The attack was to begin at daybreak with the seizure of El Caney, to which Lawton's division was assigned with the support of an independent brigade of regulars, some 7,000 in all. As soon as the sound of guns showed that Lawton was well engaged, the remaining 8,000 troops were to move down the road to San Juan Hill, with the cavalry in the lead. Guided by an observation balloon as they passed through the woods, they were to emerge and deploy, the cavalry on the right and Kent's infantry on the left. The gap on the north was to be filled by Lawton's force, coming speedily down the road from Caney to join in the general action. Most of the Cubans were also stationed on this side, to prevent the arrival of Spanish reinforcements from the northern posts; and a regiment of Michigan volunteers at Siboney was directed to detain the Spaniards on the south by an attack on the railroad bridge at the bay of Aguadores, east of the harbor entrance.

The only naval participation that Shafter invited was the shelling of Aguadores, and such demonstration as Admiral Sampson thought proper at the mouth of the harbor. He did not avail himself of the fine force of marines at Guantánamo; and, though San Juan Hill was within range of the guns of the battleships, he did not inform Sampson of the location of the Spanish works. Shafter had a poor opinion of naval bombardments—and an aversion to sharing the glory of his campaign with the rival branch of the service—and he had, besides, small interest in a cannonade of any sort. The army had four light field batteries, with black powder. Shafter always maintained that more would have been useless. One was sent with Lawton to El Caney. A second, mounted on the hill at El Pozo in front of Sevilla, was ordered to batter San Juan in preparation for the main assault. The two others were held in reserve.

Shafter was so sure of bulldozing his way into Santiago that he did not hesitate to throw his infantry, with weak artillery support, against entrenched positions. His explanations—that he knew the Spaniards did not have many heavy guns in Cuba, and that they would have been harmless against stone blockhouses and troops "in little narrow trenches with dirt thrown up in front"—were later rationalizations of the contempt for Spanish resistance with which Shafter was imbued on the day before the battle. His orders were enthusiastically received by Kent, Lawton, and General S. S. Sumner, a staunch old cavalry officer who was temporarily replacing Wheeler. In elated certainty of an easy victory, these three professional soldiers and Union army veterans did not question the most glaring defect in Shafter's plans—the dividing of his forces at the outset of a major engagement. Lawton exuberantly promised to take El Caney in two hours, though his extra brigade had been left at Siboney and could probably not join him until later in the morning.

General Chaffee, as keen as Lawton for the seizure of El Caney, had seen one serious objection to a hasty frontal assault on Santiago. Besides the road, there was only one small trail that led through the jungle forest to the open country before San Juan Hill. It was impossible for the troops to come out at two points, well known to the Spaniards and enfiladed by their rifle pits, without heavy losses. Chaffee had the idea of clearing a trail parallel with the verge of the wood, and cutting many small paths leading from it to the front, so that the whole army could march out at the same time. This movement, however, was not Chaffee's concern. If Shafter heard of his suggestion, he disregarded or forgot it. The directions to advance by the road ignored the existence of the one trail that was already there. Beyond orders to deploy the troops as they emerged, Shafter gave no instructions to his divisional commanders and accorded them no discretionary powers. Though he was funneling 8,000 men through a narrow track, bordered by high, impenetrable brush and traversed by a winding stream, he did not anticipate that his communications might be interrupted. He intended to direct the attack and deal with possible emergencies from his headquarters in the rear.

Shafter never claimed to have devised a brilliant campaign. He frankly admitted "there was no strategy about it." His business was "to do it quick." The troops were immediately placed in motion on the road. Lawton's division branched off on a trail to El Caney and bivouacked in the brush. Until long after midnight, the rest of the army went slipping and sliding over the moonlit jungle track to Santiago.

Morning found the main advance in confusion. While Lawton's guns reverberated from the north, the cavalry turned up behind the infantry, and much time was lost while the troopers jostled forward to their assigned position in the lead. The road soon became a tightly wedged mass of sweating, shoving soldiers. Regiments, pushing ahead at intervals in single file, lost contact with their officers and intermingled in disorder. In the middle of the congested line, four men towed the observation balloon, which floated glossily above the treetops and directed the Spanish fire on the helpless column. Under a hail of shrapnel and Mauser bullets, the movement came to a complete standstill, while General Sumner awaited orders from Shafter. He was at last verbally instructed to go to the last ford of the stream, at the edge of the woods. This proved to be a "bloody angle" for the advance guard of cavalrymen, exposed for a full hour to fire they were forbidden to return. The balloon was finally shot down, having made, as the only contribution of air reconnaissance, a report of the trail which Chaffee had mentioned some days earlier. It was news to General Kent, who thankfully hurried one of his brigades, old General H. S. Hawkins commanding, to a lower ford of the stream. The leading battalion of the Seventy-first New York, the only militia regiment present, was taking heavy punishment. Badly officered, the volunteers of this battalion broke and recoiled in panic. The rest of the brigade got forward by forcing them into the thickets and stepping across their legs.

Shortly after noon, two small bodies of troops had crossed the stream and deployed in their assigned positions, the cavalry on the right and the infantry on the left. Taking such scanty cover as the country afforded, they were at last permitted to return the enemy's fire; but, trapped between the rifle pits and the jungle, their predicament was desperate. Messages, begging for orders, were sent to headquarters. No answer came through the blocked road. At Sumner's instance, one of Shafter's aides authorized an attack. Two regiments of regular troopers, one of them a Negro outfit, and the Rough Riders charged and took the hill on the right, closely followed by parts of three other cavalry regiments, black and white. Some of these latter organizations had become mixed with the infantry brigade—two regular regiments and part of the New York volunteers—which Hawkins had simultaneously led up the more formidable height on the left. A battery of Gatling guns had managed to get through, and arrived in time to give valuable assistance. The ascent was temporarily arrested by the shells of the El Pozo battery, which had chosen this inopportune time to reopen on the American objective. Then the troops went steadily up until, with a last roaring volley, the Spaniards fled the blockhouse, and the Stars and Stripes and the regimental colors were planted on San Juan Hill.

There had been no massed attack; only thin lines of men in blue and a few in dusty brown, plunging across a meadow under the crackling rifle pits, trying to tear barbed wire with their hands or saw it with their bayonets. Many of them quietly sank in the slippery, waist-high grass, or stumbled to pitch forward in its depths. The others waded on to gain and climb the steep, sunny slopes. Officers and men had shown a personal courage beyond the demands of organized military action; and the Rough Riders, as well as the professional soldiers, could mark a record of unflinching discipline and a tale of dead and wounded. Colonel Wood, elevated by Young's illness to brigade command, had not been with his regiment. Theodore Roosevelt had led the troops in dusty brown. The victory of

San Juan Hill was the work of the United States regulars, valiant, expert, and uncelebrated. There was the stuff of which American heroes are made in the bespectacled volunteer officer, charging the Spanish earthworks at a gallop, with a blue polka-dotted handkerchief floating like a guidon from his sombrero.

At his headquarters in the rear, Shafter heard the crescendo of the Santiago guns, and the roar that persistently sounded from El Caney. The independent brigade had arrived from Siboney and gone to support Lawton. Shafter had no other reserves; and, in anxiety to consolidate his forces, he sent word to Lawton not to "bother with little blockhouses." But Lawton, in the midst of attack when the message was delivered, was unable to comply. The battle was still thundering on the north when the Americans charged San Juan Hill. Shafter had ridden to El Pozo for a general view of the field. "I stood on the hill, or sat on my horse on the hill," he later testified, "and about 2 o'clock I was fearful I had made a terrible mistake in engaging my whole army at 6 miles intervals." As reports trickled in from the Santiago front, Shafter knew the full extent of his error. The spate of the American attack, with all its bravery and sacrifice, had subsided on the outer ridges. The Spaniards had retired to their second line of defense, with the guns of Cervera's squadron at their backs. They might already have received large reinforcements. The Cubans had proved to be a weak reliance. The road to the north had lain open all day.

Though only three brigades had been in action at San Juan Hill, Shafter did not think of pressing on the troops that had not been engaged. In dread of a counterattack, he was wholly preoccupied by the necessity of strengthening the position he had gained. He kept the three worn-out brigades up all night, enlarging rifle pits and digging fresh entrenchments, and made still more punishing demands on Lawton's division. El Caney did not fall until late afternoon. When, exhausted and unfed, the men staggered back to El Pozo, they were at once ordered forward on the broken and mired road to close the gap on the north of the American lines. The night also brought the first jolting wagonloads of wounded from El Caney and the bloody angle of the stream at the verge of the wood. Shafter did not yet realize the severity of his losses—more than 10 per cent of the effective American force—but even a lesser estimate appalled him. One day's fighting had used up all his aggressiveness. He had broken his eggs and spoiled his omelet; and, sick in mind and body, he shrank from exposing his army to further combat.

Torrential rains set in on July 2, drenching the men who crouched in the thin arc of trenches under intermittent fire. A sense of imminent disaster oppressed their officers, discouraged by the shortage of food and ammunition, the need of artillery and reinforcements, the absence of leadership. Shafter did not visit the front that day. In the depths of despondency, he was calling on the Navy for rescue. Lying on a farmhouse door, he conferred with his generals at El Pozo in the evening. The counsel of retreat did not prevail, but the word was mentioned.

Since the news of Las Guásimas, the American public had shown signs of an adverse reaction to the Cuban invasion. The costly and meaningless little engagement seemed to imply careless handling of the troops, and some correspondents stated that they had fallen into an ambush. Shafter's reports from shipboard had been meager and belated. The perturbed authorities had been forced to depend on the press for most of their information. They had reason, however, to expect that there would be no more delays in future. The Army Signal Corps had repaired and put in operation the damaged French cable at Guantánamo Bay. It was extended to Siboney only a few hours after Shafter reached the front, and telegraph and telephone wires were quickly strung along the road to Sevilla. The Washington bureau chief, General A. W. Greely, had furnished the expedition with complete telegraphic equipment for the field. This had all been left behind at Tampa; but, with a foresight unmatched in the other supply services, Greely had provided replacements, and telephone apparatus as well. Had Shafter allowed his efficient Signal Corps a little time, his headquarters would have been in close contact with the forces in action at Caney and San Juan Hill. As it was, on the day of the battle he was in direct telegraphic communication with Washington.

On the morning of Friday, July 1, the correspondents were galvanized by the War Department's bulletin that the American forces were engaged. The hours swung slowly past without further word from Shafter. "He's fighting, not writing," Adjutant General Corbin told the newspapermen. But by evening official Washington was gravely disturbed. It was nearly midnight when the suspense was broken by Shafter's report that his troops, with heavy losses, had carried El Caney and the outer works of Santiago. A little later, another brief telegram conveyed Shafter's fears that he had underestimated his casualties, and asked that a large hospital ship be sent at once. Both of these dispatches were given out verbatim in the belief that a full disclosure of the facts would stiffen the country's morale.

The government had still received no details of the battle, and could form little conception of the army's situation. It was assumed that the attack would be renewed, and the tension became painful as July 2 passed without a message from the front. Late at night, the President sat waiting beside the telegraph with Alger and Wilson. The Morse code pattered out only an alarming rumor that Cervera had been ordered to shell Santiago as soon as the Americans were in possession of the city. At one o'clock a telegram went from the White House, asking for news to relieve the intense anxiety. Three hours later, the President retired without an answer.

Shortly before noon on Sunday, July 3, Shafter broke his silence with a dispatch that eclipsed in calamity the worst apprehensions of Washington. It was impossible, he said, to carry Santiago by storm with his present force. He was seriously considering withdrawing about five miles to a new position, where he could get his supplies by railroad. He spoke dejectedly of his losses, of the illness of Wheeler and Young. Shafter himself was sick, but—he added—he was retaining command.

In calculating the great difficulties of the Santiago campaign, the government had not dreamed that the army of invasion would be unable to reduce a remote provincial capital, tightly blockaded, in desperate straits for food, and at the mercy of the guns of the American fleet. The President had recently proclaimed the extension of the blockade to the entire southern coast of Cuba, and the closure of the port of San Juan in Porto Rico. The Navy Department had been impatiently awaiting the release of warships for this duty and for the still more important expedition to reinforce Dewey. The only hopeful note in Shafter's dispatch was that Sampson was coming to see him that very morning. It gave no satisfaction to the Navy Department to learn that Shafter was urging Sampson to try to force the entrance of the harbor.

Shafter's withdrawal from Santiago would jeopardize in every quarter the plans for ending the war. It would mean a humiliating disclosure of military weakness, a stark admission of military failure. A little group of officials sat with heavy hearts in the Sunday quiet of the Cabinet Room, where the sun burned through the awnings with a muted glare. Their efforts had culminated in placing the elite of the American Army in an untenable position, under an incapacitated commander. Washington could not take the responsibility of ordering the possible sacrifice of the troops. The decision was left to Shafter. An attempt was made to encourage him with offers of whatever reinforcements he wanted, and Alger ventured to suggest that holding on would have a much better effect on the country than falling back. In publishing Shafter's dispatch, the War Department deleted the contemplation of retreat.

Shafter had one more crushing disappointment to inflict on the authorities. Early evening brought his report that Cervera's ships had run out of the harbor and made good their escape. This rather more expansive message betrayed Shafter's relief at the removal of the Spanish guns from the vicinity of his force. He had attached no importance to the noise of heavy firing off the coast that morning, and his alacrity in transmitting a rumor of the Navy's failure added an unnecessary weight to the depression at Washington. The President was slow to believe an unofficial report, sent from Guantánamo by the chief signal officer of the army, that the Spanish squadron had been destroyed. The Cabinet members assembled at the White House with the Vice-President, Miles, Corbin, Senator Hanna, and a few others. Secretary Long, loyally certain of Sampson and the fleet, urged the President to credit the good news. A second telegram from Guantánamo soon confirmed the fact that the Sunday of July 3 had witnessed an American victory in Santiago Bay.

Shafter had eventually heard of the naval battle, and was sufficiently infected by enthusiasm to pitch in a cheering item of his own—that, in spite of his dejection in the morning, he had sent a demand for the surrender of Santiago. The authorities hastened to acquaint the country with the sudden happy reversal of fortune. Shortly after midnight, Charles H. Allen of Massachusetts, who had succeeded Roosevelt as Long's Assistant Secretary, posted the communications of the Army Signal Corps on the Navy Department bulletin board. In the small hours of that most glorious Fourth, the terse statement came from Shafter, "I shall hold my present position." Secretary Alger walked home in high gratification through streets raucous with the newsboys' shouts of the destruction of the Spanish fleet.

It had been a proud day for the American squadrons at Santiago; the day of heroic action for which they had looked for more than a month in the dazzle of sunshine and the pale glare of searchlights; the day for which their Admiral had prepared them by constant sighting, target practice, and bombardment. But, for Sampson, it was a day of impotent frustration and agonizing personal disappointment. For the Admiral was not with his fleet at the battle of Santiago Bay. He had gone to see General Shafter.

On the preceding afternoon, columns of smoke inside the harbor entrance had given rise to excited conjectures on Schley's flagship, the *Brooklyn*. The sight had caused little concern on board the other American vessels. It had long since been established that the *Merrimac* did not block the channel; but hope had been generally abandoned that Cervera, after his long refusal of the issue, would ever hazard his squadron against the superior American force. Though the *Massachusetts* had gone to Guantánamo to coal, the Admiral did not hesitate to remove his flagship from the blockade on Sunday morning. As he put on leggings and spurs for the ride from Siboney, Sampson's thoughts were bent on the coming interview at which he hoped to persuade Shafter to consent at last to a combined operation with the Navy.

At a little before nine o'clock the *New York* left her station on the extreme east of the line, flying the signal "Disregard movements of commander-in-chief." Five armor-clads were left off Santiago. The *Iowa*, on the central station directly opposite the mouth of the harbor, was flanked on the east by the *Oregon* and then the *Indiana*, while the *Texas* and Schley's flagship, the *Brooklyn*, were correspondingly situated on the west. The semicircle was completed close to shore by the converted gunboats *Gloucester* and *Vixen*. As the ships rolled gently on the long green swell, the quiet, sunny morning seemed to promise nothing more eventful than the usual weekly muster and inspection, followed by church services. On the *Iowa*, Captain Robley Evans lingered over an after-breakfast cigar with his son Franck, a naval cadet on the *Massachusetts*, who had been on picket duty the night before. Captain Francis Cook of the *Brooklyn* found his last laundered white coat, and laid it out on his bunk. A group of gossips—officers and correspondents—stood on deck, looking after the receding *New York*. Commodore Schley came out, and sat down abaft on a hatchway with his glasses.

Just after half-past nine, when the men had fallen in for the muster, the general alarm for action rang all over the *Iowa*, and Franck Evans jumped to his feet, crying, "Papa, the enemy's ships are coming out!" Leaping to the bridge on his game leg, Fighting Bob heard the crash of the *Iowa's* first shot. All along the line, the emergency flags were fluttering up the signal halyards. Sampson's standing orders to close in and engage, should Cervera try to escape, were instantly obeyed on every vessel of the fleet. In the clangor of the electric gongs, the engines began to turn, the powder monkeys tumbled to the ammunition decks, and the gunners dashed cheering to their stations, dropping their clothes as they went. "Get to your guns, lads," Captain Henry Taylor called from the bridge of the *Indiana*; "our chance has come at last." Four cruisers were rapidly moving down the chasm of the channel. They emerged, one by one, between the headlands. Even as shells pounded from the Spanish ships and land batteries, and the guns of the fleet replied, the Americans were stirred by the proud procession of the *Infanta Maria Teresa*, the *Vizcaya*, the *Cristóbal Colón*, and the *Almirante Oquendo*, with golden figureheads gleaming on their black hulls, and scarlet and yellow battleflags swinging from their peaks. The doomed cruisers came out, Captain Jack Philip thought, "as gaily as brides to the altar." The *Texas* had only the Stars and Stripes at her stern. "Where are our battleflags?" yelled a young lieutenant. "What's a battle without battleflags?" In the roar and smoke, he got a locker smashed in, and dressed the rusty old *Texas* for the conflict.

Captain Cook's only clean white coat lay forgotten on his bunk. When he reached the forecastle, he found Commodore Schley already on the conning-tower platform. From the extreme westward position of the *Brooklyn*, the *New York* was out of sight and signal distance with glasses. Schley had not been officially notified of the Admiral's absence, but he was the senior officer present with the fleet. Ready to grasp the miraculous opportunity for command in action, Schley was at first chiefly concerned with the "dangerous proximity" of his flagship to the enemy. As it quickly appeared that Cervera would attempt to avoid the battleships by running between the *Brooklyn* and the shore, Sampson's orders to head in exposed the light American cruiser to the full brunt of the attack. Schley and Cook gave almost simultaneous orders to turn her from the battle line, and the *Brooklyn* described a loop that carried her across the bows of the *Texas*, which backed water to avoid collision and temporarily came to a dead stop. Captain Clark brought the *Oregon* churning westward in a wonderful burst of speed; the *Iowa* came close behind; and, after gaining distance and the support of powerful guns, the *Brooklyn* forged ahead. As the fleet swung into an irregular column that paralleled Cervera's course, the outcome was not long in doubt. First, the flagship *Teresa*, faltering under her splendid flags, turned in flames to the beach. The *Oquendo*, staggered by the broadsides, soon followed, burning fiercely. The *Vizcaya* ran on, hard-pressed by the *Oregon*, with the *Brooklyn* in fast pursuit, until the battleship's shells set her ablaze, and she grounded on the reef at Aserraderos. Meanwhile, two Spanish torpedo-boat destroyers, hammered by the heavy guns as they streaked from the harbor, had been finished off by the armed yacht *Gloucester*, closing through shell and smoke on the dreaded little craft. Her captain was Lieutenant Commander Richard Wainwright, who had been the executive officer of the *Maine*.

An hour and a half after the proud procession had been sighted, only one ship had escaped destruction—the *Cristóbal Colón*, the best and fastest of the Spanish cruisers. Moving inside her consorts, she had been protected by their smoke, and still raced to the westward, close inshore. The tall smokestacks of the *Brooklyn* could be seen flashing ahead to cut her off. The *Oregon* blocked her flight to open sea. From Aserraderos to Santiago Bay, the bugles sounded "Cease firing," and word was passed to the magazines and engine rooms and stokeholds that the day was won. Shouts of triumph split the sudden silence, as grimy forecastles and turrets swarmed with men, naked to the waist, and black with powder and coal dust. Cheers broke out afresh on the *Iowa* when the *New York* came abreast of the battleship, and the figure of Admiral Sampson was distinguished on the bridge.

Hurrying back to the cloud and din of battle, Sampson had throbbed with a wild prayer, "Oh, that we had wings." The *New York* had arrived off the harbor mouth in time to send a few shells after the torpedo boats. She sped on past Aserraderos to join the pursuit of the *Colón*, but she was still some distance away when the Spanish cruiser hauled down her colors, and beached about fifty miles west of Santiago. Congratulatory signals were exchanged by the *Brooklyn* and *Oregon*, and their crews riotously cheered each other, their captains, and Commodore Schley. Captain Cook at last put on his white coat; and, slicking the sweat and sulphur from his hands and face, prepared to board the *Colón*. When Admiral Sampson reached the scene, the captain of the *Brooklyn* had received the surrender of the last of the enemy's ships.

It had been a grand fight for the *Brooklyn* and for the Commodore whose broad pennant she bore. With the Spanish shells chunking overhead like railroad trains, Schley had stood on the conning-tower platform, shouting, "Give them hell, bullies!" to the gunners. The swiftest vessel in the fleet, struck many times by whole shots, the *Brooklyn* was not materially damaged. She had outraced the *Colón*, and Schley was bursting with exultation. As the *New York* drew near, he had signaled, "We have won a great victory. Details will be communicated." The only reply was, "Report your casualties." Again the flags expansively fluttered, "This is a great day for our country." But Sampson's signal halyards did not stir. Beside the scarred and blackened *Brooklyn*, the *New York* appeared a stranger to the work of war. Sampson's spurs and leggings lent a touch of farce to the savage irony of his ill fortune: that on that morning hour, of all the days and hours, he should have been required to dance attendance on the bungling General; that Cervera should have chosen the westward course, carrying the battle ever farther from the American commander in chief, casting its honors to the insubordinate Commodore whose conduct he despised. The *New York* ran in between the *Brooklyn* and the *Colón*. Schley seized a megaphone, and pleaded for the surrender. He was answered by a hollow hail from the far side of the *New York*, ordering Cook to report on board. Cook returned to the *Brooklyn* with his boat emptied of the Spanish officers he had taken prisoner; but there was no prize for either of the flagships. The *Colón's* valves had been opened, and she was sinking.

When Schley went over the side of the *New York* to report, there was no doubt of his pretensions to having held the supreme command in battle, no doubt of their rejection by the Admiral of the fleet. Functioning with mechanical efficiency, Sampson asserted his authority, and made his dispositions—the *Brooklyn* was sent on a wild-goose chase after another rumored Spanish ship—but left it to his flag lieutenant to prepare and sign the official report to Washington. Schley also prepared a report, announcing the victory directly to the Navy Department. His flag lieutenant and Sampson's, each bearing a dispatch, collided at the Siboney telegraph office. Schley's officer was turned away, and the message went in Sampson's name: "The fleet under my command offers the nation as a Fourth of July present the whole of Cervera's fleet."

As the *New York* returned to Santiago Bay, the full moon lighted the wreckage of the sea power of Spain. The silver waters swirled with flotsam of charred timber and woodwork, boxes, trunks, and uniforms. The enemy's ships burned red along the beach, and the *Vizcaya's* last explosion split the night with a great chrysanthemum of flame. The triumph of Santiago had matched Manila Bay, and the American immunity had been nearly as marvelous. No ships had been seriously disabled. The losses were but one killed and one wounded, both on board the *Brooklyn*. The spirit of the captains and of their officers and men had been worthy of the highest traditions of the service, and their valor had been ennobled by compassion for the vanquished. "Don't cheer, boys," Captain Philip had cried, as the *Teresa* struck the shore, "the poor devils are dying." In their reception of the chivalrous Cervera and his officers, the American commanders had rivaled the dons in courtesy. The bluejackets, braving shark-infested waters and blazing ships on errands of rescue, had shown an enterprise beyond the call of duty. The prisoners were clothed and fed, their wounds were dressed, and their dead consigned with prayer to the sea. "So long as the enemy showed his flag, they fought like American seamen," Captain Evans wrote of the crew of the *Iowa;* "but when the flag came down they were as gentle and tender as American women."

Sampson was incapable of pride in the conduct of his command, of rejoicing in the overwhelming success in which his preparations had culminated. His face was blank. He seemed to be stunned. The broken Spanish admiral appeared less stricken by misfortune than the commander in chief of the victorious fleet.

The official report of the victory was delayed in reaching Washington, and trailed the tremendous national celebration of July 4. It was not enthusiastically received on its publication the next day. Sampson's flag lieutenant had paraphrased a famous dispatch that the Union had uproariously acclaimed—Sherman's telegram offering Lincoln the Christmas present of Savannah—but the adaptation to Independence Day impressed most people as far-fetched. The emphasis on "the fleet under my command" and the omission of commendation for Schley or any other officer struck a false note of self-conceit. Its pretentiousness seemed absurdly at variance with the simultaneously published news that Sampson had been out of the fight at every stage. As the correspondents united in lavish praise of Schley's heroic conduct, the public applauded their verdict that he had been in command, and Sampson and his dispatch were assailed with brutal ridicule.

For more than a month, the Admiral and the Commodore remained at Santiago Bay, locked in the tension of their hatred and their conflicting claims. Schley, in the first flush of popular adulation, was perhaps capable of magnanimity. In his report to Sampson and in conversation with the correspondents, he said that the victory had been big enough for all. He expressed embarrassment over his celebrity to the Navy Department, and said that the honor of the victory was due to the commander in chief. At this time, Schley was confident that his reputation was a fixed star. He did not repeat his generous utterances after he discovered that he was mistaken.

In a prolonged, acrimonious contest over the merits of the two commanders, Sampson was supported by the Navy Department and by his fellow officers in general, as opposed to the small clique devoted to Schley. The gallant Commodore had the wider backing of press and public, and also of influential politicians. The Senate opposed the Navy Department's promotions, which recognized Sampson's great services in the war. But Sampson's partisans were not powerless. Stories leaked out of Schley's incompetence and disobedience in finding and blockading the Spanish squadron. New charges were made that, by turning the *Brooklyn* from the battle line, he had nearly lost the day on July 3. His laurels were stained by censure, and even by slander of his personal courage. Published libels at length compelled him to ask for a court of inquiry, which failed to clear his reputation. Yet Schley retained to the end the loyalty of a large following, and defiantly brandished the honors of Santiago as an answer to his critics. Sampson withered away in popular neglect, failing in mind and body, like some protagonist of antique tragedy who succumbs without resistance to the malignity of fate.

Over Manila Bay, Dewey's fame shone with a pure and steady ray. The glory of Santiago was sullied by altercation. Each in his own way, Sampson and Schley had earned the name of hero, but they found a tarnished renown in the victory that was lustrous enough for all.

· 11 ·

THE PRICE OF DELAY

THE annihilation of the second Spanish squadron induced foreign skeptics to revise their opinion of the United States Navy. To the fleets of the civilized world, Santiago Bay was a lesson and a warning. European experts, impressed by the marksmanship of the American gunners and astounded by the performance of a pleasure yacht, stressed the prime importance of target practice and questioned their previous emphasis on the value of torpedo boats. European capitals, mindful of a recent announcement that a squadron of this redoubtable Navy would harry the coast of Spain, hummed with rumors of intervention. European journals broke out in effusive congratulations to the victor. Since April, foreign comment on the war had been front-page news in the United States. The American people had been informed with substantial accuracy of the international situation. England was the friend whose policy stood like a bulwark against Continental animosity to the ambitions of the American republic. Germany was the arch-enemy, more hostile even than France; jealously resentful of the extension of American influence in the Caribbean; and so avid in imperial designs on the islands of the Pacific that Berlin was secretly intriguing to secure a share of the Philippines, and openly implementing this interest by the presence of five men-of-war, a fleet stronger than Dewey's, in Manila Bay. As the German press joined the chorus of praise of Santiago, Americans recognized a rush to get on the band wagon, and preened themselves on the unaccustomed compliment of the deference due to power.

The naval victory foretold an early end of the war. Aggression on every front bade fair to speed the submission of Spain. The first Philippine expedition had reached Manila under convoy of the cruiser *Charleston*, flourishing the trophy of the unresisted seizure of Guam. Commodore John C. Watson, detached from the Havana blockade to head the new Eastern Squadron, had arrived off Santiago to organize the transatlantic expedition. But, under the tumult and vaunting of July 4, there had been a sigh of profound relief. The liberation of the soldiers in Cuba was a poignant element in the rejoicing of a people stunned by the losses of Shafter's command and the inconclusive outcome of his attack. The crowning glory of the naval triumph was the deliverance of the army.

There was no military reason for detaining troops for another day at Santiago. The fall of the city was hourly expected. The news was already overdue on July 7, when the morning papers published the President's proclamation of thanksgiving for the military and naval victories. McKinley called on the nation to offer thanks to Almighty God, who had brought nearer the attainment of a just and honorable peace, but the organ tones of his phrases were exalted, not exultant; and he solemnly invoked the country to prayers that "our gallant sons" might be shielded from harm in battle and "the scourge of suffering and disease." Although the President had waited for three days to make the proclamation, the mention of military victory was still premature.

The authorities were as impatient as the public for the final assault on Santiago. They had felt constrained to approve Shafter's delay until noon on July 5, on the grounds of the precarious situation of his troops and humane consideration for the noncombatants who were thronging out of the city. The threatened bombardment had not taken place at the appointed time. As the Spanish commander General José Toral repeatedly refused surrender, Shafter showed a considerable ingenuity in devising reasons for further negotiation: the return of a number of wounded Spanish prisoners, arrangements for the exchange of Hobson and his crew, the desire of General Toral to communicate with Madrid, and even Shafter's own reluctance to cause property damage in Santiago. The siege lasted for two weeks after the naval battle, and the national thanksgiving soured in the anti-climax of the army's inactivity.

Shafter did not doubt his ability to reduce Santiago. He was deterred by his dread of casualties. He had been unable to handle those he had already incurred. Arrangements for the care of the wounded were not, in Shafter's opinion, the province of the commander in the field. He had left everything to his small Medical Corps; but, by giving priority to quartermaster's and commissary stores, he had deprived the surgeons of most of their supplies. The single field hospital that had been set up in preparation for the battle consisted of a few tents, with a few blankets, and no cots, mattresses, or clothing. Only three ambulances had been landed out of the seventeen sent after the army from Tampa. Most of the wounded had made the journey to the coast in the jolting army wagons. Some were borne in rude litters by their comrades, and some staggered down on foot. Sampson, on Shafter's appeal, had sent Navy surgeons to relieve the emergency at Siboney. The base hospital afforded little comfort but shelter, and even this was insufficient for the eight hundred suffering men who had reached it by July 4. Old Miss Clara Barton of the American National Red Cross, arriving with a party of workers, found many wounded lying on the water-soaked ground around the wooden sheds. Evacuation to hospitals in the United States began that same day. With the aid of Red Cross litter bearers and the Navy's boats and personnel, several hundred casualties were placed on board transports. Miss Barton's supplies partially relieved the destitution of the amputees and other critically injured men who could not be moved at once.

The cost of military action had been high, but delay, too, had its price. While the white flags of truce paraded between the lines, the besieging troops lay soaking in flooded trenches and dog tents, without camp equipage or cooking utensils, or sufficient food to sustain them. Over a swampy channel of road, blocked with mired wagons, Shafter was attempting to bring up food for many thousands of Cubans—not only the insurgent force but also the hordes of Santiago refugees who had fled to El Caney. Only a day's march from plentiful commissary stores, the American troops were subsisting on a scanty ration of canned beef or bacon, hard bread, and coffee. Malaria and dysentery were prevalent in every regiment. Worse symptoms soon appeared among the teamsters and other laborers who were quartered in the shanties near the beach. Malignant disease did not begin to break out at the front until some days later. The surgeons noticed that it followed the course of the refugees, as they gradually flowed into the American lines and spilled down to the commissary dumps at Siboney. Shafter was deeply touched by the plight of these unhappy people, and permitted them to mingle freely with the soldiers. Sanitary conditions were appalling at the front and at the base; and the overworked surgeons, continually handicapped by a shortage of quinine and other medicines, were helpless to enforce preventive measures. The best they could do was to isolate the cases of virulent infection that developed among the Americans. A separate hospital building was set aside for them, and some of the heroic Negro troopers were sent back from San Juan Hill to serve as their attendants.

Shafter had ceased to reckon the cost of delay. His bout of malaria left him weakened and depressed, and he became so badly crippled by "a beastly attack" of gout that he could not climb his horse and had to mount from a specially constructed platform. He managed to ride about, with his painful foot dangling in a gunny sack, but he did not undertake tours of inspection, either at the front or the base. While every day the danger grew from the other enemy, fever, Shafter was absorbed by worry about the Spanish garrison. He was informed that, through the negligence of the Cubans, Santiago had received large reinforcements, and advised Washington that his force should be doubled before making another attack. For more than a week after the battle, Shafter brushed aside reports of broken communications and increasing sickness. He never recaptured the will to "do it quick." Preferring the losses of inaction to the losses of advance, he grasped at any excuse to prolong the negotiations for surrender.

The gloomy dispatches from the front had soon led the President to doubt the much-commended aggressiveness of the commander of the Fifth Army Corps. On July 4, McKinley called in Alger and Corbin to discuss the possible necessity of relieving Shafter on the score of ill health. As a result, the War Department was obliged to telegraph Shafter that if his health did not improve and Wheeler was also disabled, he was to order his second ranking general to succeed him. At a full-dress council held the same day, Miles was directed to go at once to Santiago. Miles was present, ready and eager to set out, and full of plans for landing on the west side of the harbor entrance, as Sampson had recommended. He had made small progress in organizing the Porto Rican expedition, on which his orders had previously been contingent. His advance force would consist of only 3,500 militia, but more volunteers would be sent after him, and on the fall of Santiago he would get the regulars for Porto Rico. Miles hurried in obvious elation from the White House to make his preparations.

As the jealous guardian of Shafter's interests, Alger had been disturbed by the trend of both these conferences. He was careful to leave the decision entirely to Shafter's own judgment. Shafter had no more intention of giving up his command than of assaulting Santiago. He returned an evasive answer, and Alger did not raise the question again. It was not so easy to dispose of the intrusion of the Major General Commanding, with his vigorous plans and his reputation for military skill. The press, to Alger's chagrin, was reacting badly to the Cuban campaign. The news stories contained allusions to Shafter's illness and the handicap of his "flesh." Some editorials broadly hinted at a military blunder. To cap the climax, Miles's departure for Cuba was acclaimed with universal satisfaction. It was taken for granted that he would assume command of the army, and shortly end the deadlock at Santiago.

Alger said that Miles, of his own accord, declared that he did not intend to replace Shafter. This was undoubtedly true. Miles made similar statements to newspapermen. It was too late to seek military honors at Santiago. Miles, moreover, seems to have felt a genuine sympathy for Shafter. In telegraphing notice of his impending arrival, he heartily congratulated Shafter on his campaign and expressed appreciation of its difficulties. Alger would have been well advised to take Miles at his word, but he could not resist forestalling the possibility of mishap. He stretched the truth in informing Shafter that Miles had "instructions" not to supersede him "in any manner" in command in the field, as long as Shafter was "able for duty." The War Department released this information to the press after Miles reached Cuba.

The guaranty of Alger's favoritism contained a strong hint that the time had come for Shafter to get better. "I am quite well," he reported on the day of Miles's arrival.

Meanwhile, the fight between the services had entered on a critical phase. Shafter's hopes of reducing Santiago without further bloodshed were obstinately centered on the battleships. In reply to petulant demands for help on July 2, Sampson had written a letter reiterating the objections to entering the harbor, but reluctantly agreeing that, if Shafter insisted, he would bring countermining outfits from Guantánamo and attempt to clear the channel. Shafter ignored this concession. On the day after the naval battle, he referred the matter to Washington; and, though an armistice was in operation, urged that "at any cost" Sampson must at once force an entrance with his whole fleet. Alger in strict confidence replied that one thing was certain, the Navy must get into the harbor and save the lives of our brave men. He added an imaginative suggestion that Shafter might, in effect, show up the rival service by sending in one of the chartered steamers, manned by army officers, to open the way for the armor-clads.

The President, on Alger's indignant remonstrance that the Navy was hanging back, once more directed that Shafter and Sampson should confer. It was a futile order. The two commanders, incompatible from the first, had become irrevocably sundered by their respective calamities. Sampson was still punctilious in offering co-operation, but he did not undertake a second trip to Sevilla. He was indisposed, and Captain Chadwick went in his stead. Chadwick, though well aware that Shafter was turning to the Navy "simply in an opportunist attitude of mind," was a diplomatic emissary. Sitting beside Shafter's cot, which had been placed in a grove of trees outside his tent, Chadwick won a grudging assent to a naval bombardment of Santiago, and finally obtained a map of the environs of the city, indicating the American positions; but this was the only progress that Chadwick was able to make. He explained that the sortie and destruction of Cervera's squadron did not reduce the danger of the electrical mines in the channel. He set forth Sampson's compromise proposal that, in preparation for removing the mines, the marines should capture the works on the west of the harbor mouth, while the army carried the works on the east. Shafter, as usual, did not discuss, or try to refute, or even appear to have heard the Navy's views. His grievance was inalterable. Chadwick, at length, halfheartedly conceded that some of the smaller ships might try to take up the mines, but the conference failed to improve an understanding between the services.

A naval bombardment of the city took place a few days later, not on Shafter's initiative, but on directions from Washington to resume hostilities. On the late afternoon of July 10 and the early morning of July 11, the fleet threw its big shells into Santiago, inflicting much property damage before receiving notice from Shafter of another truce. Firing from the Spanish lines had been returned by the American troops; but, as Shafter was unwilling to sacrifice any lives, they had not moved from their trenches. Minimizing the effectiveness of the bombardment, Shafter protested to Washington that the Navy still omitted to comply with his wishes, and again insisted—in disregard of the truce—that an effort to enter the harbor should be made at once.

The Navy Department stood squarely behind Sampson and had taken the onus of responsibility by explicitly instructing him not to risk his fighting ships. Two of the battleships had at this time been detached from the fleet. The *Oregon* and the *Massachusetts* were at Guantánamo under command of Commodore Watson, who was coaling his expedition for the voyage to the Philippines. It was soon known that the Madrid government, in fear of American raids on the Spanish coast, had recalled the reserve squadron, but the Navy Department continued to urge on Sampson the necessity of relieving Dewey. Current news reports of the hostile attitude of the German cruisers at Manila Bay were disquieting Washington. The naval strategists advised that, at the cost of stripping the Cuban blockade, the whole might of the American Navy should be displayed in European waters. As a result of a long council of war on July 13, Sampson was sent strictly confidential orders to make ready the Eastern Squadron, and himself accompany it into the Mediterranean.

Secretary Alger was intensely displeased by the priority given to the

Pacific theater and the larger aspects of the war. He had worked himself into a wrathful conviction that the army in Cuba was being ignored and victimized by the Navy in general and Admiral Sampson in particular. There was a considerable newspaper backing for Alger's point of view. Information of Shafter's complaints, published in *The New York Herald* on July 6, had provoked an outburst against the unpopular Admiral and even the Navy Department. Alger's nerves were on edge on the morning of July 13. So was the temper of Captain Mahan. When Alger began to abuse Sampson and the fleet, Mahan "sailed into" him, telling him he didn't know anything about the use or purpose of the Navy, and that he, Mahan, did not propose to sit by and hear the Navy attacked. It was "a very pretty scrimmage," Long commented. "It rather pleased the President, who, I think, was glad of the rebuke."

Alger later called on Long to apologize for his outburst. There was bad news of sickness among the troops in Cuba, and Alger seemed so downcast that Long's kind heart was touched. "He is a sanguine, generous man," Long wrote, "but the task—and it is a tremendous one—is too much for him." The personal reconciliation, however, did not alter the official differences between the secretaries, or lessen the ill-feeling at Santiago. Shafter excluded Sampson from the interviews which he held with Toral, and eventually refused Captain Chadwick's demand to sign the articles of capitulation as the Admiral's representative. The climax of the dispute was a petty and unseemly altercation over the possession of the prizes, a gunboat and five merchant ships in Santiago harbor.

The moderator between the Army and Navy had let the departments fight it out on July 13, but McKinley had not been passive in his attitude toward Shafter. The brief resumption of hostilities at Santiago had been compelled by orders from the President. He had been jolted on the night of Saturday, July 9, by a defeatist message from the front. Shafter and all of his generals concurred in recommending acceptance of a demand from Toral that he be permitted to withdraw his force intact. The President's peremptory instructions were to accept nothing but an unconditional surrender. Another telegram went from the White House direct to Shafter: "What you went to Santiago for was the Spanish army. If you allow it to evacuate with its arms you must meet it somewhere else. This is not war."

Yet the consensus of opinion was too ominous to disregard. Some other concession must be offered to Spain. The next evening, McKinley sanctioned a proposal put forward by Alger that the prisoners of war should be sent home at American expense. The negotiations at Santiago were still at a standstill when Miles arrived, presumably to imbue the jaded generals with fresh vigor. In the early hours of Wednesday, July 13, McKinley sent back an emphatic negative to another plea from Shafter on behalf of Spanish honor; but, when, towards dawn, the same plea came from Miles, the President called a meeting of his Cabinet.

Shafter had mentioned the threat of sickness, but Miles's telegram was the first official advice that severe sickness already existed among the troops. The choice lay between the risk of prolonging their ordeal and the certainty of robbing them of their victory. Total surrender was the sole remaining reward for the agony of the Santiago campaign. The newspapers were engaged in despoiling it of any other shreds of success. Details of the battle of July 1, held up by censorship of the telegraph, had begun to pour in by mail, and a number of talkative war correspondents were arriving on the hospital transports. Shafter had antagonized the press by his gruff and overbearing manners. The news stories were unsparing accounts of bungled preparations and botched attack, a ruthless expenditure of men, and a cruel neglect of the wounded. The final odium was added to the campaign by a spate of uncensored telegrams from Santiago, reporting frightful ravages of disease in the Fifth Army Corps.

The American correspondents were justly described as "the natural allies of the war party at Madrid." The dispatches from the front exposed in sensational terms the true weakness of the American position. In the festering trenches before Santiago and the steaming hospital sheds at Siboney, soldiers were burning and shivering with malaria, wasting with typhoid and dysentery; and, bright as a quarantine flag, there flashed the dreaded name of yellow jack.

The War Department had tried to counteract the newspaper scareheads by publishing the facts. The army surgeons had positively identified three cases of yellow fever, all of them at Siboney. The prevalent fever in the trenches was malaria—a serious and debilitating disease in warm climates, but too familiar to American communities to inspire great alarm. Shafter's health reports showed a low death rate and a constant return to duty of large numbers of convalescents; but they lumped all types of "fever" in one count, and the public shrank in horror from the long sick lists. Fears for and of the army mingled in a terrible apprehension of pestilence. The impulse of self-preservation triumphed over compassion. The country shuddered at rumors that the troops might be recalled. It was in an atmosphere of panic and defeat that the Cabinet met in emergency session to consider Miles's dispatch.

An incontinent withdrawal of the army was not under discussion. Plans for its disposition after the surrender were reported and approved. Miles jumped the count of yellow fever from three to one hundred cases, and stated that the surgeons believed the contagion would rapidly spread. In the military view, the significance of this information was its effect on the forthcoming expedition to Porto Rico. A considerable number of convalescents would have to be brought to a rest camp in the United States. Surgeon General Sternberg advised against moving any part of the army to either destination without strict precautions to prevent the contamination of the transports. He explained that contagion could be readily controlled, once normal conditions were restored at the front, by encamping the soldiers above the fever belt. Any regiment that remained free from infection for five days, the maximum period of incubation, could be safely sent away. Shafter was instructed to get his men into the mountains at the earliest possible moment.

On humanitarian as well as military grounds, further delay at Santiago had become intolerable; but, though the condition of the troops saddened the men around the Cabinet table, it did not persuade them to a damaging admission of defeat. The President made a forcible argument that Spain must not be permitted to chaffer for easy terms. His opinion was wholeheartedly sustained. The sense of the meeting was that, though the American generals perhaps had a good reason for evading the orders from Washington, it was probable that the Spanish commander was "tricking them along with truces and offers of terms of surrender." Distrust of Shafter's firmness was the ruling impression. Alger himself was influenced by it. He replied directly to Miles, recognizing his command, in spite of the previous arrangement with Shafter. Miles was instructed to accept total surrender, or to assault—unless in his judgment an assault would fail.

The government did not doubt that these orders would bring definite results, by one course or the other. As the Cabinet sat on Wednesday noon, Miles had already attended a meeting with Toral. The meeting broke up in confidence that the negotiations had at last been concluded on the President's terms.

The first reports, however, were conflicting. It was not until after a second parley on Thursday, July 14, that both Miles and Shafter positively reported the surrender of the city and the whole eastern end of Cuba with it. Each side had appointed commissioners to arrange the terms. "Next is Porto Rico," Alger told the correspondents; "and then, if need be, Havana." But the press was quick to note an absence of enthusiasm at Washington. In contrast with the popular applause for the unexpected gains of territory, the expressions of the government officials were perfunctory.

The President withheld his message of congratulations to Shafter and the army. He was waiting to know if his orders would be carried out to the letter. All day Friday and far into the night, telegrams rained on Shafter's unresponsive headquarters, questioning, admonishing, sternly reiterating the President's ultimatum. "It is not possible," Alger desperately wired, "that you are entertaining the proposition of permitting the Spaniards to carry away their arms." Corbin, as Shafter's friend and comrade, added his personal warning that this concession would not be approved, and had as well be abandoned once for all. "The way to surrender is to surrender," Corbin entreated Shafter. The vigil at the White House and the War Department was broken by a vague response, then by a flat denial of the imputation of Alger's message. The Spaniards were to surrender their arms absolutely, Shafter said, but they begged to have them shipped home with them, and he had agreed to intercede on their behalf. The dogwatch brought melancholy word of a misapprehension—"We may have to fight them yet"—but, in the sunshine of Saturday morning, Washington learned that delays were at an end. Madrid had authorized capitulation, and the formal surrender of Santiago would take place next day.

The American commissioners had made every atonement in their power to the pride of Toral's command. They undertook to recommend to Washington that the Spanish soldier should return home with the arms he had "so bravely defended." They had yielded to Toral's impassioned plea for a token surrender with the honors of war. They had accepted "capitulation" as a word less humiliating than "surrender," and the articles were a tissue of other verbal concessions to the chivalry of Spain. Nevertheless, the United States had unquestionably acquired all the troops and all the arms in the eastern half of Oriente Province. The President hastened to send Shafter and his gallant army the profound thanks of the American people for their brilliant achievement.

On the morning of Sunday, July 17, Shafter got his gouty foot into a stirrup, and rode out between the lines with his staff, his divisional commanders and their staffs, and his only troop of mounted cavalry. Formal submission was made by General Toral and one hundred armed men. Some 8,000 troops deposited their weapons at the Santiago arsenal, and were marched out as prisoners of war. At noon, the American flag was raised over the governor's palace in the presence of Shafter and his officers, an infantry guard of honor, the colonial dignitaries, and the city populace. As the colors ran up the masthead, a military band crashed out the American national anthem, and a salute of twenty-one guns boomed from a battery on the heights. Hoarse cheers drifted faintly down from the trenches. The guard of honor broke into three rousing cheers for Shafter.

Shafter's hour of glory had been marred by Sylvester Scovel of the

New York World. Forced to get down from the palace roof, the correspondent had slapped or nearly slapped Shafter's tired, angry, fat old face. But Shafter was well content as he stood in the sunny plaza in the din of patriotic music and his own acclaim. On his way into the city, he had seen the earthworks and barbed wire of the inner defenses. He was satisfied that he would have sacrificed 5,000 troops in an assault. His negotiations were justified, and they had been rewarded beyond his highest expectations by Toral's voluntary offer to surrender every post under his command. If Shafter's army had swept on to Santiago on July 1, he would have taken less than 8,000 prisoners. As a result of his diplomacy, he had captured nearly 25,000. The reproach of El Caney had been lifted from Shafter's conscience. He thought that, as it turned out, Providence had been on the American side on the day of the battle.

Shafter had his loyal admirers in the army and at home. Their sympathy chimed sweetly through the sneers of the press, the chorus of public censure, the mutters of some officers of the Fifth Army Corps. With a massive personal dignity and an obdurate resistance to criticism, Shafter forbore to answer his traducers. He would not stoop to defend his hard campaign. He was satisfied that it was successful because it had succeeded. In retrospect, he had no regrets and would have altered none of his arrangements.

The only military mistake that Shafter ever admitted was the providential engagement of half his force at El Caney, but he was at pains to disavow the entire credit for the negotiations. An honest old soldier did not care to claim more than his due. He frankly acknowledged that he had acted on orders from the President in requiring total surrender.

The War Department was now expected to evacuate two armies from Cuba, and send replacements for one of them. Transportation for the prisoners was provided in an ingenious, if somewhat irregular manner. Through the British ambassador, negotiations were opened with a Spanish steamship company, and a contract was signed to return the prisoners under their own flag. The government proposed to bring Shafter's force home, and occupy the conquered territory with volunteers especially recruited for their "immunity" to tropical fevers; but, apart from the shortage of shipping, the exchange would be delayed for sanitary reasons. The War Department urged Shafter to expedite the encampment of his troops above the fever belt.

Shafter had pleaded the threat of sickness and the shortage of food as grounds for compromise with Spain; but, once the surrender was concluded, he became engrossed in the responsibility of the prisoners. He took an instant liking to the tractable Spanish soldiers, and was at first chiefly concerned with protecting them from the Cuban insurgents. He replied rather evasively to instructions to move the army. He presently reported that he had placed the cavalry and artillery about three miles from Santiago, but that it was out of the question to move any more troops until the prisoners were embarked—and, he added, until the railroad was repaired. This message made it sufficiently plain that Shafter was not obeying and did not for the moment intend to obey the orders to encamp in the mountains.

The authorities were vexed and disturbed by the postponement. The "fever" lists were daily growing longer, but Shafter did not express any immediate apprehension. He reported that the new cases were mild in type and that the situation was not alarming, even that it was "somewhat improving." The Surgeon General likewise preserved a monumental calm. The sick lists were no worse than he had anticipated. He had sent everything needful, and was positive that, under normal conditions, the army surgeons could cope with the outbreak.

The war correspondents changed their tune, and chimed in with cheerful accounts of the transformation of Santiago, a bright and happy town under American rule. The troops were being placed in salubrious mountain camps. The dirty huts at Siboney had been burnt to the ground, and the area around the hospital was spread with clean white tents. Every precaution was taken to isolate the fever patients, and every attention was given to their care. The newspapers, like Shafter, belittled the severity of the new cases, and predicted that the contagion would soon be under control. The excellent health of the marines in Cuba was cited as evidence that troops need not sicken in the tropics. The orderly and strictly quarantined camp at Guantánamo had not had a single case of yellow fever.

The theme of "normal conditions" lulled the authorities as well as the public. There was no information that they had not been restored, that Shafter's subordinates did not endorse his reassuring reports. On July 25, the date of the "somewhat improving" dispatch, a personal letter was addressed to McKinley by his old friend and political aide, Charles Dick, who had gone to Cuba as lieutenant colonel of the Eighth Ohio. He wrote at the instance of a number of high-ranking officers to acquaint the President with the "appalling situation" that the army was approaching. There was no telling what might result, Dick urged, if the troops were left in Cuba until September, the fateful month for yellow fever. Colonel Hard, writing the same day to inform McKinley of the whereabouts of his nephews, also presumed to offer a suggestion about removing the army before September. He respectfully desired to impress on the President that not one moment's delay should be permitted in transporting the soldiers to some place where they would be exempt from yellow fever; but Hard was unable to confine himself to a formal recommendation. His heart ached for the magnificent army, lying there without the commonest conveniences for caring for the sick. Pity overcame discretion, and Hard bluntly told the President that, barring the matchless courage and patriotism of men and officers, the true story of the Santiago campaign would make the most shameful page in American history.

Shafter's obtuseness had brought his officers nearly to the point of desperation as they watched the rapid physical and mental deterioration of their commands. The troops were still without adequate shelter or the rudimentary conveniences of camp equipage. They were subsisting on scanty rations of fat bacon or canned beef, wormy hardtack, and coffee boiled in tin drinking cups. In their weakness, they had succumbed to a passive and self-pitying despondency, longing for home and resentful of their ostracism and neglect. The American newspapers had filled them with an abject fear of yellow fever. Orders to go to Siboney were dreaded like a death sentence. The crude regimental hospitals were filled with stricken men, tossing helplessly on the ground. Scarcely more able for duty were those who remained on their feet, feeble and apathetic soldiers unfit to march, and exhausted by the effort of pitching camp on fresh ground.

These were the troops that Washington, in total ignorance of the facts, was pressing Shafter to put in motion for a hard journey to the mountains. Dick and Hard, writing in the apprehension of imminent catastrophe, had no means of quickly getting the truth to the President. Their letters were delivered at the White House on August 12, eighteen days after they were sent.

The country had meanwhile performed the usual evolutions of triumph. Santiago had become, in the language of the press, a naval and military base of the utmost importance. An extraordinary interest attached to the President's words when he again spoke, not in the awful tones of his proclamation of thanksgiving, but in measured instructions for the government of the conquered territory. General Shafter was directed to proclaim the kindly intentions of the United States toward all peaceful and law-abiding inhabitants. They were to be protected in their persons and property, and in their private rights and relations. The transfer of authority was to occasion a minimal derangement. Municipal laws were to remain for the present in force. Existing officials and courts, on accepting American supremacy, were to continue to function under military supervision. "Our occupation," the President wrote, "should be as free from severity as possible." Editorials praised the wisdom and justice of this epoch-making document, the first of its kind ever published by an American President—but not, as was believed, the first ever prepared. The instructions, at all but one point, closely followed the as yet unpromulgated orders for the Philippines. They were presently carried out, with the newly promoted brigadier Leonard Wood commanding at Santiago; while, as the outlying posts surrendered and American control was extended, General Lawton was installed as military governor of the district.

The temporary maintenance of the existing Spanish government was the point at which the Santiago instructions differed from those for the Philippines. The omission to place the insurgents in charge was correctly interpreted as an intimation of future representative government in Cuba. A fostering interest in the welfare of the islanders had survived the strains of war, but the Cuban insurgents were nearly exempted from sympathy. The early disillusionment with their assistance had developed into active aversion and distrust. Since the landing of the Fifth Corps, the news dispatches had pictured the rebels as idle and greedy adventurers, willing neither to work nor fight; cadgers on American bounty, wanton in plundering their own land; and, as was presently discovered, ruthless in their reprisals on helpless Spanish prisoners.

The newcomers had been vastly diverted by their first sight of García's army. They snickered derisively at the rabble of dirty, tattered little black and tan guerrillas. General Lawton marked the burnished guns, and praised the transformation of the rebel bands into clean, orderly regiments, once they were furnished with gear and clothing. The doughboys despised the insurgents, and their scorn soon turned to hatred, aggravated by the shortage of supplies. Always insufficiently fed, totally deprived of the tobacco to which they were addicted, the regulars were infuriated to see the Cubans eating American Army rations, tortured by watching them smoke their own inexhaustible stores of cigarettes. But the Spanish army, after the surrender, consumed a far greater quantity of the limited commissary supplies at the front. Shafter said that the friendship between his men and the prisoners was remarkable—he could with difficulty keep them apart. Shortages were not the basis of the antipathy shown by the invaders. In dominant arrogance and prejudice, this was a white man's army, with no use for foreign "niggers."

American insolence challenged another pride: the fierce pride of poverty, of long and bitter endurance, of jealous devotion to the cause of Cuban freedom. For the sake of that cause, García had welcomed the invasion. Shafter gave him the short and surly treatment. It dashed against a dedicated spirit like gravel on a flame. The guerrillas were by-passed in the plans for battle, insulted by the suggestion they should work as common laborers.

They never gave the Americans energetic assistance. The climax came when Shafter ignored García in the negotiations with Toral; and, on their conclusion, issued blunt orders that no armed Cubans would be permitted to enter Santiago. García absented himself from the ceremonies of surrender. His forces, in open and menacing hostility, remained for a week in their encampment, and then sullenly retired into the interior.

The President's plans for Cuba placed the United States in opposition to the political ambitions of the rebel faction. The maintenance of the Spanish officials at Santiago was the ultimate offense; and, after weeks of suspicion and resentment, it seemed the ultimate betrayal. Yet a breach might have been avoided at Santiago, if Shafter had granted García a tithe of the diplomatic consideration he had lavished on Toral. Opposition newspapers protested against the exclusion of the insurgents, and some failure of tact was sensed and regretted by many thoughtful people; but the conduct of the Cubans was generally reprehended. Their hostility to the army enhanced admiration of the President's statesmanship, as the country again gave thanks for his wise refusal to countenance an alliance with the Cuban republic.

In the second half of July, the attention of the press was distracted from the health of the troops in Cuba. The excitement might have subsided altogether, if it had not been kept alight by the parties of convalescents who were returning from the front. The transports on which they traveled were destitute of conveniences. The water supply was scanty, and often foul. The only available food was the coarse Army ration, which sick men could not digest, and usually could not bring themselves to swallow. The scandals came to a climax in the very first days of August, with the exposure of conditions on board the *Seneca* and *Concho*, two antique freighters which landed at New York. The *Seneca*, which carried nearly one hundred invalids, including more than forty badly wounded veterans of San Juan Hill, had caused a storm of complaint because it was so crowded. Many of the sick had been packed into the airless hold, and left there without attendance. Protests redoubled when the disreputable old *Concho* came trailing in, overloaded with starving and neglected malaria cases.

The War Department, on August 1, had been stirred into beginning the evacuation of the army. As Shafter reported that the comparatively healthy cavalry division could be spared, it was decided to risk waiving the incubation period for the first installment. Shafter was ordered to embark part of the troopers, taking great care not to send any who had been infected with fever. On the morning of August 2, Shafter was heard from again.

He telegraphed that he was told an epidemic of yellow fever was liable to occur at any time, and he advised that all the troops be moved as rapidly as possible, while the sickness was of a mild type.

The authorities were thoroughly mystified by Shafter's sudden readiness to send off his troops. He seemed to be giving up all interest in the Spanish prisoners, though their transports had not yet arrived and only one regiment of "immune" replacements had so far reached Santiago. His recommendation seemed unreasonable as well as injudicious. Ships were not available for a large force; and a projected rest camp was in no sense ready to receive the cavalry, much less the whole army. Sternberg, called in consultation by the President, reiterated his previous advice that yellow fever was "impossible" above a certain altitude. Shafter was again ordered to move the army temporarily up to the mountains.

Shafter had not explained that his change of mind had been prompted by a dreadful apprehension. He had just found out that he would never be able to obey the government's orders. The high camp site, contrary to Sternberg's assertions, was unsuitable and sickly. The railroad was still unrepaired, and its capacity was limited. But Shafter had discovered a still more fundamental objection. When he turned his full attention on his command, he was shocked to see that only a lifeless shadow was left of the strapping, spirited army that had come to Cuba. Nourishing food and camp equipage and medicines had begun to be distributed. It was too late to revive these soldiers. It was too late to move them anywhere but home.

On receiving the War Department's orders, Shafter called a meeting of his commanding and medical officers at his headquarters at the governor's palace. There was no dissent from the view that the troops should be sent North. A recommendation in writing was discussed. Since the regular officers hung back, the initiative was taken by the volunteer, Colonel Roosevelt, who had become an acting brigadier of cavalry and a vociferous agitator for moving the army from Cuba. The understanding, according to Roosevelt, was that he should give a statement to the press, but a quiet hint from Leonard Wood persuaded him to embody it in a letter to Shafter. The general officers then agreed to write a joint letter, and the chief surgeons did likewise. Both of these communications endorsed the immediate withdrawal of the entire army, and condemned an encampment in the mountains as impracticable and dangerous; stressed the serious prevalence of malaria, and warned that a yellow-fever epidemic was unavoidable if the troops were detained in Cuba. The advice of the surgeons was emphatically but respectfully expressed. The letter of the commanding officers —composed, Roosevelt said, by Wood—was boldly dictatorial and threatening. Though addressed to Shafter, it was obviously directed against the War Department. "This army must be moved at once or it will perish. Persons responsible for preventing such a move will be responsible for the unnecessary loss of many thousands of lives." All of Shafter's divisional and brigade commanders, nine generals and one colonel, signed the paper. Only General Lawton qualified his assent, criticizing the use of "mandatory language," and ascribing much of the current illness to "homesickness and other depressing influences."

Under this pressure from his officers, Shafter told the War Department the facts. On August 3, Washington was blasted by his report that the American force was "an army of convalescents," which could be preserved only by immediate transportation to the United States. Some men would undoubtedly die on the way, Shafter said, but the loss would be much less than if an attempt were made to move to the interior of Cuba. Should the waiting plan be adopted, Shafter believed that there would be "very few to move." He submitted the two circular letters in substantiation of his statements. They were delayed in transmission to Washington, but Shafter's dispatch was strong enough to horrify the officials into instant orders for evacuation. Yellow-fever cases were excluded from the homeward movement, and Shafter was to detain a small force to make a show of authority, pending the arrival of sufficient "immunes" to guard the prisoners and administer military rule.

Overtures for peace had come from Spain. It was of vital importance to conceal the military weakness of the American occupation. The facts were rigidly suppressed at Washington. At Santiago, however, an Associated Press correspondent had obtained a copy of the "round robin" signed by the general officers. It was published in full, minus Lawton's exceptions, on August 4. Roosevelt's independent letter was also published. It was a long and spirited appeal to save the army; and, by implication, a damning indictment of the War Department. His own cavalry brigade, Roosevelt stated, was "so weakened and shattered as to be ripe for dying like rotten sheep," and he earnestly expressed his desire to avert from these brave men "a doom as fearful as it is unnecessary and undeserved."

The President, reading all this for the first time in the evening newspapers, became, according to Alger, "very much excited and indignant." The release of the round robin was the worst indiscretion of the war. In the midst of the discussions with Spain, it was advertised that the United States force was incapable of holding the only extensive territory it had gained, and that its officers were insubordinately demanding its withdrawal. The unconfirmed protest of one popular colonel of volunteers would have been sufficiently inflaming to the country. The unanimous verdict of Shafter's generals transformed a secret military withdrawal into a passionate public cause. The negotiations for peace were continued in an uproar of calamity-howling unique in the history of nations victorious in war.

· 12 ·

THE SUBMISSION OF SPAIN

The thrill of new conquest had followed hard on the fall of Santiago. While the newspapers jubilated that there would be no respite for Spain, the residue of regulars marched to the pier at Tampa, militia regiments gathered at Charleston, and General John R. Brooke prepared to move a part of the huge encampment at Chickamauga Park. Four days after the formal surrender, General Miles sailed from Guantánamo Bay to capture Porto Rico.

The delay had stretched Miles's patience to the breaking point. His stay in Cuba had been, from first to last, a series of maddening frustrations. To a mind disposed to ideas of persecution, yellow fever might well have seemed a manifestation of the will of Providence to collaborate with the enemies of General Miles.

The General's fear of yellow fever was as arbitrary as all his other emotions. Learning on his arrival of the cases at the Siboney hospital, he had at once rejected the regular force in its entirety, preferring to invade Porto Rico with a few thousand volunteers, as virgin of military experience as of tropical disease. They were not permitted to disembark, but kept well out at sea. Miles would not hear of using transports that had carried Shafter's wounded or convalescents from malaria and dysentery. He shunned, as later developed, any contact with objects that had been exposed to the infected air of Cuba. Paymasters for his command were presently sent to Porto Rico by way of Santiago, and one or two of them fell ill on shipboard. Miles declined to permit his men to receive the money; and not only a different set of paymasters, but entirely different packages of bills had to be forwarded from New York. Nevertheless, Miles's

278

dread of plague had its practical usefulness. On his way to Shafter's head-quarters, he took time to inspect the hospitals and their surroundings, and gave orders to burn the village of Siboney to the ground. By this drastic expedient, Miles cleaned up the American base—a greater sanitary im-provement than any Shafter undertook in all his weeks in Cuba.

Disappointed in his plans for a strong expedition, Miles next met with the affront of an offhand reception at Sevilla. He had told an AP corres-pondent during the ride that he did not intend to interfere with Shafter, explicitly stating that he had not come to take command; but Miles had not expected to abdicate his rank. Shafter, primed by his instructions that Miles was not to supersede him, regarded the Major General Commanding as merely a visitor, "more in an advisory character." Miles behaved with admirable self-control. His reports were uniformly complimentary to Shafter, and he did not assert himself at the conferences with Toral; but, after the second day of hanging around like a supernumerary staff officer, he left the front for good, without waiting for the formal surrender or even a definitive settlement of the terms. While he was at Siboney, he received a message from Shafter, explaining about his instructions from the Secretary of War. Miles reacted violently to this information. He was convinced that he was the victim of a "conspiracy"; and, manically deter-mined to thwart it, he made ready to leave Porto Rico, serving notice on the War Department and Admiral Sampson that he must go at once.

Washington was dismayed by this rash proposal. The regulars had been pronounced *hors de combat*. An army had to be organized for Porto Rico, and transports must be assembled to carry it. Miles was exhorted to return home, or to establish a base in eastern Cuba as a safe rendezvous for his reinforcements, but he was deaf to advice and warnings. He was determined to set forth with the few thousand militia and some artillery still on shipboard in Santiago Bay, and rendezvous and organize at his objective. This was specifically Point Fajardo, on the northeast end of Porto Rico, forty miles from San Juan, the capital and only fortress of the island. Since his force was inconsiderable, Miles was counting on large assistance from the Navy; and, in pursuance of his decision to get a power-ful convoy, he repaired to Guantánamo Bay, where the squadrons were preparing for the expedition to the Philippines.

Sampson was under urgent orders to cross the Atlantic with all the armor-clads of the fleet. Miles was already in possession of two of the Navy's armed auxiliary cruisers, and refused to move his troops from them. The Admiral did not grasp that Miles was demanding support on a much larger scale. He was dazed by the eruption of protest that resounded from Guantánamo to Washington. It sent Alger flying to the White

House in the novel role of Miles's partisan. It provoked the President to dictate severe instructions that Sampson should co-operate. It momentarily shook Long's firm faith in Sampson, and he forwarded the President's orders with an unjustified rebuke. On July 21, the expedition to the Philippines was suspended. Miles's diminutive fleet of transports departed with a majestic squadron, headed by the battleship *Massachusetts*.

Miles had swept everything before him, with one small exception. He had been assigned a brigade commander, General Guy V. Henry, who had been on Cuban soil; and Henry had requested Colonel Hard to detail as his orderlies two soldiers of the Eighth Ohio, who had also made a short stay in Cuba. Privates McKinley and Barber had received special consideration, after all. Miles did not venture to exclude the President's nephews from the Porto Rican invasion.

A brigade sailed from Charleston. Some artillery and one regiment of regular infantry got off from Tampa. The rest of the reinforcements would be delayed in starting, and Point Fajardo was only forty hours' sail from Guantánamo. The Cabinet noted the speck on a big chart of Porto Rico, and pondered the risks of Miles's headstrong movement. On the evening of July 25, the War Department still had no news for the press. On the morning of July 26, the press had news for the War Department. General Miles had circled around Porto Rico to land at Guánica on the southwest coast, opposite the point to which his reinforcements were bound. "The Secretary of War does not credit it, and yet feels it may be so," Corbin advised General Brooke, who was waiting for ships at Newport News.

"Why did you change?" Alger demanded, via the cable station at St. Thomas in the Danish West Indies. Miles replied that he had "deemed it advisable." "Spaniards surprised," he added. So, and with equal unpleasantness, was the War Department, but Alger was obliged to resign himself. A harmonious little joint operation had flourished at Guánica, and was soon successfully repeated at Ponce, the second largest city of the island, with a splendid harbor. The Spaniards were not in strong force in southern Porto Rico; and, though Miles had not been furnished with the boats promised by the War Department, landings were smoothly effected by means of captured sugar lighters. The transports from Charleston and Tampa were met and redirected, without inconvenience. Miles issued a proclamation that the United States military occupation bore the banner of freedom, and brought protection, prosperity, and liberal institutions to the inhabitants. He reported that they received his troops and saluted the flag "with wild enthusiasm." Alger, in less than a week, was beaming with official approval of Miles.

A railroad and a macadamized highway led from Ponce to San Juan. Miles had obtained accurate information of the character of the terrain; and, while awaiting the increase of his force to some 14,000 officers and men, applied himself to perfecting a plan of campaign, expert in strategy and competent in logistics. Richard Harding Davis, who had left Cuba to accompany the expedition, called the operation "a fête des fleurs" in comparison with "the Santiago nightmare." He thought it unfair that only a handful of correspondents went to Porto Rico, and that the ill-informed people at home rejoiced in Miles's good fortune, without fully appreciating his skill. A still more important reason for the rather casual quality of the public response was the parley about the termination of hostilities. On July 26, the French ambassador, M. Jules Cambon, waited on the President to communicate the first tentative overtures of Spain. While Miles was applauded for the timeliness of his landing, which had given the United States the diplomatic advantage of a foothold in Porto Rico, interest in the campaign drooped with the prospect of peace. The restive Democratic press was quick to seize the advantage, and depreciate a "military picnic," on which the War Department was wasting the public funds.

Nearly 140,000 militiamen grew fearful that the war would end without their seeing action. The War Department was pelted with appeals for service from politically influential officers and the governors of their states. Since the fall of Santiago, the newspapers had directed an intensified scrutiny on the unsanitary home camps. Porto Rico offered a tempting opportunity. By sending all the troops there, Alger could end the unwelcome publicity, and get the credit for a spectacular mass movement of volunteers. He eagerly suggested that every available regiment should be packed off to Ponce. But the President shook his head. "Mr. Secretary," McKinley said, "what do you think the people will say if they believe we unnecessarily and at great expense send these boys out of the country? Is it either necessary or expedient?" Alger's balloon was punctured. "The discussion of the subject," Cortelyou noted, "ended somewhat abruptly."

Spain had been brought to terms by defeat at sea. The military situation was unresolved in both hemispheres. General Miles was nibbling at a corner of Porto Rico. The American forces had not met the main Spanish army in Cuba, and their gains in Oriente Province were strategically insignificant. Encroachment on the territory of the Philippines had been extended from Cavite to a peanut field outside Manila. Guam was a tiny island, remote and unimportant. The empire was not yielding to the accomplished conquest of her colonies, but seeking to forestall a penetration which the destruction of her fleet made it impossible to resist.

The wish for a speedy armistice had been principally impelled by the landing of American troops in the Philippines and the approaching arrival of their commander, General Merritt. To avert the reduction of Manila, the Madrid government was, at long last, ready to relinquish Cuba. Its annexation by the United States was expected and, as a guarantee of protection to the Spanish residents and loyal native population, desired. The President's attitude on the peace terms was unknown. It had been uneasily remarked that he had been more uncompromising than his generals in the negotiations at Santiago; but, in the view of Madrid, Cuba was a liberal indemnification for a professedly disinterested victor, whose territorial gains had been negligible. M. Cambon had hopes of securing leniency for Spain, when he presented himself at the White House.

The President and Judge Day received the French ambassador in the library, and entertained the proposal with which he was charged: an invitation to attempt to reach an agreement on the political status of Cuba. Though Cambon's function was merely that of an intermediary, he expressed his personal hope that the President would feel inclined "to be humanely Christian and generous." He alluded to the fact that the pacification of Cuba had been the original cause of the war, and commented that, with the adjustment of this question, the war would cease to have any reason for existence. Judge Day in his mild way said that, if he understood M. Cambon well, Spain, while limiting herself to an inquiry on Cuba, desired to know on what conditions hostilities might be terminated "in all the points where they now exist." Bowing himself out with polite evasions, Cambon was informed that Spain had lost the first diplomatic round. The reply of the United States would not deal exclusively with Cuba.

The President applied himself to preparing the American note, on which he worked incessantly in conference and private study, until it was put in final form nearly four days later. Informal Cabinet consultations were immediately held at the White House, and continued on an excursion down the Potomac on a lighthouse tender. Attorney General Griggs was recalled from his holiday in the Thousand Islands, and arrived in time for the full Cabinet meeting which was held on Friday, July 29. Judge Day presented a rough draft, prepared with the aid of Assistant Secretary Moore, of the conclusions reached at the preliminary conferences. After two hours' discussion, Griggs took the draft and dictated to Cortelyou a concise summary of its three principal points. On the basis of this analysis, deliberations were resumed in the afternoon. Differences of opinion were at length adjusted at another session on Saturday morning.

The Cabinet unanimously endorsed the President's desire to renounce conquest in Cuba, but to accept full responsibility for directing the formation of a constitutional government. The preamble to the American note set forth the sympathy of the United States with Cuban independence, and its intention to offer aid and guidance in establishing it. The first condition imposed as a prerequisite to peace negotiations was that Spain should relinquish sovereignty over Cuba, and immediately evacuate the island. There was likewise general agreement on the second condition: that, in lieu of money indemnity, the United States must require the cession of Porto Rico and other Spanish islands in the West Indies, and also an island in the Ladrone group in the Pacific. The question of these acquisitions had already been thoroughly canvassed, and their desirability was accepted by all the members of the Cabinet. On the third condition, however, there was a fundamental division. The decision on the Philippines was the principal subject of the prolonged discussions. Neither the right to keep Manila nor the advantage of its permanent possession was disputed by the most conservative of the President's advisers. The point at issue was whether to require the cession of larger territory.

The concept of American control over the destiny of the Philippines had long since lost its first fine clarity of outline. The President's original inclination to leave the islands, apart from Manila, under Spanish dominion had soon been modified. The influential factor was the strength, in numbers and military effectiveness, of the rebel army. Thousands had flocked to Aguinaldo's standard. They had won a series of victories over the Spanish forces in Cavite, and were surrounding Manila. The insurgents, Secretary Day telegraphed Ambassador Hay on June 14, "must have just consideration in any terms of settlement." But there was another and much more troublesome aspect of native assistance in filling the military vacuum on Luzon. They were filling it with such remarkable success that they might refuse to yield obedience to the American army of occupation—might even anticipate its arrival by taking Manila for themselves.

Aguinaldo was reputedly corrupt and unreliable, but Dewey had brought him out and encouraged him, and seemed lost in admiration of his achievements. Consul Wildman at Hong Kong had been instrumental in persuading Aguinaldo to co-operate with the Asiatic Squadron. Consul E. Fletcher Pratt at Singapore, it developed, had also been active in the arrangement. The State Department learned in early June that he had made the first overtures. Pratt enclosed, without comment, a newspaper clipping which gave Aguinaldo's account of the interview, containing a mention of independence for the Philippines. This dubious communication was extremely disquieting to Washington. The authorities had recently been somewhat relieved by Dewey's denial that he had entered into an alliance with the insurgents. It was beginning to appear that Aguinaldo, from the very outset, might have been "induced to form hopes which it might not be practicable to gratify." Secretary Long ordered Dewey to report fully on his conferences and relations with Aguinaldo. Nearly two weeks passed before, on June 27, Dewey was heard from. He gave assurances that his relations with Aguinaldo had been correct, though cordial, and that the United States had not been bound by indiscreet commitments. He also expressed doubts that the natives would be able to capture Manila single-handed, though he believed that Aguinaldo expected to do so. The message did not convey a hint of apprehension about political developments. Dewey seemed, on the contrary, relaxed, approving, even indulgent. He remarked that Aguinaldo had just gone off to a meeting to form a civil government. In conclusion, he expressed the opinion that the Filipinos were far superior in intelligence and more capable of self-government than the Cubans. Having delivered himself of this unusually long dispatch, Dewey dropped the subject, except for the bare statement, received on July 7, that Aguinaldo had proclaimed himself president of a revolutionary republic.

Before this date, General Anderson had reached Manila with 2,500 men. General Francis V. Greene, a New York militia officer, presently landed with some 3,500 more. The third expedition, under command of General Arthur MacArthur and accompanied by General Merritt, would bring the invading army to nearly 11,000, a force sufficiently strong to withstand native interference. Meanwhile, according to Secretary Long, Dewey's assurances "utterly removed the fear" of American involvement in the insurgent cause. The authorities felt a natural reluctance to doubt the judgment of the national hero, and were disposed to believe that his naïve and ambiguous comments concealed, like his long silences, a cryptic sagacity. Dewey had been uncommunicative about his difficulties with the German fleet in Manila Bay. The government had learned from the newspapers that its commander had disregarded the American blockade, and was suspected of intrigues with the native forces on shore. In July, the friction culminated in an incident at Subic Bay, some miles north of the entrance to Manila harbor. When a German cruiser prevented Aguinaldo's troops from seizing an island at Subic, Dewey countered by sending two cruisers to the scene. The Admiral briefly reported that the American ships had taken the island, and the German vessel had retired. Apprehension for the Asiatic Squadron was greatly relieved by this evidence of American mastery, and the government was encouraged in the conviction that the taciturn Admiral was unmatched in resolute action.

Washington had, in fact, no choice but to trust that Dewey had shown an equal firmness in dealing with the insurgents. Fear of their pretensions had not been "utterly removed," and it was acute when the Cabinet met to consider the reply to Spain. A dispatch from General Anderson had conveyed the first unequivocal information that the people of the Philippines expected independence. A danger signal flashed in his concise warning that Aguinaldo had declared a dictatorship and martial law over all the islands. On Saturday, July 30, Washington learned that Merritt had landed five days earlier. The Spanish force might be expected to surrender, and Dewey awakened to the problem of the insurgents. The situation was most critical, he cabled; Aguinaldo had become aggressive and even threatening toward the American army. This news only confirmed the gloomy certainty of the Washington officials that the military occupation of the Philippines must inevitably crash head-on into the ambitious plans of the rebel leaders.

In one respect, Spain's overtures for peace were premature. The American government was not yet prepared to make an informed decision on future policy in the Philippines. This was the perplexing and critical question with which the Cabinet wrestled for nearly four days.

Three members of the Cabinet were in favor of United States possession of the entire group of islands. Griggs and Bliss were moved by commercial considerations, while Wilson was attracted to the expansionist orbit by pious hopes of evangelizing the native population. Three members desired to claim only the port of Manila. This course was earnestly advocated by Day and Long; and, with less positive conviction, by Gage. Alger, absorbed by his grievances about Cuba, was apparently on the fence. The new Postmaster General, Charles Emory Smith, was a Philadelphia newspaper proprietor, whose forte was political management. Like Alger, he did not take a leading part in the argument.

At the early conferences, before Griggs returned, the conservatives had an easy majority. The voice of the Secretary of State was quiet, but influential. The expansionists had vainly labored for his conversion, because of his intimate relations with the President. Even after Senator Lodge and Captain Mahan had worked on him for a whole evening, Day had remained "weak" on the Philippines. His objections were based on principle. As he repeatedly said to the President, the acquisition of an archipelago, with millions of ignorant inhabitants, seemed a very great undertaking for a country whose pride it was to rest its government on the consent of the governed. Day's rough draft of the preliminary conclusions of the Cabinet restricted the American demand to the cession of ground for a naval station. This limitation, however, was not specified in the note as eventually adopted. The third and final clause stated that the United States was entitled to occupy and would hold the city, bay, and harbor of Manila, pending the conclusion of a peace treaty which should determine the control, possession, and government of the Philippines.

At the meetings, the President had played the part at which he excelled —that of presiding. As a succession of drafts was prepared and altered, he had encouraged the fullest expression of opinion, and impartially rallied both sides. He teasingly summed up the recommendations of the State Department. "Judge Day only wants a hitching-post." He chaffed old James Wilson on his territorial acquisitiveness. "Yes, you Scotch favor keeping everything—including the Sabbath." McKinley had acted as a neutral moderator, refraining from influence or persuasion; and yet a certain parliamentary adroitness had not escaped the notice of his friend of long standing, the Secretary of State. "Mr. President, you didn't put my motion for a naval base," Judge Day said at the close of one of the meetings. "No, Judge," McKinley replied, "I was afraid it would be carried."

"The President has had his way as usual, and he is right," Charles Dawes wrote after Gage gave him a digest of the final Saturday conference. Cortelyou, keenly watching the operation of the President's "guiding hand," was less quick to see quite how firmly McKinley had directed his Cabinet. It had been a week of tremendous interest for the recently promoted Assistant Secretary, able to follow every step of the proceedings as he copied the constantly revised note. It was a good example, he remarked to the President, of the development of a state paper under discussion. By way of answer, McKinley drew from his pocket a private memorandum he had scribbled down on hearing the proposal of Spain. The terms were exactly those on which the Cabinet had finally agreed.

Cambon, notified that the American reply was ready, had hastened to the White House. He had received credentials authorizing him to act on behalf of Spain, with full powers to negotiate; and he had also been confidentially informed that Madrid was anxious to conclude an armistice without delay, and greatly reluctant to part with any other territory than Cuba. Appalled by the American demands, Cambon warmly pleaded for easier terms. His interview with McKinley and Day lasted all Saturday afternoon, and was conducted through an interpreter, M. Eugène Thiébaud, the First Secretary of the French embassy.

The rich indemnification of Cuba was still the burden of Cambon's argument. He deplored, as an excessive requirement, the cession of the rest of the Antilles and one of the Ladrones. The President replied that the first two articles of the note did not admit of discussion. Cambon turned to the subject of the Philippines. "They are very hard terms," he said, as he scanned the paragraph. In what particular? the President inquired. It might mean, Cambon pointed out, the acquiring by the United States of all of the islands. That, McKinley said, would be determined by the treaty. Cambon, seeing that the President was resolved not to modify the terms, appealed for a verbal alteration. The word "possession" might have a threatening sound in Spanish. The President entertained this objection; and in the end, though Day was opposed to the concession, consented to replace the offending word by "disposition." While Day was arranging the change in the text, the President conversed informally with the ambassador. He expressed regret that Spain had not asked for peace after the battle of Manila Bay, when the conditions would have been less rigorous; and observed that a refusal of the present American demands would lead to still harsher terms in future. Cambon put in an appeal for a suspension of hostilities. The President agreed to declare an armistice as soon as he was informed of the entire acquiescence of Madrid, and of Cambon's authorization to sign the preliminary instrument.

The French ambassador next presented himself on August 3 to transmit an entreaty that some other indemnification be substituted for Porto Rico, and a request for clarification of the clause dealing with the Philippines. The President was "inflexible" on Porto Rico. He repeated that the question of the Philippines was the only one on which he had not definitely made up his mind. Cambon improved the opportunity to ask the President for some definition of his intentions. The reply, though gracious and reasonable, was opaque. There was nothing determined in his mind, McKinley said, either against Spain or the United States. The settlement would be left to the negotiators appointed by the two countries. Cambon advanced the request of Spain that the meeting should be held in Paris, instead of Washington, for which the President had expressed a preference. In the evening he was informed that the suggestion was accepted. A second small concession had been granted, but the sage and realistic French diplomat was under no illusions that he could accomplish more. He had taken the measure of the President's firmness; and his sympathy with Spain did not blind him to the importance of the American victories at sea. He advised Madrid against vacillation, which would only aggravate the severity of the conditions.

McKinley invoked the power of a victorious nation in the knowledge that American conquest on land was imperiled in both the Philippines and Cuba. While the growing apprehensions of insurgent hostility at Manila were discreetly suppressed, the round robin broadcast to the country and the world that at Santiago there were no victors, but two defeated armies.

McKinley did not acknowledge the disastrous publication by the flicker of an eyelid. His attitude was still "inflexible" when M. Cambon called on August 9.

The response of the Spanish government revealed in every circuitous, expostulating phrase the unwillingness of its submission to the American terms. The "guidance" of Cuban independence, in lieu of annexation, was doubtfully swallowed, with a reminder of the duty of protecting the Spanish loyalists. The demands for territorial indemnity were reluctantly and, in the case of Porto Rico, protestingly met. But, aghast at the threat to the Spanish empire in the Pacific, Madrid sought to amend the clause dealing with the Philippines, on the grounds that it was indefinite and obscure. By way of clarification, the note declared that Spain did not *a priori* renounce her sovereignty over the archipelago. It was implied that the future negotiations should be limited to questions of administrative reform. The agreement was, moreover, modified by the statement that on all points, including the evacuation of Cuba, it was subject to the approval of the Cortes.

The President and the Secretary of State perused the note with visible annoyance. After a long silence, McKinley said that he had demanded the relinquishment and consequently the immediate evacuation of Cuba and Porto Rico. He had expected a categorical acceptance, not an appeal to the Cortes, and could not lend himself to entering into these considerations of domestic government. Cambon attempted to defend the Spanish position, arguing the analogy to the United States Senate which had been adduced by Madrid. Seeing that the President was on the point of breaking off the negotiations, Cambon quickly desisted, and begged to know what pledges of sincerity Spain could give. The President answered that there was a way of putting an end to equivocation. The American government could draft a protocol, setting forth the terms already formulated, and also fixing a time for the settlement. It would not, McKinley remarked, be necessary to reserve the rights of either the Cortes or the Senate in a paper which was merely antecedent to a formal treaty. He requested the French ambassador to communicate this project to Madrid, and ask for authority to sign in the name of the Spanish government. Then, but only then, the President said, would hostilities be suspended.

This was the substance of Cambon's report to Madrid. It omitted to mention the main reason for the proposal of a protocol—the ambiguous response on the Philippines. According to Secretary Day, who made notes of the conversations, this part of the reply was "denounced" by both the President and himself. Day spoke of using "pretty vigorous expressions" about the passage, and said that Cambon demurred at his reading as "too much that of the lawyer or judge," and suggested that allowance must be made for translation, Spanish phrases, and so on. The diplomat had certainly neither forgotten this discussion nor underestimated its importance. He had suppressed, in the interest of securing an armistice on the best available conditions, the details most likely to frighten the Madrid ministry into further evasions. But Cambon did not conceal from Madrid his belief that the terms of the protocol would be rigorous, or his conviction that, if the ministry declined to accept it, Spain would "have nothing more to expect from a conqueror resolved to procure all the profit possible from the advantages he has obtained."

In addition to the terms previously imposed, the protocol contained stipulations that Spain should immediately evacuate her possessions in the West Indies, and appoint and dispatch commissioners to Havana and San Juan to effect the transfer of authority in consultation with representatives of the United States. Each government was also to name five commissioners to treat of peace at a meeting to be held at Paris not later than the first of October.

To Cambon's great gratification, Spain deferred to his judgment, and unconditionally acquiesced in the American terms.

The protocol was signed at 4:23 on the afternoon of Friday, August 12, in a city lashed and dimmed by a heavy summer storm. Two copies, each engrossed with parallel versions in French and English, had been prepared at the State Department. The formalities were to have been held there, but at the last moment they were transferred to the White House. The arrangements were responsive to the President's distaste for publicity and ostentation. On his instructions, newspapermen and photographers were excluded. Judge Day, the only Cabinet member present, brought along his three assistant secretaries. The President invited four members of the White House staff to witness the historic event: Cortelyou, Pruden, Montgomery, and Loeffler. At the appointed hour of four, Cambon and Thiébaud were waiting in the library. The eight Americans had joined the President in the Cabinet Room. Rain beat against the darkened window-panes. The electric bulbs glared unsparingly on the worn, old-fashioned furnishings. A blotter and writing materials, laid at Secretary Long's place near the end of the table, were the only ceremonial preparations. The Frenchmen were ushered in. There was a delay while the seal was fetched from their embassy. Then Judge Day said, "Mr. Ambassador, the papers are ready." Cambon and Day in turn seated themselves, and affixed their signatures to the quadruple statement of the terms. The rest of the company remained standing. The President placed himself in front of James

Wilson's chair at the foot of the table, and looked down on the names "Jules Cambon" and "William R. Day," as each flowed four times from the pen. On the completion of the formalities, three officials were admitted—Secretary Alger, General Corbin, and Charles Allen, Acting Secretary of the Navy in Long's absence on holiday. They entered in time to see a cordial exchange between the President and the French ambassador. Asking for Cambon's hand, McKinley warmly thanked him and the sister republic of France for their good offices in bringing about peace, and invited the beaming diplomat to stay for the signing of the proclamation suspending hostilities.

Along the dripping telegraph wires and the submarine cables, the news of the armistice sped to the military commanders. It promptly put a stop to the flourishing campaign in Porto Rico, where a series of smart little skirmishes had cleared the way for a flanking movement on San Juan; but the notice was unavoidably delayed in reaching the only other point where active military operations were in progress. At 4:35 Washington time, which on the other side of the world was the morning of August 13, American troops were closing in around Manila. Three days before a steamer from Hong Kong brought word of the truce, the capital of the Philippines surrendered to the combined attack of General Merritt and Admiral Dewey.

Judge Day turned to the big globe in the Cabinet Room and said to Cortelyou, "Let's see what we get by this." All over the country, Americans were wondering what they had got by their rash and sentimental adventure on behalf of *Cuba Libre*. Less than four months had passed since they had essayed to test their rusted faith in their own valor. They had fought a little war: not costly, as wars go, scarcely deranging to production and trade; too bunglingly waged and too easily won for a glorious place in history. The round world seemed to spin before their eyes, as they studied the consequences of that war in a new map and a new destiny.

The Republican administration had launched the ship of state on the crowded lanes of empire. In the hullabaloo of triumph, there were voices that doubted the wisdom of the course that had been charted; but, North and South, expansionists and doubters, Americans exulted in a common pride and faith. The country, forcibly reunited before Richmond, had been fused at Manila and Santiago. It had become a sea power mighty enough to dare the enmity of a stronger empire than Spain, and to confirm, as every week of war had proved, the friendship of another. Many mistrusted the extension of the national borders. No man questioned the majesty of the national future.

The dazzle of colonial possessions would not cast an enduring light. The decision was the occasion of an event of transcendent importance—the entrance of the United States on the stage of the world. The great challenge of that advent was guessed by few then living, and would be resisted by millions in generations yet to come. While the spring ran past and the harvest ripened, the walls that had enclosed the republic, like a petty Oriental kingdom, had crumbled into rubble. The passionate young dream of untrammeled independence was not ended, but the period of American isolation had quietly drawn to a close in a shabby room on a rainswept August afternoon of 1898.

· 13 ·

THE WAR DEPARTMENT

Cortelyou was irritated by Alger's habit of going downstairs, after every conference with McKinley, to give out his own version to the press. At the beginning of August, the news reports of the *Seneca* and the *Concho* had incensed the President. The battered old hulks, stripped of furnishings, spoke plainly of loosely drawn contracts and wartime profiteering, while the scandalous overcrowding and shortages testified to chaos at the Santiago base. The President had Alger on the carpet for two days, and asked him and Corbin "many searching questions" about the steamship contracts and Shafter's arrangements. Aroused and emphatic, McKinley scattered telegrams broadcast, directed the immediate appointment of a board of inspection at Siboney, and ordered an investigation at New York.

Cortelyou observed that Alger did not share the President's indignation. On the contrary, he showed "watchful solicitude" to protect "Shafter and other personal friends" from reprimand, omitting "every sharp criticism, every word of reproof dictated by the President." (The telegraph clerk, Ingling, remembered one scorching dispatch that went to Shafter direct from the White House.) Alger also exhibited considerable regard for the steamship companies, which had taken outrageous advantage of the government's contracts. He was "a very much surprised man," Cortelyou said, when the President read him the order for an investigation. But, on his way out, Alger stopped for the usual word with the correspondents, and left them with the impression that he was responsible for the order.

Alger got what credit he could, but there was little enough to be gained from the President's belated attempts at inquiry and reform. The investigation soon fizzled out. The troops were being brought back from Cuba on any vessels that would float, and many of them rivaled the *Seneca* and *Concho* in discomfort. The interest of the episode lies in its glimpse of Alger behind the scenes, and in the misgivings which his behavior stirred in the President's fair-minded Assistant Secretary. "The President is long-suffering and slow to suspect his advisers of self-seeking," Cortelyou wrote in his diary, "but I am no judge of human nature if there is not much of it in the person of the head of the War Department; and unless drastic measures are resorted to the administration of that great department will be one of the few blots on the record of this administration."

The President's closest friends were drawing away from Alger, distrusting his character and fuddled conduct of his office. Yet Alger was called to account for a bill that far exceeded the drafts of his own deficiencies. There had been no thought of reorganizing the run-down Civil War concern over which he presided. It had been granted large appropriations of money and some increases of personnel, and summarily ordered to fill a big emergency contract. The mistakes and delays of the same old functionaries, hamstrung by the same old regulations, were the price of the national neglect to apply the lessons of business efficiency to the management of the War Department.

Alger's great excuse was the system, and his great pride the triumph of the War Department over its impediments. His unqualified commendation of the bureau chiefs was not altogether misplaced. If their abilities were not always commensurate with their exertions, their patriotic devotion was above reproach. They resolutely struggled toward the goal of military preparedness, plunging into transactions and expenditures on a scale beyond their wildest flights of imagination. In view of their narrow training and stultifying routine, it was a creditable achievement that, by August, modern rifles and smokeless powder, standard equipment, clothing, and supplies were beginning to move in volume to the volunteers.

The United States has not been remarkable for perfect preparedness at the outset of any war in which the peace-loving republic has engaged. It was Alger's misfortune to be Secretary of War in a conflict that was won in less than four months. The achievement to which he pointed came, in many important particulars, too late to be effective; and, from start to finish, it had been disfigured out of all recognition by the failure of distribution.

The Quartermaster's Department had had difficulties enough as the principal supply bureau of the Army. Its veteran chief, General Marshall Independence Ludington, was incapable of transformation into a bold executive. Yet, if he was the timid product of the system, he was its martyr, too. His aging, dutiful shoulders carried the most multifarious responsibilities of all; and his big, chaotic, paper-cluttered office was the worst monstrosity that Congress had created. It was swamped by the additional duty of handling all military transportation. Habituated to the leisurely dispatch, with ample notice given, of small bodies of troops and consignments of stores, the bureau was nearly immobilized by an eruption of orders for mass movements and huge shipments. Smothered in paper, buried in triplicate, the Quartermaster's Department was the origin of the troubles of the staff officers in camp and field.

The desk officers had not easily comprehended that the war would accelerate the jogtrot of normal procedure, or alter the frugal habits engrained by years of congressional penny pinching. With large sums at their disposal, they had at first been reluctant to send goods by express because of the expense. The freight service was slow and unreliable. Consignments vanished. There were frantic exchanges of telegrams, fruitless searches. The complete outfit for a two-hundred-bed hospital was lost for weeks. Some shipments were buried for the duration in warehouses.

Delays were extraordinary, even when the express services were used. Tampa was but the most glaring example of the railroad congestion that occurred at all the big encampments. Ludington and his subordinates had not foreseen this condition and had not the slightest idea of correcting it; nor was the department responsive to expostulations over the unsystematic packing, and entreaties for marked cars and invoices. After the Tampa embarkation, Ludington gave instructions that the cars should be marked, but his overworked clerks could not keep up with the invoices. They never did keep up, in spite of orders to work nights and increase the force. In August, thirty-six vessels out of forty arrived at Porto Rico without invoices for the tons of matériel in their holds.

The Army quartermasters knew nothing of transportation by sea. When it was decided that the War Department must acquire its own ships, Alger had called in expert assistance. He sent for a Michigan business associate, Frank J. Hecker—a railroad executive and banker of excellent reputation—and empowered him to purchase and charter troopships and other transports. Alger also asked Congress for authority to make some changes in the regulations governing the Quartermaster's Department. On receiving it in July, he issued orders which untangled many snarls of operation. The most radical innovation was the creation of a division of military transportation, with Hecker, appointed a colonel of volunteers, at its head.

It had required considerable firmness to challenge the system and brave the opposition of the Quartermaster's Department, but Alger was spite-fully censured by hostile newspapers. Hecker's commission was stigmatized as an instance of political favoritism, and also—surely a singular remon-strance from the Democracy—as a humiliation to the regular Army officers. He was roundly abused for sending the Santiago prisoners home on Span-ish ships, and he received no credit for the fine fleet of army transports that went into service soon after the armistice—steamships purchased by Hecker, and remodeled and outfitted under his supervision. The lot of the only businessman called in by the government was not a happy one, and Alger was not encouraged to repeat his attempt at reform.

The Secretary of War was scarcely more liable for the deprivations of Shafter's army than he was answerable for the system. The shortages in Cuba had been the result of the breakdown of communications in the hands of professional soldiers. Especial care had been taken to give Shafter an able staff. The Medical Corps was its weakest point; few Army surgeons had been available, and they were augmented by an insufficient number of volunteer doctors. Volunteers had also been assigned to the general staff, but there was not a quartermaster or a commissary in Cuba who was not an officer in the regular establishment. Every headquarters had a nucleus of trained officers of the higher grades, and Shafter's own staff included men of outstanding reputation in the Army. Colonel C. F. Humphrey and Colonel John F. Weston, respectively heading the Quartermaster's and Commissary Corps, were rewarded by promotion for meritorious service in Cuba.

Colonel Humphrey had worked indefatigably at a task beyond his power to do well. His supply lines had been broken by terrain and climate, by Shafter's determination to "do it quick." The landing of the cargo had been doomed from the start by the quartermasters' ignorance of their job. There had been no authority to train them, no arrangement to require the Navy to continue its voluntary aid in the disembarkation. By Army regulations, the quartermasters were in charge of military transportation, and had to muddle through as best they could.

Under the best of conditions, the regulations did not conduce to a smooth and speedy delivery of supplies. A puzzled foreign attaché ap-proached Commissary General Eagan about the American system of pro-visioning the army.

"You buy the stores in Chicago and you turn them over to the quarter-master and take them to Tampa?"

"Yes, sir."

"And they arrive in Tampa and are turned over to the commissary?"

"Yes, sir."

"And then they are turned over to the quartermaster to take them to Siboney?"

"Yes, sir."

"They arrive at Daiquirí, and you turn them back to the commissary again?"

"Yes, sir."

"And you want to get them to the troops, and you give them to the quartermaster again?"

"Yes, sir."

The system, however, had been somewhat flouted in practice. In anxiety to get off the basic ration of bread, meat, sugar, and coffee, Shafter had entrusted the task of landing them to Colonel Weston, and given him the army's only lighter for the purpose. Weston borrowed two more boats from the Navy, and set out to forage for his scattered provisions. Possibly with some dim notion of giving them priority, they had often been loaded first, and lay buried under heavy piles of camp equipment and soldiers' baggage. Weston was resourceful and persevering. He did his work so well that he was enthusiastically mentioned—with an apology for complimenting an Army officer—in the Navy's official report. Tons of food were left to rot and molder in the holds, and were finally ruined by disinfectants on the return of the ships to the Atlantic ports. Yet, though thousands of Cuban soldiers were fed and presently more thousands of refugees, the commissary dumps at Siboney always kept ahead of the daily needs of the American troops. Weston exceeded his instructions whenever possible, by landing salt and other items. But it was another matter to get plentiful stores to the front. Conveyance mainly depended on the quartermasters, with their bogged and broken wagons. In spite of Weston's readiness to co-operate, the soldiers received only a thin trickle of monotonous and unpalatable and sometimes spoiled provisions.

The surgeons were in still worse case than the commissary officers. Quantities of their stores and equipment had been left behind at Tampa, and quantities were destroyed by careless packing and rough handling. Only a fraction of the remainder was ever removed from the transports. One volunteer medical officer, seeking to emulate Weston, was peremptorily checked by Shafter himself. Large consignments of medicines and hospital supplies were sent to Cuba in July. Some were carried by Miles's transports, which proceeded to Porto Rico with their full load of cargo. Other shipments were still lying off Siboney in early August.

Shafter's expedition passed beyond the direct control of Washington when it set sail from Tampa. Had the War Department been fully informed of the army's shortages, it would have been powerless to correct them; but the round robin silenced any attempt at a reasonable explanation. The opposition press threw off patriotic restraint to demand an investigation of the conduct of the war and the instant dismissal of Secretary Alger. His love of publicity was gratified with a vengeance as Democratic newspapers abused him like a pickpocket, and maliciously cartooned his pleasant, white-bearded face. "Algerism" was the popular synonym for cynical negligence in office, loaded with imputations of corruption and venality. The onslaught resembled, in vituperation and slander, the Hearst operation against Mark Hanna in 1896, but this was a massed, all-out concentration of the opposition forces, and one to which the Republicans offered a minimal resistance. It was futile to speak in defense of the Secretary of War. Pleas of extenuating circumstances had no audience, and were scarcely attempted outside Alger's home state of Michigan. The leading Republican dailies, though less libelous than the Democrats, were nearly as censorious of the War Department, and equally insistent on a searching investigation.

The Quartermaster's Department was decried, but still worse was the condemnation of the Subsistence and Medical Bureaus. Commissary General Eagan and Surgeon General Sternberg were consigned, along with Alger, to the blackest pit of obloquy.

Charles P. Eagan was a zealous, hot-tempered Irishman, a veteran of the Civil War and the Indian fighting, who had gone into the commissary service and climbed the ladder of promotion, rung by rung, to the brigadier generalship at the top. His life had been spent at Army posts and on the plains—he did not arrive at the desk job in Washington until after the war with Spain began—and he knew and loved the regulars, and made it his study to please them. The eating habits of American soldiers were conservative. A few vegetables were the only articles that had been added to their diet since the War of the Revolution. The staples were hard bread or flour, bacon, pork, salt or fresh beef, coffee, and sugar. What the soldiers liked was good enough for Eagan. He had no fault to find with the legal ration. On the other hand, he was critical of regulations that did not serve the comfort of the men, and desirous of making a number of radical reforms in distributing and preparing the commissary supplies. Eagan had rigid, old-fashioned ideas about diet, but he was not an entirely typical bureaucrat. He thought that the soldiers were more important than the system.

When Eagan took office in early May, Dewey's victory had speeded up military planning and thrown the bureaus into a turmoil of preparations.

The small Subsistence Department, fast being shorn of its trained officers, was struggling with the supplies for the projected grand attack on Havana. Eagan pitched in, working day and night, placing the orders and rushing them to Tampa, while he was making ready to feed the volunteers at the federal camps. But the newcomer at the War Department was unfavorably noticed as soon as the volunteers were concentrated. Militiamen, accustomed to their mothers' cooking, raised a loud lament that they were being starved. There were noisy powwows in the states, the newspapers waxed indignant, and the Army menu was decried in Congress, which had prescribed the components of the ration.

Mrs. Louise Hogan, a dietetics expert who undertook an investigation, found that the camps were amply stocked with the legal ration, and that the food was wholesome and sustaining, if properly prepared. This was a large proviso. The main trouble was that the Army had no means of training cooks, and no fund for hiring them. Legislation providing for the employment of cooks was one of the foremost items on Eagan's agenda. The bill was drawn up and ready to go to Congress; but first it had to pass across the desk of General Corbin. The pampering of American soldiers was a sore subject with Corbin. They had cooked for themselves for a hundred years, and he saw no reason for change. Though Secretary Alger supported Eagan's recommendation, the bill was held up in the Adjutant General's office until Congress was on the point of adjourning.

Most of the criticism of Eagan was manifestly unfair, but he had made some mistakes in provisioning the expeditions. It did not occur to him to seek advice on a diet for the tropics—to consult with the commanding officers or the Surgeon General, or inquire about the experience of the Navy. He pushed along, as far as possible, in the groove he had always followed, and was surprised when reports came back suggesting the advisability of certain variations, such as the addition of a little dried fruit to the ration. Another astounding piece of news was that the regulars in Cuba grumbled about having their biscuits packed in wooden cases—the very same boxes they had always loved at home because they could use them around the camps. They did not love wormy biscuits, and Eagan had to adjust to the revolutionary idea of packing hardtack in tins. But, though he was hidebound and unadaptable, Eagan had ventured on one serious departure from tradition. Soon after coming to Washington, he had made heavy purchases of canned roast beef, which was scarcely known to the American Army. Though it had long been a part of the travel ration, the men had preferred corned beef for their journeys on the cars.

The fresh-meat component of the rations for the tropics was the biggest problem that Eagan faced in early May. Bacon, salt pork, and corned beef could be readily procured and shipped; but, before fresh American beef could be sent to Cuba, it would be necessary to secure refrigerated transports and to gain possession of a harbor. The puzzle was to vary the diet of salt meat in the meantime. Colonel Weston, who was on temporary duty at the War Department, thought that he had found the answer in the canned roast beef, which was "fresh" in the sense that it was unseasoned. In anticipation of war, Weston had experimented with this well-known article of commerce, which was regularly supplied to the American Navy and largely exported for the use of British and French troops. He found that it made a palatable stew, with vegetables and condiments. Eagan, on Weston's enthusiastic recommendation, opened and tasted several cans. Though they were labeled "roast beef," the meat in reality had been boiled. It was stringy and rather tasteless, and disagreeable in appearance, but Eagan thought that its quality was sound. The criteria of the two commissary officers were those of a time when the American meat-packing and canning industries were not strictly regulated by federal statute, and did not conform to high standards of processing and representation. Weston said of the canned beef, "it was the best that I knew." An inferior grade of goods was the best that there was. Eagan authorized Weston to go ahead and order a lot of it. After Weston went to Tampa, Eagan kept on buying up canned beef until he had nearly 7,000,000 pounds, including a big consignment that Armour's recalled from England.

Eagan was never able to give a convincing explanation of these immense purchases of an unfamiliar article of Army diet. He grew progressively forgetful and confused, and perhaps he himself did not clearly recall the worries of his first introduction to the Subsistence Department, the strain and effort of throwing ninety days' rations for 70,000 men into Tampa. The grand attack on Havana had soon been countermanded, but the new Commissary General had no way of knowing that a large-scale volunteer invasion would never take place; and he was, in fact, under constant pressure to supply a succession of smaller expeditions in both the Caribbean and the Pacific. A much greater mystery than Eagan's anxiety to lay in an emergency ration was its persistent distribution to soldiers who loathed it. As Shafter's chief commissary officer, Weston picked out the supplies at Tampa before the expedition sailed. He naturally helped himself to plenty of canned beef, but he also took large quantities of salt pork and bacon; and in Cuba, according to Weston, the troops had complete freedom of choice—the bacon was sometimes short, but it was generally ashore, and no man was ever refused it. Yet the hated canned beef was regularly delivered to the trenches, and numerous outfits got no other meat ration until after the fall of Santiago.

The beef was not improved by the furnace heat of the holds and the commissary dumps on the beaches. It was seldom actually spoiled, but it looked more and more repulsive, and the distaste of the men was aggravated by having to eat it, unsalted, from the cans. Many of them had gone on the ration when they boarded the transports at Tampa, eight days before the six-day voyage began. They were disgusted with cold, insipid, half-raw meat before they landed in Cuba to occupy camps and trenches that were as devoid of facilities as the ships. There was no use in Weston's furnishing potatoes and onions, since the army had no stew pans. The beef ration became a torture, as the famished soldiers sickened. They were nauseated by the very sight of the contents of the tins. They could not choke the slimy red mess down, or could not keep it down, if they did.

Eagan had heard about the transportation troubles at Santiago, and burst out cursing the quartermasters for leaving his provisions to spoil in the moist heat of Siboney. But he did not understand about the canned beef, and he was still in ignorance of its unpopularity when the round robin was published. In any case, the need for an emergency meat ration in Cuba had ended two weeks before. The first cargo of refrigerated beef had entered Santiago harbor the day after the port was opened. Millions of rations of all kinds had been sent—and then came this blast about starvation! Eagan had worked himself nearly into a breakdown. His bureau was one of the smallest at the War Department, but he had kept abundant provisions moving to more than a quarter of a million widely scattered troops. He had great responsibilities, and he took them hard. His nerves were ragged. It was enough to make a driven old man half crazy to hear it said that he had starved the regulars.

Surgeon General George M. Sternberg had fallen from an eminence of high reputation as an epidemiologist and a pioneer worker in the new field of bacteriology. He carried his brilliant attainments with a kind of remote severity, quietly authoritative and disdainful of contradiction. He was a pious Lutheran, a man of faith as well as science, and in his detached way he was as much of an optimist as Alger. Succeeding Leonard Wood as the White House physician, the distinguished scientist had seen much of the President, who leaned on his counsel in all matters of army health. Sternberg's word was law to Americans in the first weeks of the war.

Without damage to his prestige, the Surgeon General had predicted that the soldiers would get both yellow fever and malaria in Cuba. Science was ignorant of the manner in which the infections were transmitted, and inclined to attribute them to swamp exhalations and other noxious vapors of the soil. Diagnosis was frequently uncertain. Treatment, except for quinine, was merely palliative. Quinine was also given in preventive doses, and hammocks were advised to keep the sleeper off the damp ground at night. The only other safeguards were the general rules of hygiene. Mosquito nets were regarded as a luxurious refinement of camp life, designed to eliminate the annoyance of buzzing insects. Fevers were as unavoidable in tropical rains as casualties in battle, and it was the duty of the Medical Bureau to make extensive arrangements for the care of sick, as well as wounded men.

On the other hand, it had become possible to set a very high standard for the health of the troops who remained in the United States. Since "camp fever" had decimated the armies of the Civil War, science had effected the conquest of typhoid. The bacillus had been isolated and the method of its communication established. Sternberg himself had been one of the first men in America to photograph and demonstrate the organism. His presence at the Medical Bureau was accepted as a guaranty of modern camp sanitation, and he was expected to write a superlative record of army health. Cumulative evidence that this trust had been betrayed gradually undermined the respect in which Sternberg was held. The stinking camps and desolate hospitals on American soil prepared the way for the explosive public reaction to the neglect of the army in Cuba.

The work of the Medical Bureau had been hampered in every area by an insufficiency of surgeons and hospital attendants. The number prescribed by law had been scarcely adequate for the regular establishment, and the Volunteeer Act had made a haphazard expansion of the service. The President stretched his authority far beyond its intent in bestowing additional commissions, but the need remained so acute that Sternberg was finally obliged to resort to engaging "contract doctors." As the Civil War had demonstrated, the employment of these badly paid civilians was an unsatisfactory expedient. It was justified only by the stark necessity for staffing the army hospitals.

Congressional shortsightedness, however, had not shut off access to well-trained nurses. The women of the country were eager to serve the soldiers. In April, the Daughters of the American Revolution had offered to examine the applications that were piling up at the Medical Bureau, and organize a nursing corps. The offer was accepted, and the D.A.R. made up a list of eligible candidates; and there for many weeks the matter rested. A generation after their notable services in the Civil War, female nurses were still objectionable to conservative medical officers. Sternberg denied sharing the prejudice, but he treated it with respect. Even when the need for nurses became acute, he was unwilling to assign women to any hospital unless they had been asked for by the surgeon in charge. The war had ended before they were admitted in large numbers to the crowded military hospitals.

The great disgrace of the Medical Bureau was that the hospitals were crowded. Sternberg exhibited the same passivity toward the development of preventable epidemics as toward the dearth of nurses. As a young surgeon in the Civil War, he had had every opportunity of observing that volunteer soldiers tended to habits of casual filth, and that their officers were ignorant and careless in correcting them. The story was repeated a generation later. When the militia regiments were concentrated, they carried the seeds of enteric disease from their badly policed state camps. With the ostensible purpose of "acclimatizing" the men for the tropics, the federal camps were all placed in the South; and, except for Chickamauga Park, they were situated on low ground, damp and excessively hot in summer. Sternberg acted on the assumption that his responsibility for camp sanitation would be fully discharged by sending out a circular acquainting the commanding and medical officers with the strict rules imposed in the Army.

The Surgeon General next proceeded to break up the regimental hospitals. From his desk in Washington, it looked as though large divisional hospitals would make for greater efficiency than the small units, and this might have been the case if the army had had surgeons to staff the new institutions. As it was, they absorbed two-thirds of the regimental surgeons, all of them resentful of the transfer, many of them unwilling to learn their duties. The hospitals were so badly managed that they were avoided by the sick; the surgeons who remained with their regiments were overburdened with work; and the militia officers excused all neglect of hygienic precautions on the ground that their doctors had been taken away from them. The hot, swarming camps grew foul. The graph of sickness shot upward. The newspapers were noisy, and the public was alarmed. The Surgeon General remained confident that his paper of instructions had compelled the implicit obedience of a host of militia officers and civilian physicians.

Sternberg's vision was bounded by orders and regulations, nearly to the exclusion of an interest in practical execution. He disregarded the reports from the camps because they were not official. Inspection had come to a standstill, as a result of the disputed prerogatives of the Secretary of War and the Major General Commanding the Army. Alger had given the orders to Miles in May. Miles had not obeyed them, saying that it was his place to order inspections. The subject was closed for the duration of the war. The genial Inspector General, Henry C. Breckinridge, was absent from Washington. Originally assigned to Miles's staff, he finally went with Shafter to Cuba, where he sat out the campaign on one of Eagan's wooden boxes, telling stories to the officers and correspondents. The breakdown of the Bureau of Inspection was Sternberg's main excuse. It was also true that the chief surgeons and the commandants of the camps—the latter in every case regular Army officers—were derelict in reporting the disregard of the rules of sanitation. Failing an official communication, Sternberg rested on the power of his circular while the volunteers sickened by thousands and carried typhoid fever to Cuba, Porto Rico, and Manila.

When Sternberg was at last convinced that his orders had not been obeyed, he issued another circular. The tottering invalids and the pine coffins that moved to the states bore witness that more effective measures were needed to forestall total calamity. Top-level conferences resulted in the abandonment of all the old camps. New sites were chosen, and the troops were moved shortly after the armistice. A strict police was enforced, and checked by systematic inspections. After September, there was a sharp decline in the rate of disease and death; but Sternberg did not function as a competent health officer until the fatalities on American soil had far eclipsed in numbers the deaths from fever in Cuba.

Though by no means equally responsible for the calamity at Santiago, the Surgeon General made his contribution to the misery of the Fifth Army Corps. His obstinate insistence on placing the men in mountain camps was the chief reason for postponing their withdrawal. His satisfaction with Shafter's inadequate medical corps was a partial cause of the neglect of the sick. It did not prove impossible to enlarge it when Sternberg at last bestirred himself to do so. Santiago was overrun with contract doctors and "immune" women nurses just before the army was recalled. Certain Army regulations were tardily by-passed, but not at the Surgeon General's instigation. The most conspicuous case in point was the deficient invalid diet, for which the War Department was furiously taken to task. Congressional enactment had limited the provisions at military hospitals to slops—condensed milk, tea, and beef extract—and omitted authority for a convalescent travel ration. When hunger at the hospitals and on the transports finally moved Alger to commute the rations of the sick, Sternberg was not only inert, but obstructive, and the order was stubbornly hampered in operation by the surgeons.

The round robin bespattered the Surgeon General with unjust accusations. Yet Sternberg had prophesied the misfortunes of the American troops in Cuba, and there was something peculiarly repellent in the philosophic detachment with which he bore the fulfillment of his predictions.

As the scene at Santiago darkened, he had remained the only tranquil spirit at the War Department, sure that the sickness was under control, sure until nearly the end that the surgeons had everything they needed. For Sternberg had not been officially advised that his supplies were not delivered. The orders had been placed, the consignments dispatched. Contracts, vouchers, and receipts were the tangible evidence of a task completed. Sternberg's responsibility ended at his desk. There were the realities, neatly signed and docketed.

A faithful functionary of science, Sternberg availed himself of new opportunities for research after the war was over. A board of Army surgeons spent eighteen months in analyzing the records of the volunteer regiments, and drawing up a report that typhoid had been caused by the neglect of hygiene, rather than any inherent unhealthiness in the camp sites, the water, or the food. One member of the board, Major Walter Reed, showed such ability that he was pressed into service on another project in which the Surgeon General's interest had been keenly stimulated. Reed went to Cuba in 1900 at the head of a commission to investigate yellow fever. As the result of his researches, the virus-bearing mosquito was identified, and the specter of plague at long last ceased to stalk the eastern seaboard of the United States.

Americans had misunderstood the qualifications for which Sternberg was pre-eminently distinguished. His forte was abstract disease, not the relief of suffering men. He had been too inflexible and, in a humane sense, too unimaginative to rise to the demands of the war; but, in the cold, precise realm of scientific knowledge, he served humanity well.

One effect of the round robin was to splinter the morale of the War Department. Alger himself was guilty of losing his temper. He blamed Roosevelt for the publicity; and, in the blindness of anger, he struck back at the Colonel of the Rough Riders.

A weapon lay ready to hand in the shape of a personal letter from Roosevelt, whom Alger had invited to report informally from time to time. In high disgust with the performance of the militia at Santiago, Roosevelt had written that the Rough Riders and the regular regiments were each worth three regiments of guardsmen. Americans were quick to resent aspersions of the state troops, and New Yorkers were especially touchy about their gallant Seventy-first, whose prowess the newspapers had glorified without regard to the facts. The World, in an inadvertent moment, had printed a truthful account of the panic in this regiment under fire, as described by a young correspondent named Stephen Crane, who was known as the author of a cynical novel about the Civil War. The story was so vigorously denounced as an unpatriotic lie that *The World* had felt obliged to disown it. Roosevelt's slurring comment put him in a class with Crane, and Roosevelt was being boomed *in absentia* for the Republican nomination for governor of New York. Alger telegraphed the Colonel and gave the press his dispatch, which quoted and rebuked the "invidious comparisons" that Roosevelt had made. This publication created a minor sensation, but did Roosevelt surprisingly little harm. Allowance was made for his exuberant style, and he was freely forgiven an ebullient pride in his own command. Americans were destined to hear a good deal from Roosevelt about his military exploits. They laughed at Mr. Dooley's parody, "Alone in Cubia," but it was indulgent laughter.

The main reason for the miscarriage of Alger's thrust was that, by an obvious retaliation for the round robin, he had conferred on Roosevelt the accolade of saving Shafter's army. Alger vainly issued statements that the orders for withdrawal had been sent before the publicity appeared. The country could not be dissuaded from the belief that Roosevelt had forced the War Department to act. Alger was despised for using a private letter in a mean attempt to damage Roosevelt politically, and for playing into the hands of Tom Platt, who was cool to the hero's candidacy. Regretting his error, Alger privately sent Roosevelt an abject apology, which was magnanimously accepted. He never repeated the folly of his slap at a popular Republican. He translated ill temper into martyrdom, shrugging off criticism, and indicating that the facts spoke for themselves. The success of American arms seemed the conclusive answer to the railing against the War Department, and Alger stood confidently on his record, as victory came in sight.

But Alger was mistaken in thinking that victory would efface the national indignation. The War Department had so deeply humiliated the American people that they were impelled to repudiate and revile it. They were the people who had built great railway systems, constructed mammoth industrial and mercantile organizations, created the architectural and electrical marvels of the Chicago World's Fair. They were a nation of experts, and they had bragged of American efficiency to the four quarters of the globe. The War Department had betrayed that boast by its incapacity to outfit or provision or decently transport the soldiers of the United States, or care for their sick and wounded, or even, in a country whose plumbing was the admiration of the civilized world, keep the army's latrines clean.

The mortal blow which the round robin dealt the War Department was the necessity for a precipitate evacuation of Cuba. Though publicity had not prompted the orders, it forced a speedier movement than the War Department was prepared to handle.

The authorities, like the public, regarded even the medically certified elements of Shafter's army with a solicitude salted with apprehension. A certain cautious deliberation had attended the choice of a rest camp, located in an irreproachably healthful part of the North, but also isolated from centers of population. The matter had not been definitely settled until the end of July, when the lease was signed for a large, undeveloped tract at the eastern tip of Long Island. The announcement had met with general approbation. Though a few hotel owners protested, the detention of the pariah heroes at Montauk Point offered a minimal risk to the public, and steamers could land there without exposing New York to a possible whiff of infection. On August 1, when Shafter was directed to send part of his cavalry to this destination, the plans called for a rest camp for 5,000 men, with a 500-bed hospital. As there was plenty of space, a general camp was also envisioned. Alger decided to bring up the cavalry that had been left behind in Florida, and the mounts of the Cuban cavalry division. Both men and animals wanted a change of climate, and horseback drill had been advised for the Santiago troopers after their weary experience on foot.

The ensuing appearance of the round robin placed Alger in a dilemma. He badly needed to plead that the withdrawal from Cuba was unreasonably accelerated by indiscreet publicity and popular hysteria. But, in claiming credit for having recalled the army of his own volition, he could not hedge on the literal meaning of his order, or excuse the War Department's unreadiness to meet the consequences. The loss of this excuse stung Alger to fury as he faced the impending future. For, though the Department was radiating plans and good intentions, no impression had as yet been made on the grassy wastes and rolling dunes of Montauk Point.

The camp site declined in favor under the inspection of the press. It seemed doubtful that an ample water supply would be found. It was also discovered that ocean steamers could not land directly at Montauk. The nearest feasible point was Fort Pond Bay, several miles distant, and without suitable facilities. The one-horse Long Island Railroad, moreover, was absurdly inadequate. Aspersions on the greedy foresight of its management moved Mr. W. H. Baldwin, the president of the line, to a heated protest that the railroad had not offered its facilities and had never expected to haul a single soldier. Mr. Baldwin, however, was in receipt of eleventh-hour instructions to increase rolling stock and personnel, build miles of sidings for freight cars, and expand a rural depot into an important terminus.

In those days of early August, there was pathos in the desperate efforts of the War Department to race with fleeting time. It was so sadly evident that the race could not be won. At Camp Wikoff, as the tract was christened in honor of a colonel of regulars who had fallen at San Juan Hill, peaceful desolation gave place to frantic confusion. Engineers hurried over miles of empty pipe lines to push the drilling for wells. Signalmen toiled across the dunes, trailing lengths of wire. Quartermasters staked out hospital sites, and urged on teamsters and laborers. Lumber and tents lay in heaps around the disorganized little depot—there were not enough wagons to move them. The contract carpenters from Brooklyn went on strike. Warehouses had not yet been built, so the army's supplies could not be unloaded. The new railroad sidings did not work, and the freight cars were blocked as far as Amagansett.

Before a single tent had been pitched, troops picked their way through the planks and scantling at the depot—the vanguard of the cavalry that Alger had expansively ordered up from Florida and other southern points. More than four thousand men arrived, all jaded from a hot, unhealthy summer, some without travel rations, some sickening with typhoid and malaria; and behind them, restive in the boxcars, were more than five thousand ill-conditioned horses and mules, in need of stabling and forage.

Like most great failures, the preparation of Camp Wikoff had its elements of irony. One of them was the thoughtful provision of horses to exercise the depleted Santiago troopers. Another was the outstanding achievement of procuring tropical uniforms. Light duck suits had been delivered in time to clothe Shafter's veterans for the bracing climate of Montauk, where they needed flannel shirts.

Less than a week after the cavalry began coming in from the South, the first transports reached Fort Pond Bay with the cavalry from Cuba. The intervening days had been used to good advantage. The pier had been strengthened and extended. The yellow flag waved over a quarantine station, and offshore lay a disinfecting barge for the purification of the soldiers and their gear. The depot had a new station with a restaurant and a commodious platform, and numerous sheds were going up nearby. The camp was wired for electric lighting and for telegraph and telephone service. Water had at last been struck, and only a pump was needed to send it over the network of pipes. The hospitals and the detention camp for men exposed to fever were still far from completion, but the general rest camp was an impressive sight. The original specifications had been tripled and ten thousand tents dotted the sands, offering shelter, though unfurnished with floors or cots. Camp Wikoff, by the middle of August, was remarkably close to being ready for an army of able-bodied and resourceful soldiers, but it was in no sense ready for the occupancy of a force of convalescents, unable to fend for themselves and requiring, almost to a man, medical attendance and special diet.

The first arrivals told the dreary story that was reiterated throughout the rest of August. It was written in the blanketed forms on the litters and the fainting figures that were assisted into the ambulances; and, more poignantly still, in the tottering ranks of the men who had been passed at quarantine as sound. The regulars shambled into line like a retinue of ghosts with skeleton faces and blank, unseeing eyes. The road to the camp was strewn with those who fell. The strongest survivors of Shafter's campaign were not fit for a tramp of several miles, and there were too few ambulances to carry them all. New hospitals were staked out before the first were completed, but for a few days it proved impossible to care for all the sick. Men lay helpless for hours on the ground, and it was necessary to delay disembarkation from the groaning transports that inexorably, day after day, appeared on the horizon. The chief surgeon stressed the difficulty of getting lumber and tents; but, as convalescents clamored for admission, he also awoke to the want of doctors and nurses. He was directed by Sternberg to find them in the wilderness of Montauk Point. A few determined Sisters of Mercy and other nurses resolutely presented themselves before any arrangements had been made to accommodate females, and imperative telegrams aroused the Surgeon General to dispatch more women, to round up male attendants, and to engage contract doctors.

Charitable donations had enabled hospitals to purchase extra comforts, and they were stormed by the convalescents because they had delicacies, as well as medicines to dispense. Neither, in the first confusion, could be obtained elsewhere. Feuds between the hospital and regimental surgeons impeded the circulation of medical supplies. The doctors, however, were united in ignoring the new ruling for the commutation of sick rations, and without their orders the commissaries could not disburse the funds. General Joe Wheeler, placed in command of Wikoff on his return from Cuba, settled the doctors by knocking a few heads together, and cut commissary red tape by sending off requisitions for quantities of light, nourishing food and plenty of ice to keep it fresh. There were abundant supplies of the legal ration, with fresh beef and bread, but Wheeler had the highest authority for getting less Spartan fare. The President had instructed him, in most emphatic language, to make the soldiers comfortable without regard to expense.

Alger had eagerly seconded the President. The time had come for the War Department to abandon regulations and make a conspicuous display of zeal and solicitude. Congress would willingly foot the bills. But Alger had said nothing of this to General Eagan. Wheeler's supplies were on the way when the Commissary General's startled eye fell on requisitions for a lot of fancy, perishable, unauthorized stuff. Eagan was so scandalized that he ordered the shipments stopped, forbidding the Wikoff commissary to receive them at the depot.

Alger learned of this action during a flying visit to Montauk. He hastened to overrule Eagan and get the delicacies delivered; but Wheeler's loud protests over the delay and Alger's own desire to get the credit for ending it made bad publicity for the Subsistence Department at a most unfortunate moment. The well-stocked Wikoff commissary had fallen under a cloud. The provisions had not been evenly distributed because the quartermasters had allotted only two wagons for the purpose. Proximity to food, moreover, was potent to dispel the listlessness of the more able-bodied troops. New arrivals had raided the commissary wagons on the march to the camp. Troops set to guard the storehouse—which was as yet unfurnished with doors—had seized the chance to plunder the rations for themselves. The tocsin of starvation was pealing from Montauk Point.

Charity stood ready to atone for the heartlessness of the War Department. Food packages were raining on the Rough Riders and the two militia regiments. Ladies' aid societies and Red Cross workers bustled in to set up diet kitchens. Miss Helen Gould, after inspecting the hospitals, sent down a corps of chefs, some of them borrowed from the households of New York millionaires. The private cook of Mr. William K. Vanderbilt was among the *cordons bleus* who catered for the patients. The camp messes, without benefit of supervision, banqueted on lavish provisions dished up by soldiers whose culinary education had not gone beyond the frying pan and stew kettle. The volunteers, reveling in gifts of far more dainties than they could consume, gorged on squab and pheasant, washed down with flowing libations of whisky, brandy, and champagne. The regular commissaries were stocked like the larders of the Waldorf with Wheeler's supplies, and the doughboys disdained plain beef and bread to stuff themselves with rich concoctions swimming in butter and cream. A new kind of sickness mowed down the veterans of Cuba, as their craving bellies paid the sour penalty of repletion.

Never, since the triumphs of imperial Rome, had soldiers been so feasted. This was surfeit, not want; yet the tocsin of starvation kept on ringing. It was insistently sounded by the correspondents of the sensational press, and their stories were echoed by the visitors who daily descended in droves on Montauk Point. They gazed with pity at the emaciated troops, like gaunt cartoons of famine. They heard the cries of the only men who were actually deprived of food—the typhoid patients, restricted to a liquid diet by the reigning medical opinion of the day. One and all, the visitors bore firsthand testimony to the inhumanity of the War Department.

The round robin had conditioned the American public to believe the worst, but Roosevelt himself soon grew disgusted by the "hysteric nonsense" about the suffering at Montauk. In spite of the excesses of charity, it was not a bad camp after the first week. Shafter, who came home at the end of August, called it "the best camp I ever saw." The hastily improvised community, brand-new and jerry-built, looked like a western boom town that had incongruously sprung up on the Long Island seaside. The station, with its hitching rails and rough plank sheds, was lively with the traffic of mounted men and six-mule Army wagons. The rows of tents shone white along the breeze-swept sand streets, and the sinks were well removed and drenched with disinfectants. Though much typhoid was brought in, it did not become epidemic. Scares of yellow fever came to nothing. Most of the soldiers survived the slow and difficult convalescence from tropical malaria. The death rate, in this abode of universal illness, was only 2 per cent; but, in the eyes of the public, the camp was damned by the wretchedness of the troops it sheltered—damned when it kept them and when it let them go. The War Department was bitterly censured for a liberal policy of sick leaves, which all too often released men before they were fit to travel. The furloughs, nevertheless, went on. The days of Camp Wikoff were numbered as the nights grew chilly. The volunteers were all discharged. The very sick were carried from their drafty tents and moved to hospitals in the cities and suburbs. The regulars were gradually transferred to various Army posts.

The boom at Montauk was at its height in the first ten days of September. After the middle of the month, the population rapidly declined. Row after row, the tents were struck. Freight cars dwindled on the sidings. Excursionists fell off. The deserted station and the yawning storehouses were the only memorials of Camp Wikoff, as the winter sands buried the traces of the ghost town by the sea.

The President went to Camp Wikoff in early September after taking the only holiday he permitted himself in 1898—a week divided between visits to his brother and the Herricks. Night after night in the stifling White House, he had sat turning over the newspaper clippings, reading his mail. The scandals of the war washed like dirty water over his plans for peace. The "shameful page" of the Santiago campaign and the insanitation of the volunteer camps had produced a revulsion against the military service of the United States. Typhoid was rampant in Porto Rico. Montauk was a word of loathing. McKinley had studied the criticisms of Montauk and did not credit all of them—he was getting good reports direct from General Wheeler—but he had been disturbed by the haphazard feeding of the troops, and was anxious to prevent both scarcities and excesses at the new federal camps. In his usual cryptic way, he was backing the dietitian, Mrs. Louise Hogan, who had plans for diet kitchens where Army cooks and nurses could learn to prepare invalid food in bulk by her practical methods of peptonizing and pasteurizing. At Alger's request, she had gone to Montauk. She was reporting to the White House, as well as the War Department.

The sun was blistering hot at Montauk, though a fresh breeze blew from the sea, as the President drove over the miles of sand with Alger at his side and Colonel Roosevelt riding at the head of the cavalry escort. The carriage would stand waiting while McKinley walked along the rows of tents. At each entrance, an officer announced "The President of the United States, soldiers." Then McKinley stepped softly from cot to cot, pausing to smile down at the wasted faces on the pillows and speak a few words to those who were well enough to understand. It was a wearying day for a heavy, middle-aged man, sweating in a tight frock coat, sunburned under a hard straw hat. It was a painful day for a man of tender heart, and it must have been poignant in its reminders of young Jim, who was sick with dysentery in Porto Rico. General Wheeler thought that the President was on the verge of collapse when he left for the depot. Nevertheless, McKinley had been gratified by the care the soldiers were receiving. He took the unusual step of dictating a statement to that effect for the newspapers.

McKinley was still temporizing with the War Department, but he was doing so at serious risk to his policies and his party. With the approach of the mid-term elections, he was being subjected to tremendous pressures from friends and political advisers to rid his administration of the stigma of "Algerism."

The rejoicing over the military victory had at first masked the political danger of the reaction against the War Department. It had seemed un-thinkable that the exultant nation could fail to sustain the party in power. The President's expansionist policy had made him the idol of the western Republicans, and he had retained great personal popularity in the East, where there was much disaffection to the new trend. His wider hold on public esteem was tacitly acknowledged by the Democratic press. The most violently partisan newspapers did not venture to implicate the President in the libelous allegations against the War Department. The worst that was said of McKinley was that he had appointed Alger and still kept him in the Cabinet. But the smear of association alarmed Republican leaders as storm signals went up along the Atlantic seaboard and state chairmen made gloomy reports of the prospects of the autumn. There had been a good deal of private sympathy for Alger as the scapegoat of the administration, but it withered away in anxiety for the party. Fear of losing the House inspired appeals to the President to repudiate Alger and appoint a Secretary of War who would command the confidence of the country. Colonel Roosevelt was the favorite candidate, urged on the President from all sides. Though Roosevelt had been careful not to dampen the enthusiasm of his friends in New York, he preferred national affairs to state politics, and he was keenly interested in the possible vacancy at the War Department.

The President's trip to Montauk had assumed particular significance as the occasion of a meeting between him and Roosevelt. The warmth of McKinley's greeting left nothing to be desired. On arrival, he had already entered the carriage at the depot when he caught sight of Roosevelt at the head of the cavalry escort; and, jumping down, he went to shake the soldier's hand, offering congratulations and welcome home. All day, as the party pounded over the sands, men lined up to cheer the President and the Colonel. Alger came in for little notice, but his presence by McKinley's side was enough to advise Roosevelt and the public that an opening in national affairs would not be immediately available to the hero of San Juan Hill.

Not long after the President's visit, Roosevelt was mustered out, and returned to his home in Oyster Bay. Tom Platt soon yielded to an irresistible demand, and the Colonel was duly nominated for the governorship of New York.

Many of McKinley's visitors could not credit that he realized the feeling against Alger, but Cortelyou had made sure that he was fully informed. The diary of the Assistant Secretary affords the only reliable clue to the President's thoughts on the subject. One August evening, Cortelyou's budget of papers had contained an exceptionally outspoken letter from an old friend of the President, Spencer Borden. Urging the political expediency of driving Alger out and putting Roosevelt in, Borden referred to Grant's mistaken loyalty to the corrupt men of his Cabinet, and bluntly told McKinley he was making as serious a blunder in remaining loyal to Alger. "If he is not corrupt, as many believe," Borden wrote, "his incompetence has reached the magnitude of a crime." McKinley talked, after he read this letter.

"The President replied by saying that the outcry against Secy. Alger was unreasonable and unwarranted," Cortelyou wrote on the night of August 23, "that the Secy. could not be responsible for many of the conditions at Santiago and other places; that if the food, medicines, etc, were not landed from the transports at Santiago it was the fault of the regular army officers who had charge of them and that Secy. Alger could not know at the time what was going on. The President said that some of the good people who were writing to him so vigorously now—Spencer Borden and others—used to write him when he was preparing his tariff bill that it would bring ruin on the country. He cited the bitter hostility to Stanton, Grant—that Grant was called 'The Butcher;' that the people could be trusted, but were hasty and unreasonable some times. . . . He said, too, the clamor would soon be for the return of our troops from Porto Rico and Manila, that they would undoubtedly get sick in those places, but if the people expected us to hold what we had won, how could [it] be done if we withdrew our troops?"

These remarks are chiefly interesting for their comment on the instability of popular emotion. The President had been stung into speaking out on a subject which he normally glossed over and idealized. He had been less frank in implying that the only trouble with Alger was the unlucky accident of the fickleness of the mob. Without doubt, McKinley keenly felt the injustice of the attack, sympathized with Alger, and desired to stand by him, but these sentiments were utterly incommensurate with the administrative and political sacrifice of keeping Alger in office. A heavy debt of gratitude was indicated. It was usually ascribed by McKinley's critics to some election bargain, frequently involving Hanna, but such theories had the weakness of relating to Alger's appointment, not to his retention after he had become destitute of influence. The only plausible explanation for McKinley's costly loyalty lies in his own direct wartime intervention at the War Department. Alger was the screen that concealed the President's activity in army affairs, the surrogate for decisions that the President had made and lapses that he had condoned. It was not a comfortable position, and Alger came to feel resentment toward the President. Mrs. Hobart once asked him why he did not make a public statement of his difficulties. "No," Alger said, "I have been told what a Secretary of War is for."

The President's failure to respond to pressure was the confusion of political commentators in the early fall of 1898. The newspapers devoted columns to speculation about his suicidal conduct. It was said that George Washington could not have carried the load with which McKinley saddled himself by keeping Alger in the Cabinet. McKinley tacitly recognized the weight of the burden in two ways. He made plans to take a prominent part in the political campaign in the West. He gave orders for an immediate investigation of the conduct of the war.

It is improbable that the President had hoped to avoid the investigation. The demand from influential newspapers was too serious to be ignored, and McKinley had the strong motive of wishing to forestall inquiry by Congress. His decision was apparently precipitated by a series of utterances which began to emanate from General Miles while McKinley was on his week's holiday.

The armistice had cut short the conquest of Porto Rico before Miles had had a fair chance to show his military skill. So much typhoid and dysentery developed among his troops that orders were sent recalling all who were not actually needed for duty, and Miles himself prepared to return home and forward the political ambitions with which his head was rattling. Since he could no longer hope to capture the limelight by fighting Spain, he had concluded to fight the War Department. Guided by the example of the round robin, he chose the weapon of the press. He confided the history of his wrongs to the Porto Rican correspondent of the Kansas City *Star*; and, by way of documentation, he also gave out a number of official dispatches, which he declared had been "much garbled" as previously released. On arriving at New York on September 7, Miles expansively welcomed the reporters who flocked to the pier, and handed out a long prepared statement elaborating his complaints about the War Department, and stressing his own superior wisdom and judgment.

Apart from his unsoldierly conduct, Miles was becoming a good deal of a bore, but he was riding a popular hobby, and he was praised to the skies for forcing the President to act. An investigation of the War Department had seemingly become the only alternative to a court-martial for Miles.

Alger had left Washington—he paid a short visit to Michigan before setting out to inspect the federal camps—when announcements came from the White House that he had asked for an inquiry and that the President had given consent. The "request" was skeptically regarded. Sternberg wanted an investigation, and so did Corbin, who was outraged by the charge that he had "garbled" dispatches; but the public was convinced that Alger did not. He had fostered this belief by his disdainful attitude toward criticism, and his insinuations that it came from sources too disreputable to notice. "What do you want me to do?" he asked a reporter at this very time. "To get down into the sewer with these people?" Even a friendly Detroit newspaper deplored Alger's lack of frankness and his "consecrated self-righteousness."

The task of forming the investigating commission resembled that of finding open-minded jurors for the trial of a notorious criminal already condemned by the newspapers. The President met with many refusals before he succeeded in getting the services of nine estimable gentlemen, qualified—as Civil War veterans, eight Union to one Confederate—to pronounce on military matters. They were earnestly addressed by the President when they assembled in the last week of September. He invited the closest scrutiny of the accusations made against the Commissary, Quartermaster's, and Medical Bureaus; and, placing the War Department records and officers at the commissioners' disposal, he bade them seek the truth without respect to persons. "If there have been wrongs committed," the President said, "the wrongdoers must not escape conviction and punishment." Under the chairmanship of the railroad builder and promoter General Grenville M. Dodge, the gentlemen set about their arduous researches. The report which they submitted to the President the following February was a considerate appraisal of the conduct of the War Department, containing many constructive recommendations for reforming the system. It deplored the failure to prepare for war and censured Alger's want of "grasp," but found no evidence of corruption on the part of the Secretary or any of his associates.

The Dodge Commission, however, was not potent to alter public opinion. It had been called a "whitewash," and the label stuck. The President's hand-picked investigators included one of the bureau chiefs, General John M. Wilson of the Engineers; while General Dodge himself had gone so completely on record in defense of the War Department that he had at first been reluctant to serve. The sincerity of these two able men was not specifically called in question, but certain of their colleagues exhibited sufficient impatience with criticisms of the Department to earn the suspicion of bias. McKinley, moreover, had not granted the commission authority to compel the attendance of witnesses or to require them to be sworn or affirmed, though Army officers would obviously be chary of volunteering testimony that might jeopardize their careers. He later announced that witnesses would be protected from the consequences of their testimony, but soldiers still showed a tendency to reserve and discretion in giving evidence about the faults of military management.

Contemporary opinion was undoubtedly right in holding that the Dodge Commission did not uncover the whole truth about the War Department. A curtain must have been lowered over many a dimly lighted scene of pull and favoritism. It seems much less credible that actual fraud and bribery were concealed. The loose accusations evaded the diligent efforts of the commission to pin them down. Alger was acquainted with the sway of influence and the squeeze of pressure, but he was a man of large fortune, who had set his heart on becoming United States senator from Michigan. His methods in the showcase of the War Department were surely less crude and risky than jobbery in the contracts.

The "Alger Relief Commission" had at first seemed destined to a tranquil existence. In spite of ridicule and skepticism, its appointment had exerted a calming effect on the nerves of the public. Hysteria noticeably abated during the autumn, as the hearings droned on without startling exposures, and the Democrats lost face when their popular warrior, Joe Wheeler, gave testimony favorable to the Republican administration. It was not until shortly before Christmas, when General Miles appeared before the commission, that the investigation of the War Department flashed into front-page news.

Since his return from Porto Rico, Miles had spent much time in his splendid office in conference with Inspector General Breckinridge, his sole ally at the War Department. He had hit upon the commissariat as the object of his next offensive. This was a much cleverer idea than rehearsing his own grievances. It struck a popular chord. The public was so worked up about the soldiers' rations that any exaggerated statement would be believed. Miles had formed some very ugly suspicions about the army beef, refrigerated as well as canned, but he had not reported them to the President or the Secretary of War, or recommended any changes in the ration. His chief interest was not in improving the soldiers' food, but in obtaining publicity favorable to himself and damaging to the administration. Lionized by the Democrats, the General had become infatuated with his own political importance, and he was the chosen instrument of the intriguing coterie that surrounded his uncle by marriage, John Sherman. Though Miles had clashed with the Subsistence Department, it does not appear that he was strongly motivated by vindictiveness toward Eagan. The crushing of a passionate, overworked old commissary officer was merely a trivial incident in the grand design of promoting the presidential candidacy of Nelson Appleton Miles.

News quickly leaked out that Miles was prepared to make a startling exposé. The Dodge Commission, however, neglected to call him until December. On the witness stand, he declined to be either sworn or affirmed, observing that he was responsible for what he said, and proceeded to develop the contention that the food furnished by the Subsistence Bureau, with special reference to the beef, had been a serious cause of sickness among the troops. He incorrectly stated that canned beef was not part of the legal ration, and hinted at some sinister reason for its use. "The pretense," he said, "is that it was sent as an experiment."

Reports, which Miles had solicited from regimental commanders and which he placed in evidence, testified to the disagreeable appearance and flavor of the ration. Some writers believed that it contained no nutriment, but consisted of "scraps and tailings" or "refuse" from commercially marketed soups. One Major W. H. Daly, a volunteer surgeon who had been assigned to Miles's staff, offered a still more repulsive theory about the refrigerated beef—he thought that it seemed to have been treated with secret chemicals injurious to health. Miles read out a letter from Daly giving this opinion and stating that the meat had a sickening odor similar to that of a dead human body injected with preservatives.

Again and again, as Miles addressed the commission, the phrase "embalmed beef" fell gruesomely from his lips. He repeated it in talking with the reporters; and, outside the formal atmosphere of the inquiry room, positively asserted his charges as facts. The yellow press reveled again in horrors and exposures. Respectable newspapers of both parties lauded the General's moral courage, for it was not doubted that the President would at last be compelled to punish his insubordination and shut off his publicity campaign by deposing him from command of the Army, and ordering a court-martial or a court of inquiry.

Before any action was taken, General Eagan replied to the allegations. He had learned from the columns of the *New York Journal* that he was accused of experimenting on the troops with refuse and poisoning them with undertakers' chemicals. "General Miles has crucified me," he cried, "on a cross of falsehood and misrepresentation." His first thought was to prefer charges for slander, but Alger was regretfully obliged to advise that Miles was covered by the immunity which the President had promised to witnesses. Eagan then wrote to Miles, asking for verification of the statements directly quoted in the interview in the *Journal*. He also applied to the Dodge Commission for an opportunity to be heard in his own defense, and a date was appointed in January, three weeks after Miles's appearance.

Eagan passed the interval in mounting agitation, unable to sleep or eat, distraught by newspaper abuse and demands for his dismissal from the Army. He was tortured by the knowledge that he was believed to have profited financially from the beef contracts, for the use of chemical preservatives implied some sordid transaction between the Subsistence Department and the contractors. As Miles avoided an admission of his published interviews, Eagan finally formed the reckless plan of using his hearing before the commission for a vituperative tirade against his superior officer. It was a curiously deliberate act of self-destruction. Eagan spent several days in drawing up a long statement, which he dictated to his stenographer; and, in order to assure its wide circulation, he had it copied in manifold for distribution to the press.

On the appointed day, Eagan presented himself before the commission, took the stand, and rapidly began to read from the sheaf of papers in his shaking hand. A competent defense of his bureau wandered off into ranting that Miles was a liar who should be drummed out of the service, imprisoned, socially ostracized. Miles was a liar, a liar, the statement reiterated; "he lies in his throat, he lies in his heart, he lies in every hair of his head and every pore of his body. . . . I wish to force the lie back into his throat," Eagan read, "covered with the contents of a camp latrine." The commissioners listened without remonstrance, apparently stunned by Eagan's vehemence. They were recalled, in embarrassment, to a sense of the respect due to an investigating body, and declined to receive the statement until it had been revised.

More intemperately than Miles himself, Eagan had struck at Army morale and disclosed the bitter division within the War Department. His breach of discipline was too gross to overlook. Army officers and members of Congress joined in the demand for a court-martial that thundered from the press. A short delay in issuing the order was ascribed, with probable accuracy, to the Secretary of War. Though mortified by Eagan's language, Alger undoubtedly writhed under the necessity of punishing him for sentiments so congenial to his own. The order, however, was presently announced at the White House, and Eagan was tried on charges of conduct unbecoming an officer and a gentleman, and conduct prejudicial to good order and military discipline.

The court met in the red parlor of the Ebbitt House. Eagan, subdued and ashen, sat at the foot of the long table around which his brother officers were gathered in full uniform. He told of having been a Union volunteer and then a second lieutenant of regulars on the plains. He had received a wound in the Modoc War, and had been given a brevet for it. Tears came to his eyes as he pleaded the provocation of Miles's attack, and said that a soldier's honor should be as sacred as a woman's. When his counsel asked if he had received any benefit for any contract, Eagan cried no, before God, not one cent. The verdict of guilty called for dismissal from the service, but the court recommended clemency.

The country was unmoved by the tragedy in the Ebbitt House parlor. Eagan's protestations were not believed, and he had set himself beyond the pale of pity by the coarseness of his broken heart. There was much disapproval when the President commuted his sentence to suspension from duty for six years, the term remaining before his retirement. Leniency toward the agent of embalmed beef seemed an unfortunate augury for a thorough ventilation of the scandals. Hints were not lacking that McKinley's action was open to the sinister interpretation of sympathy with the meat packers.

Miles had thrust at a great American industry as well as a branch of the government. The packers were aghast at the aspersions on their products and the injury to their markets, foreign and domestic. With their effusive co-operation, Dodge and his associates had hastily transformed themselves into a beef-investigating commission, and the subject formed an important feature of their report. Miles's charges were dismissed and his conduct was censured, but these findings were generally regarded as biased and part of the War Department "whitewash." The press was calling for a special tribunal to settle the controversy, and the demand had recently been intensified by a widely circulated interview in which Miles was quoted as declaring that he had "overwhelming evidence" of the use of preservatives in the army meat. The President, before receiving the report of the Dodge Commission, had signified his intention of ordering a military court of inquiry.

Rumors of discipline for Miles had been strongly revived by his latest outburst, but the President had decided—apparently after some debate —to deny him the advantage of claiming political persecution. The motive behind the attack on the War Department was well understood in informed circles. Indeed, the activities of the Sherman faction had passed from intrigue to bold defiance. Henry Adams wrote in February that Miles's brother-in-law, Colgate Hoyt, had "actually threatened the members of the administration with electing Miles President, to their face." It was not, in the long run, a terrifying threat; but it was uttered at a time of crisis in the Philippines when the Republican government was taking heavy punishment for the policy of expansion. Miles had the administration on the ropes, to the tune of nearly unanimous applause from the press gallery. The President declined a showdown. The appearance of reprimand was avoided by directing the inquiry against Miles's allegations rather than Miles himself, and he was not even temporarily suspended from command. The "beef court" was granted ample powers and was instructed to submit an opinion on the merits of the case, with recommendations for further proceedings. The newspapers chorused approval of the President's determination to make a thorough and impartial probe.

While the country was firmly convinced of Miles's "overwhelming evidence" that the War Department had poisoned the troops, some of the General's close friends were acutely disturbed by his recklessness and folly. However the President's order was worded, Miles was being put on trial to prove his allegations, and his inability to do so was as plain to his more reasonable partisans as to the authorities of the government. Miles had muddled the public with his loose talk about the army meat. Most people mixed up the "refuse" and "pulp" of the canned beef with the "embalmed" refrigerated beef in one nauseating mess. The distinction was vital to understanding the weakness of Miles's case. He had gathered a quantity of evidence adverse to the canned product, a minor point in the charges against the Subsistence Department, since it was admittedly an article of commerce; but he had only the flimsiest support for the crux of his indictment, the employment of injurious chemicals to preserve the refrigerated meat for the army in the tropics. His suspicions had some justification—chemical preservatives were not unknown to the meat-packing industry—but they remained suspicions, which Miles was unable to prove. His charge that the fresh beef was inedible was refuted by abundant testimony, taken by the Dodge Commission, that it was relished by the troops in Cuba and Porto Rico, and that the instances of tainting and wastage were traceable to careless handling and delayed transportation.

Miles, however, was too much carried away by his own ideas to listen to people who did not agree with him. He was immersed in preparations for the inquiry, drawing up lists of witnesses and planning their examination in conference with civilian counsel and one Major Jesse Lee, who later represented him in court. Deaf to advice that he should retract and resign his command, Miles made ready to rush at the proceedings and carry the verdict by storm; "absolutely tête-montée," as Henry Adams put it, "dead-bent on breaking his head." The foreseeable result occurred. The court, after three months of exhaustive investigation, found that the Major General Commanding had no sufficient justification for alleging that the fresh beef was embalmed or was unfit for issue to the troops. His criticism of the canned beef was sustained only in respect to the enormous quantities purchased. The former Commissary General was severely criticized for this "colossal error," but no other motive was imputed than "the earnest desire to procure the best possible food for the troops." Miles himself was censured, especially for his tardiness in reporting his opinion of the beef, but the court recommended that the interests of the service would be "best subserved" if further proceedings were not taken.

The President formally approved the findings, and the great beef controversy was closed; but it was closed in an atmosphere thick with skepticism. Some weeks earlier, the newspaper campaign against the War Department had been furiously renewed. As rumor had forecast the trend of the decision, the press had changed its tune about the court. It was no longer pronounced an ideal, or even an impartial tribunal. It was said to have been packed by Alger, in particular by the assignment of Brigadier General George W. Davis as one of the three members and Lieutenant Colonel George B. Davis as recorder, or judge advocate. These two confusing Davises—who seemed to have a good many enemies of their own—were described as adepts at military politics, notoriously hostile to Miles. Their presence on the court lent plausibility to the contention that Alger had contrived to hide the blots in his copybook and baffle Miles's efforts to bring the truth to light. But the conclusion would have been drawn, in any case. The overwhelming majority of the nation's newspapers had denied a fair hearing to the War Department. A word from the President would have checked Republican editors, and sobered the judgment of a tremendous section of the country, but McKinley had nothing to say. He did not even respond to entreaties that he should give out an endorsement of the reports of his commission and the military court.

With curious inconsistency, since a strong defense of the War Department was implied, a secondary press campaign was waged against the meat packers. The testimony taken by the military court had revealed the use of chemical preservatives, and established that canned meat of every sort—including the favorite corned beef of the regulars—was wretched in quality and dubiously processed. Americans were aroused and worried, sick with suspicion of the beef on the tables of the finest homes and the best hotels and restaurants. The time was ripe for writing effective pure-food laws on the federal statute books, but the task was left to a later administration. The President refrained from any recommendation that could be construed as further interference with an important industry. The scandals had produced a disturbing reaction abroad, especially in Germany. Secretary Wilson had undertaken to restore the credit of the meat packers by exonerating their products and commending, with unwarranted enthusiasm, the thoroughness of the inspection which the Department of Agriculture was then legally empowered to make. The conservatism of the government was best illustrated by the respectful attitude of the War Department toward the packers. Never, in his hour of greatest extremity, did Secretary Alger plead the logical excuse of the beef of commerce. Eagan himself had nothing but praise for the contractors and their products.

Miles was piously honored for "the higher kind of courage"—the phrase was used by President Eliot of Harvard—and yet the beef court failed to build the General into a national leader. His testimony had been too evasive, particularly on the subject of his newspaper interviews, to make an altogether good impression, and it had subsequently appeared that his motives might be more complex than had been supposed. One intimation had come from Miles's counsel, Major Lee, while he was cross-examining Eagan about "suggestions or directions" that he might have received on the beef contracts. Did Eagan, Lee inquired in this connection, ever see or confer with, or was he ever at a conference between anyone else and Senator Hanna? "And Senator Hanna?" Eagan repeated. He had been a poor witness before this court, forgetful even of important matters, and as rambling and garrulous as a very old man. He was pretty positive, he told Major Lee, that he never spoke to Senator Hanna in his life, and he was quite confident that he would not know him if he were to come in there now. Yes, Eagan corrected himself, he thought Hanna was once pointed out to him at a distance. Then, as Major Lee pressed him, Eagan brought forth a recollection that once two gentlemen had been in the room with the Secretary when Eagan was sent for to answer some question about an award. He could not exactly recall the question, and he did not know who the gentlemen were. If Senator Hanna was there, Eagan did not know it. As he said . . . .

Hanna was raging mad, ready to prefer charges against Lee or "take it out of his hide," but the incident had consequences more damaging to Miles. It had set people wondering about the reason for this footling attempt to drag in and hurt the President. Some thought they understood when stories were printed that Miles was the next presidential choice of Boss Croker of New York City, and that an independent movement for the General's nomination was being organized in Massachusetts. Miles was a frequent caller on prominent men of both parties. His name was often seen on the programs of meetings and banquets, and he made a number of spirited speeches on home, patriotism, and the Army, as well as more topical questions. For a while, crowds gathered to watch for the Major General Commanding the Army, and cheer his carriage as it passed; but not for very long. After the beef inquiry, Miles rapidly declined into the political unimportance which he so richly merited.

· 14 ·

DESTINY IN THE PACIFIC

I f old Dewey had just sailed away when he smashed that Spanish fleet," the President said to Mr. Kohlsaat, "what a lot of trouble he would have saved us." McKinley was seeking relief from a profound perplexity in one of his little jokes. In the weeks that followed the armistice, the uproar about the War Department drummed on his preoccupation with the unsettled problem in the Pacific. He had consulted prominent men of both political parties, and scanned the leading newspapers of the country. He had let it be known that he wanted to hear from the people, and studied the thousands of letters which responded to this invitation. He had pondered and he had prayed; but he had not made up his mind about the Philippines.

The postponement of the decision had set off a lively national discussion. The press was divided into debating teams, with vehement editorials and columns of interviews and statements. The public was regaled with geographical and historical information about the hitherto unknown islands; and after August 20, when cable service between Manila and the mainland was restored, with day-by-day accounts of events there. The capture and occupation of the capital had inevitably enlarged and confirmed the sense of American involvement with the Philippines. Though the armistice had actually been signed before the attack took place, American military rule was an accomplished fact, and few people were troubled by legalistic doubts that Manila was, by right of conquest, a United States possession.

The case for annexing the whole archipelago was vigorously presented by expansionist politicians of both parties, and by two large overlapping

323

groups of citizens, commanding influential spokesmen and publications. Expansion in the Pacific was the aspiration of businessmen who, like Griggs and Bliss, looked toward the markets of the Orient. It was the prayer of churchmen who, like James Wilson, desired to spread the gospel of salvation. The propaganda met and mingled on the common ground of duty—the obligation of a great nation to guide less fortunate peoples, and bestow on them the enlightenment of her institutions and culture. Industrialists and exporters were as vocal as religious teachers for uplifting the Filipinos, and the blessings of Christianity burned with a scarcely purer flame than the torch of American enterprise and techniques. Nevertheless, the appeal to conscience encountered important resistance. Some people were crass enough to speak of grabbing land and trade, and ridicule a moral mission as sheer hypocrisy. They queried American genius for administration, as demonstrated in corrupt municipal government, and doubted American generosity, as exemplified in the treatment of the Indian and the Negro. On the other hand, very little criticism was expended on the greatest absurdity of the expansionist propaganda, its zeal for religious conversion. The Philippines were, in fact, the brightest jewel in the diadem of the Roman Church in the Far East. Practically all of the civilized population of more than six and a half millions—the wild tribes were still unnumbered—were in full enjoyment of the blessings of Christianity. But comprehension of this fact was clouded and distorted. It was known that the exactions and cruelty of the Spanish friars had been a principal cause of native revolt, and most Americans incorrectly supposed that the grievance embraced hatred of the Catholic faith. The effusions of the Protestant missionary societies were colored by bigotry and self-interest. The Roman Catholics were fully alive to the opportunities of annexation, but remained at this juncture discreetly silent.

A telling argument of the anti-annexationists was the danger of conferring American citizenship on the mongrel population of the Philippines. The other great strength of the opposition rested on American sympathy with political independence. The venerated concept of government by the consent of the governed was violated by the seizure of distant colonies, and logic and sentiment were both defied by this outcome of a war that had been fought for Cuban freedom. A few Protestant preachers refused to endorse the "gunpowder gospel" of forcible conversion. Some businessmen entertained scruples, with Andrew Carnegie as the foremost renegade to the interests of trade. Ex-President Cleveland decried the "dangerous perversions" of conquest and annexation. Honored Republican leaders, veterans of the antislavery crusade, protested against abasement of the party's high traditions. The contest was embittered by the hate-word "imperialism," the charge that the subjugation of alien peoples was odious to the ideals of the republic, subversive of the Constitution, degrading to the flag that was the symbol of freedom.

The New York *Evening Post* found it most regrettable that the President had dodged the issue, abdicating his leadership and throwing the whole matter into "a town meeting controversy." The negotiations with Spain had displayed the Chief Executive in paramount authority. He was trusted to make peace with wisdom and broad patriotism, and his prompt decision to retain only a naval station in the Philippines would have settled the question, as anti-expansionists believed, to the satisfaction of the overwhelming majority of the American people. Delay implied doubts of the conservative course, encouraged the rampant "imperialists," and beguiled the nation further along the path of ambition. It also revealed the weakness of the opposition in constructive proposals. There were ethical objections to the earlier ideas of leaving the Philippines to Spain or bartering them away to some other colonial power. Both solutions, moreover, had become exceedingly unpopular. The first was scarcely mentioned after the fall of Manila disrupted the central government. Americans were satisfied that Spanish despotism was broken and could never be restored. They were also certain that, if the islands were sold, Germany would get a share of them. Interest in this suggestion had languished in a stiff-necked determination to exclude the interfering empire from the spoils of American victory. The only feasible position for the anti-annexationists, on popular as well as moral grounds, was the support of self-government for the Philippines. But their arguments did not rest on any firm conviction that the islands were ready for full independence.

Editorial comment on this question was influenced by an article which had appeared in the July issue of the English periodical, the *Contemporary Review*. The writer, John Foreman, had long resided in the Philippines, and was considered the principal authority on the native population. Since the scanty literature on the subject was largely out-of-date, the opinions of this Englishman were widely quoted in American newspapers. The Tagalog insurrection on Luzon, Foreman said, could have no claim to a nationalist character; the Filipinos were divided by fierce racial antipathies and possessed little idea of union. A native independent government of the Philippines was an impossibility. It could lead only to chaos and ultimate intervention by one of the powers.

Foreman's statements combined with the course of events to diminish confidence in the insurgent movement. Aguinaldo, after a flare of popularity in the late spring when he was useful to Dewey, had soon fallen into disfavor as a pretentious and unreliable little upstart and autocrat, whose antipathy to the American army made him the bugbear of the American public and press. Manila had been captured without the assistance of the insurgents. They had been by-passed in the attack, and were debarred from the occupation; but native troops had succeeded in penetrating the suburbs and a section of the defenses. They were wild to loot Manila, and infuriated by their exclusion. The situation was extremely tense in the weeks after the surrender.

When Aguinaldo was ordered to withdraw his forces from the environs of the capital, and acquiesced in the expulsion, the news was received at home with general relief. As in the case of Santiago, a section of the press complained of military highhandedness at Manila. There was some feeling that the insurgents had been unfairly treated, but no responsible newspapers or public men advised that the Luzon partisans should be left in independent control of the Philippines. The critics of annexation were obliged to compromise. They recommended an American protectorate to guide and guard the beginnings of self-government and seek to nurse to life the feeble spark of union. The difficulty of the "antis" was that, as Cleveland had once remarked in another connection, it was a condition, not a theory, that confronted them. The United States was too deeply committed in the Philippines for an easy withdrawal. The root of the problem, from which all complications sprang, was the fact that old Dewey had not sailed away.

When Dewey's victory had kindled the President's imagination, the powers of Europe were advancing toward the partition of China. For the advantage of American trade, McKinley had desired to secure a foothold in the Far East. He had reached out for the port of Manila. Extensive territory in the Philippines was not essential to his object. He was amply forewarned of the political risks, administrative headaches, and international involvements which large acquisitions in the archipelago would entail. Above all else, the radical step was repugnant to the President's conscience. He had denounced forcible annexation as "criminal aggression"; had insisted on justice and humanity as the grounds for entering on war with Spain; had disowned "greed of conquest." In allegiance to American ideals and traditions, the President shrank from committing the republic to a program of colonization in the Philippines.

Night after night McKinley paced the floor of the White House, and knelt beside his bed to pray. For he had not been able to bring himself to renounce a demand for the archipelago. He had gained time to consider and consult, but he could find no course except annexation which promised peace in the Pacific and protection to the American flag at Manila.

The fundamental problem was the geographical and economic unity of the Philippines. Naval officers were urging the difficulties of defending Manila in case of war. The chief of the Bureau of Equipment, Commander R. B. Bradford—distinguished as a man who had visited Manila three times—was making a study of the islands with special reference to coaling stations and naval bases. He said that the harbor of Manila, without the rest of Luzon, would be a source of weakness rather than strength in wartime. The trouble about taking Luzon was the proximity of the other islands. They were so crowded together that any one of them would need a large force for defense, if others were in enemy possession. Their economic interdependence was another deterrent to sharing them with one of the commercial rivals of the United States. The frictions of the joint protectorate with Great Britain and Germany in Samoa seemed at last likely to be relieved by splitting up that group; but a similar separation was impracticable in the commercial organism of which Manila was the heart. The urgent whispers of German diplomacy were echoing in Washington. The State Department, deaf to the imperial aspirations of Kaiser Wilhelm, was aghast at the flagrant indiscretion with which Ambassador Andrew D. White encouraged them at Berlin. Ambassador Hay warned the President that if Germany succeeded in her ambitions, there would be "danger of grave complication with other European powers." Japan had officially communicated her interest. The dominance of Japan would specifically mean grave complication with Russia, already reported to be on the lookout for a naval base in the Philippines. Great Britain, hopeful from the first that the United States would claim the whole group, had become so alarmed for her nearby colonies that she had insisted on an option, in case of sale. The dismemberment of the islands could not be permitted. The President's choice narrowed to Spain or the United States.

McKinley was loath to abandon the islands to Spanish misrule. The American people, divided on all other proposed solutions, seemed united in opposing this one. Nevertheless, as the only feasible alternative to American possession, it was long and earnestly considered by the President. The first practical question was whether Spain could afford to hold the Philippines; whether, deprived of the revenues of Manila, the impoverished empire could support the drain of administering the immense colony. The indications were that Spain would be forced to sell. Should she be required, as John Hay had proposed, to secure the approval of the United States before alienating any part of her territory, the result might be more disastrous still. The machinery of colonial government had broken down. The Spanish garrisons were helpless, as rebellion spread like a fierce conflagration on Luzon and threatened to ignite the neighboring islands. The bond of the Philippine peoples was a consuming hatred of Spain. Her continued ownership would be a stimulus to violent disorder, an invitation to foreign intervention.

As the President's thoughts circled back to the United States, he examined and rejected the proposal of Philippine self-government under an American protectorate. Cortelyou had procured a copy of the July *Contemporary Review* from the State Department; and, though McKinley was then suffering from severe eyestrain, he had managed to read the salient portions of Foreman's article. He read that the warlike Tagalogs were representative of the masses only in their resistance to Spanish authority, and that a native independent government was an impossibility. In the Philippines as in Cuba, the President had refused alliance with the insurgent faction. He had ordered the peremptory denial of Aguinaldo's demand for a joint occupation of Manila. On grounds of justice to the Philippine people, McKinley would not consent to support the rule of an arbitrary minority; and, on grounds of national security, he would not associate the United States with a weak sovereignty, inexperienced in resisting foreign intrigues and helpless to prevent foreign interference. The President came to regard a protectorate as the unwisest answer of all: responsibility without authority, commitment without control; a constant tangle of conflict and a perpetual danger of war in an attempt to avert the calamities of chaos and intervention.

Outright American possession of the Philippines would be respected by all the powers. It was eagerly desired by Great Britain, the nation with the largest investments and commercial interests in the islands. Japan, the nearest neighbor, signified a preference for American dominion over any but her own. Germany, the most aggressive contender, would not venture to encroach on American territory. All roads but annexation led to the partition of the Philippines, on the world auction block or in the clash of racing navies; or to a guarantee that would jeopardize the sovereignty of the United States. The President's decision seemed inescapable, but he had not yet pronounced it when, in consultation with the Cabinet, he drew up the instructions for the peace commissioners. He had reached only the conclusion that the protection of a naval station at Manila required American jurisdiction over Luzon.

Judge Day was resigning from the State Department to head the Peace Commission. He gladly relinquished his office, and looked forward to a federal judgeship after the negotiations were over. The President, much as he valued Day, had no regrets. McKinley had learned a very great deal in a year and a half of acting as his own Secretary of State. He had learned that tact and common sense, combined with judicial wisdom, were insufficient qualifications for the conduct of foreign relations. He wanted an experienced diplomat to deal with the complex international questions that lay ahead. Two days after the protocol was signed, the President recalled John Hay from London to take the office of Secretary of State.

At an early date, the President had also determined to send two Republican senators to Paris. Cushman K. Davis and William P. Frye had accepted appointments in the middle of August. A few days later, Whitelaw Reid was added to the commission. For the fifth place, McKinley wanted a Democrat, and he had more difficulty in filling it. He had first turned to the Supreme Court, successively requesting the services of Chief Justice Melville Fuller and Associate Justice Edward D. White, both Cleveland appointments, both constrained to decline on the score of public duty. The President then reverted to the Senate and to a member of that body whom he had already assigned to the important Joint High Commission on the Canadian disputes. Its first session had taken place at Quebec and temporarily adjourned when McKinley offered a seat on the Peace Commission to Senator George Gray of Delaware, a conservative Democrat whom he had frequently consulted and whose support he had had during the troubled weeks of April. As a rigid opponent of expansion, Gray was reluctant to take part in making the peace treaty, but he was eventually persuaded to switch from Quebec to Paris.

The town meeting controversy had been keyed to a high pitch of excitement as the selections were gradually disclosed. The choice of Judge Day had met with general approval. His modest character and shirt-sleeve diplomacy had earned him a quiet popularity. He struck an admirable balance between the extremes of opinion; for, though Day was identified with the expansionist policy of the government, he was expected to take a prudent position on the Philippines. On the other hand, the warmakers, Davis and Frye, were counted on to go all out for annexation, while Reid was on record as desiring it. Gray, who had opposed the annexation of Hawaii, came trailing in as the only staunch objector to any colonies at all. If Judge Day stood with Gray on the Philippines, the conservatives would still be outnumbered two to three. Expansionist newspapers were jubilant and the English press applauded, but anti-annexationists took a gloomy view of the President's "strong" commission.

For quite different reasons, its membership was criticized by a number of senators, some of them Republicans. The President had recently shown a marked tendency to avail himself of senatorial abilities. Outstanding examples were the Joint High Commission and the Hawaiian Commission. In the first instance, Fairbanks of Indiana headed the American delegation, and Gray had originally served on it. (McKinley promptly filled the place vacated by Gray with another Democratic senator, Charles J. Faulkner of West Virginia.) Cullom of Illinois was chairman of the Hawaiian Commission, and another member was the expansionist Democrat, John T. Morgan of Alabama. Such appointments were seen to have set injurious precedents when the President employed three senators to make a peace treaty on which they would subsequently act—flagrantly using them as Executive agents and committing them to support Executive action.

The President was not attentive to the constitutional objections. His concern was the ratification of his treaty. It was of utmost importance, in view of the deteriorating situation on Luzon, to hurry on the negotiations, and empower the American forces to control the marauding and violence of the insurgent army. The necessity for haste would bring the subject of forcible annexation of considerable territory in the Philippines before the current session of the Senate—a body that had hesitated to accept the gift of Hawaii. Davis was the chairman of the Foreign Relations Committee. Frye and Gray were both members. The President had ensured that his treaty would be favorably reported, and improved the prospect of its confirmation.

McKinley meant to use every weapon of Executive influence in the coming contest. As he measured his strength, he could foresee the costly defection of one Republican leader—Senator Hoar, the moral voice, the respected elder statesman. Hoar had given in on Hawaii, but he had done penance all summer in addresses and published articles on the evils of a colonial policy. He would not again consent to compromise his principles. It so happened that in September the President offered Hoar the post of ambassador to Great Britain. The old scholar in politics was an irreproachable choice, a man whom McKinley revered and would have delighted to honor. It might not have been relevant that the tender was made at the time when the President had determined to require the cession of Luzon.

John Bassett Moore was to act as secretary of the commission, and his resignation went in with Day's in September. The State Department had meanwhile assembled a mass of data bearing on the negotiations. The President, at the last moment, desired the attendance of Commander Bradford at Paris to present the arguments of naval strategy. The Americans were to have the benefit of firsthand reports on the Philippines, including a conference with the Englishman, John Foreman. The most important advice on the situation was expected from General Merritt, who was to appear in person to submit his opinions and also those of Admiral Dewey, who had been reluctant to leave Manila at a critical time. This consideration did not influence the newly installed American military governor of Manila. Merritt had arranged to devote himself to his administrative duties, transferring the command of the troops to his next in rank, General Elwell S. Otis, on the arrival of the latter on August 21 with the fourth army expedition; but he had no heart for the task. His dream of colonial government had vanished on information of the terms of the armistice. The limited jurisdiction at Manila, with its enforced passivity toward insurrection elsewhere, was in painful contrast with his previous grandiose conception of his "mission." Though great powers might yet be in store for the supreme American commander in the Philippines, Merritt declined to brook the frustrations of the protocol. He requested and received permission to return home, via the peace conference at Paris. General Otis assumed the governorship of Manila, as well as the command of the Eighth Army Corps.

General Francis V. Greene, the New York militia officer who commanded the second Philippine expedition, had also left Manila on summons to report to Washington. Competent advice would soon be available, but it was lacking when the peace commissioners gathered at the Executive Mansion for a final conference with the President. It was still possible that the logical argument for American annexation was based upon some fault. The President's doubts disfigured the clarity of his confidential instructions to the commission. He was firm and explicit on all points dealing with the *fait accompli* of the first articles of the protocol. On the question of the Philippines, McKinley was pleading a case which, as it appeared, he was fearful of losing—the case for "moderation, restraint, and reason in victory" against exorbitant demands for territory.

"We took up arms," the President said, "only in obedience to the dictates of humanity and in the fulfillment of high public and moral obligations. We had no design of aggrandizement and no ambition of conquest. . . . It is my earnest wish that the United States in making peace should follow the same high rule of conduct which guided it in facing war. It should be as scrupulous and magnanimous in the concluding settlement as it was just and humane in its original action. The lustre and the moral strength attaching to a cause which can be confidently rested upon the considerate judgment of the world should not under any illusion of the hour be dimmed by ulterior designs which might tempt us into excessive demands or into an adventurous departure on untried paths."

Like a cloudy pendant on this avowal hung the tremendous "but" of the

331

obligations imposed by the presence and success of American arms at Manila. "The march of events," McKinley averred in one of his ponderous epigrams, "rules and overrules human action." The war had fortuitously brought "new duties and responsibilities," to be discharged "as becomes a great nation on whose growth and career from the beginning the Ruler of Nations has plainly written the high command and pledge of civilization." The President said a few words for the commercial opportunity, to which American statesmanship could not be indifferent, but observed that it depended less on large territorial possession than the open door for trade in the Orient. Through the guiding principles he had outlined, he believed that the present interests of the country, its future welfare, and its "exemption from unknown perils" would be found in full accord with the purpose that had been invoked in accepting war. After conducting the commissioners through this maze of verbiage, the President brought them out on a patch of open ground. He informed them, in conclusion, that the United States could not accept less than the cession, in full right and sovereignty, of the island of Luzon, and a guarantee of equal rights for American commerce elsewhere in the archipelago.

The interview was congenial, and so was the farewell dinner at the White House. In speaking with Cortelyou, the President appeared much relieved that the commission had finally started on its course and that many complex questions had "assumed shape" in the instructions. But there was depression in McKinley's heart. The next night, tired out after tussling with a batch of office seekers, he admitted to Cortelyou that the past week had been one of the hardest that he had experienced in many months.

The President, in the middle of September, was feeling the strain of the hammering of the press and the country's anger against the War Department. He was most painfully disturbed by continuing signs of antipathy to military service. Soon after the armistice, he had ordered the muster-out of 100,000 volunteers, assigning the discharges to the various states in proportion to the numbers they had furnished, with priority given to regiments that had seen action. Scarcely anyone questioned the temporary necessity of keeping troops in Cuba, Porto Rico, and Manila, and a large part of the public was bent on extending American rule over the Philippine archipelago. But cries of indignation broke from the militia regiments that were retained, and from their friends and sponsors. State officials and members of Congress, recently so insistent on getting their outfits overseas, demanded their immediate release. The inconsistencies of the popular mood defied political analysis, as Americans vaunted military success and raged against military management, bragged about new possessions and opposed the means of governing them.

The early Maine and Vermont elections had been marked by a falling off in the vote that was a warning to less rock-ribbed Republican states. Candidates everywhere were laboring under the taunts of "Algerism." The President's mail was filled with entreaties for help. His long-faced callers implored him to think of the party. McKinley had much at stake in the off-year elections. He had as yet barely launched the program with which he had entered office, and he must look to the next Congress to implement the policy of expansion. The capture of either house by the Democrats would mean the certain obstruction of all of the President's plans, and irreparable ruin for most of them.

Mark Hanna went to work on the state campaigns with an energy which national chairmen usually reserved for presidential years. It was again determined to concentrate the main effort on the states beyond the Mississippi, where the war had been popular and expansionist sentiment was strong. The West was well out of its period of hard scrabble, and the silver craze had wonderfully abated. There was a possibility of stirring up sufficient enthusiasm in this section to counterbalance the disaffection in the East. While Hanna "milked the country" for funds, McKinley examined the many invitations on his desk, and made an engagement to deliver an address at the Nebraska Peace Jubilee in October. This celebration was to be held at the Trans-Mississippi Exposition, a huge fair which had opened at Omaha in the midst of the war. Since the armistice, it had become a mecca for sightseeing farmers and industrialists, and the President could be sure of reaching a large audience from all parts of the West. He also agreed to speak at several stops on his way across Iowa, and to visit St. Louis and Chicago.

The elections of 1898 did not turn on the issues that had grown out of the war. The Democrats were campaigning on silver and Populistic platforms in states where the old issues were still live, and confined themselves to local questions elsewhere. "Algerism," in spite of much noisy jeering, was officially disregarded by the opposition party, not only because of the pending investigation of the War Department, but because the Democratic leaders were fearful of challenging the popularity of the President and of the victory. The formulation of an anti-expansionist policy necessarily waited on the final settlement of the peace terms, but this was an issue that the President intended to force. He planned to make his speaking tour the occasion for sounding out the West on taking the Philippines. He had to find out if the masses of the Republican party would support a radical and costly colonial policy, involving the detention of troops in the far Pacific.

As he turned the coin of decision, the President was still brooding over the instability of the people. There was a drop of bitterness in the irony of his mind. "We are in an anomalous position," he thought. "The people want us to hold everything but the soldiers, forgetting that without them we could not hold anything."

With the arrival of General Greene in Washington on September 27, the President had his first opportunity of consulting a man who had been at Manila, with the exception of Commander Bradford, whose latest visit had been paid in 1869. Three days later McKinley received a comprehensive memorandum from Greene on political and economic conditions in the Philippines. The press reports simultaneously pointed to an upswing in Republican sentiment on the subject. Mark Hanna, a stubborn opponent of expansion, suddenly gave out an interview at Cleveland, flatly declaring that Spain had lost the Philippines. His remarks indicated that he had not been in close consultation with McKinley on the question. He described the insurgents as "our allies" and anticipated, pending the action of Congress, a "temporary protectorate" under American military auspices. But if Hanna was talking off the cuff, he was certainly not in ignorance of the main bearing of the information that had been supplied to Washington.

The newspapers attached much importance to a dispatch from Dewey which General Greene had carried. This missive was, in fact, a reply to a month-old request that the Admiral should advise which island to select, if but one were to be taken. The obvious answer was badly out of date when Washington received Dewey's assurance that Luzon was the most desirable. Manila was situated in it, Dewey explained, and also Subic Bay, an unequalled coaling station or base, strategically commanding Manila. He noted a few random bits of data on climate, resources, and trade, such as might have been hastily gleaned from a guidebook, had such a work existed. The dispatch added nothing to the sum of knowledge at Washington, while only the purpose of confusion was served by Dewey's statement that further intercourse with the docile natives of Luzon had confirmed his earlier opinion that they were far superior to the Cubans.

On the whole, it was just as well that Dewey had not wanted to come home. The President had been lucky to get General Greene instead. The New Yorker had spent only six weeks in the Philippines and for the greater part of that time he had been busy with military duties in the peanut field outside Manila, but he had made the most of his opportunities. A former regular Army officer who had been an instructor of engineering at West Point, Greene was a businessman of broad interests, well read, observant, and articulate. His opinions were as valuable as could be expected under the circumstances, and they were the only intelligent opinions on the current situation that had ever been submitted to the President.

The machinery of Spanish government, Greene's memorandum stated, was thoroughly disorganized when the Americans entered Manila, and the central authority had fallen under the charge of the officers of the occupation. The Spanish officials feared the insurgents, who hated them and the friars with "indescribable virulence." The natives would continue to fight if any attempt were made to restore Spanish government. The result would be civil war and anarchy, leading inevitably and speedily to foreign intervention.

Aguinaldo's scheme of government, the memorandum continued, was a pure despotism, a dictatorship of the South American type. The Tagalog partisans claimed the sympathy of the Visayans, the inhabitants of the central islands, but there were many reasons to believe that the latter would oppose Aguinaldo. They had not at any time taken part in the insurrection, and were still submissive to the local Spanish officials. The educated and propertied Filipinos, of whom there were thousands at Manila, had a poor opinion of Aguinaldo's political ability. They considered him merely a successful insurgent leader. The aim of independence did not command the hearty support of these intelligent natives. All were agreed that they must have the support of a strong nation for many years. Their ideal was a Philippine republic under American protection, but they had no clearly defined ideas to offer. It was difficult to see, Greene observed, how protection could be given without leading to possession.

Greene was an enthusiast for annexation, like nearly every other American who had set foot in the Philippines, and a large part of his memorandum was devoted to a discussion of the potential wealth of the islands and the commercial advantages that would result if their resources were "explored with American energy." He could speak with some authority on the thriving foreign trade of Manila, and on the government revenue derived from it. Though Greene had spent only about two weeks in the capital, he had been chief of the bureaus of collection under the military administration, and had thus had full access to fiscal information. He believed that trade might be enormously extended under the ownership of the United States, but only on condition that the archipelago were not subdivided. The principal merchants for all the islands were at Manila, and most of the duties were collected at the customhouse there. Should duties be imposed on internal trade, the prosperity of Manila would be destroyed and the government revenue lost.

The long report was supplemented by charts, consular reports, and copies of Aguinaldo's decrees and manifestoes. After the President had studied all this and held several conversations with Greene, he had learned a good deal about the Philippines. He had learned enough to convince him that it was to the interest of the United States to take the archipelago, and that no other disposition would give peace and prosperity to the inhabitants. He had also enlarged his understanding of the conflict between annexation and the native movement for independence.

It had become plain enough that this conflict had been created and inflamed by the official representatives of the United States. The government at Washington and General Otis at Manila were the heirs of the muddle produced by three effusively annexationist consuls, a fatuously complacent admiral, and four overbearing military commanders.

Consuls Pratt and Wildman, at Singapore and Hong Kong respectively, had encouraged and aided Aguinaldo for selfishly nationalistic ends. O. F. Williams at Manila, though his attitude was less cynical and his conduct less indiscreet, was guided by similar motives. Dewey's sole idea was to protect his squadron. His military assistance to the revolutionary leaders and his indulgent attitude toward their political activities were responsible for the existence of organized rebellion on Luzon. In the view of the army officers, Dewey had imposed on the American government the obligation of suppressing it.

The military commanders had been highly indignant at Dewey's complication of the simple task of capturing Manila. General Anderson, the first to arrive, had been brusque and peremptory in his intercourse with Aguinaldo, but he was the only one of them who had condescended to deal directly with the rebel generalissimo. Neither Greene nor MacArthur had ever seen or corresponded with him. Merritt's policy was to hold entirely aloof, ignoring Aguinaldo's position and making any necessary communication through subordinates. After the Americans entered Manila, Merritt would have treated the insurgents as enemies, if he had got authority to do so, but yet he did not think that they were likely to cause any serious disturbances. Greene's report discussed the possibility of a native attack, treating it strictly as a military problem. He was confident that the successes on Luzon could not have been won against the American army. The insurgents would have been driven back to the hills and reduced to petty guerrilla warfare, and this would certainly be the result if they now attempted to attack. Native bands might give some trouble for a time, but it would not be long before they were reduced to subjection.

An armed conflict with the natives was more to the President than a military problem. It would offer, among other things, a tremendous political problem. Since Merritt and Greene had sailed, a clash had been averted at Manila, and General Otis had cheerfully cabled "no difficulty anticipated." On the other hand, the insurgent forces were in increasing strength. They had overrun Luzon, easily capturing all the Spanish garrisons. Aguinaldo, moreover, was making good progress in developing a civil government. He had established his revolutionary capital at Malolos, a large town north of Manila. The first congress of the republic of the Philippines had convened and organized. In setting up American rule on Luzon, Washington could not escape some stigma of an oppressive colonialism, and "excessive demands" for territory might work to the very serious disadvantage of the Republican party. The "subjection" of the Philippines would be a boon to the Democrats in their need of an issue to replace the tired cause of silver. Thoughts of 1900 must have been vivid in the President's mind, for he had recently had a little talk with Colonel William Jennings Bryan.

Bryan had at first been baffled by the war and the part he should choose to play in it. He had finally raised a regiment of his Nebraska adherents under the President's second call for volunteers. Since the state quota had not been filled under the first call, these recruits should properly have been used to augment two already existing regiments; but, to avoid the charge of party prejudice, an exception had been made. The Third Nebraska was mustered in with Bryan as its colonel. He had sweated out a brief, inglorious military career at Jacksonville, where his men had fallen sick in numbers that were remarkable even in the Florida encampments. Bryan was not happy in the army; and after the armistice, with the congressional elections coming on, he felt that his place was at home. The War Department, however, had declined to release the "Silver Regiment" on grounds of injustice to the First Nebraska, which had been in action at Manila.

Governor Silas Holcomb of Nebraska was a Populist, in deepest sympathy with Bryan's wishes. At the same time he did not wish to alienate the friends of the Manila veterans by giving preference to an outfit that had fought nothing but sandflies and mosquitoes. He proposed extricating battalions from both regiments, with Bryan among those favored. The War Department had ruled against breaking up regimental organizations, but Bryan was hoping for another exception. Toward the end of September, he met Holcomb in Washington, and they repaired to the White House to lay the case before the politically sensitive President. Bryan's eagerness to get out of the service was equaled by his distaste for asking a favor of the Republican administration. His presence at the interview was to be merely a tacit reminder that a denial of Holcomb's application would be open to unpleasant interpretation—that Washington was trying to keep the silver leader out of the Nebraska campaign or force him into the unpatriotic alternative of resigning from the service.

Secretary Gage was in the Cabinet Room when the two Nebraskans were admitted, and the President desired him to remain. A paper was presented, setting forth the particulars of the regiments and the proposed method of reduction. After reading this and correcting some errors of fact, the President turned to the principal beneficiary of the application, who was sitting in silence, looking fit and handsome, with a dark Florida tan. Colonel Bryan, McKinley remarked, had expressed no wish whatever. Colonel Bryan stalled, speaking vaguely of consideration for the President. But the President did not quite understand. His expressed wish, Bryan was obliged to explain, might be embarrassing to refuse in view of all the circumstances, even if the President felt it his duty to do so.

"I do not quite see it that way," McKinley replied. "If you made a request that I thought was right I should be pleased to grant it. If you asked one that I thought ought not to be granted my refusal would be based upon good reasons, and with these I should not experience any embarrassment."

Bryan must have been exasperated by this lofty rejoinder, for he took occasion to comment with some heat on the general question of Republican policy.

"Many of the Nebraska volunteers," he said, "feel that they have a right to be mustered out, on the ground that the issues of the war have changed. They volunteered to break the yoke of Spain in Cuba, and for nothing else. They did not volunteer to attempt the subjugation of other peoples, or establish United States sovereignty elsewhere."

The interview came to an end, and Bryan strode out of the Cabinet Room, leaving Secretary Gage to record the rehearsal of a campaign speech for the next national election.

On October 1, the peace commissioners of the United States and Spain held their first session in the sumptuous conference chamber which had been placed at their disposal at the Quai d'Orsay. The new Secretary of State had taken office in Washington the day before. John Hay had come back from London dragging his feet, a frail, ease-loving, fastidious man, who hated routine and political pressures, who was sure that the State Department would kill him. The President was not going to worry about it any more, and scared Hay by telling him so, but McKinley was not speaking of the settlement with Spain, which he continued to make his direct responsibility. Hay was scarcely more than the intermediary between the President and the Paris commissioners. Frequently, he did not discharge even that function, for both Day and Reid were in confidential correspondence with the White House.

Since the disposition of the Philippines was the only important question that had been left to negotiation, Day had expected to reach it quickly, and he soon cabled for full instructions. The Spaniards, however, proved resourceful in disputing the meaning of the protocol. They persisted in confounding the transfer of Cuban sovereignty with the obligation of the so-called Cuban debt, and sought to force the United States to assume the responsibility of this immense bond issue, either permanently or on behalf of a future insular government. The conference was deadlocked on this contention for nearly four weeks. The American commissioners had ample time to enlarge their knowledge of the Philippines, and to argue among themselves the pros and cons of annexation.

General Merritt had promptly presented himself, carrying a number of reports from officers of his command. His interrogation dealt with the native insurrection. His replies were restricted to conditions that had fallen under his personal observation. He assured the commission that the Luzon insurgents would fight to the bitter end against Spain, and that Spain could not reduce them. He did not fear conflict over American possession of Manila alone. Apart from these statements, Merritt's testimony was extremely guarded, but it emerged that he looked for some resistance to larger acquisitions by the United States and did not much concern himself about it. The chief impression conveyed by Merritt's remarks was one of supercilious disdain for "these people" and their negligible leader. Since he had not been granted authority to mop the natives up, Merritt seemed to regard the situation as an untidy bore, in which he had lost interest.

As the bearer of Dewey's views, Merritt was a still greater disappointment. The commissioners, awaiting competent advice on annexation, were disconcerted to find that the Admiral had fobbed them off with a mere copy of the outdated dispatch about Luzon which Greene had taken to Washington. Its tenor was ambiguous, since it had been written in reply to a specific inquiry from the Navy Department; and, deprived of this context, it suggested that Dewey was averse to claiming any territory except Luzon. Merritt was unwilling to speak for the Admiral, though he acknowledged that they had discussed the matter many times. He was cautiously inclined to believe that Dewey favored taking the archipelago, but declined to make a statement to that effect.

Ten days later, with the appearance of Commander Bradford, the commissioners were treated to a positive recommendation of annexation, with a lesson on naval strategy. Bradford roundly informed them that it would be less difficult to defend the entire group than a single island—and, if

Luzon alone were taken, it would be open to attack from almost any direction. Moreover, he was not satisfied with a coaling station at Guam. He strongly advised acquiring the rest of the Ladrones and also the Carolines, groups that were merely dependencies of the Philippines. Old Bradford represented the soaring imperialist spirit of the American Navy—he wanted to annex Cuba and would not have been averse to getting a slice of China—and he had little patience with arguments against overextension. "If we are going to inclose ourselves within a shell, like a turtle, and defend ourselves after the manner of a turtle," he sarcastically observed, "then any possession outside of our own country may be said to be a source of weakness."

Under pressure to suggest a division of the Philippine archipelago, Bradford drew a line on the map, bulging around the long sprawl of Luzon and veering back to include Mindoro and Palawan and other islands to the southwest. These were the most strategically valuable, since they commanded the entrances to the China Sea from the north end of Luzon to Borneo. If a division must be made, this was a fairly good one, offering fair protection. There was, of course, Bradford said, no reason for concern about proximity to Borneo—it was a British possession. The trend of the Navy's thinking provoked varied reactions from the commissioners.

Frye: Do you understand that Germany is trying to get Palawan?
Bradford: Yes, sir.
Gray: How do you know that Germany is trying to get it?
Bradford: It has been so reported by the press for years; their cruisers frequent the islands and their engineers have explored them.
Gray: How have they been trying to get it?
Bradford: By purchase, I presume. . . .
Reid: Would that division you have indicated there remove your objection to the dangerous proximity of the other islands if in unfriendly hands?
Bradford: No, sir.
Reid: You would consider that the least evil, on a division of the group? . . . But as not removing the evil, from a military point of view?
Bradford: Precisely.
Day: Still, you recognize the point that sometimes you have to submit to dangerous neighbors?
Bradford: Possibly. I am only advocating it be avoided, if feasible. . . .
Gray: Do you not think we would rid ourselves of the possibility of bad neighbors by keeping out of there altogether? . . .
Davis: If we should leave them in the possession of Spain we would have a very bad neighbor there?
Bradford: Most assuredly. . . .

Frye: If we should adopt your line of demarcation, what do you think Spain would do with the balance of the islands?

Bradford: Sell them to Germany.

Frye: Is not Germany about as troublesome a neighbor as we could get?

Bradford: The most so, in my opinion.

After two weeks of discussion, Davis, Frye, and Reid were confirmed in their original belief that the United States should annex the Philippines, while Gray remained in the equally logical position of desiring to have no part of them. Day alone modified his opinion. Evidently under the influence of Bradford's statements, he was considering the possible acquisition of some islands near Luzon. But Day still held back from total annexation. Besides his objections to a colonial policy, he was embarrassed by the fact that the protocol had left the question to negotiation. There was little room for negotiation, Day thought, when one party demanded at the outset all that was to be negotiated about.

While the President toured the West, the American commissioners were at odds on the main business before the conference; but they were united in apprehension that the main business might never be taken up. The peace treaty seemed in serious danger of foundering on the Cuban debt.

The President's active participation in the congressional campaigns was an event of the first political importance. He had not been west of the Mississippi since taking office, and the loyal Republicans turned out in throngs to greet him. Through the deafening cheers of Iowa, he moved to the thunderous welcome of Omaha, and on to new ovations at St. Louis and Chicago. For ten mellow autumn days, McKinley's resonant tenor voice rang over the West, and the whole country echoed with the inspiring generalizations at which he was adept. He spoke of the new national unity and the return of American prosperity. He hailed the victory of Manila Bay and the other glorious achievements of the armed forces. He talked of justice and humanity, and also "the courage of destiny"; and he said that he trusted the war would bring "blessings that are now beyond calculation." There was only one direct allusion to territorial expansion. "We have good money, we have ample revenues, we have unquestioned national credit," McKinley said at Hastings, Iowa, "but what we want is new markets, and as trade follows the flag it looks very much as if we were going to have new markets."

In his principal address at the Omaha exposition, the President admonished the people to avoid the temptation of undue aggression, and to dedicate themselves with high and unselfish aims to the problems of the peace. The United States had sought neither the war nor the resultant international responsibilities; but these could not be shirked, even if desire opposed. The heroes of Manila and Santiago and Porto Rico had made immortal history, and who would dim the splendor of their achievements? "Who will darken the counsels of the Republic in this hour requiring the united wisdom of all?" the President asked. "Shall we deny ourselves what the rest of the world so freely and so justly accords to us?" The American people would do their duty, he told the cheering multitude, and the genius of the nation would make it equal to every task.

Anti-expansionist publications complained that no definite meaning could be attached to the President's utterances, but there are communions that transcend the language of precise explanation. McKinley's hearers understood him perfectly. He was telling them that he believed the United States could not give up the Philippines, and asking them if they agreed that the acquisition was a moral obligation. With shouts for duties and tasks and burdens, the people intelligibly answered that they did.

Ten days after the President finished his tour, the country went to the polls. The returns east of the Mississippi exhibited the familiar tendency of reaction against the party in power—the outstanding Republican success was Roosevelt's election by a narrow margin to the governorship of New York—but, in state after state where the silver craze had been strongest, Republicans rallied to save the House, and to choose legislatures committed to support sound candidates for the United States Senate. The midterm elections assured McKinley of a good working majority in both houses of Congress for the two remaining years of his term.

The question of the Philippines had meanwhile been squarely posed. In hopes of concessions in that quarter, the Spanish peace commissioners had tentatively laid aside the first two articles of the protocol, and Judge Day cabled for immediate instructions. "The cession must be of the whole archipelago or none," the President directed on October 26. "The latter is wholly inadmissible, and the former must therefore be required." The progress of the Philippine insurrection had led Dewey to urge an early settlement, but McKinley was not deterred from making a demand that was sure to prolong the negotiations. He was likewise unaffected by the division among the American commissioners. On receipt of a long cable setting forth their individual opinions, Secretary Hay held up another and fuller dispatch to Paris until the President should return from an overnight trip to Philadelphia. There was, however, no modification of the instructions.

Additional dispatches soon acquainted the commissioners with the moral grounds for requiring possession of the archipelago. They were told that territorial expansion should be our least concern and that, as victors, we should be governed only by motives that would exalt the nation. Nevertheless, the President's ultimatum caused misgivings at Paris. The dissenters, Gray and Day, were not alone in objecting. Both Frye and Reid were convinced that the Spaniards could not go back empty-handed to Madrid. With little more to lose by conquest than was required at the peace table, Spain might choose the course of desperation, renewing hostilities and forcing the United States to act as the ruthless despoiler of a fallen enemy. The fear of this outcome was so strong that when the demand for the Philippines was presented, it contained a qualifying phrase. The President had observed that he was not unmindful of the distressed financial condition of Spain; and, on the basis of this statement, the American commissioners signified willingness to take over a part of the public debt of the islands. As another deadlock ensued, still greater concessions were proposed. Frye backed away from the outright claim for territory, and Reid followed him. The President was plied with a variety of suggestions for compromise, including the relinquishment of Mindanao and the Sulu group in exchange for the Carolines and all of the Ladrones. In November, only Cushman Davis adhered to a stand for total cession, desiring to deny even money compensation to Spain.

In opposition to four of his five commissioners, McKinley was immovable on territory and on the assumption of outstanding obligations in the Philippines, but he consented to a money payment and to certain minor concessions. Day, always deferential to the President's judgment, was mollified by authority to negotiate, and Davis and Gray yielded their extreme positions for the sake of securing a treaty. The sum of $20,000,000 was eventually agreed on and approved, and Spain accepted the American terms at the end of November. The negotiations were formally concluded by the signing of the Treaty of Paris on December 10.

The decision, which had germinated as a war measure and ripened under the inducement of commercial advantage, had come to full maturity in the heat of foreign aggression. McKinley had bowed to the conviction that there was no other solution for the Philippines but to "fling them, a golden apple of discord, among the rival powers." The United States, linked with Great Britain in trade policy in the Far East, was just entering on a new era of friendly *rapprochement* with Japan. The President was satisfied that, in thrusting American dominion to the China Sea, he was acting to secure peace in the Pacific. The hope of progress toward world peace was ever in his mind. Washington had promptly accepted an invitation from the Russian government to participate in a peace conference of the powers. To join in such an assemblage was a departure from American tradition, but the negotiations offered an unequaled opportunity to promote a plan for the adjustment of international disputes. The next spring, McKinley would send a strong delegation to The Hague, with a fully developed project of a permanent court of arbitration.

The American policy makers of 1898 have been sadly estranged by history. They stand on the threshold of the twentieth century like men of remote antiquity, quaintly laying their plans for establishing the trade supremacy of the United States in amity with all nations. They could not interpret the plainly prefigured alignments of World War I; far less could they guess at the ultimate enmity of Japan. The warfare of the future was sealed to their comprehension. Distance was still a factor of strategy, an element of security, and the protection of far-flung colonies seemed permanently entrusted to a fleet of proud steel ships and a chain of island stations for their banquet tables of coal. Air power and its monstrous issue, global war, were notions as fantastic as a trip to the moon, as unimaginable to the President as to young Douglas MacArthur, a candidate for West Point whose father was military commandant of Manila.

McKinley had taken his decision in the light of the knowledge of his day. His fatalistic habit was apparent in his later remarks to Jacob G. Schurman, the president of Cornell University, whom he invited to head a Philippine Commission. Schurman demurred at accepting the honor on the ground of opposition to McKinley's policy, bluntly saying that he had never wanted the Philippine Islands. "Oh, that need not trouble you," the President replied; "I didn't want the Philippine Islands, either; and in the protocol to the treaty I left myself free not to take them; but—in the end there was no alternative." The peace of the world would have been endangered, McKinley flatly told Schurman. It was an unusually barren admission. In private conversation as in his public papers and addresses, McKinley was wont to evade the bleakness of constraint by dwelling on the moral mission of America. A program of enlightened colonization was merely the extension to the political sphere of the doctrine of spiritual expansion with which he had been saturated since childhood. During the President's tour of the West, his own fervent expressions and the response of his audiences had wrought an intensity of emotion which, on his return to Washington, had reached a climax in prayer. More than a year later, McKinley described the religious experience in which his last doubts had burned away and his purposes in the Philippines had attained clarification and sanction.

The occasion was an interview with the General Missionary Committee of the Methodist Episcopal Church, which had been one of the most active of the expansionist pressure groups. As the visitors took their leave,

the President detained them. "Hold a moment longer! Not quite yet, gentlemen! Before you go I would like to say just a word about the Philippine
business." Then, to these sympathetic ears, McKinley poured out his story:
that he had not wanted the Philippines; that he had not known what to
do with them; that there were obstacles to every means of disposing of
them or leaving them to themselves. "I walked the floor of the White
House night after night until midnight," he said; "and I am not ashamed
to tell you, gentlemen, that I went down on my knees and prayed Almighty
God for light and guidance more than one night. And one night late it
came to me this way—I don't know how it was, but it came . . . that there
was nothing left for us to do but to take them all, and to educate the
Filipinos, and uplift them and civilize and Christianize them, and by
God's grace do the very best we could by them, as our fellow-men for whom
Christ also died. And then I went to bed, and went to sleep, and slept
soundly, and the next morning I sent for the chief engineer of the War
Department (our map-maker), and I told him to put the Philippines on
the map of the United States, and there they are, and there they will
stay while I am President!"

McKinley had found on his knees the argument that reconciled him to
a course he had described as "criminal aggression." He betrayed his intellectual limitations, not by the hard choice to which he had been reluctantly
led, but by an explanation which belittled a great quandary of statesmanship to resolve a dilemma of conscience. The President's political instinct
was never more sure than in adorning territorial acquisition with the bright
leaf of duty and the rose of spiritual salvation. Yet his sincerity was attested
by a faithful discharge of the obligations he preached. For the rest of his
life, McKinley placed the welfare of the Philippine inhabitants second
only to that of the American people.

The Philippine inhabitants, to the President's mind, meant primarily the
rural population of impoverished and largely illiterate peasants. They called
up a rather nebulous picture—they were known only by hearsay to the
Americans at Manila—but McKinley felt sure of one or two characteristics,
besides their political backwardness. He had learned from John Foreman's
article that they were sensitive and pliant, and that, while they had been
outraged by Spanish oppression, they could be easily molded by a just
and merciful government. It did not disturb the President's picture that
the Tagalog warriors were also inhabitants. He considered them a lawless
faction, greedy for loot, and totally distinct from and inimical to the
gentle, peace-loving masses. At the same time, he believed that the insurgents were also simple men who had been stirred up against the United

States by ambitious native politicians, and he counted on obtaining their submission as soon as they understood the kindly purposes of the American government.

Although the Washington authorities had no real apprehension that an outbreak would follow the assertion of American sovereignty, they were repeatedly disturbed by the news of insurgent successes against the Spanish garrisons. In October, Dewey had cabled that there was anarchy on Luzon and that it would probably soon spread to the islands on the south. It was judged prudent to send on the remainder of the Philippine army corps, some 5,000 troops, mainly volunteers, who had not yet sailed when the armistice was proclaimed. General Otis himself was largely responsible for the fact that the government did not feel more acute alarm about the situation in the Philippines. He asked for reinforcements, warned of dangers, reported insurgent progress, and yet his dispatches never conveyed an impression of urgency. He was always able to put in a word of cheery prophecy that was all the more persuasive because it seemed to be based on a frank recognition of the adverse factors involved; but, besides the illusions of a hopeful temperament, Otis was frequently lacking in accurate information. His opinions, like those of Dewey and Greene, were derived from one small and unrepresentative group—the upper-class, propertied natives of Manila. These educated Filipinos had supported the Malolos government out of hatred for Spain, but were not in sympathy with the aim of Philippine independence, and tended to minimize nationalist sentiment in their desire for the friendship and protection of the United States. They gradually lost ground during the autumn to the rabidly anti-American element among Aguinaldo's advisers. By midwinter, the conservatives were not only powerless to influence the insurgent program, but progressively ignorant of its trend. Yet they remained the chief source of the information supplied to Washington.

The actual conditions in the Philippines might have been arranged by the more imaginative Democrats for the purpose of falsifying the President's professions of good will. The American brand of racial superiority was not disciplined by experience in dealing with Oriental peoples. Both officers and men gave offense by rough tactlessness and discourtesy. Drunken soldiers were quarrelsome and insulting, but the boisterous ridicule of the better element provoked nearly as much resentment. The western volunteers were aggrieved and angry at finding themselves hated, and soon heartily loathed the "niggers" in return. While the two forces perpetually quivered on the verge of an incident, the Tagalog leaders at Malolos were making ready to revolt against the United States, if the peace conference should result in the cession of the Philippines. Revolutionary manifestoes

346

were posted throughout the archipelago; and hostility to the white man's dominion, under whatever flag, was spread by agitators and implemented by rifles. The fire of rebellion leapt from island to island, springing up little railroads, flickering along jungle trails. As the President had been assured, the untutored inhabitants possessed only a dim conception of nationality and union; but freedom is a more primitive idea. The name of Aguinaldo was the symbol of liberation, and the tribes arose in strength to follow him.

When news of the Treaty of Paris reached Manila in December, the American forces occupied an enclave of treachery, surrounded by violence. In the wilderness of Luzon and on the other islands of the archipelago, the brothers of the insurgents awaited the signal to drive out the invader. While McKinley's thoughts were occupied with plans for the ratification of the treaty and for the future peace and prosperity of the Philippines, events were moving toward a more obstinate and sanguinary contest than the three months' war with Spain.

· 15 ·

THE GOLDEN APPLE OF DISCORD

CHEERS rocked the gilded dome of
the state capitol, and the telegraph stuttered to the nation the news of the
greatest reception ever given an American citizen in Atlanta. The curtain
of thirty-four years dropped kindly over General Sherman's swathe of
flame, as a Union veteran addressed the Georgia legislature, praising the
valor of the Confederate dead and proffering national aid in the care of
their graves. The Republican President had gone to the Atlanta Peace
Jubilee with outstretched hands in December. Georgia rose up to greet
him, and with Georgia the whole South.

McKinley's party had come to regard him with an almost superstitious
veneration. The comparison with Lincoln was a platitude of Republican
oratory. It had taken a foreign war, but America had fulfilled the yearning
prophecy that "the mystic chords of memory" would again be "touched
. . . by the better angels of our nature." The spirit of Lincoln was Mc-
Kinley's guide on his visit to the South, though he did not mar his reception
by the allusion. He sprang to his feet when the band played "Dixie," and
waved his hat above his head. He reviewed the marching ranks of gray-
clad troops. He wore the badge of gray that was hastily made up with his
portrait and his words about the care of Confederate graves. His voice was
fervent as he said that the old disagreements had faded into history and
the nation would remain indivisible forever. General Joe Wheeler often
stood beside the President, swelling the ovation by his immense popularity;
but Shafter, too, was there, and Alger himself was among the dignitaries
who had accompanied the President from Washington. McKinley's
shoulders seemed broad enough to carry all the troubles of his administra-

348

tion, while the southern crowds hurrahed and Confederate veterans jostled to clasp his hand.

A reunited country was the President's theme, but it frequently disappeared in variations appropriate to the recent signing of the peace treaty with Spain. For example, in an address at the Piedmont Park auditorium in Atlanta, McKinley started off with praise for the contribution made by the South in the late war; proceeded via the luster thereby added to the shining stars of the old flag; and in no time at all was discussing the planting of that flag in two hemispheres. "Who will withdraw it from the people over whom it floats in protecting folds?" the President asked. "Who will haul it down?" At Savannah, a few days later, he pursued his interrogation, with strong emphasis on our duty. Who would shrink, could we leave, who would question? Should we proclaim to the world our inability to give kind government to oppressed peoples? Were we, the President inquired in a phrase more significant still, "to sit down in our isolation and recognize no obligation . . . ?" His Dixie audiences gave back a ringing negative, thrilling once more to the old expansionist aims of the southern Democracy, hailing the promise of a flourishing export trade, big markets for cotton, a full share in the new national prosperity. McKinley meant those cheers to echo in Washington, where the Fifty-fifth Congress had recently convened for its short final session. The nucleus of the opposition to the peace treaty was composed of southern senators.

More than twenty-five years had passed since the Senate had gratified the Executive by the ratification of an important treaty; and this time the President was requesting approval of a radical change in policy from a body in which the members of his party were outnumbered by the opposition and divided among themselves. Before leaving Washington, McKinley had affectionately greeted Senator Hoar and asked how he was feeling. "Pretty pugnacious, I confess, Mr. President," was the reply. Tears had started to McKinley's eyes, as he grasped Hoar's hand again and said, "I shall always love you, whatever you do." Eugene Hale of Maine, the chairman of the Committee on Naval Affairs, was another prominent dissenter. Except for Cabot Lodge of Massachusetts and Orville Platt of Connecticut, eastern Republicans were lukewarm for the Philippines, at best; while several of the Westerners, including Spooner of Wisconsin and Mason of Illinois, did not disguise their aversion to wearing the badge of "imperialism." Annexation, on the other hand, was endorsed by such influential Democrats as the diehard expansionist, Morgan of Alabama, and Gray of Delaware, who had returned from Paris a firm defender of the treaty; while the President possessed two notable advantages in the short remaining life of the Fifty-fifth Congress and the character of the treaty as a peace settlement. The November elections had ensured that, after March 4, the Senate would be responsive to the imperial trend. The existing body could interpose delays that would seriously embarrass the President's dealings with the Philippines, but it was powerless to prevent his getting approval for his treaty in the end. Many senators, moreover, would hesitate to place themselves on record as having voted to continue a state of war, detaining volunteer troops and disturbing the elated confidence of the business recovery. This was one of the arguments with which the President intended to persuade the Republican waverers; but, at the time when Congress assembled, he had still been unable to count the two-thirds majority of the Senate that was needed for ratification.

Two weeks later, the situation was altered by an unexpected development. Colonel Bryan, who had recently been a voluble critic of subjugating the Philippines, came out in favor of supporting the treaty, advising the Democratic senators to vote for ratification and then promise Philippine independence by resolution. He was seeking to exonerate his party from the blame for rejecting the peace and keeping the soldiers in the service. It was also surmised that, with an eye to 1900, the silver leader wanted to hoist the Republicans on their own imperialism as quickly as possible. The friends of the treaty were delighted by Bryan's advice and by the odor of expediency that clung to it. With the Senate opposition in confusion, the expansionist cohorts were confident of early ratification as Congress adjourned for the holiday recess.

The President, on returning to Washington, had to determine the course he would follow while Senate approval was pending. It was obviously desirable to shun any premature display of initiative, and particularly any movement outside Manila. Yet it had become necessary to begin occupying the ceded territory. The situation in the Visayas cried for action. The routed Spanish garrisons had concentrated at Iloilo, the capital of the island of Panay, and were hard pressed by insurgent forces. In dread of the surrender of this fine seaport, both Otis and Dewey had advised Washington to intervene. The President had left the matter in abeyance during his absence in the South. Finally, on December 21, he authorized an expedition, cautioning Otis to avoid conflict with the insurgents. Otis hastily embarked a regiment, but the troops arrived too late. Iloilo had fallen to the natives. Plied with admonitions from the President, Otis ordered that the Americans be held on their transports in the harbor.

On December 21, McKinley also prepared instructions for the formal announcement of the cession at Manila, and for the extension of the military government throughout the islands. A letter to Otis set forth the substance of a proclamation which, while abounding in references to conquest and sovereignty, contained guaranties of justice and protection for all who should co-operate with the new authority. The military government was adjured to win the regard of the inhabitants by assuring them of "that full measure of individual rights and liberties which is the heritage of free peoples, and by proving to them that the mission of the United States is one of benevolent assimilation. . . ." These instructions were originally sent to Manila by the slow Pacific mail. Six days later, however, the President decided to move at a faster pace, and the entire letter was rushed off to Otis by cable. The news from Iloilo had shown the risks of delay. The President had also been persuaded that his proclamation would have great psychological value. This opinion was developed by a conversation with Dean C. Worcester, a member of the zoology department of the University of Michigan.

Worcester was unknown to McKinley when he applied for an interview, with the object of giving the government advice on the Philippines. The professor had spent more than three years on collecting trips in the islands; and, though he had never visited Luzon and was not acquainted with the Tagalogs, he felt confident that he understood the situation. There was serious danger, he told the President, of an outbreak of hostilities between the natives and the Americans, but this excellent warning was negatived by Worcester's belief that the trouble had arisen from "mutual misunderstanding," which might still be smoothed over. The adjustment would be partly contingent on a firm show of authority, which the United States force at Manila was actually not large enough to support. Worcester convinced the President that the Americans should anticipate the insurgent leaders by at once taking steps to occupy strategic points. With the surrender of Iloilo, however, native troops had already seized all the Spanish stations, except for one port in the southernmost island of Mindanao.

Worcester's advice was of little value, but he was a man of good will, manifestly sincere and anxious to be of help, and genuinely sympathetic with the primitive people, many of them members of wild tribes, whom he had met on his travels. Nothing is more revealing of McKinley's own good will than the eagerness with which he listened to this well-intentioned stranger, and the trust he impulsively placed in him. The zoologist was amazed when, at the end of a long interview, the President asked him if he would go to the Philippines as his personal representative. While Worcester was debating this offer, McKinley settled on the plan of appointing a Philippine Commission, and obtained the consent of Jacob G. Schurman, the president of Cornell University, to serve as its head. Worcester was made a member of the commission, and he and Schurman started for Manila a few weeks later.

Even General Otis's hopeful spirit had been dashed by the President's instructions to announce an extension of authority which could not be enforced. Before publishing the proclamation, he had modified its language and accented the note of conciliation. But, in spite of revisions, the assertion of American intentions dangerously stimulated the ferment on Luzon. Aguinaldo issued a statement claiming American promises of independence for the Philippines. and protesting against their aggressive seizure. His words had the ring of a declaration of war.

The proclamation produced a scarcely less inflammatory effect on the President's opponents at home. His days of immunity to attack had been numbered since the report of the peace terms. Democratic newspapers, impatient to defy his policy, had settled on a strong line of propaganda, extolling Aguinaldo as a great native patriot and declaring that the Filipinos had now demonstrated their capacity for self-government. Influential Easterners had banded together to form the Anti-Imperialist League, and were preparing to cover the country with petitions of protest against the callous bargain by which a freedom-loving people had been purchased at the peace table. As news of tension on Luzon coincided with news of crisis at Iloilo, a shower of bricks flew at the President's head. He was covered with abuse for a program of military subjection and crass commercial exploitation. His address to the Filipinos was called contemptuous and insulting, and the phrase "benevolent assimilation" was derided as hypocritical cant. Both the proclamation and the dispatch of troops to Iloilo were denounced as autocratic acts which ignored the fact that the treaty had not been ratified by the Senate.

The force of this assault was partly due to the repressions suffered by Democratic editors in the preceding months. Many wrathful allusions revealed the mortification of "standing behind the President" while his followers traced resemblances to Lincoln in eulogies which, as *The Nation* crankily remarked, were comparable with the effusions of Oriental poets "in the great days of Mohammedanism," or "the flattery addressed to Louis XIV by his courtiers." Yet there was more than pent-up irritation in the dire warnings against the misuse of Executive power and the nervous anxiety over the dangers of a subservient public opinion. The violence of this attack was the violence of fear. The confidence of the opposition was undermined by the President's control of government policy and his hold on the masses of his party, an ascendancy that was illumined and confirmed by the happy financial auguries of the new year. For the jingling days of plenty had returned, and once more the nation marched in time with the throb of machines and the roar of furnaces. Factories were taxed to fill their orders. New business was crowding in. Prices were high, and dinner pails were full. Criticisms of the Republican administration were but ripples on the deep resurgent tide of American prosperity.

One resemblance between McKinley and Lincoln was not alleged. Both reduced their political enemies to a jumble of inconsistent accusations that they were absurdly weak and dangerously strong. The hostile press in 1899 endowed the occupant of the White House with a dual personality: on the one hand, an amiable, ordinary politician, befuddled by adulation; and, on the other, a self-willed dictator whose policy in the Philippines forecast his benevolent assimilation of the functions of Congress.

Soon after the treaty was transmitted on January 4, it was favorably reported by the Foreign Relations Committee, and plans were laid for its early consideration in executive session. The legal issue, however, was debated in open Senate. It had been presented weeks earlier in a resolution introduced by the distinguished jurist, George G. Vest of Missouri, that the federal government had no power to acquire territory to be held and governed permanently as colonies. The contention was justified by the silence of the Constitution on the subject, and the violation which a colonial policy would offer to the letter and spirit of that document and of the Declaration of Independence. Platt of Connecticut ably formulated and advanced the annexationist argument: that the United States as a nation is entitled to possess the inherent sovereign right to acquire territory, and that in the right to acquire is found the right to govern. This straightforward proposition was qualified by a finespun legal proviso. It was found necessary to deny that the Constitution extended automatically—or, in legal phraseology, *ex proprio vigore*, of its own force—to the new possessions. The Philippines and Porto Rico were held to be dependencies belonging to the United States, but not an integral part of the nation and hence not entitled to claim the full guaranties of the organic law. The American commissioners, in framing the peace treaty, had inserted an explicit provision that the civil rights and political status of the inhabitants of the ceded islands were to be determined by Congress. Though the warrant of the Executive branch to bestow this power seemed only less remote than that of Spain, the stipulation was destined to become a chief bulwark of the expansionist legislators.

The spokesmen of the annexationists declared that American expansion had never been hampered by scruples about the consent of the governed. They cited as precedents the Eskimos of Alaska, and the diverse inhabitants of the territories obtained by the Mexican cession and even the Louisiana

Purchase; and, forced on the defensive by jibes at colonialism, they went all the way back to the Declaration itself, and pointed out that the noble assertions of the founding fathers had not been intended to apply to Indians and Negroes. Political necessity had obliged the Republicans to turn a realistic eye on history; and the supporters of the administration likewise found themselves committed in executive session to a frank appraisal of the pressures of the international situation. Foraker stated that the disclosure of "complications with a foreign power" would fully justify the President's course, but it is doubtful that indoctrination on the tensions in the Pacific had the slightest effect on the opposition to Philippine annexation. Few senators were accustomed to weigh the bearing of foreign relations on matters of domestic policy. Some of them found the idea offensive to an independent patriotism. At least one, the senior senator from Massachusetts, was exclusively occupied with his concern for the antique values of the republic. He startled his colleagues by declaring that, if he could only prevent the ratification of that treaty, he would willingly lay his head on the block before the Vice-President's chair. "Hoar is crazy," Mark Hanna said. "He thinks Germany is just fooling."

On its higher level, the Senate contest was the struggle between a static and a dynamic conception of the Constitution, with the annexationists determined to fit the law to changing conditions, if they had to stretch the venerable document until it cracked. The legal arguments were of vital interest to the participants, but they had no more actual influence on the voting than the facts of German aggression. The real battle over the President's treaty was conducted on quite another level than the constitutional debate.

To the Washington correspondents, the early stage of the battle was a puzzle without a pattern. Bryan had visited the Capitol and urged his followers to approve the treaty; but the opposition, instead of melting away at Bryan's command, took on solidity and a markedly partisan character. The pattern of the puzzle, though not its solution, appeared in the third week of January, when Senator Arthur P. Gorman of Maryland emerged as the moving spirit of the fight against ratification. He had rallied the conservative Democrats and was talking over a number of the left-wingers. Some of Bryan's followers had not liked his Machiavellian instructions— Mark Hanna had watched him "buttonholing his men that were holding back and away from his influence." The temptation was strong to seize this golden opportunity of defeating the administration by a minority vote. Moreover, for a number of Democratic senators, the current session afforded the only opportunity of placing themselves on record against

Republican imperialism. Gorman himself was among those who would go out of office on March 4. He saw that the floating vote was large enough to reject the treaty, and he set out to capture it in a bid for the leadership of the Democratic party.

Mr. Andrew Carnegie "told" the President and the Secretary of State about these developments not long after they began to be published in the newspapers. The steel magnate was in a black mood that winter, uttering Cassandra-like prophecies of Republican doom. On a visit to the White House some weeks earlier, he had forecast that the President would have to shoot down Filipinos. The suggestion had drawn smiles from McKinley and John Hay. Hay also showed skepticism about the extent of Gorman's success. Sixty votes were needed for ratification. Hay confidentially informed Carnegie that there were ten votes to spare. But the assurance was not consoling to a man who believed that the annexation of the Philippines meant the ruin of the Republican party. Carnegie was brooding over the strength that the Democrats would muster in 1900, with the silver issue jettisoned in favor of the Declaration of Independence.

Two weeks earlier, the administration had obviously felt certain of an easy victory; but, whatever Colonel Hay was giving out, the President was certainly under this illusion no longer. Though the opposition was divided, it needed only thirty-one votes to prevail, and Gorman was an astute and experienced manager. The Washington correspondents noticed that he was about as successful in rounding up the floaters on one side as the President was on the other. McKinley had begun to hold many interviews, sending for Democrats as well as Republican waverers. Heedless of prudent advice to avoid an outright defeat, he was pressing for early action.

It was not hard to explain the unusual tremor of impatience that seemed to emanate from the White House. McKinley was still hopeful of an amicable settlement with the Philippine insurgents—the official dispatches from Manila were still optimistic—but there was manifest danger in prolonging the period of uncertainty. The risk of an incident was growing with every day of delay, and Otis, in his oddly casual way, had tossed out the disturbing comment that an outbreak in the Visayas would mean war in all the islands. Should the President call Congress in extra session in March, some further weeks must pass before the new Senate could organize and take action. There was a fighting chance for ratification by the existing Senate, and McKinley was urgent to take it.

Cushman K. Davis, who was in charge of the treaty, gave notice on January 19 of his intention to hurry things along in executive session. A Republican thunderer and the best of good fellows, the big senator from Minnesota was not gifted as a manager. All his energy seemed to be devoted to standing firm and refusing to bargain on independence for the Philippines. Reports leaked from the Senate chamber. Davis had told a delegation from the opposition that he would not consent to a vote until he was sure of ratification. Informed that there were sufficient votes to prevent, he asked for the names and was handed a list of thirty-six. A day of inactivity followed, with rumblings of an extra session. The next day, according to the news stories, Gorman arose to taunt the supporters of the treaty with their desire to avoid delay, assuring them that he agreed, that a vote might be reached within ten days. Vest joined in, urging Davis to name the day and hour—*they* were not holding up the treaty. "Let us vote now," said Nelson Aldrich, entering the chamber on an audacious line. But Davis hung back from setting a time on the plea of consulting the other members of the Foreign Relations Committee. Though the correspondents had none of this at first hand, the accurate trend of their information was established by that high-toned gossip, Mr. Henry Adams, also dependent on hearsay, but in the distinguished confidence of both Secretary Hay and Senator Lodge. Adams wrote that "the whole executive crowd" was "furious because Cush Davis let himself be bluffed in the Senate by an impudent assertion that the opposition had thirty-six votes ..." He had "lost reputation as a leader by his waste of very precious time," and had also blundered in failing to force the opposition "to take the position and the responsibility of prolonging a state of war."

Davis changed his tune after meeting with his committee. The Senate unanimously agreed to his proposal to vote on the treaty and all amendments on Monday, February 6. The ready acquiescence of the most embattled anti-imperialists was a matter of surprise. With the appropriation bills still to be passed, conditions favored a successful filibuster. The tactics of obstruction, however, would have been severely censured in the growing uneasiness over the Philippine situation and alarm for the safety of the American army. In any case, there was no advantage for Gorman in talking the treaty into an extra session. Like the President, the senator from Maryland was anxious to take a chance. On January 25, when it was agreed to limit the debate, the polling verified the "impudent assertion" of his strength. Thirty-six senators were counted against ratification, five more than the number needed to defeat. But seven of them had declined to say positively that they would persist in their opposition after all reasonable effort to amend had failed.

A single vote might decide the fate of the treaty. The Republicans had ten legislative days in which to act. Into the breach leapt Lodge and Aldrich, Hanna and Elkins and other practical politicians, men who could make a canvass, men who could make a promise. Washington began to

356

reverberate with echoes of the fighting on that scarred terrain, the cloak-rooms. There were rumors of favors to be gained by those who saw the light on the treaty, offers of patronage, and even pledges of good committee appointments and other rewards. "We were down in the engine room and do not get flowers," Lodge later wrote Roosevelt, "but we did make the ship move." Something went wrong, however, in approaching Senator Heitfeld, a stalwart young Populist from Idaho. He bawled his indigna-tion to the cloakrooms at the offer of a large bribe for his vote.

The President, according to Lodge, who was seeing him nearly every day, was "extremely anxious, but showed the greatest firmness and strength, and did everything he could do." All the Republican senators, except Hoar and Hale, were gradually led back to the fold. Spooner of Wisconsin, who thought the possession of the Philippines "one of the bitter fruits of the war," entered the constitutional debate with a brilliant defense of the right of the nation to acquire territory; and even Tom Platt, antipathetic to expansion and unused to addressing the Senate, popped up with a loyal little speech on the powers of the federal government and the benevolent purposes of the administration. Yet, in spite of the President's influence and the energy of the canvass, a total of only fifty-seven votes could be surely counted for ratification at the close of the session on Saturday, February 4.

Late on this last legislative day before the vote, Harris, a Kansas Populist, decided to come over to the treaty, bringing the total to fifty-eight. Two votes still were needed. The struggle had narrowed to four men who were vociferously protesting their detestation of imperialism: Heitfeld, the Idaho Populist; two southern Democrats, McEnery of Louisiana and McLaurin of South Carolina; and a Silver Republican, Jones of Nevada.

After a hard day of conferences, the President went into his office on Saturday night. Another week end of uncertainty must have recalled the anxious Sundays before the war. If the treaty were rejected, McKinley intended to call an extra session immediately, but he could do nothing more to affect the verdict on Monday. After chatting with Cortelyou and reading the newspaper editorials, the President began work on a speech he had engaged to make at a banquet of the Home Market Club in Boston. It was nearly half-past eleven when his dictation was interrupted by the telegraph clerk, Colonel Montgomery, bearing a dispatch which the New York *Sun* had received from its Manila correspondent. The dreaded incident had occurred. War, with American casualties, had started on Luzon.

McKinley read the dispatch carefully several times, then laid it on his desk. He sat back in his chair, and at last spoke. "It is always the unexpected that happens, at least in my case. How foolish these people are. This means the ratification of the treaty; the people will insist on its ratification."

The Republican newspapers agreed next morning that the treaty must be immediately legalized to permit the administration to act in the emergency. Expansionist senators relaxed. Lodge confidently expected that the opposition would be shattered. But on Monday Gorman's line held firm. It had gained a new recruit in Senator Heitfeld. The doubtful element was reduced to three men, two of them indispensable to the ratifiers. The vote was set for three o'clock. When the Senate went into executive session an hour earlier, the battle of the cloakrooms was still raging.

McLaurin cast his lot with the treaty at half-past two. At five minutes before three, McEnery came over. After the first roll call, Jones of Nevada registered himself with the majority, making a vote to spare for ratification. As the result was announced, Lodge felt overcome by a sudden physical exhaustion, as though he had been struggling up the side of a mountain. "It was the closest, hardest fight I have ever known," he told Roosevelt, "and probably we shall not see another in our time where there was so much at stake." Twenty years later, fighting in his stubborn old age to defeat a treaty made by a Democratic President, Lodge must have revised that opinion.

On the morning after the Senate voted, when Lodge waited on the President, he found that he had been preceded by his colleague, Senator Hoar. Lodge was struck dumb on the threshold of the Cabinet Room by the sight of the party renegade, seated at McKinley's side with a beaming smile on his Pickwickian face. John Hay, just coming in, stood staring, too. "Only a few hours before," as Henry Adams had it, "in the full belief that his single vote was going to defeat and ruin the administration, Hoar had voted against the treaty, and there he was, slobbering the President with assurances of his admiration, pressing on him a visit to Massachusetts, and distilling over him the oil of his sanctimony."

The President was loving it, that must have been what hurt. "I shall always love you, whatever you do."

The power-conscious expansionists had been exceedingly sensitive to the effect of the Senate action on world opinion. The failure of the treaty, Lodge thought, would have been a humiliating demonstration that the United States was unfit to enter into great questions of foreign policy. But the achievement of ratification seemed to have made the demonstration with sufficiently embarrassing clarity. The display of personal and factional ambition and the aroma of bargaining had debased the momentous decision. Only a handful of senators on either side had discussed the issue with intellectual force or even strong conviction, and it had been settled by the eleventh-hour action of McEnery and McLaurin, voting against the conviction they had professed. The divided Senate had bandied recriminations, each side holding the other to blame for the revolt in the Philippines; for annexationists asserted that the insurgent leaders had been egged on by the sympathy of the opposition, and the opposition retorted that war could have been easily prevented by declaring the intention to grant freedom to the islands. The cleavage was further emphasized by a tied vote on a resolution for their independence, which had been introduced by Bacon of Georgia in accordance with Bryan's advice. Annexation was definitely settled by Vice-President Hobart, to whom fell the rare opportunity of casting the decisive vote on a question of the first national importance.

A number of senators, Hoar among them, laid the success of the treaty squarely on Bryan's doorstep. Others thought that McEnery and McLaurin had been influenced by the Philippine outbreak, or overborne by Republican persuasions. According to one account, they had been respectively granted an appointment to the federal bench in Louisiana and the gift of postmasterships in South Carolina. Nelson Aldrich was said to have been the intermediary with old Senator McEnery, on the basis of their past co-operation on the sugar schedule of the McKinley Bill. Mark Hanna, however, privately claimed credit for securing both votes, advising the President, "I made myself your representative to the extent of a personal plea. . . ." It was also said that McEnery had been offered the inducement of support for his milk-and-water resolution that ratification was not intended to ensure the permanent annexation of the Philippines, or admit their inhabitants to United States citizenship. The resolution was duly passed; but, if it was actually the price of McEnery's vote, the administration had the best of the bargain. Hoar, in chagrin at the triumph of imperialism, denounced the ineffectual McEnery amendment as merely a declaration in favor of the Louisiana sugar planters.

The necessary concurrence of the House in appropriating the money compensation for the Philippines gave the members of the lower chamber an opportunity to protest against the terms of the treaty. There was a colorful but brief display of anti-imperialist fireworks. Then, under the sullen eye of the whipped dictator, Reed, all but a small minority voted for the appropriation of $20,000,000 for Spain.

The Gorman cohorts partially avenged their defeat by raiding the army bill, on which the War Department was dependent for replacements in the Philippines, as well as in Cuba and Porto Rico. The exchange of ratifications with Spain would terminate the service of all the troops, both the volunteers and the additional regulars, which had been authorized the previous year, and the administration was again seeking the permanent enlargement of the regular Army to the strength of 100,000. An appropriate bill had been passed by the House, but was stopped in the Senate. One war, with costly military lessons, had just been formally concluded; another had begun; but the perils of a large standing Army were still persuasively invoked. Only the concomitant argument was wanting, that citizen soldiers would spring to arms at their country's call. Those who had sprung the year before were impatiently awaiting their release, and the protests of their friends at their detention on tropical service grew ever more insistent as the newspapers began to print the casualty lists from Manila. The Senate Republicans were obliged to yield the principle of an effective military force in order to avert a return to the little prewar establishment. A makeshift bill, temporarily holding the regular Army at its wartime strength of 65,000 and temporarily empowering the President to raise a force of not more than 35,000 volunteer infantry, was hurriedly patched up and passed.

Partisan antagonism, in the short time remaining, also forced compromises on the naval program. The important Personnel Bill for the reorganization of the service had been passed, but last-minute amendments reduced the number of new warships and cut the authorized price of armor plate. The dominating desire was to escape an extra session. Most of the urgent recommendations of the President's annual message—for the Nicaragua canal, the government of Hawaii, a Pacific cable, shipping subsidies—were thrown aside in favor of legislation which it was impossible to postpone. The big money bills were rushed through with scarcely a pretense of serious consideration, as the Fifty-fifth Congress dashed off its business and expired.

The voice of the President had meanwhile sounded over the nationwide dismay created by the outbreak in the Philippines. The news of rebellion had shocked the American people, and thrown confusion into the loyal ranks of the Republicans. The trumpets of imperialism were opportunely blown by Rudyard Kipling, admonishing Americans in a rhymed address to "take up the white man's burden." The words were on everyone's lips; but, though the sense of an exalted duty was inspiring, the pristine enthusiasm for a colonial policy was weakened by the reckoning of its cost. So widespread was the adverse reaction that the President's detractors took heart. The more hopeful among them had prophesied that a war in the Philippines would be the end of McKinley. Baited by Miles and the beef scandals, bowed by the weight of Alger, the President could not be expected to survive the ugly necessity for turning American guns on a people struggling for freedom.

At a time of great uneasiness, while the fate of the army bill was still in doubt, McKinley went to Boston to fulfill his engagement with the Home Market Club. He left Washington with a party of dignitaries on the evening of February 15, in the wake of a blizzard that for the three preceding days had paralyzed the eastern seaboard. It was the first anniversary of the sinking of the *Maine*, and all day the flags had mourned at half-mast, and badges with the command to remembrance had been hawked in the drifted streets of the cities. Only a year had passed since the words had first aroused the passions of the nation, but it had been a year packed with more tumultuous changes of feeling than ordinary decades hold. The disaster, scarcely relevant to the problems to which it had given rise, had already slipped into history. McKinley was not traveling to Boston to speak of the *Maine* or the war. He was going to talk to the people about the Philippines, and he had chosen to do so in a stronghold of anti-expansionist sentiment. Throughout the country, the masses of his party listened for his counsel, seeking faith in the future of the republic which had so quickly assumed the oppressive role of Spain.

The banquet of the Home Market Club, held at Mechanics' Hall on the evening of February 16, was a function noteworthy for its size and its appointments. An army of Negro waiters, directed by a code of wigwag signals, served more than 1,900 guests with an elaborate, though non-alcoholic repast, and 3,800 spectators filled the lavishly decorated balconies. In an evident desire to atone for the unprogressive elements in the community, the Republican businessmen had arranged an effusive endorsement of the President's colonial policy. Behind the speakers' table hung a trio of large portraits, displaying the features of Washington, Lincoln, and McKinley, surmounted by an arch of bunting and electric lights, and captioned with the word "Liberators." This description of McKinley was at best premature, and, in view of the bloodshed on Luzon, it seemed an invitation to ridicule. Yet flippancy was rebuked by the sincerity of the lesser, living President, as he modestly stood before the portraits of his illustrious predecessors and spoke of his hopes for the future of the Philippine inhabitants; disclaimed imperial designs and declared his intention of aiding them toward self-government; and affirmed that Americans were not the masters, but the emancipators of these people.

As an unavoidable outcome of the war, the President said, the Philippines had been entrusted to our hands, and to that great trust under the Providence of God we were committed. Until a wise decision could be formed about their future government, the inhabitants must be made to understand "that their welfare is our welfare, but that neither their aspirations nor ours can be realized until our authority is acknowledged and unquestioned." McKinley derided the preachment that the United States was bound to obtain the consent of the governed. The nation had not asked the Filipinos' consent at the time of the victory over Spain, and could not now. It was not, he caustically remarked, "a good time for the liberator to submit important questions concerning liberty and government to the liberated while they are engaged in shooting down their rescuers." There were a number of other satirical comments at the expense of the critics at home—"the prophet of evil," doubters who would do nothing, men who knew everything by intuition. The President pointedly referred to the impatient warmongers of the last year, who now cried out against the consequences of their own act. Those who had tried to prevent war, he said, had dreaded its consequences, which were always beyond anticipation and control. These problems had now been forced upon the nation. They were not easy, but they must be met and an honest effort must be made to solve them.

"I have no light or knowledge not common to my countrymen," McKinley said in conclusion. "I do not prophesy. The present is all-absorbing to me. But I cannot bound my vision by the blood-stained trenches around Manila,—where every red drop, whether from the veins of an American soldier or a misguided Filipino, is anguish to my heart,—but by the broad range of future years, when . . . [that people's] children and children's children shall for ages hence bless the American republic because it emancipated and redeemed their fatherland, and set them in the pathway of the world's best civilization."

This speech was a landmark in McKinley's utterances as President. It was a fighting speech, aggressive and challenging, such as he had not made since his days in Congress. Although it had the familiar ring of moral dedication, it was direct and incisive, with a minimum of shopworn platitudes and empty generalizations. Its effect on public opinion was tremendous. The anti-expansionists were obliged to concede that war in the Philippines had not finished off the President, after all. "McKinley," *The Nation* grumbled, "is one of the rare public speakers who are able to talk humbug in such a way as to make their average hearers think it excellent sense, and exactly their idea."

The President could not make the Philippine rebellion popular, and had not sought to do so, but he had armed the people with patience to accept a bitter phase of transition, and restored their faith in the purpose and the ultimate beneficence of the national conduct.

Neither the President nor the people doubted that the phase of transition would be short. Nearly 7,000 regulars had sailed for Manila to replace the volunteers, whose time would expire on the exchange of ratifications with Spain. Meanwhile, the military situation seemed well in hand, as Otis solidified his position, and Iloilo surrendered to the Americans. Great hopes were also based on the conciliatory efforts of the five-man Philippine Commission, composed of three civilians and the military commanders, Otis and Dewey. Even the anti-expansionists were gratified by the appointment of Schurman and Worcester, both of whom were on record as opposed to the permanent annexation of the islands. There was also widespread approval of the President's third choice, Colonel Charles Denby, a Democrat who had long served as United States minister to China. The fighting had begun before these commissioners reached Manila, but it was believed that they would shortly find means of reassuring the native leaders and persuading them to lay down their arms.

Otis did not tarry in taking the offensive. He launched a campaign to the north of Manila in March, before receiving the main part of his reinforcements. Jubilant dispatches told the story as the movement rolled ahead. A column marched from flaming Malabon and seized the Tagal capital of Malolos. An expedition swept up to capture Vera Cruz. Calumpit fell at the end of April. The rebels had been driven from their strongholds, routed and scattered. Their emissaries arrived at Manila under a flag of truce to discuss terms of peace.

These events were followed with quickened emotion at home because the main stress of the fighting had been borne by volunteers. Otis's militia outfits had foregone their discharge to participate in the campaign. The American public had been stirred by the prowess of the divisions commanded by Arthur MacArthur and Henry Lawton of El Caney, and by the exploits of Colonel Frederick Funston, a little redheaded volunteer from Kansas. Yet the detention of the militiamen and their use on active service was a source of anxiety and resentment. There was a vast relief when the shooting stopped, and the War Department predicted that the end was in sight. Then came news that Otis had denied the insurgents' request for an armistice. Their emissaries withdrew, and fighting was resumed. Lawton speedily reduced San Isidro, Aguinaldo's second capital and headquarters, forcing the rebel chieftain to flee into the mountains, and sending a flag of truce again to Manila in the middle of May. This time, the American people were assured, total submission was an accomplished fact. The

President's commissioners were on hand. He had approved their proposal to offer a plan of civil government, with extensive native participation. The offer was made, but Otis once more refused to grant a truce, and negotiations were broken off.

On Luzon, the first pattering showers ushered in the deluges of summer. Americans, grown wise in the ways of tropical warfare, saw that soldiers and civilians had put forth supreme efforts to end the rebellion before the onset of the six months' rainy season; saw, with bewilderment and great anger, that these efforts had utterly failed. Bryan, backed by the Democratic press and the Anti-Imperialist League, proclaimed the collapse of the policy of subjugation and demanded that hostilities cease. Republican newspapers called for the dispatch of a large army to crush the rebellion forthwith. The country was united on two grievances, the employment of volunteers in the hard and futile campaign, and the deception of the public by a rosy official picture of the situation. There was general distrust of the War Department bulletins and disbelief of the news cables, which were gutted by military censorship at Manila. Convincing stories of disaster were told by a trickle of returning soldiers and civilians, by private letters, and by dispatches smuggled through Hong Kong. The Americans had not been in sufficient strength to hold the positions they had gained. They were exhausted by the heat; they would be destroyed in the rains. They faced a primitive and treacherous enemy, and had themselves adopted barbarous methods of warfare. The report that they took no prisoners was officially denied, but it persisted.

The breakdown of the negotiations had been a severe disappointment to the President. The authorities had been utterly misled by the elated assertions of Otis and Schurman. United in expecting rebel submission, these two were at cross-purposes on all else. The soldier advised that the war must be fought to a finish. The college president spoke for a policy of "magnanimity," the end of fighting, more concessions. Neither Worcester nor Denby agreed. Secretary Hay submitted Schurman's "long disquisition" to the President with a satirical sniff at the expense of the cable. McKinley accepted the advice of the soldier.

The President had implicit confidence in Otis, but he was mystified by his failure. Otis had said from the outset that an army of 30,000 was ample to conquer and hold the Philippines. He had had more than 20,000 troops, all told, at the time of the outbreak on Luzon. Most of them were entitled to discharge, but this had not worried Otis. He had assured Washington that a sweeping reorganization would not be necessary, because so many volunteers would re-enlist. The President was especially anxious to avoid holding troops who wanted release. Otis had been repeatedly instructed to use the transports that brought out the regulars to send off the returning outfits. He had, however, made excuses for delay. Ship after ship left Manila with only a few men on board. The embarkation of state regiments did not actually begin until June.

Otis had meantime begun to call for reinforcements. The War Department vainly tried to get an estimate of the numbers he needed. Still sticking to his figure of 30,000, Otis contrived to alter its meaning by slipping in the word "effectives." Confusion was augmented by his vagueness about the volunteer re-enlistments. He began to admit in the latter half of April that the volunteers would not re-enlist. Two months later, an unwontedly dejected cable informed Washington that Otis would probably be able to raise only the nucleus of two volunteer regiments. He mentioned 40,000 men as the maximum force he would require. He was not sanguine about the early collapse of the insurrection.

The mass withdrawal of the state troops from the Philippines meant that half of the new regular Army must be sent to the Pacific; and half would not be enough. It would be necessary to raise volunteers expressly for the Philippine service. It would take months to move a large force to Manila, and bring all the volunteers home. The President was deep in his burrow of silence, as he faced another war of distrusted management and promises unfulfilled.

·16·

FAREWELL TO SECRETARY ALGER

A<small>LGER's</small> charming smile took on a glint of defiance in the early months of 1899. The change had perhaps dated from the trip to Boston in February. Of the four Cabinet members who accompanied the President, Long and Alger had been the most conspicuous. Long, the symbol of the glorious naval victories, was a political asset anywhere, and he was welcomed in Boston with all the warmth of proud family affection. Alger was a worse liability than ever at a time when the country was smarting with suspicion of the beef contracts, and he was especially unpopular in Boston, where General Miles had a large following. Nevertheless, the President had punctiliously invited Alger to go with him, and Alger had been delighted to accept.

With indefatigable optimism, Alger was still courting public favor. He had the satisfaction of loyal applause from a G.A.R. convention, which—luckily for Alger—was meeting in Boston, but it appears that he had a disagreeable reception from the crowds that turned out for the arrival of the presidential party. According to the newspapers, the sight of Alger had been greeted with hisses and yells of "Three cheers for General Miles!" and "Yah, yah, yah! Beef! Beef!" The President, whose carriage was in the lead, heard none of this, and neither did Cortelyou. On the journey back to Washington, however, it became evident that Alger had been deeply wounded.

There at first appeared no cloud on Alger's urbanity. Congressman Grosvenor was with the little group of Cabinet officers—Alger, Long, Gage, and Smith—who gathered around the President on the train. McKinley had taken one citadel of anti-expansionist sentiment by storm. The company was in high spirits, and the conversation was lively as the warm, bright car sped through the darkening winter landscape. Smith, the proprietor of the Philadelphia *Press*, retailed some bits of newspaper gossip, highly disadvantageous to critics of the administration. Pulitzer's income from *The World*—Smith knew this for a fact—had fallen to a low figure. The *Journal*, too, was losing money every day, and the trustees of the estate had taken the paper out of young Hearst's hands. Alger contributed an animated account of Hearst's application for favors from the administration when he was going down to Santiago during the war. Hearst had got the favors, but Alger had advised him that the thing to do with a dirty sheet was to wash it. Smiling and relaxed, the President listened to the happy Republican talk. "Now and then," Cortelyou was noticing, "he will prick some bubble or turn the discussion into gentler channels when it is drifting near a point where it may become dangerous. . . ." But the discussion at one point drifted too fast. Gage brought up a certain newspaper editorial in which the beef packers were mentioned as murderers of thousands of American soldiers. Before McKinley could tactfully interpose, something was evidently said about the Boston crowds. Some word or look must have knifed through Alger's self-protective armor. He presently slipped away. His mood had changed when he joined the group again.

"I am very sorry to think," he blurted to the President, "that I have in any way spoiled the pleasure of your trip to Boston."

"What is the man talking about?" Gage exclaimed. Smith looked disgusted. Grosvenor lit another cigar. The President laughed at Alger in his kindly way, and said he believed that, next to Long, the Secretary of War had received the greatest demonstration on the trip. The awkward moment passed. Everyone followed the President's lead, chiming in to reassure and comfort Alger.

For a moment, Alger had exposed a disfigured face to the eyes of his colleagues. Their embarrassment must have been an added mortification; and, perhaps, in the whole rankling incident, there was nothing more hateful than the President's kindness. "He has many lovable qualities," Alger said of McKinley in a newspaper interview which he granted the next year, on condition that it should not be published during his lifetime; "but he lacks backbone, and nothing can make up for the lack of backbone." A sneer had begun to lurk behind the smiling deference with which Alger always treated the President.

The following week, the Secretary of War betook himself to the sympathetic atmosphere of Detroit. Local pride made western communities steadfast to their prominent sons, whatever their shortcomings. Alger, appearing as toastmaster at a Washington's Birthday banquet, was introduced as "our beloved fellow-citizen," and his conduct of the War Department was commended and cheered by his fellow Republicans, including Governor Pingree of Michigan. The response of the honored guest was markedly lacking in enthusiastic allusions to the President and the all-absorbing topic of the policy in the Philippines. Imperialism was one of several questions on which Governor Pingree was at odds with the administration. It was, however, understood that he was very well disposed toward Alger.

The presence of Hazen Stuart Pingree in the Republican party was a political paradox. He was a rambunctious crusader, dedicated to delivering the people of Michigan from the wicked trusts. His pet cause of "equal taxation" was designed to reduce the swollen earnings of the railroads and other corporations, and he inveighed as vehemently as Bryan against their control of courts, legislatures, and newspapers. As mayor of Detroit in the depths of the depression, he had provided relief for the unemployed by using the city's vacant lots for truck gardens. "Pingree's potato patches" had been a national joke, but millions of impoverished Michiganders saw nothing funny about them, or about Pingree's fight for municipal control of the Detroit street railways. His popularity had made him governor in 1896, and by 1898 he had gained control of a strong political faction. Though he declared war on the regular state organization and was hated by its leaders, Pingree was renominated by acclamation, and he had been again elected by a large vote.

The Republicans generally regarded this aberrant Populist as a kind of shameful accident, a monster to which the party had given birth. It is easy now to see that, though there was a good deal of the crank and demagogue in Pingree, he was a true forerunner of the Republican Progressives; but, at the close of the century, these gentlemen found the radical Governor a bumptious example of the species "reformer," which was as abominable to Roosevelt as to Hanna. Pingree was in particular disrepute because he had fomented party strife in Michigan. It might have been a minor discord, had he continued to confine his attention to local reforms, but he was a vociferous critic of the Washington government, which he denounced—in language frequently too pungent for publication—for its imperialist policy, its sympathy with the corporations, and its interference in the concerns of Michigan. This last and most furious complaint had been provoked by the failure of Pingree's "equal taxation" bill in the state Senate during his first term as governor. He ascribed its narrow defeat, apparently with some reason, to the manipulations of Senator Burrows, McKinley's close friend for many years. In the campaign of 1898, when

Burrows was also seeking re-election, Pingree had publicly attacked the elderly Senator, lashing out on one occasion when they were speakers on the same political platform. Shortly before Alger went to Detroit, the Governor and his faction had made a desperate attempt to prevent the Michigan legislature from returning Burrows for another term. Burrows had won, with backing from the national administration, which consistently recognized and favored the regular Republican candidates in all the states. Under these conditions, a nearly scandalous interest was attached to the signs of continued amenity between the Governor and a member of the President's Cabinet.

Alger was in the habit of declaring that he would not resign "under fire." He protested once again. The excuse might soon have worn thin as the hearings of the beef court approached their close, and it was realized that the verdict would be favorable to the War Department; but it was unexpectedly justified by the determined newspaper attack which was at its height during Alger's three weeks' absence on an inspection tour of Cuba and Porto Rico. With *The New York Herald* taking the lead, a section of the press made sensational accusations of corruption and blackmail in awarding the army contracts. The charges weighed so heavily against the credit of the administration that James Gordon Bennett, the proprietor of the *Herald*, was emboldened to attempt a little blackmail on his own account. Colonel Boynton of the Associated Press wrote General Grenville Dodge in April that the President had been given to understand that the *Herald*'s attack would stop if Alger were replaced by a candidate named by that newspaper. But Boynton took it that the President was not the man to surrender to Bennett.

This was the situation when Alger came back from his inspection tour. He later declared that McKinley three times refused to accept his proffered resignation. This was surely such an occasion. Alger was described as greatly agitated by the fresh attack, but he emerged from a White House interview in an audacious mood. He told the waiting reporters that, unless some unforeseen contingency arose, he proposed to remain Secretary of War throughout the administration, and he authorized the Associated Press to deny reports of his resignation in the strongest possible terms. One of his Detroit friends promptly issued a still more forceful statement. It asserted that, should the Secretary of War retire before March 4, 1901, it would only be at the President's direct and unqualified request; that the President had previously desired Alger to remain in the Cabinet, and Alger did not know that he had changed; and that, if he had changed, McKinley should so declare himself.

This widely published statement sounded unpleasantly like a challenge to the President to remove Alger, if he dared.

The country's hopes of a change at the War Department had been encouraged by rumors that Senator James McMillan of Michigan was about to take a diplomatic post, leaving a vacancy to which Pingree would appoint Alger. These rumors had come to nothing, but it was now reported that Alger would enter the Senate by due process of election, replacing McMillan at the expiration of his term. The suggestion seemed premature, since McMillan had two more years to serve. Moreover, he had given no intimation of a wish to retire. Though his voice was seldom heard, he enjoyed a large prestige behind the scenes as the host of the so-called "School of Philosophy Club," the coterie of old-line Republican senators whose weekly dinner meetings had much to do with shaping legislation. A man of immense wealth, esteemed for his generous benefactions to Detroit, McMillan was a dominant figure among the regular Republicans of Michigan. There was every reason to suppose that he wanted another term, and it seemed unlikely that Pingree and his set could stop him from getting it.

The press still caught at every shred of rumor. In late April, when Alger was in Detroit, the reporters were rewarded by his confirmation of his candidacy. He said that he did not credit the stories that Senator McMillan would seek re-election; he had received personal assurances a long time ago that McMillan probably would not, and would do all he could for Alger in that event. Alger thought that he would have heard if McMillan had changed his mind.

McMillan shrugged off questions with the remark that, during many conversations between himself and Alger in Washington, the subject had never been mentioned. Alger later contradicted this. In the newspaper interview which was published after his death—and several years after that of McMillan—he declared that the Senator had often come to him in Washington to reiterate his offer to retire, and had voluntarily made the promise "fifty times or more" to Alger's friends. But Alger said nothing further in the spring of 1899. McMillan presently gave out a statement that he would be a candidate for re-election. A first-rate political sensation ensued in late June. While Alger was again visiting Detroit, he and Pingree issued simultaneous announcements of their association to promote Alger's candidacy for the Senate.

The hubbub caused by the Alger-Pingree alliance was a shout of relief that, at long last, the Secretary of War would be forced to leave the Cabinet, and a shriek of raucous laughter at his conversion to reform, after a lifetime of familiarity with the trust and the machine. Alger declared himself a foe to the great amalgamations that were detrimental to the interests of the people. He came out for the direct election of United States senators as a blow to boss control. Pingree spouted sarcastic interviews on the national policies, with emphasis on the fostering of trusts. There was much disgust that this coarse demagogue should be able to use a member of the President's own household in his war on the administration. The question of the hour was, What would McKinley do?

On June 23, when Alger's candidacy was announced, McKinley was in Adams, Massachusetts. He had recently been present at Grace McKinley's graduation from Mount Holyoke, and had also attended the commencement exercises at Smith College; and, having pleasantly flurried feminist circles by endorsing higher education for women, he had taken his wife to spend a week at the home of the cotton manufacturer, Mr. W. B. Plunkett. Mrs. McKinley fell ill during this visit, and they came back to Washington early on June 27, two days ahead of schedule. Alger had already returned from Detroit. He was one of the first to greet the President, and he paid a second call at the Executive Mansion later in the day. Morning and afternoon, the correspondents watched and pounced like cats at a mousehole, but Alger waved them merrily away; his resignation had not been asked for, and he certainly did not intend to offer it. He maintained that his candidacy in no way interfered with his loyalty to McKinley—indeed, in more than one interview, he suggested that it was the part of loyalty to remain in the Cabinet, lest McKinley be reproached for opposition to the principles for which Alger and Pingree stood. The President, in other words, might appear to be championing the trusts if Alger were forced out of the administration.

The trusts, in the boom year of 1899, were fast developing into a leading political issue. Alger's insinuation was as cunningly timed as it was impudent. He was pressing McKinley hard, at a time of fresh anxiety about the Philippine war and its political repercussions. The dejected dispatch from Otis had been forwarded to the President just before he returned to Washington.

The President was alert to the political outlook in the year before the national elections. Plans for the next national convention had been prepared while he took a "rest" at Hanna's house at Thomasville in March. A number of Executive appointments had subsequently gratified the Republican organizations in troubled states. The oil of expediency glistened on the amendment to the civil service rules which had been published at the end of May. Reformers and Democratic partisans exaggerated the extent of the changes which McKinley, after many Cabinet consultations, had finally decided to make. As amended by Cleveland, the regulations had been unworkable, partly because they contained certain impractical provisions, partly because they had packed the federal offices with Democrats. It was argued by the Presidents' defenders—notably by Gage and Long, both recognized friends of the merit system—that the new order merely recognized an existing situation, and increased the efficiency of government operations. Yet the impression of a dominating expediency could not be washed away. The order was too obviously designed to expand party rewards in a season of party necessity, too obviously timed for its effect on the Ohio Republican Convention and its assistance to Hanna in clinching his control at home. The arguments of McKinley's apologists were muffled by the joyful cries of the spoilsmen.

Under heavy pressure from Congress, the President had delayed for more than two years before administering this stimulus to party solidarity and enthusiasm. His action indicated his determination to maintain Republican control of national affairs. He had another service to perform, as the fighting fiercely continued on Luzon in the torrential rains of June. Democratic newspapers were denouncing "the President's war." Every casualty was charged against the corrupt and incapable War Department. The President had to breathe new energy into the desperate little conflict, and inspire confidence in its management. He could not do it with Alger at the War Department; and Alger had furnished the occasion for his removal when he thumbed his nose at the President, locking arms with Pingree out in Michigan.

Alger had to go. Everybody seemed to know it but Alger. Adjutant General Corbin was uncomfortable. The Cabinet meetings were stiff with constraint. Alger's associates were sorry for him, but Alger himself was easy. He appeared oblivious of disapproval. He ignored the invective and derision of the press. The July days slid past without a sign from the President. He treated Alger with every courtesy—too much, as many thought. Cortelyou, taut with indignation, submitted nightly batches of newspaper clippings insisting on Alger's removal. He once ventured the comment that the demand was unanimous, but McKinley did not respond. He had never been more cryptic than in his attitude toward a matter that was commonly understood. It was clear to all of his friends that he was waiting for Alger to resign; and, in spite of his air of innocence, it was clear to Alger, too.

According to Alger's account, he did not realize that the Pingree alliance had given McKinley offense until he was told so by Garret Hobart. He went to McKinley, Alger said, and reproached him for his lack of frankness in not having spoken to him direct, and McKinley then for the first time acknowledged that he was "embarrassed" and "annoyed." This was a badly garbled story. Alger's conversation with Hobart about his resignation was preceded by a number of interviews with the President on the subject. McKinley, who found these interviews "rather trying," had fumbled an outright dismissal. With his usual ineptitude at getting rid of people, he had left it to Alger to take the initiative; but he had made his meaning plain. He had made it so plain that, early in July, Alger had sat down in the Cabinet Room and written his resignation. He had balked, however, at immediate retirement. He was fearful that the recent accomplishments of the War Department might be smeared or slighted. With the view of himself preparing the next annual report to Congress, Alger had tendered his resignation to take effect on January 2, 1900.

McKinley's strong objections are preserved among his papers in a page of private jottings, apparently the rough draft of a contemplated letter to Alger. It is not of much consequence whether or not such a letter was actually sent. Here, in the President's own hand, is the substance of what he said in the "rather trying" interviews; here is evidence of his agitation at Alger's resistance and of his incapacity to bring Alger to terms. A long postponement of the resignation would, McKinley wrote, mean "demoralization" to the War Department, which had never required more vigorous administration than at that very time. He mentioned the importance and difficulty of the new questions, and observed that Alger, with his "determination to retire," could not be expected to take them up. He spoke feelingly of the Secretary's fatigue and deplored his continuing the "onerous labor" of the Department until he was "entirely broken down"; and he declared that the report to Congress could and would be made with absolute fairness by Alger's successor. Thus far, the arguments were incisive enough, if somewhat blunted by tact. But a pleading tone crept in as McKinley recalled his "unwavering devotion" during the assault on Alger's official integrity. "I was willing to bear all," he urged, "rather than the slightest injustice should fall upon you." The President flinched, even now, from the logical consequence toward which his letter trended. "It is not for me to ask you to resign," the notes lamely concluded—"our relations should require you to spare me that painful course as well as save you from any humiliation which such action would cause. You must determine without any suggestion from me whether the time has not come for you to place your resignation in my hands."

Alger was adept at touching the weak spot in McKinley's tranquil bosom, the finicking refinement of scruple and reluctance to inflict pain. His own armor was thick. It is possible that, in spite of all that had passed and all that was at stake, Alger still believed that he could bend the President to his wishes and stay in the Cabinet until it suited him to leave. McKinley was so evidently consumed by an anguished, feminine desire to have things pass off pleasantly. Yet the President's mind was made up. He evidently spoke of his intentions to Hay and Griggs. He also made a veiled admission to the Governor of New York, who was an overnight guest at the White House in the early part of July.

Intense and vital, with his strident voice and quivering pince-nez and the big smile gleaming like a dentrifice advertisement, Governor Roosevelt was outwardly not much different from the Assistant Secretary of the Navy who had taken leave of Washington some fourteen months before. There were changes, nevertheless. The air of an incurable amateur was notably subdued. Some of his opinions had been modified. He had begun to feel very earnestly about peace and efforts for arbitration. He wanted to impress the Republican leaders, and meet them on an equal footing; for Roosevelt, not yet forty-one years old, had begun to dream of the highest office of all. The year of fulfillment was to be 1904. The interim should be employed in some conspicuous public service. The national sphere was indicated, but Roosevelt was not sure what place he would prefer—except for United State Senator, and he had little enough chance of getting that. Secretary of War? Governor of the Philippines? Vice-President, even? Garret Hobart had a serious heart ailment, and his doctors had sentenced him to a summer of absolute rest. Many rumors said that he would not be able to accept renomination. Veering like a weathervane in his feeling about the Vice-Presidency, Roosevelt was at this time well disposed toward it.

But what did the President feel? Their formerly agreeable relations had been interrupted by Roosevelt's impatience to rush into war with Spain. McKinley's cordiality had cooled. Roosevelt had been rudely persistent, using "the plainest language" to the President in front of the Cabinet and Mark Hanna. He had also been imprudent enough to ridicule the President behind his back. McKinley had been gracious since Roosevelt's return from Cuba, but Roosevelt wanted something more substantial than greetings and congratulations. He wanted to be called into conference, and recognized as the coming young man of the party. He did not want to push himself forward. On a recent trip to the West, he had been given a series of rousing ovations. He had hastened to issue vigorous statements that he was of course for McKinley's renomination. His expressions had been calculated to create a favorable atmosphere at the Executive Mansion, and Roosevelt thought that he should also get something concrete in return for them. He had decided to ask for the supreme command in Cuba for Leonard Wood, and the appointment of Francis V. Greene to replace Elwell Otis in the Philippines. A long letter conveying these requests had been sent to Secretary Hay, and also to Attorney General Griggs. In each case, the letter closed with a broad hint of Roosevelt's desire to talk over his recommendations with the President. The response was a prompt invitation to spend the night of Saturday, June 8, at the Executive Mansion.

Although Roosevelt was positive that "nothing would be done while Alger remained Secretary," he had refrained from mentioning the War Department. The President had shown "scant inclination" to listen on a previous occasion. In seeking an interview, Roosevelt had been discreet; but, as soon as he saw McKinley, he started right in on Alger. This time, McKinley listened attentively while Roosevelt vehemently asserted that the enormous majority of the American people regarded Alger as a curse, and that his retention in office was the greatest bar to the President's re-election. In the end, McKinley offered some guarded assurances that "Alger's days were numbered." Making a hasty switch, Roosevelt decided to back Frank Greene for Secretary of War. He had failed to get a favorable answer on the supreme command in the Philippines, or in Cuba. In the first case, the President turned him down flat, declaring his implicit faith in General Otis and pleasantly remarking that he had inside information that Roosevelt could not have. McKinley's interest had been caught by a minor point in Roosevelt's letter, the matter of finding the best officers for ten regiments of volunteers for the Philippine service. Arrangements were made for the Governor to give General Corbin the benefit of his advice.

The only tangible result of Roosevelt's visit to the Executive Mansion was to assist the War Department in weeding out a batch of applicants for commissions. Still, Roosevelt was not being merely polite when he wrote to thank the President for "our very satisfactory talk." He returned to Oyster Bay in elation over his reception. The President had been more than cordial; and his confidential hint about the War Department had been an acknowledgment of political services and a recognition of political weight.

The public had for some time heard very little from Alger, but he popped up again after Roosevelt's trip to Washington with another emphatic denial that he was going to resign. There was "nothing but air" in the reports, he told a correspondent of the Associated Press—he would not retire that year, certainly. Secretary Hay sent the President a clipping of the interview, accompanied by a note, unsigned and conspiratorial. "This is deplorable—after all the trouble we have taken to save his dignity." It was futile to wait any longer for Alger to take the initiative. Moreover, a new reason had arisen for getting him out quickly. A blast of sensational publicity was about to blow in from the Philippines. The Manila staff correspondents, long at loggerheads with General Otis and lately united in a formal statement of objections to the military censorship, had decided to make their joint protest public by mailing it to Hong Kong for transmission by cable to the American newspapers. Another round robin was on the way to the War Department.

McKinley bowed to the necessity for plainer speaking, but he did not personally undertake it. He first tried, it appears, to pass on the responsibility to Secretary Hay. When Hay excused himself, McKinley turned to the Vice-President. Secretary and Mrs. Alger had accepted an invitation to spend the next week end at the Hobarts' seaside place near Long Branch, New Jersey. Attorney General Griggs preceded them with the request that Hobart should wield the ax. The President did not show his usual hypersensitive regard for other people's feelings in handing over to a sick man a disagreeable task which it was his own duty to perform. Hobart's devotion to McKinley forbade his refusing the request, but he was also attached to Alger and painfully affected by his agency in the final humiliation of the Secretary of War.

Alger stopped over in New York after the week-end visit, and did not return to Washington until the Tuesday evening. Meanwhile, the Manila round robin—first published in the afternoon newspapers on Monday, July 17—had produced the expected sensation. The staff correspondents treated General Otis with unsparing hostility. The official reports, their communication averred, had presented an ultra-optimistic view that was not shared by the general officers in the field. These reports had misled the American government and public by incorrect estimates of the strength and tenacity of the Filipinos; by assertions that the American force was sufficient and the situation, "well in hand"; and by unfounded statements that the volunteers were willing to engage in further service. Otis had suppressed the actual facts on the plea that "they would alarm the people at home" or "have the people of the United States by the ears," and the correspondents had been compelled by the military censorship to participate in the misrepresentation.

Otis was already in disfavor as a general who promised more than he performed. The round robin demolished at a stroke his accomplishments, his veracity, and his judgment. The American press, hit in a vital spot, called righteously for vengeance. The instant dismissal of Otis was the second most popular act that the President could have performed, but the Washington correspondents gleaned the impression that no official cognizance would be taken of the incident.

Before McKinley was well rid of one political bugbear, he had acquired another. He had heard nothing from Alger on Tuesday night, when he sat in the Cabinet Room going over the day's portfolio of papers. Cortelyou had not been told of the approaching denouement, but a partial confidence was by chance precipitated. Among the letters was a request for an army appointment for a certain Michigan officer whose name was prominently linked with the Pingree faction. Cortelyou, stifling his irritation, inquired about this applicant. He had been "very strongly" recommended by Secretary Alger, the President remarked. Cortelyou boiled over. "The man seems to stop at nothing," he exclaimed. The President looked at Cortelyou for a moment. "I think something will happen tomorrow," he said; "something will come to a head tomorrow."

The executive offices were scarcely opened next morning, July 19, when the President told Cortelyou to get his hat and take a walk with him outside. "Well, he was over and left it with me," McKinley said, as soon as they were in the comparative privacy of the grounds. The early morning interview had been short and devoid of embarrassment. Alger's submission was unconditional. His resignation was to take place at the President's pleasure. The long ordeal was over, and Cortelyou saw that McKinley was greatly relieved, though he was "as always gentle and charitable" in his talk.

Rumors of the big story ran along the Washington grapevine and brought the correspondents swarming around Cortelyou. The President sat alone in his office, drafting his acceptance of the resignation. He set August 1 as the date on which it should take effect; and, thanking Alger for his faithful service to the country, wished him a long and happy life. It was a brief and formal note, but McKinley spent much effort on its composition, submitting it to Hay and Long, as well as Cortelyou, before he copied it off. Then he put the fair copy away for the night in his desk drawer, together with the penciled draft and Alger's resignation. It was characteristic of McKinley to "sleep on" his reply, but he showed an unusual superstitious anxiety about his own deliberateness. "I'll leave that there to-night," he said to Cortelyou, indicating the drawer of the Cabinet table, "and you will know where it is if anything happens to me to-night."

The national grumbles were temporarily drowned in paeans of rejoicing from the press. Vice-President Hobart was the hero of the hour, lyrically praised by the New York *Sun* for his "crystal insight" and "velvet tact." The only sound of dissent came from Michigan, welcoming home her insulted and injured son. Governor Pingree denounced the President for cowardice in forcing Alger out; and Senator McMillan, who had preserved a faultless suavity all along, expressed polite regrets for his friend's retirement. The President's first relief must have been threaded with contrition. He had telegraphed an affectionate inquiry for Hobart's health. Mrs. Hobart, a woman of wit and spirit, composed the telegram that went to the White House over her husband's signature: "My crystal insight is still clear, but the nap is slightly worn off my velvet tact. . . ."

Alger's memory dwelt uneasily in the minds of some of his former associates. He wore, in the eyes of a few, a faint halo of martyrdom. Some, including the Hobarts, thought that he was heartbroken. "I am sorry for Alger," wise old James Wilson wrote the President, "and will continue to be if he does not slop over; he needs a friend to tell him not to claim credit for good things done, nor lay blame on you for other things. History will credit him with much that you inspired and find little to censure in the record, provided, he does not go to talking and admonish future chroniclers that he has weaknesses incompatible with the direction of great movements. I hope for his silence." But Alger was not going to be silent. In the seclusion of his luxurious house in Detroit, he was meditating an apologia for his conduct of the War Department.

As an anticlimax to the fracas in Michigan, Alger presently announced his withdrawal from the contest for the Senate. His ambition, however, was gratified after the death of McMillan in 1902. He spent his last years as an obscure member of the erstwhile "Millionaires' Club," a representative of the rich, old-soldier type of politician that was fast disappearing from the American scene.

· 17 ·

MATTER OF U.S. COLONIES

A TELEPHONE connection was completed between New York and the Long Island village of Southampton. The mellifluous tones of Congressman Lemuel E. Quigg, one of Tom Platt's younger and more engaging henchmen, delivered a terse message.

"The President directs me to say to you that he wishes you to take the position of Secretary of War."

"Thank the President for me," said the voice at the Southampton end, "but say that it is quite absurd. I know nothing about war, I know nothing about the army."

Quigg elaborated his instructions. "President McKinley directs me to says that he is not looking for any one who knows anything about war or for any one who knows anything about the army; he has got to have a lawyer to direct the government of these Spanish islands, and you are the lawyer he wants." The demurs were evidently silenced. Three days after Alger's resignation, it was announced that the New York corporation lawyer Elihu Root had accepted the War Department portfolio.

The New York seat in the Cabinet had been vacated some months earlier by the resignation of Secretary Bliss, but the press was as surprised as Root himself at the President's selection. Neither rumor nor speculation, until just before the announcement, had touched so unlikely a choice in a lengthy canvass of names for Alger's replacement. The president of the Union League Club, active in the Republican party of his city and state, Root had hitherto had no connection with national affairs. He had not a figment of claim to the President's regard, and the retirement of the Secretary of the Interior had severed his only strong link with the admin-

379

istration. Cornelius Bliss held an "exalted opinion" of Root's abilities, and had frequently taken occasion to praise them to McKinley. Root was one of the men who had been offered the post of minister to Spain before it fell to General Woodford. McKinley had shown some eagerness in persuasion, interjecting, "I will make it an Embassy," when he saw his caller's hesitation; but Root had gone back to his prosperous law practice. The meeting would have been merely one of many inconclusive White House interviews if it had not been so deeply stamped in the President's memory. He turned to Root, as soon as he was rid of Alger, with his resolve fully formed. The telephone message to Southampton was the republican equivalent of a royal command. Exploratory conversations and discussions of policy were forgone. The President, intent on associating Root with his administration, was apparently confident that this comparative stranger would be in complete sympathy with his aims.

A good opinion had been implanted by Mr. Bliss, and John Hay said that he put in a word for Root as Secretary of War. Yet the President's extraordinary interest must have been founded on a compelling personal impression. What had he seen at the interview a year and a half before? Root was a slender, energetic, modest-looking man, with a grave intellectual face topped by a thick bang of hair. His manner was coolly deliberate. His dark eyes were sharp, as well as thoughtful. His lips sometimes widened, under his clipped mustache, in what John Hay called a "frank and murderous smile." It was not hard to read an incisive mind, a hard and resourceful efficiency, a capacity for ruthlessness. McKinley, perhaps, had discerned a quality more deeply buried—a still untested propensity for self-dedication to the public service. Root had not been tempted by the mission to Spain, even if it were made an embassy, but the whole vigorous current of his life was changed by McKinley's offer of the War Department. Pending legislation by Congress, the President as Commander in Chief remained the sole lawful authority in Cuba and the ceded islands. The powers of the Secretary of War were vast, and Root's mind was kindled by the tremendous difficulties of the assignment and its importance to the nation.

The President referred repeatedly, during a long drive with Cortelyou, to his "great satisfaction" that the matter was settled. "He said that if Elihu Root had not accepted he would have been at a loss to know where to turn; he might have found a good man but it would probably have been a very difficult task." Two days later, when Root went to Washington for his first conference on policy, the appointment had been somewhat cautiously endorsed by most of the leading Republican newspapers. The opposition press was mainly content to wait and see. As a corporation lawyer with an immensely lucrative practice, Root was vulnerable to attack, but he possessed certain recommendations, apart from the obvious advantage of succeeding Alger. He fulfilled the national ideal of self-made worldly success; the absence of political pressures suggested an appointment based on merit; and Root gained stature from the circumstance, awe-inspiring to Americans, that he was sacrificing a large income to take a government position. The combination of brains and disinterestedness was sufficiently rare in office to predispose Elihu Root's countrymen in his favor.

One voice was silent that might have wished Root well. The comment of the *New York Tribune* was bleak. Whitelaw Reid had cast covetous eyes on the vacant Cabinet seat. John Hay heard that he was "simply frantic" at the news of Root's appointment.

Though the President's choice was free from political motive, it had not been made without political consideration. The approval of Senator Tom Platt had been tactfully indicated by Lem Quigg's agency in the offer. By his own profession, Platt was in a mood of yawning indifference when he switched from his preferred candidate, General Greene, to the representative of his traditional adversary, the Union League Club. He did not care, he later wrote, whether or not Root was Secretary of War—he wouldn't go across the street to help Root and he wouldn't get out of his chair to hurt him. But the truth was that Platt was as keen as mustard to help Root, and had been for nearly a year. In September of 1898, he had gone several blocks, all the way from the office of his express company on Broadway to the office of Mr. Bliss on Duane Street, to speak on Root's behalf, and for no less a place than the ambassadorship to Great Britain. Mr. Bliss had listened in astonishment. "Wonders will never cease," he wrote the President after the boss was gone.

Root himself found an explanation in a speech he had made at the New York Republican Convention a short time before Platt's unexpected call occurred. On the eve of Colonel Roosevelt's nomination for the governorship, with the machine committed to his support, his eligibility had been threatened by the exposure of an affidavit in which, for the purpose of avoiding New York taxes, he had declared that his residence was Washington. Root—who was Roosevelt's lawyer—had eloquently defended him, brushing aside the affidavit with a quibble over the definition of "residence." The doubts of the convention were banished, and Roosevelt was enthusiastically nominated. Root was satisfied that he had won Platt's gratitude by rescuing the candidate and his backers from an awkward predicament. But there was a deeper motive for the amiability which Platt was beginning to display toward the eminent confraternity of his enemies in New York. It could be traced back to a talk with the President at the time of the signing of the protocol with Spain. There had been mention of the impending appointment of Ambassador John Hay as Secretary of State. The question of his successor at the Court of St. James's logically followed; and, in the midst of a nice, confidential interview, McKinley let drop the name of Whitelaw Reid. Platt blew up. He threatened the President that he would fight the nomination in the Senate. His call was ruined, and he took the train for home in a wretched state of nerves.

Unmistakable signs appeared that Reid was excited by John Hay's recall from London. The *Tribune* celebrated the armistice with fulsome praise of the President, provoking *The Evening Post* to jeers at the practices of expediency. Platt mailed both clippings to the White House. From his summer quarters in the Oriental Hotel at Manhattan Beach, he assailed the President with political counsels and denunciations of Reid's perfidy. Intimations of a break with the administration over this "party crime" were mingled with heartrending appeals in Platt's supreme effort, a letter that covered twenty-two pages of the Oriental Hotel's notepaper. He recalled to McKinley's mind the many New York appointments that had been disagreeable to the machine; "but I have stood by you," Platt wrote, "and have had a certain pleasure in subordinating my judgment to yours and in feeling that I was affording gratification to you by a considerate and helpful course. I had not expected that you would think it necessary to impose upon the New York Organization . . . this particular and extreme injury."

Soon after the talk with Platt, the President made Reid a member of the Peace Commission. Senator Hoar had declined the London embassy and the place was still unfilled when Platt called on Mr. Bliss, prepared to forget his feud with the Union League Club and back its very president, if he could stave off Reid. It was an ingenious plan, but it fell flat. Root's name did not figure prominently in the rumors which toyed with several distinguished New Yorkers. McKinley seemed in no haste to make up his mind. Months drifted past. Mr. Bliss might have observed a new wonder as, under the whip of continued apprehension, the boss at last began to work for the appointment of another member of the Union League Club, the urbane and witty lawyer Joseph Choate.

Platt's ordeal of suspense was matched by that of Whitelaw Reid, tantalized in the gilded conference halls of Paris by the noble vacancy across the Channel. His letters of recommendation rained on the White House. Reid's private reports to McKinley were heavily embroidered with allusions to his own proficiency, social as well as diplomatic, in guiding his less experienced associates. They drove in style in his landau, with Mrs. Reid's footman on the box. They held their private consultations in his hotel rooms, which happened to be reserved nearly every season for the Grand Duchess Vladimir. They were entertained at the Opéra in the Vicomtesse de Courval's big "box between the columns," which Reid had been fortunate enough to get. A vision of Ambassador Whitelaw Reid rose elegantly from the phrases of transparent self-seeking, so polished and so bare; but the recommendations of a footman and an indirect connection with a Grand Duchess and a Vicomtesse did not ease the political tensions of New York. When Reid came home from Paris, Secretary Hay met his eager queries with embarrassed evasions. The accomplished Joseph Choate sailed in January for London, wafted by the blessings of Tom Platt.

Had McKinley ever meant to give Reid the ambassadorship? It is possible, of course, that he was bluffing when he dropped the dreaded name. It is certain that, six months later, Platt had no reason for alarm. Reid had not the faintest chance of getting Alger's Cabinet seat. The loyalty of the *Tribune* had been shaken by Choate's appointment. More than once, it had knifed the administration. The editorial attacks on the War Department in the early summer had antagonized and disgusted McKinley. He had scathingly remarked to Cortelyou "that there was one great good resulting in such matters, and that was that you could get at a man's true character." But he did not say this in the hearing of Tom Platt, scrambling to fix up Elihu Root's appointment and concede another victory to the President in the poker game of patronage with the New York machine.

Governor Roosevelt was rather put out, though he was Root's friend and had the highest regard for him. He thought that the President's desire for a lawyer as Secretary of War was foolish—indeed, he thought that it was disingenuous, an excuse for avoiding a "sweeping reform." "He is evidently going to administer the department himself through General Corbin," Roosevelt wrote. The inference was unjust to Root, as Roosevelt soon generously recognized, and it widely missed the mark of the President's intentions. McKinley was through with running the War Department. His uniform tendency in filling Cabinet vacancies had been to replace the original members with men of superior ability and more positive character. The Department of the Interior furnished a case in point. Successful old Mr. Bliss had been something of a disappointment to the enthusiasts for getting businessmen into the government. The Pension Office had attracted the most favorable notice of any bureau under his regime. The G.A.R. pork barrel, to the surprise of the country at large and the furious annoyance of the veterans themselves, had been rationed by a conscientious commissioner, H. Clay Evans of Tennessee. The credit for the reform of the pension rolls belonged to Evans and to the President, who had appointed him. Mr. Bliss himself had jogged along like any aging politician, conventionally dispensing the patronage. His successor, Ethan Allen Hitchcock, was another elderly businessman, but he had a strict conception of public responsibility. For one thing, he was alive to the duty of guarding the Indians from exploitation and injustice. McKinley was also solicitous to protect the wards of the government, but his activity on their behalf must be partly credited to Hitchcock's vigilance. The only bill of any importance that McKinley ever vetoed was a measure opening up the Navajo Reservation to exploitation.

The Cabinet, in spite of changes, remained a "happy family," dominated by men who were personally congenial to McKinley. Hitchcock himself was an old friend whom the President had sent as minister to Russia, before recalling him to enter the closer association. Talk flowed harmoniously about the long mahogany table, and the lighthearted interludes had a sedate sparkle of fun. There was time for the President's teasing, for repartee spiced by the wit of Hay and Long; time to listen and laugh while Secretary Gage, trolling an Irish brogue through his Sophoclean whiskers, read out Mr. Dooley's latest sallies on the state of the nation. The aura of good comradeship embraced the newcomer to the War Department, but Root stood a little apart from real intimacy with the President. He was on a more purely professional basis with McKinley than any of his colleagues, with the possible exception of Attorney General Griggs. McKinley was never quite at home with men whose eyes had a cold glint, whose lips locked tight and thin. He was criticized by hostile newspapers for a prodigal use of the pardoning power. He intervened in the departments of both Root and Griggs to adjust decisions that he thought severe. "I think one duty of a President is to act as a check upon a hard-hearted Secretary," McKinley once observed to Cortelyou in denying Root's recommendation that a West Point cadet should be dismissed for having liquor in his room. The President hastily went on to say that he was speaking in general, without application to this particular case.

Though an intimacy never developed between McKinley and Root, this was a rarely close alliance, founded on common aims and reciprocal respect. Root became much impressed with the President's "unselfish self-effacement," and his indirect method of implanting his ideas in other minds. "He was a man of great power," Root told McKinley's biographer, Olcott, "because he was absolutely indifferent to credit . . . but McKinley *always had his way.*" The President, for his part, needed Root's talents, and gave them fullest scope, rejoicing in the willing spirit with which, not only at the War Department but "in many other directions," the Secretary relieved his chief of "many cares and much anxiety." Roosevelt to the contrary,

Root did not lack McKinley's backing for the "sweeping reform" which he initiated. When Root's path crossed that of Tom Platt, it was Platt who had to step aside. Hanna himself was forced to retreat from the solidarity of the McKinley-Root front. The test was met the next year on the disclosure of frauds at the Havana post office, implicating the director general, Estes G. Rathbone, who was a personal and political crony of Hanna. The charges were pressed by Leonard Wood; and Hanna, meeting Wood by chance in the Capitol, peremptorily challenged him on the subject. "If you bring *my friend* to trial," Hanna exclaimed, "you will never get to be more than a captain doctor in the Army!" Although the threat was ridiculous, in view of the advancement which General Wood had already received, it was a declaration of war from the closest political adviser of the President. Hanna, however, was unable to block the course of justice. His friend received a stiff sentence, which was later remitted by the government of the Republic of Cuba.

The President manifested his confidence in Root from the first, but the two did not begin to work regularly together for some weeks after Root's induction. McKinley had left for a holiday at Lake Champlain when the incoming Secretary moved to Washington, armed with a list of books on colonial government under English law. Alger was on hand to welcome Root and shepherd him into office. Their meetings were not marred by the constraint that the circumstances suggested. Heartbroken though Alger might be by his retirement, he was overjoyed to find that his successor had not been drawn from the crowded ranks of his outspoken enemies. He had been making cordial gestures toward Root since the first intimation of the appointment. He had also made a number of last-minute departmental reforms and Army recommendations, and evidently closed his official books with a mind relieved of apprehension about the forthcoming annual report.

Root's principal contribution to the report was to be a statement of the relation of the nation to its new possessions. The Senate debate on the peace treaty had stirred up a controversy over the question: Does the Constitution follow the flag? The President desired Root to examine the negative answer which Republican policy dictated, and formulate it in terms which would serve as a basis for legislation and meet the test of scrutiny by the Supreme Court. The Secretary of War, in other words, was to lay the foundations of the case which the Attorney General would finally plead. Roosevelt had omitted an interesting point when he demurred to the choice of a lawyer for the War Department. The President had a lawyer already, and one of outstanding competence on constitutional questions. Perhaps the thought had troubled Root himself. He had preluded his arrival in Washington by a propitiatory letter to Griggs. "I think the main feature of the change I am making is the formation of a new law firm of 'Griggs and Root, legal advisers to the President, colonial business a specialty.' "

It was a singular fact that the ever-expanding nation had not conclusively settled its relation to its successive acquisitions. Great areas of the American continent, annexed and organized as territories, had attained the goal of admission to the Union, or were still struggling toward it in the case of the future states of Oklahoma, Arizona, and New Mexico. Alaska had been rather offhandedly granted territorial status without contemplation of statehood. Congress had taken little interest in this barren, thinly populated region, far distant from the charmed field of contiguity. Tossed a few bones of legislation now and then, Alaska was still—after more than thirty years of United States ownership—virtually without an organized government. A criminal code had just been applied to the territory, thanks to the lawless elements introduced by the gold rush. Hawaii, the first of the large insular acquisitions, was slated to be another permanent territory, entitled to statehood in theory alone. The Cullom Commission had promptly submitted a report containing a bill for its organization, with an elective legislature and the privilege of sending a delegate to Congress. The measure was among the many presidential recommendations on which the Fifty-fifth Congress had omitted to act, but its passage was assured. The valuable trade of the islands and the influence of the dominant American population forbade their being treated with the prolonged neglect shown to Alaska.

The time seemed ripe for the framing of a comprehensive colonial policy, but this was not the purpose for which Root had been invited to hang out his shingle at the War Department. The former Spanish islands, according to the Republican proposition, occupied the special category of "dependencies," and the President desired that Congress should be free to legislate separately for them, without regard to precedent or consistency. The motive for this discrimination was the important trade of the Philippines—specifically, the danger to Republican doctrine of bringing Manila under the system of uniform tariffs enjoined by the Constitution. Secretary Hay was at this very time preparing to address to the nations of Europe a proposal for the open door for trade in their spheres of influence in China. The initiative of the United States in this matter implied a reciprocal equality of opportunity at Manila. Unless it were legally possible to establish tariffs between the United States and the Philippines, the whole great policy of the open door would recoil on the Republican administration, threatening the very structure of the protective system.

Root, in his own phrase, had taken the United States for his client, but the case was complicated by the interest of the Republican party. He studied the question in the soggy heat of Washington, while thunderstorms of criticism broke with renewed violence over the administration. The Democrats had become wildly alarmed by the President's retention of control over the Spanish islands, particularly the Philippines. It had at first been scarcely credited that he was proposing to hold on to his extraordinary powers during the entire nine months of the long recess of Congress. There had been many rumors of an extra session, wishfully believed in, gradually proven baseless. The Philippine war was dragging on; and, as it became apparent that McKinley meant to press a policy of subjection, Democratic newspapers redoubled their abuse of the dictator in the White House. Root was a novice in public office, unused to attack, and somewhat overwhelmed by the responsibilities he had undertaken. He soon mentioned the possibility of calling an extra session in a letter to the President; but he found McKinley unmoved by the uproar. An experienced politician was wary of tossing a vaguely defined issue into the ballground of partisan controversy. Root himself became convinced of the wisdom of delay. "Without a clear conception for thought and legislation to crystallize around," he wrote the Reverend Dr. Lyman Abbott in December, "we should inevitably drift into a hopeless entanglement of contradictions."

The clear conception, which had already been published when this letter was written, endorsed the argument of the annexationist senators: that the United States, as a nation, had the power to acquire and exercise sovereignty over the ceded islands, and that their peoples had no claim on the legal rights provided by the Constitution. Since those provisions had not been enacted for them, the new possessions had no right to be considered as states, or even as territories. Their government would be determined by Congress. Root did not make an extended argument. He confidently presented his opinion, and closed the subject with a word for justice and freedom. Wanting all human rights, the inhabitants of the islands were nonetheless possessed of the moral right to be treated in accordance with the underlying principles of the Constitution. "Congress," Root crisply asserted, "will hold itself bound by those limitations which arise from the law of its own existence."

The Secretary of War was satisfied that he had stated the only view under which it was practically possible to govern the new possessions. The practical aspect did much to reconcile the public mind to what seemed a dangerously broad construction of the Constitution. The islands had already been ceded. Peaceably or by force, American dominion was being asserted in

387

them. Root had prepared a legal justification for an existing fact. He allayed fears of the claims of native peoples, and soothed the national conscience with talk of moral right. The average citizen, indifferent to intricate legal questions, was disposed to accept any theory that promised a vigorous handling of the vexing troubles of the colonies.

On taking up his duties, Root ran head-on into the obstacle of the superannuated staff system. The War Department had necessarily continued to operate on a tremendously enlarged scale. Military warehouses were bursting with supplies of every sort, and big consignments moved with the rhythm of established routine to the camps at home and abroad. The United States Army, scattered in two hemispheres and engaged in fighting in the Pacific, was reaping the benefits of preparations that had been made too late for the war with Spain. Yet the system had survived in all its rugged imperfection. The tangle of regulations was still impenetrable. The bureaus were still pounding along on their separate treadmills. The same old piles of paper heaped the desks, and—except for General Eagan, whom John F. Weston had replaced—the same old faces were met in the offices and corridors.

The faults of the bureaus, however, had become a stale topic for the newspapers to chew on. The emotional attention of the public was focused on the Philippines, a theater which had not been connected with the scandals of government neglect. Otherwise, public interest was listless, and public judgment had calmed. The home camps were scarcely mentioned. There were good reports from the occupation forces in Cuba and Porto Rico, relishing refrigerated beef, in spite of General Miles. Their lists of sick had ceased to cause alarm. Tropical malaria was accepted as a commonplace of tropical service, while an outbreak of yellow fever in General Wood's command at Santiago had demonstrated that this infection was unavoidable, even in model camps. With the appointment of an energetic Secretary of War, Americans were ready to forget about the staff exposures, and sink back into their customary indifference to military management; but Root could not assent. The problems of colonial administration were problems of the Army. The iron ruts of the old system were hindrances to the expanded power of the United States and to the efficiency of the permanently enlarged Army that Congress must be brought to provide; and Root perceived that a still graver matter was in question. The War Department, under the *status quo*, would always defeat the reason for its being. It could not make ready for war.

Root also considered the Army and the rules of promotion that made its command top-heavy with the physically unfit. His sharp eyes marked the seniors who came to his office, middle-aged men who showed that the years had told on them, sinking down into their seats and then finding difficulty in getting up again. Their minds, perhaps, were as rusty as their joints. There were no facilities for refreshing their memories of military education, or bringing them up to date on theory and armaments. If the United States should become involved in a great war, there would be no hope of victory with such generals as these. Concern for the national security was the spur that drove Root's mind along unfamiliar roads. He started in to inform himself on the subject of the modern army, its organization and its place in a democracy. He went through the eight volumes of the report of the Dodge Commission. He studied military literature, consulted officers with progressive ideas, utilized the knowledge and the brilliant skills of General Corbin. The lawyer who had taken office knowing nothing about the Army became the military expert whose great achievement as Secretary of War was the reorganization of his Department and the fighting arm it served. The object was not easily attained. The political entrenchments of the bureaucracy were strong. Root had to enlist public opinion, to combat the inertia of custom and the drag of apathy and ignorance. It was necessary to counter the obstructive tactics of General Miles and, in the end, demolish him ruthlessly. The bill creating the General Staff Corps was not passed until 1903, but Root began his campaign of education a little more than two months after he took office. His opening gun was a speech at Chicago in which he frankly discussed the weaknesses of the War Department. The annual report for 1899 contained radical recommendations: for flexible staff appointments and the modification of the rule of appointment by seniority; the establishment of an Army War College; and the development of the obsolete National Guard into an effective supplement to the Army and a first reserve in wartime.

Only an unusual physical vitality could have sustained the working load that Root carried during his first months at Washington. While serving an arduous apprenticeship, he was daily improvising a diversity of decisions affecting millions of people. It was the President's intention eventually to set up a bureau of colonial affairs at the State Department. The War Department bore the trials of the period of transition. Rulings on policy were needed and permanent programs, both administrative and economic, but Root could not provide them. He could not even offer anticipatory assurances. His measures were stopgaps, carefully framed to avoid encroachment on the prerogatives of Congress. The destinies of the former Spanish islands had been dropped on the new Secretary's desk; and, as he examined the complex case of his client, the United States, he was at first disheartened by its difficulties.

389

The Spanish evacuation of Cuba had been tediously delayed. It had been midwinter when General John R. Brooke assumed command at Havana, and the military protectorate was established over an island devastated, disorganized, and bankrupted by years of civil war. The revolutionary leaders, gathered in the so-called National Assembly, were agitating against the presence of the American force, while the former insurgents were still under arms, unpaid and without the prospect of pay from the destitute Cuban treasury. The incendiary oratory was officially disregarded by the United States authorities, and finally blew itself out. The soldiers, however, were another matter. Their demobilization was necessary to good order and economic recovery, and, in the long run, to free political action. Some three million dollars remained of the defense fund which had been placed at the President's disposal before the war; and McKinley, by an extremely liberal construction of the intentions of Congress, used it to procure the disbandment of the idle troops. A bonus of $75 was offered to each soldier who had seen service against Spain. After much contention among the Cubans, the offer was accepted, and the insurgent army was finally disarmed and dispersed.

The Americans had meanwhile undertaken a huge program of social and industrial rehabilitation. They had fed the starving and cared for the sick. They had carried out sanitary projects in the cities. They had trained native police forces to control crime and disorder, and suppress the brigandage that flourished in the ruinous countryside. Projects had been initiated in all the provinces for reclaiming the sugar and tobacco plantations, reconstructing machinery, and rebuilding roads. The people, in contrast to the disputatious leaders, worked hard to help themselves. By summer, it was possible to give up the wholesale distribution of rations. Much had been achieved in the seven months before Root became Secretary of War, but steps had not yet been taken toward forming an independent government. Plans were just getting under way for a census, in preparation for the first Cuban elections. The political inexperience and illiteracy of the population made supervision necessary during this constructive period. The army of occupation was reduced in size; but, until a representative government was firmly established, it was not to be withdrawn.

The protective attitude of Washington was beyond the comprehension of its temporary wards. The indefinitely prolonged occupation seemed proof conclusive of imperialistic intentions. There were not, as Root said later, a dozen men in Cuba who believed that the United States would keep faith in granting independence. Except for a comparatively small element of the well-to-do, all factions were passionately averse to absorption in the colonial system of the big republic. The continued presence of American troops produced so much friction that the new Secretary of War, wrestling with rebellion in the Philippines, went in daily dread of an outbreak in Cuba.

The occupation, in spite of its great benefits, was inevitably obnoxious to the inhabitants. The Americans had been placed in authority over a foreign people, whose language they did not speak, whose customs they did not understand, and whose legal code was incomprehensible to men reared under English common law. Some of them intolerantly construed their mission as the Americanization of the island. The results, in Havana especially, took such ludicrous forms as a ban on the ringing of church bells, the proscription of gambling, and the enforcement of Puritan laws for the observance of Sunday. Even intelligent officers floundered in misunderstandings, formed alliances with unreliable Cubans, and stirred up factional antagonisms. The rank and file made no secret of their narrow prejudices, lorded it over the Cubans, and in restaurants and cafés gave them their first lessons in racial discrimination. Frequently, moreover, the poorly disciplined troops set an example of drunkenness and disorder. The worst-behaved were the "immunes" who had been rushed down for garrison duty at Santiago the year before, but there were many criticisms of the regulars—often green recruits—who later made up the force of occupation. The Army of the United States, wasted in the Santiago trenches, would again be worthy of its proud traditions. It was not yet so in 1899; and, such as it was, Cuba did not get the best of it. The most dependable regiments were sent to fight in the Philippines.

The news reports from Havana had made disagreeable reading for Americans at home. They had put themselves out for Cuba beyond the habit of nations, and the complex of motives had held something of the genuine sentiment and disinterested generosity by which they truly believed their conduct to be guided. They had innocently expected that rarest form of repayment, gratitude, and were offended beyond forgiveness when it was withheld. Many people were ready to wash their hands of Cuba, grant the promised independence forthwith, and abandon the unthankful islanders to their own devices; but others, including a good many men in public life, preferred to forget the avowals of the Teller Amendment, and acquire another colony. Both groups, as well as the diehard Cuban sympathizers, were opposed to the provisional military occupation, and their impatience to end it was increased by disgust with its conduct. Great pride had been taken in the achievements of General Leonard Wood at Santiago, and a corresponding irritation was felt when things went wrong elsewhere in the island. Only the rigorous sanitary measures rang the bell of national enthusiasm for General Brooke and his officers. Compensated for the disgrace of the dirty camps of 1898, Americans never tired of praising the cleansing of Havana. It must also have been a source of considerable satisfaction to Brooke, hitherto chiefly known to fame as the commander of the typhoid-breeding encampment at Chickamauga Park.

Brooke had not shown the qualities of a great administrator during the war, and he did not develop them afterward, but he was a devoted old officer who deserved more praise than he ever received for his constructive work in Cuba during the difficult period that followed the Spanish evacuation. Criticisms of his methods were sometimes unfair and even contradictory. It was said, for example, that his chief weakness was the failure to exert a firm central authority; but he was also insistently charged with excessive centralization of power at Havana and injurious meddling in the affairs of the several departments. This latter complaint, hotly put forward by Leonard Wood, may have been caused by Brooke's attempts to correct the first defect; or it may have simply resulted from Wood's annoyance at his subordination to Brooke, after months of virtually independent command at Santiago.

Another criticism was that Brooke gave his Cuban advisers too much freedom of action, in effect resigning his authority to an incompetent political clique. Some of his selections may have been unwise; but, in forming a cabinet of Cuban civilians and working with and through them, Brooke was following explicit instructions from the President. Similarly, his conservatism in making administrative innovations was in harmony with the President's direction to move cautiously in altering existing institutions; while Congress curtailed the economic program by forbidding the grant of franchises or concessions during the period of American control. The laudable intention of this legislation—an amendment which Senator Foraker fastened on the Army Appropriations Bill—was to protect Cuba from exploitation. Its effect, however, was to postpone the construction of public works and the development of natural resources, which were dependent on the flow of American capital to the poverty-stricken island. Like the President's instructions, the Foraker Amendment made Brooke's policies appear timid and temporizing as the occupation was prolonged.

Still, by midsummer, Brooke was sixty-one years old, and he had been in the Caribbean for a year, with only a short intermission; for, after the armistice, he had been reassigned to Porto Rico, first as head of the evacuation commission and then as military governor. No longer in the full tide of energy, he had the fatal disadvantage of a youthful and formidably efficient rival. Long before Brooke came on the scene, Leonard Wood had won the respect and confidence of the Cubans, and justified the faith of his own countrymen in their ability to produce colonial administrators of the finest English stamp. Wood had many influential friends. Governor Roosevelt was a host in himself. Brooke never had a chance against his entrenched subordinate. Wood disdained the control of Havana, disregarded Brooke's orders, and resented his consequent reprimands. He kept Roosevelt fully advised, sending him reams of complaints after Root's appointment. Roosevelt passed on the letters to Root, and Wood spoke for himself at a number of War Department conferences during a visit to the United States in November. Root, on tenterhooks over the situation in Cuba, became convinced that Wood was the man to handle it. The President appreciated Wood's value. He had also been reminded of Brooke's advanced years and his long service in the heat. Though it is hard to imagine McKinley's ever relieving the conscientious old General on his own motion, he said, "All right, go ahead," when Root submitted his opinion. In December, Brooke was transferred to the command of the Department of the East, with headquarters at New York. Wood was made military governor of Cuba, and became the instrument by which the island was guided to the formation of a representative government. Under his aegis, the first elections were ordered, and delegates were chosen for a constitutional convention. Less than a year after taking office, Wood was addressing instructions to the assemblage at Havana, but many months were still to pass before the insular government was established. It was not until May, 1902, that the Republic of Cuba was proclaimed and the United States force was at last withdrawn.

Wood's appointment did much to reconcile the American public to the protracted occupation on which McKinley had insisted. The President at all times held a steady course between the impulsive land-grabbers and the heedless advocates of immediate independence. Both groups were well represented in Congress. The strength of the Republican annexationists has been partially disguised by their acquiescence in the President's leadership. The political disunity of Cuba had uneasily recalled its strategic importance to the United States, an importance currently magnified by the plans for an isthmian canal and by rumors of German schemes for infiltrating the Caribbean. Many firsthand observers doubted that the Cubans were capable of maintaining a stable government. Leonard Wood himself believed that permanent United States possession was the destiny of the island.

The colonial fever was mildly infectious in Washington. Some of the President's closest friends and counselors came down with it. Orville Platt was outstanding among Republican senators in his positive dread of Cuban annexation. But the national policy was established by the annual message of 1899, in which the President adjured Congress that Cuba was held "in trust for the inhabitants," and that the pledge of the Teller Amendment was "of the highest honorable obligation and must be sacredly kept." He also instructed the still animated *Cuba Libre* contingent that the mission of the United States was not to be fulfilled by "turning adrift any loosely framed commonwealth. . . ." On the contrary, "we must see to it that free Cuba be a reality, not a name," McKinley wrote; "a perfect entity, not a hasty experiment bearing within itself the elements of failure."

Yet, in the international climate of that time, the President could not overlook the temptation that Cuba, like the Philippines, might offer to a predatory colonial power. As a Spanish colony, the island had drawn the United States into a long train of diplomatic troubles, and finally into war. McKinley meant to ensure that an independent Cuba should not threaten the peace in future. Unwilling to guarantee a weak state in the far Pacific, he believed that the United States must maintain its traditionally protective attitude toward the infant on its doorstep. His intention was indicated by statements in the annual message of 1899 that the destiny of Cuba was "irrevocably linked" with that of the United States, and that the new Cuba must be bound to the neighbor republic by ties of "singular intimacy and strength," whether "organic or conventional." The fixity of the President's purpose was not understood until the spring of 1901, when he whipped Congress with the threat of an extra session into demanding that the Cuban constitutional convention give formal recognition to the protective interest of the United States.

Porto Rico posed the colonial problem in its simplest form. The subject, in the first place, was not beclouded by controversy. There had been only the mildest enthusiasm for the acquisition of the island; but, if few people cared very much about owning Porto Rico, few were very much opposed to it, either. In contrast to the Philippines, it was regarded by anti-expansionists as a vaguely appropriate possession, justified by some reference to the Monroe Doctrine and the protection of an isthmian canal. Moreover, here was a place that was not only backward, but politically quiescent. Porto Rico had no history of civil war, no strong revolutionary party, and no widespread desire for independence. The inhabitants, ground into passivity by poverty and oppression, had offered little resistance to a change of flag, and were hopefully looking forward to a new era of prosperity and self-government. After the transfer of sovereignty in the autumn of 1898, the small force of occupation had had to cope with a wave of crime and banditry, but order had been presently restored with the aid of native soldiers and police. Any necessity for keeping American troops in Porto

Rico had disappeared months before Root arrived at the War Department. He lost no time in requesting the military governor, General George W. Davis—one of the army "politicians" who had figured in the beef inquiry, and who had subsequently received this appointment—to work out the details of a suitable civil organization. With the view of relieving his overburdened Department, Root was eager to have the President set up such a government in the exercise of his military authority.

McKinley's mind had followed the same course, though the political risk constrained him to deliberate. He was thinking of Charles H. Allen, the Assistant Secretary of the Navy—who had been well known to both McKinley and Long in Congress—as the first civil governor of Porto Rico. Under continued heavy pounding for his despotic usurpation of power, McKinley finally concluded to wait. Allen was, in fact, appointed, but he did not take up his duties until the next spring, after legislation had been passed to provide Porto Rico with a temporary government. This legislation closely followed the suggestions of General Davis, which had been embodied in the report of the War Department, and formed the basis for the recommendations of the President's annual message.

The first emanation of colonial planning from the Executive branch was not remarkable for its liberal character. Davis had at one point made the mistake—for which Root had taken him to task—of referring to the "Territorial government" which Congress might be expected to give Porto Rico. The error, however, was due to careless phraseology. Though sympathetic with the Porto Ricans, Davis did not find them ready for a high degree of self-government. He proposed that the administration should consist of a governor and state officers, a legislative council, and a judiciary, all to be appointed by the President. His plan also included a lower legislative chamber, to be elected by popular, though limited suffrage; but he advised that this step should be postponed, and that the natives should at first vote only in municipal elections.

Davis advanced his suggestions with some regret, but they were accepted without sentimental qualms at Washington. The President, naturally inclined to conservative procedure, was already on record with the statement: "It is easier to enlarge a grant than to contract it." Root, for his part, endorsed a "crown colony" administration with hardheaded realism. He had no desire to grant territorial status to Porto Rico, or admit the inhabitants to American citizenship. Besides, his chief concern was with the economic, rather than the political relation of the island. Under the flag of the rich republic, the Porto Ricans had been quickly reduced to a more abject poverty than they had ever suffered in all the lean centuries of Spanish dominion. Root was quite prepared to disappoint their hopes of sharing in the free institutions of the United States, but he was shocked by the idea that American sovereignty might mean mass starvation for one of the new possessions.

The fundamental difficulty was that Porto Rico could no longer profitably sell the coffee, sugar, and tobacco on which her economy depended. Her principal markets in Spain and Cuba—with which she had enjoyed practically free trade—were closed by high tariffs, while the United States tariffs continued to operate, unmodified, against her exports. Coffee, the most important crop, was not taxed, but Porto Rican coffee was almost unknown to Americans, and could not compete with the product of Brazil. Caught in a squeeze between the old regime and the new, the commerce of Porto Rico was stifled; and, shortly after Root came to Washington, a hurricane ravaged the plantations and completed the destitution of the inhabitants.

The catastrophe was of some service to the island in dramatizing its plight. On the instance of the President, there was a public appeal for relief. The country responded with its usual generosity, and war vessels went to Porto Rico with tons of supplies. Root assumed responsibility for distributing large additional quantities of army rations. Anxious to deal with the basic economic problem, he was soon writing the President that Porto Rico must be accorded free trade with the United States, either by Executive order or by action of Congress summoned in special session; but a full discussion of the subject convinced him that economic as well as administrative decisions should await the regular session of Congress, and that the risks of an Executive order on the tariff, of all things, were prohibitive. McKinley strongly pressed Congress to take action in his annual message. "Our plain duty," he wrote, "is to abolish all customs tariffs between the United States and Porto Rico and give her products free access to our markets."

At the time of that writing, the method of relieving the Porto Ricans seemed to McKinley as plain as the duty. No constitutional lawyer himself, he did not perceive the objection that, in bringing Porto Rico under the American tariff system, the government might set a precedent for the Philippines. It seems strange that his principal legal adviser, then engaged in exploring the constitutional question, had positively urged this action on the President; but the point was long missed by the legal brains of the Senate, including such specialists on the argument of "dependencies" as Orville Platt, Spooner, and Foraker. When the lawyers of the party awoke to the danger of prejudicing their case before the Supreme Court, there was an abrupt change in Republican policy. Porto Rico, neglected

stepchild of the republic, was to become a center of political agitation in
the winter that lay ahead.

The most important business on the agenda of the War Department
was the Philippine archipelago, and the first item was the rebellion. Root,
who had assumed that he would be concerned with matters of law and
government, found himself immersed in the prior claims of purely military
problems. Midsummer had brought a lull in the fighting while Otis, in
the flooding rains, gradually received his regular replacements and embarked the state regiments for home. He had quickly resigned himself to
the postponement of victory and the loss of the volunteers, and was in his
customary mood of optimism, confident that the insurgents were demoralized by defeat, merely holding out in the belief that their American
sympathizers would shortly overthrow the Republican administration.

Elsewhere than on Luzon, some progress was being made. Footholds
were being occupied in the central islands, and a number of ports had been
opened to trade; but, in spite of extending the scope of his operations,
Otis was still sticking to his estimate of 30,000 effectives, or between 35,000
and 40,000 troops. Root regarded these figures with a somewhat jaundiced
eye. The spring campaign had obviously failed because the American force
had been too small to hold its gains. News reports from Manila seemed to
indicate that Otis was again minimizing his task. Orders for ten volunteer
regiments had been published in July. During a consultation at Lake
Champlain in August, Root obtained the President's permission to raise
five regiments more.

McKinley himself had brought up the question of further enlistments,
but he would have been glad to escape the necessity, for obvious political
reasons. Though the preceding call had met with a good response, every
move connected with the Philippines was subject to unsparing criticism.
The President wanted to avoid a charge of poor judgment and reckless
extravagance in piling up preparations for a war that was nearly over. He
rather ruefully observed that if they had too many troops, it would be his
fault; and if they had too few, it would be Root's. This was not a comment
calculated to dampen Root's zeal for reinforcing Otis. On his return to
Washington, he cabled Manila for a fresh estimate of "an undoubtedly
adequate force" to ensure a prompt victory, stating that he would rather err
on the safe side in sending too many men. He suggested that Otis hold
full consultation with his general officers before submitting his conclusions.

Root's wish to hear from the other generals reflected the influence of
the Manila correspondents. It was also in line with the prevailing view at
the War Department—implanted by General Merritt—that the military

397

responsibilities in the Philippines should be divided. Otis was regarded as an armchair general; and Root, with his prejudice against the type, must have been longing to give command in the field to a more active man—possibly to the much-talked-of General Lawton, for whose "wonderful vigor" he had great admiration. The President, however, was immovably committed to Otis, convinced of his ability and sure that he was winning the war.

The response to Root's inquiry was favorable to more reinforcements, though Otis was still ambiguous. He said that the size of the force needed would depend on the outcome of negotiations then pending with the extreme southern islands. If they succeeded, as was probable, 40,000 effectives would be fully adequate for Luzon and the central islands. None of the general officers suggested more than 50,000 effectives. Indeed, as Otis explained, he could send a column through Luzon with his present half-organized force, but he had not enough men to scatter on garrison duty, which was necessary to protect the inhabitants against the insurgents. To meet such "possible contingencies" and the demands of the American public, he requested fifteen volunteer regiments besides those being enlisted, and he wanted them sent quickly. The United States, he said, overestimated the strength and cohesion of the insurgents. Organized armed opposition would cease as soon as they were overpowered.

The reassuring tone of this communication did not alter the fact that Otis was projecting operations on a far more extensive scale than ever before. He was asking for a possible 50,000 men, and at the same time, though with rather an air of yielding to pressure, he was also asking for a minimum of 60,000. Fifteen more volunteer regiments were beyond Root's legal power, but he got the President's consent to double the enlistments on which they had decided, and an order for ten volunteer regiments was issued in the middle of August. Two Negro regiments, ordered the next month, brought the volunteer force up to the total of 35,000 that Congress had authorized. The new recruits, like those secured under the July order, were carefully screened and placed under the command of experienced officers. Quickly transformed into efficient outfits, the volunteers of 1899 offered a striking demonstration of the advantage of forming a homogeneous infantry force, enlisted from the country at large in disregard of the state militia organizations. Root told the reporters that he was determined every man of them should eat Christmas dinner in the Philippines, and he was nearly as good as his word. Early in 1900, Otis's combined force of regulars and volunteers had swelled to more than 65,000 men.

Root's reputation was made in his first month in office. He soared high in public favor as the Washington correspondents, amazed by his driving energy and the length of his working day, broadcast their commendation of the new era at the War Department. Yet the outcry over the Philippines showed no sign of abating. A stream of news dispatches from Manila bore fresh testimony to Otis's faults and mistakes, and the rigid censorship by which he had endeavored to conceal them. In anticipation of the state elections, the Democrats loudly clamored for his recall, and for peace and conciliation in the Philippines. Root's rise to popularity was a badly needed asset to the administration. The mantle of Alger had fallen squarely across the shoulders of a dim figure at a desk in Manila.

The latest bugbear of the American people was a fussy, cantankerous Army officer of sixty-one, with outmoded burnside whiskers and a troublesome hole in his busy old head where a Confederate bullet had found its mark in 1864. Work was his solace and his distraction—a painkiller which he took in copious draughts, gulping big responsibilities and savoring small sips of detail. While coping with politics, jurisprudence, diplomacy, finance, commerce, business, public health, education, and religion, while planning to pacify the troubled central islands and negotiating with the islands to the south, Otis was exchanging one army for another and preparing to encircle and destroy the insurgent force on Luzon. Nothing was further from his mind than the wish to delegate an iota of his authority. He spent sixteen hours a day at his desk, but his industry was little appreciated in Manila. Very few of the people he dealt with, inside the army or out, were willing to grant him more than a grudging admission of competence and a remarkable physical endurance.

On his record, Otis cannot be slightingly dismissed. The Philippine troops were well equipped and supplied, with staff departments operating at top efficiency; and a miscellany of regiments, predominantly green militia, had been welded into a disciplined and expert fighting force. Otis's desperate efforts to hold on to his state troops had been a political, not a military blunder. They were the elite of the army in 1899. The duties of the governorship were not discharged in a narrowly military spirit. Otis was keenly interested in judicial and civic matters, promptly re-established the Manila courts under the direction of capable Filipino lawyers, and provided for setting up municipal governments in the towns that came under American control. His enforcement of a rigorous honesty in every department of the occupation set a high standard of colonial administration. But Otis was personally too much disliked to receive a fair appraisal. He repelled and maddened his associates by his stewing over trifles, his stubborn self-deception, and his surly disposition. His manner, in conference, ranged from blank indifference to snappish irritability, and his temper was quickly ignited by a hint of opposition. He had not been able to get on with Admiral Dewey. He had rowed with the interfering civilian, Schurman. He had quarreled with both of his divisional commanders, Arthur MacArthur and Henry W. Lawton. He kept up a running series of squabbles with the newspaper correspondents, threatening them with courtsmartial and expulsion from Luzon, and their antagonism was fatal in its effect on opinion at home.

The military censorship of press cables was a miracle of bad judgment, not because censorship was inadvisable—it had been instituted by Dewey before an American soldier arrived in the Philippines—but because its handling was capricious and arbitrary and, in the long run, ineffectual. The fact that the suppressed information had often been published in the Manila newspapers gave color to the charge that Otis was seeking to mislead the American public rather than the enemy. The anti-imperialists had been quick to interpret the censorship as a political instrument. There may have been some truth in the accusation. A well-attested rule of the Manila censorship was to let nothing pass that "might hurt the administration." One caution from the Executive Mansion—the importance of hushing up any differences with the Philippine Commission—is a matter of official record. It is possible that other hints were more discreetly conveyed. Yet it is also possible that Otis was acting on his own initiative. Political feeling ran high in the Philippine service. The officers were outraged by the anti-expansionist propaganda which glorified insurgent patriotism. They blamed it, to a man, for prolonging the resistance. Otis was committed to Republican policy by the nature of his task; and he was, besides, profoundly identified with McKinley's aims and devoted to carrying them out.

Otis seemed doomed by the very ardor of his loyalty to create trouble for the administration, but none of his blunders affected the warm admiration which the President had conceived for him. McKinley's good opinion was largely founded on the official reports. They were the reflection of an ideal Otis and there was much to be said for it, but it was by no means the whole picture of the man or the situation. The President could have corrected his impression by a close reading of the news dispatches, particularly the reports of conditions on Luzon and the growing discontent in the army. Otis was becoming progressively isolated in his conception of the war. He never visited the lines, but remained at his headquarters, following the telegraphic reports on a set of extremely poor maps. Yet he refused to rely on the judgment of the soldiers at the front. His hampering orders were the despair of all his generals.

In conventional military fashion, Otis directed his strategy toward the defeat of the insurgents in open combat. As his maps showed enemy concentrations broken up and native villages taken, he was entirely satisfied of success, and he brushed aside the fact that, though a few prisoners were sometimes captured, the main body of rebel troops always escaped intact. Otis had served in the Indian wars, but he was slow to apply the experience to the fighting in the Philippines. He did not recognize that his orthodox plans assumed an enemy with modern organization and equipment, or perceive the disadvantage of formal military disciplines and technological superiority in conflict with primitive and fluid bands. The fleet and self-reliant Filipino warrior had only his arms for equipment, and his commissary was a bag of rice. The American expeditions, loaded with impedimenta and tied to a railroad line or a plodding mule train, could repel but never grasp the mobile forces that dissolved like mist in the jungles and steep defiles.

The round robin of the Manila news correspondents truly stated that the generals in the field did not share the ultra-optimistic view that was presented in the official reports. The campaigns had all come to the same profitless conclusion, whether they were "picnic excursions" along the railroad line or big expeditions which saw weeks of hard combat before returning to their base. Behind the retiring Americans, the insurgent armies re-formed in strength, the villages reverted to their former masters, the jungle closed without a trace. Officers of every grade writhed at the futile cycle of advance and withdrawal. Long before Otis admitted the necessity for an extensive occupation, his army was murmurous with a demand for garrisons. An eager clique gathered around Henry Lawton, who was voluble in urging a larger army, and a freer and more spirited conduct of the war. The correspondents were his partisans, and in August their dispatches rallied the American public to Lawton's cause. The outcry against Otis was aggravated by the belief that the rebellion would be quickly ended if Lawton were in command of the army.

Lawton and Otis were both regular Army officers who had learned their profession in the Civil War and practiced it in the Indian campaigns; and each was absorbed in his military career, with a strict sense of duty and a sturdy belief in his own opinions. There the resemblance ceased. Though he was only five years younger than Otis, Lawton was a vigorous soldier, always eager for action, glorying in the excitement of "a beautiful battle." He had once been the most daring of all the young cavalry officers on the plains, and the romance of those old days still clung to the tall, erect figure with iron-gray hair cut *en brosse*. Mounted on his black horse or striding up and down the lines, Lawton always wore a big white sun helmet on Luzon; and, as he coolly exposed himself to enemy fire, he personified the disdain for personal survival that is so much admired by soldiers and by war correspondents. But in Lawton's gallant conduct there was some hidden instability, some painful tension that found release in danger—or in drink. His immoderate indulgence in alcohol had been his undoing in Cuba after the surrender of Santiago. He had not lasted very long as military governor of the conquered district, although he had wanted the job. A public scandal was narrowly averted. Leonard Wood was suddenly promoted to command of the district, and Lawton was rushed home on the pretext of ill-health. Cooling his heels in Washington, he was attached to the presidential party on several occasions, including the trip to Atlanta, and attracted McKinley's interest. Before Lawton went to the Philippines, the President privately read him a temperance lecture, exacting a promise that he would mend his ways—a promise which, in spite of reports to the contrary, it seems that Lawton kept. He must at times have had a hard struggle with temptation; for, though the assignment to Luzon was another chance for Lawton and one that he was eager to improve, it was also laden with disappointment.

When Lawton sailed in January, he believed that, in case of an outbreak in the Philippines, he was to command the forces in the field. His prospective assignment, which was bruited with much enthusiasm by the newspapers, had evidently been discussed at Washington on the assumption then prevailing that Otis would follow the precedent set by Merritt, if there were fighting to be done. But it was not the subject of orders. Otis was left free to retain command of the army or to delegate it, as he pleased. Most unfortunately—but not untypically—neither the President nor Alger had made this clear to Lawton. He landed at Manila, still expecting to have an independent command. He learned that he was to be subordinate to Otis in command of a division, and he was not long in discovering that he would be given as little opportunity as possible to distinguish himself. Otis favored MacArthur for the big spring campaign to the north, while Lawton was used for a series of minor expeditions that were scarcely more than scouts in force.

The immediate effect of these orders was to create an impression of rivalrous opposition between Otis and Lawton. The newspaper praise of Lawton and reports of his appointment had preceded him to the Philippines. It was naturally deduced that Otis had been annoyed and was jealously trying to push Lawton into the background of the war. But Lawton had a magnetic gift for attracting attention. There was a striking contrast between the impetuous soldier on the firing line and the sedentary

Commanding General, shut up with his wretched maps at Manila. Lawton's personality and his tactical skills pre-eminently fitted him for irregular warfare, and he made intelligent use of the experience he had gained on the western plains. He gave flexibility to his force, organizing it in squads of "comrades in arms," and formed a detachment of daring scouts who acted as the eyes and ears of the advancing columns. He early advocated the establishment of garrisons, and declared—in the hearing of newspapermen —that 100,000 troops would be needed to put down the rebellion. The breach with Otis widened as Lawton talked, criticizing the conduct of the war and airing his own ideas to his court of admirers. He apparently did not realize at first that his remarks would be published, and might even be exaggerated and distorted. He was abashed and profuse in denials when he discovered the storm he had created at home. As a generous-minded man and a dutiful soldier, Lawton could not acknowledge vindictive feeling, but there must have been bitterness in his heart. He had desperately needed to win honor in the Philippines. He had set his heart on a picturesque exploit, believing it would change the course of the war; and Otis had snubbed and ridiculed the enterprise, and denied Lawton his chance.

The incident occurred at the time of blackest discouragement for the Americans, at the close of May when the spring offensive was petering out, when the rains had begun and the hope of peace had died, and even General Otis was obliged to admit that most of his army was ready to go home. Lawton had just returned from an expedition to the north, designed as a diversionary operation to protect MacArthur's communications, but transformed by Lawton's initiative into an important action. He had been halted in mid-career by a spate of detailed and vacillating orders from Manila. San Isidro had been seized by the Americans, and Aguinaldo had fled. Sure that he could capture the generalissimo and the remnants of his government, Lawton had begged for permission to push on. He had received peremptory orders to withdraw. With his campaign wasted and his force broken up, he returned to confront Otis in an interview which Lawton considered so crucial that he provided himself with a witness, Professor Worcester of the Philippine Commission. It was Lawton's purpose to make a personal plea for his own plan when all else had failed. Commanding the pursuit of the Apaches in the old cavalry days, Lawton had himself received the surrender of Geronimo. He had seen the value of the symbol of leadership. He believed that the back of the Tagalog rebellion could be broken during the summer, if Aguinaldo surrendered to the Americans.

Lawton wanted only two regiments—an independent command, with permission to arm, equip, and provision his men to suit himself. If Otis would grant these requests, Lawton offered to stake his reputation as a soldier and his position in the United States Army on the claim that in sixty days he would end the insurrection and deliver Aguinaldo, dead or alive. The proposition had an extraordinary effect on Otis. It made him laugh. He was not a man given to mirth—Funston wrote that one would as soon have thought of cracking a joke in his presence as of trying to pull his beard—but he laughed at Lawton's offer. He may have been tickled by the braggadocio of the tippling officer who had attacked too rashly at El Caney. Some buried vein of irony may have been touched by talk of summer conquest at a time when the state troops were chafing to quit Luzon. Perhaps Otis was merely amused by the thought of what the newspapers at home would say if he lost a popular general and two regiments of American boys in the floods of the tropical wilderness. In any case, he thought very little of Aguinaldo, regarding him as a mere figurehead, who "never amounted to anything"; but the best opinion of the army was not in agreement. Persistent efforts were put forth in the next two years to seize the prize that had been within Lawton's grasp. MacArthur regarded the capture of Aguinaldo as an object of the first importance. When it was at last achieved by Funston in the spring of 1901, the submission of the rebel leader to the United States sovereignty was an influential factor in the pacification of the islands.

Had Otis given Lawton a free hand, it might have shortened the resistance; but, except for this bungled opportunity, it does not seem that Lawton could have fought a better war in 1899; nor MacArthur, nor Funston, nor any of the other able generals in the Philippines—S. B. M. Young, Wheaton, Kobbé, and the rest. Before the rains had ended, the great encircling movement of early autumn rolled inexorably over the inundated lowlands of central Luzon, and this time garrisons were left behind. The grasp of the Americans reached northward, as shiploads of troops crowded in, and in November Otis could announce the complete success of his plans. The rebel army was shattered beyond repair. Officers and men were reduced to the status of banditti, or had dispersed to play the part of *amigos*, with arms concealed. Some members of Aguinaldo's cabinet had been taken prisoner; others had fled to join him in the mountains. The insurgent claim to a government, as Otis jubilantly cabled the War Department, could be made no longer under any fiction.

The enemy had been overpowered, and organized opposition ceased, just as Otis had predicted; but the fighting was not ended. The disintegration of the rebel army signalized the opening of a fierce guerrilla warfare—the most savage phase of the resistance in the Philippines.

MacArthur soon got wind of the change in the insurgents' plans, and perceived the immense disadvantage which the Americans would suffer in meeting forces that could not only scatter, but vanish altogether, discarding their uniforms and becoming absorbed in the peaceful life of the villages. He urged Otis to issue a proclamation announcing a fixed period of amnesty, with payment for surrendered rifles, and declaring that all who subsequently continued in armed rebellion were subject to treatment as outlaws and murderers. Otis brusquely rejected this advice. He had a number of reasons for doing so, and one of them was a desire to avoid exacerbating the violent racial antipathies between the opposing forces. Unlike many American soldiers in the Philippines, Otis never forgot that the mission of the army was to pacify the islands. He not only feared possible reprisals by the insurgents, but dreaded the effect on the Americans themselves of a seeming license to commit "barbarities." His thinking in this respect disclosed the temperate and judicious cast of mind which so strongly appealed to the President; but Otis also had a less commendable reason for refusing to adopt severely repressive measures. He was blind to the seriousness of the new style of warfare. He was persuaded that the guerrillas would soon subside, leaving only the armed bands of *ladrones,* or robbers, which had always infested the islands; and, as time went on, he seemingly convinced himself that the transition had actually taken place. During the early part of 1900, his principal military concern was the conquest of southern Luzon, and the extension of the occupation in the Visayan group and the big southernmost island of Mindanao. He was relieved in May at his own request and left the Philippines in the belief that the insurrection was "a thing of the past," and the Filipinos were "thoroughly content to submit" to United States authority.

Though Otis's mistake was influenced by conventional military concepts, it was fundamentally a part of the still greater mistake that had plagued American policy from the first—the failure to understand that the Philippine peoples were imbued with the desire for freedom. The version of the case which Otis evolved was perhaps the most plausible of the assurances which rained on the President in 1899. Otis admitted that the ignorant masses had at first been "intoxicated by the cry for independence and self-government," but he said that the craze was passing as they became disillusioned by the oppressions of the insurgents. Fear of the United States troops, which had been instilled by enemy propaganda, would disappear on closer contact. They were received with joy in districts where they were known. Sometimes, however, the people concealed their feelings in dread of the vengeance which the insurgents visited on *amigos,* or American sympathizers. This last explanation was particularly effective because it contained a partial truth. Tactics of terror were employed by the rebel forces, and employed increasingly as elements of the population gradually became infected with discouragement and with bitter resignation to the dominance of a superior force. The confusing situation was never understood at home. By and large, the newspapers interpreted events according to their political leanings. Long after the facts began to glimmer through the dispatches of the anti-imperialist press, the President continued to maintain that American sovereignty was desired by all but a small minority of the people of the Philippines. He was obviously inclined to wishful thinking by both sentiment and expediency, but there was much justification for his adherence to a belief that had been firmly implanted by his most trusted and presumably informed advisers.

The steadfast incomprehension which Otis brought to the subject was, in the end, influenced by his confinement at Manila, but it had originally been based on his secret-service reports, and it was supported by the reports from the field throughout 1899. The American commanders were awakening in the first summer of the war to some sense of a fiercer and more amorphous resistance than they could explain. In the months before the outbreak, they had had plentiful opportunity to observe the flexible character of the insurgent army, its elements constantly shifting from warrior to farmer, from farmer to warrior again. Men of formal military training had seen "loose organization" as an evidence of weakness. They had not recognized total rebellion. At the close of the year, the dispatches from the front still reflected faith in the welcome of the villages, the gratitude of the peasants, the good will of the helpful *amigos*. Here and there, some perception was beginning to stir among the junior officers, but it had scarcely reached the generals. MacArthur apparently grew hopeful of the appeasing effect of an amnesty offer. Lawton rather vaguely and sympathetically recognized a popular aspiration for independence. He felt sure, however, that the Filipinos could be propitiated, and his admirers believed that, in chief command, he would have been able to tranquilize the islands by conciliatory methods. The claim was never put to the test, for in December the tall, white-helmeted figure went once too often within range of the enemy rifles, and Lawton met a hero's death on a sodden riverbank north of Manila. When Otis went home, he was succeeded by Arthur MacArthur, the precise, arrogant, dandified general who would finally tranquilize the islands by a policy of relentless subjugation.

MacArthur wore the badge of harshness, but he was given the harsh task of subduing a people substantially united in resistance. The eyes of the American commanders were quickly opened, as the occupation spread in a thin web over the archipelago. Hostility and betrayal encircled the garrisons that dotted the Luzon wilderness and the fringes of Panay, Cebu, Leyte, Samar, and Mindanao. The work of conquest had barely been begun. On taking command, MacArthur promptly obtained authority to make an offer of amnesty. The proclamation was published in June, 1900, without mention of the punitive features he had recommended to Otis, and it was followed by a statement of the civil rights to be expected in future. It was not until December, 1900, when these overtures had failed and MacArthur, like Otis before him, faced the loss of his volunteer force, that he was constrained to issue a proclamation enjoining "precise observance of the laws of war," with special reference to noncombatants who sent aid to the enemy from towns occupied by American detachments.

MacArthur did not seek permission to initiate a drastic policy. He had reported the conditions his army faced. In the autumn of 1900, the Washington authorities were at last advised that the enemy in the Philippines was the population, and the reception which they accorded the soldiers of the United States was the welcome of the rifle, the bolo, and the spear.

The developments of the future were unguessed in the summer of 1899, when the government confidently looked to victory in the field to settle a rebellious faction of natives. The President, with his great reliance on Otis, had no doubt that the American success would be early and complete. It was not the military problem that bore heavily on his mind, but the political problem which the struggle had created, and its bearing on the coming state elections. Although they were almost wholly concerned this year with local offices and issues, they were crucially important as indications of the voting trend in 1900. There was little indication of a spirited retort to the outcry against the war. The Republicans were on the defensive, squirming uncomfortably under the taunts of the opposition. The trouble was that they disliked the war just as much as the Democrats, and were just as indignant over the deceptions and failures of its conduct. There was nothing to choose between the two sides in antipathy to General Otis. While anti-expansionists censured him for fighting the Filipino patriots, Republican newspapers belabored him for not subduing them quickly, and even blamed him for having permitted an outbreak in the first place. The President was drawing a long breath in the comparative seclusion of Lake Champlain. After many months of silence, he was going to speak to the people again about the Philippines.

An intense political, as well as sentimental solicitude had gathered around the militia regiments which, at the end of August, were finally beginning to arrive from the islands. The objects of universal interest because of their long detention and hard service, they were regarded by many Americans as the victims of Republican policy, impressed into an unjust war waged for party ends with which they were not in sympathy; and much was made of their pitiable mental isolation, since anti-imperialist pamphlets had been barred from the army's mail. The Democrats could scarcely wait to get these unfortunate soldiers home. The President had decided to meet the challenge squarely by going himself to welcome a number of the regiments. At the end of August, before returning to Washington from his vacation, he filled the first of these engagements at Pittsburgh.

The occasion was the homecoming of the Tenth Pennsylvania Regiment, volunteers for the war with Spain, after more than a year of service in the Philippines. Lavish preparations had been made for a gala reception, and Pittsburgh was in holiday mood as the sun-tanned veterans spilled from the trains and took their place in the parade which was waiting at the station, with the President in his carriage. Crowds stood cheering along the line of march, and were massed in Schenley Park, where McKinley reviewed the regiment and made his address. It was a positive declaration that the settlement in the Philippines would be accomplished by force of arms, and not by efforts of conciliation. In an unqualified defense of General Otis, the President assumed all responsibility for the orders that had delayed the opening of hostilities, and fully supported Otis in his subsequent refusals to negotiate. There would be "no useless parley" on Luzon, McKinley asserted—no pause until American authority was acknowledged and established. The misguided followers of the rebellion he described as objects of pity. The cruel and ambitious leaders he sarcastically left to others to justify and eulogize.

The statement of policy was the stern pattern of a speech whose fabric glowed with praise for the volunteer troops. The crowd roared applause as McKinley, turning toward the Pennsylvania soldiers and at times addressing himself directly to them, commended the valor of the noble men who had served their country "in its extremity," and spoke of the special medal of honor which he had already announced the intention of asking Congress to confer on them. The President was there in Pittsburgh, he said, to express something he thought the country and the soldiers themselves might not fully appreciate—the heroism of their conduct and its important support of the government. Without the state volunteers in the Philippines, "our flag would have had its first stain and the American name its first ignominy." They had made secure and permanent the victory of Dewey, redeemed American obligations to civilization, and rescued the islands from chaos and the rule of "one man," instead of the consent of the governed.

"They were not serving the insurgents or their sympathizers at home," the President pointed out. "They had no part or patience with the men, few in number, happily, who would have rejoiced to have seen them lay down their arms. . . ." By their loyalty and devotion, the volunteers had saved the national honor, and gained for themselves imperishable distinction.

"Who resisted the suggestion of the unpatriotic that they should come home?" The President adjusted his glasses and read a list. "First California," it began. ". . . First Idaho, Fifty-first Iowa . . . Thirteenth Minnesota . . . First North Dakota. . . ." It took a long time to finish the honor roll of the nineteen state organizations that had consented to prolong their service in the Philippines. As every sonorous name rang out, the reading was interrupted by the shouts that burst from the swelling lungs of the Pennsylvania troops. The warmth of the President's praise had effaced the campfire grudges of Luzon, and turned to gilded memories of glory the torment of lethal sun and fevered rains, the skirmish in the rice swamp and the ambush in the bamboo thicket. In the grimy light of Schenley Park, they were home and they were heroes; and, with the easy nostalgia of the demobilized, they were stirred by reminders of comradeship. The Pennsylvania boys went wild for the First Nebraska and for Funston's regiment, the Twentieth Kansas. Schenley Park resounded with the Filipino yell, as they hailed the Utah Battery, their chums in jungle fighting.

The volunteers had denied, with more convincing eloquence than the President could command, that the conflict in the Philippines was a party war, reluctantly fought by men without heart for its cause. The reports of McKinley's speech and the demonstrations at Pittsburgh did not make enjoyable reading for the political opposition. He had labeled anti-expansionists "the unpatriotic" and called them "few in number," and they retaliated by heaping abuse on his policy. *The Nation* sneered that it was a long journey from the President's speech in Boston to the "no-quarter" speech in Pittsburgh—"the journey from Lincoln to Torquemada." Here was a queer admission. *The Nation* had not said anything about Lincoln at the time when the Home Market speech was delivered. It had called McKinley's utterances "humbug." Surely, some irritation over the prospects of the coming elections had betrayed the anti-expansionist weekly into the favorite comparison of the Republican orators.

· 18 ·

THE HERO'S RETURN

THROUGH the blue dusk of the early October evening a river of light ran from the Union Depot to the Capitol and poured in flood up Pennsylvania Avenue. All along its course, the dense crowds packed the pavements, and 12,000 members of civic organizations were marking time in the side streets. The District had not known a night like this since 1865, and the grand patriotic illuminations of the earlier day were dimmed by the marvels of the present—the scintillating "fairy lamps," the brilliant inscriptions, and the powerful searchlights which played on the national colors and bathed the public buildings in concentrated radiance. The façade of the new General Post Office was flaming with two famous quotations: the orders to Commodore George Dewey—always directly attributed to the President—to capture or destroy the Spanish fleet in Philippine waters; and their fulfillment in the laconic permission granted on the bridge of the *Olympia*, "You may fire when you are ready, Gridley." Floodlights dazzled on a reproduction of the prow of Dewey's flagship, projecting from the front of the reviewing stand just south of the Treasury. A blinding salutation, "Welcome, Admiral," rose above the twinkling foliage and flower beds of Lafayette Square. The candle-lit windows of the past seemed but a poor and primitive celebration, as electricity paid an incandescent homage to the sea hero of the nation, home from the sea at last.

The White House gleamed, austere and pale, between the blaze of the Treasury and the blaze of the Navy Department. The mansion marked the end of the route from the depot and, within, there were signs of expectancy. Colonel Bingham, the Commissioner of Public Buildings and

410

Grounds, was hovering in the vestibule. Secretary Long shepherded a party of high-ranking naval officers, with Generals Miles and Corbin, in the East Room. The rest of the Cabinet and one former member, General Alger, were in the meeting room upstairs. Mrs. McKinley was sitting with some friends at the end of the corridor. The President was alone in the oval library. The homecoming of the Admiral—literally "the" Admiral now, since the rank had been revived expressly for his lifetime—meant a great deal more to McKinley than an occasion for patriotic rejoicing. Some conception of its significance may be gleaned from the fact that this most conventional President, imbued with profound respect for the dignity of his office, had contemplated going to New York to meet Dewey under the apprehension that his omission to do so might be "misinterpreted" by the public. Secretaries Hay and Long had both expressed disapproval when consulted on the subject. "For you to travel all the way to New York," John Hay rather acidly commented, "to take part in a municipal demonstration in honor of a naval officer, returning from a tour of duty, would be a compliment never before paid, I think, in the world's history." McKinley had given up the idea. He still had many things to ponder while he waited in formal isolation in the library.

A faint grumble of cheers came from Pennsylvania Avenue, growling nearer and louder until it rolled like thunder around the corner of the Treasury. Hoofs clattered on the driveway, and Colonel Bingham sprang to the portico as the cavalry escort reined in before a fine carriage, drawn by four spirited bays with postilions. A short, trim man alighted and mounted the steps. He was not quite the red, white, and blue hero of the posters. He looked older and much more tired, and his face was not rosy, but darkly tanned, in startling contrast with his full white mustache. He was carrying his right arm in a queer, tenderly protective fashion. Secretary Long, bounding to the East Room door, clasped a reluctant hand. The President would instruct Dewey in the Hayes-McKinley technique of greeting ("You save yourself by not letting them get the grasp on you"), but Dewey's right arm had already been partially paralyzed in New York.

The White House reception was surprisingly unceremonious, in view of all the worry it had caused. Dewey was conducted in the elevator to the second floor, where the President came forward to give him a hearty welcome, and whisked him for a moment into Mrs. McKinley's corner before the Cabinet members were admitted to the library to make their bows. Then McKinley took Dewey downstairs again, and out by the south door. With the dignitaries in their wake, they hurried along the gravel paths to the rear of the reviewing stand. Cheers went roaring down to the Capitol as, leaning on the President's arm, the Admiral crossed the stand and seated himself on the fake white prow of the *Olympia*. If he wished himself back on the original, he was scarcely to be blamed. He had had a surfeit of celebration in the five days that had passed since the flagship entered New York harbor. Hustled into the din and glare of Pennsylvania Avenue, the jaded Admiral was obliged to review another parade—and a civic parade, at that.

Hopes of an impressive military turnout had been quashed by the refusal of General Miles to let the Army take part in a parade by night, but the President had not wanted to disappoint the eager citizens. Their representatives had called to consult him more than once. "Gentlemen, burn plenty of red fire," he had advised. The street became a scarlet inferno, as the start of the parade was announced by the explosions of giant crackers and bursting fire bombs. Bicyclists pedaled on garlanded wheels hung with Chinese lanterns. The Roman Catholic societies brandished red torches and illuminated crosses. The International Machinists were preceded by a six-inch rifled cannon from the Navy Yard, bearing the label "We make the guns for Dewey." The letter carriers had the local postal cars in line, adorned with electric greetings and a gigantic illuminated envelope, addressed to Dewey and marked "Returned to Washington." There were many equally lavish displays, but their effect was lost on the guest of honor. An interruption occurred when some of the marchers broke ranks, and spectators pushed through the ropes and milled around the reviewing stand. The center of a noisy and formless demonstration, Dewey seized the opportunity to retire. The President followed with the Cabinet and the other dignitaries.

As fast as the four horses with postilions could trot, Dewey sped to the luxurious private house which had been placed at his disposal—the K Street residence of Mrs. Washington McLean. There a quiet supper and comfortable bed awaited him, and there he found his hostess and her two daughters. It was a very happy occasion for one of them, the widowed Mrs. Mildred McLean Hazen, who had thought Dewey a hero before Manila Bay, and had been melting with pride in him ever since. Such fond, feminine welcomes have a sweetness all their own, especially for a man without wife or home. But the ladies did not long intrude. Leaving the Admiral to rest, they withdrew to Mrs. McLean's suburban estate, Beauvoir. The populace showed less consideration. Crowds, gathering to watch for Dewey's return, refused to believe that he was already inside the house. He was obliged to settle the question by appearing briefly at a window, before peace was restored to Farragut Square.

Dewey had been forewarned of the demonstrations in store for him. During his long absence, the noise of hero worship had echoed loudly across the Pacific. It had gone so far that people of both parties had been telling him that he ought to be a candidate for the next Presidential nomination. The New York *World* had been particularly insistent. The spontaneous outpouring of devotion had led to extravagant projects, like the large fund that was being collected to buy the Admiral a fine mansion in Washington, and the Dewey Arch at Madison Square in New York, a grandiose plaster structure which was to serve as the model for a permanent monument of granite and marble. A shower of golden gifts awaited Dewey's acceptance: swords and plaques and loving cups, and all manner of costly trinkets, coins and badges, eyeglass cases, paper cutters, cigar boxes. Yet he had not been fully prepared for the force of popular excitement, sustained for seventeen months in its pristine frenzy. The demonstration in New York had moved and stunned him. He had barely mustered a response to the uproar on Pennsylvania Avenue.

Was it solely fatigue that had dulled Dewey's reaction? Or had he quickly tasted the boredom of popular adulation? He had certainly not come to Washington to witness a parade that was a provincial anticlimax to the displays of the metropolis. Much grander proceedings were appointed for the morrow, when the Admiral was to be escorted by the President and Cabinet in public procession to the Capitol to receive the gold-handled sword that had been voted him by Congress. Crowds would turn out and shout for Dewey wherever he might choose to go, but the highest official distinctions could not be conferred in any city in the nation, save its federal capital alone. As he stood by the window of Mrs. McLean's house, Dewey could see the bronze statue of his former commander and lifelong ideal, sturdily planted in the square. Farragut, too, had held the rank of Admiral of the United States Navy; but the battle of Mobile Bay had not been celebrated by a national reception to the victor. Neither Farragut nor any other American had been honored as was George Dewey by the tributes of a grateful republic.

The inevitable Dewey-for-President boom had been arrested by ignorance of the Admiral's political opinions. Devout research had produced a voluminous record of his deeds and words, without uncovering any definite evidence of his party leanings. His sponsor Senator Proctor believed Dewey to be a Republican, but he did not actually know. Even Dewey's brother Charles, a stout McKinley man, was unable to speak definitely on the matter. The Admiral himself had avoided a commitment. Asked outright at Manila if he were a Democrat or a Republican, Dewey had smilingly replied, "Well, you see, I am a sailor. A sailor has no politics."

There were obvious reasons for associating Dewey with the party in power. He was a native of the ultra-Republican state of Vermont; he had been backed by the aggressively expansionist Roosevelt, as well as by Proctor; and the Republican administration had given him the appointment and the orders which had opened his way to fame. Yet it had been repeatedly said that Dewey had not favored the annexation of the Philippines, and that he now opposed the war, advocating a conciliatory policy and a grant of self-government. Though he had asked for troops with which to hold Manila, he had later professed friendship for Aguinaldo, and praised the fitness of the Filipinos for self-government. The country had heard little else of Dewey's opinions. Anti-expansionists had readily assumed that his silence was an indication of disagreement with the government. The impression was confirmed in the course of his leisurely voyage home on the flagship *Olympia*. According to an interview which appeared in the London *Daily News* shortly after he reached Gibraltar, he had never been in favor of violence toward the Filipinos. "I should like to see autonomy first conceded, and then annexation might be talked about," he was quoted as saying. If this interview were genuine, the Admiral not only opposed the war, but denied that United States sovereignty had been definitely established by the ratification of the peace treaty.

The Republicans put on a brave face, pooh-poohing the idle rumors of the press, but there was trepidation among the more nervous political experts. The national conventions were less than a year away. It was not naïve to suppose that, as an avowed opponent of Philippine annexation, Dewey might secure the Democratic nomination for President. The party of opposition was still profoundly divided. A movement was stirring in the East to dislodge Bryan from leadership, unload the obsolescent silver cause, and battle out the national elections on the contemporary issue of imperialism; and interest in this program had been whetted by the obvious dread with which it was regarded by the Republican strategists. In spite of the invigorating effect of the President's speech at Pittsburgh, the party was feeling the strain of the war. The injury might be irreparable if the Democrats should appropriate Dewey, with his unique appeal to popular emotion and his incomparable title to speak with authority on the Philippines. He would be a strong presidential candidate, far harder to beat than Bryan.

Another factor in these gloomy forecasts was the tense situation which had unexpectedly developed in the contest for the governorship of Ohio. Mark Hanna had handily controlled the Republican convention in June, and his chosen nominee, George K. Nash, was marked for a walkover. Late in the summer, however, the Ohio Democrats retaliated with a peremptory attack on the national administration. Their candidate, John R. McLean, the proprietor of *The Cincinnati Enquirer* and the Democratic boss of the state, was running on a free-silver, anti-imperialist, anti-trust platform, which also included a denunciation of the "secret and vicious alliance" between the Republican administration and England. Secretary Hay hastened to prepare an elaborate defense, reminding the Ohio Republicans of the unprecedented power and prosperity of the country, and denying the "ghost story" of a secret alliance. The local contest was magnified in importance as a test of the national issues. Mark Hanna, returning after a summer spent in Europe, took personal charge of Nash's canvass. Yet, on the formal opening of the campaign in late September, it was by no means certain that Hanna could marshal sufficient strength to win. He had come home to find a formidable revolt against his political methods and dictatorial control. Under an outward aspect of harmony, the party was dangerously split, with the Foraker crowd burning to avenge their recent defeats. A third, independent candidate for governor, standing on a reform platform, was attractive to many voters. McLean was prepared to spend money, and had plenty of money to spend. The "dusty arena" was set for a typical dirty, cut-throat Ohio fight, and the eyes of the whole country were riveted on its progress.

One result of this situation was to raise for the first time a question of McKinley's renomination in 1900. Americans had recently been chary of continuing their Presidents in office. A Chief Executive had not been chosen to succeed himself since Grant's second election, more than a quarter of a century earlier. McKinley, however, had been regarded as a special case, distinguished from his immediate predecessors by his immense popular following and his particular claim to the allegiance of the business community. His position was still dominant in spite of the Philippine rebellion; and, if peace were restored in the next three or four months, he could not be seriously hurt by the dissension in Ohio and the reproach of "Hannaism." But what if the war went on? Political commentators were asking if the President could sustain a party disaster in his home state, in addition to a massive party revulsion against his policy of expansion and its bitter fruit in the Philippines.

The President was never numbered among the fainthearted. He entertained no doubts of a speedy settlement on Luzon. He continued to believe that Philippine annexation was ratified by what he called the "masterful public opinion of this country." Nevertheless, as an experienced political weatherman, McKinley had become acutely concerned about the elections, and especially the forecast of calamity in Ohio. He was planning to make another speaking trip in the West, but first he had to meet the challenge of Dewey's return. Whatever the enigmatic Admiral was about to say or do, it was necessary for the President to efface the impression of discord between them, and maintain the Republican administration in the sunshine of the victory of Manila Bay.

When the *Olympia* dropped anchor in New York harbor, the public impatience to hear from Dewey was partially gratified by an enterprising reporter of the New York *Evening Post,* who boarded the flagship and succeeded in obtaining an exclusive interview. One of its notable features was a repetition of the opinion—which Dewey never seemed to drop— that the Filipinos were more fitted for self-government than the Cubans. The ructions at Havana had robbed the comparison of much of its earlier impact. To estimate anybody's political capacity as superior to that of the Cubans had become very faint praise indeed. Still, the statement implied a criticism of administration policy, and as such it was headlined by the anti-expansionist *Post* and by Democratic papers throughout the country.

The interview, for the most part, was somewhat inconclusive. Dewey was not taciturn. He ran on merrily to his visitor, as he sat on the deck of the *Olympia,* fondling his sickly "Chow Chow dog," Bob. These Filipinos were a queer lot, Dewey observed, a very queer mixture, some quite civilized and good people. He would not say they were fit for self-government just yet, but they probably would be in a little time. They had been so badly treated by the Spaniards that they were distrustful. He was sure that they would take kindly to the Americans, once they understood they would be well treated. Aguinaldo was the tool of abler men and lacked "the brains," but also he was "a pretty smart fellow." He and Dewey had been great friends, and still were, for the matter of that. The man from the *Post* was shown a carved black cane, a present to Dewey from Aguinaldo. Dewey had thought that "this thing in the Philippines" would have been over long ago. But, of course, there was the rainy season; and then "the great trouble" was that General Otis tried to do too much. Dewey had told him so. Otis wanted to "have hold of all the irons."

The flow of chatter was stemmed by questions about foreign affairs and domestic politics. Dewey refused to comment on his troubles with the German navy in Manila Bay or on the rumored alliance between the United States and England, and he remained ambiguous on the subject of his party preference. He laughed at a report that his son had called him "a dyed-in-the-wool Republican," and said that his son knew nothing about it. He really laughed outright, when asked about his presidential candidacy. Tugging at his heavy mustache, Dewey exclaimed with a sigh and a quizzical glance that the politicians didn't know him. "I am perfectly satisfied to live and die a simple sailor, who tried to do his duty," he said. "I am not a politician."

While this interview was being copied and eagerly read from coast to coast, another conversation with Dewey was reported to the President in a private letter from Murat Halstead. This elderly journalist, who had long been an influential figure in the Ohio Republican party, had latterly turned his talents to writing books. A vapid but complimentary biography of Dewey had earned him a gracious reception on the *Olympia* and an invitation to accompany the Admiral on "a ride" to the Navy Yard. Since Halstead had recently been in touch with the President, it may be assumed that he was acting on instructions in sounding Dewey's attitude toward the Philippine policy. Dewey, it developed, had spoken about McKinley in the "most hearty" and indeed "boyish" manner. Halstead brought up the speech to the Tenth Pennsylvania, asking if Dewey had read it. Dewey had, and thought it "jam up," "spang up," and "bang up." Halstead was emboldened to probe more deeply. He made scathing allusion to the "cranks" who were opposed to keeping the Philippines, and declared— borrowing the President's phrase—that the "masterful public opinion of this country" was against giving up what Dewey's victory had won. "Give it up!" the Admiral cried. "Never! Never! Keep it forever!"

Here was something a good deal more positive and explicit than the trivial remarks in the *Post*. Halstead, moreover, agreed with the opinion which the *Post* reporter had expressed, that Dewey was not politically ambitious. Charles Dawes, too, had a word of reassurance on this score after a talk with Charles Dewey in New York. Yet the various reports did not carry much weight. Dewey had said nothing that could not readily be unsaid. He had never at any time been free and open in communicating with Washington. McKinley did not forget that Dewey had entirely omitted to report on one subject of vital interest to the United States government—the friction in his relations with the commander of the German squadron in Manila Bay. While newspaper correspondents were nervously discussing the tension between the two fleets, the Admiral had been silent. There was still no record of the facts in the Navy Department files.

The President was in suspense on the night of Dewey's arrival in Washington. The time was at hand when the Admiral must rise to his full heroic stature and declare himself to the people. Democratic hopes were throbbing at the thought of the presentation ceremonies at the Capitol. There was high gratification among the President's enemies that the Admiral had spurned the official hospitality of the White House in favor of the residence of Mrs. Washington McLean. For Dewey's chosen hostess was the mother of that John R. McLean who was stirring up Ohio in a desperate effort to strike down Republican power and reverse the decision on the Philippines. As the grand illuminations were quenched and the darkened streets grew quiet, a long distance seemed to stretch between the White House and the mansion on Farragut Square.

The next morning, in full fig, with the crisp sunlight glinting on his gold braid and four stars, the Admiral made his triumphal progress to the Capitol. He was seated beside the President. The Cabinet members attended him in their carriages, and the governors of eight states rode with their staffs in his train. General Miles headed the military escort of distinguished officers of the Army and Navy, and marching ranks of soldiers, sailors, and marines. But, in all this impressive retinue, only the jackies of the *Olympia* drew an echo of the din of applause that traveled down Pennsylvania Avenue with the passing of the Admiral, ceaselessly vibrating his gold-laced chapeau. It was said that governors had never been so neglected in Washington. Even Pingree of Michigan went unrecognized, though his horse curveted from curb to curb, and finally threw him in the street. Strangest sight of all was the President of the United States, driving through the cheers of the national capital with his hands folded and his silk hat firmly settled above his smiling face. It had been announced that on "Dewey Day" he would not respond to any salutations. He was paying to heroism the ultimate honor of abdicating his prerogatives, and appearing as a symbol of the national homage.

McKinley had chosen to efface himself, but not as completely as he had at first intended. He had made two last-minute changes in the original program, one providing that Dewey should ride with him, and the other that Dewey should receive the sword of honor from his hand. The stellar role in the presentation belonged to the Secretary of the Navy, and the President had not previously proposed to participate, except by lending his presence. He and Dewey were to sit apart from the other dignitaries on a small raised stand, which Long would enter to deliver his address. For Dewey to remain seated while Long stood over him, complimenting him on his victory, was a sufficiently awkward arrangement without the added constraint of the President's lack of function. McKinley had undoubtedly realized that his attitude might seem aloof and ungracious, rather than deferential. In any case, he had finally concluded to figure more prominently in the day's proceedings.

The decision about the sword struck exactly the right note, and met with general approbation. The change in the apparently minor matter of the drive was actually much more daring. In the protocol hastily devised for the occasion, it had been decreed that the Admiral should ride in solitary state. It was, moreover, settled that he should ride in Mrs. Mc-Lean's carriage. J. Addison Porter, still the arbiter of White House elegancies, wanted to keep to this plan. He insisted that the Admiral should go to the Capitol alone, and advised that it would be "in best taste" for the President and Cabinet to precede him "as quietly and unostentatiously as possible." He also spoke feelingly of Mrs. McLean's four horses with postilions, but the President had gone ahead with his own plan. Mrs. McLean's showy equipage had been left behind, and Dewey was bowling along Pennsylvania Avenue in the modest White House carriage, drawn by McKinley's new team of bays.

At the Capitol, the President and the Admiral were the first to alight, passing into the lobby of the Senate, with the official party following behind them. Two distinguished gentlemen owed their presence directly to the President. It is improbable that anyone else would have thought of including ex-Secretary Alger, who was publicly honored this morning by a seat beside Long in his carriage. Still more striking was the appearance of an ascetic-faced churchman who was to take part in the program. It was not remarkable that the ceremonies were to be opened by the prayer of a Methodist minister—McKinley's Washington pastor, Dr. Frank M. Bristol—but it was nearly sensational that the benediction was to be pronounced by Cardinal James Gibbons of Baltimore in his scarlet robes. The President was always serenely indifferent to the forces of bigotry; and perhaps he thought it timely to recall the fact to his Roman Catholic friends. Vexing ecclesiastical questions were bound to arise in the Philippines. Angry criticism had already been provoked by stories alleging the desecration of church property by American soldiers on Luzon, and Cardinal Gibbons had defended the administration in a published interview.

While the dignitaries were waiting for the signal to proceed, an immense throng was surging around the east front of the Capitol, where a commodious platform had been erected. The gallery around the dome and the roofs of both wings were laden with spectators, mostly ladies, and it was remarked that the naked Greenough statue of George Washington was decently clothed, for once, with the swarming figures of his countrymen. The focus of attention was the presentation stand. Situated at the front of the platform and surrounded by a flag-draped railing, it contained two leather easy chairs and a narrow oaken case. Except for the Marine Band, which occupied a low platform of its own, the foreground of the crowded plaza was pre-empted by photographers. Several large, important-looking cameras—including three of the new Biographs for taking pictures in motion—were ranged on a high scaffolding. Others were mounted on stepladders which rose like derricks from the asphalt. Two photographers had squeezed on the bandstand, among the scarlet-coated musicians. On every hand, a host of pestiferous amateurs—the "camera fiends" who had recently become a nuisance at all outdoor events—pointed their lenses like guns at the historic scene.

Shortly before noon, the sailors of the *Olympia* posted themselves on the Senate steps, with their big blue banner waving. There was the distant boom of a gun. The Marine Band struck up a preliminary flourish and a deafening shout was raised, as the head of the procession appeared. To the strains of "Hail to the Chief," the President, with the Admiral on his left, came slowly down the steps, crossed the platform, and climbed into the presentation stand. A polite fracas ensued. The President moved to the left, with the intention of yielding the honors of the occasion. Dewey resisted by edging still farther left. But, taking the Admiral by the arm, McKinley propelled him firmly to the right, and stepped behind him. Dewey stood alone for a moment, bowing in all directions. The solitary central figure in gold-braided uniform created a strange impression. The east front of the Capitol was the traditional setting for presidential inaugurations, and the association was vivid in everyone's mind. Here were all the sights and sounds of inauguration day, with the President in the background, and some thoughtful men were moved to meditate on the queer predilection of Americans for being governed by their military heroes.

The frock coat and the uniform presently occupied the easy chairs (with Dewey once more on the left); and, after prayer and the compliments of civic welcome, Secretary Long advanced to make his speech. Addressing himself to the Admiral, he began by reading out the orders that had been sent from the Navy Department on April 24, 1898. Though the matter had become an old story by this time, it was to be expected that the Secretary of the Navy should stress the responsibility of Washington for victory. Many fluent phrases later, Long gradually disclosed the intention of making an extremely broad interpretation of the responsibility that the victory had entailed. Clouds might linger about the Philippine Islands now, but Long envisioned the dawn of a glorious new day—not of "any mere selfish imperial dominion," but of "the imperial moral and physical growth and expansion of all the peoples . . . under the broad shield of the United States of America." From this glorious dawn, Long skipped nimbly to a conclusion that ignored the anti-expansionists of Congress, participants all in the vote of money for Dewey's sword. He declared that the gift represented the country's recognition, not of the rich fruits of victory alone, but also of "her own responsibility to . . . fulfil the destiny of her own growth and of the empire that is now her charge." In conclusion, Long drew the gold-handled sword from its oaken case and passed it to the President, who rose and in his turn very briefly addressed Dewey. McKinley joined with all his heart in the affectionate welcome home of the people. "There was no flaw in your victory," he said; "there will be no faltering in maintaining it." He held out the sword with a bow, and Dewey got up to receive it in a swelling roar of applause. The Admiral appeared greatly moved, but managed to murmur a few words of thanks, saying that the beautiful gift should be kept as an heirloom in his family forever, as an evidence that republics were not ungrateful. The Marine Band played "The Star-Spangled Banner." Cardinal Gibbons invoked the Divine benediction, and the ceremony was over.

While the police cleared the plaza, Dewey obligingly brandished the gleaming sword in the sunshine, and perched with it on top of one of the stepladders to have his photograph taken. Then the military escort marched before the stand in review, and the President and the Admiral retired. As the platform gradually emptied, another demonstration was set off by calls for Commodore Schley. Dewey's reference to the gratitude of republics must have rung ironically in the ears of one gaunt old naval officer, who withdrew unnoticed. The Senate blocked promotion for Rear Admiral Sampson and all the officers of his fleet because the recommendations of the Navy Department gave the commander in chief at Santiago Bay a higher grade than Schley. The Commodore was enjoying a reign of popularity second only to Dewey's. With professional alacrity, he climbed into the vacated presentation stand, and smilingly responded to the plaudits of his admirers.

The President's carriage rolled rapidly back to the White House, where Mrs. McLean's coach and four stood waiting. Dewey was to return in the evening for a grand dinner in his honor. The farewells were quickly spoken, and he drove off to Farragut Square. The Admiral had carried off all the tributes of the morning, but the President was smiling as he went up the steps of the White House. There was a little flush in his usually pale cheeks. Dewey had been outspoken in his cordiality, offering personal "protestations of regard." At the Capitol, he had appeared to be positively overcome with gratitude; and Long had moved in on his fame with the whole load of the administration and its Philippine policy on his back.

"There was no flaw in your victory; there will be no faltering in maintaining it." McKinley had a fancy for the little speech he had made. He had summed up all Long's verbosities in one simple, gracious phrase.

The next hurdle to be taken was a consultation with Dewey on the Philippines. A month earlier, McKinley had received another firsthand report, not as momentous as this one, but still of great importance. The head of the Philippine Commission, Jacob Schurman, had come home a convert to annexation. Under the influence of the Manila *Americanistas*, he had adopted a tenderly proprietary attitude toward the native peoples, called them "my dear Filipinos," and was longing to educate and elevate them. In spite of his disagreements with Otis, Schurman was willing to concede that force should be used, if necessary, to maintain American sovereignty. He effusively endorsed the President's policy, and assured McKinley that he could also count on Worcester and Denby for full support.

Schurman's account of the Philippines repeated the errors of the military reports, but he differed from the soldiers at one point. He did not consider the Army a suitable instrument of government, or believe that it could inspire trust in the President's purposes. He looked toward a civil administration, with self-government in local affairs, to reconcile the Filipinos, and proposed that Congress should be called in special session to offer such assurances, or even to take immediate action. The President, of course, was not thinking of a special session. He was most anxious to avoid hasty legislation for the Philippines, of all things; but he was deeply troubled by the continuing gap between his professions and his performance in the islands. As a step toward initiating civil government, McKinley determined to expedite the report of the Philippine Commission, and not long after the talk with Schurman he cabled to recall Worcester and Denby from Manila.

The President was counting on the other commissioners to enhance the favorable reaction produced by Schurman's addresses and interviews. The theme of national duty was held before the public, as the college president stressed the salvation of the Philippines from division among the nations of Europe, and discussed the liberal government which McKinley designed for the inhabitants. Schurman spoke with a moral voice that the anti-expansionists were reluctant to disown. Except for McKinley's speech at Pittsburgh, his utterances gave the Republicans the greatest tonic they had had since the failure of the spring offensive on Luzon. Denby and Worcester were due to arrive in October, too late to prepare the report before the state elections, but in ample season to put out a summary of its conclusions. It would be an effective campaign document—provided that the Democrats failed to draw Dewey into the opposition ranks. He was regarded as the supreme authority on the Philippines, and his concurrence with his colleagues of the Philippine Commission was indispensable to the prestige of their report.

Dewey's golden opportunity for political power lay in these early days of his homecoming. He had already let more than a week slip past without committing himself. He could not delay much longer, if he meant to assert his leadership. There were risks in pinning Dewey down, but a conference could not be deferred. The President was about to start on his campaign trip in the West. It had been announced that he would first seek Dewey's advice, and the meeting was appointed for the morning after the presentation ceremonies.

McKinley did not wait until morning to clear up one puzzle. He took the first opportunity to ask Dewey about the stories of friction with the German commander in Manila Bay. The files, he remarked, had no record of this at all. "No, Mr. President," Dewey later recalled that he answered. "As I was on the spot and familiar with the situation from day to day, it seemed best that I look after it myself, at a time when you had worries enough of your own." McKinley had surely observed by this time that, in calling himself a simple sailor, Dewey had not understated the case; but, combined with a fatuous self-esteem, this simplicity was not altogether reassuring. At least, the President's mind was not at ease as he prepared to interrogate Dewey about the Philippines.

Before the morning meeting, McKinley jotted down a questionnaire on a piece of Executive Mansion notepaper, spacing out the headings so as to leave room to fill in the replies. The memorandum, at the close of the conference, read as follows:

> SELF GOVT—are they capable?
> No & will not be for many many years.
> The U S must control & supervise giving
> Philipinos participation as far as capable
> WHAT DOES AG REPRESENT? in population & sentiment.
> He has no more than 40000 followers
> of all kinds out of 8 or 10 millions
> WHAT IS OUR DUTY?
> Keep the islands permanently
> Valuable in every sense
> HOW MANY TROOPS NEEDED?
> 50000
> HAVE WE SHIPS ENOUGH?
> Ought to send some more. Recommends
> that Brooklyn go & smaller vessels
> SHOULD WE GIVE UP THE ISLANDS?
> Never—never
> THE STORIES OF CHURCH DESECRATION & INHUMANITY.
> [no notation]

Here was seemingly the end of equivocation. Dewey's opinions were worthy of the most ardent expansionist. McKinley had not heard the ring of true Republican metal, but the Admiral was committed to the use of force in the Philippines. Before the President left for the West, it was given out that he had adopted Dewey's plan of sending naval reinforcements to the Philippines, and was hurrying off the *Brooklyn* and other smaller vessels.

The campaign tour took the President and the members of the Cabinet as far as the Dakotas. They moved erratically across the western plains: barnstorming through the industrial cities of Illinois; slipping back into southern Indiana, then veering up to Minneapolis and St. Paul; forging on to North and South Dakota; and turning eastward again by way of Milwaukee and other Wisconsin cities. McKinley had made nearly a hundred speeches when, after two weeks, the tour ended at Youngstown, Ohio. His utterances were a test of the national issues, and intended for national consumption. Ohio and South Dakota were actually the only states on the itinerary that were holding elections of any importance in 1899.

Many sorts of people turned out to greet the President and hear what he had to say: industrialists, bankers, merchants, and other businessmen; farmers and laborers and mechanics; veterans of the Civil War and young soldiers just home from the Pacific. McKinley talked to them about expansion, and maintaining American sovereignty, and a liberal government for the Philippines. He talked about the busy mills and factories, and the balance of trade in manufactured products that had inclined, for the first time, in favor of the United States. He discussed the reciprocity agreements and the need of a strong merchant marine. He spoke of good crops and good prices, of good money and plenty of it. He said that we were on a gold basis, and meant to stay there. He dwelt on the fraternal unity of North and South; and at a banquet in Minneapolis he referred to a larger unity—the hope of world peace inspired by the recent convening of the powers at the Hague Conference. Wherever he was and whatever he said, he always came back to the glorious old flag that now floated over two hemispheres; to the destiny of the American nation and its responsibilities in the Pacific.

Once more, the country heard the applause of the loyal Republican West. The President had become rather excessively celebrated for his oratory. It was true, as Cortelyou had approvingly noted, that he was constantly gaining in vigor and directness, and a growing facility of expression enlivened his studied compositions. Yet the speeches scarcely deserved John

Hay's encomium, "political classics." It was more to the point that, as always, people liked the plain, earnest style in which McKinley spoke. The warm response from audiences of workingmen was of particular interest, for 1899 was a year of ominous labor unrest, rumbling turbulently under the surface of the industrial recovery. In the spring, striking miners in Idaho had engaged in such destructive violence that the President had complied with the request of the Democratic-Populist governor to send federal troops to the Coeur d'Alene district. The troops were still there. Chicago, where the presidential party stopped for a long weekend, was a center of trade-union activity, conspicuous for radical agitation. To the indignation of the anti-labor press, it had been reported that the Bricklayers' and Stonemasons' Union would refuse to permit the President to fulfill the main purpose of his visit, the laying of the cornerstone of the new Federal Building. In the end, McKinley plied the trowel as an honorary member of the Chicago union, wearing its button and carrying its card. He also attended a meeting of the union, which he called "our organization" in addressing the members. Crowds in the manufacturing centers repeatedly testified to McKinley's singular attraction for the workers. Even at a time of seething antagonism toward management, they were drawn to his fine presence and pulpit charm, thronging around the rear platform of his train to shake his hand, or salute him with the dinner pails that were the emblem of the promise he had kept. They applauded when he spoke of the flourishing export trade. They burst into cheers when, with one of his swift transitions, he said that we not only sent our goods abroad, we had sent our flag abroad; that we had a duty in the Philippines, and that duty unperformed was dishonor.

Every step of the President's progress was closely followed by the press. Its interest reached a climax when, as the trip drew to a close, he entered Ohio. The gaping cracks in the Republican organization could no longer be concealed. Some leaders of the faction hostile to Hanna were almost openly defiant; and, though Foraker himself would stand by Judge Nash, it was rumored that he would not greatly regret a Republican defeat. Hanna, crippled by rheumatism, was fighting hard. He had gone on the stump in the rural districts, and his blunt little speeches were liked by the staunchly Republican farmers; but he was hated in the cities, and his campaign funds were fast being used up. McLean was boldly fishing in the troubled Republican waters. The energy and the extravagant outlay of his canvass indicated confidence of victory, but the Democrats dreaded the visit of the President. Hanna's personal following was insignificant. He owed his power to McKinley's influence, and would retain it, if he could retain it, by grace of McKinley's position and his deep hold on popular affection in his home state. The President was coming to Hanna's rescue, and the McLean newspapers heralded his arrival with raucous, desperate attacks on his speaking tour in the West.

McKinley, of course, said nothing about the local campaign during the day he spent in Ohio. The impression was that of a grateful glimpsing of old scenes, a happy reunion with old friends. The morning was spent at Cleveland. Hanna was a member of the welcoming committee, met the special train, and took part in the official program. After luncheon at Colonel Herrick's, McKinley left for Youngstown, stopping en route to greet the crowds at Warren and at his birthplace Niles, and making his scheduled address in the late afternoon. He talked, in his customary vein, about the hum of industry and our flag in the Philippines, but there was a more personal, intimate note in his speeches than had been sounded elsewhere on the journey. He told of his pleasure in the welcome of the workingmen of Ohio, waving their shining dinner buckets from the mills and factories along the railroad line. He alluded to sacred memories and lifetime friendships, and the faithful constituents to whom he had never appealed in vain. The Republicans of Ohio responded, like a chorus, to his words, thrilling with affectionate pride in their great man, approving his sentiments with hand and voice, and answering No and Yes, as he wanted them to do.

McKinley went back to Washington, invigorated, as always, by his contact with the people; but he was not confident about the Ohio election. While he greeted Worcester and Denby, and conferred with them and Schurman, he was thinking about the revolt with which Hanna was threatened. Before October ended, McKinley had concluded that practical assistance was indicated. The seriousness of the emergency was very quietly explained to a few men in the East. One of them was John A. McCall, the president of the New York Life Insurance Company, who had already contributed heavily to Judge Nash's campaign. He arranged for William C. Beer to go to Ohio and do what he could, especially among the transportation companies. Before leaving, Beer received confidential instructions from the President. He was to report daily by letter, addressed to the White House executive clerk, Colonel Montgomery. He was also requested to report to the President by long-distance telephone, in case of "anything startling," and once did so, after investigating the disturbing situation in Cincinnati.

Only six days before the election, Beer presented himself to Hanna and told him that President McKinley was anxious about Ohio. "He has —— good reason to be," Hanna replied. Beer dashed off letters to railway and express officials, urging them to get out the votes of their employees.

McCall and others bestirred themselves in New York. Colonel Herrick also managed to procure some "substantial" assistance from friends in the East. A magical change came over Republican prospects in Ohio in the last week of the campaign. Many prognostications were upset when, on November 7, John R. McLean went down to defeat. Though the Republican ticket took a bad beating in Cleveland and Cuyahoga County, the returns elsewhere added up to a comfortable victory for Nash, and Beer was well content with the results of his eleventh-hour efforts. He remarked that Tom Platt's telegraphed orders to the superintendents of the United States Express Company changed 25,000 votes, but he gave the most credit to McCall, both for his direct contributions and his influence with the corporations.

Ohio was numbered with the majority, for the Republicans carried eight of the twelve states voting. A preliminary report from the Philippine Commission, published four days before the elections, was credited with having influenced the vote in doubtfully expansionist states. Its effectiveness was largely enhanced by its nonpartisan character, and especially by Admiral Dewey's signature. It was understood that he had had little part in preparing the report, but he had let it be known that he was in full agreement with his colleagues. This meant that he held the opinion that the rebellion was confined to the Tagalogs, that its outbreak could not have been prevented and must be suppressed; and that he joined in a vigorous defense of the annexation of the Philippines. Dewey was at last, although in a rather offhand way, fully pledged to Republican policy.

McKinley was about to lay the whole troubled question of the Philippines before Congress. His annual message of 1899 advised that legislation should be deferred until the end of the rebellion, but suggested that essentially popular governments should be inaugurated as fast as territory was held by American troops. He believed that reconstruction should not begin by establishing one central civil government at Manila, but "by building up from the bottom" through municipal and then provincial governments. In short, the President was still not ready to yield up the extraordinary powers he had so long exercised. While courteously deferring to the jurisdiction of Congress, he would ask it merely to approve an edifice he would erect. The proposal was audacious, but it was assured of Republican support as a means of shutting off agitation and interference by the minority in the new Congress.

Early in 1900, the President had "a most interesting talk" with Dewey at a dinner given by Secretary Hay. The political pressures on the Admiral must have been annoyingly persistent, for he had developed an aversion to the anti-expansionists. Referring to the forthcoming report of the Philippine Commission, he said that "they were going to make it so comprehensive that the opposition would not have a leg to stand on." He also spoke of the Democrats as "Those rattled-pated* people who are doing so much wild talking." This was the substance of the President's report to Cortelyou later in the evening. He commented, with manifest satisfaction, that "Dewey evidently realized that public sentiment and his own fame were safer in the hands of the Republicans than in those of the opposition."

The next month, the Philippine Commission submitted a report which, with its accompanying exhibits, filled four fat volumes. It presented a scheme of government, with local home rule, and urged that it be substituted for military command; but the commissioners advised that, pending complete pacification and final action by Congress, the plan should be gradually put in operation by the President. McKinley had got precisely the recommendations he wanted. There had probably never been any reason to doubt that his commissioners would unanimously sustain him. His misgivings about Dewey had been caused by a flaw of logic. He had assumed that since Dewey was not a Republican, it followed that he must be a Democrat. The President had been baffled by a political vacuum.

Dewey had meanwhile given his popularity a seismic shock by getting married. His fall from eminence had been inevitable, in any case. Only a superman could have fulfilled the expectations of his delirious fellow citizens, and Dewey was a quite ordinary man of specialized professional competence. A lifetime of naval routine had circumscribed his outlook and absorbed his capacity for serious attention. The mystery about his political opinions was easily explained—they were nonexistent. Off duty, the Admiral was a nice, garrulous old dandy, naïvely conceited, devoted to society, and very fond of the ladies. His heroic lineaments had begun to blur as soon as he came home. The news of his engagement merely accelerated the process. Incidentally, it cleared up another mystery, that of his connection with Mrs. Washington McLean. Dewey had not been remotely concerned with the political activities of her son. He had merely had his eye on her daughter, Mrs. Hazen.

The news was an intensely disagreeable surprise to the public. The possibility of Dewey's marrying had not been faced, though he had been for many years a widower. In his splendid solitude, the grand old Admiral had belonged to the nation. Plans to enshrine him in bachelor state at

* The spelling is Cortelyou's.

Washington had swept the country. Subscriptions, large and small, poured in to make up a fund of more than $50,000, and the purchase of a mansion on Rhode Island Avenue had recently been concluded with Dewey's approval, and to his presumed gratitude and delight. The American people, palpitating with a sense of their own munificence, felt betrayed when they discovered that the nation's sweetheart had been engaged in private courtship. The basic primness of the American character was disclosed in a general disapproval of such foolishness in a man of Dewey's age. It was implied that there was something ridiculous and even a little distasteful in the union of a bridegroom of nearly sixty-two and a bride of forty-nine. Dewey's choice of a rich and fashionable widow made his offense much worse. Mildred McLean Hazen was reputed to be cold, haughty, and ambitious, and another disqualification was presently added to the list. On the quiet solemnization of the marriage in November, it became known that the new Mrs. Dewey was a convert to the Church of Rome. Her religious faith was a flagrant occasion for public displeasure in the stiffly Protestant atmosphere of America. Yet the root of the matter was the money, after all. Everyone knew about the fabulous wealth of the McLeans. They could buy any number of houses for Dewey. The marriage had diminished the national generosity, and made the gift of the people seem superfluous and unappreciated.

Soon after the newlyweds returned from their honeymoon, the notice of a legal transaction in Washington made headlines throughout the United States. There was high indignation at the news that the title of the house on Rhode Island Avenue had been transferred to Mrs. Dewey. In vain, it was explained that Dewey desired to deed the property to his son, and was complying with the law in conveying it through his wife. He had discarded the gift of the people; and, to the people, it was a gesture of rejection too contemptuous to be forgiven. Dewey was bewildered and wounded by an outburst of cutting criticism, but amenities were presently restored, and a civilized politeness replaced the ardors of love. A number of publications came to the Admiral's support, expressing regret for the cruel things that had been said in the heat of anger, and pointing out that he had the right to make what disposition he pleased of his own property. In the official world of Washington, there was nothing to suggest a change in Dewey's status. He was naïvely unaware that the great social phenomenon of his celebrity was over.

On thinking over the Presidency, the Admiral concluded that he had been too hasty in waving it aside. His wife liked the idea of his being President, and he was confident that he was equal to the duties of the place. Early in April, 1900, Dewey received a reporter for the New York

World; and, with probably the most embarrassing gesture ever made by a dignified public figure, tossed his gold-laced chapeau into the political ring. He announced that he was willing to be a candidate for the Presidency, and would gladly assume that office, if the people cared to elect him. Evidently by way of affirming his qualifications, the Admiral added that he did not think it was a very hard position to fill.

The fatuity of this announcement was enhanced by the peculiarly cut-and-dried political situation in the spring of 1900. In the memory of men then living, there had never been a preconvention season so devoid of the interest of speculation and the excitement of contest. The presidential nominations had been settled by the autumn elections. It had been conceded in November that the President's renomination by acclamation was assured. Bryan, too, had confirmed his claim to leadership. Barnstorming across the country, he had shown that he was still the idol of Democrats, Populists, and Silverites. Like McKinley, he had had a significant victory in his home state, for the Fusion ticket had for a second time swept Nebraska, in spite of threats of regained Republican control. Moreover, Bryan now dominated the Democratic managers. The last glimmerings of diehard rebellion were quenched in the East. Bryan embodied the new, radical Democracy, and would be its undisputed standard-bearer in the campaign of 1900. Whether or not Dewey was willing to be a candidate was a matter of almost farcical irrelevance to the contest.

It seems curious, under the circumstances, that Dawes should have expected McKinley to show some discomposure. After calling at the White House, he noted with apparent surprise, "The President exhibited no feeling whatever of resentment toward Dewey." Cortelyou, who was in the Cabinet Room at the time, recorded the President's views. With respect to the candidacy, McKinley said that the only time when Dewey might have been strong was immediately after his return. He admitted that the Admiral might then have caused some Republican concern, at least temporarily, by taking ground against the retention of the Philippines. A couple of nights later, McKinley was still turning over his thoughts about Dewey, as he sat alone with Cortelyou. He recalled a story about General Grant's telling Admiral Porter that "this was a land fight and he'd beat him out of his boots." The President also said that "if Dewey had originated the idea of going to Manila there might be some force in some of the claims of some of his friends; but the orders came from *else-where.* . . ." He observed that, while the people laughed at Dewey's candidacy, there was "an undercurrent of pity." McKinley reverted rather ironically to the matter of the Admiral's fame. It was more secure, he again said, with the Republicans. "They had made him what he was."

Into the deep waters of the national life, the pebble of Dewey's availability had dropped with scarcely a trace but the widening ripples of laughter. The risibilities of the American people were tickled by anticlimax and conceit, by the incongruous difference between the man they now saw and the man they had worshiped yesterday. But, if cause for merriment existed, the bitter jest was at the expense of the people themselves. They had conducted themselves with a cosmic absurdity that was a theme for some despairing social philosopher. They, not Dewey, had altered. He remained the same simple sailor who had won the victory of Manila Bay.

The subscription drive for the permanent Dewey Arch in New York City had begun at about the time of the Admiral's marriage. A large sum was needed to erect the imposing memorial of granite and marble on Madison Square. Money came in slowly, then ceased to come in at all. The project was abandoned while, beaten by wind and rain, the temporary arch decayed. At last, the plaster wreckage was carted off to the dump heap, a sorry symbol of the gratitude of republics. But, for many years, Dewey lived on in the cocoon of his renown, spun of salutes and ceremonies, the place of honor at the banquet, the deference paid to gold braid and four stars. He lived to see war convulse the nations of Europe, and threaten the involvement of the United States. In the perils of that era, the glory of Manila Bay had faded out of sight. When the Admiral died early in 1917, he was merely a reminder of some bygone incident of history, like the statue of a forgotten hero in the dusty corner of a hall.

FIRST LADY

I<small>N ACTING</small> as the official hostess of the White House, Mrs. McKinley had disclosed the nature of her infirmity to a very large number of people. Every precaution was taken to protect her. At dinner, she was seated on her husband's right, convenient to the veil of his napkin. A relative or friend stayed at her side when she received callers, and two or three nieces were usually hovering nearby during the social season. On state occasions, her maid was always on call to take her out, if necessary. Careful arrangements were made at the evening receptions to leave a way open for whisking her through the Red Room and the state dining room to the elevator. Mrs. McKinley's seizures were rendered as inconspicuous as possible, but they could not be entirely concealed. As long as the season lasted, she was on display at the White House functions and at other official parties. Her symptoms became well known to Washington society, and to persons from all parts of the country who saw her at the big receptions. Yet, in spite of so many eyewitnesses and a pervasive murmur of gossip, Mrs. McKinley's malady was not generally known to the public.

By denying his wife's illness a name and by treating its manifestations as normal routine, McKinley had largely succeeded in keeping the gossip in the realm of conjecture. His friends followed his lead in appearing to ignore the seizures. Ida's own relatives did not frankly discuss her affliction even in the privacy of the family circle. Pina Barber's youngest daughter, Kate, did not suspect that her aunt was an epileptic, and resented the statement, when she heard it in later life, as a slander spread by the Democrats. The conspiracy of disregard was sometimes more startling to an acquaintance than the lady's sudden collapse. Judge William Howard Taft, during an informal dinner with the McKinleys at Canton, had occasion to ask for a pencil. As the President put his hand to his pocket, "a peculiar hissing sound" came from Mrs. McKinley's lips. With his left hand, McKinley nonchalantly swept his napkin over her face, while completing the gesture of producing a pencil and passing it to Taft. The Judge was in bewilderment at the President's composure and the lack of concern shown by the other guests.

As though by an extension of the President's personal influence, the buzz of talk about Mrs. McKinley was always muted. He was greatly revered for his devotion to his delicate wife. Unpleasant clinical details were inappropriate to the sentimental gratification which the marriage afforded the country. The words "epilepsy" and "fits" were spoken only in whispers. The press, of course, could not touch the subject. Opposition newspapers, when not restrained by taste, were muzzled by expediency. Any crude exposure of the facts would have outraged propriety and induced an out-pouring of sympathy for the President. Besides, there was very little curiosity about the facts. That Mrs. McKinley was "delicate" was explana-tion enough. Invalid ladies were not a rarity in that day. They were well-known figures in every American community, lingering victims of some weakness of heart or lungs, or the "female trouble" which covered a multi-tude of disorders, physical and emotional. People seldom insisted on a precise diagnosis of the vague complaints and still vaguer "nerves" of the sufferers. In spite of the vogue of the daring bicycle girl, ill health had not yet lost its romantic nineteenth-century aura. The pathetic mistress of the White House had quickly become an object of national solicitude. Many photographs had acquainted the public with her beautiful brow and dreamy, unfocused eyes. An impression of charming fragility was enhanced by the grace with which she posed, drooping in velvet in the Green Room with a fan, or languishing in lace in the conservatory, holding a single rose.

The country saw Mrs. McKinley just as she liked to see herself—a frail and gentle lady, martyred by the demands of her position, but sweetly resigned to meeting them because of her love for her husband.

Mrs. McKinley's martyrdom was completely self-imposed. Her assump-tion of the position of First Lady was a cause of embarrassment to all who participated in the official functions. There would have been general relief if she had been willing to absent herself, while her long-suffering husband would have been spared an ordeal which must often have taxed even his stoical endurance. But Mrs. McKinley had "set her head" on appearing with the President at every possible opportunity, and only utter

433

physical prostration could alter her fixed intention. Its obsessive character was variously interpreted. Mr. Kohlsaat baldly called it "the persistence which was a part of her disease." Politer language was usually employed, at least within hearing of the McKinleys. Captain H. O. S. Heistand, intimately associated with the household for several years, once wrote the President, "I believe her determination to be with you is the sustaining factor in her strength." This explanation, with its suggestion of a heroic bearing-up, was the sort of comment to which Mrs. McKinley was used. Her title to devotion was indulged by her husband and affirmed by those who sought to please her.

Living in an atmosphere of hothouse affection, always coddled and flattered, Mrs. McKinley would have been the last one to hear the disagreeable details of her disease. Yet she had a certain acuteness of observation, and by 1898 she had been an epileptic for a quarter of a century. Unavoidably, she had discovered that there was something odd about her "fainting spells." It was her habit to appear ignorant of having lost consciousness, but she betrayed her knowledge on occasion. She once blanked out in the middle of a euchre game with the Hobarts. The President automatically dropped his handkerchief over her face and, as it was her turn to play, selected a card from her hand. "Who played that card for me?" she sharply demanded a second later. Even if she were actually unaware of a lapse, she could not help noticing that she had been hooded in a handkerchief or napkin. She must have seen, when it was removed, that the eyes of her friends were studiously averted from her face, and over the years she must surely have sometimes surprised a stranger's glance of apprehension, curiosity, or disgust. While paying a call at the White House, Mr. Kohlsaat had the misfortune to find himself alone with Mrs. McKinley in the throes of an attack. His natural desire was to escape from the distressing sight, and he wanted to look for her maid, but he was afraid to leave the helpless woman. With commendable presence of mind, Kohlsaat rose to the emergency, standing behind Mrs. McKinley's chair and pressing her temples, as he had often seen her husband do. Later, she apologized for making "a scene," thus indicating that she not only knew about the seizure, but realized that it had been an unpleasant experience for Kohlsaat.

Mrs. McKinley evidently understood much more than she ever admitted about the embarrassment caused by her "fainting spells," but her plans were not affected by the thought of other people's inconvenience, or even by distaste for making a public spectacle of herself. Her mind was concentrated on mustering the strength for the appearances that entitled her to be recognized as official hostess. So long as she was present, conscious

434

or unconscious, the position was hers. No trumped-up hostess could usurp her prerogative of receiving the guests with the President, and no strange woman could be honored by the place on his right at dinner.

The fact that Mrs. McKinley was incapable of performing the duties of her position created an awkwardness that was partially relieved by the accomplished wife of the Vice-President. Soon after coming to Washington, the Hobarts rented the old Tayloe mansion on Lafayette Square, diagonally across from the White House, and a peculiarly informal and neighborly relationship sprang up between the two couples. McKinley and Hobart fell into the habit of dropping in on each other, and Mrs. Hobart ran over to the White House almost every day to see Mrs. McKinley. "Her health made it impossible for her to assume the heavy social burdens of First Lady," Mrs. Hobart wrote; "the President constantly turned to me to help her wherever I could—not because I was Second Lady, but because I was their good friend." McKinley, who seldom had an opportunity for friendship with a woman, was on unusually intimate terms with Mrs. Hobart. "Oh, if you could have seen what a beauty Ida was as a girl!" he often used to say to her. The ultimate proof of his esteem was his willingness to entrust Ida to her care. "You will remain by Mrs. McKinley," he would caution Mrs. Hobart, if obliged to step out of the room while they were together in the evening. Ida was the main bond between them, but the President grew extremely dependent on Mrs. Hobart's support at White House entertainments. He frequently sent an emergency call for her to attend some dinner on the plea that her presence "gave him confidence." It is hard to conceive of the discretion and tact that could disarm Ida's jealous suspicions, but Jennie Hobart was equal to the task. In spite of her active duty at the White House in the winter seasons of 1898 and 1899, she was always high in Mrs. McKinley's favor.

A further difficulty arose from Mrs. McKinley's avoidance of having a woman companion at the White House. There were many services which could not be performed by her maid, Clara Tharin, and for which it was troublesome to rely on her various friends. She obviously needed someone regularly on hand, to be sociable with her during the hours when the President was engaged, to escort her on her morning drives, and to protect and assist her in receiving callers. In the early months of the administration, this post was filled by Ida's aunt-by-marriage, Mrs. Maria Saxton, a mild, retiring widow with whom she was on affectionate terms. The arrangement, as W. E. Curtis of the Chicago *Record* remarked, settled a matter that had agitated "the Canton mind" for months. But it did not settle it permanently. Quiet old Aunt Maria faded back into Canton in the first summer. A still more promptly eliminated companion was Mrs. Heistand. Though this case lacked the delicacy of a family connection, it may have required more drastic handling than that of Aunt Maria. Captain Heistand had received an appointment in Washington, and the newspapers had announced that he would act as military aide to the President. His wife had entrenched herself in the Canton household, taking charge of all entertainment, running the errands, and finally helping to pack up the family effects. Her brusque manners, aggressive personality, and glossy black topknot were regarded with disfavor by one female reporter who was assigned to North Market Street. Edith Sessions Tupper of *The New York Journal* sniffily wrote that Mrs. Heistand had made herself indispensable to Mrs. McKinley by "cleverness and push." But Mrs. McKinley soon exposed the myth of Mrs. Heistand's indispensability. The glossy black topknot was not in evidence at the White House. Secretary Long mentioned Mrs. Heistand's presence at one of the Sunday evenings of sacred music which were so dear to the President. She "sang psalm-tunes at the piano in a melancholy voice," Long wrote, "and the rest of us grumbled a faint accompaniment." The couple may have been invited on other occasions, for Captain Heistand was attached to the Adjutant General's office for more than two years, and his relations with the President were always cordial. But the duty of military aide did not materialize, and their close association was never renewed.

Many house guests were entertained at the White House, and Mrs. McKinley saw much of her particular friends in Washington, but these ladies came to the mansion at her wish and stayed by her sufferance, and none of them was there for very long. Although she had her great favorites, it could not be said that she was dependent on any one of them. She was dependent only on her husband. McKinley never had the relief of shifting a little of the responsibility for cheering and comforting Ida.

Mrs. McKinley made her nearest approach to having a companion by often desiring the presence of her niece, Mary Barber, at the White House and on trips. It was a relief to Pina, a home-loving woman, busy with the care of a large family, that her eldest daughter could often take her place. Ida was extremely fond of having girls about her. The ardor of her affection for them was sometimes unpleasing. When the President's friend John J. McCook brought his blooming daughter Martha to call, Mrs. McKinley greeted her with a hard kiss on the lips. Martha kept a disagreeable memory of the pressure of the flabby mouth. Mary Barber, for her part, did not like to be with her Aunt Ida, and was quaintly unimpressed by her own popularity in Washington. Petite and graceful, with dark, curly hair and large, sympathetic brown eyes, she was the loveliest

436

ornament of many official parties. Her charms became nationally celebrated, and she fluttered a number of distinguished pulses. General Corbin,
a susceptible widower, was among her conquests. But social success did
not turn Mary's head, or even set her dreaming of a grander future than
any she might find in Canton. She candidly appraised the imposing functions, elderly beaux, and newspaper publicity, and found them insufficient
compensation for dancing attendance on a querulous invalid. Her frequent
appearances in Washington were prompted by the double duty of obliging
her aunt and sparing her mother.

Not many girls were as sensible and unworldly as Mary Barber, and no
other was subject to the trying demands which Mrs. McKinley made on her
favorite niece. The President's wife was able to gather plenty of young
people about her, at least during the Washington season. Her much-
publicized affection for her "little friends" also attracted many children.
The Easter Monday egg rolling drew the biggest crowds, but every week
children came privately to call, under escort of mothers who were eager both
to show off their treasures and to give them an experience they would always
remember. Unfortunately, they often remembered a frightening face,
quickly covered by a twitching cloth. Pretty Mrs. Joseph Stanley-Brown—
who as little Molly Garfield had been the White House pet in years gone
by—once brought her boy, Rudolph, to see Mrs. McKinley. That lady,
attended by a friend from Ohio, received them in the Red Room. She took
Rudy's hand and welcomed him sweetly, but presently her face became
rigid, and her friend threw a large silk handkerchief over it. "What is it?"
Rudy wailed in anguish. "What's the matter with her?" Mrs. Stanley-
Brown explained, as soothingly as she could, that Mrs. McKinley was not
well. Then, almost at once, Mrs. McKinley was better. The handkerchief
was removed, and she went on with the conversation as though nothing
had happened.

Calls at the White House were often uncomfortable, but Republican
matrons kept on taking their children with them, because it was expected
and desired, because they wanted to please the President's wife and hoped
to see the President. McKinley's love of children was well known in
Washington. He never lost an opportunity to attend Children's Day and
other Sunday-school celebrations. His pastor, Dr. Bristol, thought that he
seemed his happiest on these occasions. The East Room swarmed with
youngsters of all ages on the days of his public receptions. The mothers
approached him eagerly, pushing forward toddlers and holding up infants,
as though there were a blessing in his handclasp or caress. Some lucky
child was sure to get the bright pink carnation he habitually wore. The
President's buttonhole had become a valued souvenir of a visit to the

mansion. There is a charming story of a call paid by Mrs. Cortelyou with her sons, Bruce and Win. They were sitting in the Red Room with Mrs. McKinley when the President came in. He found two expectant little boys, but he had only one buttonhole. Taking the flower from his coat, he gave it to Bruce, the elder. Then he selected another carnation from a vase for Win; but, before giving it, he wore it for a moment in his lapel, so that Bruce would not be able to lord it over his brother. The incident recalls a comment that Taft made about McKinley. "He had such a good heart that the right thing to do always occurred to him." Half a century later, Bruce Cortelyou would remember his first instruction in the true meaning of tact, that diplomacy of the heart in which McKinley was so delicately skilled.

The McKinleys loved to surround themselves with flowers as well as children, and took much pleasure in the conservatories which sprawled on the west side of the mansion. A maze of small hothouses held vines and ferns, tropical foliage plants, a miniature "grove" of potted orange trees, and some small beds of pineapples. Most of the flowers were in the main conservatory, which had been erected on the site of the former west portico, and could be entered from the first-floor corridor. By walking a short distance from the elevator, Mrs. McKinley could step into a warm, fragrant bower of roses, carnations, lilies, and hyacinths, and the collection of rare orchids that had been introduced by Mrs. Garfield. The President shared her delight in the profusion of blossoms that were theirs to see and smell and wear, to give to callers and send to friends. Their living rooms and the President's office were always adorned with bouquets, and elaborate arrangements were designed for their big dinners and receptions. In previous administrations, floral decorations had been chiefly confined to set pieces for the dining table. The emblems of the republic hung in wire framework from the rafters of the gardeners' workroom in the basement: American eagles and Ships of State, the star, the anchor, and the Scales of Justice. The McKinleys used them all, and inspired the gardeners to fresh efforts and inventions. Palms, crotons, rubber plants, and maidenhair ferns continued to be in evidence on formal occasions, but the signature of this occupancy of the White House was the lavish display of flowers that brightened the noble, shabby rooms.

The pattern of Mrs. McKinley's days had been quickly established. She drove in the morning and afternoon when the weather was fine. She furiously crocheted red worsted slippers for favored children, or for charitable bazaars that besought her assistance. Two or three of her intimates stopped in for a chat or a game of cribbage. Besides Mrs. Hobart, she frequently saw Mrs. Gage and Mrs. Dawes, and also two friends of long standing: Mrs. Stephen Rand (Sue), the wife of an officer on duty at the

*Ambassador Cambon watches as Secretary Day signs the Peace Protocol.
Standing, left to right, are: Montgomery, Thiébaut, Corbin, Moore, Adee,
the President, Cortelyou, Pruden, Cridler, and Loeffler.
The photograph was posed the week after the signing took place.*

The Cabinet, 1899. On the President's right, Hay and Root;
on his left, Gage and Griggs; standing, left to right,
Long, Wilson, Hitchcock, and Smith.

The ladies of the Cabinet grouped beside Mrs. McKinley's chair: on the left, Miss Flora Wilson, Mmes. Root, Long, and Hay; on the right, Mmes. Gage, Smith, Griggs, and Hitchcock.

A group of American officers at Manila in 1899. In the foreground,
left to right, Generals MacArthur, Otis, and Funston

A volunteer outfit "laying low" outside Manila in 1899.
General Otis stands in the background.

The conservatories at the west front of the White House

Carriages waiting before the south portico during a New Year reception

The President standing protectively beside his wife   *"drooping in velvet in the Green Room . . ."*

Culver Service

Several photographs of McKinley and Hobart, taken in the late summer of 1899, were so much admired that the next summer a photograph was issued of McKinley and Roosevelt in a similar pose. McKinley's identical clothing and a faint line down the middle of the later picture suggest that it was actually a composite.

Brown Brothers

The President in a thoughtful pose as he faces a second term

"holding a single rose . . ."

North Market Street was again crowded for the notification ceremonies in July, 1900. The octagonal extension of the front porch of the McKinleys' house can be seen on the right.

McKinley's second inaugural address was delivered in the rain

Cardinal Gibbons pronouncing the benediction after the presentation of the sword to Admiral Dewey. The participation of a Roman Catholic prelate in a ceremony at the Capitol was unprecedented.

The President entering the carriage at the Milburn house

The President and Mrs. McKinley driving through the Pan American Exposition with Mr. Milburn

Frances B. Johnston, Library of Congress

"The period of exclusiveness is past."

The President visits Goat Island, Niagara Falls, dogged by the Secret Service agent Foster.

Dunlap, The Canton Repository

(Above) The automobile ambulance of the emergency hospital at the Ex

*(Below) The new President in serious conference with Senator Hanna
after the death of McKinley*

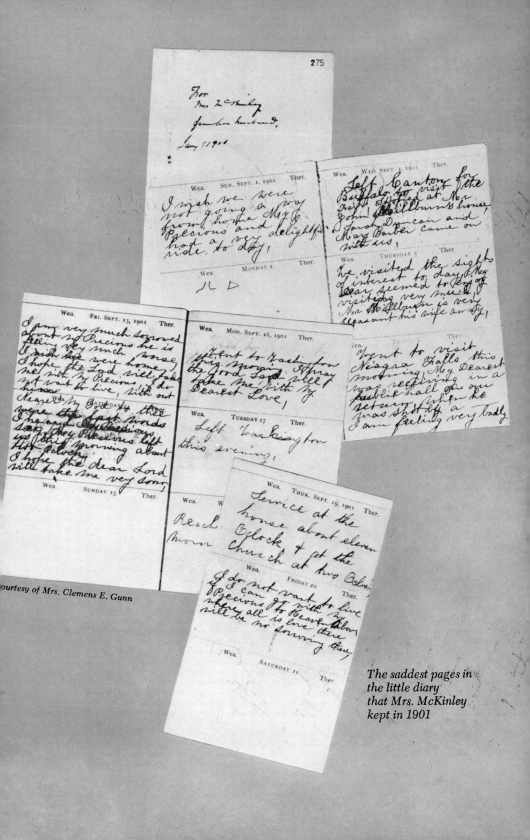

For
Mrs McKinley
from her husband,
Jany 1 1901

Wea. SUN. SEPT. 1, 1901 **Ther.**

I wish we were
not going a way
from home My
Precious and
had a very delightful
ride to day,

Wea. MONDAY 2 **Ther.**

M D

Wea. WED SEPT 4, 1901 **Ther.**

Left Canton for
Buffalo to visit the
Fair Stopped at Mr
John Milburn's house,
Sarah Duncan and
May Barber came on
with us,

Wea. THURSDAY 5 **Ther.**

We visited the sights
of interest to day My
dear seemed to enjoy
visiting very much
Mr Milburn is very
pleasant his wife is very

Wea. FRI. SEPT. 13, 1901 **Ther.**

I am very much sorrowed
about my Precious he is
failing very much I wish
I wish they were home,
I hope the Lord will take
me with My Precious if I do
not want to live, with out
him

Wea. SATURDAY 14 **Ther.**

Nearer My God to thee
were the last words
I heard My Precious
say, My Precious left
us this morning about
two o'clock,
I hope the dear Lord
will take me very soon,

Wea. SUNDAY 15 **Ther.**

Wea. MON. SEPT. 16, 1901 **Ther.**

Went to Washington
this morning I pray
the good Lord will
take Me with My
Dearest Love,

Wea. TUESDAY 17 **Ther.**

Left Washington
this evening,

Wea. W **Ther.**

Reach
Morn

Wea. F **Ther.**

Went to visit
Niagara Falls this
morning My Dearest
was receiving in a
public hall on our
return when he
was shot by a
I am feeling very badly

Wea. THUR. SEPT. 19, 1901 **Ther.**

Service at the
house about eleven
O'clock & at the
church at two O'clo

Wea. FRIDAY 20 **Ther.**

I do not want to live
if I can go with My
Precious to Heaven above
where all is love there
will be no sorrowing there

Wea. SATURDAY 21 **Ther.**

*The saddest pages in
the little diary
that Mrs. McKinley
kept in 1901*

Mrs. McKinley alone with her mementos and memories in Canton

Navy Department; and Abner McKinley's sister-in-law, Miss Katharine Endsley (Kitty), whom the President had given a clerkship in one of the departments. At stated hours, Mrs. McKinley formally received a procession of ladies, strangers for the most part, who had applied for permission to call and been granted an appointment. The McKinleys seldom ate their big hot meals alone. The President liked to issue hospitable invitations to lunch and dinner. He often played a game of euchre in the evening before going back to his office.

In the first months, there was nothing to tax the energies of a normal woman, but the pace went far beyond anything Mrs. McKinley had attempted as an invalid. The excitement had seemed to be the tonic that she needed. She had begun to gain in strength and spirits as soon as she was installed in Washington. She thoroughly enjoyed the summer holiday at the Hotel Champlain in northern New York, spent with the Hobarts and other friends in a round of informal outings, drives and picnics, and visits to Lake Placid and Ausable Chasm. Later the McKinleys went to Ohio. The President had engaged to attend the reunion of his regiment at Fremont, the old home of Rutherford B. Hayes. As Fanny Hayes was going to be married, McKinley had asked that the date should be set a day in advance of the veterans' meeting, so that he and his wife could be present. "A union should always precede a reunion," he had written Fanny in the jesting tone he took with young people. The McKinleys stayed at the Hayes homestead, Spiegel Grove, for the wedding of this "little friend" of earlier years. There were other reunions in Ohio, other nostalgic scenes, before they traveled back to Washington. In late September, they were off again for a glimpse of autumn in the Berkshire Hills of western Massachusetts.

Casual acquaintances might not have been struck by the improvement in Mrs. McKinley's condition. Those who talked about her being "better" were all people who had known her to be far worse. Cortelyou became much impressed with her steady progress. It is revealing that, at a time when he found her "vastly better," he observed, "Now she can almost walk alone." At the top of her form, Mrs. McKinley was feeble and lame, subject to severe headaches, and constantly going off into stiff little swoons. Her nervous instability made her hypersensitive to the slightest shock, and any agitation brought on an aggravated attack. The hazards of upsetting her were naturally multiplied on journeys, and particularly on visits to households in which her peculiarities were not known. The difficulty was illustrated during this trip to the Berkshires. The chance of untoward incidents was minimized at the home of W. B. Plunkett, a cotton manufacturer of Adams, Massachusetts. The Plunketts had entertained Mrs. McKinley before, sympathized with her frailty, and loved McKinley for the devotion with which he treated her. The President felt so much at home with this kindly, unaffected family that he would lift Ida in his arms, if she grew tired in the evening, and carry her up to bed. But the McKinleys entered a much more formal atmosphere when they went on to stay on an estate at the fashionable resort of Lenox. Mr. and Mrs. John Sloane were merely acquaintances, and under their roof Mrs. McKinley was very badly startled by a "surprise."

The responsibility for the surprise rested on the slender, animated shoulders of Auguste Chollet, a butler whom the host had borrowed from a neighbor for a dinner in honor of the President and his wife. Auguste was a clever young Frenchman, noted for his original table decorations. Asked to prepare a suitable patriotic display, he had secretly completed an ingenious arrangement, which involved boring a hole through the Sloanes' dining-room floor and threading it with a piece of string attached to the mechanism of a large clock in the cellar. When the President and Mrs. McKinley led the way into the dining room, followed by the Sloanes and thirty or forty guests, they saw a huge mound, covered by a silken flag, in the center of the long, resplendent table. The suspense was prolonged while the ladies and gentlemen found their places, and a bishop said grace. Then Auguste flipped off the flag, and disclosed a stuffed American eagle, which at once began to move, bobbing its head and flapping its wings in a jerky but lifelike fashion. Much to the amusement of Jim Barnes, the son of Auguste's regular employer, the bird seemed to be nodding and winking at Mrs. McKinley, whose chair it directly faced. She stumbled in terror to her feet, without her husband's arm to grasp, for the Sloanes knew so little of her habits that she had not been seated beside the President. He hurried to her side, and supported her from the room, while Auguste's masterpiece was snatched from the table and deposited on the lawn in disgrace.

Mrs. McKinley's venture into society did not augur well for the coming season in Washington. There would be no clockwork eagles at the White House, but the presidential entertainments were affairs of extraordinary discomfort. Even though McKinley had sanctioned limiting the numbers at the receptions, the crowds would be large. There would be bustle and commotion, mishaps and maladjustments. McKinley did not discourage his wife's plans—crossing Ida would have provoked her worst symptoms—but he must have looked forward with some apprehension to their first season in Washington.

The winter of 1898 was Mrs. McKinley's great test, and she met it with decks cleared and colors flying. As the event proved, the season was abnormally short. The opening was postponed until the middle of January because of thirty days' official mourning for the President's mother—thus obviating the traditional New Year's Day visitation of several thousand handshakers—and the last of the four card receptions was canceled on receipt of the news of the *Maine* disaster. But for a month the White House was in a constant uproar, the scene by day of scurrying gardeners, extra footmen, and an army of laborers, and thronged night after night with guests. Colonel Bingham had effected some improvements at the evening receptions. For one thing, the shaky floor beams were supported by a forest of stout posts. For another, there was a notable increase in the checking facilities. Previously this need had been inadequately met by a few hat-and-cloak boxes, set up in the corridor. Colonel Bingham bought six secondhand hookracks and a quantity of additional boxes, which he resourcefully adapted for placement in the main vestibule. He procured a lot of used velours curtains (sixty cents a yard), and contrived a means of hanging them by running segments of gas pipe along the top of the cloak boxes destined for the uppermost tier. Thus, for the first time in its history, the Executive Mansion was supplied with sightly and convenient repositories for the outer garments of about 1,200 persons.

The fundamental improvement was the reduction in attendance, notable in the first two seasons of the McKinley era. With the assistance of J. Addison Porter, Bingham had applied himself to eliminating duplication in the invitations. The White House lists included the members of the diplomatic corps, the officers of the government, and all officers of the armed services who were resident in the capital; and the "Hard Pan List," a register of the Washington elite, which owed its label to the influence of the Alaskan Gold Rush. Bingham operated on the principle that, while none of these people could properly be left out, there was no good reason to go on asking them repeatedly every season, in many cases to all four of the receptions. He and Porter divided up the lists, and arranged for each person, including each member of Congress, to be invited once and only once. The first reception was in honor of the diplomatic corps, the second was for the Cabinet and the Supreme Court, and the third was for the Army and Navy. The fourth and last—eventually canceled in 1898—was intended to serve as a mopping-up operation.

On paper, the reformers succeeded in keeping the attendance down to a thousand at a time, but there were never less than two thousand guests, even in the very first season. The issuance of the invitations brought howls of protest from personages who had been omitted. Explanations were of no avail. The dividing-up of the lists was condemned as un-American. Requests for exceptions and special invitations streamed in from quarters that could not be ignored. It became necessary to ask Congress in a body to the second reception, as usual. Besides, there was the problem of the gatecrashers. Since the President flatly refused to sanction a demand for cards of admission, Bingham had recourse to the employment of "spotters," experienced doorkeepers from the Capitol, a White House usher who knew the President's callers, and a man familiar with the appearance of the Washington socialites. The arriving guests were scrutinized at the entrance. The names of the unidentified were checked against the typewritten invitation lists; and, if they had not been asked, their addresses were taken down. But it was another matter to turn away intruders who failed to wilt under this treatment. Not all of them could be classed with "the scum of the city," against whom Bingham's wrath was directed. Some accredited guests were in the habit of bringing relatives and friends to shake hands with the President. It was embarrassing to leave shivering ladies with their escorts on the doorstep. Custom, moreover, had bred confidence among the members of the populace who frequented the receptions. As a result of years of sufferance, they had established a sort of squatters' rights at the mansion. The bolder spirits among them pushed past the attendants or sailed in complacently under the protection of congressmen. Bingham at first sent severe reprimands to all concerned in these irregularities, but the spotters were soon withdrawn, and the gatecrashers gradually returned in their usual numbers to the White House.

Bingham and Porter, in the long run, largely failed in their laudable enterprise of cutting down the crowds at the card receptions. They had been eminently successful in provoking ill feeling and ridicule, and they had contrived to paste a label of snobbery on the mansion, though never on the President. It was impossible to associate McKinley with exclusiveness or prejudice. He had the same shining welcome for everyone. An ideal of republican simplicity was an anachronism in modern America, but McKinley could never quite give up the old-fashioned notion that the Chief Magistrate and his dwelling should be accessible to the people.

Long before the firstcomers arrived, the mansion had been put in readiness, with posts, cloakboxes, and hookracks in place. The corridor and parlors were swept and polished and garlanded, and crash was laid over the floors. The Blue Room was divided by a rank of sofas, arranged to close off the area "behind the line," which was reserved for especially invited guests. By eight-thirty the preparations were complete. A fireman was in the attic. The Marine Band was in the conservatory. Trays of ice water were set out in the state dining room and the Red Parlor. The doorkeepers and footmen went to their stations, and the carriage wheels began to roll to the portico. Bingham's efforts were rewarded, as he preceded the President down the stairway. Ladies and gentlemen in full evening dress were flowing smoothly from the vestibule, after a handy disposal of their wraps. The light from the crystal chandeliers glittered on banks of flowers, serried plants, and trailing smilax. Strains of music were softly wafted from the west end of the corridor. The members of the receiving party aligned themselves in front of the upholstery fence in the Blue Room, and the procession of guests advanced. Tall and handsome in his impeccably tailored uniform, with his blond mustache neatly pointed, Bingham stood on the President's left and made the presentations. When the hands had all been shaken and the crowd had gone, there was a choice little supper, with wine, for the receiving party and a few friends.

Bingham deserved credit for his efficiency and knew it, but he also suffered the agonies common to perfectionists. Hard experiences were in store for him during his faithful service at the White House: the admittance of huge crowds beyond his power to control, bleak receptions held before the carpets were laid in the autumn, the irritating day when sand was tracked in from the snowy paths and scratched the vestibule floors, one humiliating evening when the mansion was pervaded by a smell of cooking, like burnt cheese. Invaders penetrated the enclosure "behind the line," and had to be chased out, or tolerated with glares of indignation. Even when things went well, Bingham's satisfaction was sure to be clouded by the sight of some dowdy landlady or vulgar office seeker—persons not in evening dress, females wearing hats. But the worst trial of all was the behavior of the official hostess, and her husband's indulgent attitude toward her. Bingham was constantly mortified by Mrs. McKinley's ill health, and constantly vexed by the courtly attentions the President paid her, in seeming obliviousness of her social inadequacy.

The entrance of the presidential couple, traditionally made by the stairway on formal occasions, was a conspicuously awkward performance. Mrs. McKinley painfully negotiated the descent, clinging to her husband's arm —clinging, as Bingham was horrified to discover, to his *left* arm. It was obvious that Mrs. McKinley's right was her "bad" side, on which she wanted support, but Bingham was unable to imagine a good explanation for the singular habit. He could only conjecture that the President wanted to be prepared for possible handshaking as he passed along. His disapproval was dreadfully justified at a subsequent stag dinner at the White House. Although McKinley correctly offered his arm to other ladies, the sway of habit proved too much on this particular evening. In the absence of his wife, he gave his left arm to the guest of honor, the President of Costa Rica.

Once delivered to the Blue Room, Mrs. McKinley took her proper place, but again her behavior was highly unconventional, for she could not stand and was unequal to the strain of shaking hands. Seated in a large blue velvet chair, with Mrs. Hobart on her farther side, she responded to the greetings with a bow. The President made a point of introducing people to her. At Mrs. Hobart's suggestion, she held a bouquet of flowers to indicate that she would not give her hand, but the hint was not always understood. An embarrassed lady once remained so long with hand outstretched that Mrs. Hobart came to the rescue, saying, "Won't you shake hands with me instead?" In the midst of his rhythmic performance, reaching to the left, swinging to the right, the President "flashed" Mrs. Hobart "a look of heartfelt gratitude." She said that thereafter he took care to swing each guest clear across Mrs. McKinley into her clasp. It is not easy, though, to see how this maneuver was combined with the presentations to his wife, a practice in which McKinley certainly persisted. It was one of Bingham's chief grievances that the office was taken away from his first assistant, Lieutenant Curtis Gilmore, who hovered before Mrs. McKinley in a posture of perpetually frustrated readiness to perform it. McKinley intensely disliked being hedged around by soldiers. As Bingham put it, he was "particularly impatient of military retinue." He could not dispense with the officers assigned to duty at the White House; but at all his receptions, public as well as official, he was at pains to avoid an impression that he was shut off from his visitors and desirous of protection.

The influence of Mrs. McKinley's invalidism on the state dinners was still more drastic than in the case of the receptions, for those functions repeated all the irregularities of the larger gatherings and embellished them with the greatest impropriety of all, the unconventional seating at table. The progress from the Blue Room was usually—though not invariably—made in proper style, with Mrs. McKinley on the arm of the guest of honor, preceded by the President with the gentleman's wife, and at times a promenade was made in this fashion by way of the East Room. But, on reaching the table, the President showed the lady he escorted to the seat on his left. Then he drew out the chair on his right for his wife, and assisted her to take her place. Objections to the arrangement were by no means confined to Colonel Bingham. As a breach of protocol, it was startling to official Washington and shocking to the more rigid members of the diplomatic corps. McKinley was somehow persuaded to permit a formal dinner to be seated in the customary manner. This meant that he was separated from his wife by the width of the board, for, according to the European fashion traditional at the White House, the President and his wife sat opposite each other at the center of the table. On the evening in question, McKinley faced Ida across a comparatively narrow expanse of flowers and napery and silver; but he was helpless to reach her quickly, in case of need, and Mrs. Hobart said that "he was anxious to the point of distraction and never took his eyes from her." Later, with touching simplicity, he appealed to this sympathetic friend, "Could it possibly offend anyone for me to have my wife sit beside me?" Mrs. Hobart warmly assured him that it was the privilege of the Chief Executive to do as he pleased in his own house. Ida was never displaced again. The only conventionally seated dinners at the mansion were the stag parties given from time to time by the President.

In contrast to their receptions, the McKinleys' dinners were unprecedentedly large. Very few of them could be held in the state dining room, which accommodated at a tight squeeze only fifty. The increasing representation of foreign governments at Washington had compelled the Clevelands to hold their last diplomatic dinner in the main corridor. The Tiffany glass screen formed the only shelter from the draughts of the vestibule. A gale roared through the improvised banquet hall whenever the front door was opened, and the floor was so cold that the divans were robbed of cushions to make footstools for the ladies. Nevertheless, the Clevelands' innovation became the McKinleys' rule. In their first winter, they broke the record of the mansion with a dinner of seventy-one covers for President and Mrs. Sanford B. Dole of the Republic of Hawaii. A similarly grand, though somewhat smaller party was given for ex-President and Mrs. Harrison. All the usual White House banquets were wedged into the single, crowded month, and the President and his wife were also guests at eight dinners respectively given by the Vice-President and the members of the Cabinet.

There was a tedious monotony about the solemn, protracted feasts. They were served promptly at eight, and lasted for an hour and a quarter. Mark Hanna used to sit with watch in hand, timing the service when it was slow. John D. Long pronounced the Washington dinners "horrible." "Language cannot express the reluctance with which I stretch myself out on the altar of these sacrifices," Long groaned. ". . . The same food; same dishes; same waiters, each ejecting the same breath over your right [sic] shoulder; the same courses; the same long hours; the same men and women; exactly the same conversation; and the same everything. Nobody wants to give them. Nobody wants to attend them." But there was one exception, at least. Mrs. McKinley could not have been kept away. Night after night, she willingly stretched herself out on the altar of those sacrifices; and, when the month of the Washington season was over, she was off to Philadelphia to attend a banquet held before the President's Washington Birthday speech to the University of Pennsylvania. In her first winter at the Executive Mansion, she silenced reports of her withdrawal from social life. She appeared on every occasion beside the President.

Their hospitality was more than generous. By the standard of their decorations, it was elaborate. At every formal dinner, the ranks of pink-shaded candelabra shone on multiple arrangements of blossoms, clustered in graceful bouquets and in ornate plaques twinkling with electric bulbs. Orchids dressed the table at the parties for the Doles and the Harrisons, and there were corsages or boutonnieres of the same exotic flowers at each place. For the diplomatic reception, the Blue Room was completely canopied in greenery, studded with red, white, and blue incandescent lights; and, besides the wealth of the government greenhouses, four hundred roses had been ordered from New York. The reception to the Army and Navy was another notable event. The entire first floor was festooned with American flags, interspersed with floral garlands, and stars and anchors of roses. On the occasion of a large party for Prince Albert of Belgium, the East Room was transformed into "a jungle of tropical plants and exotics, in which the yellow striped chairs and fauteuils lurked like so many Bengal tigers."

The Marine Band played Sousa's new march, "The Lady of the White House," and, in her thronelike blue chair or her honored seat at table, Mrs. McKinley was the cynosure of attention. She wore her handsome gowns—the pearl-gray brocade, the black velvet with point lace, the pale blue satin, the white satin embroidered in silver. Diamonds sparkled in her frizzed hair, at her ears, and on her fingers and bosom. With her faded and refined beauty, she did not look unsuited to her position, but she was drained by the exertion of putting in an appearance, and could rarely make the effort of carrying on a conversation. Dosed with bromides, she sat with tense hands and dazed eyes, vaguely smiling and bowing. *Harper's Bazar* selected an unfortunately apt metaphor in praising the President's wife as "a needed gentle sedative to the typical woman of to-day who aims to do too much."

Mrs. McKinley had her success in the White House, but it was the purely personal triumph of her indomitable will. The receptions were more than ordinarily dreary occasions for the ladies who dragged their heavy trains to the enclosure "behind the line" in the Blue Room. Uneasiness dulled the spirits of the diners in the drafty corridor, awaiting the premonitory hiss and the flash of the President's napkin.

Though the *Maine* disaster brought the official season to a premature close in 1898, festivities were temporarily revived in March, when Prince

Albert of Belgium, the nephew and destined heir of King Leopold II, spent a long week end in Washington. A slender young man with bashful manners and a curly blond pompadour, he had come to the United States to study American industries, and was traveling with two aides as the Comte de Rethy. In spite of his incognito, an effort had been made by the Belgian minister, the Comte de Lichtervelde, to have the President recognize the future ruler by returning his formal call. The attitude of the legation had created some confusion. Vice-President and Mrs. Hobart, in issuing invitations to a dinner and reception, inscribed "To meet H.R.H. Prince Albert of Belgium" on their cards. Invitations to a similar function at the Executive Mansion skirted the difficulty by omitting mention of the guest of honor. The precaution, however, was taken of extending an offer of royal honors on Albert's arrival at the station. Since the offer was declined, the State Department confidently drew the conclusion that Albert's incognito was to be strictly observed. The application of the Belgian minister had earlier been denied, with certain polite concessions. Colonel Bingham was to escort the Comte de Rethy to call at the Executive Mansion. The President, in lieu of a return call, was to invite the youth to accompany him on a drive; and it was finally settled that he should alight at its conclusion and momentarily enter the vestibule of the Comte's hotel, the Arlington, thus paying a sort of call with one foot.

In the forenoon, after the Prince arrived, Bingham presented himself at the Arlington in full uniform, and conducted Albert and the Belgian minister to the Executive Mansion in the President's open landau, followed by the aides in another carriage. The program of two drives, with a call in between, was bristling with problems of etiquette, and its awkwardness was accentuated by the condition of the mansion. The party for the Prince was to take place that evening, and the house was in a turmoil of preparations for the biggest dinner to date. Besides the dignitaries of the government and the diplomatic corps, it had been thought suitable to invite a number of young girls. The main corridor was in such disorder that, contrary to custom, the landau was driven to the south portico, and Albert was brought in by the back door, which opened directly into the Blue Room and was ordinarily kept locked. Nor was the situation relieved by the deportment of the President, who appeared to be preoccupied and in haste. He was already engrossed by the crisis in American relations with Spain. Quite possibly, he was impatient because Albert's call had been arranged for noon on a Friday, when the Cabinet regularly met. In any case, McKinley displayed something less than his usual charm. He was, to begin with, late in coming down. Albert stood cooling his heels for several minutes in the Blue Room, with no one more consequential than Lieutenant Gilmore to bid him welcome. Then, when the greetings and presentations were over, the President was obviously in a hurry to terminate the interview. He did not offer the Prince a seat—a neglect which caused some muttering among the Belgians—but shortly broached the matter of the drive, and made off to get his hat and coat, which a servant was holding in the Red Parlor. Albert, compliantly following, made polite inquiries for Mrs. McKinley while the President was being helped on.

Colonel Bingham had already experienced the crisis of entering the carriage. The ordeal was again at hand, complicated by the participation of the President. On emerging from the south portico, he found the landau standing with the right-hand seat on the side away from the house, and directed that it be turned around. After making the conventional motion of courtesy to Albert and receiving the conventional remonstrance, he entered the carriage first and took the "seat of honor" on the right. The result was that Albert was obliged to step over the President's feet to reach his place. Bingham, for his part, walked around the rear of the carriage to avoid squeezing between the knees of the President and the Belgian minister. But, whatever agony Bingham suffered, there was no trace of displeasure on the bland, blond features of the Prince. Perhaps McKinley's charm had triumphed, after all. When the farewells were spoken just inside the front door of the Arlington, Albert seemed positively reluctant to end the meeting. Not to be outdone in condescension, he popped out again with the President, and saw him off at the curb.

Albert was not presented to Mrs. McKinley until he returned to the mansion. He had asked to pay his respects to her in the morning, but the President had "excused her as not being very well and having the fatigue of the day before her. . . ." The fatigue of the evening bade fair to be extreme. It was to open with a grand promenade by the Presidential party, passing down the stairs to the state dining room and thence proceeding to the East Room. This was a greater exertion than Mrs. McKinley had previously essayed at one stretch, but she was planning to undertake it without her husband's assistance. She would not only go in to dinner with Albert but also make her entrance with that royal stripling, descending the stairway and marching through the parlors on his arm. When he arrived at a few minutes before eight, he was taken in the elevator to the second floor. The President came to meet him, and led him to Mrs. McKinley, who was sitting in her own bailiwick at the end of the corridor.

The use of the elevator was, in itself, a mark of distinction. Dinner guests were obliged to climb the office stairs to reach the improvised cloakrooms, gentlemen in the Cabinet Room and ladies in the oval library. The elevator was not at their disposal because, like the main stairway, it was situated in the west wing. On this occasion the bars had been somewhat lowered. The ranking officials of the administration, assembling for the promenade, saw a good many unfamiliar faces in the private part of the house. The Prince was attended by his aides and the secretary of the Belgian legation. The Belgian minister and his wife were also present. The first guests to arrive, they had been sent up by the office stairs; but the Comtesse de Lichtervelde had been invited as an extra lady to balance the promenade, and they had firmly made their way from the cloakrooms into Mrs. McKinley's alcove. The ambassadors and their wives, on discovering the privileged position of the Belgians, did not hesitate to crash the family wing. An exclusive little levee took place in the upper hall, while the other guests waited below. The President soon gave his arm to Mrs. Hobart, and the procession formed: Albert and Mrs. McKinley, the Vice-President and the Comtesse de Lichtervelde, and the members of the Cabinet in order of precedence. The supernumeraries hastened down to join the rest of the company, while the official party traversed the mansion.

There was, said Colonel Bingham, a "little hitch" at the beginning of the presentations, because the ambassadors naturally came first, and they had already been in the "family party" upstairs. But Bingham was tolerant of such distinguished irregularities. On this notable evening, the White House had been brought into an unprecedentedly intimate relationship with the representatives of the European governments. He was gratified, too, by the Prince's constant "amiability and evident satisfaction at his stay. . . ." The disciplines of royalty are severe, and Albert had smilingly survived what must have been one of the least enjoyable promenades in history; but, in spite of the Washington buds and a famous violoncellist, he did not linger in the East Room when the gentlemen joined the ladies after coffee and cigars. There was one good thing to be said for the White House dinners—it was not necessary to stay late at them. They broke up informally, "American fashion." Albert promptly availed himself of the permission to leave. Sustained by some private discipline, Mrs. McKinley sat on in her blue velvet armchair, enjoying the musicale.

The next weeks of increasing national tensions were an unsuitable time for merrymaking at the White House, but Mrs. McKinley went right on entertaining. The mansion was filled with visitors, many of them young girls; for, besides summoning all the nieces, she had scattered invitations broadcast to the daughters of friends in Canton and elsewhere. She resumed her afternoon receptions, greeting callers by appointment in the Red Parlor. She had another musicale at the end of March, again engaging the violoncellist, Leo Stern, who had performed after the dinner for Prince Albert. There were euchre games, and a series of theater parties.

As the last hope of peace waned in early April, Mrs. McKinley gave an elaborate "red, white and blue luncheon" of fifty young ladies. Ten days later, she was hostess at a luncheon of more than a hundred alumnae of her old boarding school, Brooke Hall. She also showed unusual initiative in making excursions without her husband. She went to Baltimore to attend the benefit for the *Maine* Monument Fund; and, when the outbreak of war occurred, she was spending the week end in New York.

Mrs. McKinley's pursuit of pleasure contrasts painfully with her husband's acute distress during this period. She showed concern for his nervous state, saying to Cortelyou that the President was not sleeping well and needed rest; but like a child, self-centered and unable to comprehend the adult predicament, she saw only that he ought to "get away." There was no privacy for McKinley at the White House. He went through his ordeal in an incongruous bustle of festivity, obliged to welcome visitors and make small talk at dinner. At least once, he had to put in an appearance at a formal function—Mrs. McKinley's musicale, the occasion on which he was so unstrung that he burst into tears in the Red Room. His nervousness, moreover, was aggravated by worry about his wife. Mrs. McKinley was certainly doing too much. On one day in March, for example, she received several hundred callers in the Red Room, and then played euchre in the evening—with the President taking a hand. Yet it is impossible to believe that she was in poorer health than usual, as Kohlsaat reported that McKinley told him on the night of the musicale. According to the standards by which her health was judged, Mrs. McKinley was "better"—stronger, livelier, and more cheerful. Cortelyou thought in April that she seemed "quite well for her," and particularly remarked her "deep interest" in the preparations for the Brooke Hall luncheon. Her physician, Dr. Bishop, found her "well and happy" when he saw her in New York.

The improvement continued during the quieter life imposed by the war. It was in June that Cortelyou pronounced Mrs. McKinley "vastly better." She remained well through a summer of peculiarly oppressive heat, entirely spent in Washington except for another independent jaunt to New York and the single week of the President's vacation. September found the White House prepared to lodge a succession of guests, and already humming with plans for an evening reception in honor of the delegates to the forthcoming Protestant Episcopal Convention. Mrs. McKinley enjoyed a long visit from her sister, whose son John Barber had contracted typhoid fever in Porto Rico and was taken to Garfield Memorial Hospital in Washington on his return. There is an agreeable glimpse of the First Lady at this time in a letter written by Charles Bawsel, the former clerk at Columbus, who had been given a minor federal appointment. He had had a "most delightful visit with Mrs. McKinley," and was elated at having found her "so gracious." Evidently after an interval of coldness, she had been "like her old self" with Bawsel, and called him "Charlie."

The party for the Episcopalians in early October was one of the most elegant of the McKinleys' entertainments. A formal, full-dress affair, with refreshments served in the state dining room, it was attended by a throng of clerics and prominent laymen, including the New York banker Mr. J. Pierpont Morgan. The President shook hands with more than a thousand of these gentlemen and their ladies, and was pleased to accept a bishop's invitation to unveil a Peace Cross in Washington. McKinley's blend of dignity, joviality, and spiritual warmth made him an ideal host for such an assemblage. He struck precisely the right note. So, in her own way, did the genteel invalid in a gown of white satin with a high collar held close to the neck by a circlet of diamonds. Several house guests from Ohio were dressed in plainer fashion. Pina was able to be present. The thoughts of the two Saxton women were surely far removed from expectation of tragedy when, in the midst of the high-toned festivity, a telegram from Canton announced the murder of their only brother George.

McKinley did not break the news until the front door had closed on the last departing bishop's coat-tails. A long-distance telephone call to Canton arranged for a private funeral at the old Saxton house on South Market Street, where George had made his home with Pina. The next evening, the White House party left for Ohio, accompanied by John Barber on a stretcher.

The murder of George Saxton was an artistically fitting climax, as pat as the ending of a moral tale, to his shabby career as a Lothario. For more than six years, Canton had followed with morbid interest the clashes between Saxton and Mrs. Anna George, the pretty dressmaker whom he had rejected after breaking up her marriage and ruining her reputation. A series of lawsuits, brought by both Anna and her divorced husband Sample C. George, and obstinately contested by Saxton, had kept the affair before the public; and Saxton had also attracted local attention by appealing to the police and the postal authorities for protection against his former mistress. Outside Ohio, however, the scandal had been little noticed, and it had recently seemed likely to subside. The last of the outstanding litigation, Sample George's suit for alienation of affections, had been settled just three days before Saxton came to a violent end. The crime reopened the whole story, and spread it far beyond the previous confines of its interest. The disgraceful life and death of Mrs. McKinley's brother suddenly became a topic that competed with the Philippines in the headlines of the nation.

Early on the evening of October 7, George Saxton had sallied forth, nattily dressed in his bicycle cap and a light-colored overcoat, and pedaled smoothly through the dusk to a quiet residential street not far from the Barber house. He parked his wheel before the dwelling of Mrs. Eva Althouse, an attractive widow—who was incidentally away from home—and crossed the sidewalk to the steps that ascended the terraced lawn. As he started up, a volley of shots rang out, and Saxton fell, mortally wounded in the belly. Neighbors, running to their windows at the noise of gunfire, glimpsed a tall, slim woman in black in the Althouse shrubbery. The Canton police lost little time in finding and arresting Anna George. Though she had received some small remuneration in settlement of a suit for breach of promise, her vengeful feelings had not been satisfied. The lovely dressmaker had repeatedly stated in the presence of witnesses that she was going to shoot George Saxton if he did not stop calling on Eva Althouse.

Charles Dawes was with the President the next morning, and remarked that he seemed depressed. Apart from the cruel shock to Mrs. McKinley, the bad news had come at a peculiarly inopportune time. The President was in the throes of his momentous decision on the Philippines, and had expected to leave Washington two days later on the trip to sound out the West. The first part of the schedule was altered, but his business in Canton did not delay his tour. McKinley drove to the cemetery and bowed with due solemnity beside George Saxton's grave. He also conferred with the judge and county prosecutor, and an announcement was made that the state would follow the usual routine, without expediting the case. Two days after the McKinleys reached Canton, the campaign train from Washington halted in the yards, the President's private car was attached, and he went on to the rousing welcome of Iowa. Mrs. McKinley was unable to accompany her husband, but she did not tarry long among her friends at home. She took refuge with Mary McWilliams in Chicago, and awaited the President there.

Though Canton pitied George Saxton's relatives, there was small regret for the taking off of the elderly libertine himself. On the contrary, the crime started a wave of sentimental sympathy for the beautiful woman he had wronged. Anna George was an appealing figure after her arrest. Saxton's death had seemingly purged her of vindictive passions. Her composure was perfect. She made no damaging admissions, refusing to answer the questions of the county prosecutor, Atlee Pomerene. She calmly pleaded not guilty to a charge of first-degree murder, and conducted herself with ladylike dignity throughout the long ordeal of the hearings and the indictment by the grand jury in January, 1899. The trial did not take place until April. Freed on bond, Anna took a room at the centrally situated Williams Hotel, and engaged in embroidering sofa cushions for sale. The front window of the ground-floor parlor often framed a picture that drew and held the eyes of passers-by. Little Gretchen Groetzinger used to stand outside the hotel in hopes of the thrill of an answering smile from the "gorgeous-looking creature" who sat pensively working the brightly colored strands of silk floss. Canton romanced over Anna, but her position grew increasingly precarious as the prosecution built up a case of exceptional strength.

The President had sought to avoid the role of George Saxton's avenger, letting it be known that he would abstain from interference and desired only that justice should take its course. By the end of the winter, it was plain that the course of justice might not serve his interests, but he continued to hold himself aloof. His friends were fervently hoping for Anna's acquittal. A verdict of guilty would enable sensational Democratic newspapers to keep the sordid story before the public, while the possibility of a woman's receiving the death sentence for a crime connected with the President's family was nothing short of a political nightmare. Some two weeks before the trial opened, McKinley was confidentially informed of another hazard, involving his good personal friend, the Democratic prosecutor of Stark County. Atlee Pomerene—later United States senator—was in 1899 an ambitious young lawyer, pushing himself forward at a time when political strife in Ohio was peculiarly tense and bitter. The trial, with its national news coverage, was a big opportunity, and Pomerene had been tempted to turn it to partisan ends. A letter from Canton informed McKinley that unsavory evidence might be introduced about several of his friends, two of them then holding public office. The writer, James J. Grant, was a reliable informant. Formerly George Saxton's attorney and thoroughly acquainted with the background of the case, he was being urged to take part in the prosecution and had been made privy to its plans. But Grant hung back, worried by "the possibility of *nasty things*," and fearful of incurring the disfavor of the President. Except for this warning letter, the facts have been obliterated. Grant was evidently reassured, for he accepted an appointment as assistant counsel for the state, and figured prominently in the trial. A court record has not been found, but newspaper accounts suggest that the revelations of "nasty things" were confined to George Saxton. The President and Pomerene continued to be the best of friends.

The fate of Anna George hung in suspense until nearly the end of April. For Canton, it was a month of titillating entertainment. Spectators packed the courtroom to gaze at the accused, and admire the modesty of her bearing; to hear the Saxton name smeared by the defense in testimony too salty to be printed in the newspapers; and to appreciate the battle of wits between Pomerene and his neighbor and crony, the attorney who acted for Anna. It was generally admitted that her guilt was solidly established; but the jury, after more than twenty-four hours, found otherwise. The verdict of not guilty was cheered by the spectators and by the crowd that had assembled in the street outside. A free woman, Anna left the courtroom, and vanished forever from public view.

The Canton lawyer, Harry Frease, always privately doubted that the President's detachment had been as complete as was believed. One day while the trial was in progress, Frease was surprised to run into the Heistands. Their visit seemed suspiciously timely to Frease, since Heistand had been confidentially associated with McKinley, and knew everyone in Canton "from the judge down." Such speculation, however, was not commonly indulged in. Most people were satisfied that sympathy with a woman wronged was an adequate explanation of the verdict. The President's attitude was formally cited by the members of the Stark County bar as illustrating his high ethical standards and personal integrity.

The Saxton family ties were close, but George was mourned in secret. He had been gay and vital, a lady-killer and a dashing wheelman; the kind of man who slides into middle age without having quite grown up. Pina, it would seem, had taken his mother's place. George had strayed, but he had never married. He had always come home to the Barbers and their seven children, and borne his share of the expenses of the big old house in which he had been reared. Less intimately a part of Ida's life, he had felt an obligation toward his invalid sister. In 1890, he had made a will leaving her an annuity of $3,000, if she needed or desired it; and not until 1898, when Mrs. McKinley's future was financially secure, had George altered this provision in favor of Pina's children. However harshly his sisters censured his conduct, they must have grieved for him, and their sorrow must have been hot with anger at the woman who had taken his life. Yet their natural emotions were rigorously repressed. In the available family letters, the references to George are of the most formal character, dealing mainly with the settlement of his estate. Family ties and tenderness had ostensibly been expunged when he was shot down in his bicycle cap. The Saxton name had been dragged in the mud, and the response of the entire connection was a proud, oblivious silence.

At the time of the funeral, Mrs. McKinley had seemed so oblivious that people thought she had not been told the facts. "Do you mean to say that Mrs. McK does not know George was shot?" Charles Bawsel wrote his wife, in reply to a letter retailing the talk of Canton. "What care and grief she is spared by the ignorance. I too feel very sorry for Mrs. Barber. She is a proud high spirited woman and must feel this keenly. Mrs. McK's is truly a bed of roses." But Mrs. McKinley was not always as dull as she appeared. Ignorance was a protection, and she had a talent for feigning it. Amid all the clatter of newspaper publicity and court proceedings, she must surely have learned or guessed the truth, and the studied indifference of her demeanor is proof that she had done so. Mrs. McKinley not only seemed ignorant of her brother's murder, but heedless of his death. She disregarded the strictly prescribed conventions of mourning. On her return to Washington, she at once began receiving callers, making up games of euchre, and taking parties to the theater. William C. Beer heard her rattling on about the Philippines a scant two weeks after the funeral. She had caught the craze for uplifting the natives, and quite prematurely selected the wild tribes of northern Luzon as subjects for missionary teaching. Beer drily wrote that "Mrs. McKinley talked ten to the minute about converting the Igorrotes," and wanted his children to pray for them.

But, if Mrs. McKinley was sometimes overexcited, she showed no sign of physical weakening. Her life grew ever more animated. She was present in November at a grand White House dinner in honor of the Joint High Commission, which had removed from Quebec to Washington. She made another trip to New York before setting off with the President for Atlanta. Christmas was celebrated with many offerings of slippers and cravats, and New Year's Day of 1899 brought callers streaming past the First Lady's chair in the East Room. She intrepidly faced the social season, again appearing at all major functions with her husband and holding a number of receptions of her own, besides entertaining a house party of young people. In March, the McKinleys went back to Georgia for a stay of two weeks, mostly spent at Thomasville, with side trips to Tallahassee and Jekyll Island. Mrs. McKinley kept on going at full speed, but her physical endurance is a deceptive gauge of her emotional state. Several bits of evidence indicate that, throughout this period of apparent sprightliness, she was under severe and increasing nervous tension.

It is probably pertinent that, on the visit to Atlanta in December, the President had begun to treat her with more than ordinary solicitude, fussing over her in front of a formal caller, the editor of the Atlanta *Constitution*. Clark Howell was an expansionist and an admirer of the President, but he was not a personal friend and had not come on a personal errand. He had called to discuss a suggestion which he had originated and which McKinley had adopted—that of affording federal care for Confederate graves. When Howell presented himself at the President's private parlor at the Kimball House, he found Mrs. McKinley sitting beside the fire. The President repeatedly interrupted his talk with Howell to go to his wife and fasten her shawl around her shoulders and pat her on the cheek. Even for an affectionate husband, these attentions seem odd and excessive. Yet the implied point, that Mrs. McKinley was in such a bad mood that her husband had to admit an acquaintance to their domestic intimacies, is somewhat blunted by the still odder circumstance that McKinley was shaving during the consultation. A looking glass had been placed on the center table of the parlor, and the President received the visitor with a towel around his neck and his face covered with lather.

Other glimpses, however, establish Mrs. McKinley's extreme nervousness beyond a doubt. In late January, her temper was so ragged that she spitefully attacked the wife of the Secretary of War at a White House dinner party. As Henry Adams reported it, "the other evening when going to dinner, she suddenly turned on her ladies, and said: 'I know one of you who wants to be in my place, and that's Mrs. Alger.'" Adams rather admired Mrs. McKinley's insight. "The poor woman is not so imbecile," he wrote, "but that she sees some things intensely. . . ." Nevertheless, she was a worse trial than usual to those about her. She was sharp with Mrs. Foraker when she called, and spoke crossly of the young visitors at the mansion. Adams pitied Hay because of "the court work" which sat him next to Mrs. McKinley.

After the close of the season, the mansion was in the doldrums. The President was engrossed by public business, harried by the situation at the War Department and chained by a cast-iron schedule to his desk. He was always on call to go to his wife, but he could not remain beside her, and, except for one theater party, she did little to amuse herself. Visitors had been invited to stay at the mansion—Mary Barber served a long term in 1899—but there were times when Mrs. McKinley was cast on the bare rocks of her own devices, and became resentful and hard to handle. It was on such a day that two strangers were impressed into the task of diverting Mrs. McKinley.

Charles S. Hamlin was a Democrat, a clever young lawyer who had been Assistant Secretary of the Treasury in Cleveland's second term. He had become a specialist on the question of the Alaskan seal fisheries, and was retained as an adviser in the McKinley administration. Recently he had been attached to the Joint High Commission. On its adjournment in late February, the President offered Hamlin a position in the Treasury, and asked him to stay on and work on a treaty. The appointment was the occasion for a formal call which Hamlin paid at the White House with his bride of less than a year. The mild weather had tempted them to take a drive in one of the small open carriages that stood outside the Arlington. They were simply going to leave their cards at the door. Charlie had met the President only at conferences, Gertje had never seen him, and neither of them was acquainted with Mrs. McKinley, but they were mistaken in thinking that they had no personal connection with the White House. As the door opened, a man rushed out with glad cries of welcome, and the surprised callers recognized the inferior half of a couple once temporarily employed by Gertje's mother at her house in Albany. In his execrable English, Charles Tharin explained that Clare was now Madame McKinley's maid, and would be heartbroken if the Hamlins did not come in. "Madame McKinley," he said, "liked to see visitors."

The Hamlins hung reluctantly on the doorstep, but they were overborne. "The two men stationed by the door joined in saying that we must come in," Mrs. Hamlin wrote, "and it would do Mrs. McKinley good to see us. There was nothing to do but go in and Charles ushered us into one of the reception rooms and ran off upstairs only to return at once and breathlessly assure us that Madame as well as Clare were 'enchanted.' We followed him up the old stair case to the large hall and there in the center in a small rocker sat a fragile little figure rocking vigorously and Clare rushed out to meet us with voluble exclamations and Mrs. McKinley in a nasal voice said—'Friends of Clara's are always welcome—please be seated.'"

The Hamlins took chairs on either side of the rocker, and Mrs. McKinley inquired if they had been sightseeing, but the pose of polite hostess was not sustained. Hamlin's reply, mentioning an earlier residence at the capital, evidently alerted Mrs. McKinley to suspect the presence of a Democrat. "She said," Mrs. Hamlin reported, "that if we had been here before that she hoped it was not in the time of Pres. Cleveland—that he had been a poor man when he became Pres. but he had made enough money to be able to buy a fine place at Princeton and that her husband was the only honest man who ever was Pres." Clare, in distress, ran down the hall, while Mrs. McKinley rambled on that "the American people did not deserve such a Pres. as her husband—they did not deserve such a man. . . ." The door of the partition must have been open, for Mrs. Hamlin saw a face suddenly look out from a room in the east wing. In a moment, the President joined the little group. It was obvious to the Hamlins that he had been called to the rescue, and they could see how much the occasion distressed him. "We both said later—we never had seen a face with such a piteous expression as if he hoped we would understand the situation." McKinley pulled another chair close to Ida's little rocker. He took her hand

and held it, as he told the young people how glad he was they had called. He spoke for a few moments about the treaty on which Hamlin was engaged. Then, turning to Mrs. Hamlin, he inquired about her family, and began to talk of his old days at the Albany Law School. She listened in astonishment. For how had the President heard that Gertje came from Albany? How could he possibly have known that she was the granddaughter of that Judge Amasa J. Parker at whose reception he had first tasted ice cream? He had always remembered her mother's sister, Grace Parker, and the sweet way in which she had corrected his blundering idea that "the custard got frozen." Sitting close to Ida and calming her with the firm clasp of his hand, McKinley could say that a lovely girl had "won his heart completely." Grace had been dust for more than thirty years.

There were other times when Ida's demons were not exorcised by her husband's touch, when she demanded his undivided attention and could not brook competition and intrusion. During the trip to Jekyll Island—a visit to the estate of Cornelius Bliss—she was unable to control her hysterical behavior at a reception. The arrival of the President caused a ripple of pleasurable excitement at the exclusive winter colony off the coast of Georgia. The residents represented American privilege at its worthiest and best. They were thoroughly estimable people, well-mannered, churchgoing, and philanthropic; and they were so solidly and reliably rich that they had no need for display, but enjoyed the luxury of simplicity in their expensive island paradise. Everyone went down to the dock to meet the McKinleys and to see them into a landau merrily trimmed in red calico, with a small Negro boy for footman, and everyone, of course, turned out for the reception in their honor. The President's cordiality was irresistible as always, but his wife could scarcely bring herself to acknowledge the introductions. Her faced sagged in peevish, fretful lines. Her eyes clung to her husband. If anyone detained him in conversation, she tried to attract his notice by pulling at his arm and twisting his sleeve. At the Washington receptions, Mrs. McKinley's standard of ladylike deportment had kept her bowing and smiling to the point of exhaustion. This breakdown in polite company was a much more serious lapse than any private tantrums.

Yet, though her emotional instability had become critically aggravated, she seemed physically as well as usual. "They are both apparently much benefited by their vacation," Charles Dawes rather cautiously wrote in late March, after calling to welcome the presidential couple home.

The trial of Anna George opened on April 3, the week after the McKinley's return. Ten days later, the President dictated a letter to the erstwhile invalid, John Barber, who was handling the details of the family business.

"I got your letter enclosing the leases," the President wrote. "Your Aunt Ida has signed them, they are enclosed. Sorry your mother was not well. I hope she is standing the great strain through which she is now passing as well as she could expect. She has our sincere sympathy and our thoughts are with you. Your Aunt Ida herself has not been very well for the last ten days." Here was a guarded, but clear admission that "the great strain" of the trial had painfully affected Mrs. McKinley since the very day it started, though she had remained, in seeming indifference, in the public view. The acquittal of Anna George, however, was the signal for her retirement. A week end in New York was passed in unusual seclusion. In May, the McKinleys left Washington to spend ten quiet days at Virginia Hot Springs, accompanied by Dr. Presley M. Rixey, a Navy surgeon who was the new White House physician. Sternberg was retained as a consultant, but Rixey had taken his place as a regular attendant on the presidential couple. He had the keenest interest in Mrs. McKinley's symptoms, and devoted himself to her care.

The President was looking very worn, but Mrs. McKinley's deteriorating nervous condition was undoubtedly responsible for the sudden trip to Hot Springs. The next month, while visiting the Plunketts, she suffered a severe epileptic attack, and sank into a hysterical depression such as she had not known for ten years or more.

Without pleasure in her position or heart for her favorite pastimes, she concentrated on her husband, making insatiable demands on his attention. Even when she let him go, McKinley was not free from the reproach of her need and her waiting. Cortelyou heard something of his difficulties one summer evening when he told the President that the balance of the papers before him could wait until the next day. "He said he was glad of that, for he was afraid Mrs. McKinley might be waiting for him; that this afternoon when he went out he, by some mis-calculation of time, was gone longer than he expected to be and found her 'sobbing like a child,' fearing that 'something might have happened to him.'"

Soon after, there was a short interlude of relief. In early July, the President bought their old home in Canton, paying $14,500 in cash for the little property. He thought the price was large, but both he and Ida were joyful over the purchase. The house was theirs to fix up as they pleased, and it belonged to them in a peculiarly intimate way because they knew exactly what they wanted to do. For three days—the happiest, McKinley told Long, that they had spent for a long time—the two of them were engrossed in planning how they would lay out $3,000, which was all they could afford, on repairing and improving the house. It was just as if they were newly married, McKinley said, and were going there on their honeymoon. Long was touched by the sentimental confidence, and by the way in which the President spoke of looking forward to the happy days when he and Mrs. McKinley could lead a quiet life by themselves, free from all these public pressures.

"I could easily see the extreme satisfaction it gave the President to get back his old place," Cortelyou wrote at this time. "He said, pathetically: 'We began our married life in that house; our children were born there, one of them died and was buried from there. Some of the tenderest memories of my life are centered there, and some of the saddest. I am as happy as a child to have it back. It's a fine old place.'

"He sat at the end of the Cabinet table, almost musing to himself, tapping on the table as he talked. As he touched first upon one feature and then another of the desirability of the purchase his eyes filled and his voice became soft and low. He was evidently much affected. Taking a telegram—it happened [to be] one from President Schurman of the Philippine Commission just received—he drew hastily an outline of certain improvements he would make; extending the hall, adding to this room, enlarging here and there, and he said, 'Now I shall have a home, what I have wanted for so long; a home I can go to. If I have a place like that I can get away any time, and could take you with all the help we need, and we could transact all the executive business there.'"

For three days, Mrs. McKinley's tears dried in the glow of her husband's emotion, in the tenderness of their memories and the eagerness of their plans. Then the decisions were made and the novelty of owning the house wore off, and the President's work reasserted its claim. A life of uninterrupted companionship was a dream of the future for the McKinleys. Once more, Ida sank deep into the wretchedness of the present. McKinley thought that a change of scene was the only remedy. He decided to take her to Bluff Point on Lake Champlain, where they had enjoyed their holiday two years before. Preparations for their departure were inconspicuously made. Besides Dr. Rixey and his wife, the party included only Cortelyou, a few members of the office staff, and the personal servants. The usual carload of correspondents was omitted, by request. It was made known, said the Washington *Evening Star*, that McKinley was to travel as a husband, not as "Mr. President."

McKinley did his best to create an atmosphere of domestic privacy at the Hotel Champlain, declining numerous invitations, and staying close to his wife, but he could not escape the pressures of his office. Telegrams flashed from Washington. Cabinet members and other officials arrived for consultation. Delegations, sightseeing parties, and press correspondents sprang up like weeds around Bluff Point. The hotel was filled to capacity. Tents were erected on the lawn. McKinley was finally induced to greet a few callers, speak a few words, hold a couple of receptions, and review one of the new volunteer regiments for the Philippines. Garret Hobart had insisted on joining the President, but he grew so exhausted by the excitement that McKinley cut short his stay, and took the sick man back to Long Branch.

The President was at once engulfed in an uproar that made Bluff Point seem peaceful by comparison. A week end at Long Branch brought public appearances and duties, including a speech to a large crowd at Ocean Grove, while the important address on the Philippines at Pittsburgh was attended by a swirl of ceremonies, a reception, and a banquet. The McKinleys headed for Ohio on a late train, dispatched from Pittsburgh with a deafening salute of cannon and received by East Liverpool with blazing red fire and huzzaing citizens. They spent two nights with the President's friend, Colonel Taylor, before going on through the cheering villages of Stark County to the tumultuous shouts of Canton, where they were to pay a short visit to Pina. As the train approached the outskirts of the city, McKinley sprang into action, bowing and waving to welcoming throngs on both sides of the track. "They seem glad to see you," someone in the car remarked. "They're no gladder than I am to see them," McKinley fervently replied. For the next two days, the Saxton house bulged with callers from town and country, and such large crowds gathered on the lawn that McKinley twice made a speech from the piazza.

Part of McKinley would always belong to the people. He responded with warm emotion to the affection of his neighbors, but Ida was scarcely seen. She had been badly upset by the firing of the cannon in the Pittsburgh station. She did not even go with her husband to see the little house for which they had made such happy plans. The remedy of a change of scene had been a total failure. The vacation, from start to finish, had merely demonstrated that quiet and privacy were luxuries that the President of the United States could not afford.

· 20 ·

WINTER OF DECISION

THE shadow in which McKinley walked had tightened his hold on faith. In the midst of heavy cares, a part of his mind had been occupied with a fresh assessment of his religious belief. A signed paper, dated May 26, 1899, was inserted in his letter book: "My belief embraces the Divinity of Christ and a recognition of Christianity as the mightiest factor in the world's civilization." The record, so formally preserved, suggests the solemnity with which the President had resolved to strip from his personal creed the last traces of dogma. The paper was purely private. It did not imply or contemplate an estrangement from Methodism. This man who did not like to be alone—wanting at night the comfort of another breathing presence, the sociability of small talk on awakening—had not the temperament of a solitary mystic. McKinley, in the truest sense, "belonged" to the Methodist communion, drawing inspiration from the connection and the fellowship.

McKinley needed sustainment, for the state of his wife's "nerves" had plunged him into an eddy of uncertainty. The fact was unguessed by the newspaper correspondents, but the President shrank from the thought of a second term. He talked longingly to several friends during the summer of his desire to return to private life. He spoke very positively on the subject after coming back to Washington in September. One Sunday evening while he was sitting with Cortelyou and Dawes in the Cabinet Room, he received a call from his former secretary, James Boyle, who was on leave from his post as consul at Liverpool. Boyle had been in Ohio, and had much to say about the political situation there. He was doing most of the talking, with Dawes occasionally chiming in; but, as the conversation led to the national field, McKinley entered the discussion and "expressed himself quite forcibly." The President did not seem at first to notice that both Dawes and Boyle were assuming as a matter of course that he would be renominated. He "suddenly straightened himself in his chair ... and, looking squarely at Boyle," delivered a statement which Cortelyou set down on paper the same night:

If what you gentlemen are saying implies that I am a candidate for renomination next year, I want to say to you that I would be the happiest man in America if I could go out of office in 1901, of course with the feeling that I had reasonably met the expectations of the people. I have had enough of it, Heaven knows! I have had all the honor there is in the place, and have had responsibilities enough to kill any man. You [turning to Mr. Dawes] have heard me say this repeatedly, as have you [turning to myself]. There is only one condition upon which I would listen to such a suggestion, and that is, a perfectly clear and imperative call of duty; and it is only upon that condition that I will listen to any suggestion of my renomination. I would be perfectly willing to have any good Republican, holding of course my views on the great questions that have come before the Administration—for I would not want anyone in this office hostile to them in the main—to occupy this place; and I repeat that when the time comes the question of my acquiescence will be based absolutely upon whether the call of duty appears to me clear and well defined.

The President's statement conveys emotion, but does not carry conviction. The yawning loophole in his protestations is "the call of duty." He is arguing so repetitiously because he is trying to deny the belief that it will be necessary to acquiesce. In spite of current worries over Dewey and the Ohio elections, it is overwhelmingly probable that he will be renominated. It is idle for him to talk of "any good Republican"—his successor would first have to get himself nominated and elected. And where could McKinley pretend that this good Republican was to be found? The eligible candidates were even fewer than at the last convention. Tom Reed had been ruined by his hostility to the expansionist trend, and had permanently retired from politics. The elderly favorite sons of 1896 had grown still older, with progressively weakening claims on popular enthusiasm. One new figure had emerged since the gathering at St. Louis, but Roosevelt's star would not rise to the zenith in the next year. He was regarded as radical and unsafe by Hanna and his associates. The men who would control the Republican National Convention were united on the President as the only hope of the party in 1900.

Republican success in 1900 meant a very great deal to McKinley. It meant the achievement of his cherished plans for an enlightened colonial policy, world-wide reciprocity agreements, and the extension of American commerce in every quarter of the globe. It meant the fulfillment of another aspiration, all-absorbing, though still imperfectly defined: the assertion of the influence of the United States for good—above all, for peace—among the nations. The President was exceedingly conscious of a turning point in American destiny. During the Sunday evening discussion, Boyle spoke of the respect and admiration that Americans now encountered abroad, and remarked that the Spanish war had placed the United States in a new light. "Yes," the President said. "From the time of the Mexican War up to 1898 we had lived by ourselves in a spirit of isolation." He had measured a period and marked its close, as he sat in the Sunday evening stillness of the Cabinet Room, seeing his administration as a milestone in the national history.

Almost as though he were thinking aloud, McKinley briefly rehearsed the events of the war and the peace making; "and one of the best things we ever did," he put in, with a surprising dry inflection, "was to insist upon taking the Philippines and not a coaling station or an island, for if we had done the latter we would have been the laughing stock of the world. And so it has come to pass," he continued, "that in a few short months we have become a world power; and I know, sitting here in this chair, with what added respect the nations of the world now deal with the United States, and it is vastly different from the conditions I found when I was inaugurated."

The President had been the humble instrument of a great design. By every motive of conviction and public obligation, he was impelled to carry it forward. Yet his mind, in the next months, remained divided. Even after the elections had announced his renomination, Cortelyou often heard him speak of his reluctance to go before the people again, as though it were a course that might somehow be avoided.

Mrs. McKinley made a spirited effort to recover during the autumn. She resumed her social appearances and, of course, accompanied her husband wherever he went; but her strength was unequal to the pace. She grew alarmingly weak and exhausted, and a rest cure, prescribed in November, did not bring improvement.

The President practiced an almost childish self-deception in shunning the Republican National Committee, ignoring the approach of its meeting, and refusing to express an opinion on the business before it. The Wisconsin committeeman Henry C. Payne was vigorously advocating a resolution to alter the basis of representation at Republican conventions. It had long been obvious that the existing basis, population, conferred undue power on the Solid South, and Payne regarded the condition as a scandal and a menace to party harmony. In conversation and by letter, he had presented his plan to the President, but he had not succeeded in eliciting an opinion.

The President, in fact, was intensely disapproving. Payne was moving to antagonize the South, and the cries of the wounded Republicans would echo throughout the section which McKinley had striven to conciliate. There was another, more practical objection. The implied recognition of disfranchisement was obnoxious to Negro leaders in the North, and might adversely affect the Republican vote in certain states the next year. This was the danger that at length forced the President to abandon his passive role. On December 15, the night before the National Committee met, Payne was invited to a conference in the Cabinet Room. Three politicians from Ohio were also present. Two of them, Major Dick and Governor-elect Nash, were opposed to Payne's resolution.

McKinley disposed of the difficulty with his usual suavity. Cortelyou thought that the discussion showed the President "at his best, as a clear-headed and conservative man." After Payne had had his say, McKinley spoke in favor of the fullest discussion and a fair hearing of both sides. He said that he would not allow his own personality to play a part; he was simply a member of the party. And then, very gently and reasonably, he raised the fatal question of expediency. "Was it wise, asked the President [as Cortelyou wrote it down], to introduce new questions unnecessarily at this time, when everything was running along so harmoniously? If the adoption of the resolution would lose a single State it should not be adopted." Payne stoutly defended his measure, but he was answered by Dick and Nash, shaking their heads over Ohio, Indiana, and Kentucky. The President finally came up with a suggestion. He thought the best thing to do was for Payne and Dick and Senator Hanna and a few other members of the committee to get together at once, that night, and come to some conclusion. He urged that it would be a great mistake to go into the meeting the next day and have a long and heated discussion. It should be settled ahead of time. McKinley, in short, was asking Payne to bury his reform and keep the funeral private.

Payne's courteous acquiescence evidently caused the President a twinge of compunction, for he said that it was important that Payne should not be hurt or embarrassed. McKinley's personal problem recurred, as he spoke. He protested that he would not allow himself to be put in the position of saying to the committee what they should do on this or any other proposition. He reminded them that he had not said a word to any of them about the time and place for the convention, and other such matters. At this point, Will Osborne entered the room. He had come back from London in poor health, and painfully changed in appearance. Mc-

Kinley turned to his cousin and called him to witness—as though it proved an important point—that, during a week's visit at the White House, he had not once heard the President mention these subjects. "He repeated his statement, made many times lately," Cortelyou wrote, "that nothing but the clear call of duty would induce him to go before the people again; he would be infinitely happy to retire at the end of this term. . . ." But perhaps his callers did not go away in much disquiet of mind. Before they left, McKinley paid "a handsome tribute" to the administration of Benjamin Harrison, and took occasion to remark that it would have been "criminal" if the Republican party had not renominated him. Though the President was not finished with his demurs, he was drawing closer to the admission that the call of duty would prove to be imperative.

McKinley showed the strain of worry over his wife. His temperament was hopeful and his trust in God was strong; but, like any man of nearly fifty-seven, he heard the toll of passing time, and thought of the uncertainty of human existence. Hobart had gone in November. McKinley had been in constant touch with the sickroom, and had often received an affectionate message from the dying man. "Please send this message with my love to the President," Hobart said to his wife shortly before the end. "Tell him for me that he has not only done well, but that he has done the best." Hobart's death was a painful loss, personal and official. Now Will Osborne was home, with a pitifully shrunken face. McKinley said "poor fellow," when he spoke of his cousin. The holiday season was always saddened by memories of little Katie, who had been born on Christmas Day. This year, McKinley seemed more than usually solemn, as the wreaths were hung in the hushed and unfrequented mansion. "The President said one should feel *holy* at this season," Cortelyou wrote; "that the time should be one of resolution and reflection; the spirit of self-sacrifice should dominate everything."

"I don't know what in the world to give Mrs. McKinley for Christmas," the President exclaimed one evening. "She has about everything she needs." She loved diamonds, as the New York jewelers, J. Dreicer and Son, had been gratified to discover. There had been two diamond rings for her fifty-second birthday in June, two diamond bracelets the preceding Christmas, a pair of diamond side-combs the year before that. She had taken pleasure in the costly presents, but this year she had lost interest. She had asked her husband not to give her anything expensive, and he was at a loss to know what to get. He seemed to be thinking very deeply on the subject. He brought it up again while he was working with Cortelyou. It was still on his mind when he went to bed. As he reluctantly moved toward the admission of his impending renomination, the President was perplexed by a personal problem. He had given his wife everything she needed—everything but the undivided attention that she craved, everything but the quiet and privacy which might preserve her reason and prolong her life.

But the steward Sinclair settled the question of Christmas. He went to Galt's jewelry store and brought back a beautiful vase and—a still more inspired selection—an exquisite little blue picture frame, set with jewels. The President put Katie's photograph in the frame, and Mrs. McKinley was "delighted" with the pretty enshrinement of their sorrow.

The end of seclusion was foretold by the passing of florists and workmen, the ubiquitous presence of Colonel Bingham, and the stacks of cloak boxes in the hall. On the morning of January 1, 1900, the corridors and parlors were densely filled with dignitaries waiting in the order of their progress; while on the snowy street outside, a long line of handshakers inched patiently toward the sawdust-covered path. The Marine Band played "Hail to the Chief," and the President appeared on the stairway with—marvel of marvels—Mrs. McKinley on his arm. Frail but undefeated, she made her way through the throng, and took her place in the blue chair in the East Room.

Mrs. McKinley was able to bow and smile for only an hour—the President took her upstairs himself—but Cortelyou thought that she stood the reception well and seemed improved in the evening.

The reception had not been an entirely happy affair. It had witnessed the climax of a one-sided feud which had arisen between the naval officers and the Executive Mansion, in spite of the President's endeavors to keep things running smoothly. There was something very pathetic in the situation of the busy, troubled Executive, striving singlehanded to maintain an atmosphere of gracious hospitality at the mansion. Yet the basic fault was McKinley's own. He could have avoided much embarrassment to others and irritation to himself if Cortelyou had possessed the authority of Secretary. As matters stood, Cortelyou kept clear of the field which Addison Porter had marked for his own. During Porter's increasingly frequent absences, Bingham operated independently, under the President.

In a practical way, Bingham's arrangements deserved high praise—the McKinley's card receptions were called the most comfortable and seemly that the mansion had known for more than a generation—but his very virtues created antagonism. He ran the mansion with parade-ground precision. He was in the habit of announcing his plans and rulings in peremptory paragraphs, like a series of military commands, in the society column of *The Evening Star*. People were quick to sense the snobbishness that lay beneath his spit-and-polish efficiency. Bingham, however, was also in trouble with the snobs. The Washington socialites regarded him as an iconoclast, and he was loathed by the naval officers.

Bingham was not to blame for the distrust which the Navy instinctively felt for the Army, but for a blunder which had inflamed a prejudice into a swollen grievance. The matter dated from the McKinley's first season, when Bingham had selected his two aides, traditionally representing the two branches of the service. There had been no objection to the first assistant, Lieutenant Gilmore, a correct artillery officer, who had learned his duties at the Cleveland receptions. The fatal error was the choice of the Navy representative. Captain Charles L. McCawley was an admirable young man, witty and well bred. It was to be proved at Guantánamo Bay that he was also brave. The trouble was that he did not belong to the Navy proper. He was a captain of Marines.

Navy circles buzzed with the news that officers of the line had been passed over at the Executive Mansion. The officers themselves felt the insult keenly. There was possibly no other group in Washington to whom the dividing-up of the reception lists was so grossly suspect, or who so jealously scrutinized the invitations for evidences of discrimination. It was openly hinted that White House hospitality was governed by the coarsest motives—the social standing of an officer or the amount of his wife's fortune. Feeling was too bitter to admit the possibility of a respectable incentive, or even to make allowance for the personal acquaintance of the President and his wife. The Navy Department was boiling over with resentment, and at last Crowninshield came to the Secretary "with a long face," and recited the grievances. John D. Long got the President's consent to augment the introducing party by a naval officer. The assignment was "rather snobbishly" declined by two young lieutenants. A dependable ensign was finally detailed to the obnoxious duty, but his ordeal was soon cut short by the *Maine* disaster. In the next months, the naval officers had something besides social trivia to occupy their minds; but Bingham had created a grudge which strongly survived the war, and led to frigid hostility in the winter of 1900.

The exacerbating influence in that season was Admiral Dewey's residence in Washington. The victories at sea had so inflated the arrogance of the naval officers that they expected the Executive Mansion to recognize Dewey's presence by abolishing the rule of Army precedence on occasions of state. The Admiral himself grew worried that he might have to play second fiddle to General Miles. Egged on, it was said, by his ambitious wife, he determined to arrange the matter. Shortly before New Year's, he had waited on the Secretary of War to discuss the question of his preceding the Army at the reception. But Elihu Root did not acknowledge the existence of a question. He simply informed Dewey that the War Department ranked the Navy, and would consequently take precedence. On New Year's Day, General Miles and the Army officers came after Congress, as usual, with Dewey and his contingent in their rear.

Mrs. Dewey, for her part, contrived to bring off a clever little stratagem, and precede all the other ladies present. While the diplomats were passing through the Blue Room, she went to Secretary Long "with many pleasant words," and asked him as a special favor to take her down the line, since she was obliged to leave early with the Admiral. John Hay overheard these advances, saw what was afoot, and mischievously urged Mrs. Dewey on. Thus encouraged, the guileless Secretary of the Navy escorted the Admiral's bride past the receiving party in the wake of the last diplomat. Long was not enlightened until later in the day, when he met Hay again at the Hitchcocks'. "He said the wife of the Major General Commanding and the other military ladies were quite aggrieved," Long wrote, "and intimated it was all a shrewd movement of Mrs. Dewey's to get ahead of the Army. . . ."

The tale of Dewey's rebuff had enlivened the gossip of Washington. The President, as Cortelyou saw, had been "rather amused at Admiral Dewey's anxiety as to his position. . . ." But there were no smiles on the frozen faces of the officers who stalked down the line behind Miles and the Army. The affront sealed the estrangement which Bingham had initiated. McKinley attempted conciliation by directing that every Navy officer in Washington should receive a special invitation to the Army and Navy reception; but few deigned to accept. Bingham was informed of the comment of one commander, that the Navy was no longer recognized or wanted around the White House, and he saw no use in its taking the trouble to go.

Numerically, at any rate, the huffy officers were not missed in the season of 1900. More than 3,000 cards had been sent out for the Army and Navy reception, and three ladies fainted in the crush. Secretary Porter, under pressure, had "rather let down the bars." He had returned from an extended sick leave to find ruin overtaking the laboriously partitioned lists. The restrictions were being swept away like flimsy dikes in floodtime. Congress poured through the breach, invited all four evenings. The uninvited, too, thronged the parlors in their frumpy street clothes, increasing the congestion and lowering the tone. Porter and Bingham were helpless. They could not keep down the attendance without the support of the President, and that had obviously been lost.

McKinley had all but abandoned a reform he had gladly endorsed. To "let down the bars" was the answer to the persistent accusation of exclusiveness at the White House. Irritation with his two social arbiters had been building in the President's breast. He was sick of etiquette, and surfeited with fashion. His temper had been rubbed raw by complaints. He was tired of Addison Porter's ineptitude, and impatient to get rid of him; but he still could not ask him to resign. McKinley would probably not have expressed his annoyance at all, if in January he had not been given extraordinary provocation.

Porter and Bingham were defeated in their contest with the uninvited guests, but, like veteran troops, they prepared to attack from a new position. They felt that some ground might be retrieved if the gatecrashers were suitably garbed. In preparing the instructions for the second card reception, they included a few suggestions designed to shame the intruders into dressing themselves up—or perhaps into staying away, if they did not possess the proper garments. The following paragraphs formed part of the bulletin which was sent from the White House to the Washington *Evening Star*:

It may seem unnecessary information to those acquainted with the customs which are ordinarily followed to state that women should not wear bonnets at evening receptions at the White House. While this practice has grown less and less frequent of late years, there are always a few who transgress against the law of evening dress which implies an unbonnetted head. . . . A violation of this rule only subjects the offender to unnecessary observation and criticism.

Precisely the same thing applies to men who do not follow the accepted fashions of dress and appear in other than evening clothes. Every offender in this regard helps to detract from the fitness and harmony, to say nothing of the brilliancy of the most important of all our social functions—a presidential levee. . . . Notables or those who are apt to reach that class never run any risk by violations of accepted customs in dress or anything else.

The President's eye fell on these paragraphs as he glanced over the social notes in the *Star* one January evening. He uttered a cry, "I can stand anything around me but a fool." He was "incensed and disgusted" with the fatuous, sneering publication—clearly identified by its context as having emanated from the mansion—and spoke severely on the subject of "snobbery." "It would seem as though I might be relieved of such embarrassments with all my other perplexities," McKinley fumed. "Some people are always putting their foot in it. It would be well and we would get on better if they had something else to do than attending to social functions."

McKinley then wrote out a statement of his own. It declared that the President did not prescribe what guests should wear when invited to the White House, nor had he authorized anyone to do so for him; and that he was always glad to see them in whatever apparel might be most con venient and comfortable. He appended his signature, and paused. He asked if Porter was in his office, but the Secretary had left. McKinley decided to put the paper in his desk, and call Porter and Bingham in next morn ing. "I'll give some one a hauling over for this," he promised.

The President's statement was never sent to the *Star*, but the "hauling over" must have been effective. The reign of fashion terminated at the White House, and its dictates were heard of no more. Addison Porter's failing health compelled him to retire in the spring. A new era of efficiency dawned in the east wing, and Bingham performed his duties with a chastened spirit, as George B. Cortelyou at last assumed the authority of Secretary to the President.

The state dinners were another story. The many contretemps that centered around them were largely the result of the peculiar conditions of Washington society and the President's own household. For one thing, an apparently constant surplus of male guests made it necessary to seat some of them between two members of their own sex, incurring their displeasure and, not infrequently, their remonstrance. Dread of their wrath hung gloomily over the east wing. Extra ladies were eagerly seized upon and distributed, like choice tidbits, among the more prominent stags, and so nice were the decisions that they were sometimes carried to the State Department. But, in a society governed by a strict observance of precedence, there was a still more vital problem than that of "the gentlemen who go out alone." The diagram of the White House table was bedeviled by puzzles of protocol. The death of the Vice-President increased the confusion. At the first state dinner of 1900, the honors went to the presiding officer of the Senate, William P. Frye of Maine. This brought a heated protest from the new Speaker of the House, General David B. Henderson of Iowa, who claimed to rank a mere Vice-President pro tem. Opinion was divided, with a third faction taking up the cudgels for Secretary Hay. It was not, however, suggested that Hay himself was aggrieved. He was having troubles enough as a substitute for the hostess at the dinners.

The prime consideration at table was the degree of proximity to the President and his wife, who were customarily seated across from each other at the center of the board, with the ranking guests beside them. The places progressively diminished in importance until they reached the young aides and attachés at either end. The McKinleys had badly upset this scheme by sitting together. Two places of honor were cancelled at one swoop, and it was possible to put only the principal guest in the usual position on the right of the hostess. A new scheme had been devised in the first season.

The Secretary of State occupied the vacated chair across from the President, and the first three ranking ladies were assigned in order to the President's left and the right and left of the Secretary. The queer arrangement was not challenged by Americans, but it was extremely unsatisfactory to the European diplomats and their wives, who took a condesending view of the Secretary of State as an appointed official. The ill-feeling had been intensely aggravated in the second season by the *affaire* Cassini.

Count Arthur Cassini, the Russian ambassador, had long served as minister to China, and was a vigorous proponent of Russian designs on the territory and trade of that empire. Secretary Hay's policy of the Open Door was as detestable to him as the whiff of pro-Japanese sentiment which his nostrils detected at the State Department. His mission in Washington was to sow distrust of England and intrigue against the extension of American influence in the Orient. An elderly aristocrat, monocled and pomaded, Cassini cut a fine figure in the parlors, but his private character made him an odd choice for a capital strictly ruled by propriety. He was a notorious gambler and libertine, he had been twice divorced, and the circumstances of his domestic life were irregular in the extreme. His family consisted of a sixteen-year-old daughter, Marguerite, who was represented to be his niece, and her mother, a former singer and actress, who posed as the girl's governess. Marguerite later explained that a legal marriage had taken place, but was not acknowledged because her father feared the ruin of his career if it should become known at St. Petersburg that he had contracted a union unsuited to his rank. Cassini, however, had no intention of keeping Marguerite in the background. It was soon made known that she would act as his hostess, with the standing and privileges of an ambassadress.

The young unmarried hostess was not entirely strange to Washington society. Flora Wilson presided with dignity over the household of the Secretary of Agriculture, and was accepted as her father's companion at all official functions. Helen Long usually substituted for her stepmother, who suffered from a nervous illness and seldom came to the capital, and other daughters of Cabinet members often assisted their fathers. Yet Cassini's motive is obscure. Himself a high-tempered stickler for protocol, he must have known that the diplomatic wives rejected the claim of rank for an unmarried girl. Marguerite was absurdly young, and a mere "niece," at that. Nevertheless, Cassini persisted, and his wishes were observed by Colonel Bingham in seating the diplomatic dinner of 1899. The wife of Ambassador Pauncefote, the dean of the diplomatic corps, had an unassailable title to the place on the President's left, the best that was to be had, but Miss Cassini got the right of the Secretary of State, taking precedence over all the other ladies present. There was no balm for outraged feelings in the charming appearance of the minx herself: a dressed-up child in a pearl dog collar, with lustrous dark-red curls brushed high above a face as round and pretty and inscrutable as that of a little cat. The Baroness von Hengelmüller of Austria was enraged by the seating at the White House. Lady Pauncefote herself was said to be seriously vexed. The portly German ambassador, Dr. von Holleben, had been doubly injured—by Miss Cassini's place and by his own place next to her.

The fracas did not subside with the end of the 1899 season. It had blown up the whole smoldering question of the prominence given to the Secretary of State. The objections extended to his entire side of the table. The places opposite the McKinleys had come to be regarded by the ambassadors as a sort of no man's land, to which it was a degradation to be assigned. The matter was carried over Bingham's head to the State Department. Secretary Hay gravely entertained the protests, and personally supervised the arrangement of the diplomatic dinner of 1900. The method was, as Bingham remarked, to a certain extent unusual. All the ambassadors and their wives were squeezed together on the McKinleys' side, while the Secretary of State was flanked by the envoys of lesser kingdoms and South American republics. Hay also demoted the unmarried girls, with the exception of Miss Wilson. The agitating agent, Miss Cassini, was not present—she had conveniently fallen ill—but Baroness von Hengelmüller met a blow from another quarter. The Secretary of State had apparently failed to consider the fate of the ill-starred Hapsburg, Maximilian. He partnered the wife of the Austrian minister with the Mexican ambassador, and she flatly refused to go out with him.

Except for this lapse, Hay's handling of the diplomatic crisis was admirable. The European representatives were fully reconciled with the White House. The next year, to be sure, brought a passing flare-up of anxiety about Count Cassini's intentions. He had decided to attempt to regularize his daughter's position; and, during a visit to St. Petersburg, he braved the displeasure of the Czar, and made a full confession. It was indulgently received, and Marguerite returned to Washington as his acknowledged daughter, created Countess by imperial ukase. Apprehension that Cassini might be maneuvering for a fresh assault on the White House dinner table sent Baron von Hengelmüller flying to Colonel Bingham, but Marguerite did not repeat the triumph of two years earlier. At the diplomatic dinner of 1901, the little Countess found her place on the inferior side of the board, between the ministers of Portugal and China.

Mrs. McKinley was not concerned with the worries that eddied around her in her third social season. Untouched even by the troubles she occasioned, she performed her prescribed routine: was helped in, bowed, smiled, fainted, was helped out. The President repeatedly employed the device of the stag dinner to spare her, but, whenever wives were included, Mrs. McKinley was present. The effort was often hard. She never regained the comparative strength and serenity that she had known in 1898, but she did not again meet the world with anger, nor retreat from it into depression. Some anguish in her breast was lulled, and, between sieges of blinding headache, she was content to put on her sumptuous dresses, and share her husband with the crowd. The physical discomfort of the White House functions did not affect her. She was in uncommonly good form on the night of the diplomatic dinner of 1900, when something went amiss with the furnace and the guests wilted in sickening heat. She appeared to take pleasure in the card receptions, though the house was filled to suffocation, and the fashionable length of the ladies' trains slowed the line to a snail's pace. Her enjoyment was particularly noticeable at the Army and Navy reception, the one at which three ladies fainted.

The call of duty had whistled imperatively in the President's ears, and Mrs. McKinley was ready for another four years in the White House. There was courage and perhaps some selflessness, too, in her cheerful postponement of a private life. She seemed brushed with a new grace as she sat beside her Dearest, holding her delicate bouquets—white rosebuds with the white moire antique gown; lilies of the valley with the black velvet, cascading with falls of lace. Her eyes were bright with interest, and she chatted animatedly with her acquaintance. Her drawn face sometimes attracted admiring glances. A dress of Russian lace over pink taffeta was pronounced extremely becoming. She always had a sweet smile for a child, and it was often possible to see, in a fleeting expression of gaiety or kindness, how very pretty she had been.

Mrs. McKinley lurks in the background of history, screened by the veil of her silence. Not many traces of her spoken words survive. There are no letters at all. There is only a little book in which, surprisingly, she made a few entries in 1901. "I am feeling very miserable," one notation ran, "head ache most of the time, I will go out with my Dearest and enjoy it." Here is surely more than willful vanity and jealous attachment. The scratchy characters, formed by a shaking hand, speak of a will to disdain self-pity. For more than a quarter of a century, Mrs. McKinley had clung tenaciously to her husband's love. In the end, perhaps, she learned to yield as well as take, giving thought for his happiness and fulfillment, and granting a loving acceptance to the necessity of his heart, which belonged in part to the people.

· 21 ·

THE REPUBLICAN LAWMAKERS

EARLY in 1900, a boyish-looking man, with a pale, tense, pugnacious face, arose in the Senate Chamber and with practiced art rolled out the cadences of a carefully prepared address on the Philippines. Albert J. Beveridge of Indiana was a stranger on Capitol Hill, but he was well known as the apostle of an extreme imperialism, who for nearly two years had been holding to the nation's lips a brimming cup of power and riches, laced with the heady doctrine of a master race. Thirty-seven years old and a complete novice in politics, he had been elected to the Senate in the postwar Republican sweep of the Middle West, and had taken his seat at the recent opening of the first session of the Fifty-sixth Congress. He was speaking, this January day, on behalf of his joint resolution declaring that the Philippines were territory belonging to the United States, and would be retained as such.

Although Beveridge was a newcomer, he could assert some claim to be heard. He was the only member of Congress who had visited the Philippines. His trip had awakened a general interest, stimulated into strong curiosity by the reticence he had preserved since his return, and by the knowledge that he had been in close conference with the President. He had a passionate conviction, a melodious voice, and a little red notebook, and the floor and galleries of the Senate were packed for his maiden speech.

Beveridge did not linger over the unsettled question of constitutional power. In his fervid opening, he drove straight to the illimitable markets of China. His keynote was American dominance of world trade, and his favorite adverb was "forever." Most future wars, he said, would be conflicts for commerce. The Pacific was "our ocean." The power that ruled the

Pacific was the power that ruled the world. To surrender the commercial throne of Manila would be treason to American supremacy. Besides, the Philippines must be held because they were so valuable themselves. No man on the spot could fail to see that if the United States retired, the archipelago would fall to England, Germany, Russia, or Japan. Should we abandon our great base in the Pacific? Beveridge asked, and had the answer ready. "That man little knows the common people of the Republic, little understands the instincts of our race, who thinks we will not hold it fast and hold it forever. . . ."

There was, incidentally, the matter of subduing the rebellion. The fighting must end in the absolutely final defeat of the enemy. Then definite plans of government would at once be needed, and Beveridge had plenty of suggestions; but there should be no question of treating with the insurgents. Kindness to them had been our mistake. Every effort of the civil commissioners had only delayed peace, while the chief factor in prolonging the war had been the Philippine sympathizers (i.e., Democrats) at home. In sorrow rather than anger, Beveridge told these Americans that the blood of our wounded boys was on their hands, and the flood of all the years could never wash that stain away.

A soaring edifice of rhetoric rested on the hard, concrete facts that Beveridge had gathered on his trip. He could report on the war, for, unlike General Otis and the President's civil commissioners, he had gone to the front and seen action with Lawton and MacArthur. He could generalize on conditions in the archipelago, for he had visited some of the southern islands, as well as Luzon, and he had talked with European residents and upper-class natives everywhere that he went. He read excerpts from his notes about the copious resources of the Philippines, the salubrity of their climate, and the political incapacity of their inhabitants. The masses, Beveridge could positively state, were stupid and incurably indolent. It would be better to abandon "this combined garden and Gibraltar of the Pacific" than to apply any academic arguments of self-government to these children. "What alchemy," the speaker cried, "will change the oriental quality of their blood and set the self-governing currents of the American pouring through their Malay veins?" The question was deeper than party politics, deeper even than any question of constitutional power. It was elemental. It was racial. God had made the English-speaking and Teutonic peoples adepts in government, that they might administer it among savage and senile people. God had marked America as His chosen nation to lead in the regeneration of the world.

In the name of peace, Beveridge bade the Senate adopt his resolution, and give the deluded children of the Philippines the final word of Con-

gress. Two hours of oratory had not fatigued his audience. His conclusion—
"How dare we delay when our soldiers' blood is flowing?"—brought thundering applause from the galleries. Senator Frye, the presiding officer, was
slow in checking the demonstration. The floor was in confusion. Pitchfork
Ben Tillman of South Carolina bounded to the Republican orator's desk,
and many others were on their feet, crowding forward with outstretched
hands. Charles Dawes, an admiring friend, looked down with emotion on
"a great scene and a great triumph for Albert." He had heard the whole
oration twice before, and run through the revised portions only that morning, but he was spellbound by the "power and matchless grace" of the
Senator's delivery. Correspondents dashed from the press gallery with
stories to empurple the front pages of the newspapers and set off a shower
of star-spangled editorials. The voice of American youth had sounded, and
its accents arrested attention. For Beveridge knew the facts. He had been
in the Philippines.

Beveridge had been in the Philippines, but his observations, like those of
many travelers, had merely confirmed the beliefs with which he had started
out. His speech was essentially the same speech that he had been making
since the spring of 1898. With a shrewd perception of the value of his little
red notebook, an Indianapolis lawyer had stepped on the stage of the
Senate to sound the bugles of imperialism in the dawn of the presidential
year.

Dawes believed that Beveridge made no mistakes in the eyes of the
people, but the eyes of the Senate were undeniably another matter. Beveridge was far from popular with the members of the gentlemen's club he
had lately joined. He had arrived, as Cabot Lodge icily remarked, "with a
very imperfect idea of the rights of seniority in the Senate, and with a
large idea of what he ought to have." He had wanted to get on the Foreign
Relations Committee, though there was only one vacancy and it was the
most coveted of all assignments, and he had also aspired to the chairmanship of the new Committee on the Philippines, which was expected to
exert an important influence on policy. His mind was alight with a double
conviction, that the Fifty-sixth Congress should at once make a declaration
for the permanent retention of the Philippines, and that Beveridge was
the man to see that it was done.

Beveridge was ignorant not only of the traditions and courtesies of the
Senate, but of the whole intricate etiquette of political life. He was a parvenu, elected by the Indiana legislature in defiance of the regular Republican organization, including ex-President Harrison and the senior United
States senator, Charles Fairbanks. He had pushed himself forward at home

and, with crass naïveté, he supposed that push was the method to use in Washington. While he was in the Philippines, making ready for his duties, his devoted friend, George W. Perkins of the New York Life Insurance Company, had worked tirelessly on the committee assignments. Charles Dawes was another ardent partisan, eager to serve Beveridge in any way he could. Theodore Roosevelt was taken into camp at first meeting, just after Beveridge returned from the Pacific. He warmly recommended the congenial imperialist to Cabot Lodge, and wrote again to suggest him for the vacancy on the Foreign Relations Committee. It must have been a glittering intelligence that seduced these active, keen young men, and distracted them from the boredom inseparable from an intensely egoistic personality. Various in forensic style, Beveridge was wont to dwell in private on a single favorite theme, his own tremendous abilities and the great career in store for him. The Republican leaders, however, were not impressed by the genius of the much-publicized rookie, who was lobbying like a sugar-beet farmer to promote his own interests. Many stories were flying around, including a report that certain "eulogistic matter" about Beveridge had actually been sent out by the Senator himself. Perhaps the keenest irritation was not felt by the all-powerful veterans of the upper chamber, but by their seconds in command who had recently risen to leadership and did not yet take for granted the great prizes of authority. Cabot Lodge had not been on Foreign Relations very long himself. During his first four years in the Senate, he had not been on any committee that ever met. He sent a testy reply to Roosevelt's recommendation of Beveridge.

Beveridge, as he believed, had a trump card to play—his friendship with the President. Eager for news from the Philippines, McKinley had sent for the traveler, and listened with flattering attention to his firsthand impressions of the islands—which, incidentally, confirmed much of the gross misinformation supplied in previous reports to Washington. Beveridge felt so secure in this new relationship that it had taken the combined efforts of Dawes and Gage to dissuade him from submitting his speech to the President before the session opened. He haunted the White House in early December, soliciting McKinley's influence for his committee assignments, and perplexing Mr. Cortelyou by his unrealistic view of his prospects. One day, when Beveridge had sent in several notes to the President, Cortelyou urged the aspirant "not to get his hopes too high, as he might be disappointed." The sensible warning was needed, though Beveridge fared very well for a new senator. The place on Foreign Relations went to Wolcott of Colorado. Beveridge was made a member of the Committee on the Philippines, but the chairmanship was "forced" on Lodge.

The disappointing outcome did not basically alter Beveridge's program.

While Lodge was tentatively laying his own plans—"I have now got the Philippines in my especial charge," he importantly wrote Roosevelt— Beveridge was pressing to introduce his resolution. Much to his frustration, the opportunity did not come until after the Christmas recess. For the first time, he then finally showed the resolution to Lodge and two of the weightiest men on the Philippine Committee, Cushman K. Davis and Allison. None of them was precisely enthusiastic, and Lodge seemed downright indifferent. He remarked, in effect, that "he really was somewhat at sea as to just what should be done and just what form a resolution should take." Appealing to Cortelyou at the eleventh hour, Beveridge was advised to consult a number of other senators, including his colleague, Fairbanks, and the rest of the Republicans on the Philippine Committee. In the short time that was left, Beveridge scurried around to the men whom Cortelyou had named, and obtained some offhand or conditional approval from all of them but Hale of Maine.

The President was always well informed, and the new Senator's conduct had given him some concern. He had told Dawes of his fears that Beveridge "was hurting his standing here by his unwise methods of securing recognition." McKinley was not dazzled by Beveridge's cleverness—he found him, on the contrary, "sometimes tiresome"—but there was great kindness in his feeling, nevertheless. He thought that Beveridge was a manly young fellow, honest and courageous, and feared to see him rashly provoking the Senate. After the Philippine resolution was introduced, the President told Cortelyou he was most sincerely hoping that Beveridge would make a brilliant speech. "The President said he wished him [Beveridge] well and hoped for his triumph," Cortelyou again noted. "He hoped he would make a great speech and that he would not be disappointed."

Beveridge had his triumph, but the President's mind was not entirely relieved. It was immediately apparent that Beveridge's great speech on the Philippines had increased the number of his critics in the Senate.

Senator Hoar had been profoundly shocked by the address. While the air of the Senate still quivered with its impassioned peroration, Hoar had risen to welcome to the public service the new Senator's enthusiasm, his patriotism, and his "silver speech." Yet Hoar had listened in vain for certain words—Right, Justice, Duty, Freedom. He could think of but one occurrence, as this brave young republic of ours listened to what Beveridge had to say; and Hoar recited the passage of Scripture beginning, "Then the devil taketh Him up into an exceeding high mountain," and ending, "Get thee behind me, Satan." He forbore to labor the comparison between his honorable friend and the tempter, but he left no doubt that, in emulation

479

of the Saviour, he had the advantage of Beveridge.

The moderate expansionists squirmed under Hoar's rebuke. They were conscious that a candidly avowed materialism snatched the moral cushion from their position. Wolcott of Colorado, who thought it a gloomy duty to hold the Philippines, spoke for many of his associates in repudiating the sordid idea of rich conquest. He also confessed his shrinking at the references to God and His dealings personal with nations, and commented skeptically on the role of America as his chosen people. The doctrine of racial superiority was, of course, particularly repugnant to all old-line Republicans who cherished the ideals on which the party had been founded.

Beveridge was freely castigated outside the Senate, and some of the comment suggested a spiteful motive. Secretary Hitchcock told McKinley that the criticism had been instigated by another new senator, Chauncey M. Depew, formerly president and currently chairman of the board of the New York Central Railroad. For one thing, Depew had stated at an evening reception that "the fundamental objection" to Beveridge's speech "was that he had pretended to speak for the administration." By making this allegation in front of a member of the Cabinet, Depew had ensured that his words would reach the President. He was not yet perfectly sure of his own welcome at the White House. Three years earlier, when he was avidly seeking the ambassadorship to Great Britain, he had been so tactless as to make a speech containing a patronizing allusion to the simplicity of McKinley's house in Canton. The story had naturally traveled to Canton at lightning speed, and Depew believed that his "desperate break" had lost him the ambassadorship and the good opinion of the President.

The attempt to undermine Beveridge was conceived in guile. The President, as everyone understood, was not in complete agreement with his restless political bedfellows, the extreme imperialists. Conservative expansionists trusted McKinley to protect the interests of the Philippine inhabitants—to develop the liberal plans of which he had often spoken, but of which Beveridge had said little. The President was stung into an emphatic denial by the statement that Beveridge had pretended to speak for the administration. He told Hitchcock it was not so, Senator Beveridge had done nothing of the sort.

Depew's enmity to his eloquent associate did not go unnoted, or want a ready explanation. He had been a Commencement Day orator at Yale before Beveridge was born. He was a celebrated wit and raconteur, whose bald pate and big, bleak, canny face had been gracing the most distinguished banquet tables for more than a generation. Yet his maiden speech in the Senate, a eulogy of Hobart, had been barely noticed by the press. Depew had been steeled to meet some vulgar prejudice against railroad magnates in Washington, but a far more unlikely thing had happened. His polished fluency had been outshone by the "silver speech" of an upstart from Indiana.

A little later, Depew himself took the Philippines as his topic on the Senate floor. These questions of the nation's right to acquire and govern territories were purely academic, he said. They reminded him of the gatherings every year in London to protest against the beheading of Charles I. Depew elaborated his point with apt citation and nice analysis. It was an accomplished discourse, and about it there was the faintest aroma of brandy and cigars. Depew did not excite. He could scarcely be said, in any vital sense, to interest. The habit of a lifetime had made him an aid to digestion. He had donned the toga of an elder statesman, but his importance in Washington was largely derivative. He was deferentially treated on Capitol Hill because he was a senator from the Empire State and the familiar of his colleague Tom Platt.

Beveridge, with ardent faith, was launched upon the river of the times, but he had not sounded the deepest currents of Republican policy. In his headlong impatience to present his resolution, he had failed to notice that the leaders of the Senate were avoiding ineffectual declarations on the future of the Philippines.

The Fifty-sixth Congress had assembled in a spirit of tranquillity. For the first time since 1883, the Republicans were in control of every branch of the government, and they rejoiced in an exceptional unity. The President's ascendancy lay like a quiet hand on the legislative program. His administration stood in the prestige of a dramatically expanding foreign trade, and the whole country was applauding Secretary Hay's negotiations for the Open Door in China. Men who had campaigned in the confusion of the postwar months took their seats in an atmosphere of acquiescence and almost languid calm.

The salient difference in the House was in the Speaker's chair. Tom Reed was gone, with his cankered heart and his loathing of White House policy, and his gavel was wielded by a Union veteran, Henderson of Iowa, a stout, one-legged, politically tractable old Scot. On the rostrum of the Senate, Frye of Maine replaced the lamented Hobart, but the significant evidences of change were on the floor. The seating had been drastically altered to accommodate the Republicans, who had overflowed their own side to plant a strong colony on the extreme left of the opposition. Many strange faces among them proclaimed, no less than the shrunken and surrounded forces of the Democrats, the dissolution of the silver bloc. A declaration for the gold standard was at last certain to pass the upper chamber, and the Republicans were also free to take action on the President's policy in the new possessions. In conformity with his advice, legislation for the Philippines was to be postponed, but Congress would promptly prepare to establish a temporary civil government in Porto Rico, with free trade between the islands and the United States, and to pass the still pending Cullom Bill, providing a territorial government for Hawaii.

The minority lost no time in taking its revenge. Lacking a constructive program and impotent to prevent legislation on which the majority united, the Democratic leaders resorted to opposition in its meanest form, seeking by every device to divide and delay the Republicans, and goad them into premature and controversial declarations. The constitutional question was posed in a flock of resolutions adverse to the President's policy, and McKinley and his advisers were pilloried for mishandling the Philippine situation and suppressing the facts from the public. The charge of censorship was spitefully pressed by Pettigrew of South Dakota, a former Republican who had broken with the party over silver in 1896. Majority leaders would have shut off his demagogic tirades, but their purpose was defeated soon after the Christmas recess when Hoar came to Pettigrew's support, and himself cantankerously demanded that all relevant papers be submitted to the scrutiny of the Senate. Administration senators were insidiously drawn into defending the President; and in a furious, intermittent debate the opposition repeatedly proved successful in diverting the Republicans from their heavy schedule of legislation and emphasizing their differing opinions on the subject of expansion.

This tendency was already apparent when Beveridge was making ready to introduce his resolution. Lodge's negative attitude was not purely a matter of pique. He was genuinely doubtful of the wisdom of a declaration which was, in any case, futile to control the future action of Congress. But Lodge was not quite truthful in saying that he was "at sea" about the form that a resolution should take. His considered opinion was accurately set forth, only two days after Beveridge made his speech, in a bill introduced by Spooner of Wisconsin. It did not refer to the ownership of the Philippines or the intentions of the United States respecting them, but simply provided that, after the end of the insurrection and pending action by Congress, the President should be endowed with all military, civil, and judicial powers necessary to govern the islands. The Spooner Bill was the text of the cogent and scholarly address in which, a few weeks later, the chairman of the Committee on the Philippines presented his views to the Senate.

The proposal to clothe the President with broad legislative powers was outrageous to the Democrats. Indeed, it seemed dangerously radical to many Republican senators. Yet its source was a guaranty that it had been sagaciously framed—it was actually modeled on the act by which Congress had authorized Jefferson to govern Louisiana—and it was, moreover, an indication of government policy on the very highest level. Homely little Spooner, with his long, untidy hair, his bulging brow, and his large eyes squinting behind pince-nez, was called the most brilliant member of the upper chamber. His legal attainments were rivaled only by the superbly able Orville Platt of Connecticut. His versatility was unique and his influence with his colleagues, uncontested. It was well known in Washington that he was also a valued adviser of the President. With the private reservation "too argumentative," McKinley held the oracle of the Senate in the greatest respect, and few weeks passed in which Spooner was not called into consultation at the White House.

The Spooner Bill was a logical step toward the civil government of the Philippines under Executive direction. Schurman had refused to return to the islands; and, as the President moved to replace him, he was contemplating a much bolder assumption of authority than his annual message had implied. His commissioners were to begin "building up from the bottom" in the areas under American control; but they were also to adopt a plan of central government and, as soon as was feasible, put it into operation at Manila, themselves assuming the direction, with their head as civil governor. The war powers of the Executive were plainly insufficient for the tremendous undertaking McKinley had in view.

For the head of the new commission, the President wanted a man of unusual qualifications, not only administrative and judicial, but moral as well. He wanted someone as sincere and disinterested as Schurman, yet possessing the extraordinary tact and patience that would be required to bridge an interim period of joint control with the military government. Soon after the middle of January, the President telegraphed to Judge William Howard Taft of Cincinnati, politely asking him to call.

Taft was a likable man of forty-two, jolly but impressive, with a big body and a big smile and a big judicial brain. He had been for the past eight years a judge of the United States circuit court at Cincinnati. But, though Taft was a prominent jurist and one of the most respected of the younger Republicans, he had not been well acquainted with McKinley, during the governorship or later. Taft had mingled in politics without ever becoming a typical politician. He was too fastidious for the compromises and the bargains, not quite at ease in the backslapping, *quid pro quo* commingling of the clans. Then, too, Cincinnati was Foraker territory, and Taft was used to breathing the air of the Foraker faction.

He had not had a high opinion of McKinley's ability when Hanna first put him forward. Recently, however, Taft had heard a different story from his new associate on the bench, Judge Day, and Day had soon arranged to bring the President and Taft together. The meeting occurred on the night of the Ohio elections of 1899, when the McKinleys took dinner at the Days' house in Canton. Besides Taft, the only other guest was General Corbin. It was a pleasant informal evening of conversation, and McKinley and Taft improved the opportunity to know and like each other.

Less than three months later, Taft received the invitation to call at the White House. His one consuming ambition was to be appointed to the Supreme Court. He was puzzled by the President's telegram, for he had not heard of a vacancy; but still he went to Washington in hopes.

Root and Long were with the President when Taft was ushered in. McKinley came straight to the point. The Judge, in blank astonishment, heard the President saying that he wanted him as a member of a commission for the Philippines, and intimating that he might be its head. The following account of the conversation was given by Taft in a speech that he made in 1908 as President-elect:

" 'Judge,' he said, 'I'd like to have you go to the Philippines.' I said, 'Mr. President, what do you mean by going to the Philippines?' He replied, 'We must establish a government there and I would like you to help.' 'But, Mr. President,' I said, 'I am sorry we have got the Philippines. I don't want them and I think you ought to have some man who is more in sympathy with the situation.' 'You don't want them any less than I do,' replied the President, 'but we have got them and in dealing with them I think I can trust the man who didn't want them better than I can the man who did.' "

Taft remembered the sense and spirit of this conversation, though he may not have had it verbatim after eight years. His report gives a clear glimpse of McKinley, meeting his biggest colonial problem dryly and philosophically, and feeling free, among friends, to take a poke at the Republican imperialists. The interview, in which Root also bore a leading part, was evidently prolonged. McKinley wrote that he had "gone over the whole ground" with Taft, and there was considerable ground to cover, though it proved to be an area of agreement. Taft subscribed to the Republican tenet that the Constitution did not automatically extend to the new dependencies. He was opposed to free trade with the Philippines, and had no scruples about denying United States citizenship to their inhabitants. He had, on the other hand, a strong feeling of the national obligation to give the islands a good administration; but he could find no fault in the outlined plans, with their guaranty of an efficient civil service and promise of a broad educational program. As the discussion went on, Taft's first amazed resistance weakened. His interest was engaged by the "large powers and wide jurisdiction" which the President held out to him, and he was vulnerable to the argument of duty and the inspirational appeal which McKinley made. "I never came in contact with a more sweetly sympathetic nature nor one more persuasive in his treatment of men," Taft said of McKinley in recalling this interview.

Another effective argument was that the post was only temporary, and would not seriously interrupt the judicial career on which Taft's mind was set. Root, indeed, suggested that it might advance his career. Taft turned to the President for some assurance about the Supreme Court, and received a conditional promise. "If I last and the opportunity comes, I shall appoint you," McKinley said. "Yes, if I am here, you will be here." In the end, Taft asked for a week in which to consider the offer, and went back to Cincinnati.

The President felt sure that Taft was interested, but he was fearful of discouraging influences, and his uneasiness was increased when Taft asked for a little more time. The stated reason, as McKinley wrote Judge Day, was Taft's wish to "consult with his brethren." The reference was not to Taft's actual blood brothers—whom he was, in fact, earnestly consulting—but to the other judges of the circuit court, who were expected to oppose his leaving. Root wrote Taft, expressly urging him not to yield to his colleagues, and dread of their interference inspired the rather severe admonitions which McKinley addressed to Day. "I want you to appreciate, Judge, that this is a very important matter and I invoke your aid to get the consent of Judge Taft to go. It is a great field for him, a great opportunity, and he will never have so good a one again to serve his country. I think he is inclined to accept. You must not make it harder for him to accept." The President's wishes prevailed. After the conference with his "brethren," Taft at once resigned his judgeship. That same night, accompanied by Day, he took the train to Washington to accept the appointment to the Philippines.

"I went under the influence of Mr. McKinley's personality," Taft later said, "the influence he had of making people do what they ought to do in the interest of the public service." On his second visit, Taft was fully indoctrinated in the plans of the Washington government. He sat in on a regular meeting of the Cabinet—he arrived on February 6, a Tuesday—and spent several hours in discussion with the President. Taft was much gratified to learn on this occasion that McKinley meant to give him "the full power of appointment" in the Philippines. A favorite device of the opposition press was to dwell on the rich harvest of government jobs which awaited the faithful in the colonies, and to depict the Philippines in particular as the future home of a host of needy Republicans. The grant of appointive power to Taft, combined with the provision of an efficient civil service, was McKinley's answer to the charge that the administration of the islands would be crippled by the patronage.

Taft's appointment was in itself a pledge of the President's intentions. Its importance in this aspect had been emphasized in the letter invoking the aid of Judge Day. After alluding to the "great good" to be accomplished in the Philippines, the President stated a second compelling motive for obtaining Taft's consent. "Besides, a Commission made up of men of the character of Judge Taft will give repose and confidence to the country and will be an earnest of my high purpose to bring those people the blessings of peace and liberty. It will be an assurance that my instructions to the Peace Commission were sincere and my purpose [is] to abide by them." No time was lost in publishing Taft's acceptance. The announcement of a second Philippine Commission was necessarily vague —two months were still to pass before it was formally appointed—but Taft's name deeply impressed the public. Amid general approval, he was prematurely hailed by leading newspapers as the first civil governor of the Philippines.

A month later, the President again acted to secure the "repose and confidence" of his fellow citizens by disowning the opprobrious epithet of "imperialism." Beveridge's speech had undoubtedly been in part responsible for an increasing tendency to identify the expansionist policy with the commercial exploitation of the colonies. His sensational utterances had been applauded by Republican organs, and it was frequently inferred, not only by unfriendly publications, that Beveridge was the spokesman of the administration. The tag of imperialism dismayed the President's large conservative following. For once, he met an accusation squarely, and made a ringing denial.

"There can be no imperialism," the President said at the banquet of the Ohio Society of New York in early March. "Those who fear it are against it. Those who have faith in the republic are against it. So that there is universal abhorrence for it and unanimous opposition to it. . . . Let us fear not! . . . It is not possible that seventy-five millions of American freemen are unable to establish liberty and justice and good government in our new possessions. The burden is our opportunity. The opportunity is greater than the burden."

What McKinley's address wanted in factual accuracy and close reasoning was offset by its stately moral tone and strong note of common sense.

His words were an inspiration to the army of his adherents. The significance of the speech was enhanced because it was delivered at a time of great uneasiness about the colonial policy. The Philippines were not, for the moment, in question. The eyes of the country were riveted on the Caribbean. All unexpectedly, the question of free trade for Porto Rico had exploded like a land mine under the Republican majority in Congress, and cast the gravest doubts on the intentions of the Washington government.

With every outward evidence of alacrity, both houses of Congress had taken steps to carry out the President's recommendation to abolish customs tariffs between the United States and Porto Rico. An appropriate fiscal measure was in the hands of Congressman Sereno E. Payne of New York, one of McKinley's lieutenants in the lower chamber, and chairman of the Ways and Means Committee since the death of Nelson Dingley the year before. The Senate bill for the temporary government of Porto Rico, embodying a provision for bringing the island within the American tariff system, was in charge of Foraker of Ohio, the chairman of the new Committee on the Pacific Islands and Porto Rico. Governor General Davis had been called from San Juan, and Foraker held several conferences with him and Root, as well as the President, in December. The bill was put together with all speed. Foraker was ready to introduce it immediately after the holiday recess.

The country watched these preparations with approval. The President's counsel of "our plain duty" had been commended by the press of both parties. Americans were anxious to help the impoverished Porto Ricans, and pleased that they could do so at very small expense. Since trade was insignificant, abolishing tariffs would put no one out of pocket. Moreover, the step was in line with the reciprocity program. The big upswing in foreign trade had accented the high retaliatory duties which the Dingley rates provoked. Republican, as well as Democratic exporters were looking for substantial relief from the batch of commercial treaties—including an important exchange of concessions with France—which the President had submitted to the Senate. Free trade for Porto Rico was generally popular because it was identified with reciprocity.

For precisely the same reasons, one section of the public detested the proposal. Reciprocity was the bugbear of the protected agricultural interests, with the sugar-beet growers in the lead. The arrangement with Hawaii would be perpetuated by the grant of territorial status, which the President had urged Congress to enact. Three of his pending treaties gave a preferential duty to sugar from the British West Indies. Free trade with Porto Rico was altogether too much of a trend for the sugar planters.

The embattled farmers had good friends in Congress. There was a hidden rift in Republican harmony, a secret fault in party solidarity. The protectionist diehards in the Senate meant to block the President's treaties. They did not like the advice on Porto Rico, and also feared that it might set a precedent for the Philippines. The keen lawyer Orville Platt of Connecticut was much concerned as a lifelong devotee of the protective system. Besides, he was a senator from a tobacco-growing state. He wrote Foraker a strong letter during the Christmas recess.

Foraker introduced his bill on January 3, but he dawdled about bringing it up. It was said that he was waiting for the outcome in the House. Payne was slow to speak. Yet no resistance was apparent. Everything seemed quiescent until January 19, when Payne at last arose with a straightforward proposal to extend United States customs and internal revenue laws over Porto Rico. The syllables might have been an incantation for the confusion of the government. Sugar-beet and tobacco planters dinned a protest from California to Connecticut, and loud cries came from the sugar-cane belt and from the growers of citrus fruits and early vegetables. Lobbyists went flying among the committees. Foraker scrutinized his bill, and struck out every reference to the Constitution. The Republicans of the Ways and Means Committee, after holding a secret conference, decided to report a substitute for the free-trade bill. A second Payne Bill, introduced on February 2, provided for duties equal to 25 per cent of the Dingley rates on trade with Porto Rico. Foraker made the same provision in an amendment to the Senate bill. The revenues, in each case, were to be expended for the insular government.

The dubious struggle on Capitol Hill had amazed and disgusted the public. The constitutional problem did not seem valid. The people were mainly interested in the moral problem, and many Republican newspapers supported that position. The unjust taxation of a colony was a wrong peculiarly shameful to Americans. A demand arose that Congress should cease truckling to the farmers' groups, and follow the President's admonition of "our plain duty."

The situation at Washington had a number of obscure and puzzling aspects. How, in that rumorous city, did the obdurate attitude of the Republican protectionists remain for so many weeks concealed? Why had the politically cautious President gone overboard for Porto Rico without ascertaining the sentiment of the leaders of Congress? What obtuseness had prevented his principal legal adviser on the colonies from perceiving the risk of a precedent for the Philippines? These questions have not been answered. It is only known that the President, with Root's urgent endorsement, committed himself to a recommendation of free trade with Porto Rico; and that he subsequently reversed himself, with Root's full concurrence, and exerted himself to secure the enactment of tariff legislation.

The President was not immediately affected by the overturn in Congress. There is uncommonly good evidence of what he was thinking in the middle of February. Not the least peculiar happening of the whole queer sequence was the publication of an exclusive statement of the President's views in the New York *World*.

It was sufficiently unusual that McKinley had talked at all, but on one previous occasion he had modified his strict rule against being interviewed. While at Lake Champlain in the preceding summer, he had ventured to express some opinions, though with a prohibition of direct quotation, to Henry Loomis Nelson, a former editor of *Harper's Weekly*, who had recently engaged in free-lance journalism. Nelson was an old-time Democrat, a man of good education, with a dignified style. His article, which appeared in *Harper's*, had been so discreet that McKinley was emboldened to try the experiment again. This time, it did not work as well. *Harper's* rejected the article. Nelson thereupon recast it "in a less intimate way," and hastily placed it with the *World*, writing to advise the President after he had done so.

This second "interview," though disfigured by some mischievous interpolations, was mainly characterless. It came alive only in mentioning the serenity and self-assurance on the President's face when he spoke of Porto Rico. He was proud, McKinley told Nelson—if it were proper for him to feel pride in any act of his own—of his recommendation that the Porto Ricans have free access to American markets. Without it, he felt sure that Congress would have imposed the full Dingley rates, and the resultant misery would have been appalling. He had not favored free trade at the start himself. He had to be satisfied first that it would work no harm on any American interests. Congress, he believed, would yet come to the same conclusion.

These remarks, made during the week before the House debate on the tariff, show that the President had taken the withdrawal of the first Payne Bill with composure, and regarded the substitute as a partial victory for his recommendation. His attitude explains the reactions of his congressional callers at this time. To men eager to follow the President's leadership on "our plain duty," his neutrality seemed almost like indifference. A large number of Republicans disliked the compromise bill, and were angered by the secrecy with which the switch had been made. One member of the Ways and Means Committee, McCall of Massachusetts, had refused to sign the majority report. Payne and his colleagues, Dalzell and Grosvenor, also called on the President. They were vastly relieved to learn that he would not urge his views on Congress, and would sign the Payne Bill, if it passed.

Congressman Payne brought up his bill with a pleasant, chatty talk about the need of revenue for the Porto Rican government. Internal revenue taxes would work great hardship on these poor people, and Payne made a touching plea to leave them their cheap supply of rum. He also referred to American interests, avowing his concern for the beet-sugar industry, which had been "something of a pet" of his, and stating his wish to set a good precedent for the Philippines, and serve notice on Cuba, too, that Congress had the power to impose a tariff on trade with a possession. This speech produced a strong effect, though some criticized its note of expediency and the deplorable reference to rum. Payne was followed by Dalzell, who expounded the constitutional argument in a learned speech which emphasized the peril of free trade with the Philippines.

The Republicans had made a respectable beginning, but their deep division appeared as the battle was joined. The trouble was not with the high-tariff men—they proved to be amenable, as long as the tariff principle was maintained—but with the free-trade advocates, who clung with unexpected tenacity to the recommendation of the message. It was a heaven-sent opportunity for the opposition. The minority leaders were hastily performing a somersault of their own. Instead of groaning over the island acquisitions and shrinking from incorporating them in the American system, the Democrats boldly seized the position that the Constitution (*ex proprio vigore*) had indubitably followed the flag, and that the Union must shortly be augmented by the states of Porto Rico and the Philippines. This premise afforded a logical basis for crying down the Payne Bill. In addition, the Democrats possessed the unusual advantage of loyalty to the President's instructions. Party discipline could not restrain the Republicans who made it a point of conscience to join the opposition. Many bolters were urged on by their constituents and the party press of their states. Republican newspapers of the Middle West were nearly unanimous in their protests. Feeling for free trade was intense in the wheat-growing states of the Northwest, which had anticipated a good market in an island obliged to import most of its breadstuffs. The tariff bill was threatened with a humiliating defeat. On the second day of the debate, the House leaders appealed in consternation to the President.

McKinley sent for Payne, Dalzell, and Grosvenor in the evening. He had wanted to hold aloof and let the will of the Republican majority prevail; but there had ceased to be an operative Republican majority in the lower chamber. The first attempt to legislate for the new possessions had resulted in a shameful exhibition of disunity. Unless the party lines could be restored, the Democrats would take control of the House. After a long conference, the President consented to permit the House leaders to suggest that he had receded from his original recommendation. Whispers began to circulate next day. Grosvenor pushed the matter bluntly in a speech on February 22, saying that he thought "nothing would give the President greater sorrow and regret than the defeat of this bill. . . ." But the disaffected Republicans refused to be convinced. At the last minute, the vote was postponed for two days, until February 28, and the President was entreated to save the bill by sending for some of the bolters. A number of interviews were quietly arranged. McKinley explained that he had formerly believed in free trade for Porto Rico, but had changed his mind. He now thoroughly endorsed the tariff bill, and hoped that every Republican would vote for it in the name of party solidarity. Undoubtedly, the President also spoke of the danger of affecting the verdict of the Supreme Court, a point which had finally been brought home to him and to his legal adviser Root.

Meanwhile, the President had furthered agreement on the bill by drafting two amendments. One of them cut the tariff from 25 per cent to 15 per cent of the Dingley rates—committing, as a Democratic congressman remarked, petit larceny instead of grand—and the other changed the bill to an emergency revenue measure, limited to two years' duration. The additional concession was made of entitling it a relief measure for Porto Rico. These modifications were accepted by the Republican caucus, and dispelled much of the antagonism. Until late on the night of February 27, the party managers were out in carriages, accounting for every member. Men on both sides were brought next day from sickbeds, and two were carried from hospitals. As the chamber filled up for the big decision, the President could look back on a morning of accomplishment. Four representatives had called. He had won over four votes. While he was out driving with Mrs. McKinley in the afternoon, he told her he thought the bill would pass by either six or eleven votes. The second figure was correct.

Without the President's intervention, the tariff bill would have been defeated, but this fact was not as yet generally known. The result was widely received by the Republican press as a party misfortune. Most Republicans found their only cause for pride in the six irreconcilables who had voted with the minority. "I regard it as a most inauspicious omen," McCall of Massachusetts had written in his dissenting report on the bill, "that our first legislative act should be framed on the theory that freedom does not follow the flag." "Our flag should be an emblem of human rights," Little-field of Maine had declared in an eloquent protest against unequal taxation. These were voices that expressed a deep American impulse to do justice. The rest was political maneuvering. Good Republicans accepted the need of revenue for Porto Rico with a sigh; wished for some word from the President, and defended his right to keep silence.

Two days after the vote in the House, the President was heard from, though not in a form that shed light on his views. A special message to Congress recommended that a sum of more than two million dollars, representing the customs collections on trade with Porto Rico since the Spanish evacuation, be appropriated for the benefit of the island as the President might direct. The minority leaders of the House were taken by surprise, and a suitable bill was rushed through before they regained their balance.

Atonement seemed to follow fast on the heels of the tariff bill, and the country was consoled by the knowledge that means of immediate relief for Porto Rico had been devised. Yet there was an incongruity about the President's message, and the eager haste with which the House Republicans had complied. The appropriation nullified the pressing need of revenue, the only excuse for the tariff which had been seriously considered by the public. An impression spread that perhaps the whole story of the Payne Bill had not yet been told, but it was still not understood that the tariff was the adopted policy of the government. Washington correspondents discerned bright prospects that, in face of the overwhelming demand of the press, the Senate would pass a measure providing for free trade with Porto Rico.

The two bills on Porto Rico gave the Senate opposition a double opportunity for attack in March. The second of them did not slip quietly through the upper chamber. The appropriation was derided as pretended benevolence and a concession to public indignation but the gibes were merely the political oratory suitable for election year. While loading the bill with amendments, the Democrats had no serious inclination to block the emergency fund. The President intervened to compel an agreement in conference on substantially the original provisions, and the measure was quickly adopted. The real contest centered around the substitute for the Payne Bill, which was brought up on March 2, and remained the unfinished business before the Senate until it was passed five weeks later.

The issue was presented in a peculiarly involved and shapeless form. Foraker had attached his civil-government bill as an amendment to the House bill, thus encumbering the fiscal measure with an unwieldy load of administrative machinery. He exhibited a somewhat more liberal tendency than Secretary Root, notably by providing for a legislative assembly chosen by restricted native suffrage, and by stipulating that the Porto Ricans be granted United States citizenship. Otherwise, he had mainly followed the "crown colony" proposals of the War Department. His bill had the weakness of leaving the legal status of Porto Rico undefined, and many of its complex provisions were highly debatable. But, while Foraker had blanketed the House bill with subsidiary controversies, he had not succeeded in smothering it. The imposition of a small temporary tariff remained the vital point in dispute.

The division of the Senate majority was as marked as in the House, and it was rendered even more striking by the prominence of some of the dissenters. Redfield Proctor and Cushman K. Davis were among the irreconcilable enemies of the revenue clause. The opposition within the party was so impressive that the correspondents believed that Foraker might yet revert to his free-trade measure. It soon appeared, however, that he was sold on the tariff.

Foraker was preparing to carry out the President's wishes, but he started with some feelings of resentment. The grievance of Hanna's regained control of Ohio was the matrix which enclosed his minor differences with the President on Porto Rico, and his pique at not being more closely consulted. In early March, his irritation quivered so close to the surface that he once betrayed it in the Senate. Tillman of South Carolina was goading him to explain the ambiguous attitude of the President. Foraker sarcastically retorted that he would have to refer the Senator to his colleague from Ohio. "I do not know. I am not the keeper of the President's opinion." He hastily recovered himself, adding that he had no doubt the President knew more about the subject now, and, if he had changed his mind, it was to his credit.

"I do not know whether the President has changed his mind," Foraker still huffily insisted. "I know nothing about that; I do not pretend to know. . . ." The lapse was speedily corrected. Foraker was in close and confidential touch with the President thereafter. The gibes of the opposition did not ruffle him again, as he masterfully steered his bill through a trying contest. He was a smart constitutional lawyer, and an audacious fighter, but he also displayed qualities uncommon in a high-strung, clever man: patience in exposition, alacrity in compromise, poise under attack. McKinley felt a professional admiration for Foraker. He approved of him

because "he did things." The President's confidence was justified by
Foraker's management during the Senate debate on Porto Rico.

Under the gloating eyes of the Democrats, the Republicans locked in
a deadly internal struggle. The drama removed, in the middle of March,
to the caucus and the conference. Foraker was ready to accept amendments to his plan of government, but implacable dissension centered
around the little hook of revenue on which the structure hung. The high
protectionists would make their utmost concession in assenting to 15%
of the Dingley rates—Platt of Connecticut wanted 80%—but the insurgents
refused to vote for any tariff at all. Foraker became suspiciously courteous
about laying the unfinished business aside. The Democrats began to fear
that the bill would be permitted to drift into oblivion, but the suspicion
was unfounded. Porto Rico had become the test of Republican
dominance of Congress. Almost any bill would be better than the ignominy
of failing to unite on a program. Foraker was marking time, but he meant
to get legislation in some form. He knew the value of bluff, and had the
nerve to risk it. On March 22, after a talk with the President, he went
jauntily to the Senate, prepared to play a bold hand. At the first complaint of his dilatory tactics, he asked for an agreement on a time to
vote, declaring that he was ready and would like an early day.

Foraker, as everyone knew, was very far from ready. His bill was buried
under a rubble of amendments. The senators of the opposition—who
were not ready, either—redoubled their attack. Allen of Nebraska, a
Populist, excitably charged that the Republicans had no intention of
bringing the bill to a vote—the Senate would not touch the tariff before
the national election. The taunt rang out, "You do not dare," and the Fire
Alarm sprang to his feet. He asked unanimous consent to withdraw his
substitute bill, and vote that very day on the revenue measure of the
House, the tariff pure and simple. The opposition, on both sides, was
thunderstruck. It seemed incredible to the Democrats that Foraker would
take so great a risk if he were not sure of his strength. When Allen mutely
appealed to them for help, they floundered in confusion. Proctor, the
spokesman of the Republican insurgents, reluctantly assented to a day in
the following week. Democratic objections threw the onus of delay on the
discomfited political minority.

Four days later, the effrontery of Foraker's tactics was disclosed by
reports of the Republican caucus. The diverse elements of the majority
were incapable of coming together. The only display of unity had been
a common resistance to Foraker's plea to take up the tariff bill separately.
Some senators frankly acknowledged their discouragement, but Foraker
himself was still confident. He had been hurriedly whipping his measure

into shape. The President had recently suggested still another amendment when he "laid down the lines of a compromise" by again shortening the existence of the tariff. It was to terminate as soon as the prospective insular government should have devised means of raising revenues, and the President was empowered to issue a proclamation of free trade at his discretion. There was also a provision for the uninterrupted extension of the Executive free list of food and other commodities entering Porto Rico from the United States. With these modifications, the imposition of a nominal tariff was reduced to a mere perfunctory obeisance to the protective principle. On March 27, the day after the gloomy caucus, Foraker drove on with his measure as vigorously as though he had not just solicited its partition. A close study of the new compromise cleared the air on the Republican side. The preliminary voting verified Foraker's optimism. Except for the constitutional diehards, opposition within the party crumbled, while the political minority looked on in helpless frustration.

The outcome had not been entirely unanticipated. The week before, Allen of Nebraska had paid a satirical tribute to the "vast and well-disciplined army" of the Republican party. "Whatever the head of that party thinks," said Allen, "it makes no difference who he may be, every man rolls his eyes to heaven, and says 'Amen'; he bows his own convictions and his own will in subordination to the wishes of the chief." It had not always been as Allen said; but he spoke with envy, as well as satire, and his exaggeration was pardonable. In the case of the Foraker Bill, he was very nearly right. The final vote could have been safely taken on Saturday, March 31. Foraker adhered to the appointed date, April 3, to allow time to finish the speeches that had been scheduled. Then the Senate passed the bill by a vote of 40 to 31, with only eight Republicans holding out to align themselves with the minority.

The chastisement of Senator Beveridge was a minor incident of the contest. His forwardness on the Philippine question might have been forgotten, if he had been content to subside on the laurels of his January speech, but Beveridge had been unable to resist thrusting himself into the thick of the Porto Rican controversy. He was opposed to the tariff on principle; and, conscious that he had the Republican party of Indiana at his back, he entered into the insurgent movement with righteous zeal. It became known that he was preparing an exhaustive speech in advocacy of free trade with Porto Rico.

Senators of every shade of sentiment were annoyed by Beveridge's outbreak. In a long interview with the President on Sunday, March 18, he regretted his impending break with party policy. Cortelyou reported the

President's remarks that Sunday evening. "He said Beveridge was a most loveable [sic] young fellow, that he was bright and courageous but handicapped himself by his egotism. At the interview the President said he had part of the time treated him as a superior and then again had advised him as though he was a boy; told him not to lose his head; keep cool; not be swayed by popular clamor. Matters were coming out all right." Beveridge told Cortelyou afterward that he "had never had so lovely a talk with a man." He thought that he and the President differed very little on the matter of Porto Rico. Nothing, he added, must arise to disturb the relations between them. But the lovely talk did not have the effect of calming Beveridge down. The next morning, without consulting the Committee on the Pacific Islands and Porto Rico, he introduced a free-trade amendment, and gave notice that he would speak three days later.

The disregard of senatorial courtesy was the last straw. Foraker and his committee were furious, and the other Republican senators with them. The President's fatherly kindness had no counterpart in the Senate. Such parental feelings as Beveridge stirred in his colleagues pointed to the birch rod of discipline. All factions readily united on a scheme to call up his amendment as soon as he made his speech, and summarily vote it down. The conspiracy was a well-kept secret, but Dawes heard of it, probably from the President, on the eve of Beveridge's speech, and hastened to warn his friend of the move "to read him out of the party." Beveridge was daunted. He had already sent his oration to the press. It was an emotional appeal to do justice to Porto Rico. Its peroration reverberated with all the considerations of right and duty which he had been criticized for neglecting in the case of the Philippines. But now Beveridge thought that he would wait. He paid another call on the President in the morning. Then, amid snickers from the opposition, he put off his address until March 30.

Beveridge passed the next week in an agony of indecision. He felt that loyalty to party would mean the betrayal of his conscience, and there was no doubt that it would entail some loss of popularity at home. His mental anguish was climaxed by news that his wife was suffering from a fatal illness. To enable him to go to her a day earlier, Proctor yielded his time on March 29. On the preceding night, Beveridge composed a new ending to his speech, supporting the latest compromise on the tariff, but he was uncertain whether he would deliver it. He was in great agitation when Dawes and George W. Perkins called and pleaded with him to stand with his party. In the morning, he sent word to the press to cut short his speech, omitting the exalted sentiments with which it closed.

During the last days of the Senate debate on the Foraker Bill, the

importance of the proceedings was amplified by a solemn sense of legislative history in the making. The chamber was filled to capacity, and
spectators crowded the galleries to hear the Republican lions roar on both
sides of the question. One of the largest audiences of the session was
present when Proctor announced that he was giving up his place, and
Beveridge arose. Foraker expressed a chill surprise. The Senator from
Indiana desired now to address the Senate? Had he an amendment to
offer? Beveridge said he understood that he had already offered an amendment. But it developed that he desired to speak on the general subject.
"I hope we may dispose of these amendments," said Foraker, in the character of a busy man greatly tried by interruption. "They must be disposed
of at some time." Then he turned away, and Beveridge began to speak.
Pale-faced and tense, he uttered again the polished phrases of a carefully
rehearsed oration, lucid in exposition and shining with conviction. But this
time the Senate did not wait to hear him. As period followed fervid period,
the Republicans made a concerted movement toward the cloakrooms, with
most of the Democrats trailing after them. Only half a dozen men remained on the floor to hear Beveridge plump for the tariff bill at the close
of a free-trade speech. Foraker sat unheeding at his desk, whispering with
a passer-by or riffling through his papers.

There was pathos in the situation of the proud young man, wounded
by personal grief and shamed by public submission, delivering his gelded
speech to deserted ranks of seats. But the Senate was well pleased with
his discomfiture. It was perhaps particularly gratifying to Senator Depew.
A loyal and industrious member of the administration team, he had long
since been reassured about his reception at the White House, and he
lost no time in laying his account of the boycott before the President.
When Dawes called to express indignation over the treatment of his
friend, he learned that Depew had already been there with "the anti-
Beveridge side of it." The general disposition of the Senate was that of a
crowd of practical jokers, tickled by their prank, without a twinge of pity
for their victim. The venerable Pettus of Alabama, droning out his views
on the constitutional question, startled his audience out of a drowse by an
ironical allusion to "our great orator." A ripple of merriment ran around
the floor, and echoed back from the galleries. "When you get a genuine
orator," Pettus declared, "he is absolutely absolved from all rules of logic
or commonsense." The old man solemnly pursued his theme, stopping
now and then to mop his head with a big silk bandanna and look quaintly
about him, as if surprised by the hilarity he was causing. And well might
Pettus have been surprised. The Senate had abandoned all pretense of
dignity and decorum. Red-faced, convulsed, and gasping, Republicans and

497

Democrats united on the issue of Beveridge, as party antagonisms vanished in the great solvent of laughter.

Beveridge was at the bedside of his dying wife. He had left Washington in abject humiliation, believing that his political career was ruined. His bumptiousness had merited rebuke, not crabbed insolence and the titter of elderly spite. There had been no boycott of Cushman Davis, thundering out an indictment of "this pernicious mockery of a tariff." Redfield Proctor was given a respectful hearing when he bluntly carried the issue to "the judgment and conscience of the American people." A political novice from Indiana had wanted, like these privileged seniors, to declare himself for principle. He had been coerced, had yielded, had been punished all the same. The Senate had given Beveridge, as well as Porto Rico, a painful lesson in the processes of American politics.

The Foraker Bill had been open to criticism as it came from committee, but a hodgepodge of amendments made it an object of ridicule. Foraker himself particularly regretted the failure to grant United States citizenship to the Porto Ricans. While evasively calling the island "the People of Porto Rico," his committee had felt that the inhabitants must be given some political status. If they were not to be American citizens, they would be either subjects or aliens, and Foraker found both terms inadmissible. He had settled in the end for the meaningless designation "citizens of Porto Rico," with a declaration that as such they were entitled to United States protection. Yet, in the eyes of all practical Republicans, the defects of the measure weighed lightly against the achievement of getting it passed. Showered with congratulations by the party dignitaries, Foraker took pride in his assertion of the practically unlimited powers of Congress to deal with the insular possessions. He believed that the verdict of the Supreme Court would sustain the hodgepodge at every point.

The action of the Senate was generally accepted as decisive. The protests of the lower chamber had ceased to figure in the press. The Republican leaders had made ready to force through a party measure with dispatch, and their well-drilled battalions acquitted themselves with a discipline that the Senate could never match. A caucus, with substantial unanimity, endorsed the Senate bill as it stood. A special rule was adopted on April 11, fixing the hour of five in the afternoon for the vote on a motion to concur in all the Senate amendments. After a lively debate, the motion was passed. The President signed the measure the next evening.

Thus, over the passionate objections of press and public and against the sincere conviction of a majority in both houses of Congress, the Foraker

Bill became the law of the land. The President at once began to implement the plan of civil administration. Even before signing the bill, he offered the governorship to the Assistant Secretary of the Navy, Charles H. Allen. Though he had been destined for the place since the summer before, Allen was hesitant to accept. It was well known that the President had him in mind for the projected bureau of insular affairs in the State Department. He would have preferred to remain in Washington, but, like Taft, he was vulnerable to the appeal to patriotic duty, and could offer little resistance to McKinley's persuasions. Allen was a modest, conscientious man and an able public servant. The ensuing appointments of other officials for Porto Rico confirmed the promise of a clean and competent administration, barred to the intrusion of the patronage. The public was also assured that the island would be protected from commercial exploitation. A belated amendment, regulating the granting of corporate franchises, was initiated by the House in a flurry of self-expression. The Senate balked at its provisions, but it went through conference committee with a celerity that bespoke administration pressure.

Allen sailed for San Juan ten days after the Foraker Bill was enacted. By way of instructive reading matter on the voyage, he carried a volume of Napoleon's letters to his brother Joseph, the gift of Charles Dawes. More importantly, he bore a message from the President, pledging a just and honest government to the people of Porto Rico. It had been quickly realized that officials of the requisite caliber could not be obtained on short notice, and Congress had been asked for additional legislation. Allen, as he thought, was making a preliminary trip to consult with Governor General Davis and line up the Porto Ricans who were qualified for appointments. But, on seeing the urgent need to stabilize conditions, restore prosperity, and win popular confidence, Allen decided to remain. He was inaugurated on May 1 as the first American civil governor of Porto Rico.

The anomalies of Republican doctrine were well illustrated when Allen took the oath to support and defend the Constitution as governor of an island over which the Washington government contended that the document did not extend. But the absurdity of the circumstance was glossed by the happy auspices of the ceremony. The passions of the tariff controversy were dying out, in Congress and in the country. It was seen that some of the violent partisan assaults on the Republican position—notably the accusation that the majority in Congress was acting in obedience to the sugar and tobacco trusts—were deliberate falsifications. It was recognized that the economy of the insular possessions was not as yet adapted to the federal system of taxation. It was admitted that the temporary imposition of a token tariff, under the stipulations of the Foraker Bill, could not be seriously condemned as oppressive. The Republicans had failed to conduct their first essay at colonial administration with wisdom and consistency. They had been guilty of fumbling, mystification of the public, and hocus-pocus with the protected interests. But, in practical terms, they had been generous in their treatment of Porto Rico.

The legion of McKinley's loyal champions had been slow to place credence in reports that he had backtracked on the tariff. They had adhered to the policy of free trade in the conviction that they were siding with the President against Congress and a noisy little farmers' lobby. They refused to believe that he would have reversed himself without informing the country. But the evidence that McKinley had "changed his mind" accumulated; newspapers in several widely separated cities printed interviews with representatives whom he had urged to vote for the tariff bill. A chill of disillusionment crept over his devoted popular following.

The opposition in both houses had made the most of the President's want of frankness. The debates had resounded with demands that he send another message to Congress, if he had turned his coat; and with false professions of incredulity that he was capable of such deceit and connivance. After rumors of his intervention in the House were confirmed, the more aggressive partisans indulged in rude mockery, insolently twitting the Republicans with the President's instability and double-dealing. The embarrassed Republicans could only bluster and equivocate. They had not been authorized to speak for the President who refused to speak for himself.

For two years past, there had been scarcely a respectable reminder of the earlier sneers at McKinley. His policies had been fiercely assailed, but his personal character had been all but immune to reproach. It was generally forgotten that he had once been described as the timeserving friend of the business interests, and the creature of Mark Hanna. His ambiguity on the Porto Rican tariff created an atmosphere in which scurrilous insinuations once more flourished. McKinley's enemies again dared to hint that he was not his own man, but the puppet of secret influences: a politician without a policy, pliant and opportunistic.

McKinley had not stumbled blindly into the slough of unpopularity. He had accurately forecast the consequences of his course. He had seen that, by standing on his message, he could win a great victory over the House leaders. He had known that, in modifying his policy, he would sacrifice personal prestige and incur charges of inconsistency and weakness. He had deliberately chosen "to stand the abuse and to maintain the right position as he saw it." So Dawes noted in his diary on March

7, after hearing the President argue out the whole question in detail, first in a discussion at which Gage and Fairbanks were also present, and later in a confidential "man to man" talk alone with Dawes in the Cabinet Room. McKinley accepted the loss of public confidence with his usual stoicism, treating it as a passing phase, but his distress was revealed in the hours he spent in going over the subject with Dawes, and in the enduring resentment he bore his old friend, Kohlsaat. The Chicago *Times-Herald*, one of the many party organs in the Middle West which supported free trade with Porto Rico, published a scornful editorial referring to "the mysterious influence that has pushed the Republican party to the verge of a precipice over which lie dishonor, injustice, and disaster." The clipping was lying on the side of the President's desk when Dawes arrived on one of his frequent visits. McKinley also had before him a letter he had previously dictated to Kohlsaat, mildly rebuking his newspaper's policy. He read the latest clipping after Dawes came in. All that he said was, "Well _____." Then he tore up the letter he had written. He was never friendly with Kohlsaat again.

In private conversation, the President was ready to explain the reasons for his course. He said that the decisive influence on his mind had been the necessity for asserting the right of Congress to govern the colonies, especially the Philippines, with a "free hand." The Democrats of the House had unexpectedly made the legal question paramount in the debate by postulating that the Constitution automatically extended to the island possessions. The President had then felt compelled to recede from his free-trade recommendation. He spoke gravely to Dawes of "the danger of the slightest weakening" on the constitutional position. "I think after all," Dawes wrote, "that the strongest man is the one who dares to incur the charge of weakness when it is necessary in order to accomplish the right." Under the spell of McKinley's earnestness, Dawes uncritically accepted the view that the President had no alternative to standing on his message except a dumb endurance of the odium of repudiating it. But there was obviously another choice. McKinley could have openly declared a change of policy. He could have strengthened his friends and discomfited his enemies by a vigorous and outspoken message to Congress. He had yielded, instead, to his ingrained habit of indirection and passivity. He had taken refuge once more in his old burrow of silence.

Nor was McKinley entirely candid in implying that a tariff on trade with Porto Rico was the only possible means of safeguarding the Republican position. Commercial reciprocity did not necessarily imply that the island was entitled to the privilege. The President's annual message had made no mention of legal right. The allusions to the Constitution had been introduced in Congress. He could have requested Congress to grant reciprocity to Porto Rico by special enactment, without reference to the Constitution. There would have been a very different scene in the Cabinet Room on the night of February 20, when the President had his crucial interview with Payne, Dalzell, and Grosvenor. Confronted by a resolute Executive, the Republican leaders would have been compelled to bow to the party insurgents, and bring in a free-trade bill in the form the President required. Such legislation, as McKinley well knew, would have passed the House by a large majority. He had not wanted to win personal prestige at the expense of his friends, but it is probable that a still stronger deterrent was the obstructiveness of the Old Guard of the Senate. McKinley was facing a stiff battle for his whole reciprocity program. He declined to fight it in the year of the national elections.

The President had made his decision for the sake of party unity, but the political wisdom of his action was sharply challenged. It was said that he had sacrificed his popular leadership to conciliate the reactionaries of Congress. McKinley's strength was his affinity with the people. He had been the instrument of their ideals of national duty. He had come to represent, to a degree scarcely known before, the conscience of the country. His reversal on the tariff seemed a betrayal too massive for repair. Many Republicans trembled to think of the consequences that might flow in November from the President's compromise on justice for Porto Rico.

Yet, in his own circuitous and accommodating way, McKinley had contrived to get what he wanted—or at least as nearly what he wanted as might be expected by a reasonable Chief Executive of the conglomerate Union of the States. He had authority to set up civil government in Porto Rico, and a generous appropriation from the Treasury to meet its immediate expenses. He had obtained a nominal tariff, with all revenues accruing to the colony on its trade with the mother country, and he had been granted the power to terminate the operation of the tariff at his discretion. The bitterly disputed impost had a short existence. Under the administration of Governor Allen and his associates, Porto Rico soon enjoyed an economic recovery that warranted the insular government in introducing a system of local taxation. The President issued a proclamation of free trade between the United States and the island in July, 1901, less than fifteen months after the Foraker Act went into operation. The Supreme Court had then already justified the foresight of the Republicans in protecting their constitutional position. In May, 1901, the verdict was pronounced that the United States had the right to acquire territory by treaty and that the Constitution did not automatically extend to territory so acquired. It was held that the new possessions could not be considered as foreign, but they were not to be regarded as entirely domestic, either. Confronted by an accomplished political and commercial fact, the majority of the Court rather tortuously sustained the right of Congress to treat the islands as not fully incorporated into the United States, and found the Foraker Act to be valid and constitutional.

"Whether th' Constitution follows th' flag or not," runs Mr. Dooley's often quoted dictum, "th' Supreme Court follows th' iliction returns." Months before the verdict was handed down, the nation had had its say on Republican policy. Popular clamor over Porto Rico had been only a passing phase, as McKinley had predicted. His true friends, the people, had not deserted him for long. Yet there was a subtle change in the estimate of his statesmanship. This most beloved of Presidents had failed to meet the test of greatness. Americans did not forget that, in an hour that called for steadfast leadership, some banner had been lowered in surrender, and political expediency, *ex proprio vigore*, had won a quiet triumph.

· 22 ·

AFFAIRS OF STATE

THE British ambassador, his broad face glowing between the twin snowdrifts of his side whiskers, strode up the high flight of stone steps with the attaché who was engaged to his daughter, Lillian. They were a few minutes early for an eleven o'clock appointment, but the Secretary of State was waiting in his spacious office at the south end of the State, War and Navy Building: a nervous, civilized, sensitive man, spruced to the tips of his mustache and beard, with eyeglasses pinching his fastidious little nose. John Hay had many uncongenial duties, but this meeting was not one of them. He had found Lord Pauncefote—for Her Majesty's grateful government had elevated Sir Julian to the peerage—an effective ally in his own great object of strengthening the ties between the United States and England. This morning of early February, 1900, was to mark the successful close of a difficult negotiation. Lord Pauncefote was in receipt of instructions to sign a treaty according to the United States the exclusive right to build and control an isthmian canal.

The formalities were rapidly completed. On Pauncefote's entrance, the chief of the Diplomatic Bureau spread the engrossed copies of the convention on the Secretary's desk, and the seals were placed in readiness. The veteran messenger, William Gwin—said to have witnessed the signing of every treaty since the days of Hamilton Fish—stood by with sealing wax and lighted candle. The plenipotentiaries signed. The wax dripped, and puddled around the impress of the seals. As Gwin blew out the candle, Hay felt for his watch, and announced that it was just eleven o'clock. The cause of more than forty years' dissension between the English-speaking countries had been diplomatically adjusted in the space of five minutes.

Americans had soon resented the Clayton-Bulwer Treaty of 1850, which bound the two governments to joint control of a neutralized canal through Nicaragua; and their feeling had been intensified by their growing national power and more vigorous assertion of the Monroe Doctrine. With passing time, moreover, the waterway had become a predominantly American concern. The interest of Great Britain had declined, while that of the United States had been stimulated by the conquest of the Far West and the development of the Pacific trade. The failure of various attempts to build a canal under private auspices established the necessity for government financing and management. Washington had repeatedly applied for a revision of the agreement, but Great Britain had been unresponsive to the plea of changed conditions and the increasing indignation of Congress and the press. The dead hand of an obsolete treaty still rested on the plans for an American-controlled canal, when the events of 1898 made it a matter of the first strategic and commercial importance to the United States.

The State Department renewed its overtures in December, soon after Congress assembled, breathing impatience to get on with the project. The President had advised Secretary Hay to approach the British government "in a frank and friendly spirit," but he was exceedingly anxious to avoid further delay. His annual message had asked for legislation as soon as the Nicaragua Canal Commission should complete its report. The request had led Pauncefote to interrogate the State Department. Secretary Hay had been profuse in assurances that the President did not intend to disregard the treaty; yet the information was conveyed that the United States meant to proceed with the canal. Her Majesty's Government was not slow to perceive that the Anglo-American *rapprochement* would not be served by a refusal to recognize the paramount interest of the United States in the Caribbean. Negotiations were reopened, and Pauncefote was empowered to conduct them in Washington. Two factors, however, interrupted their progress. One was the attempt of Great Britain to strike a bargain for the Canadians by securing a concession on the Alaskan boundary—an irrelevant demand which the American government regarded as entirely unjustified. The other was the President's conversion to the belief that canal legislation should be postponed pending further investigation of the route.

It had usually been taken for granted that the canal would be built in Nicaragua. A somewhat shorter route through Panama was cluttered with debris and tainted by the fevers and failure of a French construction company, and it had not been seriously considered by the Washington authorities until early in 1899, when its advantages were persuasively set forth by William Nelson Cromwell, a New York lawyer who had been retained by the French stockholders to sell the rights in the collapsed enterprise to the United States. The Nicaraguan plan had strong backing in Congress. The President's commission unanimously reported that it was practicable, and there was considerable agitation in favor of going ahead with it. Nevertheless, sufficient interest in Panama had been generated to prevent a firm decision. Congress passed a joint resolution authorizing the appointment of a second commission to examine both routes and determine which was the more feasible.

The President had been impressed by Cromwell's arguments, and was satisfied that they warranted the delay of another year or more. In search of expert advice, he also asked Mark Hanna to post himself on the business and technical aspects of the matter. Hanna had not been prominently associated with the policies of the administration, excepting the merchant marine program; but a commercial waterway was a congenial specialty for a practical man with experience in shipping and construction. He became a useful member of the Senate Committee on Interoceanic Canals, and was soon immersed in the subject, conferring with Cromwell and making a thorough study of the Panama route.

The negotiations with Great Britain were meantime at a standstill. They might well have been suspended until the second commission made its report, but for the threat of reckless legislation by the Fifty-sixth Congress. The opening session was preluded by lively reports of a bill which entirely ignored the Clayton-Bulwer Treaty in providing for the immediate construction of a fortified canal in Nicaragua. Its sponsor, Congressman William P. Hepburn of Iowa, felt assured that it would pass the House, and it was attracting favorable notice in the upper chamber. Among those most avidly interested, as the President was privately informed, was Senator John T. Morgan of Alabama, the foremost authority in Congress on the canal question. A Democratic expansionist of the old school, Morgan had devoted more than twenty years to fighting for a waterway which would open Pacific markets to the South. His convictions had led him into strange company since the war with Spain. He was perhaps on more confidential terms with the President than any other member of the political opposition; and his Republican colleagues had recognized his independent character and special knowledge by giving him the chairmanship of the Committee on Interoceanic Canals. Morgan was committed to the Nicaraguan route, and regarded Cromwell's interference with furious suspicion. The enthusiasm for the Hepburn Bill filled him with eager hopes. Though he had a bill of his own, he was ready to yield to Hepburn's leadership. Morgan did not want credit or prestige. He wanted the canal. If the House should pass its bill, there was every probability that Morgan would get it through the Senate.

Though the President's annual message of 1899 advised that time was needed for the important examinations then being made, it was shortly apparent that impetuous expansionists in both houses were in headlong haste to act. Secretary Hay became acutely alarmed. He was not concerned about the locality of the canal, supposing it probable—as most people still did—that it would go through Nicaragua, but he was shocked by the prospect that Congress might disregard the international obligations of the United States, and keenly apprehended the awkward position in which such action would place the Secretary of State. The American embassy in London was instructed to urge the desirability of concluding the revision of the treaty. This time, Her Majesty's Government, coping with a troublesome and unpopular war in South Africa and disturbed by unfriendly relations with the Continental powers, proved entirely sympathetic. The American proposals were accepted without a change, and Pauncefote was cabled instructions to sign.

Thus, when William Gwin blew out the candle at precisely eleven o'clock of a February morning, Hay marked the hour with a flourish of satisfaction. He had obtained generous concessions from England without yielding so much as an Alaskan glacier in return. He had won the race with Congress, and cleared the administration of "complicity in a violent and one-sided abrogation" of an existing treaty. There still remained, to be sure, the necessity of submitting his diplomatic triumph to a legislative body notorious for its tendency to override Executive agreements. Hay himself had sourly said that an important treaty would never again be ratified. But he had no fears on this occasion. He had positively assured Lord Pauncefote that the treaty would pass the Senate. Nearly every member of the Foreign Relations Committee, as Hay firmly believed, had signified approval and promised support. He had taken care to eliminate controversial details, and it did not enter his mind that "anyone out of a madhouse" could object to the convention, which had been prepared by the United States and was altogether to the American advantage.

Hay, however, was wrong. Masses of sane Americans were going to object to his treaty. Its handling by the Senate would bring him to offer his resignation before many weeks had passed.

The American copy of the instrument was immediately carried to the White House, and thence dispatched with a brief letter of transmittal to the Capitol. The President had made a point of sending it at once. The night before, when the knowledge of Great Britain's assent was scarcely twenty-four hours old, McKinley had spoken elatedly to Cortelyou of the "great achievement" which had finally been brought off, and expressed the hope that the news would not "leak out" prematurely. The coup of the State Department was to take the Senate by surprise, and startle the whole country into admiration of its success.

All seemed to go well at first. The treaty was widely applauded by the conservative press. In the Senate, the prevailing impression appeared to be one of gratification that Hay's diplomacy had obtained so much; but objections sounded louder as the provisions were studied. Hay himself was quick to take alarm. Two days after the treaty was signed, he was worried about its fate, and appealed to Lodge to oppose amendments in committee.

The objectionable features of the agreement were not novel. That was precisely the trouble. Except for the one imposing alteration, the Clayton-Bulwer terms were little changed. The United States repeated the former pledge to refrain from fortifying the canal, or restricting its free access to the ships of all nations, even in time of war; and both signatory powers once more united in guaranteeing the policy of neutralization, and in inviting other maritime powers to adhere to the agreement. The retention of these provisions antagonized the ultra-expansionist Republicans, and was denounced by the political opposition. The zeal of the Democrats to destroy the treaty seduced them into a defense of imperialist tenets, but their attack was no less fierce because it was illogical. Its practical basis was the exploitation of anti-British sentiment. As the Ohio Democrats had shown in the campaign of 1899, the historic colonial suspicion of England was still alive and politically useful. The canal was not the only cause of ill feeling. The embers of hostility had been fanned by the failure to settle the disputes with Canada, and strongly stirred of late by the war in South Africa. Americans sympathized warmly with the Boers, seeing Lexington and Concord in the velds and kopjes where embattled farmers defied the khaki-clad counterparts of the redcoats. The first great successes of the rebels had had immense newspaper coverage, and by February their stout assaults on Ladysmith were all but crowding the Philippine war from the front pages. The atmosphere was favorable to the propaganda of the dependably embittered Irish-Americans and the recently disaffected German groups, who loudly protested against the neutrality of the Washington government and called for intervention on behalf of the Boers. Democratic partisans bracketed the South Africans with the persecuted Filipinos, and denounced the cordial understanding between that brace of imperial tyrannies, the British Empire and the McKinley administration. No just consideration of a treaty with England could be expected from these irreconcilable elements, and none was forthcoming. They greeted the new convention with howls that American interests had been surrendered, and the Secretary of State was held up to scorn for his unpatriotic truckling to Great Britain.

Though Hay winced under the attack, he had grimly anticipated the tactics of election year. For the antagonism within his own party, he was utterly unprepared. His frustration was acute as he watched the distortion of the treaty. Lodge had not responded to the appeal to oppose amendments. He was, as Hay disgustedly commented, "the first to flop." The other Republicans on the Foreign Relations Committee followed suit. The chairman Cushman K. Davis sponsored an amendment declaring that the stipulations of the treaty should not apply to measures which the United States might find it necessary to take for the national defense or the maintenance of public order. Hay sneered that Davis, a convinced advocate of neutralization, was "too indolent to make a strong fight," but it is fair to say the Senator had correctly judged opposition to the treaty, and had put forward his compromise in the belief that it would answer all objections. Nevertheless, the amendment was a serious alteration. Ambiguous though its language was, it clearly annulled the principle of neutrality; and its inclusion invalidated the report from the committee, commending the treaty and urging its ratification.

Hay claimed that the treaty was changed because of the fears inspired by the newspaper attacks, but he well knew that the highhanded behavior of the Senate was not a phenomenon of election year. The situation, moreover, had not been mitigated by the attitude of the arrogant and hypersensitive Secretary of State. Hay had a scornful opinion of the Senate, and had not troubled to conceal it. Finding it irksome to associate with men of inferior culture, he made no effort to cultivate pleasant relations with the Republican leaders. The canal treaty affords an illustration of his indifferent treatment of the Foreign Relations Committee, with which a friendly alliance was so obviously important. Although he claimed their promises of support, the members were not fully acquainted with the provisions of the treaty until it went to the Senate. Hay had obviously assumed their acquiescence in all particulars of an arrangement which seemed beyond criticism to himself. The tactless omission of consultation in advance was especially offensive to Senator Davis. The treaty, incidentally, was not accompanied by the usual letter of explanation from the Secretary.

But, fundamentally, the opposition to Hay's terms was inherent in the ruling imperialist spirit of the Senate. The Secretary of State had not drawn up, nor had the President sanctioned an agreement which ignored the traditional policy and the vital interests of the nation. A neutralized canal was a conception which had seldom been questioned, and which was in line, as John Bassett Moore pointed out, with the other great American policy, the freedom of the seas. The best naval opinion disapproved fortifications on the isthmus, holding that the proper defenses of the canal were the proposed naval bases at San Juan and Pearl Harbor. Nevertheless, in 1900, the neutrality provisions were repugnant to most Republican senators, and there was considerable support in the party for their view. Governor Roosevelt's disapprobation of the terms was splashed across the front page of the Republican New York *Sun*, which was as sharply critical of the treaty as the Democratic New York *Journal.* Many aggressively patriotic citizens believed with Roosevelt that the national security depended on freedom to fortify the canal, or to close it in wartime. A still larger element objected to the formal prohibition to do so. They disliked an engagement with Great Britain in an exclusively American concern, and indignantly repudiated the idea of dragging in other maritime powers. The Senate majority represented a spirited expansionist sentiment which would be satisfied with nothing less than an acknowledgment by Great Britain of American naval supremacy in the Caribbean.

Hay saw none of this, but only an unparalleled "exhibition of craven cowardice, ignorance and prejudice" on the part of "the howling fools in the Senate." Shortly after the Foreign Relations Committee reported the treaty with the Davis amendment, he wrote out his resignation "in profound disgust." An accompanying letter to the President stated that the divergence between his views and those of the Senate made him fear that his usefulness was at an end. "I cannot help fearing also," he added, "that the newspaper attacks on the State Department, which have so strongly influenced the Senate, may be an injury to you, if I remain in the Cabinet." Hay's thin skin had been burned by the slaps of the press. His "first experience of filthy newspaper abuse" was a painful contrast to the great applause for the policy of the Open Door. McKinley, himself under fire in March on account of Porto Rico, had no suspicion of the impending resignation. When the Secretary of State called him to one side at the close of a Cabinet meeting, he innocently accepted the letter which Hay handed him with the remark, "Mr. President, here are some communications which I hope you will read at your leisure."

That evening, after disposing of the business on his desk, McKinley took a paper from his pocket; and, saying to Cortelyou, "You are the only one who knows about this," read out Secretary Hay's letter. Then he read the reply he had already sent, returning the formal resignation and stating that, had he known the contents of the letter, he would have declined to receive it. The President talked for a while about the treaty with England, which he said "would live in diplomatic history as one of the greatest achievements of the sort." He spoke, too, of the propaganda of the opposition, and mentioned reports he had had of funds being spent on "disseminating the stuff" in the press.

"Nothing could be more unfortunate than to have you retire from the Cabinet," the President had written Hay. "The personal loss would be great, but the public loss even greater. Your administration of the State Department has had my warm approval. As in all matters you have taken my counsel, I will cheerfully bear whatever criticism or condemnation may come. Your record constitutes one of the most important and interesting pages of our diplomatic history." Before signing himself, "Yours devotedly," the President added a few words which poignantly revealed his comprehension of Hay's ordeal. "We must bear the atmosphere of the hour. It will pass away. We must continue working on the lines of duty and honor. Conscious of high purpose and honorable effort, we cannot yield our posts however the storm may rage."

Hay was deeply affected by this letter—"a most touching and beautiful letter," as he thought. "I cannot express my feeling of gratitude and devotion," he wrote the President next day. He had been strengthened by McKinley's praise and warmed by his sympathy; and it is evident that he had been influenced by the example of fortitude. "But all this will pass away," he wrote a few days later in telling his son, Adelbert, of the newspaper abuse to which he was being subjected.

A singularly close relationship had grown up between McKinley and Hay. One reason for its intimacy was fortuitous. On Hobart's death, the Secretary of State had become next in line of succession—in his own phrase, *héritier présomptif*—to the Presidency. Hay was inevitably conscious that, until March 4, 1901, the office entailed a special responsibility. The thought may have aggravated his sensitiveness to criticism. A fundamental assumption of McKinley's foreign policy was that a natural compatibility existed between the United States and England, but he did not give it predominant importance. He thought of the sympathy between the English-speaking peoples as one aspect of a grand design of world peace, with all the nations linked by the ties of trade and commercial treaties. Hay's consuming ambition was an Anglo-American alliance. He railed against the political deterrents, and seemed incapable of accepting them as final. But McKinley was not worried by the pro-British inclination of the State Department. He saw a different man from the polished trifler Henry Adams knew, or the autocratic official who rebuffed the Senate. He saw Hay's modesty, his high sense of public duty, and his sincere patriotism. Speaking to Cortelyou of a sneer that Hay had been "educated in the English school," the President remarked, "I wish some one had replied to that by saying, 'Yes, he was trained under Abraham Lincoln.' "

Hay, for his part, had come to feel deep respect, as well as affection for the President. Foreign policy was less cramped by political solicitude than Hay had anticipated. He had been "greatly struck" with the "coolness and courage" which the President brought to international problems. Though McKinley was eager for advice, he was never deferential. He did not hesitate to edit the Secretary's writing, amend his proposals, or gently rebuke his intolerance of frustration. Hay showed his susceptibility to this influence by a *volte-face* on the Davis amendment, which he promptly decided was ridiculous, but acceptable enough, and in the self-control with which he bore the further mutilation of his treaty.

The Foreign Relations Committee had overestimated the efficacy of the Davis compromise. More amendments were demanded by the Senate after the treaty was reported. The committee adopted two that had been drafted by Foraker, and submitted them to the President as "relatively innocent"; but the President could not agree. They summarily altered Executive policy; and defied Great Britain by declaring that the new treaty superseded the Clayton-Bulwer agreement, and by striking out the article that invited the adherence of other powers. In an effort to work out some adjustment, the President asked Secretary Hay to meet a committee from the Senate.

Lodge, Foraker, and Aldrich presented themselves at the Executive Mansion, and laid down the alternatives. Without the two additional amendments, the treaty would be rejected. With them, it could be carried, and canal legislation could be staved off pending further negotiations. The treaty was right as originally drawn, the President retorted, and ought to be ratified without amendment; but, as this seemed impossible, they were willing to do their best to persuade the British government to accept the Davis amendment. He did not think the other two could be accepted. "That puts the onus of rejecting the treaty on England!" Lodge crowed. Hay should have known where an eager chauvinist would stand—they were old friends, joined by the bonds of a hostile intimacy—but he did not give Lodge credit for convictions, describing him as a timid man who had "lost his nerve" under pressure.

The senators pointedly stressed the diplomatic embarrassment that would result from the rejection of the treaty. They were agreed that it would be impossible, in that case, to prevent a repudiation of the Clayton-Bulwer Treaty by act of Congress. The warning was not needed. It had been evident for weeks that the House was out of control, champing to vote for the Hepburn Bill, while the Senate impatiently awaited the opportunity to concur. So forceful was the trend that the extreme recourse of a presidential veto would not avail to halt the threatened action. The President's callers were delivering an ultimatum. To avoid legislation insulting to Great Britain, the administration would have to yield to the Senate. The President made no reply on this occasion, but an understanding must have been reached. Lodge took the lead in blocking consideration of the Hepburn Bill when it came from the House in May.

The canal treaty, laid aside until after the election, was marked for destruction in the next session. Two other treaties, however, had passed the Senate unscathed. One was the convention, concluded with Germany and Great Britain, which gave the United States possession of the eastern half of the Samoan group. The other was the peace convention signed at The Hague by the delegates of twenty-six nations. German militarism had nearly wrecked the program, but the conference had had one practical result. It had created a Permanent Court of Arbitration to which international differences might be referred. The delegates of the United States had been chiefly responsible for this achievement. They had gone to The Hague with a well-developed project, and persuaded the German government to accept it in a modified form. The President based high hopes on establishing the machinery for arbitration, and the people heartily approved it, proud that their delegates had won the respect of the conference, and that their jurists would sit on the bench of the Hague Tribunal.

The first assemblage of the nations in the cause of peace had not accomplished very much. It had been found impossible to reach any agreement on the primary object of the conference, the limitation of armaments; even the vaunted system of arbitration was not compulsory; and, before signing the limited declarations of the convention, the United States delegates had appended a reservation for the Monroe Doctrine. A momentous departure from the traditions of the republic had come to an unalarming conclusion. Americans would not forget the precedent of their participation in the conference at The Hague. It had been a small advance on the road of international co-operation, a small defeat for the isolationist spirit.

Secretary Hay had to wait until the next spring before reopening the canal negotiations. When his first treaty had run its predestined course of failure, he at once engaged in framing another draft. It was designed to meet the irreconcilable objections of England to the Senate amendments, and at the same time accord with the prevailing views of the Senate. He wrote a number of Republican senators to ask just what they would agree to, and later submitted the text to several of them. The revised treaty embodied a joint agreement to abrogate the Clayton-Bulwer Treaty. It dropped the British guaranty of the neutrality of the canal, and also the invitation to the other powers. The Davis amendment was eliminated by the expedient of omitting the prohibition of fortifications and the reference to neutralization in wartime.

The principal importance of the second Hay-Pauncefote Treaty lay in what it left unsaid. The United States was made the sole guarantor of the neutrality of the canal, without restriction on the right to fortify it. The concession was larger than Hay's diplomacy might previously have looked to obtain; but, in the autumn of 1901, drained by the Boer War and chilled by the growing hostility of the German Empire, England recognized the obdurate determination of the Senate and unqualifiedly acknowledged American dominance of the Caribbean.

John Hay was never able to form a really cordial relationship with the Senate. His autocratic and fastidious temperament was suited to the foreign office of an absolute monarchy. He chafed under the restraints imposed on an American Secretary of State. His nerves were rasped by the frictions and intrusions of the legislative partnership. He was jealous of the prerogatives of his office, and prone to impugn the motives of those who opposed him. Yet, after his first disappointment, he conducted himself with excellent self-discipline in the canal negotiations. He broke through the trammels of impatience and irritability to come to terms with the Senate, and tolerate the third and unseen party at his conferences with Pauncefote. The fate of the second Hay-Pauncefote Treaty was never in doubt. It went a long step beyond the Senate's demands, and it was promptly and enthusiastically ratified.

The superseding of the Clayton-Bulwer Treaty was one of three large questions of Anglo-American diplomacy under discussion during the years in which Washington resolutely maintained neutrality in the South African War. The Alaskan boundary dispute, another principal cause of resentment in the United States, was also eventually settled to the disadvantage of England. But the development of a joint policy toward China was attended by happy omens from the start. The hidden irony of John Hay's popular doctrine of the Open Door was that it served the interests of Great Britain as well as those of his own country.

The Open Door in China had long been a primary object of British diplomacy. A keen participant in the race for treaty rights and grants of privilege, England had become fearful that the determined aggressions of other European countries would cause the partition of the Chinese Empire and lead to the exclusion of English commerce from ports under rival jurisdiction. In March, 1898, these apprehensions had suggested the desirability of an alliance with the United States, but the President had rebuffed a tentative proposal to join England in opposing the Continental powers in China. Nor was there a favorable response to a letter from John Hay, then American ambassador to Great Britain and alerted to the alarms of London. Trade with the Far East was far down on McKinley's agenda at a time when he was absorbed in the effort to avoid war with Spain; but he was beginning to think very deeply about it before the short war was over. Judge Day, in writing Ambassador Hay in July that the British proposal was still inopportune, took occasion to speak of the possible need of extending American interests in Asia. Day had, in fact, already recommended an appropriation for a commission to study the question of enlarging United States markets in China.

When Hay became Secretary of State at the end of September, revolutionary changes had occurred in the attitude of the government. The President soon determined to acquire the entire Philippine archipelago, and made the extension of American markets in the Far East a leading policy of his administration. Washington viewed with intensified dismay the rapacity of the European powers in China, and the new Secretary of State longed to find some means of collaboration with Great Britain.

Hay was entirely untrained in Far Eastern affairs. There was no specialist on the subject at the State Department; and, as all the offices had been filled before Hay's return, he had to resort to a roundabout method of obtaining advice. The man he most wanted was W. W. Rockhill, a former secretary of the American legation at Pekin, who had studied and traveled widely in the East. He was currently pining at Athens, having been made minister to Greece, Rumania, and Serbia in the shuffle of diplomatic appointments. A vacancy had been created at Washington by the death of McKinley's faithful friend, Joe Smith. Hay contrived to have Rockhill —who was incidentally a Democrat—appointed to this place, the directorship of the Bureau of American Republics. It was as uncongenial to a scholarly Orientalist as Athens, but it was much more convenient to the State Department, and from it Rockhill began to operate as Hay's unofficial adviser early in 1899.

Rockhill was lacking in the important qualification of recent, firsthand observation of his field—he had not been in China for seven years— but the western world did not suppose that the Empire was capable of radical inner change. Since her humiliating defeat by Japan in 1895, the inertia of her people was believed to be permanent and complete Anti-foreign demonstrations at Pekin were not seen as socially significant. To Washington, they merely represented disorder, an additional incentive to protecting American interests. Rockhill, however, did not come up with a plan until summer. Hay was well impressed with the proposal that, while realistically accepting the spheres of influences enjoyed by the various powers in China, Washington should seek to obtain from each of them an undertaking not to interfere with existing commercial treaties. Mention of the territorial integrity of China was deliberately excluded in order to avoid a flagrant imitation of British policy, and possibly also because the American naval strategists were clamoring for a coaling station in China.

A little deception was practiced in submitting the plan to the President. It had originated with an elderly Englishman, Alfred E. Hippisley, who was in the Chinese customs service, and who had renewed an old acquaintance with Rockhill while visiting the United States. On the ground that Hippisley's name would "require additional explanation," Rockhill represented the project as coming from himself alone. The State Department was far from hopeful of obtaining the President's agreement, especially at a time when the Democratic press was loudly strumming the anti-British theme, but McKinley determined to go ahead. A draft of the notes was prepared, and shortly approved. They were addressed to England, Russia, and Germany on September 6, and subsequently to France, Italy, and Japan. The governments were in each case informed of the desire of the United States to see them make a formal declaration that there would be no commercial discrimination in their respective spheres of influence in China.

Newspaper reports of these notes produced an unexpectedly strong effect on the American public. A broad construction was instantly placed on the action of the government. The purely commercial proposals, with their uncritical acceptance of the aggressions of the powers, were hailed as the expression of a liberal and farsighted policy. The applause reinforced Hay's influence, and led the President to outspoken advocacy of the preservation of China. Soon after the New Year of 1900, the news was permitted to slip out that the State Department was assured of unanimous assent to its proposals. The country was exultant. This was a kind of diplomacy that appealed to Americans. There was no question of a complicated treaty, riddled with damaging concessions and dangerous ambiguities. The trick had been turned by writing letters. The United States had given nothing away, and asked only for fair and equal treatment for all nations; and the nations had seen the justice of the request, and followed American leadership. Much satisfaction was derived from the fact that frank, straightforward American methods had brought results for which English diplomacy had long striven in vain. John Hay was praised to the skies for his Open Door policy. The familiar catch phrase graced his achievement with overtones of confidence and generous hospitality. Hay had not used it in his notes, but it was a glib description of the object of his diplomacy, and his countrymen thenceforward associated it exclusively with his name.

The notes had been a bold diplomatic move, but far bolder was Hay's assumption that they had been answered in the affirmative. His sheaf of answers veiled in polite circumlocutions the strong reluctance of the powers to commit themselves. All were profuse in lipservice to the principle of equal treatment; but each made its agreement conditional on that of the other governments, and some were evasive to the point of negation. Even England hedged, reserving a sphere of special privilege. Hay endured many weary interviews with Count Cassini, raving against the American "demands," before Russia grudgingly consented to make a written reply. The German foreign minister, though he had verbally complied, could not be persuaded to put anything on paper until after the middle of February, when he was assured that satisfactory letters had been received from the rest of the powers.

On March 20, Secretary Hay posted off six more letters to the capitals of the world. Each was informed that, as the others had accepted, its agreement would be considered "final and definitive." Unhampered by legislative interference, Hay had brought off a diplomatic *coup d'état*. With his canal treaty in ruins and the yellow press at his throat, he had shown how skillfully he could negotiate when he was free from "the howling fools in the Senate."

The President was hopeful that the unanimous agreement of the powers would abate Chinese distrust of their purposes and tend to quell the anti-foreign movement, but such hopes bore no relation to the realities of the situation. In the summer of 1899, there had been a formidable re-crudescence of the secret patriotic organizations which had for years been hostile to the foreign occupations and to the feeble and compliant Manchu dynasty. The Boxers, a society long since placed under imperial interdict, had inflamed the people of northern China to appalling acts of violence. Bands of fanatical revolutionaries swept through the province of Shantung, whose control and exploitation by Germany had particularly incensed the Chinese. The land was reddened by the murder of mission-aries and their converts, and charred with the smoking ruins of their houses and colleges. The Chinese authorities responded to protests with

517

empty assurances and ineffectual decrees, and it was correctly concluded that the government contained elements sympathetic to the uprising. Evidence appeared in midwinter that the powerful and reactionary Empress Dowager had commanded war on the foreign invaders. But the western capitals, while indignant over the outrages, viewed them as an old story and were slow to give up confidence that the disorder would be suppressed.

The State Department was incapable of interpreting the storm signals, though full reports were made by the American minister, Edwin H. Conger. A former congressman from Iowa, and an old friend of the President, Conger had had no training in Far Eastern affairs before his arrival at Pekin in the summer of 1898. According to the opinion he then formed, the old China was not worth preserving. He thought in terms of westernizing China and developing its material resources, and had advised Secretary Hay that the United States should get "at least one good port" in the process. His warnings about the outbreaks did not conform to Rockhill's observations of eight years before. The out-of-date views of the expert easily outweighed those of the political appointee on the spot. Hay was skeptical when Conger telegraphed him in March that the situation was critical.

The other powers were sufficiently alarmed to propose a combined naval demonstration. The United States declined to participate, but had detailed a warship for the "independent protection" of the Americans in China. In April, a sizable international fleet was assembled off Taku, the fortified outer port of Tientsin, a city seventy miles from Pekin and connected by rail with the capital. Conger was much gratified, but his spirits sank when the Navy Department abruptly transferred the American ship to Shanghai. The arrangement was that, in case of emergency, he was to communicate with Rear Admiral Louis Kempff, second in command of the force on the Asiatic Station. He telegraphed in the middle of May, when the Boxers were swarming around Tientsin and thrusting close to the capital. Kempff promptly sailed from Yokohama on the *Newark*. Some days later, the State Department rather grudgingly acceded to Conger's request to provide a legation guard, as the other governments were doing. The railroad had been attacked, bridges were down and stations burned, but all the guards got through from Tientsin. Conger was proud that the Americans were the first to arrive, fifty marines and seamen from the *Newark*, with an automatic gun.

The European capitals grew excited as the news from Pekin lagged, and the diplomats at Washington visited Secretary Hay's office with worried inquiries; but Hay himself was calm. After examining a packet of Conger's recent dispatches, Rockhill still did not believe that the uprising would cause "any serious complications." When this report was made, June 1, the countryside around Pekin was aflame and Boxers were rioting and burning within the city walls. The imperial troops were fraternizing with the revolutionaries; the Cabinet was divided and impotent. As communications with the coast were repeatedly severed, the commanders of the squadrons in Taku Bay resolved to organize an expedition to go to the relief of the legations and repair the railroad on the way. A force of about two thousand marines, mainly Russian and English, but including a hundred Americans under Captain Bowman McCalla of the *Newark*, started out from Tientsin on June 10, and soon lost contact with the fleet. For a few days, the frail thread of a government telegraph still bore messages from Pekin. Then, with a last call for help, the legations were silent.

The Cabinet meeting on June 15 was entirely devoted to China. Kempff was being reinforced, in spite of remonstrances from Admiral Remey at Manila. It was reluctantly decided to bring an infantry regiment from the Philippines, in spite of equally strong protests from MacArthur. A few troops of cavalry were to sail from San Francisco. Secretary Hay had been plying Conger with cautions against co-operating with the other diplomats, but this uneasy Cabinet meeting prompted a different concern. Hay sent a cable directing Conger to communicate with Kempff and report. The unfortunate minister would have liked nothing better. He could no longer speak to the seacoast, or the outside world. The Chinese troops were out of control. They had murdered the chancellor of the Japanese legation, and were vying with the Boxers in arson and pillage. The foreigners, besieged in the Inner City of Pekin, were praying for the arrival of the relief expedition.

The siege of the legations lasted until August 14, when a second relief expedition succeeded in fighting its way to Pekin. The weeks of suspense were a time of strain for the Washington officials. Their natural feelings of distress and responsibility were magnified by having to tread a slippery path between the chasm of embroilment with the European powers and the abyss of indifference to American citizens and interests. The dangers of breaking with tradition were enhanced by the untimely political season at which the siege occurred. A voluminous flow of press releases, both before and after the two national conventions, emphasized the limited character of the intervention in China, and assured the public that the government had not entered a concert of the powers and would avoid joint action with their forces. While convincing the people that the

United States was acting singly, Washington also had to demonstrate that it was acting energetically. The silence of the legations oppressed the country with horror of Boxer atrocities. Newspaper columns were lurid with tales of anarchy at Pekin. The propaganda of the church groups, with more than a thousand American missionaries in China, kept fear and anger burning. "The drama of the Legations," Henry Adams wrote, "interested the public much as though it were a novel by Alexandre Dumas." But Adams's educated blood ran colder than that of common folk. While American lives and property were in danger, the country seethed with impatience for effective intervention.

The scale of the military preparations was tremendously increased as the result of an incident at Taku on June 17. The allied admirals had decided to safeguard their communications with Tientsin by occupying the port installations. When the Chinese commander refused to surrender, the fleet bombarded and captured the forts. This engagement— in which Admiral Kempff did not take part—inflamed Chinese hostility. It was followed by fierce assaults on the foreigners at Pekin and Tientsin. War between the powers and China seemed imminent. Among the American ships that converged on China were the *Oregon* and the *Brooklyn* of Spanish War fame. Admiral Remey himself proceeded to Taku. Peremptory orders to MacArthur speeded the departure of the infantry regiment from the Philippines. General Adna Chaffee was appointed to the command of the American forces on land, and sailed on July 1 from San Francisco. Meanwhile, the sense of crisis had been deepened by news of the expedition which had set out for Pekin. It had been severely handled by imperial troops, who swarmed to the aid of the Boxers after the action at Taku; and, compelled to fall back with heavy losses, it was finally rescued by another mixed force of marines who had battled their way through Tientsin. The mauling suffered by this small but spirited column and the stiff resistance at Tientsin altered the concept of "prostrate China." At a conference of the foreign admirals on July 5, it was nervously estimated that 60,000 troops would be needed to march on Pekin, besides 20,000 required to hold the line from the outer port to Tientsin.

Russia was pouring soldiers into China from nine warships in Taku Bay, and there were large reserves at her "leased" harbor of Port Arthur. Japan, the only other nation with a large force available, had offered to send an army to Pekin, and settle the Boxer uprising singlehanded. The Japanese admiral was asked to bring on 13,000 troops known to be waiting at Hiroshima. The greater part of the force that assembled in July and early August was thus supplied by the two powers that were in hostile rivalry over their respective occupations in Manchuria and Korea. A quota of 10,000 troops had been assigned to the United States. Root succeeded in getting more than half that number to China before the relief of the legations, but only about half again saw action. Two American infantry battalions, a mere token force, were in the army that captured the native city of Tientsin on July 13. The expedition that entered Pekin a month later contained 2,100 Americans out of a total of about 20,000. But they represented the new military power in the Pacific, with an army of more than 75,000 in the Philippines; and their participation was an assurance that the intervention was limited and disinterested in character. In the policy of maintaining the Chinese Empire, the United States had the support of Japan as well as England. The friendly attitude of the Tokyo government greatly simplified the task of supplying two armies in the Far East. The port of Nagasaki, which the Americans were permitted to use as a redistribution point, was the secondary base of the China Relief Expedition of the United States.

To retain the friendship of China was the President's paramount desire. His tolerant mind was quick to comprehend the distress and confusion of an isolated people, whose homogeneity and seclusion had been disturbed by the inroads of the powers. Though keenly worried about Conger and the other members of the American legation, he refused to acknowledge doubts of their survival even in the dark days of July, when it was known that the German minister had been murdered by Chinese soldiers, and almost universally believed that the entire foreign colony had perished. The reports of a general massacre came from an apparently reliable source, but they were insistently denied by the Chinese minister at Washington, and the President continued to hope. His optimism was a matter of policy, as well as personal inclination. To abandon hope for the legations was to divest the intervention of the motive of rescue and relief. When Secretary Hay submitted the draft of a telegram to Kaiser Wilhelm, conveying the President's condolences on the murder of the German minister, McKinley took care to delete a reference to "the only too real apprehension that the other foreign representatives may have shared his fate."

The aim of cordial relations with China was advanced by Admiral Kempff's refusal to take part in the bombardment at Taku. The advantage had not been immediately recognized at Washington. In spite of all the warnings against co-operating with other powers, the Navy Department was startled by the news that American warships had been inactive under fire. (One old tub, the *Monocacy*, was actually struck by Chinese shell.) But the authorities rallied to Kempff's defense on realizing that the Chinese officials regarded his attitude as an evidence of American friendship. Through the Chinese minister, Wu Ting Fang, many messages were exchanged between Washington and the viceroys of the central and southern provinces. There were repeated proposals from the powerful old statesman, Li Hung Chang. He was deeply involved with Russia and John Hay regarded him as "an unmitigated scoundrel," but the Earl Li exercised a dominant influence at Pekin, particularly after his recall to the capital in July. It was expedient for the State Department to appear to trust him, and the War Department named him as a friendly official in the instructions sent to General Chaffee at Nagasaki. Dealing with the viceroys was a frequently wearisome business, productive of misleading information and fruitless correspondence, but it served the resolute assumption of the United States government that the anti-foreign demonstrations were merely local outbreaks and that the intervention of the powers did not imply a state of war with China.

In furtherance of this policy, Hay addressed another circular to the powers on July 3. It declared the wish of the United States to remain at peace with China, reaffirmed the principle of equal and impartial trade, and emphatically declared for the permanent peace and preservation of the Empire. It did not expressly renounce the desire to acquire Chinese territory. As John W. Foster later heard from Hay, the omission had been directed by the President. So much the Navy Department had accomplished. While bending every effort to prevent the partition of China, McKinley had a mental reservation in case it became inevitable.

The foreign governments did not reply to the circular. The rousing response came from the people at home when it was released to the press. Vindictiveness toward China had swollen as the suspense was drawn out, and Kempff's inaction had provoked a din of outraged protests. But the spirit of retaliation was calmed by Secretary Hay's pronouncements. The diplomatic notes of July 3, always popularly confounded with the Open Door proposals, were regarded by Americans as an example to the whole world of unselfish national purposes.

Acclaim for the Secretary of State was amplified by one of the most dramatic incidents of the summer, the receipt on July 20 of a message from Conger. On learning that the Chinese legation at Washington had been in touch with Pekin, Hay had asked Minister Wu to try to get through a cipher dispatch to Conger, asking for news. Some ten days passed before the reply was delivered. It was a message of impending massacre and a prayer for quick relief; but, after a month of silence, it seemed miraculous that Conger still lived and that his cry for help could be heard. The authenticity of the message was at first doubted, but Hay established that he was in actual communication with the American minister by ask-

ing for the name of his sister and obtaining the correct answer, "Alta."
Americans were delighted by the homeliness and ingenuity of this method
of identification. They probably gave Hay more credit than he deserved
for hastening the advance of the relief force. His success was not unique.
The Japanese soon found means of communicating with their legation.

General Chaffee, arriving at Tientsin at the end of July, found the
generals ready to take the aggressive with the forces that were available.
At their conference on August 3, it was decided to move the next night in
a double column—the Japanese, British, and American troops on one
side, and the Russians with a small French force on the other—against the
Chinese entrenchments about twenty-five miles from Tientsin. The action
was successful. The international army pressed on, and entered Pekin
after a campaign of ten days.

In dealing with the Chinese officials, Washington had insisted on the
reopening of direct communications between the legations and their
governments, and this result was attained in early August, after the relief
expedition started. The other American stipulation, that the Pekin government should co-operate with the expedition, was then repeated to Wu
Ting Fang as a virtual ultimatum. But the fearful rulers fled before the
invasion of marauding soldiery. The allied commanders were deprived of
any authority on which to enforce submission, or with which to treat;
and even the liberated diplomats seemed superfluous, lacking a government
to which to be accredited. The drama at Pekin lapsed abruptly into anti-
climax, as the Chinese capital succumbed to foreign occupation and the
plunder of the fabulous spoils of its ancient palaces.

Neither the President nor Secretary Hay was in Washington when the
news was received. Shortly after his renomination by the Republican
National Convention, McKinley had gone to Canton. The idea of repeating the "front porch" visitations of 1896 was not in his mind. According
to his strict, old-fashioned view, it was improper for the President of all
the people to enter into a contest for his own re-election. He had set up
temporary offices at the North Market Street house, which was connected
with the Executive Mansion by long-distance telephone, and intended to
remain there in quasi-retirement until the political campaign was over.
The crisis in China, however, had interfered with McKinley's plans. He
had twice gone to Washington for special Cabinet meetings before the
capture of Pekin, and the illness of Secretary Hay doubled his responsibilities thereafter.

The Secretary of State had stayed at his desk in deepening depression
of strength and spirits. His labors in the muggy July heat carried a delicate

man of nearly sixty-two to the verge of collapse. The week before the relief of the legations, Hay fled to his summer place in New Hampshire, and was invalided there for the next two months. He kept in touch with the State Department, writing daily to Alvey A. Adee, who was Acting Secretary during the absence on leave of the First Assistant, David J. Hill. Hay also occasionally telegraphed the President, or penciled a note from his bed. But, even with the telephone connection, McKinley was not satisfied to stay away from Washington. He returned to the White House in the middle of August for a stay of four or five weeks, and went back for important conferences later in September.

The President's chief consultant on China during the first month of Hay's absence was Secretary Root. Adee, as Cortelyou commented, was "wonderfully well versed in all the technical details of international correspondence and negotiation . . . very fertile in resource, a man of ready wit, keen and incisive in the conduct of a diplomatic interview." But his deafness was a handicap in discussion, and precluded conference over the long-distance telephone; and Cortelyou also noted the lack of "a certain initiative." These deficiencies were amply compensated by the "vigor and assertiveness" of the Secretary of War. Root plunged into his first experience in diplomacy with boyish enthusiasm. Captivated by the new game, he brought zest to all its problems, including that of serving as intermediary between the Acting Secretary of State and the President, when the latter was in Canton. First, Root had to "yell at Adee," and then go to the White House and "yell at the President" over the telephone. "I feel as if China had me by the throat," he blithely wrote his wife.

One of the important questions discussed by long-range communication was raised a few days before the relief of the legations. A large German force was on its way to China, under instructions to take revenge for the murder of the German minister. The Kaiser proposed that its commander, Field Marshal Count von Waldersee, should become the generalissimo of all the foreign troops in China. Root drafted an evasive acceptance, which the President criticized as "rather formal and doubting," and "not quite as generous as it ought to be." "If we are going to do it," McKinley said after hearing the draft read over the telephone, "it seems to me the more graciously we do it the better and with the fewest ifs and qualifications."

The President's first reaction—somewhat modified as the conversation went on—is interesting on two scores. It shows a desire to cultivate the good will of Germany—and perhaps salvage German-American votes in the approaching election—and a considerable indifference to the command of the international army. Since Count von Waldersee could not reach

China for another six weeks, his appointment was actually little more than a courteous formality in the view then taken at Washington. Long before his arrival, it was expected that the legation staffs and other foreign residents would have been evacuated from Pekin to the seacoast, and that negotiations would be under way for a settlement with China.

These hopes were dashed by the flight of the Pekin officials and the dissension among the European powers. Washington temporized. The desire of the State Department was to back England and the Open Door with military force until satisfactory peace terms were arranged. Chaffee, however, was instructed to hold himself in readiness to move. McKinley and Root were inclined to evacuate the Americans as soon as possible.

The tortuous diplomacy of St. Petersburg supplied an unlooked-for occasion for a statement of policy. The President was in command at Washington when on August 28 a note from Russia was received, disclaiming territorial designs, and inviting the United States to follow her in withdrawing her troops and legation staff to Tientsin. Russia was transparently seeking a trading point for new concessions from China in Manchuria; but, even at the risk of estranging England, as well as Germany, Washington could not refuse the opportunity to set forth the American position. In this view, a conditional acceptance was endorsed even by Acting Secretary Adee, who was satisfied to leave only the American legation and "an adequate mixed military police guard" at Pekin.

The Cabinet members who were in Washington—Root, Gage, Smith, Hitchcock, and Wilson—were called to a special middle-of-the-week meeting, and spent an entire day in considering the reply. They were furnished with copies of two drafts which had been dictated the night before, one by the President and the other by Root. After the morning's discussion, these two retired and separately prepared new versions. Cortelyou, always a curious observer of methods of work, was amused by the "exceedingly deliberate, one might almost say labored" performance of the Secretary of War. The dictation of Root's second draft consumed forty or fifty minutes, while the President in ten minutes rolled off wordage two or three times as long. During the afternoon session, the two versions were combined and edited. The finished product was signed by Adee. Though present at most of the discussion and in agreement with its conclusions, he had been overshadowed by Root. Cortelyou's account does not mention the tentative reply which Adee himself had prepared in advance of the meeting.

The American note was the vapid fruit of multiple collaboration. It may have owed some of its turgidity to Root's inexperience in diplomatic correspondence, but its ambiguities also suggest the cautiousness of the President. Obscurity thickened as it reached the crux of the Russian invitation. In plain language, what the President wanted was to get out of Pekin, not with Russia alone, but in co-operation with all the powers. This idea was involved in so many circumlocutions, provisos, and qualifications that it baffled the press. London and Berlin were startled by the information that the United States had concerted with Russia to withdraw.

The President, in fact, grew increasingly impatient to follow the Russian example. Political interest urged the removal of Chaffee's force before the national election, but the campaign issue of "McKinley imperialism" did not tell the whole story. The involvement in military occupation was on every count objectionable to the President. He was informed of the atrocities which some European troops inflicted on the Chinese people, and of the difficulties of supplying a large force at Pekin during the winter. Both Chaffee and Conger strongly advised withdrawal. The military situation in the Philippines pressed for the same conclusion. There had been an unexpected recurrence of sharp insurgent attacks, and MacArthur was in serious need of reinforcements. McKinley was much impressed by a letter from Senator Morgan, urging that Chaffee's expedition be held in the Philippines. Above all, the jealous quarrels among the powers made the President anxious to extricate the American troops from an equilibrium of tensions which might momentarily break into violence, invasion, and world war.

On Sunday, September 9, McKinley dashed off an abrupt query to Hay about reducing the Pekin force to a legation guard, or alternatively bringing Conger and his staff to the coast. The handwritten note suggests a melancholy picture of the President, brooding over his problems in the deserted Executive Mansion, without the assistance of Cortelyou, or even a stenographer. McKinley had now been deprived of his substitute consultant on China. Root had developed a carbuncle on his left breast. That same Sunday he was undergoing an operation at Southampton, and would be confined to his room for the next two or three weeks.

McKinley had virtually made up his mind when he went to Ohio a few days later—"I know of no way to get out but to come out," he wrote Hay on September 14—but Washington was in receipt of dispatches which argued against the decision. Conger had become reluctantly convinced of the unwisdom of entirely abandoning the occupation, and now advised that some military force at Pekin was absolutely essential to successful negotiations. Attorney General Griggs, just returned from his vacation, undertook to telephone the President. A decision was once more postponed.

The important business which soon brought McKinley back to Washington was a note from Berlin, suggesting that, as a condition antecedent to entering on negotiations, the guilty officials at Pekin should be turned over to the powers for punishment. Griggs was the only Cabinet member at the White House dinner meeting which considered the reply. Adjutant General Corbin, designated Acting Secretary of War, appeared in place of Root. The State Department was represented by Acting Secretary Hill, who had finally returned from leave, and his next in command, Adee. A blunt statement was framed that the United States was not disposed to join in the German demand, since the punishment of the guilty throughout China should be carried out by the supreme imperial authority. The immediate result of this rebuke to the spirit of reprisal was a hubbub of disapproval in western Europe. Even England hung back from supporting the United States. Germany, however, eventually receded from the demand.

The President did not again advert to removing the legation from Pekin; but, to the satisfaction of the American public, the United States force was reduced to a sizable guard. There was a certain irony in the fact that the course Adee had recommended was adopted mainly on the advice of a minister who was lightly esteemed by the State Department. Secretary Hay had dispatched Rockhill to Pekin in anticipation of the peace discussions. Adee had been scandalized by two cables which Conger sent in August, violently denouncing the Chinese authorities, especially Li Hung Chang, and demanding their severe punishment. These outbursts—which were carefully concealed from the press—had persuaded Adee that Conger's mind had been unbalanced by the strain of the siege, and that he was unfit to represent the United States in the negotiations. But the President had confidence in Conger, and trusted him to regain his balance, even though he had to deal with Li Hung Chang at the peace table. Conger served with credit as American plenipotentiary in the preliminary discussions; and, like Rockhill, who succeeded him, consistently exerted the influence of the United States to moderate the penalties imposed on China.

The doctrine of the Open Door lingered in American mythology as a powerful assertion, but its cogency was gone with the withdrawal of the United States army. Unessential to the national interest, the policy had not been destined to a vigorous survival. The people had been pleased to utter a wish for the preservation of China. Keeping their soldiers on Chinese soil was quite a different matter. Yet, in the negative sense of forswearing encroachment on that soil, the wish was entirely sincere. The vast majority of Americans would have been outraged by the knowledge that the Navy Department was grasping at a coaling station in China.

Shortly after the national election of 1900, the State Department was persuaded to raise the question of a concession in the southeastern province of Fukien. A more awkwardly timed or futile inquiry could not have been imagined. Conger himself was reluctant to pursue it, in view of the declarations that had emanated from Washington. The United States, moreover, had abstained too long from the feast. Everything was gone. The Fukien coast had recently become a Japanese sphere of influence, and the American inquiry was politely rebuffed by Tokyo.

· 23 ·

THE RUNNING MATE AND THE ISSUES

GOVERNOR ROOSEVELT had gone to Washington in June to deny that he was a candidate for the vice-presidency. He heard no objection from the highest officials of the government. The President observed that he would be far more valuable in New York. Elihu Root, "with his frank and murderous smile," told Roosevelt: "Of course not,—you're not fit for it." John Hay thought that "Teddy" was "more fun than a goat." "He came down," Hay wrote Adams, "with a somber resolution throned in his strenuous brow, to let McKinley and Hanna know, once for all, that he would not be Vice-President, and found to his stupefaction that nobody in Washington, except Platt, had ever dreamed of such a thing. . . ."

It was well known that "the McKinley people" had not encouraged talk of Roosevelt's candidacy, but plenty of Republican politicians had dreamed of it besides Tom Platt. The hero of San Juan Hill was an Easterner with a national reputation. He was popular in New York, which wanted the nomination and was always a hard state for the Republicans to carry in the national campaign; and he had the uncommon advantage of an enthusiastic following in the West. The reticence of "the McKinley people" had failed to suppress the opinion that the ebullient, hard-hitting Colonel of the Rough Riders would make a good running mate for the President.

The nomination was a subject of exceptional interest, and not only for the obvious reason that everything else about the Republican convention had been settled in advance. The vice-presidency had taken on a notable prestige during Hobart's time in Washington. The significance of his intimate association with the White House had not been fully appreciated until his death. Then it was remarked that, by making the Vice-President a functioning member of the administration, McKinley had restored to the office an importance that had actually been the design of the framers of the Constitution. The "true greatness" of the vice-presidency had been expounded by Senator Cabot Lodge in a memorial address in January. Hobart, he said, had lifted out of neglect a place that too often had been treated as a convenient and honorable shelf, or a consolation prize. The office should be one of the great prizes of political life, to be desired by "our most ambitious men . . . as a stepping stone to higher honors."

Lodge was addressing the Senate, but he meant his voice to carry to Albany, New York. Roosevelt's next move would be crucial to his presidential aspirations. Turning from one preference to another, he had sometimes expressed a wish for two more years as governor, but Lodge was aiming at a national position. Roosevelt's hopes of the War Department had recently vanished for a second time. Elihu Root had been the first choice of the Republican National Committee for the vice-presidential nomination, but McKinley had objected to losing his Secretary of War, and Root was to stay in the Cabinet. The civil governorship of the Philippines was the only suitable appointment that remained, and Lodge determined to clear the matter up by "a very frank talk" with the President.

The interview took place in late January. Lodge asked McKinley "point blank" if he were thinking of sending Roosevelt to the Philippines. Not at present, McKinley replied. When civil government was fully established, he thought that Roosevelt was the ideal man for the first governor. There was no one he thought so well fitted. He had said so to Schurman. But the war was still going on. The President did not think it fair to make Roosevelt governor until he could have control of everything. Lodge was obliged to admit the force of this. Incidentally, the President had already sent for Judge Taft when the "very frank talk" took place. If the chairman of the Senate Committee on the Philippines was told of the summons, he did not mention it to Roosevelt in advising him of this second disappointment. Lodge certainly was given no conception of the scope of the President's plans for the new civil commission.

The question of the vice-presidency was explored before the interview ended. Lodge wrote Roosevelt that McKinley seemed "perfectly content" to have him on the ticket. The time had come for Roosevelt to make up his mind between the national candidacy and a second term in New York. He concluded to stay where he was. In spite of Lodge's arguments, Roosevelt was leaning toward the shelf, rather than the steppingstone theory of the Vice-Presidency. He was carelessly confident that he could have another term as governor; but, though Roosevelt had made many compromises with Platt's machine, he had refused to play ball with the corporations and the big insurance companies. Platt had been given his orders to get Roosevelt out of New York.

Roosevelt had at first been naïvely puzzled by Platt's enthusiasm for making him vice-president. When he learned that the moneyed interests were behind it, he still thought that he could fight it out in New York. The information had whetted his aversion to the national office. He proceeded to issue a statement that under no circumstances could he or would he accept the nomination. As time passed, the dismal truth was borne in on Roosevelt that he was likely to end up without any office at all, but pride made him stick to his statement. There was only one condition that would enable him to eat his words with self-respect: an overwhelming party pressure, totally unrelated to the machinations of Platt.

In early March, Nicholas Murray Butler of Columbia University went to Washington at Roosevelt's request, to find out what was "up" about the vice-presidency. He was expressly charged to tell the President and Hanna that Roosevelt would not accept the nomination. McKinley was amused, and laughed pleasantly with Butler "about some of T. R.'s characteristics." Hanna received the emissary with expletives. He banged on the table and told Butler that he was going to control the convention at Philadelphia and Roosevelt would not be nominated. It seems odd that, after this report, Roosevelt should have persisted in going to Washington himself; and odder still that he was disappointed by his reception. Foraker said that the indifference of "the McKinley people" stung Roosevelt into deciding to accept the nomination.

Roosevelt's public utterances, however, did not bear Foraker out. The press was blaring the news that Platt and Quay had formed one of their familiar coalitions, and were planning to stampede the convention. Roosevelt expostulated more strenuously than ever after his trip to Washington.

McKinley had mystified his party by adopting a neutral position on the choice of his running mate. His support had been claimed by the friends of John D. Long and Cornelius Bliss, of Senators Fairbanks, Allison, and Spooner, and young Representative Jonathan Dolliver of Iowa. The President had beamed assurances that the field was open to all. Most of them had withdrawn. The western states, the main battleground of the coming campaign, had shown little energy in promoting their favorite sons. The politicians were waiting for a sign, skeptical of the President's impartiality and convinced that an Easterner was slated. Secretary Long, a passive candidate from the firmly Republican State of Massachusetts, was for some weeks believed to be the favorite; but the sign had not appeared, and Long's candidacy failed to make progress outside New England. Bliss, who had Hanna's backing, was indisposed to run. Another New Yorker was the only aggressive candidate who had come forward. Lieutenant Governor Timothy L. Woodruff was a prosperous Brooklyn businessman and a loyal member of Platt's organization. He had shown a daring eccentricity by wearing a brightly colored vest at the convention of 1896. No one took Woodruff's busy canvass seriously.

Ten days before the convention opened, the President held a long conference with Hanna and Charles Dick, the secretary of the Republican National Committee. An attempt was made to stimulate some activity in the West by putting out an announcement of the President's neutrality. McKinley also appealed to the candidate of his secret choice to reconsider. This was Senator Allison of Iowa, now "the father of the Senate," and proud of his twenty-eight years of unbroken service in that body. Determined to stay in an honorable and accustomed place, Allison declined to listen to persuasion.

The President's obvious anxiety about the nomination was described by Senator Foraker as active opposition to the choice of Roosevelt. Years later, Foraker told of a conversation he had with the President on the eve of the convention. He had as usual been requested to nominate McKinley, and was incensed by an eleventh-hour newspaper report that Hanna had arranged to replace him with Allison. Calling at the White House on his way to the train, Foraker disclosed his grievance and offered to stand aside. The President reassured him, and smoothed him down. Then, as Foraker was leaving, McKinley abruptly said, "I hope you will not allow the convention to be stampeded to Roosevelt for Vice-President."

Apart from the prejudiced character of the source, the accuracy of this recollection is open to question. It is in direct conflict with the most reliable testimony that the President refused to influence the delegates. Possibly Foraker distorted some censure of the threatened coalition of the bosses. There can be no doubt that McKinley dreaded Roosevelt's nomination at the hands of Platt and Quay. He abhorred such deals, and had shunned them throughout his political life; and at the same time he may have feared some taint of association with this one. There was no mistrust of his connection with the thoroughly discredited boss of Pennsylvania. Quay had been ousted—temporarily—from the Senate, and blamed Hanna for casting the decisive vote which lost him his seat. But the President's cordial relationship with Platt had caused unfavorable comment, recently aggravated by the appointment of Platt's friend, John R. Hazel, to a federal judgeship in western New York. With the repercussions of this case still sounding, McKinley had more than ordinarily strong reasons for wishing to avoid the scandal of machine control at the convention.

A spontaneous movement for Roosevelt would be quite another matter. Had McKinley wished to block it, he had no need to apply to Foraker's dubious loyalty. Most of his conservative advisers were anti-Roosevelt. Hanna had set his heart on naming a "safe" candidate, identified with the policies of the administration, and fitted to carry them out, if need should arise. "It must always be remembered," he told the newspapermen at Philadelphia, "that there is only one life between the Vice-President and the Chief Magistracy of the Nation. . . ." But such arguments did not persuade McKinley. He needed a united and enthusiastic party organization. He needed a running mate who would strengthen the ticket in the West. Roosevelt would not be a second Hobart, smoothly enfolded in the councils of the administration, but he was a coming man, a potential nominee for President in 1904. If the convention wanted Roosevelt, McKinley was ready to smile his approval, in spite of his advisers.

Hanna was no longer confident of his standing with McKinley. He had passed the month of May in an agony of doubt that he was to remain as chairman of the Republican National Committee. He was badly crippled by rheumatism; and, nursing his painful knees, he had complained that he was not well enough to manage the campaign. He was not coaxed, or told that he was indispensable and must sacrifice himself for the President and the party. McKinley appeared to have taken him at his word. Hanna glimpsed the possibility of being shorn of his command. His face grew haggard. His friends thought that he was sick with worry. He had a heart attack, and fainted away at his desk. McKinley drew out the suspense until the very end of May before he spoke to Hanna.

McKinley had been displeased by Hanna's pretensions to paramount influence at the White House, but the injury had not affected his treatment of his friend. His uncharacteristic coldness implies some fresh cause of offense. An open disagreement is suggested by Hanna's oddly passive, desperate misery. It is impossible to accept the theory that McKinley had been antagonized by Hanna's increasing power in the Senate and before the people. Hanna owed his prestige in the Senate to his hold on the federal patronage. He enjoyed that hold by favor of the President, and was sick with fear of losing it. The timing is wrong for a reference to his popular "leadership." Except by sinister reputation, Hanna was still almost unknown outside Ohio. Most of the delegates at Philadelphia had never seen him before the convention opened. McKinley's renomination was, in any case, assured; political rivalry could not touch him. But he was exceedingly sensitive to the slur of association with a coarse standard of public morality. The approaching campaign had revived the partisan outcry that he was Hanna's man. In the month before the Republican convention, the post-office scandals in Cuba were creating intense excitement in Congress and in the press.

The Department of Posts in Cuba—as in Porto Rico and the Philippines—had not been placed under the direction of the military government, but was controlled by the Post Office Department. The arrangement was not an altogether happy one. It gave some color of validity to Democratic charges that the Republicans were manufacturing jobs abroad. The Post Office, moreover, was peculiarly vulnerable to criticism. In preceding administrations, corruption had crept insidiously through the huge, politically dominated Department. The situation had not been improved by Hanna's wholesale appointments, made in flagrant violation of the civil service regulations. Postmaster General Smith, though never implicated in dishonest practices, had been as complaisant as his predecessors in overlooking laxities in the bureaus. The President, of course, was responsible for Hanna's operations. He must, at least tacitly, have condoned them; but he took a very different attitude toward evidence of fraud in the public service. Governor General Wood's report of the embezzlements at Havana had stirred the President to action. He not only supported Wood in pressing charges, but ordered an investigation from Washington. In the middle of May, he called in the Fourth Assistant Postmaster General, Joseph L. Bristow, a highly competent investigator of the fearless, fanatical type. Bristow shortly left for Havana with instructions from the President to clean out the Department of Posts, and spare no man, regardless of his political influence.

Hanna's anxiety to protect his friend, Director General Rathbone, was a sufficient reason for a break with the President. The delay in the matter of the chairmanship possibly indicated a measure of discipline, as well as an estrangement. "Anticipation is sometimes a good regulator," the President once said with emphasis, in another connection. Hanna grasped at the eventual offer in relief, though he was never reconciled to Bristow's interference. In earlier days of hero worship, he had gloried in McKinley's scruples. Now he was nearly sixty-two, rheumatic and cross, enamored of the exercise of power. He would always love McKinley, but the bloom of romance had faded. Scruples had lost their charm.

Hanna was not resigned to the President's impartiality on the Vice-Presidency, either. He went off to Philadelphia in a mood of sullen resistance to leaving the delegates without an intimation of the way the patronage might be expected to flow. Even in the week before the convention, a hint from the White House would have brought a legion of federal officeholders into line. Their confusion was confounded by the diversity of opinion among the President's friends. Some favored Long;

some still talked of Fairbanks. Grosvenor and Dawes were both for Dolliver. Delegates crowded around Hanna, begging for a clue. He could only profess that he, too, was impartial, twisting his mouth around the phrase "May the best man win."

Meanwhile, the Roosevelt backers were skirmishing for position. Quay led the forces in the field, eager to avenge himself on Hanna for the loss of his seat in the Senate. Platt was to remain in the rear in technical fulfillment of a promise made to Roosevelt that he would not force his nomination. Actually, Platt took to his bed with a broken rib. But, corseted in plaster of Paris and drugged with opiates, he was still a formidable adversary, and he had a score of his own to pay. By attempting to build up Bliss, Hanna had committed a trespass on Platt's private domain of New York.

Governor Roosevelt had accompanied Senator Platt to Philadelphia. Three days before the convention opened, he was on the scene of action with an ache in one of his famous teeth and an aggressive objection to receiving the vice-presidential nomination. Only two circumstances seemed to belie his assertions. One was his presence in Philadelphia. A delegate at large from New York, he had been repeatedly warned by Lodge to stay away from the convention if he did not want to be nominated. The other inconsistency was Roosevelt's conspicuous appearance as he strode through the hotel lobbies and the headquarters of the various delegations. In June, nearly all the Easterners had laid aside their derbies and curly-brimmed little fedoras, and donned the hard straws that were the summertime badge of the American male. Roosevelt had dug out a broad-brimmed black felt hat which closely resembled the headgear of the Rough Riders. He had worn this hat when he campaigned for governor in 1898. It had recalled to every beholder the gallant charge of San Juan Hill, and it did so once again in 1900. This was a dull convention, unusually barren of colorful personalities. Roosevelt, with his wide brim raked at a military angle, was the most picturesque figure to be seen. Appreciative smiles greeted the quip of one of the delegates, "Gentlemen, that's an acceptance hat."

The news correspondents remarked how greatly Hanna had changed since 1896. His full face had shrunk, and the snapping brightness had faded from his red-brown eyes. He was so lame that he had to be helped up and down the front steps of the Hotel Walton, where the Republican National Committee had its headquarters. There was also a limp in his generalship. He did not recognize the genuine sentiment for Roosevelt, and had planned no strategy to meet it. He was still sticking to Cornelius Bliss, who did not want the nomination, and could not get the support of the New York delegation, if he tried.

The convention was to open on Tuesday, June 19. During the preceding week of meetings, Hanna stayed at Haverford at the house of the big shipowner, Clement A. Griscom. He returned there on the Saturday evening, when most of the delegations had reached Philadelphia, to pass a quiet Sunday, ending in a dinner meeting of Republican grandees who had been invited to discuss the platform. A Roosevelt boom started while Hanna was out of town. Quay's deputy, Senator Boies Penrose, called on Roosevelt at the Walton on Sunday morning, to convey assurances of the support of Pennsylvania. He was followed by the chairman of the California delegation, whose unanimous endorsement had been arranged. The idea of conscripting a popular candidate quickly caught on. Excitement flashed up in the western delegations, and even some of the southern delegations, which Hanna controlled. Crowds milled in Broad Street, enlivening the dreariness of the dry Philadelphia Sabbath, and Bim the Button Man did a brisk trade in the McKinley-Roosevelt badges which he had had the foresight to provide. A procession of callers turned in at the Walton to protest their loyal support. The Governor of New York gave them his dazzling grin, and expressed regret that they should have decided to force him into the field. He still said that he did not want the nomination, but his resistance was evidently weakening. Platt and Quay were shrewdly exploiting the enthusiasm. Lodge—officially the manager of Long's canvass—was doing what he could to promote it. Veteran politicians and correspondents thought that Roosevelt was as good as nominated. "I think up to this moment Roosevelt was against it, but they have turned his head," Charles Dick told Cortelyou over the telephone at ten-thirty in the evening.

Tidings of the day's developments had been borne to Haverford by Mr. Griscom's dinner guests. Senator Lodge was among them, and so was Platt's suave old lieutenant Depew. Hanna must have spent an evening of grim repression. Dick had found him "quite unhappy" when he called him on the telephone. The phrase was an understatement. Hanna saw the convention slipping out of his control. The defeat was too cruel for him to accept. He desperately looked to the President for help in crushing Roosevelt's candidacy. Dick questioned the wisdom of attempting to do so. A hasty canvass of "our friends" had been discouraging. There was no alternative candidate to whom they could rally their delegations. Most of them had bowed to the inevitable, and were ready to climb on the band wagon. But, obviously at Hanna's request, Dick laid the question before Cortelyou. He asked to know that night, if possible, "what the sentiment is at that end of the line," and twice suggested that a telephone conference be held between the White House and the country home of Mr. Griscom. The conference, however, did not take place. Cortelyou relayed the message to Dick at midnight. "The President has no choice for Vice-President. Any of the distinguished names suggested would be satisfactory to him. The choice of the convention will be his choice; he has no advice to give. . . ."

On Monday morning, Hanna moved into the Walton with blood in his eye. A scene in his private room was witnessed by a well-known Washington correspondent. Hanna came out of the telephone booth "in a towering passion." The national committeeman from Wisconsin had dropped in with a question to ask. "Do whatever you damn please!" Hanna shouted at Payne. "I'm through! I won't have anything more to do with the convention! I won't take charge of the campaign! I won't be chairman of the national committee again!" This was also the occasion of Hanna's wildly indiscreet comment on Roosevelt: "Don't any of you realize that there's only one life between that madman and the Presidency?" Payne—a Roosevelt supporter—blandly pointed out that Hanna controlled the convention. "I am not in control!" Hanna stormed. "McKinley won't let me use the power of the Administration to defeat Roosevelt. He is blind, or afraid, or something!"

But Hanna would not give up. He made for Roosevelt, and accused him of bad faith. Roosevelt could not gainsay that his eleventh-hour entry in the race would be unjust to the other contestants, or that it would wear some aspect of collaboration with Platt and Quay. Under the pounding of Hanna's reproaches, he consented to make another public denial. While Roosevelt consulted with his advisers, Hanna held a series of interviews with state leaders. Posing as the champion of fair play and Roosevelt's protector from base intrigues, he whipped the Southerners into line, and rebuked the impetuosity of the western delegations. At four o'clock, Roosevelt issued a rather wishy-washy statement, alleging that he could best help the national ticket if he were renominated for the governorship of New York, and appealing to his friends to respect his wish and judgment. The jubilation of the Roosevelt men was subdued on Monday evening. Their councils were in confusion. The New York caucus adjourned without taking action. Yet Hanna's gains were by no means as solid as they appeared to some of the correspondents. He still needed a substitute candidate. Long and Dolliver were the strongest men available, but it was questionable that either was strong enough to unite the opposition.

Hanna received an ovation the next morning when he mounted the rostrum of the big boxlike exposition building in West Philadelphia, and called the convention to order with peremptory thwacks of his gavel. The unfamiliar compliment should have been gratifying, but Hanna was in sore trouble on Tuesday. He could dictate to the southern delegations, but the Westerners were hanging back and refusing to commit themselves. Dawes thought that Hanna seemed ready to defy both the President and the convention, and give out that Long was the choice of the administration. As a Dolliver man, Dawes was in close touch with the western delegates. He knew the force of the sentiment for Roosevelt, and the antagonism which Hanna's strong-arm methods had already created. He had "almost an altercation" with Hanna in an effort to prevent a further attempt at interference. It was nevertheless with Hanna's approval that Dawes telephoned Washington, and arranged to talk with Cortelyou while McKinley listened in on the extension. The fiction was preserved that the President was isolated, like a Tibetan lama, from the worldly commotions at Philadelphia, and Dawes wanted to be able to say he had not talked with him.

The call was completed in the evening. After hearing the report, McKinley dictated a message to Cortelyou for Dawes to give to Hanna. Dawes had no paper on which to take it down. Fishing in his pocket, he found a guest card of the Union League Club of Philadelphia, and scribbled the President's instructions on the back.

The Presidents close friend must not undertake to commit the administration to any candidate. It has no candidate. The Convention must make the nomination. The administration would not if it could. The Prest close friend should be satisfied with his unanimous nomination and not interfere with the Vice P nomination. The administration wants the choice of the convention and the Presidents friend must not dictate to the convention.

Hanna appeared "a little perplexed" when Dawes gave him the "ultimatum," but he said he would follow the President's instructions. He had, however, already called a conference to decide whether to make a final effort to concentrate the anti-Roosevelt forces. It was to take place at ten-thirty that night in Mr. Bliss's rooms at the Stratford, and Hanna now invited Dawes to attend as representing Dolliver. Dawes soon heard enough to convince him that no conclusion would be reached. He left the meeting before one o'clock to make another report to Cortelyou. As Dawes went out, Hanna whispered a message in his ear that he would do exactly as the President had requested.

Yet Hanna had not admitted defeat. He was encouraged by a second caucus of the New York delegation. Mr. Bliss had come back to his rooms with the news that Roosevelt had defied Platt. The New York delegation had voted to endorse Woodruff. "Roosevelt is out of it, and will not be nominated," Hanna had assured the reporters after hearing the story from Bliss. But Hanna was surveying the convention through a distorted glass. The actual result of Roosevelt's bold conduct was to make his nomination inevitable. His defiance of the New York machine fired the western delegates with new admiration for his courage and independence. On the second day of the convention, the boom for his nomination was roaring. Wisconsin and several Far Western states declared for Roosevelt in the morning. An outbreak of applause rippled over the hall when he entered—still wearing his Rough Rider hat—and he was again acclaimed when he ascended the platform to perform the duty of escorting the permanent chairman, Senator Lodge, to the desk.

The opposition to Roosevelt scarcely needed the *coup de grâce*, but Matt Quay delivered it in style. His weapon was a resolution to alter the basis of representation at Republican conventions—the much-discussed reform which Payne had dropped at the President's wish. Such vociferous cheers greeted the boss of Pennsylvania that he was finally obliged to take the platform. Many Northerners were genuinely in favor of shearing the undue influence of the South, and Quay was on home ground, in a hall packed with adherents of his machine; but the sensation of his proposal was its challenge to Hanna's control of the southern delegations. Aghast at Quay's threat and its enthusiastic reception, the Dixie delegates had sprung to their feet, and were tramping about in disorder. They were finally quieted by Quay's urbane offer to let his resolution go over until next morning.

The platform came as an anticlimax to the excitement. It was read to an inattentive and diminishing audience, and adopted with perfunctory bays of approval. While Senator Fairbanks was intoning the monotonous phrases, Tom Platt had slipped from the convention hall in the jostle of departing delegates. His work well done, he was going home to New York to nurse his aching side. Behind him, a tidal wave for Roosevelt pounded in, laden with southern leaders. Dolliver requested that his name be withdrawn. Long telegraphed assent to the abandonment of his canvass. Roosevelt was nowhere to be found—he had gone into hiding at the house of a relative—but Benjamin B. Odell, the chairman of the New York Republican Committee, was closeted with Hanna in the evening. At about eleven, Odell came out and told the correspondents that a statement would soon be forthcoming; the vice-presidential matter had got in such a snarl that it had been left to Hanna's arbitration, and he had given assurances that the nomination would go to Roosevelt. But

Hanna still delayed the humiliating admission of his misjudgment and defeat. He talked with Roosevelt's secretary and with Nicholas Murray Butler. At one o'clock, he at last called in the champing correspondents. He announced that, as all the candidates and Governor Roosevelt also had put their affairs in his hands, he had concluded to accept the responsibility. Hanna's decision was that Roosevelt should be nominated with the same unanimity as the President.

Roosevelt had resigned himself with a good conscience to the will of the convention. The only remaining question in his mind on Wednesday night concerned the attitude of the President. His doubts were dispelled at a late hour by a conversation with his friend George W. Perkins of New York, who had made an inconspicuous trip to Washington for a talk with Cortelyou. He brought Roosevelt cordial assurances from "the friend in Washington," and acquainted him with the part that Dawes had played as intermediary between Hanna and the President. McKinley obviously felt apprehensive that Roosevelt might be lukewarm in his acceptance. Perkins emphasized in flattering terms the great responsibility and honor that had been added to the vice-presidency. Roosevelt, in his turn, gave assurances that "he saw the wisdom of the friend in Washington," and that "he was going into it with his whole heart." He earnestly asked Perkins to telephone Washington, and express his appreciation of the message.

The convention sprang to life on Thursday morning. The price of tickets quadrupled. Carriage rates to West Philadelphia were up. McKinley-Roosevelt buttons were selling by the gross. Thousands of spectators pushed their way into the din of the convention hall, where volunteers were distributing huge plumes of red, white, and blue pampas grass among the seats on the floor. Delegates eddied around their standards with cheers bubbling in their throats. The Kansas delegation, decked with yellow silk sunflowers, marched down the aisle bearing the first Roosevelt banner. The Grand Army Band from Canton, present as usual for McKinley's nomination, rendered the national anthem. Senator Lodge thumped for order, and Archbishop Patrick J. Ryan of Philadelphia offered prayer. Quay withdrew his resolution, to the tune of joyful shrieks from the Dixie delegations. The call of the states began. Cheering started in earnest, when Alabama yielded to Ohio. Foraker mounted the platform, and nominated McKinley with the warmth of professional passion. The ultimate mention of the President's name brought the delegates to their feet with frenzied hurrahs. State standards were brandished on high, with red, white, and blue umbrellas and pampas plumes, as the dense ranks

540

paraded deliriously around the platform. Above them, an elderly man rushed out and grabbed a gaudy plume. Mark Hanna, his rheumatism and his grievances forgotten, climbed on a chair, and "yelled like an Apache" for McKinley.

A fresh outburst was released by the appearance of Governor Roosevelt to second the nomination of the President. It was a moment of tremendous emotion for Lodge. Roosevelt himself was in complete control. His forcible speech for the President was in effect his own nomination. Hurrahs for McKinley and Roosevelt were with difficulty silenced. The convention was now at a frantic pitch of impatience to start the roll call. The other seconding speeches were interrupted by demands for the vote. The balloting at last began. Its ceremonious progress was followed with a curiously strained interest, punctuated by one minor opportunity for the surcease of cheers—the history-making call on Hawaii. The announcement that the President had been unanimously nominated once more plunged the convention into riotous celebration, while the bands blared "Rally 'Round the Flag" and "There'll Be a Hot Time in the Old Town Tonight," and a big fake elephant, borne aloft, came swaying down the aisle to join the circus parade. A temporary decorum was necessitated by the formality of choosing the vice-presidential candidate. Roosevelt was given another ovation on his nomination by Iowa; and the announcement that he had received every vote but one—his own—set off a final parade, hurrahing and clanging around the hall with looming elephant, jiggling standards, and waving pampas plumes. The convention wound up its business and adjourned in a mood of unanticipated elation.

Hoarse and happy, the delegates piled into hacks and streetcars, and went to pack their grips, while the telegraph sounded throughout the nation the noise of Republican harmony. Senator Platt, confined to his rooms at the Fifth Avenue Hotel, was asked for his comment on the outcome. "I am glad that we had our way," he told the reporters who gathered beside his lounge. "The people, I mean, had their way."

Ohioans were prominent in the throngs that crowded the trains to Washington. All evening in the festively decorated White House, the President beamed on the procession of guests: congratulatory party leaders, an assortment of devoted delegates, a merry party of Cantonians, the Grand Army Band, and an irrelevant gathering of the American Institute of Homeopathy. When the reception was over, he took Dawes upstairs to the Cabinet Room, and got the whole story of the vice-presidential contest. "The President thinks all has come out for the best," Dawes wrote in his diary.

Hanna was not among the jubilating Ohioans who went to Washington, but he did not sulk over his discomfiture. He seemed grateful for the "taffy" of a formal letter of compliment from the President, crediting him with "the courage and sagacity of true leadership" at the convention. "Well it was a nice little scrap at Phila," he wrote McKinley, "not exactly to my liking with my hands tied behind me. However we got through in good shape and the ticket is all right. Your *duty* to the Country is to *live* for four years from next March."

A startling aftermath of the convention was the revelation that the platform, as adopted, was lacking in certain declarations which had been sanctioned at the highest level. A good many collaborators had been engaged on the statement of party principles. Postmaster General Smith had carried to Philadelphia a draft approved by the President and Cabinet. Foraker had substantially completed the revision in advance of the organization of the Committee on Resolutions, with Fairbanks as chairman. The constitutional relationship of the new possessions—not yet decided by the Supreme Court, and an inevitable campaign issue—had been covered by a plank affirming the powers of Congress; but, before the platform was submitted to the convention, this important plank had vanished in a subcommittee of a subcommittee, together with all mention of Foraker's hard-won act for the government of Porto Rico, and a discussion of colonial government extracted from the President's latest annual message. The treacherous raid temporarily disfigured the effect of Republican harmony. Congressman Grosvenor apoplectically pointed the finger of suspicion at Congressman Lem Quigg of New York, who had acted as secretary of the subcommittee in charge of the final revisions; but much more powerful influences had obviously been involved. Whoever the culprits were, they were not friends of Mark Hanna. They had also contrived to water down the recommendation of his favorite project, government subsidies for the American merchant marine.

The deficiency of the Republican statement on expansion was underlined by the declarations adopted by the Democratic convention. The ratification meeting for William Jennings Bryan, held at Kansas City in the first week of July, had a sentimental redolence of 1896. The radical principles of the previous platform had all been retained. The majority of the delegates would have liked to soft-pedal the money tune, but Bryan had insisted on repeating the demand for silver at 16 to 1. His running mate was Adlai E. Stevenson, the dignified old Illinois silverite who had been Vice-President in Cleveland's second term. (A baby grandson had recently been named for him.) The main attack, however, was directed at "imperialism," which was declared to be the "paramount issue" of the

542

campaign. Proclaiming that no nation could long endure half republic and half empire, the Democrats denounced the colonial policy of the administration, and roundly insisted that the Constitution followed the flag. The indictment was completed by blasts against militarism, land-grabbing in Asia, and the Republican alliance with England.

It was the President's task to repair the omissions of the Philadelphia platform in his only speech of the summer—the response to the formal notification of his renomination. The calendar seemed to have rolled back four years in Canton on the July morning when the ceremonies were held. Once more, crowds filled the lawn and the sun-dappled breadth of North Market Street. Once more, the McKinleys' porch was busy with Republican dignitaries from East and West. Senator Lodge, the chairman of the notification committee, took his place at one side of the porch steps. The President came out in a thunder of full-throated cheers. He mounted a plain little stand in front of the flag-swathed awning, and gave his attention to Lodge. Then, in a ringing voice, the President delivered his reply. Free silver was the vulnerable article of the Democratic creed, and McKinley did not neglect to name the currency as the principal issue before the country. He touched on a number of other subjects—the tariff, "prosperity at home and prestige abroad," the Open Door, and the protection of Americans in China—but the significant part of his speech was its answer to the indictment of "imperialism." He asseverated the power of Congress over the island possessions, and cited the beneficent government which had been provided for Porto Rico. He repudiated the suggestion of a premature peace in the Philippines—"There must be no scuttle policy"—while disowning the purpose of severity, and promising to give a just, representative government to the islands, with liberal amnesty for the insurgents. Republican doctrine, the President said, would never be used as a weapon for oppression. The party of Lincoln had bravely met another supreme opportunity in the liberation of ten millions of the human family from the yoke of imperialism.

The crowd went on cheering after the President retired. There were calls for more speeches. Hanna, Fairbanks, and others said a few words. Loath to leave the scene, the people lingered on the lawn, while the dignitaries partook of a collation in a tent erected in the backyard. Hanna and his national committeemen caught the late afternoon train for Cleveland to hold their preliminary consultations. The task this year was less difficult than the desperate fight of 1896, with its mammoth educational program—a smaller outlay was required, and the corporations were ready to pay up—but there was plenty of work to be done before the red fire started burning. The people had forgotten the alarms which had been potent to defeat Bryan in 1896. It would not be easy to arouse them in the rich and confident America of 1900.

Hanna had no use for the cloudy issue of "imperialism." He was of the opinion that Bryan would force the trust issue to the front, and he planned to make the business recovery the keynote of the Republican campaign. The slogan of a "full dinner pail" was language that every workingman could understand, even if he could not swallow the rest of Republican doctrine.

Though expansionism was not a clean-cut issue between the two major parties, it had obvious political advantages for the Democrats. The American people were growling over the trouble and expense of the new possessions. Two years after the victory over Spain, they were still paying war taxes, and they were testy about the uses to which their money was put. The Republicans suffered from the handicap of all parties in power. They had been obliged to act. Wherever the attack might fall—the Philippines, Porto Rico, Cuba, China—the Washington government had to vindicate a costly policy in which the American mission of liberty and justice was nowhere strikingly exemplified.

Yet, in the broad sense of expanding American power, Republican policy had become the policy of the nation. The President had made the point in one of his Iowa speeches the year before. "It is no longer a question of expansion with us; we have expanded. If there is any question at all it is a question of contracting; and who is going to contract?" The Democrats had not dreamed of proposing a course so unpopular. On the contrary, the Kansas City platform favored "expansion by peaceful and legitimate means." It neglected to include the annexation of Hawaii in the roster of Republican mistakes; it tacitly condoned the acquisition of Porto Rico; and its pronouncements on behalf of the Monroe Doctrine and the isthmian canal were strong enough to suit Governor Roosevelt. Only in the case of the Philippines was the controversy clearly, if not forcefully indicated. The platform called for a declaration that the islands would be eventually granted independence under an American protectorate.

To replace the burning currency issue of 1896, the political opposition had gone to the distant Pacific, relegating to a secondary place the problems of capital and labor at home. The class division between the two major parties was still more deeply trenched than it had been four years earlier. The Democracy was fully identified with the proletarian cause. Conventions of Populists and Silverites automatically embraced Bryan as their candidate. He was the unanimous choice of the great consolidating unions of the American Federation of Labor, restive in strikes and hostile demonstrations, and clamorous for a larger share in the national wealth. The fusion of the Republicans and the money interests had been similarly confirmed. Under the indulgent eye of the government, railroads freely violated the Interstate Commerce Act, and corporations merged without regard for the Sherman Act. The administration had shown no disposition to test the Supreme Court decision which had emasculated the anti-trust law before McKinley took office. Attorney General Griggs had brought only a few minor suits. The growth of monopolies of unprecedented size and power—vast aggregations of capital, organized as holding companies— was the conspicuous accompaniment of McKinley prosperity. The party of business was the champion of colossal, titanic, megatherian business, cowering from attack in the bosom of political protection.

The Kansas City platform assailed "dishonest paltering" with the evil, and pledged "unceasing warfare" against all private monopolies. It declared that the trusts had been fostered by Republican laws, and were protected by the administration in return for financial support. The indictment found a wide response. Public opinion had been vehemently aroused for more than a year, and the Republicans were wary of the issue. In contrast to the Democrats, they avoided a wholesale condemnation of big business, making a careful distinction between legitimate corporations and harmful monopolies; but hand-wringing over the second group had become indispensable to respectability. Even extreme reactionaries paid lip service to some form of control, though without spreading much conviction of their impatience to begin. The attitude of right-wing Republicans toward the trusts was much like that of "good" Southerners toward the Negro problem. They loudly lamented the situation and expressed a desire to correct it, but not in any specific way, nor at any foreseeable date.

The impediments to action were real enough. By prohibiting federal interference with production within a state, the Supreme Court had tied the hands of the Washington government; while the state laws, to which Cleveland had looked for remedy, were too diverse to afford an effective national control, even if liberally interpreted by the courts. The failure of the resort to legislation had prompted an extensive inquiry in 1898. Congress had authorized the appointment of an Industrial Commission of nineteen members—partly named by Senate and House, and partly by the President with the consent of the Senate—which was to investigate "the growing concentration of economic power," and also the problems of labor and management. The Republican-dominated body thus assembled was not generally distinguished by intellectual attainments, or broad knowledge of the industrial field. In some instances, of which Senator Boies Penrose of Pennsylvania was the most flagrant, they were predisposed to antagonize all proposals of reform. The majority, however, was guided by a sense of public duty. Much credit for earnest effort must be given the chairman, Senator James H. Kyle of South Dakota, a Congregational minister, an educator, and a quasi-Republican independent. The trust question had been tackled first. Expert advice was obtained by engaging the services of a political economist, Professor Jeremiah W. Jenks of Cornell University. The commissioners had held a large number of hearings, at which representatives of the corporations were examined on "trust topics." The testimony of the magnates was not without interest. For one thing, it abounded—to a degree perhaps unexpected—in opinion adverse to the protective tariff. The record of these proceedings had been included in a preliminary report, published on March 1, 1900, well in advance of the political conventions. The conclusions were admittedly incomplete—the final report of the Commission would fill nineteen ponderous volumes—but recommendations were immediately made for legislation to provide public access to information necessary for intelligent investment and subsequent control of the property. It was also advised that the larger corporations, or so-called trusts, should be required to publish an audited report annually. Finally, there was a recommendation that the authority of the Interstate Commerce Commission be enlarged. The question of freight rates had arisen at the hearings, and it had come as a surprise to some—though not to all—of the commissioners that discriminatory favors were still being granted by the railroads.

The Republicans of the House had likewise bestirred themselves to offer some solution. Shortly before adjournment, they had recognized the need of strengthening the Sherman Act by bringing in a number of bills, one of which was passed but failed in the Senate. They had also supported a joint resolution for a constitutional amendment expressly giving Congress the power to regulate the trusts. The Democrats were under obligation to uphold states' rights by opposing all consideration of possible federal controls—a serious defect in their position on the trust issue—and they duly defeated the resolution in the House. The gestures of the Republicans were decried as impracticable and transparently insincere, but they furnished some talking points in the campaign. The party in power claimed a record of constructive effort to cure the ailments of capitalism, as contrasted with mere sorehead agitation on the part of the Democrats. Yet the effort had not made much progress to date, and there was considerable skepticism in the country about how far the Republicans would ever go. The President, at this crucial juncture, had nothing at all to say.

A year earlier, McKinley had expected to be ready with a program for action on the trusts. In March, 1899, he had confidently told Dawes that he would "lead in a movement for their proper restriction." The leadership, however, had failed to materialize when he laid the question before Congress in his next annual message, warning that the trusts were justly provoking public discussion and should early claim attention. The President had circled inconclusively around the subject, like a worried man thinking aloud. There were many divergent views, he wrote, but it was universally conceded that these combinations were obnoxious to the public welfare. A remedy must be found. If the present law could be extended to control them, it should be done without delay; but all federal legislation might fall short because of the character of our governmental system. It was to be hoped that state legislation might be strengthened, and that a means might be found for Congress to supplement it.

The weakness of the President's statement—and it was the only statement he had made about the trusts—was the absence of moral vigor. He did not arraign the corporations which had set their private interests above the national welfare. He neither condemned specific abuses nor praised the more enlightened state laws. Indeed he did not seem to have observed the abuses himself, but rather to have learned of them through the complaints of the public; and it was plain from his cautious tone and a reference to the still incomplete report of the Industrial Commission that he did not expect prompt action from Congress. McKinley's decision to seek another term only partly explains his temporizing on the trusts. Wading confidently into the question, he had found himself in deep waters of economic and governmental theory, and prudently backed out. He was bound to deny that combinations of capital were intrinsically injurious. Consolidation was the dominant tendency of industry, not only in the United States, but in Europe. It had resulted, according to one theory, from the operation of natural laws of commercial evolution; and unavoidable errors in the process would tend to disappear in time, if business remained self-regulating. Dawes, for one, discussed this idea with McKinley. "The President said that he didn't know," Cortelyou wrote on a winter evening after Dawes had called, "but that he 'guessed' combination must necessarily control largely in the near future; that as a gentleman had said to Mr. Dawes, the great need in such matters was protection to the companies as well as to consult the interests of the people at large." This puzzled conclusion, with its uneasy allusion to the people, did not settle the question, but it guided McKinley's conduct in the months before the convention. He turned a deaf ear to Senator Cullom's appeals for help in obtaining an amendment to the Interstate Commerce Act. He sanctioned a routine trust plank for the platform—a vague statement of disapproval, whose authorship was claimed by both Hanna and Foraker. Though the preliminary report of the Industrial Commission was in his hands, the President was not yet ready to endorse even the limited recommendations of Senator Kyle and his associates.

Before the summer was over, McKinley firmly condemned the trusts. It was unfortunate that he could not have done so earlier. His silence in the spring was a strategic error, not only because it appeared politically timid—as it was—but because it laid him open to the old accusation of subservience to Hanna. The yellow press gladly welcomed the opportunity. Even before the Republican convention, the New York *Evening Journal* had started its popular series of Opper cartoons, "Willie and His Papa." Little "Willie" was McKinley in a velvet Lord Fauntleroy suit. His pot-bellied, bediamonded "Papa" was labeled "The Trusts." Hanna was a hovering "Nursie" in cap and apron. The first drawing set the pattern of the series. It showed Willie sitting on Papa's lap. Underneath was the caption:

"Whose ittle boy is oo?"
"I's oor ittle boy."

When the Democrats assembled at Kansas City, the stage had seemed set for a full-dress drama of class conflict. But Bryan had been defeated on a platform of radical reform in the lean year of 1896. In the plenitude of 1900, he carefully tested a plank that would bear his weight. His main attack was not aimed at McKinley, the tool of the money interests, but McKinley, the usurper of imperial power and the destroyer of human liberty.

· 24 ·

THE VERDICT OF THE PEOPLE

B RYAN opened his grand offensive at
the Democratic notification ceremonies, which took place at Indianapolis
in early August. A very small part of his long and studied speech was concerned with the proposal that the United States government should promise
the Philippines eventual independence under a protectorate. Gliding over
the assumption that all difficulties in the islands would thereby be composed, Bryan briskly pledged that, if elected, he would convene Congress
in extraordinary session to take this action. The principal part of his address
was devoted to a denunciation of the Republican conduct of Philippine
affairs, to the sordid motives by which the administration was dominated,
and its design to lead the republic down the path of "militarism," a sinister
new term of French derivation. The Democratic candidate scathingly in-
dicted the party which, forsaking its early ideals, had violated the Constitution and ignored Filipino rights. The Republicans, he asserted, did not
dare even to take the people's side here at home against the great monopolies. How could they be trusted to protect the Filipinos against the corporations that were waiting to despoil them? The promises of the administration
would not be kept, not even the deceitful promise of education. "We dare
not educate the Filipinos," Bryan thundered, "lest they learn to read the
Declaration of Independence and the Constitution of the United States."

To the new crusade for equality, inalienable rights, and the consent of
the governed, Bryan called the illustrious dead: the founding fathers, Patrick Henry, Washington, and Lincoln, whom the Republicans could ill
afford to spare. In tones scarcely less imperious, he enlisted God on the
side of the Democrats. God Himself placed in the human heart the love

of liberty, and never made a race so low it would welcome a foreign master; to say that He denied to any people the capacity of self-government was a reflection on the Creator. The arguments that the imperialists addressed to the missionary spirit were false to the teachings of Christ. The command, "Go ye into all the world and preach the Gospel," had no Gatling-gun attachment. Bryan drew an inspiring picture of American missionaries who should go forth, seeking souls, not sovereignty; and, in his peroration, he imaged a still grander ideal of the future of the whole American people. He rejected the complacent and helpless "destiny" of the Republicans as "the subterfuge of the invertebrate." He envisioned a national destiny of surpassing glory. Behold a republic, Bryan cried, in which every citizen is a sovereign, but no one cares to wear a crown! Behold a republic whose flag is loved while other flags are only feared! Behold a republic, increasing in population, wealth, strength, and influence, solving the problems of civilization, and hastening the coming of universal brotherhood, which shakes thrones and dissolves aristocracies by its silent example! Behold a republic becoming "the supreme moral factor in the world's progress and the accepted arbiter of the world's disputes. . . ."

Nothing in Bryan's previous fulminations had prepared the Republicans for a speech of this elevated tone. It had obvious defects of demagogic harping and rhetorical cant. Its consistency was not improved by Bryan's defense of his action on behalf of ratifying the peace treaty with Spain. There was no little absurdity in his assumption that the Democratic party was in exclusive possession of civic virtue, and particularly in his marshaling the South under the banner of human rights. Nevertheless, the challenge to the party in power was a tremendous political achievement. Bryan had carried the attack to the heart of the Republicans' position, and compelled them to fight on the defensive.

The peroration, to be sure, represented another notable triumph for McKinley's policies. All but silenced on the currency, acquiescent in peaceable expansion, the Democrats had now embraced the conception of the moral mission of the United States. But the President could take small comfort in their conversion. Bryan had boldly appropriated McKinley's aspiration for the American future, along with his reverence for the American past, and indeed his devotion to the principles of Christianity. He had avoided a direct allusion to the President—though, by this time, McKinley's backbone should have quivered at the reference to "the subterfuge of the invertebrate"—but the effect of the Indianapolis speech, at every point, was to malign the President's motives and impugn his sincerity. It was William McKinley who was flouting the sacred documents, behaving like a crowned monarch, reflecting on his Creator, and betraying the commandments of Christ. It was, specifically, William McKinley who was deluding the Philippine people with false promises, while he planned to keep them in ignorance and servitude, and sacrifice their interests to the corporations.

The President's indignation at these charges and his recognition of their political impact were disclosed a month later, on the publication of his letter of acceptance. Though the gold standard was duly placed first, two-thirds of this lengthy missive consisted of a justification of his course in the Philippines. The unavoidability of American involvement in the islands was the subject of an extensive review, heavily documented with extracts from official papers, of the events since the battle of Manila Bay. The inconsistencies of the Democratic stand, both on the ratification of the treaty and the broader question of human rights, were caustically treated. The purpose was declared to establish in the Philippines a government suitable for the inhabitants, and to prepare them for self-government, and to give them self-government when they were ready for it and as rapidly as they were ready for it.

McKinley gave considerable space to examining and rejecting the plausible scheme of an American protectorate. The "exaggerated phrase-making" of the campaign, he wrote, threatened to divert us from the real contention. We were asked to yield our authority to "a minority of the Filipino people," guerrilla bands in active rebellion against the United States, and then support "the murderers of our soldiers" in setting up and maintaining their government. Our obligation would continue, but our title would be surrendered to a weaker power. The protective relationship would afford only embarrassment, drawing us into troubles that we would be impotent to prevent, giving provocation for conflicts and possibly costly wars. "A military support of an authority not our own is the very essence of militarism . . ." the President stated. "We will not give up our own to guarantee another sovereignty."

Once more disclaiming the creed of imperialism, McKinley declared that every effort of the Executive had been directed for the benefit of the islanders, "not for our aggrandizement nor for pride of might, not for trade or commerce, not for exploitation, but for humanity and civilization. . . ." It was in proof of this statement that he laid the official record before his countrymen. The bulky paper was labored in presentation. It bore some traces of hasty organization. It had its own examples of cant and inconsistency, and it was marred by the assumption, which events made decreasingly credible, that the majority of the Filipinos welcomed the American occupation. But the President's letter was still an immensely convincing document. Its accumulated evidence conquered respectful attention. Its very awkwardness carried an emphatic accent of sincerity.

The impression made by the letter was supplemented by the ensuing publication of the full text of the President's instructions to the Taft Commission. All provisions of the Bill of Rights, except trial by jury and the right to bear arms, were guaranteed to the Philippine people. They were to select their own local officials, and natives were to be preferred, whenever possible, for positions of public trust. Stress was laid on a sound educational system and an efficient civil service. The paper, which had been drafted by Root, provided the administrative structure which had been forecast in the President's annual message. It was a model for colonial administrators rather than a project of representative government, but it supplied the basis for a transitional regime and a charter of liberties for the Philippines.

The civil authority had already begun to function when the instructions were made public. The Taft Commission, on September 1, had been constituted by Executive order the legislative body of the archipelago. The power of the military arm had been diminished, and would steadily contract with the progress of pacification. The facts were the President's answer to Bryan's challenge. Here, McKinley was plainly saying, were the things he was doing in the Philippines; what other, if elected to his place, would Bryan do? Yet the President was very far from confident that his record would command the support of the people. He had omitted to make the conclusive reply to the accusation of imperialism: the avowal of a purpose to prepare the Philippines for ultimate independence.

McKinley had considered declaring this purpose. He had had before him a letter from Senator Hoar, who urged that the pledge would assure Bryan's defeat. Three days before giving out his letter of acceptance, McKinley had dictated to Cortelyou a statement based on Hoar's suggestion; but in the end he had left it out, and substituted the promise of self-government. The decision should not be taken as evidence that the President did not desire the eventual freedom of the islands—Hoar was convinced that he did, and Cortelyou was much struck by the direction his thoughts were taking—but rather as a sober recognition of the military unwisdom of issuing the politically advantageous declaration. Insurgent hopes of Democratic success in the election were blamed for the flat failure of MacArthur's offer of amnesty. Bryan's announcement of the "paramount issue" had set off a renewal of heavy fighting. Washington could not appear to weaken at a time when the American force was strained to the utmost.

The fact that McKinley had been momentarily tempted to follow Hoar's advice was an indication of his anxiety about the election. His hopes were at low ebb after his choice was made. The very next day, he discussed the possibility of Republican defeat with Corbin, Dawes, and Cortelyou, meditating the action he should take in that event, especially with reference to the Philippines. Even though he should succeed in moving most of Chaffee's force to Manila in the next few weeks, the status of MacArthur's command was as insecure as Otis's had been. On July 1, 1901, the regular Army would revert to a total of 28,000, and the volunteers must all be disbanded on or before that date. Root had prepared a measure providing for a standing Army of 60,000, so elastically organized as to permit its expansion to 100,000. A bill containing this provision—though only partially responsive to Root's recommendations for Army reforms—had been passed by the Senate in the spring. Whatever the result of the election, it would be McKinley's duty to arouse Congress to the emergency in the Pacific, and obtain legislation without delay. "He said," Cortelyou wrote, "immediately upon Mr. Bryan's election he would bend every energy to have the army placed on a proper footing, say 100,000 men, so that Mr. Bryan could not complain that he did not have a large enough force to do the work required in the Philippines." Conditions, the President added, would be "infinitely worse" in the islands, in case of a Democratic victory.

The President's doubts were untypical of his optimistic temperament, but not of the despondency that had engulfed the Republicans. Their confidence had wilted in midsummer. Panic fears of Democratic success had caused a slump in business. Idle men mocked the slogan of "the full dinner pail." A threatened strike in the anthracite mines of Pennsylvania brought dire visions of rioting and bloodshed, and apprehensions of a fuel shortage. Heavy Republican losses were anticipated in the East on account of the Philippines. Nearly every day, the New York *Evening Journal* hammered the theme that the President was the child of the trusts and the helpless nursling of Hanna.

Hanna was not much troubled about the outlook. He counted on the fundamental prosperity of the country to win the day, but he kept his confident thoughts to himself. His aim was to punish the Democrats by a smashing, decisive victory; and, inveighing against "General Apathy," he drove the party workers unsparingly to prepare for a hard contest. He took a summer cottage at Elberon, New Jersey, and stayed close to the New York headquarters until the early part of September. After two weeks in the Middle West, he returned to New York for one week more. Thereafter, until the election, he was based on the Chicago headquarters, and concentrated his attention on the western states.

On at least two occasions, Hanna was provoked to extreme resentment against the President. The first cause for offense grew out of a question of campaign methods. A letter from Hanna to the President—dated August 3, but delivered by Dawes to Canton apparently some days later—transmitted a protest from New York that men were being laid off at the Brooklyn Navy Yard and that Democrats were being employed at a depot for naval ammunition. Another letter, addressed to Hanna and forwarded by him to McKinley, complained that the Treasury Department was keeping a strict surveillance over travel expenses for its employees. It is not possible that Hanna actually expected that the President would use his influence to obtain co-operation from the departments in the campaign. The fact that he raised the question was in itself a sign of a perverse and needling attitude toward McKinley.

Hanna shortly received an exceedingly polite answer from the President, rebuking political pressures on the departments and declaring his opposition to the use of public money for party expenses. McKinley's views were spelled out with much patience and persuasion—perhaps a trifle too much; the tone slightly suggested that of a kindly lecture to a child. Though he had been at pains to except Hanna from any reproach, the letter so enraged the recipient that he threw it on the floor, and sneered that it had been written for the President's biography. A main cause of Hanna's annoyance was that the letter had been dictated, and therefore copied for the White House files. This, of course, was standard procedure for McKinley, yet in this case it seemed to indicate a nervous desire for the protection of the record. He would not ordinarily have discussed the delicate matter of campaign ethics in explicit detail on paper.

There was more than appeared on the surface of this exchange. The obvious clue is again to be found in the investigation of the Havana post office. Hanna's friend, Rathbone, had just been arrested. Though his collusion in the embezzlements was still to be proved, evidence had been found that Rathbone had appropriated government revenues for his personal expenses. Two weeks earlier, moreover, another of Hanna's good friends had been eased out of his influential place in the Post Office Department at Washington. Perry S. Heath, a former newspaperman, had been made First Assistant Postmaster General as a reward for his campaign service in 1896. His office had been a principal source of Hanna's political appointments until Heath quietly went back to his old press job at Republican campaign headquarters in Chicago, and succeeded Charles Dick as secretary of the National Committee. In the light of later disclosures of irregularities at the Department, it is clear that Heath's removal was a precaution inspired by fear of the repercussions of the Havana investigation; but the transfer had been discreetly arranged and it did not excite suspicion at the time.

Hanna had not mentioned the investigation in writing to the President, but he spoke insultingly of Bristow in a letter to Dawes, intended for the President's eye. Though its main concern was extremely serious, a warning of a threat of assassination, Hanna had dragged in his grievances about the departments, chiefly the fact that Bristow had just fired an official who hailed from Maryland, a doubtful state in the election. Hanna exploded to Dawes: "it seems as if he [Bristow] had no political sense or else is vicious—I think the latter as I have no use for him." This comment, taken in conjunction with the requests to the President, illuminates Hanna's hair-trigger irritability and McKinley's exaggerated concern to dissociate himself from questionable practices. Hanna was the one in whom "political sense" was lacking. For at the bar of public opinion the Republicans had only one answer to the disgraceful conduct of the officials in Cuba: their prompt removal and punishment through the honorable efforts of other Republican officials, the vigilance of Leonard Wood and the zeal of Bristow and his assistants. The President's letter to Hanna was an argument addressed to a stubborn contempt for decent administrative standards.

This is a time when every effort will be made to have the administration do questionable things [the letter concluded]. It is a period of great temptation, just the sort that will require the highest courage to meet and resist. If elected I have to live with the administration for four years. I do not want to feel that any improper or questionable methods have been employed to reach the place, and you must continue, as you have always done, to stand against unreasonable exactions, which are so common at a time like the present.

Hanna's second cause for offense was the President's lack of enthusiasm for his stumping tour. The previously unobtrusive National Chairman had become stage-struck. The Ohio speeches had brought him a number of invitations to speak in other states, and he accepted as many as he could. He was greatly tempted by requests for his services from Bryan's home state of Nebraska, and from South Dakota, the stamping ground of the renegade Republican, Senator Pettigrew. Many of Hanna's friends were opposed to his appearing in Populist centers, where he was known only through the pen and tongue of slander. They were fearful that he would risk unpleasantness and possibly rough treatment if he injected his personality into two excessively embittered contests. But Hanna was obstinately confident of his ability to handle the situation. He especially wanted to punish Pettigrew, who had repeatedly attacked him and who was a candidate for re-election. In defiance of all advice to the contrary, Hanna arranged to make the tour. Soon after his decision was taken, Postmaster General Smith arrived in Chicago, and called at Republican headquarters. The members of the Cabinet disapproved of the proposed trip, but it is a fair assumption that not all of the concern at Washington was for Hanna's comfort and safety. He had emerged from the back room to advertise an unvarnished material philosophy, and declare that the issue of the campaign was "a business proposition purely." As the Democratic appeal to class prejudice sounded louder, Hanna's speeches had been closely scrutinized, and he had blundered badly at the big Chicago meeting by spouting a denial that any trusts existed. The holding companies had, of course, been organized to evade the letter of the law. On a fine point of definition, Hanna's statement could be defended. But, tossed off brusquely in the course of a political speech, it all too plainly betrayed his impatience with talk of business regulation, and opposition newspapers had made much of it. The publicity would have been especially irksome to the President in view of Hanna's reputed domination over his own opinions. His letter of acceptance had contained the strongest language he had yet used about the trusts. "They are dangerous conspiracies against the public good," McKinley had written, "and should be made the subject of prohibitory or penal legislation." Hanna's injudicious remark could be uncharitably construed as a correction of the President by the leering "Nursie" of the cartoons.

Hanna was probably feeling guilty when Postmaster General Smith walked in. He was certainly feeling suspicious and antagonistic, for he cut off Smith's expressions of solicitude about his trip with the query, "The President sent you, didn't he?" The story runs that, when Smith admitted the fact, Hanna cried, "Return to Washington and tell the President that God hates a coward." There is nothing improbable in the idea that Hanna lost his temper. He may well have uttered this melodramatic command, or something very much like it; and it is altogether credible that, as has also been said, his first thought was to send in his resignation. But the story is incomplete without the sequel of his early meeting with the President—a meeting which it may have been part of Smith's errand to arrange. Both McKinley and Hanna were about to go to Ohio. A luncheon engagement was appointed at the North Market Street house. When Hanna returned to Cleveland, he took occasion to correct the unfortunate impression he had created at Chicago. He had meant, he explained to the reporters, that there were no trusts within the meaning of the law, not that there were no combinations that worked injustice to the people. An inexperienced campaigner had learned the importance of choosing his words with care. Hanna made his tour of the West in October, and established himself as a popular stump speaker.

Face to face, the two friends had reached a good understanding. Time had brought its changes to both of them, and Hanna would not recapture the intimacy of their simpler yesterdays; but there are no other tales of rebellion against the President.

To offset Bryan's energetic campaign, Hanna chiefly relied on Roosevelt. The vice-presidential candidate had volunteered to go on the stump during a conference at Canton in early July. He told the New York reporters that he was "as strong as a bull moose," but he was hoarse and haggard before he finished the grueling tour which Hanna sent him to make in the Northwest. From start to finish, Roosevelt was an immense success. His spread-eagle nationalism, as Hanna had realized, was a valuable asset with expansionist audiences. Roosevelt had another political asset, which Hanna was not equipped to appreciate—his outspoken criticism of the offenses of corporate wealth. The future "trust-buster" was not a radical by any standards but those of blind reaction. His practical proposals at this time were limited to state legislation for a franchise tax, such as had recently been enacted in New York, and for the protection of investors along the lines recommended by the Industrial Commission. But Roosevelt strongly felt that means must be found to make the corporations subordinate to the national interest, and that the initiative in their control should be seized by the conservative party. His forthright censure of the trusts did much to counterbalance the deference to business which paralyzed Republican leadership on economic questions, and to attract the enthusiastic support of younger and more progressive elements of the party.

Hanna made his greatest single contribution to the Republican cause in the mediation of the Pennsylvania coal strike. The miners had gone out in September, demanding a 10 per cent wage increase and recognition of their union. They were strongly organized under the presidency of the able young labor leader, John Mitchell, but the operators flatly refused to arbitrate. The tension in the coal fields snapped in an outbreak of disorder. The Pennsylvania militia was called out. The price of coal soared. At the height of the political contest, the war between labor and management was thrust violently to the fore. All the advantage accrued to the party of protest. The attitude of the operators had disgusted the public, and sympathy with the strikers was widespread.

Fortunately for the Republicans, Hanna knew the coal-mining industry like the inside of his pocket. He believed that the men were right, and bent every effort to compel the reactionary owners to arbitrate. During the week of September when he paid a return visit to New York, a number of prosperous Pennsylvanians appeared in the city, and made their way to Wall Street. The reporters were alert. They noted that Hanna went to Wall Street, too. Their curiosity was whetted when he and J. Pierpont

Morgan were one day observed to enter the same office building; but their questions went unanswered, and Hanna's important part in the conferences was not publicly admitted. Reports began to rumble that the coal operators were yielding. It was confirmed that they had decided to arbitrate, after all. Behind closed doors, John Mitchell agreed to withdraw—for that year—the demand for recognition of the union, and obtained the full wage increase of 10 per cent. News of a great victory for labor was published in the middle of October.

Bryan's campaign, in the meanwhile, had failed to gain momentum. Barnstorming through the West, he had largely shelved the "paramount issue" in favor of diatribes against plutocracy and the trusts. The anti-imperialist crusade had failed to stir expansionist sections of the country, and the President's letter of acceptance had been well received. Moreover, as the nominee of the Populists and Silver Republicans as well as the Democrats, Bryan was eventually obliged to underscore the radical declarations of the Kansas City platform. He had not one, but three letters of acceptance to write, and the issue of free silver, which he had markedly neglected, came back to nag the public with its dreary obsoleteness. Some dignity of national leadership which Bryan had attained in August was lost in the shifts of a politician who changed his emphasis to suit his audience. His demagogic tirades had produced a still more drastic reaction. For the second time, he had frightened off the conservative wing of his support. The have-nots, bitterly aligned against the haves, would vote for Bryan or for Eugene V. Debs, the obscure candidate of a Socialist organization; but the election would be decided by the great mass of voters who had a little, and a large element of these voters retreated in alarm from the promise of an indiscriminate attack on capital.

Even in his hostility to the trusts, the average American was confused. While he execrated the veteran offenders, Standard Oil and American Sugar, he could not deny that their commodities had never been as excellent or as cheap. In the industrial co-operation which was fast replacing the wasteful, individualistic methods of the past, he recognized progress, a movement in which he most devoutly believed. He wanted to see the power of the monopolies curbed; but he repudiated a deranging and futile attempt to return to a primitive economy. Nor was this average man of 1900 susceptible to the slogans of class hatred. He was proud of the multiplication of fortunes estimated in seven figures. American millionaires were a part of the national brag. They were the romance and the daydream of capitalism, and the substitutes for royalty in the republic. They had no attribute of a permanent privileged "class." They were hustling individuals who had fought their way to the top of the heap. Any poor man's son might do the same. In the marvelous fluidity and abundance of American life, there was little scope for the hatred that fear breeds. On the contrary, the men to be feared were the men who hated the rich: Socialist laborers, foreign subversives, plotting anarchists. This was the class which Americans regarded with deepest hostility. These were the ranks, swelling in size and boldness, which seemed to menace the nation with the scarlet flag of nihilism.

So it came about that business was poised for recovery when the coal strike was settled in October. Factories were reopening to fill a rush of orders. Men trooped back to work with swinging dinner pails. Glowing reports began to pour in from Republican managers in the doubtful states. Apathy had been succeeded by feverish excitement. Anti-expansionists resigned themselves to the Philippines. Old-school Democrats sheepishly plumped for prosperity. Republican laughter celebrated the final joke on silver coinage—odds of 16 to 1 on McKinley, given in a wager at the Union League Club of New York.

The verdict on November 6 was the greatest victory that the Republicans had won since 1872. Of the 447 electoral votes, McKinley received 292, with a popular plurality of nearly a million. Outside the Solid South, Bryan carried only four silver-mining states, losing even his native Nebraska. The epoch-making decision administered a final quietus to the Populists; while the Democrats were so routed and discredited that twelve years would pass before they put a candidate in the White House, in the tumult of new, convulsive issues and a split in the Republican party.

Hanna's emotional attitude toward McKinley had been complicated by another emotion than anger. He had become apprehensive of danger to the President in the excitement of election year.

The precautions taken for the President's safety in 1898 had been gradually relaxed. There were still extra Secret Service guards at the White House on September 13 of that year when the head usher, Dubois, made an early-morning inspection at Cortelyou's request. One of them was a night watchman in the domestic wing. Hunting through the empty bedrooms, Dubois found him soundly sleeping on a lounge. Cortelyou's vigilance at this date can be readily explained. Two days earlier, the Empress Elizabeth of Austria had been fatally stabbed by an anarchist. It was only four years since President Carnot of France had met the same fate. The Spanish premier, Cánovas del Castillo, had been assassinated the year before. The murder of the Empress had shocked the civilized world, and shaken the nerves of those concerned with the protection of its rulers. Cortelyou's anxiety, however, had been lulled as time passed without an untoward occurrence. In 1900, the only "guard" on duty at the White House was the artless manservant, Charles Tharin, who slept with Clara in a bedroom in the west wing.

Though Hanna was not moved to change this casual arrangement until midsummer, he had betrayed an unusual nervousness about McKinley at the time of the Philadelphia convention. In dwelling on the importance of the vice-presidential nomination, Hanna had persistently suggested a haunting fear that McKinley might not live out a second term. The implication had been so marked that Mr. Hearst's *Evening Journal* was led, in retrospect, to deduce that the President was in doubtful health; but a different explanation had appeared in Mr. Pulitzer's *World*. In July, that newspaper reported a plot by Spanish-Cubans, with headquarters in New York City, to assassinate the President. The story sounded fictitious, and Hanna's uneasy remarks at Philadelphia afford the only hint that he might ever have believed it. Yet, if there was no truth at all in the rumor, it is an odd coincidence that Hanna shortly received a warning on which he felt impelled to act.

Between July 29 and August 2, a Secret Service agent named Ralph D. Redfern advised Hanna that steps should be taken to protect the President, and supported his recommendation by a memorandum of certain information in the files of the Intelligence Bureau. It had been furnished about two years before by one E. Moretti, an Italian-American who had been temporarily employed by the Intelligence Bureau because he had access to the proceedings of a grotto of anarchists at Paterson, New Jersey. Through their underground organizations in the various countries, Moretti had stated, the anarchists were plotting to rid the world of its rulers in the following order: the Empress of Austria, the King of Italy, the Czar of Russia, the Prince of Wales or the Queen of England, the President of the United States, and the Emperor of Germany. This old report was all that Redfern had to offer, but it struck Hanna with stunning force. The anarchists had just ticked off the second name on Moretti's list. King Humbert I had been shot dead on July 29 at his summer palace at Monza; and his assassin, Gaetano Bresci, was a silk weaver who had been until recently employed at Paterson, New Jersey.

The crime had startled Americans like a shout of danger. What comrades had Bresci left behind when he sailed on his bloody errand? A searchlight was beamed on Paterson, on New York, Chicago, and other cities where foreign laborers congregated. Detectives ranged through sour tenements. Reporters kept watch on dingy meeting halls. Newspapers recalled the details of anarchist crimes and attempts—the Prince of Wales in April had escaped an assassin's bullet in the Brussels railway station; his assailant was still at large—and circulated rumors of more outrages to come. The rich and peaceful landscape of the national life seemed undermined by violence. Assassination was an un-American crime, and Americans did not care to think about it. They liked the idea that their Chief Executives behaved like ordinary citizens, going freely about their occasions, sitting in a theater or walking through a railway station. Now, in guilty confusion, men asked themselves if another President were to follow Lincoln and Garfield.

Hanna forwarded Redfern's memorandum by special delivery to Dawes at Washington. He felt it his duty to suggest caution in the pre-election excitement, when the class issue was being revived. "There are many diseased minds in the country," he wrote Dawes. The letter, with its enclosure, was delivered only a few hours before Dawes left for Canton in the President's party. Much worried, he took the papers to the President and insisted with all his power that McKinley show less indifference to his personal safety. Dawes then talked to Cortelyou, and saw his fellow official at the Treasury, Chief Wilkie of the Secret Service Bureau, about increasing the President's guard.

Hanna had not divulged the name of his informant, but Redfern soon made himself known to Dawes, with whom he was well acquainted, and whom he bound to conceal his identity, particularly at the Treasury Department. The motive for Redfern's unauthorized disclosure had been a simple one. The memorandum had been part of his credentials in applying for a campaign appointment with the Republican National Committee. Hanna had repaid Redfern's zeal for the President's protection by asking Henry C. Payne to appoint him Assistant Sergeant at Arms on special duty at the Chicago headquarters. Dawes, for his part, was to supply a letter of introduction which Redfern could present to Payne. It was the enterprise of a job-seeker that had unearthed Moretti's forgotten report, and caused the assignment of another guard to the President.

The new Secret Service operative was named George E. Foster. He was a solid tub of a man, with a solemn, jowly face and a pair of downcast mustaches. His derby hat was tipped well forward on his brow, and he wore a minute bow tie, like a clipping from one of the President's big cravats. The nature of his calling was as unmistakable as though he had been uniformed in brass-buttoned blue, with high helmet and nightstick. Stout, flat-footed Foster was every inch the cop.

Where the President went, there went Foster—in theory, at least. There were irregularities in practice. At Canton, McKinley lived, as far as possible, like a private citizen. He continued to walk unattended to church or the business district. At Washington, he often slipped off for a stroll in the White House grounds. Foster would have been *de trop* on the drives with Mrs. McKinley, and he was not asked to share them. In fact, there is no evidence that Foster ever sat in the President's carriage, even on public occasions, when the streets were crowded; though one photograph shows him, during a ceremonial progress at Buffalo the next year, trudging doggedly beside the horses.

McKinley's yielding to the solicitude of his friends was a purely formal submission. He remained utterly—perhaps fatalistically—indifferent to warnings of physical danger.

McKinley was deeply sobered by the election. Dawes thought him more impressed with his responsibilities than his triumph. He modestly told his Cabinet that the victory was as much theirs as his, and asked them all to stay with him. Among the exultant Republicans, the President seemed an oddly solitary figure, estranged by gravity and reflection. His most notable public comment on the election was, in effect, a wish that it should be forgotten. "It has to me no personal phase," he told a Union League banquet at Philadelphia. "It is not the triumph of an individual, nor altogether of a party. . . ." The new problems, McKinley said, were "too exalted for partisanship"—their settlement was the task of "the whole American people."

The President was contemplating the emerging design of the next four years. He was thinking about the reciprocity treaties and the isthmian canal; liberal governments in the former Spanish islands; a merciful settlement with China; the Hague Court of Arbitration, "the noblest forum for the settlement of international disputes." He was foreseeing the influence which the United States might wield through the artifacts of peace: the strong skeins of commerce, the torch of moral principle, and the balanced scales of justice. The President's vision was not altogether fanciful, but he was not going to see its fulfillment. His plans would drop, half-finished, for the use of a man very different from himself: a man who, with great abilities, was often rash and wrongheaded; a belligerent, excitable man who was just beginning to accept an ideal of peaceful arbitration. It was a queer twist of history that such impetuous hands would mold the design that McKinley had traced for the future of America among the nations.

· 25 ·

THE SECOND ACT BEGINS

T HE specter of social unrest had been
exorcised by the election; and, at Christmas of 1900, the menace was all
but forgotten in the fat contentment of plenty and the pride of commercial supremacy. Railroads, manufacturing concerns, and shipping companies flaunted the statistics of a record-breaking year of profit. New York
dared to challenge the financial pre-eminence of London, as the governments of Europe looked transatlantic for help in floating their loans. A
bull market was soaring on Wall Street, with capital stocks at sensational
heights, and there were rumors of more gigantic combinations forming in
railroads and in steel. Rich men were growing richer. Brand-new fortunes
were made overnight. In the generosity of the holiday spirit, corporations
and banks and mercantile establishments made handsome presents to their
employees, and the feasts of charity were bountifully spread before the
poor. Socialism, the *New York Tribune* commented, would not easily
secure a foothold in a country where capital willingly shared its profits with
labor; and Americans might be pardoned for emulating the Pharisee in
giving thanks they were "not as other men."

Americans, at this season, were peculiarly conscious of their unique
and transcendent destiny. The sands of the old century were fast running
out, and it was a time of recapitulation and of prophecy. In comparison
with preceding history, the tale of the last few years was an astounding
record of progress, not alone in wealth and productivity, nor in those other
tokens of national power, the mighty sheathed battleships that busied
the shipyards and boomed the steel industry; but in the enlargement of the
horizons of men's minds. The Philippines, Cuba, Porto Rico, and Hawaii

had become as familiar to Americans as the distant parts of their own Union of the States. There was scarcely a community that had not read the letters or listened to the tales of some new-fledged traveler—soldier, sailor, civil servant, prospector, promoter, trader, teacher—who had seen jungles and palm-fringed beaches, walked in strange cities, and deferred to alien customs. Americans, almost unawares, had come to inhabit a less parochial world, and their broadening interest in foreign affairs was reflected in their newspapers and magazines and in the new books and lecture courses. A great tide of tourist traffic was turning toward Europe. People were beginning to talk of new opportunities for cruises nearer home. Yesterday, it had been a novelty that Easterners were seeking the mild climate of Florida for a winter vacation. Now that the army had cleaned up Cuba, it was predicted that Havana would be a pleasure resort of the future.

The excitement of opening vistas was intensified by the acceleration of technological progress. Modern machines were speeding and simplifying the processes of industry. Electricity was lighting more and more streets, public buildings, and houses. The use of the telephone was increasing, and the improvement in long-distance service gave promise that it might soon be possible to hold conversations from coast to coast. The trolley had revolutionized transportation in cities, great and small. The propulsion of streetcars by electric current, transmitted by overhead wires with dangling pulleys, had already made the horsecar seem old-fashioned. The system was expected to produce most important results in relieving the housing congestion in the larger cities and in drawing nearby communities within their orbit. Its eventual vast extension was anticipated by the well-known authority on electrical phenomena, Professor John Trowbridge of Harvard University, in preparing an article for a special centennial number of the *New York Tribune*. Invited to foretell the probable uses of electricity in the next hundred years, the scientist had no hesitation in stating that a network of trolley lines would undoubtedly cover the entire American continent.

Trowbridge's article omitted mention of the electric automobile, though the queer, elegantly finished little carriages were a not infrequent sight on level, paved city streets. New York had three electric stages which traversed Central Park, and ran up Riverside Drive as far as Grant's Tomb. General Miles, in his erratic way, had seized on the idea that automobiles might be useful to the Army—for carrying dispatches, and for the movements of staff officers and small reconnoitering parties. Three electric vehicles, tried out at Fort Myer in Virginia, had not proved quite satisfactory because of a lack of facilities for recharging the batteries, but Miles was stubbornly experimenting with automobiles propelled by steam and

gasoline. It had been tentatively suggested that, at the centennial celebration of the founding of the District of Columbia, the President should
ride in an electric victoria as a feature of the parade. This was a rather
frisky proposal for McKinley, apart from the not inconsiderable danger
of his being ignominiously stalled in the middle of Pennsylvania Avenue.
He had declined. Under more private conditions at Canton the next summer, he went for a spin in a Stanley Steamer.

Horseless carriages of some sort were obviously there to stay—they had
invaded and taken over the bicycle shows, and started a new sport of
automobile racing—but only a few wild-eyed inventors and other eccentrics
dreamed that they would ever be anything more than a hobby of the rich.
They went scooting and hooting about the countryside at a speed that
transformed a pleasant rural road into an intermittent hell of noise and
choking dust, rearing horses and suicidal chickens. The discommoded
public took a rather meek revenge in ridicule. The automobile was fast becoming the great national joke, as Americans guffawed at the freakish,
foreshortened machines and their grotesquely goggled occupants, and
exultantly shouted, "Get a horse!" at the stranded wrecks by the wayside.
The contraptions were treated with phenomenal indulgence because it
was so remarkable that they ran at all. They were a marvel of invention, as
amazing—and just as impractical—as Edison's kinetoscope, which so rapidly
reproduced a continuous series of photographs that they conveyed a
startling illusion of real motion.

Since the American brain could devise ingenious toys like these, what
might not be expected in fields of larger utility and more direct application to industry? In that Elizabethan age of discovery and expansion, no
conquest seemed impossible to man. The new science of electrochemistry
foretold a revolution in agricultural methods. Electrophysicists were asserting that the atom was not the smallest particle of matter, but would some
day be subdivided. Marconi's recent experiments suggested a coming
practical use of wireless telegraphy. Dr. Walter Reed's announcement
that he had identified a mosquito as the carrier of the yellow-fever virus
meant an incalculable benefit to public health in the southern states,
in Cuba and other tropical places. The discovery of the Roentgen ray had
opened limitless possibilities for medical diagnosis, and Edison was already
building machines that could be installed in hospitals and doctor's offices.
With such accomplishments and such prospects, America faced the year
of 1901, the greatest New Year of her history. The thrill of transition had
an element of solemnity. Reminders had not been wanting that, in the
majestic march of the nineteenth century, moral progress had been laggard.
Mistakes had been made in education, in programs of social reform, and

in the treatment of crime and disease. The boasts of civilization were mocked by the prevalence of poverty; by the worsening clash between capital and labor; by the failure to outlaw war. These were thoughts which sobered, but did not deflate the national exaltation. Faith in the moral grandeur of the future was secure. Whether they rioted with tin whistles in the streets, or heard in family parlors the fateful din of bells, or knelt at solemn High Mass and meetings of watch and prayer, Americans confidently welcomed the glorious twentieth century as the millennium of the brotherhood of man and peace among the nations.

The President had lingered in the Cabinet Room, chatting with his brother and Cortelyou. At midnight he exchanged with them the compliments of the season, and retired to rest. Below, in the scented dark, the parlors were dressed and waiting. A great crush of callers was expected in the morning, for the President had been unwilling to limit the admission of the public on the first day of the new century.

The people began to gather outside the gates in the dull light of early morning, and were marshaled four abreast in an ever-lengthening column. They shuffled patiently in line while the dignitaries arrived and departed. Then they streamed toward the East Room to gain their moment with the President, to blurt their good wishes and feel the warm handclasp that swept them rapidly along. When one o'clock marked the customary close of the reception, the line still reached into the street, and the President directed that the doors should be left open until everyone had been admitted. He had been shaking hands continuously for three hours when the last caller passed and he turned to conduct his wife to the elevator.

It was one of Mrs. McKinley's "good" days. She had appeared almost lively in conversation with Mrs. Takahira, the wife of the Japanese ambassador. Her pleasure was manifest at the presence of many children in the crowd. She had tossed them white roses from her big bouquet; chucked a baby under the chin, kissed the chocolate-smeared face of a chubby boy, shaken hands with a little girl's doll. In a pale blue gown of embossed satin and velvet, she had remained firmly seated in her throne-like blue chair. She had ignored the preparations made for slipping her out, and kept her place until the end. It was a red-letter day on which she made the first entry in the diary that the President had given her as a New Year's remembrance.

The little book was one of the standard, pocket-size diaries, bound in stiff black cloth, and closed with a triangular flap, like an envelope. On the flyleaf, the President had formally inscribed "For Mrs. McKinley from her husband." What hopes, what tender discipline had suggested a present so ill suited to the confused mind and awkward penmanship of the recipient? Her interests had small variety: the weather ("rain rain" or "Cold, Cold, Cold"), her headaches and the health of "my Dearest," the drives and the callers, the evenings of euchre ("I was the successful one"), the numbers at the big receptions. This is a very sad little book, sad in its all but illegible scribbles, sad in its many blank pages; sad in the entries, purporting to be Mrs. McKinley's, which were encouragingly made in the President's neat hand. His desire for a continuous record was not to be fulfilled, but she took up her pen with elation on New Year's Day. There had been 5,350 callers. She wrote the number twice. No reference was made to her own feat of endurance; but "My Dearest was tired out," Mrs. McKinley slyly scrawled in her diary.

The President came down with a heavy cold, which developed into grippe. Epidemic influenza was especially severe that winter. For the only time during his occupancy of the White House, McKinley was ill in bed, seriously ill for a few days, though the fact was concealed from the press. Mrs. McKinley remained constantly at his side, except for one anxious night which Dr. Rixey spent in the sickroom. The President escaped the dreaded sequel of pneumonia, but his strength came back slowly, and he did not fully resume his duties for a week after getting out of bed. Official appointments were canceled, and social invitations withdrawn. McKinley passed the days of convalescence quietly with his wife, scarcely leaving the domestic wing of the mansion except for a drive when the weather was fine.

The Cabinet met, after two weeks' intermission, on January 22. With a single exception, the members were all to stay for the second term. Attorney General Griggs had made known his wish to return to private practice, but he had remained for the hearings on the "Insular Cases," which would determine the status of the new possessions. His masterly arguments before the Supreme Court had won him national applause, and he would retire full of honors in March. The President was thinking of appointing his old friend, Philander C. Knox of Pittsburgh.

Others around the mahogany table had less reason than Griggs for self-congratulation; yet the discussion was not all of the difficulties of the several departments, harassed by problems of administration and the harsh struggle with Congress. News had come from England that the old Queen was sinking. Victoria Regina had been a constant in a variable world. More than a monarch, an epoch was felt to be passing. "Why, gentlemen," the President said, "she began to reign before we were born." It was unanimously agreed to half-mast the flags on the White

House and the Executive departments on the day of the Queen's death and again on the day of the funeral. The expected news was received before the meeting adjourned, and the White House flag soon plunged ruefully down the staff. The mourning of Washington for a foreign ruler was a small but significant marker on the turning pages of history.

Of an evening, the President did not confine himself as strictly as usual to the papers on his desk. He had become much interested in, of all things, a book—*Hugh Wynne*, Dr. S. Weir Mitchell's well-told tale of the American Revolution. Cortelyou found him reading it at eleven o'clock at night. But this was the only distraction that McKinley enjoyed, unless a belated round of official entertaining could be covered by the term. With returning strength, he was closely involved in the difficulties of the War Department. Root had been having a bad time over the Army Reorganization Bill, embodying his first recommendations for reform. It had been defaced by the House under pressure from the lobbyists of the staff corps. Root had refused to compromise, in spite of military necessity in the Philippines. Appearing before the Military Affairs Committee of the Senate, he had argued so cogently for a flexible staff system, as well as the immediate increase of the standing Army, that the excrescences were lopped from the bill. Two weeks were consumed in debate before it was passed by the Senate, and two weeks more in conference before the House yielded. It was February 2 when at long last the War Department was empowered to recruit replacements for the regiments that were being withdrawn from the Philippines. The contention and suspense had told on Root's nerves. The Army bill was a victory for him, the President observed, but he also noticed Root's careworn face. He privately remarked that Root was not accustomed to the hard knocks of a public career; was not (in the jargon of the day) "immune."

On other business before the War Department, the President was moving to take the lead himself in dealing with Congress. He saw with intense disapproval the botch that the Senate was making of the River and Harbor bill. "If they send me a whopper of a bill with a lot of bad things in it, I'll veto it," he briskly said to Cortelyou. But McKinley was not thinking merely of the veto power. There was need for legislation on which the Fifty-sixth Congress could improbably take action in the closing weeks of its existence. Talk of an extra session had begun to vibrate from the White House on the President's return to the east wing.

The Senate, on January 25, had been most unpleasantly surprised to receive a sheaf of papers from the Philippines, including a formal report from the Taft Commission. The disagreeable feature was the emphasis laid on the disadvantage to the commission, in its legislative capacity, of functioning under the war powers of the Executive. Judge Taft urged the passage of the still pending Spooner bill, and he desired that the grant of extraordinary powers to the President should be made operative at once, without awaiting the complete suppression of the rebellion. This request was strongly supported by the Secretary of War and the President.

The first reaction was that compliance was out of the question. The Spooner bill had been dropped in the preceding session because of Republican as well as Democratic objections that the grant was unwise and unconstitutional. The Senate was badly behind schedule. To bring up a controversial measure and attempt to rush it through seemed a hopeless undertaking. In the consternation caused by the suggestion, little credence was at first given to rumors that the President would also require legislation for Cuba. These rumors, however, were shortly confirmed. By February 8, when Spooner attached his bill—duly altered to be made operative at the President's discretion—as an amendment to the bill for Army appropriations, the attention of both houses was unexpectedly fixed on Havana.

The Cuban constitutional convention, which had been sitting since November at Havana, had been charged by Governor General Wood with a double duty: to formulate the governing principles for an independent republic, and to prepare a formal recognition of the protective interest of the United States in the foreign affairs of Cuba and in its domestic order. But in late January, when work on the constitution was nearing completion, the War Department was informed that it would entirely ignore the latter subject. If the draft should be submitted to Washington with this omission, the President had determined to call an extra session. "He wants some of the pending questions settled," Cortelyou wrote on January 30; "says that the Philippine question will have become acute in the next year and that he does not want both that and the Cuban situation on hand at the same time."

Signs of the President's intention caused nervous strain on Capitol Hill. An extra session was dreaded, especially by the Senate. Yet it seemed utterly unavoidable, if action on Cuba were required. Legislation had not been contemplated, and Republican opinion in both houses was fragmented on the matter. One seemingly insuperable obstacle was the ambiguous status of the island which had been fostered by the Teller Amendment. The Supreme Court had recently affirmed that Cuba was a foreign country. How, then, could Congress claim the right to pronounce on the form of the future republic, or regulate its relations with the United States? A nucleus of Republican senators stood ready to trample on legal niceties. Others hung back in uncertainty, while the Democrats jeered at the idea that Congress could deal with the constitution of a foreign country as if it were a bill.

The question remained open for more than three weeks of February. The President made no secret of his determination that Congress must share the responsibility for Cuba. He was repeatedly quoted as saying that he did not see how an extra session was to be avoided. A challenge seemed to lurk in the negative phrase, and it had been accepted by Senator Orville Platt, chairman of the Committee on Cuban Relations. He had found a warrant for congressional action in the military intervention of 1898, and its direct relation to the military occupation. Since Congress had authorized the intervention, Platt concluded that Congress possessed the right to declare on what terms the resultant occupation should cease. But this resourceful argument did not raise the hopes of the Republicans. Though they had grown eager to bury their differences, they had no faith in a last-minute resolution on Cuba. The fatal announcement of a filibuster had sounded from the opposition. Majority leaders began to draw up plans for an extra session.

Meanwhile, the President had been in conference with Orville Platt and the invaluable Spooner, who was a member of the Cuban committee. The two senators were privately furnished with the Executive requirements. Another amendment was framed, empowering the President to negotiate with the Havana delegates. When it was unanimously reported from committee on February 25, the attitude of the Senate underwent a sudden, spectacular change. The conditions prescribed for Cuban independence were enthusiastically approved by the Republicans, and commended by some of the Democrats.

Bryan made strenuous efforts to rally his forces against both the Platt and Spooner amendments, but the demoralized opposition was incapable of coherence even in obstruction. It was common knowledge that the complacency of several leading Democrats had been purchased by special appropriations in the River and Harbor Bill and other legislation. The threatened filibuster dwindled into a few face-saving speeches. The amendments came to a vote on February 27, and were adopted by the Republican majority. The Spooner resolution, however, was disfigured by Senator Hoar's amendment, limiting the power to grant franchises and other commercial rights in the Philippines. The restrictions, similar to those which had been imposed in the case of Cuba, would handicap Taft's plans for economic development, but the President discouraged the House leaders from contesting them. On ascertaining his wishes, the House took up the heavily laden appropriations bill, and expeditiously voted to concur.

The President had accepted compromise with his usual realism. A qualified resolution on the Philippines was the best that he could get. The antagonism of many Republican senators to the Spooner resolution had been carefully concealed by a smoke screen of party loyalty, but it had stubbornly endured to the end. Shortly before the vote was taken on the amended amendment, Senator Fairbanks had reported the situation over the private telephone wire to the White House. "Is the President really anxious about it? Does he want this?" Fairbanks agitatedly asked Secretary Cortelyou. If so, there would be no difficulty about sustaining it, but many seriously doubted the propriety unless it was deemed essential. . . . After speaking to the President, Cortelyou gave Fairbanks the answer: "For your confidential information, Senator, I will say that the President most emphatically desires it in its present shape. He thinks it would be the gravest of blunders, having gone so far, to now recede."

To obtain extraordinary powers in the Philippines, the President had exerted the full influence of his office. He had done so because of his decision to end military rule without waiting until pacification was complete. Plans were already matured to inaugurate a civil administration, with Taft as governor. The announcement of the impending change had been published two weeks before the Senate adopted the Spooner Amendment.

Taft had quickly recognized that pacification was not a purely military task. Even in the orderly conditions that now prevailed at Manila, the American army was hated—hated for its insolent attitude toward friendly Filipinos, hated for the color line drawn by the officers and their wives on social occasions. Wise and tolerant in his dealings, democratic and genial in manner, Taft had demonstrated his ability to win the confidence of the people and give them hope for the future. The President's decision to hasten the civil program had obviously been influenced by Taft's urgent recommendations. But another influence had also been at work. Since the preceding autumn, Washington had been in possession of Governor General MacArthur's report that the population of the Philippines was united in sympathy with the insurrection. There is no direct evidence of the impression which this statement made on the President. The indirect evidence suggests that it was not wholly credited. Skepticism was to be expected in the case of information which shook the very groundwork of the government's beliefs; which contradicted the observations of Otis and Schurman; which disagreed with statements made by Taft himself. (Though latterly less optimistic, Taft also had been beguiled by the upper-class Filipinos at Manila.) Moreover, MacArthur's florid and pompous style was not the most persuasive means of communicating new and unwelcome ideas.

What, for example, was McKinley to make of the purple-tinted suggestion that "the adhesive principle comes from ethnological homogeneity, which induces men to respond for a time to the appeals of consanguineous leadership . . ."? At one point, the General expressed the opinion that the Filipinos had been "maddened by rhetorical sophistry." A similar fate might have seemed to threaten McKinley and Root, as they studied MacArthur's report.

Nevertheless, the report could not be brushed aside. Two years of service in the field had entitled MacArthur to speak with incomparably greater authority than any previous official informant. His statement supplied a logical explanation for the vitality of the rebellion, after American victory in the field. It accounted for the failure of his offer of amnesty, and justified the adoption of a policy of severity, in which the Taft Commission was co-operating. The Washington authorities could no longer doubt that popular sympathy with the insurgent cause must be far more widespread and passionate than they had been given to understand; but this realization had manifestly had an effect quite other than MacArthur had intended. It had undermined the assumption that the army must remain in supreme control as long as hostile activities persisted. The hatred of the Philippine people for American rule made it urgent that the United States government should be represented by men dissociated from the military in dress and tradition and habit of mind.

The decision to make Taft governor meant that MacArthur must be replaced. That able soldier was a pre-eminent exemplar of the caste system of the regular Army: rigid, autocratic, and utterly incapable of subordination to civil authority. He had jealously resented the appointment of the commissioners, and, from the first, had made Taft's life unbearable by acts of obstructiveness and even petty hostility. Like many jolly fat men, Taft had a smoldering temper. He had controlled himself in his intercourse with MacArthur, but his protests showered the War Department. He had bluntly intimated that the government must choose between retaining him or MacArthur at Manila.

MacArthur, for his part, was well satisfied to be relieved. His promotion to major general in the regular service had been confirmed by the Senate. In due course, he returned home to exercise various departmental commands, and attend the higher honors in store for him. It must have seemed above all things unlikely that his career might be affected by his high-handed treatment of a meddlesome civilian who had crossed his path in the Philippines. In 1904, however, Taft became Secretary of War, and four years later he was elected President of the United States. MacArthur was made lieutenant general during Taft's time at the War Department, but he did not assume the chief command to which his rank entitled him. His instructions were to await orders at his home in Milwaukee. He was still waiting on the September night of 1912 when he suffered a fatal heart attack while addressing a veterans' banquet.

The first inauguration of the twentieth century was also the centenary of the first inauguration held in the Federal District. On the cloudy morning of March 4, Washington was conscious of offering a splendid contrast to the waste of mud and sheds in which Thomas Jefferson had taken the oath of office. The street decorations had been elaborately conceived. The buildings along the route of the parade blazed with the national colors, and uniform banks of seats, trimmed in white and yellow, bordered Pennsylvania Avenue from the Capitol to the Treasury. The east front of the Capitol was to be, as usual, the scene of the main ceremony; but this year the location had been shifted from the Senate wing to the central portico. The House, rebelling against the pretensions of the upper chamber, had insisted on the transfer to common ground. The huge platform, bearing a miniature Greek temple, was an imposing sight, but still finer were the arrangements in the vicinity of the Executive Mansion. A white-columned Court of Honor embraced the front lawn and the adjacent strip of Pennsylvania Avenue in one handsome architectural design. A glass-enclosed reviewing stand had been erected near the State, War and Navy Building, and that massive gray pile was adorned with great illuminated badges of the two Civil War corps in which the President had served: the six-pointed star of the Eighth Corps, and the crossed gun and anchor of the Ninth.

The grand march in review was scheduled for the afternoon, but the President's drive to and from the Capitol attracted an equal interest, and the crowds were out at an early hour. The tunes of the bands clashed jubilantly as troops and marching clubs went swinging to their stations in Pennsylvania Avenue and Fifteenth Street. The grand marshal, General Francis V. Greene of New York, posted himself at the Treasury, with his staff. A group of Grand Army veterans assembled glumly in the Court of Honor. They were not going to take part in the grand march. They had been insulted by General Greene. He had asked them to bring up the rear of the procession, behind the state organizations. So they had refused to march at all. The President had done his best to smooth things over. The old soldiers had been invited to furnish his personal escort in the morning, and they were to have their own private review in the Court of Honor, after the big parade had passed. Comrade McKinley was loyal (though he had a mean pension commissioner in H. Clay Evans), but he

573

would be the last of the Union soldiers to sit in the White House. They were being pushed aside by the upstart veterans of a war without a Cause, a contest embittered and ennobled by scarcely a major engagement on land. The angry futility of old age oppressed the President's personal escort, as they waited in the damp colonnade. A Rough Rider band charged up to rend the air with a boisterous cowboy concert.

The first of the official party to enter the mansion was General Corbin, Mrs. McKinley's squire for the inaugural ceremonies. Admiral Dewey arrived soon after; then Senator Hanna, quickly followed by the Cabinet members, and by Dr. Rixey, who was to assist Corbin in supporting Mrs. McKinley. The cavalry escort from Cleveland clattered smartly into the driveway. General Miles walked over from his headquarters. The party was completed by Representatives Cannon of Illinois and McRae of Arkansas. At ten-thirty, the President's carriage drew up before the portico, with his blacks in the lead and his favorite bays at the wheel. McKinley came out, accompanied by the select committee of Congress, and, in the bravery of prancing horses and marching troops, made a ceremonious progress to the Capitol.

Congress had sat all night. The air of the Capitol was stale with contention and compromise. The yield of the legislative debauch was stacked on the desk in the President's Room. Four great appropriation bills awaited his signature, but the River and Harbor Bill was not among them. Senator Thomas Carter of Montana, formerly McKinley's colleague in the House, was engaged in talking the "whopper" to death, to the bewilderment of strangers arriving to witness the inauguration of Theodore Roosevelt. The filibuster was finally interrupted by the opening of the vice-presidential ceremonies in the fusty Senate Chamber, hastily pushed to rights, and barren of decorations.

Republican luck had not held in the weather. The lowering skies turned leaden while Roosevelt was inducted into office. A drizzle quickened to a downpour as the President emerged at the east front and, with head bared and overcoat collar carelessly turned up, sprang lightly down the steps. He had never appeared more vigorous and spirited than at this hour when, for the second time, his choice was ratified by the cheers of the host in the Capitol Park. He firmly repeated the words of the oath, and in a strong, chiming voice delivered a brief inaugural address. He spoke of the abundant production of America, of larger foreign markets and broader commercial relations. He referred to the obligations imposed by the war with Spain, and fervently prayed for the rule of peaceful arbitration, that the nation might in future be spared the horrors of war. Appealing to Americans to renew their ancient faith in the principles of the republic,

McKinley asked for the co-operation of men of all parties in discharging his great responsibilities. The storm thickened while the President spoke, but the blows of sleet and hail did not diminish the enthusiasm with which his audience gave back, point by point, the thunderous noise of approval.

The President's coachman and footman had donned their rubber coats, and closed his carriage for the return to the White House; but the drenched crowds were still massed along the route, waiting to see him pass. As the rain began to slacken, he had the top thrown back before turning into Pennsylvania Avenue. Under lighter skies, the President drove up the glistening river of asphalt between the banks of the people, whose shouts traveled with him to the White House in a sustained roar of acclamation.

A great swing around the country was to be the first public action of McKinley's second term. He planned to leave Washington at the end of April, and spend six weeks on the road, traveling to the Pacific coast by the southern route and returning via the Northwest. The high point of his stay in San Francisco was to be the launching of one of the new battle-ships, the *Ohio*. The trip would conclude on June 13 with the celebration of President's Day at the Pan-American Exposition at Buffalo. It was a far more extensive tour than McKinley had previously taken. Unlike his other visits to the West, it was not designed to influence elections. The President was going to talk to the country about two subjects which had previously been overshadowed by the postwar issues: the control of trusts and the extension of commercial reciprocity. His choice of these subjects implied that, in the political freedom of his second term, McKinley was prepared to pit the power of the Executive against the power of the Senate.

The antagonism to the reciprocity program was as unavowed as the antagonism to regulating the monopolies. Republican senators could not openly denounce the established party policy of widening American markets abroad; but the conservatives on the tariff would smother any specific proposal for lowering the rates. The President had submitted seven commercial treaties—as distinguished from the limited trade agreements, which the Executive himself was empowered to make—for ratification by the Senate. On the adjournment of the Fifty-sixth Congress, all seven were languishing in the oubliettes of the Foreign Relations Committee. With the exception of Senator Cullom, the Republican members of the committee were hostile to the President's policy. Hanna was implacable in his opposition to ratifying the treaties. It would require tremendous pressure merely to get them laid before the Senate.

Without minimizing the trust question, to which he had been giving much study, the President intended to place his main emphasis on reciprocity in this first open conflict with the reactionaries of his party. Here was a clearly defined issue on which his program was well advanced, and on which the obstructiveness of the Senate, especially in the case of the important treaty with France, had disappointed and angered the public. McKinley was extremely eager to develop his long-postponed program of trade expansion. The approaching independence of Cuba, moreover, raised a special aspect of the question. As a matter of simple justice, the United States was bound to conclude a generous trade agreement with the republic. The President gave assurances of this intention to five commissioners from the Havana convention, who came to Washington in doubt of the meaning of the Platt Amendment and in apprehension for the economic future of Cuba. An inevitable battle with the American sugar and tobacco interests made it desirable for the President to consolidate public support for the reciprocity principle.

The important addresses on policy were reserved for the return journey from the Pacific coast, and were to culminate in the Buffalo speech. On his way through the South, the President would develop the theme of foreign markets, speaking, with John Hay at his side, about an Open Door for cotton in the Far East. But it was not McKinley's intention to appeal to self-interest alone. Foreign trade was inseparably linked in his mind with the aspiration of international unity. It was with this larger view that he composed the speech he would make at the launching of the *Ohio.* "There is nothing in this world that brings people so close together as commerce. There is nothing in this world that so much promotes the universal brotherhood of man as commerce. . . . The nations are close together now. The powers of the earth are tied together. We have overcome distance."

A party of forty-three—officials, friends, members of the Executive staff, personal servants, and newspaper correspondents—joined the President and Mrs. McKinley on the special train which left Washington on the morning of April 29. McKinley had originally meant to take his entire Cabinet, but the plan had not proved to be feasible. The new Attorney General, Philander C. Knox, was just becoming acquainted with his duties; Root was snowed under by the complications in Cuba and the Philippines; and Gage was detained at the bedside of his wife, whose heart had been weakened by a severe attack of grippe. Secretaries Long, Hitchcock, and Wilson arranged to join the party at San Francisco. Secretary Hay and Postmaster General Smith were the only Cabinet members who traveled with the President through the plaudits of the expansionist South to the riotous welcome of Los Angeles.

Mrs. McKinley was in her usual dubious health, but her pleasure in travel was unflagging. She enjoyed the affectionate greeting which she was sure of receiving wherever she went. Her maid Clara was on hand to take care of her, and her favorite niece Mary Barber had been persuaded to keep her company. Best of all, she had her devoted physician. Mrs. McKinley always had a sweet smile for Dr. Rixey, and he noticed and appreciated it. The President, too, warmly approved of his treatment. For one important thing, Rixey had cut down the bromides on which Mrs. McKinley had formerly been so dependent. He had made a special study of her case, and was tireless in his attendance. McKinley had the utmost confidence in his professional judgment.

The second week of May was fiesta time in Los Angeles. Enormous crowds hailed the McKinleys in the gaudily decorated streets. At the head of a splendid floral parade, the President's carriage was drawn by six white horses, caparisoned in yellow satin. He stood ankle-deep in showered rose petals on the reviewing stand. Mrs. McKinley did not watch the parade, but arranged a little triumph of her own by driving out just ahead of it. Her popularity seemed to nerve her to extraordinary exertions, for she was in excruciating pain. A bone felon on her forefinger had become so inflamed and swollen that Dr. Rixey had lanced it while the train was crossing the desert. The operation had failed to bring relief. Mrs. McKinley was beginning to run a fever. She had also developed a bad case of diarrhea. Nevertheless, she persisted in attending the social functions that had been scheduled in Los Angeles.

The party was due to reach San Francisco on Tuesday, May 14, and left Los Angeles on the preceding Friday. Arrangements had been made to spend a quiet week end at Del Monte, in anticipation of five days of celebration to follow. On the way, the train was stopped for nearly an hour while Dr. Rixey again lanced Mrs. McKinley's finger. Though exhausted and feverish on arrival, she forced herself to accompany the President while he drove out to make two speeches in nearby communities. Then she collapsed. On Sunday, she was so ill that the President made an exception to his strict rule against travel on the Sabbath, and took her at once to San Francisco. Mr. H. T. Scott, the head of the Union Iron Works, which had built the battleship *Ohio*, had placed his house at the President's disposal, and there Mrs. McKinley was put to bed, with trained nurses in attendance.

During the next three days, Mrs. McKinley's condition grew progressively worse, but Dr. Rixey made light of the trouble in his statements to the press and in the official bulletins which Cortelyou prepared for publication. The invalid's sufferings had evidently brought on more than one heavy epileptic attack, and Rixey was evidently looking for the usual recuperation. Local physicians, called in consultation, were reported to take a more serious view. They probably made the diagnosis which was later confirmed—that Mrs. McKinley had a blood infection resulting from the felon on her finger. But, as late as Wednesday, Cortelyou, in his capacity of official spokesman, was talking to reporters about Mrs. McKinley's "sinking spells" and her powers of rapid recovery, and giving the assurance that Dr. Rixey expected to have her out before long.

The President must have longed to trust the comforting opinion of the physician who understood Mrs. McKinley's "case" so thoroughly, but he could not fail to see that she was critically ill. Subsisting on a little beef broth and brandy, she was alarmingly weak, and at times unconscious. On Wednesday, McKinley gave up all thought of continuing his tour. He stayed close to his wife, prolonging his watch through the night. Before dawn, her pulse failed and she sank into a stupor. A medical consultation was hastily called, and heart stimulants were administered. The Cabinet members and their ladies gathered at the Scott house. The President's San Francisco relatives, Marjorie McKinley Morse and her husband, were summoned. In the suspense of early morning, tentative plans were made for the departure of a funeral train for Washington. But Mrs. McKinley at last showed her famous capacity to rally. As her heart responded to stimulants, the new treatment of intravenous injections of salt was tried with good effect. Before noon on Thursday, Mrs. McKinley regained consciousness, smiled, and spoke a few words.

The improvement held, and on Saturday the President attended the launching of the *Ohio*. His relief burst from his lips, as he arose to address the men at the shipyards: "I am inexpressibly thankful to the Ruler of us all for His goodness and His mercy, which have made it possible for me to be with you here today." But keeping this engagement was a painful effort for McKinley. The visit to the Union Iron Works entailed a boat trip across the bay, and during the two crossings he was removed from the direct telegraphic connections with the Scott house which had been installed at both the San Francisco wharf and the shipyards. His nervousness became so intense on the return trip that he did not wait for the gangplank to be lowered at the landing. Stepping over the side of the pier, he almost ran to his carriage in his haste to reach the sickroom.

With more ease of mind, the President left his wife for short intervals during the next week. The citizens of San Francisco had earned his fervent gratitude. His trouble had seemed to cast a pall over the whole city. Day after day, crowds had gathered in Lafayette Park, across from the Scott house. They had waited quietly through the hours of gravest anxiety, with eyes raised to the drawn blinds of the sickroom. Still more touchingly, on news of Mrs. McKinley's improvement, they had restrained any expressions of rejoicing which would have disturbed her rest. When the President came out to go to the *Ohio* launching, the men in the crowd respectfully uncovered. There was no other demonstration in the vicinity of the house; but, once his carriage was well on the way to the wharf, joyful shouts broke wildly from the curblines. McKinley responded with a full heart to this display of affection and spontaneous delicacy of feeling. He spent his last days in San Francisco in a strenuous effort to atone for the disappointments caused by the cancellation of most of the official program.

The press had made the President's ordeal a vivid reality to the country. He had been seen in a more intimate light than ever before, as a suffering man, putting aside his personal grief to perform his public duty. His reputation as a model husband had credited him with a formal virtue. A curtain of privacy had been drawn across his life with Ida. But at San Francisco the curtain had been lifted, and the anguish of the disclosure deeply moved the people. Their prayers were with the McKinleys in the last week of May, while the special train made its swift and silent journey eastward. The President's national influence had never been so potent as when he returned from his tour without having made one of his important speeches on policy.

Mrs. McKinley stood the journey well, and Dr. Rixey pronounced that she was slowly improving, but a disquieting verdict was in store for the President at Washington. After a medical consultation, in which Surgeon General Sternberg participated, the opinion was given that Mrs. McKinley could not be considered out of danger. The principal cause of anxiety was her heart. Mrs. McKinley's heart had always been strong—its soundness had enabled her to withstand her bad attacks. The sickroom held the President in a renewed grip of apprehension. He met with his Cabinet to discuss a hitch in the Cuban settlement, but denied himself to all but a few callers, and left the house only to take a breath of air. His state of mind can be read in the memoranda which he made of the daily consultations: notes, scrabbled down on medical prescription blanks and frequently corrected in a painstaking effort to get the record exactly right. On June 8, after the results of a blood analysis had been received, the doctors summed up their findings. A blood infection, resulting from the bone felon on Mrs. McKinley's finger, had caused an acute endocarditis, or inflammation of the lining of the heart. This condition did not appear to be progressive; and, since there had been an improvement in the diarrhea and in the patient's general condition, the doctors rather cautiously admitted that the case presented a more hopeful aspect.

Coming back with a lightened mind to the world of public affairs, the President was jolted by certain recent developments on the political scene. The demonstrations of his hold on popular affection had started a buzz of talk about a third term. Premature though the discussion was, it was regarded as significant because of the outgivings of Senator Depew and Congressman Grosvenor, who were believed to be in the confidence of the President. His wife's condition obviously made the suggestion peculiarly odious to him, but he had other than personal reasons for the vehemence of his reaction. While the reception of his deferred speeches would largely depend on public confidence in his disinterestedness, the Democratic press was now accusing the President of a third-term mania. Such suspicions, if unrebuked, would cast on anything that McKinley might say the shadow of selfish ambition and partisan purpose. He vented his indignation to Dawes while walking in the White House grounds on Monday, June 10. The substance of his comment, as noted by Dawes, was that the Depew and Grosvenor interviews were "unkind and uncalled for, though possibly well meant." McKinley spoke of silencing the talk by making a public statement.

The statement, in fact, had already been prepared. The President had written it out himself the day before, but he was doubtful that he should give the matter notice, and fearful that a denial "might appear strange or ridiculous." He consulted Hay and also Long in the course of the Monday afternoon. Then, at quarter past six, he suddenly directed Cortelyou to ask the Cabinet members to call on him after dinner. His impulsive decision to consult the rest of the Cabinet, without waiting for the regular Tuesday morning meeting, had probably been crystallized by the conversation with Hay, who had shown signs of being "a third termer."

Hay would not be present at the evening meeting. He was taking the train to Buffalo, to attend the Pan-American Exposition, in partial amends for McKinley's cancellation of his appointment. Root had already left on the same errand, but the rest of the Cabinet members were in Washington. In response to the President's summons, they went to the White House, examined what he had written, and ratified the proposal to publish it. McKinley handed the paper to Cortelyou before he went to bed, with instructions to give it out the next day.

The Washington correspondents were in a fever of unsatisfied curiosity about the emergency meeting. As experienced newspapermen, they could not admit the naïve idea that the President would consult the Cabinet about a political matter. They were startled to find, when Cortelyou passed

THE SECOND ACT BEGINS

out the releases on Tuesday, that the President had done something more irregular still—he had actually signed his name to a political statement. "I will say now, once for all, expressing a long settled conviction," McKinley wrote, "that I not only am not and will not be a candidate for a third term, but would not accept a nomination for it if it were tendered me." A short concluding paragraph followed the main statement. "My only ambition is to serve through my second term to the acceptance of my countrymen, whose generous confidence I so deeply appreciate, and then with them to do my duty in the ranks of private citizenship."

There was no possibility of distorting the sense or questioning the sincerity of this unqualified denial. The public responded with instantaneous approval. McKinley had at last forsaken caution, and promptly and vigorously spoken out his mind. By doing so, he raised himself about the ruck of partisans, and ensured a sympathetic hearing for his utterances on policy.

The President was looking forward to taking his wife to Canton, but the move was postponed for three more weeks. These weeks foretold the speedy passing of the issues which had arisen from the war with Spain. The Havana convention unconditionally accepted the terms of the Platt Amendment, clearing the way for the withdrawal of the occupation force. The Supreme Court's decision had recently been handed down, and arrangements were proceeding without interruption in Porto Rico and the Philippines. A good fiscal report from Governor Allen justified the President in proclaiming free trade with Porto Rico, and the assembly was called in special session at San Juan to invite this action. Formal orders were issued for the civil administration of the Philippines. Governor Taft took office, under hopeful auguries, on July 4. The capture of Aguinaldo and his submission to United States authority had taken the heart out of the rebellion. Soldiers would be needed for years to come in the islands, but Taft's inauguration was a promise that the real work of pacification had begun.

Sometimes in the sultry evenings, The President sat very late in the Cabinet Room. One night, he told Cortelyou about a visit he had had from General Fitzhugh Lee. The former Confederate's son was now an officer in the Army of the United States. One of Lee's daughters was engaged to an officer of the Seventh Cavalry, and another was going to be engaged to another officer of the Seventh Cavalry. "Mr. President," Fitz Lee had said, "you have knocked the old gray all to flinders." McKinley observed to Cortelyou that not in their day would the Democrats of the South have the courage to nominate an ex-Confederate as vice-presidential candidate, but the Republican party would have the courage, and could elect him. On another night, the President talked about the tariff. He remarked that it would be "intensely amusing" to have the issue revived; but any tariff revision would have to be done by the Republicans. The Democrats had "made a mess of it." All they had ever done on the subject, McKinley said, was display "economical ignorance."

The President was relaxed and discursive, as Mrs. McKinley grew stronger, and the time neared for their removal to Canton. No crisis, in China or elsewhere, disturbed the prospect of a peaceful summer in the North Market Street house, with a miniature executive office installed in the library. Leaving on July 5, the President intended to spend three months away from Washington, the longest absence he had ever made. One plan for his official household was altered in late June by a tragic accident. He had taken a great liking to John Hay's son, Adelbert; had appointed the young man United States consul at Pretoria; and, after his return, had offered him the position of Assistant Secretary to the President. Only a few days before Del was to have started work, he was killed by a fall from a hotel window, while at New Haven for his Yale reunion.

McKinley had perhaps been hoping to groom Del Hay for the position of Secretary. Cortelyou had a growing reputation, and was entitled to higher honors. Before leaving Washington, the President was pointedly reminded that Cortelyou should be given his opportunity. Dawes, who had senatorial ambitions, resigned as Comptroller of the Currency, and suggested Cortelyou as his successor. McKinley at once called the Secretary in, and offered him the appointment; but Cortelyou was not yet prepared to leave the place in which he was so badly needed. He chose to stay with the President.

Cortelyou was like a member of the family at Canton. It was Cortelyou who helped the President to push Mrs. McKinley's rolling chair; who drove the carriage to the station to meet the visitors; who entertained them in the evening by playing on a kind of piano, the Caecilian. It was Cortelyou who managed the executive office, scheduled the daily appointments, and discharged the heavy routine business. It was of course Cortelyou who, without bothering the President with details, made the final preparations for the trip to Buffalo. For McKinley had never relinquished the idea of making his speech at the Pan-American Exposition. He had supported since its first inception the project of a fair dedicated to the spirit of hemispheric unity; and it offered an exceptionally appropriate setting for a declaration on behalf of reciprocal trade agreements. He was planning to be in Cleveland in the second week of September to attend the National Encampment of the G.A.R. The visit to Buffalo could be conveniently made the week before. In early August, after a committee of prominent Buffalo gentlemen had spent the day in Canton, it was announced that September 5 had been chosen as President's Day at the Pan-American Exposition.

McKinley's enjoyment turned an uneventful holiday into a village idyl. He was brimming over with pleasure in the life of the town, with pride in his property. He would step out in the morning for a stroll about the small grounds, a talk with the gardener, or a neighborly exchange with the passers-by on the brick sidewalk beyond the fence. Roosevelt had been amazed, when he went to Canton the year before, by the modesty of the President's house. To a prosperous Easterner, with stuck-up eastern standards, this had appeared the kind of little house that might belong to a retired division superintendent of a railroad. The slur implied by the comparison would have been lost on McKinley. He was innocently content with just the house he had. This year, there were more alterations to marvel at. A pillared porte-cochere roofed the driveway on the north side, and that end of the porch had been extended to form an octagonal gazebo that overlooked lawn and garden. McKinley's satisfaction welled up when he surveyed these improvements. "I don't suppose you can possibly appreciate," he told an old friend who stood beside him, "how much it means to me to have a home of my own." His happiness was doubled because it was mirrored in Ida's face. The return to Canton had wonderfully revived her. Still attended by a trained nurse, she followed a strict regimen of rest, but she was so much better that Dr. Rixey had felt able to pay a visit to his farm near Washington. In spite of his errors of diagnosis, he remained the beloved physician and the ultimate authority on Mrs. McKinley's health. He was separated from his patient only for a short vacation.

After Rixey came back to his post, the President twice made excursions in Myron Herrick's private car. One day was spent at the picturesque hamlet of Zoar, founded by German religious refugees, and until recently vowed to the practice of a primitive communism. The other trip had the purpose of inspecting the farm at Minerva which had passed to the McKinleys on the death of Ida's father. The tour was conducted by the gnarled old farmer, Jack Adams, who had gone to Washington for the inauguration and been entertained at the White House. After the President and his party had looked over the fields and the stock and the outbuildings, they sat down in the kitchen to a dinner of country-cured ham. Except for these two outings, McKinley stayed close to home. He and Ida went for many drives among the rolling wheatfields of Stark County; enlivened many evenings with music and euchre and talk with old friends. As Ida grew steadily stronger, the McKinleys gave a little dinner party. On another evening, she was wheeled over to a musicale at the house of a neighbor. Four tuneful young Canton ladies entertained the company with song. The President was particularly pleased with the display of "home talent." He put in a request for "Louisiana Lou" before taking Mrs. McKinley home.

The approaching absence of ten days would interrupt the sojourn at Canton, but the President was looking forward to the trip. His important speech was much on his mind. One evening, as he sat smoking beside an open window in the library, he suddenly said to Cortelyou, "Expositions are the timekeepers of progress." Another sentence was added to the Buffalo address. McKinley was hopeful that his visit would promote interest in the Pan-American Exposition, and swell the gate receipts. Besides, he was looking forward to the sights. The electrical illuminations, created by Henry Rustin, were said to surpass in beauty those of the recent Paris exposition. A gorgeous display of fireworks was scheduled for the evening of September 5. On the following day, there were plans for an excursion to Niagara Falls. These diversions were to be enjoyed against a background of privacy and comfort in the mansion of Mr. John G. Milburn, the president of the Exposition.

The program, as submitted to Cortelyou, did not make excessive demands on the President, but there was one item of which the Secretary intensely disapproved. On the second and last day of McKinley's stay, after the trip to Niagara Falls, he was to go back to the fairgrounds to hold a public reception in the Temple of Music. His presence at Buffalo, widely advertised by the managers of the Exposition, was sure to attract immense crowds. Cortelyou was less concerned about the gate receipts than the President's security. He was flicked by anxiety, even in the summer peace of Canton, with Foster "always on hand." Other friends worried, too. It made them nervous to see the President sitting in the evening near the windows, with the shades up. If someone ventured a comment, McKinley might get up and draw the shades. Or he might simply change the subject. "I have no enemies. Why should I fear?" he said to people who pressed the point.

The public reception had been twice taken off the program; twice put back at the President's direction. The second time, Cortelyou said, "the direction was wellnigh imperative," but he ventured a last appeal to McKinley to give up this appearance. "Why should I?" McKinley replied. "No one would wish to hurt me." Cortelyou tried another tack. Thousands of people, he argued, would want to greet the President, and it would be impossible for him to shake hands with more than a few of them. "Well, they'll know I tried, anyhow," McKinley said.

Cortelyou took out his dissatisfaction in a telegram to Buffalo, enjoining that thorough precautionary measures be discreetly taken during the President's stay. It was a superfluous warning. Both the city authorities and the Exposition management were alive to their responsibilities. The Buffalo chief of police had written his Washington counterpart, and punctiliously followed his advice. City patrolmen, Exposition guards, railroad detectives, and Pinkerton men would augment the two extra Secret Service operatives whom Chief Wilkie, at Cortelyou's instigation, had agreed to provide; and various detachments of troops had also been assigned to escort and guard the President. Special officers, in uniform and in plain clothes, would be posted night and day around the Milburn house. Whenever the President drove out, his carriage would be preceded, flanked, and followed by a phalanx of soldiers and police. Nothing could have been more uncongenial to McKinley than the conspicuous arrangements made to protect him during his visit to Buffalo.

Measures for the protection of the President's wife had figured largely in Cortelyou's correspondence. For Mrs. McKinley was going on the trip, with a full retinue of doctor, nurse, maid, and nieces, and it was necessary to ensure that she be spared overexertion and disturbance. Mr. Milburn's house was sure to afford the same opulent and upholstered luxury as the Herricks' and the Hannas', where she was to stay in Cleveland. Cortelyou was concerned with protecting Mrs. McKinley when she was exposed to the crowded fair. He warned against noisy demonstrations which might frighten the horses, and suggested—with the unfortunate incident at the Pittsburgh station in mind—that any salutes should be fired at a distance. He frowned on social invitations, and telegraphed the Board of Women Managers of the fair, who had planned a luncheon in Mrs. McKinley's honor, that she would probably not attend any of the Exposition exercises. No formal evening engagements had been made for the President. The trip promised to be exceptionally restful and pleasant, but for once Mrs. McKinley did not desire a change of scene. Some impulse led her to confide her feelings to a neglected little book, the pocket diary which the President had given her on New Year's Day. Four months of blank pages lay reproachfully beneath her fingers, as she wrote of the "lovely time" they were having in Canton, and made the plaintive entry, "I wish we were not going away from home."

But the hours slipped through Mrs. McKinley's clutching fingers. The trunks were packed. The office files were stacked in the traveling cabinets. The special train pulled into the Canton depot, and McKinley went to Buffalo.

APPOINTMENT AT BUFFALO

Above the festive crowds, the decorations blazed in the sunshine, and a soft breeze rippled the Stars and Stripes and the massed colors of the neighbor countries. September 5 was a holiday in Buffalo. By nine o'clock, the streets were full of people. They jammed the sidewalk across from Mr. Milburn's vine-smothered brick mansion on Delaware Avenue, and lined the Lincoln Parkway, the highroad to the fairgrounds. The biggest crowds of all were flocking past the clicking turnstiles of the Pan-American Exposition. More than 116,000 people would visit the fair that day, and 50,000 of them gathered in the Esplanade to hear the President's speech.

The Esplanade was packed to suffocation, with the earliest arrivals wedged against the purple-swathed speakers' stand, and latecomers overflowing into the Court of Fountains and the open space before the Government and Horticulture Buildings. As the sun grew hot, parasols and umbrellas domed the throng like giant mushrooms, and the swish of waving hats and fans and handkerchiefs mingled with the animated buzz of conversation. The holidaymakers were easily diverted from the discomforts of waiting by the interest of the preliminaries. Military bands were blasting out martial airs, while regiments of smart-stepping soldiers marched up the Triumphal Causeway toward the Lincoln Parkway entrance. Ticket holders gradually filled the purple rectangle of the stand, like personages on a stage. The crowd gaped at exotic figures among the diplomatic corps: the monocled Duke of Arcos, who had represented Spain since the peace; the Turkish minister in a red fez; and a contingent of Chinese in fine blue and gray silk robes.

All eyes were raised to the Triumphal Causeway and cheers began to sound, as noon approached and the booming of the President's salute announced that the head of his cavalcade had entered the grounds. Two rows of officers snapped to attention, forming a gold-laced aisle from the Causeway to the stand. An escort of horsemen came into distant view, and then an open carriage in which the President was seated, with Mrs. McKinley at his side. The carriage moved to the crest of the Causeway in a silence so profound that the tiny crackle of hoofs was clearly audible. It halted, and the President stood up. He raised Mrs. McKinley, gowned in gray, with a black lace face shade, to stand in the circle of his arm. For a moment, he looked around him, gazing off at the golden goddess on the summit of the Electric Tower that dominated the long central basin of the grounds; letting his eyes travel over the panorama of gleaming domes, dancing fountains, and sparkling ornamental waters. Then he alighted, and lifted his wife down. She did not lean on the President for support as they walked to the stand, but he kept his left arm about her waist, and his right hand held hers, as well as his silk hat.

Mr. Milburn made a short introduction, and the President stepped to the edge of the stand. Beside a flag-draped stanchion, he stood erect and solid, with his black satin neckcloth knotted around a high collar, and his open frock coat disclosing an amplitude of white piqué. He bowed and smiled in response to a tumultuous demonstration, but the raised sheaf of papers in his left hand indicated that he awaited silence. The lines of earnestness deepened in his face as, thrusting his right hand into his trousers pocket, he began to deliver his speech.

Two themes were interwoven in the President's forcible recommendation of a broad and enlightened policy of commercial reciprocity: the unity of the modern world and the "almost appalling" prosperity of the United States. Distance, he reminded his hearers, had been effaced by the telegraph and cable, by swift ships and fast trains. A larger share of the world's business was the urgent need of an enormous and diversified production that far exceeded the demands of home consumption. No narrow, sordid policy would subserve this vast and intricate business. "We must not repose in fancied security that we can forever sell everything and buy little or nothing." Reciprocity treaties were in harmony with the spirit of the times; measures of retaliation were not. In phrase after ringing, emphatic phrase, the President pointed to the trend of the future. "Isolation is no longer possible or desirable. . . . God and man have linked the nations together. . . . The period of exclusiveness is past."

As the pattern of the address emerged, the intermissions of applause increased in volume and enthusiasm. At the conclusion, an invocation of blessings on all neighbors of the United States and all the peoples and powers of the earth, a tempest of cheering swept the Esplanade. The crowd pushed wildly against the stand, shouting for McKinley and seeking to clasp his hand. The uproar was still deafening when the President returned to greet the diplomats, after escorting his wife to the carriage. He held an impromptu public reception at the front of the stand before he went on to a military review at the Stadium.

McKinley's progress through the fair was a prolonged ovation. He complimented the commissioners of the neighbor countries by a tour of their various buildings and exhibits. He attended a luncheon at the New York State Building, and a card reception at the Government Building. Hailed by excited crowds wherever he went, the President sought to dispel the undemocratic impression made by his heavy guard. He encouragingly noticed those who managed to break through the lines of soldiers and police, laughed at the antics of his more eccentric admirers, and honored the whooping popcorn boys with a special bow. Departing informally from his program, McKinley sat down to sip coffee at the Porto Rican Building, and posed for a photograph at the Agricultural Building with Secretary Wilson and a group of Latin American commissioners.

The President was weary when he went back to the Milburn house in the late afternoon, but he had greatly enjoyed his day. He found Mrs. McKinley in a sprightly mood—a surprising thing, in view of a nervous upset she had had on their arrival the evening before. Though Cortelyou had given explicit instructions about the presidential salute, the guns had been laid so close to the track that the concussion blew out the windows of one of the cars. But Mrs. McKinley had recovered from the shock. She had attended the luncheon given in her honor by the Board of Women Managers of the Exposition, and she was quite ready to enjoy the display of fireworks that had been arranged for the evening. After an early dinner, the McKinleys returned to the fairgrounds. They stopped on the Triumphal Causeway to watch a thrilling sight—the coming-on of the electrical illuminations. In the blue dusk, the first traceries were dimly pricked in dots of orange, which brightened to diamond points and then merged in dazzling lines. The shaft of the Tower soared in splendor, and, beyond the glittering domes of light, the Midway was a channel of flame. Descending into this brilliance, the carriages moved on to the Park Lake, where boats were waiting to carry the official party to the vantage point of the Life Saving Station. A water-nymph ballet glinted in the black waters. Pain's fireworks burst gaudily across the darkened sky, twenty-two battleships in pyrotechnic line, and Niagara Falls gushing liquid fire. A portrait of the President blazed on high, with the burning legend "Welcome to McKinley, Chief of Our Nation."

The gasps of wonder died away, the company re-embarked. Through the cheering populace, the presidential carriage rolled back along the Lincoln Parkway. The lights in the McKinleys' bedroom were quickly extinguished, and the Milburn residence stood in a silence broken only by the footfalls of the police detail, keeping their nightlong watch.

Early on the morning of Friday, September 6, the President again arrayed himself in the livery of his office: boiled, bestudded shirt, iron-starched collar and cuffs, black satin cravat, gleaming piqué vest, pin-striped trousers, and frock coat. He slipped over his head the fine chain on which his eyeglasses hung, and stowed in various pockets his small possessions, useful or sentimental. He had a gold watch and pencil; a wallet with bills and papers, and $1.20 in small change; three knives; a nugget and two other pocket pieces; and nine keys, two of them loose, six on a steel ring, and one on a heart-shaped ring. He took a pair of gloves; and, since cloudless skies presaged another day of heat, he added three handkerchiefs to the collection in his pockets.

This was to be, the President said, "the restful day" of his visit. A special train of parlor cars carried the members of his party, the diplomats, and other distinguished guests on an excursion to Niagara Falls. Transferring to four trolley cars at Lewiston, they viewed the scenic wonders of the gorge. At the town of Niagara Falls, they entered carriages for a tour of the environs. A halfway trip was made across the suspension bridge, to let the President glimpse the view from the Canadian side, without leaving American territory. Mrs. McKinley had taken the gorge in her stride, but she began to feel unwell in the broiling heat of the bridge, and the tour was interrupted while she was driven to the International Hotel. The President saw that she was made comfortable in the suite of rooms reserved for their use, and resumed his sightseeing. He left the carriage at Goat Island to toil up the steep ascent in his heavy coat and silk hat. He ate a hearty lunch in the hotel ballroom, and smoked a cigar on the veranda. He then escorted Mrs. McKinley to the train, where she rested until the President and the rest of the party returned from an inspection of the powerhouse.

As the train approached the Exposition station, the President called Charles Tharin and asked for a fresh collar. He wanted to "brush up a bit," he told his companions, in preparation for the reception at the Temple of Music, which was to take place at four o'clock. He would not be long detained, since the allotted time had been cut down to about ten minutes.

589

Mrs. McKinley had intended to accompany him, but it was decided that Dr. Rixey and Clara should take her straight to the Milburn house. The President saw her to the carriage, leaning over to say good-by and hand her her bottle of smelling salts. "Good afternoon, Mrs. McKinley," he said, "I hope you will enjoy your ride; good-by." He stood back to wave, and watched her drive away; waited until she turned to smile at him; waved again and raised his hat. Rejoining Mr. Milburn and Secretary Cortelyou, the President entered a victoria, and they started off through the fairgrounds. There was half an hour to spare before the reception, and McKinley stopped for refreshments at the Mission Building before he went on to fulfill his last engagement at Buffalo.

The managers of the Exposition had had no hesitation about holding the President's public reception in the Temple of Music. Major Louis L. Babcock, a Buffalo attorney and the grand marshal of the Exposition, considered it an ideal place for the event. The ornate confectionery edifice of faintly Byzantine inspiration was one of the magnificent sights of the fair; and, in its central situation near the Esplanade, it was easily accessible to the crowds. Its spacious, galleried auditorium, with a pipe organ on a dais at the east wall, had doorways on all four sides. The hall was furnished with rows of chairs, and the galleries could also accommodate a large number of spectators; while the slightly raised platform afforded an excellent position for the President. It had been decided to station him at the corner of the dais, and admit the greeters by one of the doorways on the east.

Babcock had spent a busy morning superintending the preparations. Chairs were removed to make a wide aisle running from the entrance past the dais, and then turning to the south doorways, which were to serve as exits. The chairs bordering this right-angled aisle were trimmed with blue bunting. A big frame was set behind the corner at which the President would stand, and hung with a large American flag. The primary purpose of this arrangement was to screen the President from the rear, but it also served the end of decoration. With the addition of potted palms and two bay trees, a pleasing background was created. Well content with his morning's work, Babcock went with another Buffalo attorney, James L. Quackenbush, to get a bite of lunch in one of the restaurants that bordered the Esplanade. His complacency was soon disturbed by a flippant remark. Over sandwiches and imported Pilsener beer, Quackenbush casually suggested that it would be Roosevelt's luck to have someone shoot the President that afternoon.

Three Secret Service men were on duty with the President: George Foster and two other agents on detail for the Buffalo visit. In addition, a special guard had been provided for the public reception by assigning a squad of Exposition police to the entrance door and posting several Buffalo detectives in the aisle. Yet it was common knowledge that the Chief Magistrate of the United States was exposed to physical danger by his traditional obligation of shaking hands with the public. The statement was frequently made that no precautions could avail against a reckless and determined assassin who was prepared to forfeit his own life. Quackenbush's smart remark rankled so uncomfortably in Babcock's mind that he determined to increase the guard when he got back from lunch. Ten enlisted artillerymen and a corporal had been ordered to report at the Temple of Music. Attired in full-dress uniform, they had been meant for decorative purposes, but Babcock put them in the aisle, between the Exposition police and the Buffalo detectives, with orders to close up on both sides, and prevent any suspicious-looking persons from approaching the President.

Since the artillerymen were unarmed and untrained in police work, their presence could serve only to narrow the aisle and obstruct the detectives' view of the oncoming line. Babcock, with the best of intentions, had violated a cardinal rule of police protection: that a large space must be kept clear in front of, and on either side of the President. The disadvantage was to be aggravated by the positions eventually taken by the Secret Service agents. The appropriate place for George Foster—the place from which he could scrutinize every hand that was outstretched—was on the left of the President, and just behind him. On this occasion, however, Mr. Milburn was to stand on McKinley's left, in order to introduce acquaintances in the line. Foster and an agent named Samuel R. Ireland were to stand opposite the President. The third Secret Service man would be at some distance to the right.

Conditions, as it developed, were far from ideal for a public reception. Nevertheless, a goodly number of police and detectives would have the opportunity of inspecting the people in line, as they moved from the entrance to the corner of the dais. Another cardinal rule for the President's protection was that the hands of those approaching him should be plainly visible, and that they should be empty. This rule, for some incomprehensible reason, was ignored at the Temple of Music. It was a hot day, and handkerchiefs were much in evidence. That was the only explanation ever given for the universal indifference to the appearance of a right hand that was bulkily swathed in a handkerchief.

By the middle of the afternoon, sightseers were swarming to the Temple of Music by thousands. Some pushed their way through the unguarded doorways to pack the already well-filled floor and galleries of the auditorium.

Others mingled with the crowd on the outside of the building, and many of them optimistically joined the long queue that had formed on the east. These latecomers could have no realistic expectation of shaking the President's hand. Only the earliest arrivals, who had been standing for hours under the blazing sun, could be sure of gaining admission before the reception was over.

Not far from the east entrance stood a short, slender young man whose big muscular hands and decent black suit stamped him as a skilled mechanic on holiday. His face was clean-shaven, with sensitive, almost feminine features. The vacuous expression of his large eyes was aggravated by a cast. His aspect was too negative to attract an interested glance, much less to provoke suspicion or alarm, but this mild-looking young workman was bound on a mission of violence. In his pocket he was carrying a short-barreled, .32-caliber Iver-Johnson revolver. Leon Czolgosz had come to the Temple of Music for the purpose of killing the President.

The record of Czolgosz's life is bleak and scanty. The fourth child of immigrants newly arrived from Poland, he was born in Detroit in 1873, and grew up in various Michigan towns where his father worked as a common laborer. His mother died, after bearing her eighth child, when Leon was twelve. The father subsequently remarried. For a time, he settled his family in a town near Pittsburgh, and then moved to Cleveland. He was never able to get ahead, but he had six sons, and a little money accumulated after they went to work. During the depression, their combined savings bought a small farm not far from Cleveland and a shabby store in the city itself.

In Leon's impoverished childhood, there must have been injuries which had dislocated an emotional adjustment too delicate for rough handling. The man who went to the Temple of Music was sane only within the meaning of the law. But, until three years earlier, Czolgosz had still been capable of outwardly normal behavior. Employed at a Cleveland wire mill, he had been an exceptionally good worker, who kept his job through the depression years. Though unsociable, he was not quarrelsome. He stayed by himself, reading many radical newspapers and magazines, and attending some Socialist meetings. In revolt against the injustice of the social order, Czolgosz was strongly attracted by the doctrines of anarchism. He came to hate the American system of government, and to believe that all rulers were the enemies of the working people. He learned that it was right to kill the enemies of the people.

Leon had a breakdown in 1898, left the wire mill, and went to live on the family farm. He avoided heavy work, but sometimes tinkered with wagons and machinery, or tramped off to shoot rabbits. Most of the time he lay around, sleeping or reading newspapers. His temper was cranky. He wanted to be let alone, and was always fighting with his stepmother. It is evident that his mental condition progressively deteriorated. In his last year at the farm, he became more and more withdrawn and irritable. He began to eat apart from his family, fixing his own food and carrying it up to his room. He seems to have spent an abnormal amount of time in sleep. His reading sometimes excited him intensely. He took a newspaper account of King Humbert's assassination to bed with him for weeks.

In the spring of 1901, Czolgosz developed a wild impatience to get away from the farm. He dunned his family for the money he had contributed toward its purchase, keeping up his demands until, in July, he obtained a partial payment, and cleared out. Meanwhile, he had made a number of trips to Cleveland. On one of them, he heard a lecture by the rabble-rousing anarchist leader Emma Goldman. At this time and later, he attempted to approach anarchist groups in Cleveland and Chicago, but his obviously superficial knowledge of their ideas and his vague revolutionary talk aroused suspicion. He was also unsuccessful in efforts to talk to Emma Goldman, whom he sought out in Chicago shortly after he left home.

Czolgosz next moved, for some unknown reason, to the vicinity of Buffalo. He spent several weeks in a boardinghouse at West Seneca, an outlying town which was connected with the city by a trolleyline. He gave up this lodging in late August, when he paid a flying visit to Cleveland. On August 31, the Saturday before Labor Day, he returned to Buffalo, and took a two-dollar-a-week room at John Nowak's saloon, a Raines Law hotel in the heart of the city. It was understood that he had come to see the Exposition. Every day, in his solitary, secretive way, Czolgosz went out, presumably to ride on trolley cars, eat at lunch counters, shoulder his neighbors at the exhibits. Hundreds of people must have seen him, but no one remembered doing so. The record of nearly a week is blank. It rests on his unsupported statement that he was in the Esplanade when the President made his speech, and that he aimlessly followed McKinley to Niagara Falls the next morning.

According to the account he later gave, Czolgosz did not plan the assassination until, some days after reaching Buffalo, he read a newspaper announcement of the President's public reception. But the magnet which pulled him back to Buffalo was certainly not a fair which he could have seen at any time in the six preceding weeks. McKinley's coming visit, heralded by great publicity, was known to everyone who followed the news. Perhaps Czolgosz had been drawn toward the hated ruler without a conscious plan. Perhaps the opportunity of the reception created the design.

The actual sight of the living, smiling man, the idol of the crowd, may have been the shock that finally transmuted his fantasies into action. "I didn't believe one man should have so much service," he stated afterward, "and another man should have none."

Czolgosz made his preparations with the utmost calm. He bought a short-barreled revolver, which was easily contained within his large hand. He decided to conceal the weapon by wrapping his hand in a handkerchief; and it is likely—though his statements were contradictory on the point— that he practiced folding the cloth and securing it at the wrist. Since he could not hold the revolver for a long period in his sweating palm, Czolgosz would have to perform this complicated adjustment in public, but he was certain of reaching his victim, and of shooting to kill. A number of anarchist attempts in Europe had recently failed because their perpetrators thought of their own safety. Czolgosz was free of the handicap of self-preservation. He would fire at close range, through the handkerchief, and offer no resistance to arrest. His crime would be his willing martyrdom to the workers' cause: an act of suicide, the ultimate destruction.

When Czolgosz went out on the morning of September 6, the revolver was in his right pocket under the handkerchief, a square of coarse white cotton with a wide machine-stitched hem. He had no intention, he said, of trying to shoot the President at Niagara Falls. His mind was riveted on the public reception, and he returned to the Exposition in good season to take his place near the head of the line. He was not going to draw the revolver and wrap up his hand until he was actually inside the Temple of Music. He would then be under the scrutiny of the police. Nevertheless, as he noted the flutter of handkerchiefs around him, Czolgosz decided on a bold elaboration of his plan. After he had covered his hand, he would raise it negligently now and then, exposing his bulging palm as he pretended to mop his face. He did not fear that the gesture would attract attention. People had never paid attention to Czolgosz. There was bleak self-revelation in the alias which he had often used, and which he would use again when the time came for the police to question him: Fred Nieman, Fred Nobody. But on this September afternoon, for the first time in his thwarted twenty-eight years, Czolgosz was going to be somebody.

The line stirred expectantly. A noise of cheers came from the other side of the Temple of Music, and through the stucco wall sounded the organ peal of the national anthem. Czolgosz waited, as cold as the steel in his pocket; without pity for his victim, or apprehension for himself.

At four o'clock, the President stepped from the victoria with a pleasant word for Major Babcock, who had sprung forward to open the door. In a blare of applause from floor and galleries, McKinley walked rapidly across the auditorium. Appraising the arrangements at a glance, he took his place at the corner of the dais. Mr. Milburn went to his left, and Cortelyou to his right. Foster and Ireland stood opposite him in the aisle. The President nodded to Babcock, and said with a smile, "Let them come." The east doorway was flung open, and the greeters began to enter the noisy confusion of the hall, admitted two abreast and then formed into single file as they advanced along the narrowing aisle. Their progress was too slow for the speed with which the President was accustomed to shake hands, and twice in the first few minutes Cortelyou sent word to Babcock to hurry them along. But, in spite of Babcock's instructions to expedite admissions at the door, the line still moved in jerks. The rhythm of the President's pendulum swing was broken; and, in his eagerness to greet as many people as possible, he was working to the left, reaching out for the next hand. The two Secret Service agents had only a fleeting glimpse of each newcomer, as he was drawn with suddenly accelerated pace past the dais.

Tense with anxiety to have the ordeal over, Cortelyou kept his eye on the time. Five or six minutes after the reception began, he sent word to Babcock that he would raise his hand as a signal for closing the doors. Babcock had gone to stand across from the President. He observed Cortelyou closely. Seeing the Secretary take out his watch, Babcock started to work his way toward the entrance, so that no time would be lost in transmitting the signal when it came.

At seven minutes past four, while a Bach sonata was purling under the din of the crowd, the President's reaching hand was struck aside, and a man lurched forward. Two shots cracked sharply. There was a moment of dead silence. In that suspended instant, the President and Fred Nobody faced each other, with a thin veil of smoke between them. The President's fixed stare might have expressed reproach or scorn, or simply astonishment. The assassin's eyes were empty. Only two smoking holes in his handkerchief told that he had been capable of action. He was knocked down, pinioned under a heap of assailants, and then dragged to the center of the hall. As McKinley was assisted to a chair, his eyes followed that other man. A blow landed on the vacant face. "Don't let them hurt him," the President said.

The scuffling had broken the stupefaction of the crowd. A mutter swelled to a roar of panic, pierced by hysterical screams. Stampedes toward the doorways were blocked by excited throngs shoving in from the outside. The chair where the President sat was like the eye of a cyclone. A few men stood about, fanning him with their hats. Cortelyou bent close, while the President fumbled at his breast and belly. There was blood on the hand he raised to Cortelyou's shoulder. "My wife," he whispered, "—be careful, Cortelyou, how you tell her—oh, be careful."

Police reinforcements shouldered through the dense press around the Temple of Music, Czolgosz was removed to an inner office, and the auditorium was cleared. A motor ambulance clanged up, discharging doctors bearing a litter. The crowd fell back as the President was carried out. At the sight of his ashen face, a great moan went up—a keen of horror and anguish that was the last greeting of the people to McKinley.

At eighteen minutes after four, the President was received at the emergency hospital of the Exposition. Though scarcely more than a first-aid station, it had an operating room, and the President was at once laid on the table. He was in severe shock, but conscious and entirely composed. As the attendants undressed him, a bullet fell from his underclothing. The shot fired at his breast had caused only an angry graze on the ribs; but the serious nature of the abdominal wound was immediately apparent to the doctors who gathered around the operating table. The medical director of the Exposition, Dr. Roswell Park, was at Niagara Falls. It was judged inadvisable to wait for his return, especially since the afternoon light was failing in the small room, and the electric lighting was inadequate. The arrival of another prominent Buffalo surgeon, Dr. Mathew D. Mann, settled the decision to operate at once. Dr. Mann and three assistant surgeons hastily made ready. The President's lips were forming the words of the Lord's Prayer when ether was administered.

On opening the abdomen, the surgeons found that the shot had passed straight through the stomach, lacerating the front and rear walls. The operation consisted mainly of suturing these tears, and cleansing the peritoneal cavity. The bullet was not found. No use was made of X ray, though one of the new machines was on exhibition at the fair; and an attempt to probe was abandoned because of the patient's dangerously weak condition. Dr. Rixey, who had arrived soon after the operation began, used a looking glass to reflect the rays of the setting sun on the surgeons' work, and succeeded, toward the end, in rigging up an electric light. The incision was finally closed, without drainage, and covered with an antiseptic dressing. It was agreed that the President should be immediately removed to the Milburn residence. Rixey hurried back to prepare Mrs. McKinley, who was still in ignorance of the attack.

Mrs. McKinley was told very little, but the news was shocking at best, and she took it with remarkable self-control. She was denied the only prayer she uttered, that her husband should be brought to her. After he was carried, unconscious and moaning, up the stairs, he was placed in a separate bedroom, with doctors and nurses in possession. They let Mrs. McKinley go in for a moment. Then the door was closed behind her. She had brought her diary to Buffalo, and on that lonely evening she took up her pen to note the major events of the day. "Went to visit Niagra Falls this morning," she wrote. "My Dearest was receiving in a public hall on our return, when he was shot by a . . . ."

Poor Mrs. McKinley was stunned and uncomprehending—she could not spell the queer word "anarchist" that everyone was using—but the knowledge that her Dearest was suffering pierced sharply through her confusion. She was feeling very badly, she confided to the diary he had given her.

The news of the attack on the President spread horror throughout the nation. The bare statement, sent over the AP wires only two or three minutes after Czolgosz fired, had reached the cities in time to make the last editions. Apprehension that McKinley had been killed outright brought silent throngs to the newspaper bulletin boards in the evening. Their worst fears were relieved by two releases, signed by Cortelyou: the bulletin prepared by the doctors after the operation, and later a statement that the President was rallying and resting comfortably.

The week end passed in keen suspense. The press uttered warnings of the danger of peritonitis, and recalled the long ordeal that Garfield had suffered. Yet, after the reprieve of Friday night, the temper of the public was hopeful. Faith was placed in the President's strong constitution, invigorated by a restful holiday; in the promptness with which he had received surgical attention; and in the antiseptic methods which, since Garfield's time, had made successful abdominal operations a routine matter. In their anxious concentration on the Milburn house, Americans were wonderfully conscious of a unity which had effaced their political differences. Its solidarity was matched by the other current of national feeling—the wave of vindictive anger that surged toward the Buffalo police headquarters. The newspapers of Saturday morning had reported that the President's assailant was an anarchist, who boasted that he had done his duty. The excited emotions of the country found vent in demanding reprisals against all anarchists everywhere. It was not for an instant credited that Czolgosz had acted alone. The deed had the menace and the insolence of conspiracy. A hunt for his accomplices was pressed in Cleveland, Chicago, Detroit, and other industrial centers. Hundreds of anarchist sympathizers were questioned, and some were arrested and detained. Second only to Czolgosz in popular odium was Emma Goldman, whom he had spoken of with admiration to the police. She was generally supposed to have instigated his crime, and there was high satisfaction when she was tracked down and arrested in Chicago.

Meanwhile, high officials of the government had assembled at the Milburn house. Secretary Wilson was the only member of the Cabinet who had gone to the Exposition with the President. Not one of his colleagues, on that week end of early September, was in Washington. The first weight of the emergency had fallen on Cortelyou's shoulders. A long-distance telephone connection with the White House was rushed through, and the Secretary dictated instructions which brought Vice-President Roosevelt—reached on an island in Lake Champlain—and the members of the Cabinet, except Hay and Long, to Buffalo on Saturday. Cortelyou also had to find and notify the relatives and privileged friends. Hanna and Dawes were among the first to arrive. They were followed by Herrick, Day, Fairbanks, Grosvenor, and others. The President's two sisters came from Cleveland. Abner McKinley and his wife sped back from a vacation in Colorado. Pina Barber, Mary McWilliams, and Sue Rand gathered around Mrs. McKinley.

The Milburn house had lost the character of a private residence. The second floor was a hospital, with its waiting room occupied by Mrs. McKinley and her circle. Downstairs, there was a continuous subdued reception, graced by dignitaries and consulting physicians. The stables accommodated an improvised executive office, outfitted with a telegraphic apparatus. The house next door took in the overflow of clerks and stenographers who had been summoned from Washington to handle the heavy mail. Ropes, manned by police, were stretched across Delaware Avenue to shut off the traffic. The sidewalk was patrolled by a detachment of regular infantry. On the opposite corner, a big election booth and several tents sheltered the members of the press on their twenty-four-hour watch.

By Tuesday, however, the agitation was noticeably subsiding. Monday's medical bulletins had broken the spell of anxiety. The President's temperature had gone down, and nourishment had been given by enema. Dr. Charles McBurney, an eminent New York City surgeon who had been called in consultation, added his signature to the medical bulletin which announced that the patient's condition was satisfactory. The bulletin on Tuesday morning confirmed the improvement, and stated that, if no complications arose, a rapid convalescence might be expected. An exodus from Buffalo was already under way. Secretary Gage and Attorney General Knox had gone to Washington, the one recalled to the Treasury by the financial uneasiness of the country, and the other bound to confer with the legal experts at his Department about the possibility of reaching

Czolgosz under federal law. Colonel Herrick took the Ohio relatives home on his private train. Vice-President Roosevelt, who conducted himself with great good taste and feeling, left for Oyster Bay. Hanna and Dawes were making ready to go, and so were Secretary Root and Postmaster General Smith.

On a day of anticlimax, the Secretary of State made his appearance at Buffalo. His mood was obdurately despondent. Major Babcock, who met him at the station with a good report from the sickroom, was flatly told that the President would not live. Hay had no sensible reason for this belief. The secretary of Lincoln, the close friend of Garfield, he was merely indulging a morbid fancy that he had the touch of death. If, before going on to Washington, he talked to others as he talked to Babcock, his superstitious fears would have made little impression. No one, on Tuesday, was disposed to listen to gloomy forebodings. The correspondents were flooding the press with happy auguries. Thanksgiving celebrations were being planned at Buffalo and Cleveland. Callers at the Milburn house came out with smiling faces. Dr. McBurney took a trip to Niagara Falls. Mrs. McKinley went for a drive. The President was getting better.

It is difficult to interpret the optimism with which the President's physicians looked for his recovery. There was obviously the most serious danger that his wounds would become septic. In that case, he would almost certainly die, since drugs to control infection did not exist. Yet the risks were persistently minimized by the doctors in charge. The whereabouts of the bullet was a question chiefly interesting to the press. The aid of X ray was declined, even after Thomas Edison, in response to a telegram from Cortelyou, sent a new machine with a trained operator to Buffalo. The most frequently expressed medical opinion was that the bullet had lodged in the muscles of the back, without inflicting further injury on the vital organs—a guess which, by dint of repetition, seemed to assume the accent of certainty. Dr. McBurney was by far the worst offender in showering sanguine assurances on the correspondents. As the only big-city surgeon on the case, he was eagerly questioned and quoted, and his rosy prognostications largely contributed to the delusion of the American public. But, while the local doctors showed more professional reserve, they did not conceal their confidence in private. Roosevelt, on the day after the shooting, was given to understand that the President was "coming along splendidly" and "on the highroad to recovery." When he left Buffalo, the Vice-President was so firmly convinced that the emergency was over that he went on to join his family at a camp in the Adirondacks, twelve miles from telegraph or telephone.

The hopeful view had naturally been confirmed by the President's rally from the shock of wounds and surgery. His temperature went down, though his pulse remained abnormally fast. His mind cleared, and he wanted to talk. In all his fifty-eight years, he had never been without people to talk to; but the doctors and nurses discouraged his sociable attempts to open a conversation, and Mrs. McKinley—to her own frantic unhappiness—was not allowed to stay with him. Cortelyou was the only other caller admitted to the sickroom. "It's mighty lonesome in here," the President told him, with a smile. Forbidden to see the newspapers, McKinley had two eager questions: "How did they like my speech?" and "How was it received abroad?" He beamed with satisfaction when Cortelyou reported the tremendous impression made by his advocacy of commercial reciprocity, and the enthusiastic approval expressed in both the American and foreign press.

The President's improvement was remarkable, but it did not indicate recovery. It was merely the resistance of his strong body to the gangrene that was creeping along the bullet's track through the stomach, the pancreas, and one kidney. The intensity of the struggle became marked on Thursday, the sixth day after the shooting. McKinley had been able to take a little liquid nourishment. As it had seemed to agree with him, he was given toast with coffee and chicken broth for breakfast on Thursday morning. His ensuing intense discomfort and racing pulse were ascribed to indigestion. He was dosed with purgatives and digitalis. After the evening consultation, most of the doctors dispersed, only to be recalled in the early hours of Friday by the patient's collapse. For a time, the end seemed at hand. Heart specialists were summoned. Telegrams were sent to bring back the departed officials, family, and friends, and urgent dispatches went to the Vice-President, whose recent host, Mr. Ansley Wilcox, was fortunately supplied with his address. Yet the doctors continued to hope that McKinley had a chance, if he could survive the "complication" of a weakened heart. It was six o'clock on Friday evening when they admitted that hope was abandoned, and the telegraph instruments in the press tents clicked out the message that the President was dying.

In the late afternoon, the President came out of the stupor in which he had lain for hours. "It is useless, gentlemen," he said to the doctors, "I think we ought to have prayer." As the twilight deepened, he asked for his wife, and Cortelyou led her in. Her anguished wish was granted at last. There was no longer any need for McKinley to rest. She leaned over the bed, holding his hands, kissing his lips. A little group of family and friends stood in the shadows of the darkening room. The President said in a feeble voice, "Good-bye—good-bye, all." In a moment, he went on, "It is God's way. His will, not ours, be done." He put his arm around Ida, and smiled at her. His lips moved, and he began to whisper, ever more faintly, the words of a favorite hymn. "Nearer, my God to Thee, Nearer to Thee."

Those were the last words she heard him say, but his arm still lay around her, his hand held hers, he smiled at the face she bent close to the pillow. So Dawes found them when he came from the railway station at nearly nine o'clock. He stood hand in hand with Abner beside the bed. Looking at Dawes in his kindly way, the President did not at first seem like a dying man. His senses slowly dimmed. He muttered, and moved his head restlessly. Mrs. McKinley was led away, and Dr. Rixey took her place. The President held Rixey's hand instead, reaching out for him like a child in the dark, Dawes thought. High officials of the government were again gathered downstairs. Now and then, there was a soft stir at the doorway, as one of them took a long glance at the deathbed. Secretary Long reached the house in time to bid a last farewell. The New York heart specialist, Dr. Edward Janeway, arrived just before midnight. He could only pronounce the verdict that the end was very near. For more than two hours, McKinley's heart faltered on, and the harsh rattle of his breathing filled the room. At last, the noise ceased. There was one more labored gasp. Dr. Rixey adjusted his stethoscope, and raised his head to say, "The President is dead."

Before the black-columned newspapers thudded against the doorways, the people had heard the bells tolling heavily in the night. Saturday, September 14, was a day of grief and fear. There was a panic on Wall Street. Men of business, great and small, wore troubled faces. A cold wind of change seemed to blow with McKinley's passing. Americans anxiously queried whether plenty and prosperity were destined to endure, while they waited for some word from the new President, the unknown quantity, the X in the equation of the American future.

For more than twelve suspenseful hours, the nation had no President. Theodore Roosevelt was speeding on Saturday morning across the breadth of New York State. He had not learned of McKinley's relapse until late the day before. High on Mount Marcy, a guide had met him with a batch of telegrams that brought him scrambling down the rest of the slope, and then clattering all night, with three relays of horses, over the mountain roads. At dawn, in a little railway station, Roosevelt had learned that McKinley was dead. A special train had been sent to carry the Vice-President to Buffalo. Closing himself in a compartment, he refused to see the reporters who mobbed his car at Albany, Amsterdam, Utica, Rome, Syracuse. He avoided demonstrations on his arrival at Buffalo, and peremptorily dismissed the mounted escort that tried to accompany his carriage on the short drive from the Wilcox house to the house of mourning. After paying his respects to the dead President and his family, Roosevelt quietly returned to await his induction into office in Ansley Wilcox's library. Root, as the senior Cabinet officer present, took charge of the arrangements. The judge whom he brought to administer the oath was, ironically enough, that John R. Hazel for whose appointment McKinley had been so sharply censured. A small company gradually assembled: the Cabinet members, except Hay and Gage, who had remained in Washington; a few other officials and invited guests; and finally, at Roosevelt's request, the representatives of the press. The solemnity of the dim room, in a summer desolation of dust covers, was enhanced by the evident emotion of the two principals, who stood conversing in whispers. Root stepped forward to pay an affectionate tribute to the late President in a voice choked with tears. Then, in the name of the Cabinet, he asked Roosevelt to take the oath of office without delay. Roosevelt, his youthful features stern and stiff, responded in terms suggested by Root as needful to allay the national disquietude:

"I will show the people at once that the administration of the government will not falter in spite of the terrible blow. . . . I wish to say that it shall be my aim to continue, absolutely unbroken, the policy of President McKinley for the peace, the prosperity, and the honor of our beloved country."

There were five more days of mourning, of crepe-shrouded buildings and tolling bells and newspapers barred in black, while McKinley's bier traveled from the services at Buffalo to the rites at Washington and then to the resting place at Canton. The circuitous journey was a cruel ordeal for the woman who huddled in a compartment of the funeral train, praying that the Lord would take her with her Dearest Love; but pity for Mrs. McKinley had been overborne by the grief of the nation. Never in history had the Union of the States been joined in such universal sorrow. North and South, East and West, the people mourned a father and a friend, and the fervent strains of "Nearer, My God, to Thee" floated, like a prayer and a leavetaking, above the half-masted flags in every city and town. When at last McKinley's casket was carried from the white frame house in Canton, five minutes of silence ruled the land, all traffic and business suspended, while the people bowed in homage to the President who was gone.

The new President was in office. The republic still lived. Yet, for a space, Americans turned from the challenge and the strangeness of the future. Entranced and regretful, they remembered McKinley's firm, unquestioning faith; his kindly, frock-coated dignity; his accessibility and dedication to the people: the federal simplicity that would not be seen again in Washington. The eulogies reverberated, as orators and journalists and poets extolled the virtue of an upright life, a death of Christian fortitude. Uncelebrated among the tributes was the farewell of Chiefs Geronimo, Blue Horse, Flat Iron, and Red Shirt, and the seven hundred braves of the Indian Congress at the Pan-American Exposition. They had thought of President McKinley as their good friend. Many of them had gone to see him lying in state at the Buffalo City Hall. Like visitants from an earlier day, the men with painted faces had filed past the flower-banked casket, sharing the nation's grief; and, among the gathered cards, was the big crudely lettered square of pasteboard that had come with their wreath of purplish evergreen leaves.

"The rainbow of Hope is out of the sky. Heavy clouds hang about us.

"Tears wet the ground of the tepees. The palefaces too are in sorrow. The Great Chief of the Nation is dead. Farewell! Farewell! Farewell!"

Epilogue

Cortelyou had the personal belongings packed and shipped to Canton: the closetsful of costly dresses, all the presents and souvenirs and photographs, the oil painting of little Katie, the two small rocking chairs. Delivery wagons rattled up to the Executive Mansion with loads of rugs and furniture, with crates of toys and cases of books, with saddles, stilts, and bicycles. Dogs arrived, and guinea pigs. Hunters and hacks pranced in the driveway. Shrieking children rode ponies on the lawn. A large blue macaw came to live in the conservatory where Mrs. McKinley had lingered, holding a single rose.

The big shabby house began to look cozy. Every bedroom was in use. Even the attic was opened. Colonel Bingham was busy with the arrangements for Alice's coming-out ball. A telephone switchboard was going to be needed to take care of the calls from one of her beaux—or so the clerks in the east wing whispered, laughing behind their hands. Fresh supplies of stationery were informally headed "The White House," instead of "Executive Mansion." Almost any late afternoon, the President might be surprised in an unconventional posture, lounging in boots and spurs after a hard ride, or in brogans muddied by a scramble up Rock Creek; often flinging a well-aimed pillow, or playing bear with the little boys. Old men came to the mansion on errands of state and politics, but their primacy was disputed by the young men crowding forward. The nation felt another leadership, nervous, aggressive, and strong. Under command of a bold young captain, America set sail on the stormy voyage of the twentieth century.

ACKNOWLEDGMENTS

A NUMBER of people have aided me in gathering the information for this book. Mr. George B. Cortelyou, Jr., generously took the time to speak of his childhood impressions of President McKinley and the White House, and permitted me to examine his father's diary for the years 1898–1901, with accompanying memoranda and appointment books. The diary, originally written in shorthand, contains transcriptions made by the elder Mr. Cortelyou or by his secretary. It was sporadically kept under the pressure of heavy duties, but it is nearly always enlightening, and it is invaluable to the study of a President so formally presented to the public as was McKinley

I have been under deep obligation to the late Honorable Charles G. Dawes, who welcomed me to his Chicago office and his house at Evanston, and talked freely and illuminatingly of the McKinley years. He let me read the manuscript of his journal—at that time unpublished—and showed me letters and mementos in his possession. I also had the pleasure of meeting the late Mrs. Dawes, who had been an affectionate friend of Mrs. McKinley.

The reception of Canton was wonderfully hospitable. Mr. Clayton G. Horn, executive editor of Brush-Moore Newspapers, Inc., had old bound volumes of The Evening Repository and The Sunday Repository brought from storage for my perusal. The publisher of Brush-Moore Newspapers, Mr. John D. Raridan, furnished me with many photographs, several of which are reproduced in this book. Especial thanks are due to that lively reporter Mrs. George F. Putnam (Gretchen Groetzinger), who was one of Mrs. McKinley's "little friends" in her last years, and who is well informed about both the McKinley and Saxton families. Through Mrs. Putnam I met a number of older Canton residents—now no longer living—all of whom had interesting reminiscences: Mrs. E. E. Esselburne (Mary Harter), Mrs. Henry Belden (Kate Barber), Mr. Harry Frease, and Mr. William T. Kuhns. Mrs. Belden lent me the diary kept by her mother Pina Saxton (Mrs. Marshall Barber) during the European tour of 1869, and the two letters from McKinley to his wife which are reproduced on pages 18 and 29. It was also through Mrs. Putnam that I met the late Miss Lucy Alexander, and obtained access to the 1869 diary and letters of her aunt Miss Jeannette Alexander. Another acquaintance made in Canton was that of Mr. Edward T. Heald, now of The Stark County Historical Society, and the author of two published monographs cited in the "Notes and References" that follow. He should also be credited with the "Heald MS.," a selection from the letters of Charles Bawsel and an essay, "A Day in a Governor's Life," based on that correspondence. I obtained a copy of this material through the kindness of Miss Helen L. Bawsel of Washington, D.C.

High on the list of my indebtedness are Mrs. James F. McKinley and Mrs. Helen McKinley Heidt Magee of Washington, D.C., Mrs. Clemens E. Gunn of Cleveland Heights, Ohio, and the late Mrs. Ralph Hartzell of Denver, Colorado. Mrs. Hartzell (Mary Barber), nearing seventy when I saw her, still vividly recalled the pretty, frank, and spirited girl who had been the belle of the White House in the McKinley administration. A totally unexpected find was the diary which the President's wife kept in 1901, now the property of Mrs. Gunn, the daughter of Ida Barber Day. I take this opportunity of thanking Mrs. Gunn for permitting me to borrow and photograph the little book, and also of thanking my niece, Mrs. William C. Weir of Cleveland Heights, through whose alertness in my interest the connection was made. Mrs. James F. McKinley, the widow of the President's nephew and ward "Jim," and Mrs. Magee, the daughter of the President's niece and ward Grace, received me with charming cordiality and showed me a quantity of family letters and photographs.

Particular acknowledgment is due to Mr. Opha Moore, who made a day spent at Columbus enjoyable and rewarding; to the late Mr. Clarence E. Ingling, who went to the White House as a young telegraph clerk in 1898 and remained on the staff until 1949; to Mrs. Charles S. Hamlin, who told me about the Tharins, and sent me her notes of a social call at the White House in 1899; to the late Mr. James R. Garfield and his lovely sister, the late Mrs. Joseph Stanley-Brown; and to Mr. Everett Willson, who filled in the Hartford background of Secretary J. Addison Porter. Other segments of information were supplied by Miss Irene Poirier, the late Mrs. Eliot Cross, the late Miss Annie Hegeman, and the late Mr. Auguste Chollet; and by Mr. Luther Day, Mr. Leland S. Briggs, Mr. Donald S. McWilliams, and Mr. William P. Kelly. I am indebted to Miss Mary A. Deibel for allowing me to refer to her thesis, "William McKinley as Governor of Ohio"; and to Professor Phillip A. Shriver for directing me to an interesting chapter in his doctoral dissertation, "The Making of a Moderate Progressive, Atlee Pomerene." I have to thank Mr. Lawrence K. Miller for making available to me the files of *The Berkshire Eagle* for 1896–98; Mr. Frederick H. Meserve for assistance in procuring photographs; and Mr. Joseph Halle Schaffner for entrusting me with his copy of *Letters of John Hay and Extracts from Diary.* Mrs. Ann C. Whitman, personal secretary to President Eisenhower, very courteously supplied we with information about the painting of the signing of the Peace Protocol with Spain.

Professor Allan Nevins, with his habitual generosity, read the manuscript of this book, and I am under the greatest obligation to him for his comment and criticism. I have to thank Mrs. Joseph Brewer of Queens College, who came to my rescue on several questions of research, and Mrs. Halsey Munson of Harper & Brothers, who has shown an enthusiasm beyond the call of duty in coping with editorial and other problems.

Mr. Watt P. Marchman of The Rutherford B. Hayes Memorial Library was good enough to furnish me with copies of letters exchanged by Hayes and McKinley and with other information in his possession. This library, at Fremont, Ohio, has recently acquired seven volumes of diaries, kept for President McKinley by the White House telegrapher. They should be valuable to future students of the period.

Among the many librarians who have been helpful are: Dr. C. Percy Powell, Dr. Elizabeth G. McPherson, and Mr. John de Porry of the Manuscript Division, and Mr. Hirst D. Milhollen and Miss Virginia Daiker of the Division of Prints and Photographs of the Library of Congress; Miss Shirley Dekin, Mr. F. Ivor D. Avellino, and Mr. S. J. Riccardi of the New York Public Library, and Mr. Sylvester L. Vigilante, formerly of that library; Miss Sylvia Hilton and Miss Helen Ruskell of The New York Society Library, and Mrs. Frederick Gore King, recently retired.

Among those who have assisted me in research are Mr. Edward Pessen, Mrs. Stanley Cogan, Mr. James F. McRee, Jr., Mrs. Thomas S. Shaw, and Mr. Ralph K. Spencer, the courthouse reporter of *The Canton Repository.* For an arduous task of typing, with checking of sources, I have to thank Miss Y. B. Garden and Miss Eleanor Wallis.

Margaret Leech
New York
August 31, 1959

SOURCES

Besides the unpublished material in the mentioned acknowledgments, I have consulted a number of manuscript collections. First in importance are the McKinley Papers in the Library of Congress, comprising 86 bound volumes, 84 letterbooks and other books, and 101 manuscript boxes. This collection naturally includes much that is of minor interest. Its striking feature is its impersonal character, a formality and discretion that are typical of McKinley. There is little information bearing on his policies as President, still less that reveals the inner thoughts and motives of the man; yet these papers remain the chief clue to an understanding of McKinley and his administration, and an examination of their contents is not infrequently rewarding.

The Theodore A. Bingham Collection at the Library of Congress has been utilized for descriptions of the official entertainments at the White House. I have also made a limited use of several large collections in the same library: the William E. Chandler Papers, vols. 115-16; the Theodore Roosevelt Papers, 1897–1901, Personal; the Elihu Root Papers, 1894–1904, Personal; the John Sherman Papers, Accessions 2019 and 2199. One reference is made to the Benjamin F. Tracy Papers, Box 14.

At the National Archives in Washington, I examined vols. 125-29 of the *Consular Letters*, Department of State, 1896–97. The Myron T. Herrick Papers, deposited at the Library of the Western Reserve Historical Society at Cleveland, contain a number of McKinley's letters, particularly interesting because of their intimate tone. This pleasant library possesses a few additional McKinley items.

Among the publications of the United States government consulted in my research were: *Annual Reports of the War Department*, 1898–1900; *Annual Reports of the Navy Department*, 1898; *Annual Reports of the Post Office Department*, 1900; *Papers Relating to the Foreign Relations of the United States*, 1898–1900 (noted as *For Rels*); *Correspondence Relating to the War with Spain*, 2 vols. (noted as *Corres Rel*); *Spanish Diplomatic Correspondence and Documents*, 1896–1900 (noted as *Sp Corres*). Senate and House reports and documents are usually identified in the references, but four of the latter have been designated by short descriptive titles:

Sen Doc 62, 55/3 (two parts, 1899), *Treaty of Peace and Accompanying Papers*. Cited as *Treaty Papers*.

Sen Doc 221, 56/1 (8 vols, 1900), *Report of the Commission Appointed by the President to Investigate the Conduct of the War Department in the War with Spain*. Cited as *Dodge Comm.*

Sen Doc 270, 56/1 (3 vols, 1900), *Food furnished by the Subsistence Department to the Troops in the Field*. Cited as *Beef Court.*

House Doc 485, 57/1 (2 vols, 1902), *Record of the Proceedings of a Court of Inquiry in the Case of Rear-Admiral Winfield S. Schley, U.S. Navy*. Cited as *Schley Court.*

In a desire to avoid a useless multiplication of references, I have omitted allusion to conventional or obvious sources, and to a large number of newspapers and magazines. The *New York Tribune* has been often cited, partly because the files were more readily available to me than those of any daily newspaper except *The Evening Post* of New York, but also because of its flair for "Republican news" and its usually well-informed Washington correspondence.

In addition to the books mentioned in the references, I have been particularly interested in the following:

Theodore E. Burton, *John Sherman* (Boston and New York, 1906); Andrew Carnegie, *Autobiography* (Boston and New York, 1920); W. Cameron Forbes, *The Philippine Islands* (2 vols., Boston and New York, 1928); John W. Foster, *American Diplomacy in the Orient* (Boston and New York, 1903); F. D. Millet, *The Expedition to the Philippines* (New York and London, 1899); Walter Millis, *The Martial Spirit* (Boston and New York, 1931); R. B. Mowat, *The Life of Lord Pauncefote* (London, 1929); Allan Nevins, *The Emergence of Modern America, 1865–1878* in *A History of American Life* (New York, 1927), VIII; Capt. W. D. Puleston, USN, *Mahan: The Life and Work of Captain Alfred Thayer Mahan, USN* (New Haven, 1939); Ida M. Tarbell, *The Nationalizing of Business, 1878–1898* (New York, 1936); Frank W. Taussig, *Free Trade, Tariff and Reciprocity* (New York, 1920); Edwin Wildman, *Aguinaldo* (Boston, 1901); William F. Willoughby, *Territories and Dependencies of the United States* (New York, 1905).

The following abbreviations have been used: *McK* for *McKinley; McK P* for *McKinley Papers; GBC* for *George B. Cortelyou*, also *Cortelyou diary; JAP* for *J. Addison Porter; TR* for *Theodore Roosevelt; Repos* for *The Evening Repository* or *The Sunday Repository* of Canton, Ohio.

NOTES AND REFERENCES

CHAPTER 1

THE MAJOR AND HIS WIFE

The Life of William McKinley by Charles S. Olcott (2 vols, Boston and New York, 1916) has been largely used for this chapter. For McKinley's ancestry, childhood, Civil War record, law studies, and early life in Canton, use has also been made of the *Life of William McKinley* by Robert P. Porter and James Boyle (Cleveland, 1897). Except for the inclusion of ten not very informative chapters by Boyle, this book differs very little from Porter's campaign biography of the same name (Cleveland, 1896). Although a prolix and tiresome writer, Porter interviewed many people who had known McKinley in childhood and youth, and the 1897 edition reproduces a letter from McKinley, commending its historical accuracy. (See also McK to R. P. Porter 2/28/96, McK P, Letbk 87.) Two special issues of *The Canton Repository*, March 31, 1940 and January 24, 1943, were devoted to items about the McKinley and Saxton families and the Canton background. Impressions of the sentiment and gossip of the community were derived from the lively memories of Mrs. Putnam, and the late Mrs. Esselburne, Mr. Frease, and Mr. Kuhns.

pages

1–4   RETURN TO CANTON: *Repos* 1/16,17,19/96. *The house:* McK to H. W. Harter 7/24,28/95, 8/25/95, to E. Harter 9/9/95, to M. G. McWilliams 12/21/95, McK P, Letbk 87; J. N. Taylor to McK 1/18/96, McK P, vol 1; McK to C. P. Herrick 12/5,12/95, H. O. S. Heistand to C. P. Herrick 1/15/96, Herrick Papers; Phila *Press* 6/11/96. *McKinley's sentiment:* GBC 7/5/99; Lawrence S. Mayo, editor, *America of Yesterday, As Reflected in the Journal of John Davis Long* (Boston, 1932), 216. *Grand Army Band:* William T. Kuhns, *Memories of Old Canton* (privately printed, Canton, 1937), 57; see letterhead, McK P, Box 214. *A country town:* E. T. Heald, "Young McKinley's Canton," in *The Stark County Story*, I (Canton, 1949).

4–5   PARENTS AND EARLY LIFE: *Bridal tour:* Statement by Wm McK Sr, *Repos* 1/7/92. *William's childhood:* "The Mother's Story," by Julius Chambers in NY *Journal*, nd, quoted in Charles H. Grosvenor, *William McKinley* (Washington, 1901), 175-76. *Barefoot:* Julia B. Foraker, *I Would Live It Again* (New York and London, 1932), 264-65. *Father's bankruptcy:* John Johnson to McK 9/5/00, McK P, Box 214. *Poland:*

With the industrial development of Youngstown, Poland changed from a village to a residential suburb.

6–9   THE SOLDIER: quoted remarks of William McK Osborne, *Ohio Archaeological and Historical Society Quarterly*, July/01.

McKinley and Osborne were mustered in on June 11, 1861, at Camp Jackson, Ohio. Osborne was discharged on certificate of disability November 4, 1861.

In camp: McK to W. K. Miller 8/11/61, quoted in Olcott, I, 29-32. *Indifference to danger:* Samuel L. Powers, *Portraits of a Half Century* (Boston,

1925), 163-64. *Sought promotion:* J. T. Webb to R. B. Hayes (recd) 10/5/62, *Diary and Letters of Rutherford Birchard Hayes*, edited by Charles R. Williams (5 vols, Columbus, 1922-26), II, 361-62. *Praised by Hayes:* Hayes to Lucy W. Hayes 12/14/62, to Birchard Hayes 11/4/64, ibid, 374, 534; speech by Hayes 7/30/91, quoted in Porter and Boyle, 61-63. See statement by Russell Hastings, ibid, 90-97. *Correct young officer:* McK to James McK 4/13/99, McK P, Letbk 90. *Statement of military service:* McK P, vol 7; see *NY Trib* 9/14/01. *Masonry:* McK P, vols 25, 45; Harry L. Haywood, *Famous Masons and Masonic Presidents* (Chicago, 1944).

In 1899, McKinley interrupted a train journey through the Shenandoah Valley to call at the lodge at Winchester and visit the graves of the Confederate dead (*NY Trib* 5/20/99).

Anxious parents:

William's father wrote him a letter filled with affectionate solicitude on June 8, 1864. (Original in possession of Mrs. Magee.) At this time young Abner was serving for 100 days in the militia.

9-14   THE LAWYER: Statement by W. R. Day, McK P, Box 259; Heald, "Young McKinley's Canton"; Repos 3/31/40, 1/24/43.

A clipping in Mr. Luther Day's scrapbook told of finding McKinley's letters of introduction among the effects of the late Mrs. Sarah Belden Frease (*Repos* 1/28/40).

Hayes's advice: Hayes to McK 11/6/66, *Diary and Letters*, V, 149. The original letter is in the possession of Mrs. Magee. *Meticulous transactions:*

McKinley's letterbooks repeatedly illustrate punctilious attention to business matters, often of small importance. In 1899, he smilingly dismissed the prospect of finding oil on his farm at Minerva, Ohio, saying, "I have been so near wealth so many times, Cortelyou, that I don't get excited over these things nowadays." Nevertheless, Cortelyou thought that McKinley was more than usually interested, and recalled his having spoken of expecting a large fortune from oil found on this property. A previous report had, in fact, prompted McKinley to make inquiry of his farmer, but he had received a discouraging reply (GBC 6/12/99; W. F. Faas to McK 2/18/99, W. J. Adams to McK 3/6/99, McK P, vols 25, 26).

Defense of striking coal-miners: Herbert Croly, *Marcus Alonzo Hanna* (New York, 1912), 92-94; Thomas Beer, *Hanna* (New York, 1929), 78-80; *Repos* 9/24/93. *Political activities:* Heald, "Young McKinley's Canton." *Knox's testimony:* GBC 7/3/01. *Three cigars:* Information from the late Charles G. Dawes, a non-smoker who succumbed to temptation soon after entering politics.

10-12   PERSONAL DATA: *Decorum:* Statement by G. F. Arrel, quoted in Olcott, I, 57-58; McK to James McK 11/1/98, McK P, Letbk 90. *Had not tasted ice cream:* Information from Mrs. Hamlin, to whom McKinley related the incident in 1899. See p. 458. *Minstrel show:* Kuhns, 55. *Sigma Alpha Epsilon:* NY *Journal* 3/4/97. *Wore badge and rosette:* Sketch by Jessie M. Baker, McK P, Box 259. YMCA: Heald, "Young McKinley's Canton." *Favorite hymns:* Rev. Dr. Frank M. Bristol, "William McKinley," *The Sunday School Times* 10/12/01; Charles G. Dawes, *A Journal of the McKinley Years* (Chicago, 1950), 282; Marcus A. Hanna, "William McKinley as I Knew Him," *The National Magazine*, Jan/02.

14–16 IDA SAXTON:
The youthful group photograph was in an unidentified clipping in Mr. Luther Day's scrapbook. Mary Goodman, later married to Lafayette McWilliams of Chicago, remained Ida's intimate friend throughout her life.

Brooke Hall: Wash *Eve Star* 1/22/98. *"the beloved Miss Eastman":* Mrs. McK to Harriet F. Gault 4/15/97, McK P, Box 225.

Mrs. McKinley had offered to help Miss Gault obtain the position of postmistress at Media (H. F. Gault to Mrs. McK 4/5/97, above cited). A letter in McKinley's files mentions that he and his wife often visited Miss Maria L. Eastman during the congressional years (E. A. Angier to Fred C. Bryan 9/12/99, McK P, vol 3).

European tour: Pina Saxton's diary, 1869; Miss Jeannette Alexander's diary and letters, 1869. *Marshall Barber:* Kuhns, 55. *Ida in love:* Edwin A. Lee, "William McKinley's Wedding," *National Magazine,* cited. *Chilly toward a rival:* Information from Mrs. Esselburne.

According to "A McKinley Romance," a narrative poem by Alice Danner Jones (Akron, 1901), Ida first became attracted to McKinley at a lecture at which he introduced the speaker, Horace Greeley. The story of McKinley's proposing while on a drive is told by Olcott (I, 68-69). Mr. Heald heard that it occurred during one of the meetings between the Sunday schools.

16–20 MARRIAGE: *The wedding:* Edwin A. Lee, cited; Miss Alexander's diary 1/25/71. *Illness:* Information from Mrs. Esselburne. *Reason for cropping hair:* Information from Mrs. Belden. *Katie left to Pina:* Information from Mrs. Hartzell. *"God'll punish Mamma":* Beer, 102. *McKinley stared, was forgetful:* Ibid., 108-9. *Often sat in the dark:* Information from Mr. Dawes. *Pressed temples:* H. H. Kohlsaat, *From McKinley to Harding* (New York and London, 1923), 155.

McKinley's anxiety when parted from his wife is illustrated by his letter to her of March 17, 1880, reproduced on page 18 (photographed through the courtesy of Mrs. Belden).

20–22 THE WASHINGTON YEARS: *Friendship with Hayes family:* Hayes-McKinley correspondence, 1869-1896, Rutherford B. Hayes Memorial Library; Hayes, *Diary and Letters,* II, 524-25. *"quite thrilling":* Mrs. Fanny Hayes to Mr. Watt Marchman 1/16/47, copy by courtesy of Mr. Marchman. *Friendship with Garfield:* Information from Mr. James R. Garfield. *Hard worker:* A. B. Atkins, "McKinley's Washington Life," *Bklyn Eagle* 5/3/96. *After-supper cigar:* O. O. Stealey, *Twenty Years in the Press Gallery* (New York, 1906), 31. *Leisure spent with wife:* Porter and Boyle, 153; "McKinley in Washington," *NY Trib* 6/21/96. *The Wattersons:* H. Watterson to A. K. McClure 1/24/97, McK P, vol 5. *Dreary times at Canton:* Kuhns, 56; Beer, 103. *"I knew you would come":* Olcott, II, 362.

McKinley was granted indefinite leave of absence from the House in August, 1888, on account of the serious illness of his wife (*Congr Rec,* vol 19, 8074). Letters in the possession of Mrs. Magee indicate that Mrs. McKinley's recovery was slow, and that her dependence on her husband limited his participation in the autumn campaign.

21–22 FINANCES: Olcott, I, 244. *Borrowed money:* See p 58. *Refused position with railroad:* GBC 12/23/00. *Mrs. McKinley's inheritance:*

Her fortune was appraised at $70,000 in 1893, but much of it was tied up in questionable mining stock (*NY Trib* 7/24/01). James Saxton had taken a second wife, Mrs. Hester B. Medill, in 1882 (*Repos* 3/31/40).

23–26   PERSONALITY OF A POLITICIAN: *Non-committal*: Information from Mr. Garfield. *Chewed Garcías*: Information from Mr. Opha Moore. *Liked a joke*: Hanna, cited. *Disgusted by vulgarity*: Mr. Moore. *Practiced orator*: Joseph B. Foraker, *Notes of a Busy Life* (2 vols, Cincinnati, 1916), I, 119; GBC 2/16/99. *"Song of the Mystic"*: quoted in Olcott, II, 369-71. *"Recompense"*: McK to Herrick 11/29/92, Herrick Papers; *Repos* 11/27/92. *Critical of modern education*: McK to D. E. Hawkins 3/21/96, McK P, Letbk 87; *Speeches and Addresses of William McKinley* (New York, 1893), 303; Porter and Boyle, 474. *Read two books*: McK to Herrick 12/31/94, Herrick Papers. *Method of shaving*: Information from Mr. Moore; see also speech by Governor A. L. Harris quoted in Thomas A. Knight, *Tippecanoe* (A History of the Tippecanoe Club, Cleveland, 1940), 111. *"matinée idol's virility"*: William Allen White, *Autobiography* (New York, 1905), 335. *"a mediaeval knight"*: Maria L. Storer, *In Memoriam Bellamy Storer* (privately printed, Boston, 1923), 17. *Not impeccably neat*: Information from Mr. Garfield.

Mrs. Putnam also heard this from her father, but William Allen White said that McKinley was neatly dressed on his campaign trip in 1894 (*Autobiography*, 251).

24–28   THE GOVERNORSHIP: Information from Mr. Moore; Heald MS, "A Day in a Governor's Life." *Appointment given Bawsel*: Ibid. *Heistands*: Wash *Eve Star* 3/8/97. *Neal House*: *Repos* 11/11/95. *Rejected offers*: Olcott, I, 244-45.

In spite of his comfortable income, McKinley's financial straits obliged him to raise $18,000 on his Canton property in 1894 (McK to A. H. Welch, 8/15/94, McK P, Letbk 87).

Ida's middle age: J. N. Bishop to McK 9/22/96, McK P, vol 3; Chi *Record* 3/3/97, quoting Dr. T. H. Phillips; Albert Fisher, Osteopathist, to McK 9/16/98, McK P, vol 18. *Week-end visits*: Hanna, above cited. *Crocheting*: Information from Mrs. Esselburne. *Neckties*: Information from Mr. Dawes and Mr. Moore. *Jewelry cleaning*: Mr. Moore.

28–31   INTIMACY AND TENDERNESS: Olcott, II, 361-62, 364; information from Mrs. Hartzell, Mr. Dawes, Mr. Kuhns; Storer, 19. *"always your lover"*: McK to I. McK 12/11/96. See p 29. *Fancy-work*: McK to C. P. Herrick 3/10/93, Herrick Papers. *Mrs. McKinley's Loyalty*: Information from Mr. Kuhns. *Loved children*:

McKinley's way with children was emphasized by Mrs. Hartzell, Mrs. Belden, and Mr. George B. Cortelyou, Jr. Kohlsaat (pp 155-56) wrote that Mrs. McKinley wept over a sleeping infant. Mr. Moore told the story of her emptying her jewels on the carpet for his baby.

31–33   HOMECOMING: *"pleasure of a schoolboy"*: *Repos* 11/17/95. *James and Grace*:

McKinley's wards went to live with their grandparents in 1888 after their mother's death. Their father also returned to Ohio before his death the next year. (Letters in the possession of Mrs. Magee.)

Major:

Pina and Marshall Barber both called McKinley by this name. Mr. Dawes said that some members of the family called him "Will," but he did not remember ever hearing any man friend do so.

Gave up chewing: Information from Mr. Garfield and Mrs. Putnam. *Silver wedding celebration:* George Charters to McK, nd [1896], McK P, vol 4; *Repos* 2/5,6/96.

CHAPTER 2
CHAMPION OF PROTECTION

McKinley's early political career and his prominence at the Republican convention of 1888 are treated in detail in both Olcott's biography and that by Porter and Boyle. For the Ohio gerrymanders, see Olcott, I, 82-85.

35–39   NEW CONGRESSMAN: Robert M. La Follette, *La Follette's Autobiography* (Madison, Wis, 1913), 127; Atkins, *Bklyn Eagle* 5/3/96; *NY Trib* 6/21/96. *"practical":* Repos 1/22/96. *Background:* Heald, "Young McKinley's Canton," above cited; *Repos* 3/31/40. *First speech on tariff 4/15/78: Speeches and Addresses of William McKinley* (1893), 1-22; Atkins, cited. *Not regarded as first rank:* clipping of article by Henry MacFarland in McK P, vol 6. *As a speaker:* Atkins; La Follette, 92-93; information from Mr. Moore.

39–42   RISE TO PROMINENCE: *Speech on Mills Bill 5/18/88: Speeches and Addresses* (1893), 290-335; Allan Nevins, *Grover Cleveland* (New York, 1948), 390-91; Shelby M. Cullom, *Fifty Years of Public Service* (Chicago, 1911), 444-45, quoting letter from J. Medill 8/5/88. *Convention of 1888: Official Proceedings of the Republican National Convention* (Chicago); Walter Wellman in *Chi Trib* 6/24,25/88; Foraker, I, chaps 21-23, also pp 385-88; Everett Walters, *Joseph Benson Foraker* (Columbus, 1948), chap 5. *Foraker's personal machine:* Walters, 61. *Hanna's relations with Foraker:* Croly, chap 12; Walters, 80-83; Julia B. Foraker, above cited, 86-90, 105-8. *"violent profanity":* Beer, above cited, 110. *"the wrong horse":* James F. Rhodes, *The McKinley and Roosevelt Administrations* (New York, 1922), 4.

43–44   SPEAKERSHIP CONTEST: *Reed:* Henry Cabot Lodge, *The Democracy of the Constitution and Other Addresses and Essays* (New York, 1915), 187-89, 192-98, 206; Samuel W. McCall, *The Life of Thomas Brackett Reed* (Boston and New York, 1914), 148, 165; Arthur W. Dunn, *From Harrison to Harding* (2 vols, New York and London, 1922), I, 23-25, 300; Croly, 150. *McKinley wanted to win:* Governor J. J. Geer of Oregon, quoted in Grosvenor, 130-31. *Concealed disappointment:* See McK to Herrick 12/10/89, Herrick Papers. *Reed's faithful ally:* NY Times 6/19/96.

  Dunn, however, said that "McKinley had to be pushed hard to stand for all the Reed methods in the Fifty-first Congress" (Dunn, I, 164).

44–47   TARIFF OF 1890: Ida M. Tarbell, *The Tariff in Our Times* (New York, 1912), 185-208; Frank M. Taussig, *A Tariff History of the United States* (New York, 1923), 251-84. *Preparation of bill:* La Follette, 102-3, 110-11. *McKinley's speech 5/7/90: Speeches and Addresses* (1893), 397-430.

  McKinley himself thought some of the schedules too high. He later told Herrick that he had consented to them to get the bill passed (Olcott, I, 127).

Blaine: Edward Stanwood, *James Gillespie Blaine* (New York and Boston, 1908), II, 327-78; Dunn, I, 44; John W. Foster, *Diplomatic Memoirs* (2 vols, New York and Boston, 1909), II, 2-18; Reed to McK 1/30/92, McK P, vol 1.

  John W. Foster succeeded Blaine as Harrison's Secretary of State. He had a little namesake born in 1888, his daughter's baby John Foster Dulles.

48–49   DEFEAT: *Campaign*: *Repos* 11/1,4/90; Olcott, I, 180. *"In the time of darkest defeat"*: Olcott, I, 186. *"Protection was never stronger"*: Ibid, 187-89; cf *Repos* 11/13/90. *Newspaper comments*: *Repos* 11/11/90; comments of other newspapers quoted in *Repos* 11/7,8,10,22/90. *Meeting with Cannon and Carter*: Report of a speech made by Senator Carter in 1901, Arthur W. Dunn, *Gridiron Nights* (New York, 1915), 117. *"defeat . . . for the best"*: McK to Hanna 11/12/90, quoted in Croly, 158. *"full of grasshoppers"*: William Allen White, *Masks in a Pageant* (New York, 1928), 155-56.

CHAPTER 3

REPUBLICAN SUCCESS STORY

The two biographies previously discussed deal extensively with the Republican convention of 1892 and McKinley's part in the presidential campaign of 1894. Olcott also has much material on the labor troubles of McKinley's second term as governor of Ohio. Miss Mary A. Deibel's thesis, "William McKinley as Governor of Ohio" (Columbus, 1939), has been a useful guide to the events of the governorship.

50–51   NOMINATION FOR GOVERNOR: Walters, 99; *Repos* 6/16,22/91.
McKinley had returned to Canton on May 6 (*Repos* 5/6/91).
Hanna: Walters, 101; Croly, 159-60. *"frying the fat"*: Nevins, *Cleveland*, 417-18.

51–52   THE CURRENCY: *Repos* 11/9/91, 9/12/93; *The Nation* 8/27/91, 5/7/96. *"We cannot gamble"*: Porter and Boyle, 356.

52–55   ADMINISTRATION: *Inaugural address*: *Repos* 1/11/92. *Franchise tax*: Walters, 124. *Influence on arbitration*: Information from Mr. Frease and Mr. Moore; McK to R. P. Skinner 9/22/94, McK P, Letbk 87.
McKinley told Mr. Skinner, a Massillon newspaperman who later held various diplomatic posts, that he had personally urged arbitration on the operators and some of the miners' representatives, but asked that his letter should not be published.
Labor troubles: *Repos*, 1894, passim; quotations from *Chi Herald* and *Cld Plain Dealer* in *Repos* 6/12/94. *McBride interview*: Information from Mr. Frease. *His speech on lawlessness*: *Repos* 6/20/94. *Massillon miners*: *Repos* 11/4/95.
The *Repository* reporter who accompanied McKinley on his second campaign tour wrote that a group of miners waited on the Governor at Somerset, and said they would now raise the money he had formerly refused. "You helped us once and we have not forgotten it," the spokesman told McKinley with tears in his eyes. "If you ever want any body to die for you call on us" (*Repos* 9/24/93).
Ohio banks: McK to Herrick 6/27/94, Herrick Papers. *"outrages must stop"*: Deibel MS. *Personal contribution*: McK to Thomas McDougall 4/26/94, McK P, Letbk 87.

55–57   CONVENTION OF 1892: *Proceedings of the Tenth Republican National Convention* (Minneapolis, 1892); Minneapolis *Trib* 6/5-12/92; *Repos* 3/2,17,29/92, 6/8-10/92; Croly, 165-66; Dunn, *Harrison to Harding*, I, 85,

92-93; Walters, 105-6; Nevins, 487-88; Kohlsaat, 9; Foraker, I, 447; Hanna, *National Magazine*, Jan/02, above cited. *McKinley snubbed by Harrison:* Olcott, II, 343-44. *Kohlsaat's room:* Kohlsaat, 8-9. For a similar account, see Nicholas Murray Butler, *Across the Busy Years* (2 vols, New York, 1939), I, 221.

> Kohlsaat, as a traveling salesman for a wholesale bakery firm, had met McKinley late in 1876. He purchased a half-interest in the Chicago *Inter Ocean* in 1891, and sold it in 1894. The next year, he bought the Chicago *Times-Herald* and *Evening Post.*

57   CONFIDENT PLANS: Croly, 66-67; Powers, above cited, 163.

58-60   BANKRUPTCY: Kohlsaat, 10-16; Croly, 169-70; Powers, 167; Storer, above cited, 18-19; *Repos* 2/18,20/93, 3/14/93; *NY Trib* 2/18,22,23/93; *Bklyn Eagle* 5/1/96. *McKinley on way to New York:* Heald MS. *"not a beggar": Repos* 2/24/93, quoting Herrick.

> A copy of a rather incoherent letter from Walker, dated March 22, 1893, expressing gratitude and regrets to McKinley, is pasted in the back of McKinley's Letterbook 87.

61–62   CAMPAIGN OF 1894: *Repos* 10/6/94-11/8/94.

62–63   THOMASVILLE: Croly, 175-76; Dunn, *Harrison to Harding*, I, 171-74. See E. T. Heald, "McKinley and Thomasville, Georgia," in *The Stark County Story*, IV, part 3 (Canton, 1959). *"ridiculous" construction:* McK to T. McDougall 12/19/94, McK P, Letbk 87. *"rest and outing":* McK to A. E. Buck 2/1/95, ibid. *"consent of my mind":* McK to J. F. Hanson 2/27/95, ibid.

63   HARTFORD: *"The sentiment . . . favorable":* McK to J. Hay 4/13/95, ibid.

63–64   OHIO: Foraker, I, 452-54; Walters, 109-10; Croly, 176-77; see A. S. Bushnell to Herrick 8/23/95, Herrick Papers. *Campaign: Repos* Oct, early Nov/95.

64   NORTH MARKET STREET: *NY World* 6/16/96; *Phila Press* 6/11/96; *NY Trib* 9/13/96.

CHAPTER 4
FRONT PORCH

The estimate of Hanna's character has been influenced by Herbert Croly's biography and by the paragraphs in Charles G. Dawes's *Journal* (pp 365-66), written on Hanna's death in 1904. The account of "the front porch campaign" is taken from the files of *The Evening Repository* and from three pamphlets: *McKinley as a Candidate; McKinley's Speeches in August;* and *McKinley's Speeches in September* (compiled by Joseph P. Smith, Canton, 1896).

66-68   MCKINLEY'S FRIENDSHIPS: *Hanna's attitude:* William Allen White, *Autobiography*, 294 (cf *McClure's Magazine*, Nov/00); information from Mr. Dawes and Mr. Frease; Dawes, *Journal*, 368; Kohlsaat, 96; La Follette, 128; Hanna, *National Magazine*, Jan/02, above cited.

> An impression of McKinley's quiet dominance was formed in 1896 by the correspondent of a hostile newspaper, William Shaw Bowen (*NY World* 6/17/96).

Expressed regard: McK to Herrick 3/20/93, 6/15/94, Herrick Papers; to Dawes 4/30/96, Dawes, 81; George F. Hoar, *Autobiography of Seventy Years* (2 vols, New York, 1903), II, 315.

69   DISLIKE OF PUBLICITY: McK to T. McDougall 4/26/94, to R. P. Skinner
9/22/94, to W. E. Curtis 12/2/95, McK P, Letbk 87. *"a patent medicine"*:
Beer, above cited, 165.

69–75   PRE-CONVENTION CANVASS: *"a better man"*: Croly, 208. *Quay*: Dunn, *Harrison to Harding*, I, 333; La Follette, 58; Harry Thurston Peck, *Twenty Years of the Republic, 1885-1905* (New York, 1906), 282. *Platt*: W. A. White, *Masks*, 42, 58, *Autobiography*, 335. *Disappointed by Harrison: The Autobiography of Thomas Collier Platt*, edited by Louis J. Lang (New York, 1910), 206. *McKinley's refusal to trade*: Kohlsaat, 30. *Struggle for control*: Osborne to McK 1/6/96, Grosvenor to McK 2/19/96, Hay to Hanna 1/27/96, McK P, vol 1. *Reed's equivocations: The Letters of Theodore Roosevelt*, edited by Elting E. Morison (8 vols, Cambridge, Mass, 1951-54), I, #626. *Ohio*: Walters, 127-29; McK to Foraker 1/29/96, McK P, vol 1. *Illinois*: Kohlsaat, 21; Dawes, 65-69, 73-82; Dawes to McK 3/13,14,16/96, McK P, vol 1; Cullom, above cited, 272.

Dawes was active in persuading McKinley to reach an agreement with Cullom (Dawes, 75). See also letters to McKinley from P. S. Grosscup and J. C. McNulta, April 9, 1896 (McK P, vol 1).

Nomination assured: Bklyn Eagle 5/1/96. *Quay at Canton: Repos* 5/23/96. *Success of Hanna's strategy*: Dunn, *Harrison to Harding*, I, 171-74, 178-79; McCall, above cited, 222-24. *Fund for the canvass*: Croly, 183-84; Osborne to Hanna 3/11/96, McK P, vol 1; P. C. Knox to McK 2/26/96, ibid; Hanna to McK 2/28/96, ibid. Cf Dawes, 66.

75–78   ATTACKS ON CANDIDACY: *"shuffle him and deal him," "gambling for a White House"*: NY *Journal* 5/4/96, 4/30/96. Hanna *"at the flanks of labor"*: Ibid, 8/3/96.

Homer Davenport, meeting Hanna at the close of the campaign, made his apologies in the form of a cartoon of the real Hanna arm-in-arm with his gross likeness. Davenport told Hanna that he had treated McKinley with consideration because he had met and liked him. Murat Halstead was responsible for taking Davenport to Canton (NY *Journal* 11/8/96). APA: McK P, vol 2 and Letbk 87, passim; McK to Osborne 4/17/96, Letbk 87; Kohlsaat, 18; Louis A. Coolidge, *An Old-Fashioned Senator, Orville H. Platt of Connecticut* (New York and London, 1910), 503-4. *"made papists of us"*: Hanna to McK 4/21/96, McK P, vol 2. *Foraker linked*: Walters, 128. *Asked by McKinley to nominate him*: McK P, Letbk 87.

For a general discussion of the APA movement, see Hoar, II, 278-93.

78–79   MCKINLEY'S SILENCE ON MONEY: NY *World* 5/12/96; NY *Times* 6/19/96; *Nation* 5/14,21/96. See McK to J. F. Laning 5/27/95, Letbk 87; to Sherman 3/22/96, Sherman Papers, Ac 2019. *Hanna also silent*: Hanna to McK, nd, McK P, vol 4.

79–80   THE MONEY PLANK: *Official Proceedings of the Eleventh Republican National Convention* (St Louis, 1896); Croly, 192-204; Olcott, I, 311-14; Foraker, I, 463-82; Dawes, 85; Kohlsaat, 33-37; Beer, 143-44; Walters, 130; Dunn, *Harrison to Harding*, I, 174-79; Peck, 485-86; Letter from Horace Porter, NY *Trib* 6/19/96. A proposed draft, edited by McKinley, is in McK P, vol 4. See also Butler, above cited, 222-23. *St. Louis described*: Walters, 129. *"Silver . . . wept over"*: *Nation* 6/25/96. *Bryan*: Dunn, *Harrison to Harding*, I, 179-81.

80–83   THE NOMINATION, CANTON: *Repos* 6/11-21/96; NY *Trib*, Phila *Press*, 6/19/96; William Shaw Bowen, NY *World* 6/16-19/96; Foraker, I, 486-88, quoting Murat Halstead; *McKinley as a Candidate*, 5-7; Kuhns, above cited, 59-60.

84–85   CHANGED OUTLOOK: Rhodes, above cited, 17-19; Croly, 204-5, 209-10. *"a chestnut"*: *Bklyn Eagle* 7/15/96. *McKinley an illogical candidate*: *Nation* 6/11/96.

85–93   THE REPUBLICAN CAMPAIGN: *Hanna*: Croly, 211-23; Hay to H. Adams 9/8/96, *Letters of John Hay and Extracts from Diary* (3 vols, privately printed, Washington, 1908), II, 74. *Campaign fund*:

> Dawes was in charge of all campaign accounting. On November 21, 1896, he submitted a statement of the expenditures of the Chicago head-quarters, totaling $1,960,188.48, with unpaid claims estimated at $4,820. Receipts in the amount of $1,565,000 had come to Chicago from New York (Dawes, 106).

McKinley: Hanna, *National Magazine*, cited; Croly, 215-16; *Cld Plain Dealer* 9/8,12,19,20,28/96; information from Mr. Frease. *Special church service*: *Repos* 6/22/96. *Mrs. McKinley sent away*: Beer, 150. *McKinley averse to bringing crowds*: McK to [?] Ford, nd, McK P, Letbk 88. *"a good pull at the tariff"*: *Nation* 8/6/96. *Luther Day*: Information from Mr. Day. *"your pink dress"*: Information from Mrs. Esselburne. *Height of silver craze reached*: McK to W. F. Wakeman 8/7/96, McK P, Letbk 88.

90–92   LETTER OF ACCEPTANCE: *Proceedings, Eleventh Republican Convention*, pp 151-59. See Osborne to McK 9/1/96, McK P, vol 3.

94–95   RECONCILIATIONS: Foraker, I, 496; Quay to McK 10/25/96, McK P, vol 3; Hay to Adams 10/4,29/96, *Letters and Diary*, above cited, II, 77-78.

96   ELECTION: *Kohlsaat's telephone call*: Kohlsaat, 53.

CHAPTER 5
PRELUDE TO HIGH OFFICE

97–99   CUBA: *Cleveland "likely to dump"*: Reid to McK 12/5/96, repeating McK's expressed opinion, McK P, vol 4. See Hay to McK 12/28/96, ibid.

99, 100   ALLISON: Dawes, 105, 108; W. M. McFarland to McK 12/29/96, McK P, vol 4. *McKinley still hoping*:

> Allison wrote on December 30, acknowledging an invitation to stop in Canton on his way to Washington (McK P, vol 4).

99–101   HANNA: *Postmaster Generalship*: Dawes, 105, 108, 114; McK to Hanna 11/12/96, McK P, vol 4; same 2/18/97, Letbk 88. *Not offered Treasury*: Dawes, 108. *Desire for Senate*: Croly, 231-33. *Foraker's protest*: Foraker, I, 496-501.

> Allowance must be made for a prejudiced source in considering the state-ment that McKinley was "thoroughly committed" to the idea of appoint-ing Senator Sherman a "few days after the election."

100–102   THE STATE DEPARTMENT: McK to Sherman 1/4,11/97, 2/11/97, Sherman Papers, Ac 2019; Hanna to Sherman 2/6/97, ibid; Sherman to Hanna 12/15/96, Hanna to McK 12/24/96, 1/13/97, Sherman to McK 1/7,13/97, W. M. Osborne to McK 12/11/96, 1/6/97, R. A. Alger to McK 1/11/97, McK P, vol 4; Sherman to McK 1/16/97, to A. S. Bushnell 1/16/97 (copy), Hanna to McK 2/1/97, Alger to Foraker 2/1/97 (copy), Sherman to McK

2/10,15/97, Sherman's memo on Cuba 2/15/97, Bushnell to McK 2/21/97, McK P, vol 5; McK to J. Medill 2/8/97, Letbk 88. See Foraker, I, 501-4; Walters, 136-37; Croly, 233-41.

Sherman first mentioned doubts about his appointment in a letter to Richard Smith, February 9 (copy, McK P, vol 5). By this time, his failings had been widely advertised. Later letters, to W. S. Ward, April 28 and July 27, 1898 (Sherman Papers, Ac 2199), and the unmailed draft of November 8, 1898, reproduced in Foraker's Notes (I, opposite page 508), were expressions of the grievance which became entrenched after Sherman's resignation from the Cabinet.

Hanna was not actually handed his commission until the morning of March 5, the day after McKinley's inauguration. Foraker thus became the senior senator from Ohio by precedence of one day.

102-104   THE WAR DEPARTMENT: Alger to McK 1/11/97, McK P, vol 4; J. C. Burrows to McK 1/20,25/97; T. C. Platt to Burrows (copy) 1/18/97, H. V. Boynton to McK 1/18/97, McK P, vol 5; memo on Alger, nd [March ? 1899], McK P, vol 28; McK to J. Medill 2/8/97, cited; Chi Record 2/1/97; Wash Eve Star 3/1/97. See Nation 9/15/98; William D. Orcutt, Burrows of Michigan and the Republican Party (3 vols, New York, 1917), II, 97-100. Convention of 1888: John Sherman, Recollections of Forty Years (2 vols, Chicago, 1895), II, 1029. See also Foraker, I, 363; Walters, 70; NY Herald 6/28/88, 7/3,6/88. Hanna's comment on War Department: Alger to Foraker 2/1/97, cited.

104-105   THE TREASURY: Dingley: Dawes, 108; N. Dingley to McK 12/22/96, McK P, vol 4; Edward P. Mitchell, Memoirs of an Editor (New York, 1924), 98-99. Gage: Kohlsaat, 56-58; Dawes, 112-14; Dawes to McK 1/21/97, McK P, vol 5; "A Day with Mr. Gage," Wash Eve Star 4/3/97; Moses P. Handy, "Lyman J. Gage, A Character Sketch," The Review of Reviews, Mar/97. Cullom:

McKinley did not consider Cullom seriously, though the Senator himself had received a different impression (Cullom, cited, 130).

The Dawes dilemma: Dawes, 82, 105, 108, 112-14.

105-106   THE POST OFFICE: Pressure for Payne resisted: La Follette, 128-30. Criticism of Payne: McK to Hanna, nd, Letbk 88. Cf NY Journal 7/23,29/96.

Payne was appointed Postmaster General by Roosevelt, who greatly admired him. (See TR, Letters, III, #2684, 2688.)

106   NAVY DEPARTMENT: John D. Long: Powers, above cited, 128-32; Chi Record 1/23/97; Wash Post 3/5/97; Harper's Weekly 3/13,20/97.

AGRICULTURE: James Wilson: Chi Record 1/13/97; Wash Eve Star 3/1/97; NY Trib 3/4/97; Rev of Revs, Aug/97.

106-108   INTERIOR AND JUSTICE: Joseph McKenna: NY Journal 2/23/97; NY Trib 3/4/97; Wash Post 3/5/97. Switched to Attorney General: Kohlsaat, 59; McKenna to McK 1/20/97, 2/5,17/97, McK P, vol 5; McK to McKenna 2/11/97, Letbk 88.

Harrison had been reluctant to make McKenna a circuit judge because of his religious faith (Dunn, Harrison to Harding, I, 82-84). Several protests against the appointment were addressed to McKinley in February (McK P, vol 5).

Tom Platt and Bliss: Platt to B. F. Tracy 2/2/91, Tracy Papers; W. Reid to

McK 12/5/96, 1/2/97, McK P, vol 4; C. M. Depew to Reid 12/28/96, ibid; Reid to E. Root 2/2/98, McK P, vol 11; Platt, *Autobiography*, cited, 510-11. *Bliss declined:* C. N. Bliss to McK 1/8/97, McK P, vol 4; McK to Bliss 1/11/[97], Letbk 88. *Woodford and McCook:* Platt to Alger 1/31/97, McK P, vol 5. *McCook:* Alger to McK 2/9/97, ibid; McCook to McK 2/27/97, McK P, vol 6.

An interview between McKinley and McCook developed a strong sympathy between them. Their friendship was not disturbed by the upset over the Attorney Generalship. McCook attended the inauguration with his beautiful daughter Martha, and, in some interval of private confidence, heard McKinley recite a Bible text (information from Mrs. Eliot Cross).

108–109   THE REID DILEMMA: Reid to McK 12/5/96, 1/2/97, Hay to McK 12/26/[96], 2/2/[97] C.M.D. [Depew] to Reid 12/28/96, Hay's drafts of two letters to Reid (enclosure of 2/16) McK P, vol 4; Hay to Hanna 1/15/[97], to McK 1/31/[97], 2/8,13,16,19/[97], McK P, vol 5; S. B. Elkins to McK 2/16/97, ibid; McK to Reid 12/26/96, 2/19/97, Letbk 88; Reid to McK 3/3/97, vol 6.

Platt also made an effort on behalf of Levi P. Morton, who declined to be considered (Hanna to McK 1/18/97, T. C. Platt to Morton 1/18/97 [copy in McK's hand], Morton to McK 1/26/97, McK P, vol 5).

108–110   THE AMBASSADORSHIP: W. M. Osborne to McK 12/11/96, Hay to McK 12/28/96, McK P, vol 4; Hay to McK 2/19,22/97, vol 5; same, 4/13/[97], vol 6. See Hay to Samuel Mather 2/25/97, quoted in William R. Thayer, *The Life and Letters of John Hay* (2 vols, New York and Boston, 1915), II, 754-55.

Hay was so pleased with the idea of the ring that eight years later, having procured some hairs from the head of Abraham Lincoln, he had them similarly mounted as a present for Theodore Roosevelt (Tyler Dennett, *John Hay*, New York, 1933, 348).

Platt had another flurry of trying to get the ambassadorship for Morton, who again declined (Morton to McK 2/6/97, McK P, vol 5. See McK to C. M. Depew 1/30/97, Letbk 88).

111–115   CANTON TO WASHINGTON: *Repos* 3/2/97; Chi *Record* 3/2,3/97; Wash *Eve Star* 3/2/97; Wash *Post* 3/2,3,4/97. *Mrs McKinley's wardrobe:* Chi *Trib* 1/26,27/97, 2/1,6/97; Chi *Record* 1/26,28/97; Chi *Times-Herald* 1/26-28/97, 2/2/97. *Another "mother's boy":* Walter Wellman in *Repos* 3/2/97. *Mother McKinley:* Chi *Record* 3/5/97. *"better than a bishopric":* Ibid. *George Saxton: Repos* 11/17/95; information from Mrs. Esselburne; report by Ralph K. Spencer of *The Canton Repository. Abner McKinley:* Information from Mr. Frease and Mr. Dawes; Perry S. Heath to Hanna 5/29/[96], McK P, vol 2; B. C. Faurot to McK 12/3/97, McK P, vol 10; NY *Eve Post* 5/27/99; Dawes, 318.

Mr. Ingling said that Benjamin F. Montgomery—executive clerk and later White House telegrapher—used to get railroad passes which he handed on to the President's brother.

115   DINNER WITH CLEVELAND: Cleveland to McK 2/3/97, McK P, vol 5; McK to Cleveland 2/7/97, Letbk 88; Wash *Eve Star* 3/2,3/97; Wash *Post* 3/4/97. *"sadness and sincerity":* George F. Parker, *Recollections of Grover Cleveland* (New York, 1909), 250. *Pink canopied bed:*

A photograph of the bed is in the Division of Prints and Photographs at the Library of Congress. A note states that it brought $160 at the sale of the Ebbitt House furnishings.

116–120 INAUGURATION DAY: *NY Trib*, Wash *Post*, Chi *Record* (W. E. Curtis), 3/5/97. *McKinley's shoes*: Kuhns, *Old Canton*, above cited, 58. *His suit*: George Sykes to McK 2/4/97, McK P, vol 5. *Mrs. McKinley*: Dunn, *Harrison to Harding*, I, 208.

The Hockanum Mills of Rockville, Connecticut, were widely advertised as the manufacturers of the cloth worn by the President for his inauguration. Mrs. McKinley's blue velvet dress is at the Canton Art Institute.
Inaugural address: *Congr Rec*, vol 30, 2-5. *The ball*: Wash *Eve Star* 3/5/97; *Harper's Wkly* 3/13/97. *Mrs. McKinley's attack*: Information from Mr. Kuhns.

120 ATTACK ON GÜINES: A. del Castillo to McK 3/5/97, McK P, Box 211.
This letter, with translation attached, was enclosed in a letter from F. V. Alvord Jr. to McKinley, dated Havana, March 13, 1897.

CHAPTER 6
HONEYMOON PERIOD

121–123 THE MANSION: Benjamin Harrison, "A Day with the President at His Desk," *The Ladies' Home Journal*, Mar/97; W. H. Crook to JAP 3/19/97, McK P, Letbk 89; Ira R. T. Smith, *"Dear Mr. President. . . ," The Story of Fifty Years in the White House Mailroom* (New York, 1949), 172.

The most revealing account of the defects of the White House is contained in the report of McKim, Mead, and White, the architects in charge of the alterations and repairs undertaken in the Theodore Roosevelt administration (*Sen Doc* 197, 57/2, 1903).
A public park: Benjamin Harrison, "The Domestic Side of the White House," *LHJ* May/97. *Cleveland closed path*: *The Review of Reviews* Apr/97. *McKinley moved office*: Wash *Eve Star* 3/26/98. *Furniture from Lincoln's time*: The desk and table are now in the Museum of The Rutherford B. Hayes Library at Fremont, Ohio. Webb C. Hayes bought them for $10 when the White House was renovated in the Roosevelt administration (information from Mr. Marchman).

123–125 THE STAFF: Harrison, *LHJ* May/97, cited; G. B. Williams to McK 1/11/97, W. E. Curtis to McK 1/12/97, McK P, vol 4. *Tharins*: Information from Mrs. Hamlin, Mr. Ingling; I. R. T. Smith, 137-38.

Clare or Clara had temporarily left Mrs. McKinley in 1895 because her husband could not get a place in Columbus (McK to C. P. Herrick 1/11/95, 2/27/95, Herrick Papers). This was evidently not the first such parting. Charles Bawsel wrote, October 21, 1894, that Clare was "again" with Mrs. McKinley (Heald MS). Ike Hoover contributed the information that Tharin drank (Irwin H. Hoover, *Forty-two Years in the White House*, Boston and New York, 1934, 339).
Sinclair: Nevins, *Cleveland*, 74, 127, 213, 521; Wash *Eve Star* 3/8/97; W. E. Curtis to McK, cited; H. Kengla to McK 1/3/98, McK P, Box 212. *Electric wiring*: Hoover, 3-4.

Hoover's book contains remarkably little of interest about President and Mrs. McKinley or the White House in their time.

Jerry Smith: T. A. Bingham to JAP 5/18/98, 1/24/99; Jerry Smith to McK 1/29/99, McK P, Box 212. *"too frivolous and flirty":* W. E. Curtis to McK, cited. *"cuisine à la Canton": Town Topics* 2/9/99 (clipping in Bingham Coll, Box 16).

125–128   THE OFFICE FORCE: Information from Mr. Ingling; William H. Crook, *Memories of the White House,* edited by Henry Rood (Boston, 1911), 244, 250; I. R. T. Smith, 33-34. *"fine 'form' ":* GBC 12/19/99. *J. Addison Porter:* Information from Mr. Willson, Mr. Ingling; I. R. T. Smith, 41; Wash *Post* 3/5/97. See JAP to McK 9/15/97, Josephine E. S. Porter to McK 2/22/99, 4/21/99, McK P, Box 216. *"Secretary to the President": Rev of Revs* Apr/97.
Mr. Willson correctly stated that McKinley would have been glad to see Porter get the governorship of Connecticut. In the summer of 1899, he inspired the suggestion of the consul-generalship at Cairo, but Porter— then in Europe, having been away from his job for many months because of illness—declared his intention to "be back at the side of the President" (GBC 7/1/99).
"over mental strain": Amy Porter to McK [Dec ? 1900], McK P, Box 216.
Newspaper obituaries on Porter's death, December 15, 1900, indicate that he had suffered from an intestinal cancer.
George B. Cortelyou: Dawes, 272; Dunn, *Harrison to Harding,* I, 208-10; Stealey, above cited, 34-35; I. R. T. Smith, 41.

128–131   COLONEL BINGHAM: JAP to McK 2/18/97, McK P, vol 5; memos, Bingham to McK, May, Nov/97, Bingham Coll, Box 18. Cf Benjamin Harrison, "The Social Life of the President," *Ladies' Home Journal* Apr/97.
Mrs. McKinley's receptions were frequently noticed in the Washington newspapers. (See *Eve Star,* 3/13/97. For the Cabinet dinner, ibid, 3/25/97.)

131–133   THE NEW PRESIDENT: *Afternoon walks:* Wash *Eve Star* 3/8,13/97. See JAP to T. S. Clarkson 5/7/97, McK P, Letbk 91. *Never photographed with a cigar:* W. A. White, *Autobiography,* cited, 333. *Piqué waistcoats:* John J. Kennedy to McK 6/2/97, McK P, Box 212. See also other letters from Kennedy, Box 212. *Visits of barber:*
The White House barber from 1898 to 1901 was John W. Dabney, a Negro who had a small shop in an F Street basement (*NY Trib* 2/24/01).
Diamond brooch: F. F. Bonnet to McK 8/4/97 (enclosing statement of $366.20), McK P, Box 212. *Investments:*
McKinley steadfastly refused to invest in any business affected by the tariff. When his friend, W. B. Plunkett, set apart $5,000 worth of stock in his cotton mills for the President, McKinley returned the certificate. See draft of letter, McKinley's hand nd (McK P, vol 48) and Plunkett's reply 5/22/00 (vol 49).
Riding: JAP to Charles Fleischmann 4/20/97, Letbk 91; Wash *Eve Star* 8/12/99. *Bible text:* Information from Mrs. Cross. *Church attendance:* Frank M. Bristol, *Sunday School Times,* above cited.
The only deference paid the President was that the congregation remained standing at the close of the service until he had passed out.
Dawes an habitué: Dawes, 116. *His musical interests:* Bascom N. Timmons,

Portrait of an American: Charles G. Dawes (New York, 1953), 16. *Smoking-room story:* Information from Mr. Dawes.

133–138   THE PATRONAGE: *Cleveland's civil service order:* See TR to Carl Schurz, 12/24/97, *Letters*, cited I, #887; to Frank P. Blair 12/30/97, TR Papers; to Charles J. Bonaparte 12/31/97, ibid. *McKinley tired:* T. McDougall to McK 7/13/97, McK P, vol 7; *America of Yesterday*, above cited, 147-48. *Liked modesty:* GBC 1/22/99. *Lost his temper:* Information from Mr. Dawes. *"that never failing remedy":* Hanna to McK, nd [1897], vol 10. *Senator Mason quoted:* Kohlsaat, 5. *Labor leader melted:* Ibid, 5-6. *Senator Wolcott quoted:* Mrs. Garret A. Hobart, *Memories* (privately printed, Mt. Vernon, NY, 1930), 18. *Senator Frye offended:* W. P. Frye to McK 3/31/97, McK P, vol. 6; McK to Frye 3/31/97, Letbk 90. *McKinley with Cullom:* Cullom, 276-79. *With Tom Platt:* Platt, *Autobiography*, 397-98; De Alva S. Alexander, *Four Famous New Yorkers* in *The Political History of the State of New York*, IV (New York, 1923), 149, 289-90; TR to P. T. Sherman, *Letters*, I, #855.

On the subject of Bliss, however, Alexander is wrong, and Platt (pp 398-99), disingenuous.

Roosevelt's appointment: Selections from the Correspondence of Theodore Roosevelt and Henry Cabot Lodge, 1884-1918 (2 vols, New York, 1925), I, 241-47, 252-54, 260-63; *NY Sun* 4/5,6,8/98. *Foraker and Storer:* Walters, 145, see 119-23. See also news clipping, signed Henry MacFarland, McK P, vol 6; Maria L. Storer to Herrick 3/19/97, ibid. *Professor Williams:* Foraker, I, 81-82.

138–140   HANNA: *Hard fight in Ohio:* Croly, chap 18; Walters, 138-40; Hanna to McK 11/8/97, McK P, vol 9; McK to Hanna 10/14/97, 12/30/97, 1/7/98, Letbk 90; McK to J. L. Carpenter, 12/30/97, to J. C. Schmidlapp, 1/7/98, ibid.

McKinley attempted to make at least one direct appeal for a vote for Hanna (Dawes, 138, 139). He also agreed to address the Commercial Club of Cincinnati on October 30 because Hanna thought that his appearance in Ohio would be helpful (McK to Hanna 10/14/97, cited).

Regained control in Ohio: Croly, 291. *Took leadership in Senate:* Cullom, 281; Dunn, *Harrison to Harding*, I, 205-6. *Gained in self-importance:* Information from Mr. Dawes. *Complained of lack of co-operation:* Dawes, 365.

140–142   DINGLEY TARIFF: Taussig, above cited, 321-60; Tarbell, above cited, 242-52; Rhodes, 37-39. *McKinley converted to reciprocity:* Joseph P. Smith to McK 7/31/97, McK P, vol 8; McK to W. E. Curtis 12/2/95, Letbk 87; La Follette, 114-15; Speech, Commercial Club of Cincinnati, *Speeches and Addresses of William McKinley* (New York, 1900), 52-55.

143   MOTHER MCKINLEY: Helen McK to McKs 6/19[97], McK P, Box 211; Dawes, 130, 134. *McKinley's tears:* Information from Mr. Dawes.

ANNUAL MESSAGE OF 1897: *Congr Rec*, vol 30, 2-9. *"not a prime minister living":* Hay to McK 12/7/97, McK P, vol 10.

143–144   THE CURRENCY: Rhodes, 36-37; Olcott, I, 353-59; McK to Hay 5/29/97, 7/27/97, McK P, Letbk 90; Hay to McK 10/11/97, McK P, vol 9; Dawes, 128, 129, 133, 134.

The friends of bimetallism were convinced of McKinley's sincerity, but deplored the antagonistic views of some members of the administration, especially Secretary Gage (W. E. Chandler Papers, vols 115, 116, passim).

144–145   SEALING CONTROVERSY: Foster, II, 22-50, 183-86. *Importance to President:* McK to Hay 7/27/97, McK P, Letbk 90. *Great Britain:* See Hay to J. W. Foster 12/27/97, quoted in Foster, II, 185. *Foster in charge:*

> Thoroughly experienced in the negotiations, Foster was not always diplomatic in conducting them. (See Dennett, *Hay*, 185; Hay to McK 7/16/97, McK P, vol 7.)

145   MIDWAY ISLANDS: See speech by Senator Orville Platt, *Congr Rec*, vol 32, 291.

145–147   HAWAII:

> The tariff of 1890 had robbed the American sugar magnates of their advantage in the American market, and goaded them to seek a status that would assure their profits in future (Thomas A. Bailey, A *Diplomatic History of the American People*, New York, 1950, 469). McKinley had had a personal reason for interest in the islands. His eldest brother, David, had acted as U.S. consul at Honolulu, and later served the Republic of Hawaii as consul at San Francisco.

Treaty of Annexation: Foster, cited, 275-76; L. B. Shippee and R. B. Way, "William Rufus Day," in S. F. Bemis, *The American Secretaries of State and Their Diplomacy*, IX (New York, 1929), 34-37. *Protest of Japan:* Ibid, 38-40; A. Whitney Griswold, *The Far Eastern Policy of the United States* (New York, 1938), 339-41; T. A. Bailey, "Japan's Protest Against the Annexation of Hawaii," *The Journal of Modern History*, III, 46-61. *Sewall:* Mitchell, cited, 338-39, quoting letter written by Sewall 12/14/97.

> Sewall's father Arthur M. Sewall had been Bryan's running mate in 1896, but approved his son's decision to vote the Republican ticket. In writing to Mitchell, Harold Sewall gave the credit for his instructions to Senator Frye of Maine, but Lodge and Roosevelt had also been at work on the President (TR to A. T. Mahan 5/3/97, *Letters*, I, #718).

147–150   CUBA: Shippee and Way, cited, 42-61. French E. Chadwick, *The Relations of the United States and Spain: Diplomacy* (New York, 1909), 495-527. *Cuban relief:* Chadwick, *Diplomacy*, 529. See Clara Barton, "Our Work and Observations in Cuba," *The North American Review*, May/98.

CHAPTER 7
CUBA

151–155   THE STATE DEPARTMENT: Henry MacFarland, "William R. Day, A Statesman of the First Rank," *Rev of Revs*, Sept/98.

> McKinley laughingly spoke of having been his own Secretary of State at this time (GBC 2/4/00).

Sherman: Photograph of Cabinet, 1897; *America of Yesterday*, above cited, 186; Foraker, I, 506. For later expressions of resentment, see letters above cited: Sherman to W. S. Ward 4/28/98, 7/27/98, Sherman Papers, Ac 2199; draft, 11/8/98, Foraker, I, opposite 508. *"a paramount ruler":* Foraker I, 508. *Lapse with Japanese minister:* Foster, above cited, II, 173. *Day:* MacFarland, cited; Kohlsaat, 64-65; NY *Eve Post* 8/9/98; GBC 4/16/98; Dawes, 156. *Adee:* Alfred L. P. Dennis, *Adventures in American Diplomacy*, 1896-1906 (New York, 1928), 7; Dennett, *Hay*, 197, 199-200. *Falsetto voice:* Information from

Mr. Ingling. *"The head . . . knows nothing"*: Dunn, *Harrison to Harding*, I, 204-5.

The Third Assistant Secretary of State was Thomas W. Cridler, a political appointee. (See TR *Letters*, III, #2189.)

Gossip of subordinates: Foster to JAP 8/11/97, McK P, vol 8. *Sherman's indiscretion:* NY *World* 8/4,7,10/97; Sherman to McK 8/16,21/97, McK P, vol 8; McK to Sherman 8/18/97, Letbk 90. *Sherman clan:*

A prime mover in opposition to the administration was General Nelson A. Miles, who had married Mary Sherman, daughter of John's eldest brother, Charles. Mary's sister Lizzie, wife of ex-Senator Donald Cameron of Pennsylvania, was McKinley's bitter critic. Colgate Hoyt, husband of a third sister, Lida, was an active ally of Miles. Allegations of an "intrigue" against Sherman were widely credited (H. Adams to Elizabeth S. Cameron 12/11/98, *Letters of Henry Adams, 1892-1918*, edited by Worthington C. Ford, Boston, 1938, p 196). Even so good a friend of McKinley as John Hay was influenced by them (same, 1/16/99, 203).

155–156   LONG: Adams (Mass) *Freeman* 10/15/03; *America of Yesterday*, 156, 157, 194, 217.

156–158   ROOSEVELT: *"a bully time"*: TR to F. Remington 8/18/97, TR Papers. *Failed to influence appointments:* TR to W. E. Chandler 8/12/97, Chandler Papers, vol 115. *Increase in Navy:* TR *Letters*, I, #746, #790, #792, #810. *Long not "converted"*: Ibid, #848.

159–161   DEWEY APPOINTMENT: Chandler to Long 9/25/97, 10/14/97, to TR 10/13/97, Chandler Papers, vol 116; Long to Chandler 10/12,16/97, ibid; TR to Chandler 9/27/97, *Letters*, I, #827; same, 9/29/97, TR Papers; TR *Letters*, II, #1118, #1288; TR, *An Autobiography* (New York, 1913), 231-32; John D. Long, *The New American Navy* (2 vols, New York, 1903), I, 176-77; George Dewey, *Autobiography* (New York, 1913), 167, 168-69, 173.

161–162   TR AND MCKINLEY: TR *Letters*, I, #810, #819, #826. *Thought JAP "a trump"*; TR to L. N. Littauer 6/17/97, TR Papers.

162   "THOSE DARNED ISLANDS": Kohlsaat, 68.

162–163   FITZHUGH LEE: Department of State, *Consular Letters*, Cuba, vols 125-29; Cleveland to Olney 4/26/98, cited in Dennis, 89; JAP to Sherman 3/15/97, note in *Consular Letters*, vol 129; Day to Woodford 3/2,3/98, *For Rels*, 1898, 676, 681. *Havana riots:* Lee to Day 1/12,13/98, *For Rels*, 1898, 1024-25; Chadwick, *Diplomacy*, 531.

164–166   SENDING OF MAINE: *America of Yesterday*, 155; Long, *Navy*, I, 134-37; Chadwick, *Diplomacy*, 533-35; *Sp Corres*, 1898, #48-#50, #55; *For Rels*, 1898, 1026, 1028. *Lee changed his mind:* *For Rels*, 1898, 1027.

165–166   DUPUY DE LÔME: *Diplomatic dinner:* *Sp Corres*, 1898, #54.

This dinner was actually held on the night of January 26, although Dupuy's dispatch of January 28 says "last night."

The letter: Chadwick, *Diplomacy*, 538-39; *Sp Corres*, 1898, #60, #61. *Day's call:* *Sp Corres*, #61; NY *Eve Post* 8/9/98.

166–170   THE DISASTER: *America of Yesterday*, 163; GBC 1/22/99; NY *Times* 2/17,20/98; NY *Sun*, NY *Trib* 2/17/98. *President's speech:* *Speeches and Addresses* (1900), 67-68. *Unanimity of support:* Lodge to McK 3/21/98,

McK P, vol 12. *Talk with Fairbanks:* Olcott, II, 12-13.

In preparing his biography, Olcott talked with Fairbanks and saw a manuscript of his reminiscences (Olcott, I, ix-x).

TR's rampage: Long to TR 2/25/98, TR Papers; *America of Yesterday,* 168-70.

McKinley's backbone:

The "chocolate éclair" remark has been attributed to Roosevelt at a variety of dates. It seems probable that it belongs to this period of his intense disgust with McKinley's reluctance to go to war, rather than to a later date, when Roosevelt's political ambition made him consistently discreet in referring to the President. Dunn says that at this time Roosevelt compared McKinley's backbone to "a jellyfish." (*Harrison to Harding,* I, 234.)

Hostile Spanish note: For Rels, 1898, 657.

A synopsis of this note had been telegraphed to Washington by Woodford on February 8.

170–172 HOPE OF PEACE: Chadwick, *Diplomacy,* 544-48; *For Rels,* 1898, 686, 692. *Lee's explanation: America of Yesterday,* 171-72. A *"peace measure":* Ibid, 172. *"power to control":* Dawes, 146. *President wanted Congress:* Ibid. *His mail:* GBC, Mar/98, passim. *"it has stunned them":* For Rels, 1898, 684.

172–173 PROCTOR'S SPEECH: *NY Times* 3/18,26/98. *"market for gravestones":* Dunn, *Harrison to Harding,* I, 234. *Roosevelt urged Day:* Dawes, 146-47.

Roosevelt had offered the same advice to the President on March 15 (TR *Letters,* I, #957).

173–178 MAINE REPORT: *McKinley's nervousness:* GBC 3/18,20,24/98. *Conferences with opposition:* GBC 3/23,24; NY Trib 3/24,25. *Arrival of report:* Wash *Times, Eve Star,* 3/25/98; *NY Times* 3/25-26. *Cabinet:* GBC 3/25/98. *Griggs:* Ibid, 4/16/98. *Alger:* Alger to Grenville M. Dodge 3/19/98, quoted in Jacob R. Perkins, *Trails, Rails and War: The Life of General G. M. Dodge* (Indianapolis, 1927), 315-16.

Alger's increasing trend toward war made it advisable to assure the public that the Cabinet was in harmony. A statement signed by Alger—though actually prepared by Long—was given to the press after the meeting of March 29 (GBC 3/29/98).

"We are not prepared": William S. Hawk, "President McKinley, Recollections of an Intimate Friend," *Leslie's Weekly* 10/31/01. *President's message: Congr Rec,* vol 31, 3278-279. *Leakage of report:* GBC 3/25,26,28/98.

A serious leakage had previously occurred in the case of the President's Annual Message of 1897. The report of the Secretary of the Treasury, important for its effect on Wall Street, had been prematurely published in the Washington *Post* and New York *Sun.* Gage had given copies to five Cabinet members. He was satisfied that three of them—McKenna, Bliss, and Gary—were not responsible for the publication (Gage to McK 10/31/97, McK P, vol 9). The leakages of official information persisted after these three and also Sherman had resigned. Alger, Long, and Wilson were the Cabinet members who continued to serve. For confidential relationships of the correspondents with public men, see Stealey, *Twenty Years,* cited, 1-10.

178–179 EFFECT OF REPORT: *NY Times* 3/30/98; *NY Trib* 3/30/98; *For Rels,* 1898, 721. *"My whole life":* Olcott, II, 342.

180   REPLY OF SPAIN: NY *Trib* 4/1/98; *For Rels*, 1898, 727-28.

181–182   MCKINLEY'S STATE OF MIND: Mrs. Hobart, 62; *America of Yesterday*, 175, 176; GBC 3/26/98; Dawes, 148; Kohlsaat, 66.

The occasion on which Kohlsaat recalled that McKinley broke down must have been the recital given by the violoncellist Leo Stern on March 30. The Dawes journal (p 150) confirms McKinley's brief appearance on this occasion. See pp 449-50.

182–187   MESSAGE OF INTERVENTION: *Congr Rec*, vol 31, 3699-702; Alger to McK 4/5/98, McK P, vol 12; *America of Yesterday*, 176, 177-78; GBC 4/6/98; Olcott, II, 28; *NY Times* 4/7/98. *Griggs assisted:* GBC 4/16/98.

The argument of "humanity" as a ground for forcible intervention was in accord with the moral conception of "international law" then held by American legal authorities.

183   IRELAND AT WHITE HOUSE:

Ireland saw the President on April 3 and 4 (Polo to Spanish Minister 4/4/98, *Sp Corres* 1898, #117).

183–187   SITUATION IN CONGRESS: *Nation* 4/21/98; Mrs. Hobart, 60; Olcott, II, 27-28.

In the vote on the Turpie Amendment, taken on April 17, only 19 Republican senators voted to sustain a policy explicitly recommended by the Executive.

House Republicans: See Dunn, *Harrison to Harding*, I, 232-33. *"Dissuade them!":* NY Times 4/7/98.

186   PRESIDENT'S REPLY TO POWERS, 4/6/98: *For Rels*, 1898, 741. NY *World* 4/8/98, quoted in Bailey, 513.

GRANT OF ARMISTICE: Woodford to Day 4/9/98, *For Rels*, 746. The President's note and memo by Webb Hayes are contained in a special file, GBC, McK P.

188   VETO MESSAGE: Dawes, 154-55.

DISCIPLINE RESTORED IN HOUSE: See Walter Wellman, *Berkshire Eagle* 5/4/98.

189–193   PRESIDENT'S ORDEAL: GBC 4/12,13,16/98.

190   SENATOR FRYE: Information from his grandson, Leland S. Briggs. *"only fifteen minutes":* GBC 4/20/98.

191   PRESIDENT'S WALK: *America of Yesterday*, 183.

DAY APPOINTMENT: Hay to Adams 5/9/98, quoted in Thayer, II, 173. *Had hoped to retire:* Dawes, 145.

There was at no time an open breach between Sherman and the President. When Sherman fell ill during a trip to the Caribbean in 1899, his nephew-by-marriage, Colgate Hoyt, telegraphed an appeal to McKinley, who sent a warship to bring the old man home. Sherman sent a grateful acknowledgment of McKinley's constant kindness and generosity. Shortly before his death at Washington, October 22, 1900, he indirectly applied to the President for a commissionership, but his doctor advised against granting the request. The Forakers stated that Sherman's family refused to accept flowers sent from the White House at the time of his death. But McKinley, then just leaving for Canton, paid his respects to the family, and arranged to attend the services at Mansfield, Ohio. The funeral train was stopped at Canton to permit the President's car to be attached. (GBC to B. F. Montgomery 3/15/99, B. F. Montgomery to

McK 3/16/99, McK P, vol 27; Sherman to McK 3/25/99, ibid; W. M. Parker to McK 2/8/00, McK P, vol 45; Dr. W. W. Johnston to McK 2/11/00, ibid; Foraker, I, 506; Julia Foraker, above cited, 233; *NY Trib* 10/18/00; McK P, Box 213.)

191–192   DEWEY'S ORDERS: Long, *Navy*, I, 181-82; *NY Trib* 7/5,9/01.

Dewey, forced to leave Hong Kong, went to Mirs Bay and awaited the arrival of O. F. Williams from Manila. The American consul, however, had little valuable information to report. To Dewey's surprise, he returned to Manila with the Asiatic Squadron. See Dewey's statements before the Senate Committee on the Philippines (*Sen Doc* 331, 57/1, 3 parts, 1902, part 3, pp 2933, 2950).

192–193   WAR DECLARED: GBC 4/25/98; Webb C. Hayes's statement, special file, GBC, McK P.

The White House pen and inkstand are now in the Museum of The Rutherford B. Hayes Library at Fremont, Ohio.

CHAPTER 8

MANILA BAY

The best-documented history of the naval campaigns is French E. Chadwick's *The Relations of the United States and Spain: The Spanish American War* (2 vols, New York, 1911). John D. Long described the preparations of the Navy Department, and Alfred T. Mahan analyzed the strategic problems in his *Lessons of the War with Spain* (Boston, 1899). The proceedings of the Schley Court disclose in detail the movements of the Flying Squadron in the Caribbean. In considering the Sampson-Schley controversy, it should be noted that Long, Mahan, and especially Chadwick—captain of the flagship *New York*—were warm admirers of Sampson. Schley has been less fortunate in the record left by his partisans, George E. Graham, *Schley and Santiago* (Chicago, 1902), and James Parker, *Rear-Admirals Sampson, Schley and Cervera* (New York and Wash, 1910). Graham was the AP correspondent on board the *Brooklyn*, and Parker was a former lieutenant-commander in the United States Navy who had resigned to become a lawyer, and was one of counsel for Schley before the Court of Inquiry.

195   MAHAN: *America of Yesterday*, 191, 194.

196–197   SAMPSON: Long, *Navy*, I, 211-12; Chadwick, *Spanish War*, I, 21; Alfred T. Mahan, *Retrospect and Prospect* (Boston, 1902), 291.

197–198   SCHLEY: Long, *Navy*, I, 212; TR *Letters*, II, #1288.

198–201   THE WAR DEPARTMENT: Philip C. Jessup, *Elihu Root* (2 vols, New York, 1939), I, 226-27, 241-43; Lodge, *The War with Spain*, 108; *Rev of Revs* Oct/98; *NY Eve Post* 3/28/99; *NY Trib* 4/17/99, 6/12/99; *Nation* 2/13/02. See the Report of the Dodge Commission which summarizes the findings of the investigation made in 1898 (vol I, pp 107-233). Alger: *NY Times* 3/27/98; Long, II, 145; *America of Yesterday*, 188; *NY Trib* 7/20/99.

Alger's frail health was repeatedly mentioned in the press. He had a long illness early in 1898 (see McK's note to Alger 1/13/98, McK P, Letbk 90). His obituary notices stated that he had suffered for many years from valvular heart disease. (See NY *Eve Post* 1/24/07.)

Miles, "a brave peacock": Henry F. Pringle, *Theodore Roosevelt* (New York, 1931), 446. *Army bills*: Russell A. Alger, *The Spanish American War* (New York, 1901), 16-18; NY *Trib* 4/21-24/98, 5/1/98, 6/16/98.

A provision of the volunteer legislation authorized a limited recruitment from the nation at large, and resulted in the formation of three volunteer cavalry regiments. Additional legislation on May 11 provided for a volunteer brigade of engineers and a force of not more than 10,000 men "immune" to tropical diseases.

201   JOINT CONFERENCE: Nelson A. Miles, *Serving the Republic* (New York and London, 1911), 273-74; Miles, *Dodge Comm*, vol VII, 3240-264; *America of Yesterday*, 182-83. "*I do remember*": Draft of letter (McK's hand, nd), McK P, vol 34. This seems to be an answer to Alger's letter of 12/28/99 (McK P, vol 44).

202   SHAFTER: *White House call*: Information from Mr. Ingling. *Miles recommended*: Alger, 35; William R. Shafter, "The Capture of Santiago de Cuba," *The Century Magazine* Feb/99.

Corbin, asked to explain Shafter's selection, instanced his rank, ability, vigor, good judgment (NY *Herald* 6/5/98). See *Nation*, 2/13/02.

203–209   DEWEY AND MANILA: *Autobiography*, 168; NY *Herald* 5/3/98; Wash *Eve Star* 5/7/98; NY *Trib*, Extra, 5/8/98. "*Anglo-Saxon valor*": NY *Trib* 5/10/98. *The war correspondents*: NY *Herald* 5/8/98; Mark Sullivan, *The Turn of the Century in Our Times* (6 vols, New York, 1922-35), I, 318-20. *Dewey craze*: Adelbert M. and Louis M. Dewey, *The Life of George Dewey, Rear-Admiral, U.S.N.* (Westfield, Mass, 1898), 124-28; NY *Herald* 5/28/98; NY *Trib* 9/24,28/99. *President's Message*, 5/9/98: *Congr Rec*, vol 31, 4689.

210–212   TROOPS FOR PHILIPPINES: Miles to Alger 5/3/98 (notation, McK to Alger 5/4/98), *Corres Rel*, II, 635; ibid, 643 ff; Merritt to JAP 5/17/98, McK P, vol 14; NY *Trib* 5/17-19/98, 7/18/99; Wash *Eve Star* 5/17/98; James A. LeRoy, *The Americans in the Philippines* (2 vols, New York and Boston, 1914) I, 177. *President's instructions*:

While the instructions were dated May 19, 1898, the War Department did not forward them to Merritt at San Francisco until May 28 (*Corres Rel*, II, 676-79). It was evidently intended at the outset to keep the real nature of Merritt's task a secret. He was ordered on May 12 to command an expedition to the Philippines, but assigned on May 16 to the command of the new Department of the Pacific, with the confidential information that this meant the Philippines only (*Corres Rel*, II, 637, 649). However, the creation of the department was generally interpreted to mean the extension of the military organization beyond United States boundaries.

211   MOORE'S APPOINTMENT: MacFarland, *Rev of Revs*, cited.

212–214   HAWAII: Dennis, above cited, 76, quoting Hay to Day 5/3/98; Tyler Dennett, *Americans in Eastern Asia* (New York, 1922), 625-26; GBC 5/31/98, 6/8/98; Wash *Eve Star* 5/31/98; Hoar, above cited, II, 305-7; TR-Lodge, *Corres*, I, 330.

213 SPEAKER REED: See Wash *Eve Star* 5/27,28/98; NY *Eve Post* 6/27/98; Dunn, *Harrison to Harding*, I, 288-91, 298-99; McCall, *Reed*, 235-36.

215-216 GRAND ATTACK ON HAVANA: *America of Yesterday*, 188-89; Dawes, 158; GBC 5/15/98; Miles, 272-73, 275-76; Miles, *Dodge Comm*, vol VII; Eagan, *Dodge Comm*, vol VI, 2938-968.

  On May 24, Alger announced he had 75,000 men ready for Cuba, but backed down two days later (*America of Yesterday*, 196-97).

216-218 UNPREPAREDNESS: Ludington, *Dodge Comm*, vol VII, 3138-158; NY *Trib* 4/27/98; Alger, 8-9, 11, 74. *Alger's concern about coast defense:* See Alger to Chandler 10/18/97, Chandler Papers, vol 116. *President's supervision:* Dawes, 188.

218-219 WAR BOARD AND TELEGRAPH: NY *Herald* 5/22/98; Wash *Eve Star* 5/24/98; Herbert W. Wilson, *The Downfall of Spain* (Boston, 1900), 427-28. *Dispatch re Porto Rico:* Chadwick, *Spanish War*, I, 221.

220 ATTACK ON SAN JUAN: Chadwick, I, chap 7; Robley D. Evans, *A Sailor's Log* (New York, 1901), 418-21.

220-223 SCHLEY'S DELAY:

  A detailed account is given in Chadwick, I, chapters 9-11. Schley's considered defense is contained in his testimony before the Naval Court of Inquiry and his book, *Forty-five Years Under the Flag* (New York, 1904), 261-85. This book was published nearly three years after the court, which had been called at Schley's request, had given a verdict censuring him for dilatoriness and disobedience in May, 1898.

Long, *Navy*, I, 275, II, 189-94 (Appendix A); *America of Yesterday*, 232-33; Evans, 427-28. *At Santiago:* Evans, 430-32.

  The presence of Cervera's entire squadron in the harbor was confirmed— after Sampson's arrival—by a reconnaissance made by Lieutenant Victor Blue.

Impression on Brooklyn: G. E. Graham, cited, passim.

223-224 BLOCKADE OF SANTIAGO: Chadwick, I, chaps 14-16; Mahan, *Retrospect*, 306; Evans, 433, 437-41; "The Story of the Captains," *Century* May/99. See Wilson, 254-58. *Urgency for troops:* Chadwick, II, 17-18; Long, II, 8, 10.

  The description of the fighting at Guantánamo is based on the AP dispatch which was published in the *New York Tribune* on June 13, 1898.

225 MILES: *Recommended delays: Corres Rel*, I, 264; Alger, 59-61, 73-74. *Applied to accompany expedition:* Alger, 69; Miles, 275-76. *Liaison with García:* Miles, 276-80; White House memo, García to Miles, nd, McK P, vol 14; NY *Trib* 4/28,30/98, 5/27,31/98, 9/6/98.

  Lieutenant Andrew S. Rowan had carried "a message to García," later celebrated by Elbert Hubbard, on a trip to Oriente Province in late April.

225-227 SHAFTER'S EMBARKATION: John D. Miley, *In Cuba with Shafter* (New York, 1899), chaps 2, 3; *Report of Dodge Comm*; Shafter, *Dodge Comm*, vol VII; Miles, ibid; Alger, chap 6; TR, *The Rough Riders* (New York, 1904), 54-62; TR *Letters*, II, #1027, #1030; Richard Harding Davis, *The Cuban and Porto Rican Campaigns* (New York, 1898), 86-98. *Leonard Wood:*

  The Army doctor had taken the post of White House physician on the death in 1897 of Captain Newton L. Bates of the Navy Medical

Corps, who had been the McKinleys' physician during the congressional years. Wood was in turn succeeded by the Surgeon General of the Army, George M. Sternberg.

CHAPTER 9
The President and the War

228–229   MCKINLEY'S POPULARITY: GBC 6/8/98. *In England:* Osborne to McK 3/22/98, 5/17/98, McK P, vols 12, 14.

229   WAR REVENUE BILL: *NY Trib,* passim, May, June/98. *Costly delay, "Populistic" temper:* Ibid, editorials 6/6, 6/10. See Dunn, *Harrison to Harding,* I, 239-40.

RECIPROCITY WITH FRANCE:
The agreement, signed by Ambassador Jules Cambon and Commissioner John A. Kasson on May 28, was proclaimed by the President on May 30 (NY *Trib* 5/31/98).

230–231   RELATIONS WITH PRESS: James E. Pollard, *The President and the Press* (New York, 1947), 552; Ida M. Tarbell, "President McKinley in War Times," *McClure's Magazine,* July/98; S. Scovel to McK 12/22/98, McK P, vol 21; Albert Halstead, "The President at Work," *The Independent* 9/5/01; GBC, March, April/98, passim; also entries of 7/26, 7/30, 8/2/98.

The press releases were at first sometimes handed out by Secretary Porter. The article in *McClure's* was written under the misapprehension that he was responsible for the good relations with the press.

McKinley attended the Gridiron dinners in 1897 and 1898 (Dunn, *Gridiron Nights,* 61, 74).

231–232   PRESIDENT'S SAFETY: GBC, 3/25/98, 4/2/98; Bingham Coll, Box 5; Wash *Eve Star* 5/21/98. *Laughed at Griggs:* NY *Trib* 9/7/01.

232–234   COMMANDER-IN-CHIEF: *War Room:* GBC 5/3/98, 6/17/98; NY *Herald* 5/15/98; information from Mr. Ingling. *Telegraph moved:* GBC 4/22-24/98.

Mr. Ingling chuckled reminiscently over Secretary Porter's audible discussions of his private affairs in the green flannel booth.

Military direction: Dawes, 188; GBC 5/3/98, 6/8,17/98. *Long wavered:* GBC 5/15/98. *"we must not scatter":* Alger to McK 5/26/98, McK P, vol 14. *"unconditional surrender":* See p 266. *Gathmann torpedo:* Herrick to McK 7/30/98, McK P, vol 16. *Hanna's interest:* Hanna to McK 6/30/98, 7/6/98, McK P, vol 15; Croly, 280-81.

234–236   COMMISSIONS: GBC 5/15,31/98, 6/8,17/98. *Loeffler:* Information from Mr. Ingling. *Navy:* Long, I, 159. *Army:* Alger, 32-36; Corbin, *Dodge Comm,* vol VII, 3272-300; NY *Trib* 5/23/98. *Regular army depleted: Dodge Comm,* vol I, 113; Alger, 16-17. *Praise for President:* See NY *Trib* 5/4,5,27/98, 6/1/98; NY *Eve Post* 6/2/98.

The Secretary of War was glad to acknowledge that he had selected the officers of the three volunteer cavalry regiments, which included the popular Rough Riders, but minimized the considerable part he must have had in making the much criticized staff appointments.

236–237   CORBIN: *Called down by President:* GBC 5/3/98; Corbin to McK 5/3/98, McK P, vol 14; Mrs. Hobart, *Memories,* 34. *Efficiency: Dodge Comm,* vol I, 120; Dunn, *Harrison to Harding,* I, 251.

237–238   PERSONAL GLIMPSES: GBC 5/15,22/98, 6/17,19/98; Long, I, 276; I. R. T. Smith, cited, 35; Dawes, 163.

238   LARGER DECISIONS: *"keep what we want"*: Olcott, II, 165. *Terms of peace*: Dennis, 99, citing Day to Hay 6/3/98, Hay Papers; see Hay to Day 6/5/98, McK P, vol 15. *Address to Russian ambassador*: GBC 6/21/98.

239   LITTLE RELAXATION: *"You have always been a marvel"*: Osborne to McK 5/17/98, McK P, vol 14. *Dinners*: GBC 6/8,22/98. *Marine Band*: Ibid, 7/30/98. *"standing the hard work"*: McK to Helen McK 7/15/98, McK P, Letbk 90.

239–240   MCKINLEY AND JIM: J. F. McK to McK 6/5/98, McK P, Box 211; McK to J. F. McK 6/9/98, Letbk 90, to Col. C. V. Hard 6/23/98, ibid; Hard to McK 6/23/98, McK P, vol 15; GBC 6/22/98. *"straightened him up"*: McK to H. McK 7/4/98, cited. *"as dearly as his own child"*: McK to J. F. McK 11/1/99, Letbk 90.

James McKinley, as a second lieutenant of cavalry, served with distinction on the staff of General S. B. M. Young in the Philippines. He was Adjutant General of the United States Army when he retired, with the rank of Major General, in 1935. His death occurred in 1941.

CHAPTER 10
SANTIAGO BAY

The events of the Santiago campaign are set forth in the reports of Shafter and Sampson and other officers (*Annual Reports of the War Department* for 1898, vol 1, part 2; Appendix to the *Report of the Chief of the Bureau of Navigation, Annual Reports of the Navy Department* for 1898, part 2), but for enlivening detail it is necessary to consult the firsthand accounts which were later published in books and magazines, and the testimony given before the Dodge Commission and the Schley Court of Inquiry. Chadwick's *The Spanish American War*, above cited, is an excellent work of reference by a man well acquainted with the military actions, although not actually an eyewitness of either the land or the naval battle. His statements, on all points touching the chief command at Santiago Bay, have been disputed by the partisans of Schley. As in the case of the delay of the Flying Squadron in the Caribbean, the evidence for both sides is contained in the proceedings of the Schley Court.

241–242   TROOPS AND STORES FOR SHAFTER: Memo, Alger to McK 6/18/98, McK P, vol 15.

This paper twice makes the point that the cruisers must be shortly returned. A notation, initialed by McKinley, reads, "Dictated at my suggestion—the result of a previous [*sic*] agreed programme."
"unthrifty neighbor": America of Yesterday, 201.

242–244   ARMY VS. NAVY: Shafter, *Century*, cited; Miley, cited, 52-58; Alger, 49, 88; Chadwick, II, 22-26, 48-49; Long, *Navy*, II, 22-23. *Long had foreseen*: Long, II, 26-27.

On inquiry, Long had been informed by Alger that Shafter would land his own troops.

244–245   LANDING THE ARMY: Report of Capt. C. F. Goodrich, Appendix, *Bureau of Navigation*, cited, pp 685-88; Evans, above cited, 438; Shafter, *Dodge Comm*, vol VII; Miley, 59-70, 76-79; TR, *Rough Riders*, 70. *Shafter praised the Navy:* Corres Rel, I, 53-54.

245–246   LAS GUÁSIMAS: Shafter, *Dodge Comm*, vol VII; Wheeler, *Dodge Comm*, vol III, 3-56; Lawton, *Dodge Comm*, vol IV, 944-53; Shafter to Corbin 6/25/98, *Corres Rel*, I, 54-55; TR, *Rough Riders*, 73-108; R. H. Davis, above cited, 170-72; Lodge, *War*, cited, 117. See Miles, *Dodge Comm*, vol VII.

246–247   HASTY ADVANCE: Breckinridge, *Dodge Comm*, vol V, 1758-793; Miley, 84-89. *"to do it quick":* Shafter, *Dodge Comm*, vol VII.

247–250   PLAN OF ATTACK: Shafter, *Dodge Comm*, vol VII, and *Century*; Shafter to Sampson 6/26/98, quoted in Chadwick, *War*, II, 61-62. *El Caney:* Lawton, *Dodge Comm*, vol IV. *Conference at Sevilla:* Miley, 101-6. *Ignored Navy:* Ibid, 58, 67-68. *Chaffee's idea:* R. H. Davis, 181-82. *Barbed wire:*

> The use of barbed wire by the Spanish army was a matter of keen interest when it became known in the United States. (See *NY Trib* 7/10/98.)

249–252   SAN JUAN HILL: Shafter, *Century*; TR, *Rough Riders*, 113-41; R. H. Davis, 188-223; Miley, 105-15; Lodge, *War*, 124-29. *71st New York:*

> The volunteer regiments, except for the cavalry, had only black powder. The 2nd Massachusetts was withdrawn from the battle of El Caney because the smoke of their rifles made them a target. Shafter's artillery was under the same disadvantage (TR, *Rough Riders*, 104; Alger, 455. See Lodge, *War*, 120-21).

"a terrible mistake": Shafter, *Dodge Comm*, vol VII. See also Shafter, *Century*. *Discouragement:* TR, *Rough Riders*, 145-47; TR, *Autobiography*, 1265, *Letters*, II, #1034, #1036, #1037. See also R. H. Davis, 247-50.

252   SIGNAL CORPS: Report of the Chief Signal Officer, *War Dept Reports*, 1898, vol 1, part 1, pp 880-88; Miley, *In Cuba with Shafter*, 93-94; Miley, *Dodge Comm*, vol VII, 3132-240.

252–254   REACTION AT WASHINGTON: Alger, 172-79; Alger to Shafter 7/3/98, *Corres Rel*, I, 74, 75; *America of Yesterday*, 202; Long, *Navy*, II, 42, 149; Lodge to TR 7/23/98, *Corres*, I, 329; *NY Trib* 7/2-5/98; Chadwick, *War*, II, 84. See Miley, 127.

254–259   NAVAL VICTORY:

> The description of the fleet on July 3, before the alarm was given and on the appearance of Cervera's squadron, is drawn from the various accounts in "The Story of the Captains," *The Century Magazine*, May, 1899. It was a singular fact that the *Brooklyn* was the only American vessel alerted on the preceding evening by the suspicion that the Spanish ships might be firing up. (See Schley, *Under the Flag*, 296-97; *Schley Court*, II, 1384; Graham, cited, 275-78.) The signal quartermaster of the *Iowa*, however, had been sufficiently alarmed to leave the flags signaling "Enemy's ships coming out" on the halyards, ready to hoist (Evans, 441-42). For Schley's testimony about the battle, see *Schley Court*, II, 1384 ff. The *Gloucester* had formerly been Mr. J. P. Morgan's *Corsair*.

Sampson's return: Rear-Admiral W. T. Sampson, "The Atlantic Fleet in the Spanish War," *Century*, Apr/99; Evans, 448; Schley, 310-11; James Parker, above cited, 327; Graham, 339-43; "The Story of the Captains," cited.

Schley's gallantry: G. E. Graham, 294, 355-59; testimony of Lt. Edward McCauley, Lt. Edward Simpson, Carpenter G. M. Warford, Chief Boatswain W. L. Hill, *Schley Court*, I. *Announcement of victory*: Sampson to Long 7/4/98, *Corres Rel*, I, 81; Long, II, 42; Schley, 316-17; James Parker, 218-19. For Sampson's report of the battle, 7/15/98, see Appendix, *Bureau of Navigation*, pp 506-11. For Schley's report to Sampson, 7/6/98, ibid, 517-20. *Conduct of Americans*: Long, II, 39; Evans's report, Appendix, *Bureau of Navigation*, p 539. *Schley's attitude*: Schley, 318-20, 322-26, 335.

The report which Schley made to Sampson was formally correct, but repeated references to "the squadron under your command" have a suspiciously mocking ring.

259   SAMPSON WITHERED AWAY: See *America of Yesterday*, 208-9, for a pathetic description which Long wrote in December, 1898. Sampson died in 1902.

CHAPTER 11
The Price of Delay

The trends of American public sentiment during July and early August, 1898, have been mainly drawn from the New York newspapers, the *Tribune* and *The Evening Post*. Many references have been omitted to the chronologically arranged *Correspondence Relating to the War with Spain*, volume I. The failure of supplies for the Fifth Army Corps is covered in the references for Chapter 13.

262   SUFFERINGS OF WOUNDED: *NY Trib* 7/13/98, 8/9/98; cable from Miss Clara Barton, ibid, 7/7/98; Chadwick, *War*, II, 102-5.
        FEEDING CUBANS: Miles, *Dodge Comm*, vol VII; Alger, 293; Chadwick, II, 198-99.
262–263 SHAFTER'S DISABILITY: Shafter, *Dodge Comm*, vol VII.
263–264 PRESSURE FROM PRESIDENT: *Conference of July 4*: Corbin to Shafter 7/4/98, *Corres Rel*, I, 82.

For samples of tone taken by Alger himself, see his telegrams to Shafter of July 4 and 9 (*Corres Rel*, I, 82, 114).

Miles sent: Miles, above cited, 282-83.

The *New York Tribune*, July 8, stated that the decision to send Miles to Cuba was reached by the President after a long conference attended by Miles, Alger, Long, and the members of the Naval War Board. The Washington correspondent of the *Tribune* marked Miles's "elated demeanor," as he left the White House.

Miles not to supersede: Alger, 204; Corbin to Shafter 7/8/98, *Corres Rel*, I, 110; *NY Trib* 7/8/98. *Information published*: *NY Trib* 7/12/98.

264   ARMY VS. NAVY: Alger, 188-91, 224-41; Corbin to Shafter 7/5/98, *Corres Rel*, I, 91; Long, II, 23-26; *America of Yesterday*, cited, 203-4; Chadwick, cited, II, 191-204.

Chadwick, in spite of Shafter's obstructiveness, had a personal liking for the gruff General (Chadwick, II, 6).

264–267 PRESIDENT'S DIRECTION: Corbin to Shafter 7/9/98, *Corres Rel*, I, 116, 119; Olcott, II, 50; Dawes, 164; Shafter, *Dodge Comm*, vol VII. *Returning Spanish army*: Memo, vol 21, McK P; Alger, 197-98; *NY Trib* 7/24/99. *Emphatic negative*: Alger to Shafter 7/13/98, *Corres Rel*, I, 134. *Official advice of yellow fever*: Miles to Alger 7/13/98, ibid, 134. *Emergency Cabinet meeting*:

America of Yesterday, 203-4; Corbin to Shafter 7/13/98, *Corres Rel*, I, 135; Alger to Shafter 7/13/98, ibid, 134; to Miles 7/13/98, ibid, 134-35, 136.

267   NEWSPAPER CORRESPONDENTS:

The flood of newspaper criticism of Shafter's campaign began in the middle of July, but a few dispatches got through at an earlier date. See Richard Harding Davis's sensational story in *The New York Herald*, July 7, 1898. The quotation "natural allies . . . Madrid" is from a London dispatch to the *New York Tribune*, July 10, 1898.

268–269   SUSPENSE AT WASHINGTON: Alger, 214-16; *Corres Rel*, I, 142-50. *"Next is Porto Rico"*: NY *Trib* 7/15/98. *President withheld congratulations*: Dawes, 164.

The President conferred with Alger and other Cabinet members until early on Saturday morning. Corbin was called in shortly before midnight.

269–270   SURRENDER: *Concessions to Spain*: Miley, *In Cuba with Shafter*, cited, 166-68, 178.

The delays in arranging the terms are explained in Miley's account. He was a participant in the conferences with the Spanish commissioners, appointed to act with Generals Wheeler and Lawton on behalf of the United States.

Shafter had expected the surrender of some 8,000 troops. The Spanish offer of large additional territory and its army of occupation was a complete surprise. In all, nearly 23,500 prisoners were included in the surrender. Cuban elements did not desire transportation to Spain, but provision had to be made for wives and children of Spanish officers, and a number of priests and Sisters of Charity. Nearly 23,000 embarked from Santiago on ships of the *Trasatlantica* line in August and September, 1898 (Chadwick, II, 264; Qm Gen's Report, 1898, *War Dept Reports*, 1898, vol 1, part 1). Credit for the efficient performance of the War Department in this case belongs to Secretary Alger's wartime appointee, Colonel Frank J. Hecker. See pp 294-95.

Ceremonies: Shafter, *Century*; Miley, 185-86. *Scovel*: Shafter to Alger 7/24/98, *Corres Rel*, I, 176-77. *Shafter's thoughts*: Shafter, *Dodge Comm*, vol VII; Shafter to Corbin 7/23/98, *Corres Rel*, I, 172; to Rev. Dr. C. O. Brown, quoted in NY *Trib* 9/9/99.

270–271   WASHINGTON MISLED: Shafter to Corbin 7/18,23,25/98, *Corres Rel*, I, 158, 174, 178. *Spanish soldiers*: Ibid, 8/4/98, 204. *"normal conditions"*: NY *Trib* 7/20/98, quoting Sternberg. *Guantánamo*:

Yellow fever began to appear in the marines' camp in the middle of August (*Navy Dept Reports*, 1898, part 1, p 787).

271–272   ACTUAL CONDITIONS:

Shafter's troops were unfitted for any physical effort by recurrent bouts of tropical malaria, combined with exposure and malnutrition (see TR, *Rough Riders*, 194-99). The evidence is that they went to pieces very fast after occupying the trenches. Colonel Weston thought that their vitality had already been lowered by the heat in Florida (testimony before the *Beef Court*, vol I, pp 162-63).

Letters reporting: Charles Dick, C. V. Hard to McK 7/25/98, McK P, vol 16. The notation that they were received August 12 is in the President's hand. Dick had written in a less alarming vein July 18 and 20.

272–273 INSTRUCTIONS FOR GOVERNMENT: *Corres Rel*, I, 159-61.

273–274 CUBANS:

American prejudice was strongly reflected in the news dispatches in July. (See NY *Eve Post* 7/19,21/98; editorials, NY *Trib* 7/7,20/98.) The Cubans' inadequate performance on July 1 was a basic cause of resentment. They had, however, been helpful in Shafter's landing and on scouting expeditions (Breckinridge, *Dodge Comm*, vol V). A small body, assigned to Lawton on July 1, had done good service at El Caney (Miley, 105). Cubans had also been of great assistance at Guantánamo (Sampson to Long 6/18/98, McK P, vol 15).

García:

American feeling was briefly excited by reports of a letter from García to Shafter complaining that he had not been asked to attend the ceremonies of surrender. This letter was soon found to be a forgery (see NY *Trib* 7/23,24/98). The fact was that Shafter had verbally invited García to witness the formal surrender, but García had declined to enter Santiago because the Spanish civil officials had not been removed (Shafter, *Century*; Shafter to Alger 7/29/98, *Corres Rel*, I, 185). The Cuban patriot must have gained a different impression of Americans during a visit to Washington in the following December, when he was most warmly received and entertained at the White House. He again met Shafter at the Gridiron Club dinner, attended in 1898 by many notables, including the President (Dawes, 175). García died suddenly at the Raleigh Hotel in Washington on December 11, 1898.

274–275 TRANSPORTS: NY *Eve Post* 7/20/98, 8/1/98; NY *Trib* 7/20/98, 8/1/98; Corbin to Shafter 8/1/98, *Corres Rel*, I, 190.

One reason for the overcrowding on the *Seneca* was the refusal of the new army hospital ship *Relief* to take fever suspects on board (Shafter to Alger 8/3/98, *Corres Rel*, I, 199). The rule was always strictly enforced by the Navy.

275–277 RECALL OF THE ARMY: Alger, 261-65; Shafter to and from Alger and Corbin 8/1-4/98, *Corres Rel*, I, 189 ff.

Shafter had once previously suggested the speedy recall of his troops (Shafter to Corbin 7/23, *Corres Rel*, I, 173). Anxiety also appeared in his dispatches of July 29 and August 3 complaining of the Medical Department (*Corres Rel*, I, 186, 197-98).

Release of round robin: TR, *Autobiography*, 267-68; TR, *Rough Riders*, 203-4; Alger, 265-73; Shafter, *Century. President "excited and indignant":* Alger, 271.

Responsibility for the publication was never officially fixed. Roosevelt gave Shafter full credit for the indiscretion. Shafter disclaimed all knowledge, and condemned it as "a foolish, improper thing to do" (Shafter to Alger 8/4/98, cited in Alger, 271). Obviously, neither man was entirely frank. Wood and Roosevelt were admittedly desirous of bringing pressure on the War Department. Roosevelt took the AP correspondent with him when he called on Shafter with the letter which he had written himself. He said that Shafter "shoved" the letter toward the correspondent, and the correspondent said that it had been "handed" to him by Shafter (NY *Trib* 8/5/98). In his overwrought state of mind, Shafter apparently succumbed to the dominance of two forceful personalities, and the acquisitiveness of a newspaper reporter eager for a scoop.

Besides sending the telegram of August 3, Shafter arranged for a verbal report to the President at the earliest possible date. His emissary, Lieutenant-Colonel Charles Dick, left Santiago on August 4, but was quarantined for five days in Louisiana and did not reach Washington until the 14th (Dick to McK 8/14/98, McK P, vol 17).

CHAPTER 12
THE SUBMISSION OF SPAIN

278–280 MILES IN CUBA: Miles, *Dodge Comm*, vol VII, *Serving the Republic*, 293. *Refused money, Porto Rico*: Corbin, *Dodge Comm*, vol VII. *With Shafter*: NY Trib 7/14/98; Shafter to Corbin 8/1/98, *Corres Rel*, I, 218-19; Wash Post 8/25/98; Shafter, *Dodge Comm*, vol VII. *Preparations for Porto Rico*: Miles to and from Alger and Corbin 7/17-20/98, *Corres Rel*, I, 280-97; McK to Long 7/20/98, ibid, 297-98; Alger, 304; Chadwick, *War*, II, 266-83. *President's nephews*: Guy V. Henry to McK 7/13/98, C. V. Hard to McK 7/25/98, C. V. Hard to Corbin 8/3/98, [J. C.] Gilmore to Corbin 8/3/98, McK P, vol 16.

280–281 PORTO RICO: *Landing*: NY Trib 7/26,27/98; Corbin to Brooke, Alger to Miles, Miles to Alger, 7/26/98, *Corres Rel*, I, 318, 320, 322; Miles to Alger 7/30, ibid, 337-38; Miles, *Serving the Republic*, 296-97; Alger, 304-5.

Miles gave two explanations for his change, the importance of deceiving the enemy and the failure of his landing craft to arrive. He was also influenced by the information supplied during the voyage by one of his aides—Lieutenant H. H. Whitney, U.S.A., who had traveled through Porto Rico in June, disguised as a British seaman (Chadwick, *War*, II, 285, 358-59).

Campaign: Miles's Report, *War Dept Reports*, 1898, vol 1, part 2, pp 1-38; R. H. Davis, above cited, chap 8; Alger, 307-17; Lodge, *War*, 188. *"with wild enthusiasm"*: Miles to Alger 7/29/98, *Corres Rel*, I, 330. *President's rebuke to Alger*: GBC 7/30/98.

281–282 OVERTURES FROM SPAIN: *For Rels*, 1898, 202-3; GBC 7/26/98. *Cambon's report on call of July 26*: For Rels, 1898, 206-7.

The diplomatic exchanges with the Madrid government were conducted through the Spanish ambassador to France.

282–286 THE AMERICAN REPLY: *For Rels*, 1898, 211-12. *Cambon's further report, call of July 30*: For Rels, 1898, 213-14; GBC 7/29-30/98; Olcott, II, 61-63.

Among the men whom Olcott interviewed in preparing his book were Day, Griggs, Long, and Cortelyou.

Day "weak" on Philippines: TR-Lodge, *Corres*, I, 313, 324. *His objections*: Day to McK 10/28/98, McK P, vol 19. *President had his way*: Dawes, 166. *President's memorandum*: McK P, vol 16; GBC 7/31/98.

The important Cabinet consultations occurred during one of Secretary Porter's many absences from Washington. He had gone to New York to meet his wife, who was returning from Cuba. She had done relief work with the Red Cross at Siboney, Caney, and Santiago (NY Trib 7/30/98).

283–285 THE PHILIPPINES: Day to Hay 6/14/98, quoted in Dennis, 99. *Dewey's assurances:* Appendix, *Bureau of Navigation,* cited, p 103. *Revolutionary republic:* Memo for War Dept from Navy, *Corres Rel,* II, 720. *Pratt:* Day to Pratt 6/16/99, *Treaty Papers,* p 354; LeRoy, I, 180-81, 187. *"utterly removed" the fear:* Long, *Navy,* II, 110.

286–289   *Negotiations: Cambon's report, call of August 3:* For Rels, 1898, 216-17. *Call of August 9:* For Rels, 1898, 220-21. *The protocol:* For Rels, 1898, 221-22.

The idea of drafting a protocol had originated with Day (Olcott, II, 70). *Day's notes:* Day to McK 11/18,19/98, McK P, vol 21.

Cambon's dispatches are, of course, translations, and direct quotations from them represent the sense, rather than the actual wording, of what was said. Day's notes were made at the time of the conversations, and were transcribed after correction by the President.

289–290   SIGNING THE PROTOCOL: GBC 8/12/98; NY *Trib* 8/13/98.

The photograph of the "signing" by Francis B. Johnston was actually taken a week later (NY *Trib* 8/20/98). General Corbin appears among the spectators, although not actually present on August 12. On April 17, 1899, the participants were again asked to pose for a painting by the French artist Théobald Chartran (GBC appointment book, 1899). This picture was given to the White House by Henry C. Frick and still hangs in the ground-floor corridor (information from Mrs. Ann C. Whitman).

CHAPTER 13

THE WAR DEPARTMENT

292–293   TRANSPORTS: GBC 8/3,4/98; Alger to Shafter 8/1/98, *Corres Rel,* I, 190; NY *Trib* 8/3,4/98.

293–295   QUARTERMASTER'S DEPARTMENT: Qm Gen's Report, 1898, cited; *Report of Dodge Comm;* Ludington, *Dodge Comm,* vol VII. *Purchase of ships:* Alger, 456; Alger to F. J. Hecker 6/20/98 (copy), Root Papers; NY *Trib* 6/25/98.

The legislation requested by Alger was passed on July 7. The division of transportation was created on July 18, but not published until a month later (Qm Gen's Report, cited). *The Evening Post* of New York had reports on August 3 and 22 of friction in the Quartermaster's Department. Frank J. Hecker had long been associated with Alger, and had managed his presidential canvass at the Republican convention of 1888 (NY *Trib* 6/14,20/88). Theodore Roosevelt knew Hecker's good business reputation, but, as President, hesitated to appoint him to the Panama Canal Commission because of criticisms made of his performance at the War Department. (TR, *Letters,* III, #2655.) After inquiry, Hecker was appointed. Roosevelt called him the "best man I got" on the Commission (TR, *Letters,* IV, #3431).

The System: Eagan, *Dodge Comm,* vol VI.

295–297   SHORTAGES IN CUBA: *Report of Dodge Comm;* Breckinridge, *Dodge Comm,* vol V; Roosevelt, ibid, 2255-272; Weston, vol VI, 3106-115; Miley, *In Cuba with Shafter,* cited, 87-88; R. H. Davis, cited, 173-77. *Shafter's staff:* Shafter, *Dodge Comm,* vol VII. *Weston's good work:* NY *Trib* 8/6/98; TR, *Rough Riders,* 110-11, 184; Report of Capt. Goodrich, Appendix, *Bureau of Navigation,* p 688. *Medical supplies:* See NY *Trib* 8/8/98.

297–300 SUBSISTENCE DEPARTMENT: Alger, 379-80; *Report of Dodge Comm. Army diet: Report of Beef Court*, vol II, pp 1855-895; *Report of Dodge Comm. Eagan's plans:* Eagan, *Dodge Comm*, vol VI. *Corbin's opposition:* Ibid. Cf Corbin to Merritt 6/9/98, *Corres Rel*, II, 695. *Canned beef:* Eagan, *Dodge Comm*, vols VI, VII; Weston, *Beef Court*, vol I, pp 151-65; II, pp 1795-1804, 1814-818; Alger, 385, 388-89. *Defense of Eagan's purchases:* Alger, 594-95.

300–304 MEDICAL DEPARTMENT: *Personnel inadequate:* Alger, 12.

    This was a standard—and valid—excuse, and it was volubly put forward by the Surgeon General. A long, self-vindicating letter from Sternberg was published in the New York *Medical Record* of August 6, 1898, in reply to sharp comment on conditions on the *Seneca*, which had appeared in the July 30 issue. Another letter enumerating his excuses was addressed to the *Philadelphia Medical Journal*, and was published on August 20.

Women nurses: Dr. Anita N. McGee, *Dodge Comm*, vol VII, 3168-181.

    Dr. McGee, who was in charge of the D.A.R. project, had endorsed only graduate nurses, but the same high standard was not maintained in the case of the "immune" nurses who were sent to Santiago in mid-July or those engaged in the emergency at Montauk Point. Trained or untrained, the women were paid a monthly wage of $30, out of which they had to pay $4 for laundry. In late August, when several hundred of them had been employed, Surgeon General Sternberg bowed to the inevitable and made Dr. McGee an acting assistant surgeon, with rank of first lieutenant, in charge of matters relating to women in the Army, especially nurses.

Sternberg's circular: Alger, 412-14. *Divisional hospitals: Report of Dodge Comm. Breakdown of inspection:* Ibid. *Breckinridge in Cuba:* R. H. Davis, 258.

    Breckinridge's assignment to Shafter was obviously a move in the struggle between Alger and Miles.

Invalid diet:

    Alger's order of August 10, authorizing the expenditure of $.60 a day per soldier, was neglectfully handled by the Medical Bureau (NY *Eve Post* 8/26/98; NY *Trib* 8/27/98; Detroit *Sunday News-Tribune* 8/28/98;

304–305 ALGER AND ROOSEVELT: TR, *Autobiography*, 278-79; NY *Trib* 8/5/98.

    Cortelyou noted on August 10 that the President dictated a letter for Alger to send to Roosevelt. This may have been the original of the "manly letter" which was handed to Roosevelt on his return from Cuba.

306–312 MONTAUK: Alger, 259-62, 424-32, 436-48; Alger to Shafter 7/28/98, *Corres Rel*, I, 185; *Report of Dodge Comm*; correspondence between Surgeon General's office and Col. W. H. Forwood 8/4/98-9/22/98, *Dodge Comm*, vol II, 739-770; letter from W. H. Baldwin, NY *Trib* 8/9/98; Louise E. Hogan to McK 8/25/98, McK P, vol 17. See also L. E. Hogan to GBC [Sept?] 98, vol 18, [Oct?] 98, vol 20, and 2/2/98, vol 24. *Wheeler's supplies:* NY *Trib* 8/26,28/98; Eagan, *Dodge Comm*, vol VI. *President's instructions:* NY *Trib* 9/4/98.

    Wheeler had the benefit of advice from Colonel Weston, who returned to the United States in early August and was assigned to Montauk, though physically unfit to work. Weston had been taken sick on the way to

Porto Rico under orders from Miles, detaching him from Shafter's command. (Weston, *Beef Court*, vol II, pp 1825-26; *NY Eve Post* 8/16/98.) *"hysteric nonsense"*: TR-Lodge, *Corres*, I, 344. *"best camp I ever saw"*: Shafter, *Dodge Comm*, vol VII. *Western town*: *NY Trib* 9/9/98. *McKinley's visit*: *NY Trib* 9/4/98; TR *Letters*, II, #1060. *Roosevelt and the War Department*: Pringle, *Roosevelt*, 201-2; TR-Lodge, *Corres*, I, 338, 347-48; *Rev of Revs*, Oct/98.

312–314   MCKINLEY AND ALGER: Spencer Borden to McK 8/22/98, McK P, vol 17; GBC 8/23/98; Mrs. Hobart, *Memories*, 67.

314–316   WAR INVESTIGATING COMMISSION: *Alger's request, President's address*: *Dodge Comm*, vol I, 5-6. *"consecrated self-righteousness"*: Detroit *Sunday News-Tribune* 9/11/98. *Dodge reluctant to serve*: Perkins, above cited, 323. *Exemption promised*: *NY Trib* 1/14/99. *"Alger Relief Commission"*: *Congr Rec*, vol 32, 678.

The chief accusations against Alger were connected with the selection of the camp sites and the award of the beef contracts. The Dodge Commission could find no evidence of dishonesty in either case (*Report*, vol I, 116). Its censure of Alger for "want of grasp" seems fair to a later judgment, although it was too mild for the prejudices of the time. The report was made public in February, 1899, but there was delay in issuing the eight volumes, which included testimony and correspondence. The printing of 5,000 copies, on which the President and General Dodge had agreed, was held up in the late spring of 1899 on the score of the expense. General Dodge was informed that the real reason was hesitancy to make the evidence available to Germany, a large purchaser of American meats (Perkins, 328; *NY Trib* 5/29/99).

316–317   MILES'S ATTACK: J. D. Whelpley in Kansas City *Star*, quoted in *NY Eve Post* 8/24/98, Wash *Post* 8/25/98, *NY Trib* 8/30/98. *Statement on return*: *NY Eve Post* 9/7,8/98; *NY Trib*, Chi *Trib*, 9/8/98. *"embalmed beef"*: Miles, *Dodge Comm*, vol VII.

The Dodge Commission may have deliberately postponed asking for Miles's testimony. There were rumors that he was offended by the delay. In the end, he professed reluctance to speak, and agreed to appear only on the personal solicitation of General Dodge. (See W. E. Curtis, Chi *Record* 9/30/98.)

W. H. Daly: See testimony, *Dodge Comm*, vol VII, 3707-736. *Effect on Eagan*: Alger, 380; testimony at Eagan court-martial, *NY Eve Post* 1/26/99, *NY Trib* 1/27/99.

317–319   EAGAN'S REPLY: *Dodge Comm*, vol VII; Alger, 380-83; *NY Trib* 1/13/99. Since the commission's version of the statement was expurgated, Eagan's insulting references to Miles can be found only in the press. It appears from testimony given at the court-martial that the newspapers did not have all the offensive material that was actually read before the commission. Eagan's own copy of the statement, deposited with the commission and later returned to him, had disappeared by the time of his court-martial.

The court-martial: *NY Eve Post* 1/25,26/99.

The delay had been critically noticed by the *New York Tribune* on January 17. This newspaper was vehement in attacks on Eagan and regrets for the President's clemency. (See issues of 2/2,8/99, 8/12/99.) In 1900, Eagan was retired on his own application, and the unexpired portion of his suspension from duty was remitted. John F. Weston, who had been in acting charge of the Subsistence Bureau, succeeded to the office of Commissary General (*NY Trib* 12/7/00).

Major W. H. Daly, whose report to Miles had started the "embalmed beef" scandal, presently shot himself at his home in Pittsburgh (*NY Trib* 6/10/01).

319–321 MILITARY COURT OF INQUIRY:
On February 20, before the first meeting of the court, the President read to the members a list of twenty points as a guide to their investigation. The list concluded with three admonishments: If the packers of the country were guilty, it must be known; if commissary officers were guilty, it must be known; if any officer of the army were guilty, it must be known (2/20/99, McK P, vol 26).
Report of Beef Court, vol II, cited. *Weakness of Miles's case*: H. Adams, *Letters*, 216. *Widespread use of chemicals*: See editorials, *NY Trib* 1/25/99, 12/9/00. *Eagan forgetful*:
Eagan's poorest showing before the Beef Court was his confusion about the length of time that the beef was guaranteed to keep fresh after leaving refrigeration. (See G. M. Dodge to H. V. Boynton 3/28/99, McK P, vol 27.)
Censure of canned beef purchases:
Nevertheless, with a small allowance for wastage, Eagan's 7,000,000 rations were all consumed, partly as an army travel ration, partly by destitute Cubans (Alger, 395).
Charges the court was packed: See *NY Trib* 5/9,11/99. *Appeals to President to endorse reports*: G. M. Dodge to McK 4/20/99, McK P, vol 29; H. V. Boynton to McK 4/25/99, ibid.

321–322 POLITICAL IMPLICATIONS: H. Adams, *Letters*, 203, 217; Perkins, cited, 325-27; G. M. Dodge to H. V. Boynton 3/28/99, McK P, vol 27.
Dodge wrote "I think someone should go to the President. This attack is not on beef—it is on the administration." According to Perkins, McKinley considered relieving Miles of his command, but was dissuaded from doing so on the ground that the action would play into the hands of his political enemies. An undated memorandum (McK P, vol 23) asserting the President's power to select the Commanding General of the Army, suggests that McKinley had weighed the subject carefully.
Hanna enraged by Lee: Hanna to McK 4/1/99, McK P, vol 28.

CHAPTER 14
DESTINY IN THE PACIFIC

323–328 THE PHILIPPINE QUANDARY: *"If old Dewey"*: Kohlsaat, 68. *Pressure groups*: Julius W. Pratt, *Expansionists of 1898* (Baltimore, 1951), 267-78, 290-315. *"a town meeting controversy"*: NY Eve Post 8/27/98.
The Philippine section of the protocol had been dictated by McKinley's desire to acquire full information on the subject without, as Dawes understood from a conversation on July 30, "the consideration involving

the loss of any present advantage" (Dawes, 166). Dawes believed that the American public would not have tolerated a hasty settlement of the question (Dawes to McK 8/10/98, McK P, vol 16).

Geographical unity: Statement of R. B. Bradford 10/14/98, *Treaty Papers,* pp 472-90. *The colonial powers: Hay to Day* 7/14,28/98, A. D. White to Day 7/30/98, Day to A. D. White 8/15/98, cited by Dennis, 93-96, 99; Bemis, *Diplomatic History,* 464-65; Dennis, 81. *Foreman article:* John Foreman, "Spain and the Philippine Islands," *The Contemporary Review,* London, July/98.

McKinley had read this article on August 1 (GBC 8/1/98). Foreman described the Filipinos as "pliant" in character. Former Consul O. F. Williams, now once more resident at Manila, had written that the insurgents were "submissive," and friendly to the United States. After the formation of the provisional government on June 12, Williams reported Aguinaldo's personal assurances that he and his friends were hoping that the islands would be held as a United States colony (O. F. Williams to Day 6/16/98, *Treaty Papers,* pp 329-30).

McKinley's matured objections to an American protectorate were expressed in his Annual Message of 1899 (*Congr Rec,* vol 33, 24-37), and his Letter of Acceptance of his second nomination, published September 8, 1900 (*Proceedings of the Twelfth Republican National Convention,* Philadelphia, 1900, pp 156-79). These opinions could not be expressed in the Annual Message of 1898, which was sent to Congress on December 5, five days before the Treaty of Paris was signed. The treaty was transmitted to the Senate a month later with only a brief message.

328-332   THE PEACE COMMISSIONERS:

Mr. Justice White was for some days believed to have agreed to serve. As a Roman Catholic, he was undoubtedly under heavy pressure to accept. Archbishop John Ireland had seen the President on August 19 (*NY Trib* 8/20/98), and Cardinal James Gibbons wrote commending the appointment to McKinley on August 22 (McK P, vol 17).

Senator Davis at St. Paul and Senator Frye at Boston had recently been quoted as favorable to expansion in the Pacific (*NY Eve Post* 7/15/98; *NY Trib* 8/28/98). An article of imperialistic trend appeared over Whitelaw Reid's signature in the current issue of *The Century Magazine.*

For a protest against appointing senators, see the letter from W. E. Chandler to the President, August 17, 1898 (McK P, vol 17). It was reported that objections were made in executive session by Senators Hoar, Bacon, and Vest (*NY Trib* 12/8/98).

President's instructions: For Rels 1898, 904-8.

Washington at this time maintained that Manila was held by right of conquest as well as by virtue of the protocol. The contention was later discarded on the unanimous advice of the peace commissioners.

Senator Gray was not present at the conference with the President or at the White House dinner. He was detained in Philadelphia by legal business, and joined the other commissioners in New York in time to sail on September 17 (*NY Trib* 9/15-17/98).

President appeared relieved: GBC 9/16/98.

331   MERRITT: See Albert G. Robinson, *The Philippines, the War and the People* (New York, 1901), 56-57.

Before leaving the United States, Merritt had had his force designated the Eighth Army Corps, and obtained authority to transfer its command. This devolved on General Otis on August 23 (*Corres Rel*, II, 701, 703, 705-8). Merritt's request to return home was dated August 26 (ibid, 764). See his reference to "the prestige and importance of my mission" (6/22/98, ibid, 710).

332-334   POLITICAL WORRIES: *McKinley's hard week*: GBC 9/17/98. *Hanna "milked the country"*: Croly, 293. *"anomalous position"*:

The President dictated his thoughts on this subject as part of a personal letter to Hobart, but ultimately omitted them (GBC 9/19/98).

334-336   GENERAL GREENE'S ADVICE:

A short memo, written August 27, 1898, was among the papers which Merritt submitted to the American commissioners at Paris. Greene's important memo for the President is also included in *A Treaty of Peace and Accompanying Papers*, pp 404-29. It was partly based on conversations with Señor Felipe Agoncillo, emissary from Aguinaldo to the Washington authorities. Greene, who spoke Spanish, had invited Agoncillo to travel with him to Washington. The President declined to recognize Agoncillo in an official capacity, but agreed to receive him informally. The meeting took place on October 2, with Adee acting as interpreter. Agoncillo, who was accompanied by his secretary, later went to Paris to try to obtain a hearing before the American peace commissioners. The attempt was unsuccessful. The President had refused to commend the Filipinos to Judge Day (Memo, F. V. Greene to Hay 2/3/00, McK P, vol 45; Hay to Day 10/4/98, McK P, vol 18).

Hanna's interview: NY Trib 10/1/98. *Dewey's dispatch*: to Long 8/29/98, *Treaty Papers*, p 383-84.

336-337   THE MILITARY COMMANDERS: *Thomas M. Anderson*: "Our Rule in the Philippines," N Amer Rev, Feb/00. See *Senate Document* 208, 56/1, 3 parts, 1900, for correspondence with Aguinaldo and other relevant papers. *Merritt*: Testimony at Paris, *Treaty Papers*, pp 362-70. For a documented discussion of the subject, see LeRoy, I, 219-25.

Dewey's naïveté was revealed in his testimony before the Senate Committee on the Philippines in 1902 (*Sen Doc* 331, 57/1).

Cheerful news: Otis to Corbin 9/16/98, *Corres Rel*, II, 791.

337-338   BRYAN'S CALL: Signed statement by Lyman J. Gage 9/24/98, McK P, vol 18. *Not happy in army*: J. W. Keifer to McK 9/10/98, McK P, vol 17. *Efforts for his release*: McK P, vols 17, 18, passim.

Bryan finally resigned on December 10, 1898 (R. C. Ainsworth to Root 5/25/00, McK P, vol 49). The Third Nebraska was shortly sent to Cuba, and served there until April 7, 1899 (*Corres Rel*, I, 603). For reported circumstances of Bryan's enlistment, see *New York Tribune* (10/4/00).

⎰338-341,⎱ THE PEACE NEGOTIATIONS:
⎱342-343⎰   The official correspondence with the United States commissioners is contained in *Foreign Relations*, 1898, pp 904-66. For private letters to the President from Reid and Day, see McKinley Papers, vols 18-21. See also McKinley to Day, October 25, vol 19. The making of the Treaty of

Paris is discussed in detail by LeRoy (I, chap 9) and Chadwick (*War,* II, chap 21). Some interesting facts are added by Royal Cortissoz in his biography *The Life of Whitelaw Reid* (2 vols, New York, 1921).

The unoccupied atolls of Wake Island were appropriated by an American naval vessel in January, 1899. The United States subsequently purchased from Spain two small islands, near the Philippines but not included in the cession. Spain sold the Carolines and the Ladrones or Marianas, exclusive of Guam, to Germany in 1899.

Hay held up instructions: Hay to McK 10/27/99, McK P, vol 19. *"little room for negotiation":* Day to McK 10/28/99, ibid.

341–342 PRESIDENT'S WESTERN TOUR: *"the courage of destiny"; "blessings . . . beyond calculation":* NY Trib 10/12/98. *"new markets":* NY Trib 10/14/98. *Speech at Omaha:* NY Trib 10/13/98.

343–345 MCKINLEY ACCEPTS THE INEVITABLE: *With fatalism:* J. G. Schurman, *Philippine Affairs; A Retrospect and An Outlook,* An Address (New York, 1904), 1-3. *With religious conviction:* Olcott, II, 109-11, citing article from *The Christian Advocate* 1/22/03. *As a duty:* Additional instructions to peace commissioners 10/28/98, 11/13/98, Letter of Acceptance, 9/8/00, cited, pp 165-66; instructions to Philippine [Schurman] Commission 1/21/99, *Sen Doc* 208, 56/1, pp 149-50; instructions to Taft Philippine Commission 4/7/00, *War Dept Reports,* 1900, vol I, part 1, pp 72-76. *"a golden apple of discord":* Annual Message, 1899.

345–347 SITUATION AT MANILA: *Americans hated:* Robinson, cited, 57-59, 384-85; T. M. Anderson, cited; Leroy, I, 267-69; NY Trib (Hong Kong dispatch via London) 8/30/98. *Anarchy on Luzon:*

Dewey's dispatch had been forwarded to the President at Chicago on October 18 (McK P, vol 19).

CHAPTER 15
THE GOLDEN APPLE OF DISCORD

348–349 VISIT TO ATLANTA: NY *Eve Post* 12/15,19/98; NY *Trib* 12/16,18/98; Clark Howell to H. Kohlsaat 12/22/21, quoted in Kohlsaat, 24-26.

The suggestion of national decoration of Confederate graves had come from Clark Howell, the editor of *The Atlanta Constitution,* who had learned to know McKinley during the Thomasville visit in 1895. McKinley had made Howell's father a member of the War Investigating Commission. Misleading reports that McKinley had had "a Confederate badge" pinned to his lapel caused some criticism in the North. (See CBC 1/3/99.)

349–350 OUTLOOK FOR THE TREATY: William S. Holt, *Treaties Defeated by the Senate* (Baltimore, 1933), 176. *Bryan:* Paxton Hibben, *The Peerless Leader: William Jennings Bryan* (New York, 1929), 222; Morris R. Werner, *Bryan* (New York, 1929), 121.

Lodge, writing on December 23, did not expect "serious opposition" (TR-Lodge, *Corres,* I, 372). Bryan's visit to Washington closely followed his resignation from the army. Thereafter, he devoted himself to attacks on the expansionist program, especially the acquisition of the Philippines. *Hoar's opposition:* Hoar, above cited, II, 315. *Gray's support:*

Gray's conversion to the Republican concept of duty toward the Philippines was expressed, outside the Senate, in a speech at the dinner of the Ohio Society of New York (*NY Trib* 2/26/99). There were some sneers when McKinley appointed Gray to a judgeship of the circuit court. (See *Nation* 3/9/99.)

350–352   EXECUTIVE ORDERS IN THE PHILIPPINES: *Iloilo: Corres Rel,* II, 853 ff; LeRoy, I, 399-402; John H. Latané, *America as a World Power* (New York and London, 1911), 88; Charles B. Elliott, *The Philippines; To the End of the Military Regime* (Indianapolis, 1916), 442-46. *Proclamation: Corres Rel,* II, 858 ff; Otis's Report, *War Dept Reports,* 1899, vol I, part 4, pp 66-70.

The President's instructions to Otis and Dewey reflected the anxiety caused by Otis's dispatch of January 8, with its dismal report on the proclamation and its startling statement that war in the Visayas would mean war in all the islands. (See LeRoy, I, 399-406.)

Worcester's call: Worcester, I, 2-8. See Alger to Otis 12/29/98, Otis to Alger 12/30/98, *Corres Rel,* II, 863-64. *Abuse for the President:* See *Nation* 5/4/99.

353–359   THE TREATY IN THE SENATE: *Legal issue:* See *Congr Rec,* vol 32, speeches by George G. Vest 12/12/98, Orville Platt 12/19/98, George F. Hoar 1/19/99, Joseph B. Foraker 1/11/99. *Hoar startled his colleagues:*

"So Cabot told me with a gasp," Adams wrote on January 29 (*Letters,* cited, 209).

"Hoar is crazy": W. C. Beer to G. W. Perkins 2/19/99, quoted in Beer, 212. W. C. Beer, then on a visit to Washington, was reporting a conversation in which Hanna had stressed the importance of keeping the Philippines out of German control. The impression in Washington, Beer found, was that Hanna was not much in favor of holding the islands, but had been talked over by Hay and Orville Platt.

Battle for ratification: Lodge, *War,* 230-31; Andrew Carnegie to McK, Sunday [2/5/97], McK P, vol 26. See Andrew Carnegie, "The Opportunity of the United States," *N Amer Rev,* May/02. See *NY Eve Post* 1/21/99, *NY Sun* 2/9/99. *Bryan "buttonholing his men":* *NY Trib* 9/16/00, reporting a speech by Hanna at Delphi, Ind, 9/15. *A fighting chance:*

Had the treaty failed, the President would have immediately called an extra session (Lodge to TR 2/9/99, TR-Lodge, *Corres,* I, 391-92). A motion to reconsider required only a simple majority to prevail.

Davis no manager: Lodge to TR 2/9/99, cited. *Leakage from Senate:* Holt, cited, 167; *NY Trib* 1/22,25,26/99; *NY Eve Post* 1/25/99; H. Adams, *Letters,* 209-10. *"the engine room," McKinley active:* Lodge to TR 2/9/99, cited. *The vote:* Ibid; Holt, 169. *Heitfeld:* Holt, 172. *McEnery and McLaurin:* Dunn, *Harrison to Harding,* I, 282. *Hanna claimed credit:* Hanna to McK 2/7/99, McK P, vol 25.

Gorman spoke indignantly about the methods of Hanna and his friends, instancing especially "the railroad influence" worked through Elkins of West Virginia (Dunn, I, 182). C. K. Davis thought that they could not have ratified without Elkins (Davis to McK 2/9/99, McK P, vol 25).

McKinley and Hoar: H. Adams, *Letters,* 217.

359–360 THE ARMY BILL: See NY *Trib* 2/16,20,28/99.

> Ratifications of the treaty were exchanged with Spain on April 11, 1899. Lodge wrote that, if the bill had gone over until an extra session, it would not have been passed before May, at the earliest (TR-Lodge, *Corres*, I, 395).

357–365 REBELLION IN THE PHILIPPINES: *President's reaction*: GBC 2/4/99.

> Although McKinley called the outbreak "unexpected," he had been for some weeks fearful that it might occur. On January 10, when General Greene was again in Washington, he was called to the White House and questioned about the possibility of persuading Agoncillo to advise Aguinaldo against an attack. Greene agreed to try. He prepared an appropriate telegram, and, after it had been edited by the President, translated it into Spanish; but Agoncillo, fearful of the consequences when he returned home, refused to sign it. He told Greene with tears in his eyes that there was no way to prevent conflict, unless the United States would grant the Philippines absolute independence under an American protectorate (memo, F. V. Greene to Hay 2/3/00, McK P, vol 45 cited).

Small effect on Senate vote: Lodge to TR 2/9/99, cited; Holt, 170, 175; Bailey, *Diplomatic History*, 523. *"the white man's burden"*: *McClure's*, Feb /99. *Home Market Club dinner*: GBC 2/16/99; *Speeches and Addresses of William McKinley* (1900), 185-93; NY *Trib* 2/17/99; NY *Times* 3/23/99; *Nation* 2/23/99. *The spring campaign*: Otis's Report, *War Dept Reports*, 1899, vol 1, part 4, pp 1-165; LeRoy, II, 30-48; Elliott, 462-67. See Frederick Funston, *Memories of Two Wars* (New York, 1914). *The civil commissioners*: LeRoy, II, 82-84; Elliott, 473-74.

> Colonel Denby, the third member of the commission, did not reach Manila until April 4, a month later than Schurman and Worcester (Worcester, I, 8-9). A Democratic expansionist, Denby had been warmly welcomed by the Republican administration. The President had made him a member of the War Investigating Commission and he was detained in Washington by its closing sessions.

Plan of government offered: Sen Doc 208, 56/1, pp 155-56; Schurman to Hay 4/4,13/99, McK P, vol 28; same, 5/23,30/99, ibid, vol 31; Schurman, *Philippine Affairs*, cited, 8-14. *Otis refused armistice*: Otis to Corbin 4/29/99, 5/3/99, *Corres Rel*, II, 978. See R. M. Collins to C. S. Diehl 6/29/99 (copy), McK P, vol 33.

> News reports of disagreement between Otis and the President's commission prompted anxious inquiries from Washington in May. Otis's response suggested a general impatience with civilian interference, but the principal cause of his irritation was Schurman. Both he and Schurman were admonished, on instructions from the President, to suppress information of any differences between them (Otis to Alger 5/29/99 (recd) 6/4/99, Corbin to Otis 6/4/99, *Corres Rel*, II, 996, 1002. See NY *Eve Post* 6/5/99, 7/18/99).

"long disquisition": Hay to McK 6/3/99, Schurman to Hay 6/3, McK P, vol 32. *The volunteers of 1898*:

> The President had been reassured by a cable from Otis, stating that he believed the majority of the volunteer organizations would re-enlist for a period of six months. By the middle of June, however, the news had

become discouraging. The dejected cable was received June 26 (Montgomery to McK [at Adams, Mass.] 6/26/99, McK P, vol 33). Three volunteer regiments, one of cavalry and two of infantry, were eventually organized in the Philippines.

CHAPTER 16
FAREWELL TO SECRETARY ALGER

366–367   ALGER AT BOSTON: NY Times 2/17,18/99; NY Trib 2/17/99. Scene on train: GBC 2/17/99.

Just before going to Boston, Alger had been well received at the Lincoln dinner of the Union League Club in Brooklyn (NY Trib 2/14/99).

367–369   MICHIGAN: Alger as toastmaster: NY Trib 2/23/99. Pingree: TR, Letters, I, #884; Detroit Trib 8/23/98; Chi Record 9/22/98; NY Eve Post 8/11/98; NY Trib 9/22/98, 10/24/98, 6/26/99, 7/4/99; ibid, 7/6/99, quoting Detroit Eve News 11/?/98.

369–370   ALGER'S PROTESTATIONS: NY Trib 2/25/99, 4/15/99; NY Eve Post 4/15/99. Alger had made a mystery of his departure for the West Indies in the latter part of March. He had apparently been offended by newspaper talk of a "junket" (NY Trib 3/18/99). It was said in late February that the trip had been dropped altogether. The Washington correspondent of the New York Times at this time transmitted a report that, since his return from Michigan, Alger had felt that some members of the Cabinet were hostile to him (NY Times 2/26/99).

Herald's attack: Perkins, above cited, 327. Statement published in Detroit: NY Eve Post 4/18/99. See Dawes, 187-88.

370   THE SENATE: McMillan's seat:

The diplomatic post was that vacated by John Hay at London (Wash Post 8/20/98; NY Times 8/24/98; Chi Record 9/29,30/98; NY World 11/14/98). An alternative report was that the President would create the Senate vacancy by giving McMillan Alger's place at the War Department (NY World 9/5/98).

Alger to run: NY Times 5/1/99. Statement about McMillan: NY Trib 1/25/07, quoting posthumous interview in Milwaukee Journal 1/24/07, obtained from Alger 3/4/00. McMillan's statements: NY Trib 5/12,19/99. Pingree's backing announced: NY Times, NY Trib, 6/24/99. See NY Trib 6/25-28/99, 7/11/99.

371   ALGER SEES THE PRESIDENT: NY Trib 6/28/99. McKinley's trip: NY Trib 6/17-27/99.

371–372   THE CIVIL SERVICE AMENDMENT: Defended: Lyman J. Gage, "The Civil Service and the Merit System," The Forum, Aug/99; NY Trib 5/30/99, 6/1,3,6,10/99; Olcott, I, 363-66. See GBC 6/8/99, 7/13/99. Cabinet consultations: NY Trib 3/30/99, 5/23,27/99.

At the meeting of April 11, the President had asked each member to prepare a statement on the proposed modifications (President's memo, McK P, vol 28).

See TR, Letters, II, #1285, #1287. See also Hanna to McK 5/15/99, Grosvenor to McK 5/22/99, McK P, vol 31.

Rather oddly, in view of the attacks, the question of the civil service

did not figure in the campaign of 1900. The Democratic platform did
not assail McKinley on the issue, and the Republicans paid their usual
tribute to the merit system.

⎰ 372–374, ⎱ ALGER'S RESIGNATION: *President courteous, cryptic*: GBC 7/13/99. *Alger's*
⎱ 375–377 ⎰ *account*: Posthumous interview, above cited. *Actually tendered a resignation*:
Note, McK's hand 7/19/99, McK P, vol 34. *McKinley's plea*: Rough draft,
McK's hand, McK P, vol 33. *"rather trying interviews"*: GBC 7/19/99. *Admission made to TR*: TR, *Letters*, II, #1305. *"nothing but air"*: NY Trib
7/13/99. *"This is deplorable"*: unsigned note to McK, Hay's hand, marked
7/13/99, clipping enclosed, McK P, vol 34. *McKinley applied to Hay, then
Hobart*: Mrs. Hobart, *Memories*, 68; David Magie, *Life of Garret Augustus
Hobart* (New York and London, 1910), 208-11. See NY Trib 7/22/99. *Scene
with Cortelyou*: GBC 7/18/99. *President relieved*: GBC 7/19/99. *His
acceptance*: Ibid.

374–375 ROOSEVELT'S VISIT: NY Trib 7/9/99; TR, *Letters*, II, #1288, #1300,
#1305, cited. *Earnest about peace*: TR to Maria Storer 10/28/99, *Letters*, II,
#1370. *Persistent in 1898*: TR, *Letters*, I, #962, #974. *Pro-McKinley state-
ments*: NY Trib 6/29,30/99. See TR, *Letters*, II, #1287. *Hobart's illness*:
Magie, cited, 203-4.

376–377 MANILA ROUND ROBIN: NY Eve Post 7/17,18/99; NY Trib 7/18/99; LeRoy,
II, 56-64; Robinson, above cited, chap 6; R. M. Collins to C. S. Diehl
6/26,29/99 (copies), C. S. Diehl to C. A. Boynton 6/28/99 (copy), McK P,
vol 33; Melville Stone to Charles E. Smith 8/7/99, McK P, vol 35; Root to
M. Stone 10/27/99, Root Papers; Otis to Corbin (recd) 7/20/99, *Corres Rel*,
II, 1036; Corbin to Otis 7/27/99, 9/9/99, ibid, 1041, 1065. *Washington
forewarned*: NY Trib 7/20/99.

377–378 AFTERMATH: Mrs. Hobart, 68-69; Hobart to McK 7/21/99, McK P, vol
34; James Wilson to McK 7/30/99, McK P, vol 35. *McMillan's regrets*: NY
Trib 7/21/99. *Pingree's comment*: NY Journal 7/22/99. *Alger welcomed
home*: NY Trib, Wash Eve Star, 8/3/99. *Retirement pathetic*: Dunn, *Harrison to Harding*, I, 246-47. *Withdrew from Senate contest*: NY Trib 9/17/99.

CHAPTER 17
Matter of U.S. Colonies

379–383 ROOT'S APPOINTMENT: *The summons*: Jessup, I, 215-16.
Root arrived in Washington on the night of July 24, expecting to see
the President next morning; but McKinley, who was about to leave for
Lake Champlain, called Root at once to the White House, in spite of
the late hour. Before returning to New York on July 25, Root called at
the War and Navy Departments, and was introduced to the full
Cabinet, in session at the White House, by the President (Root to
McK 7/24/99, McK P, vol 35; NY Trib 7/26/99).

"exalted opinion": Bliss to McK 9/30/98, McK P, vol 18.
Bliss had originally recommended Root for the Attorney Generalship
(memo from Bliss 1/9/97, McK P, vol 4). He himself retired from the
Cabinet November 28, 1898.

Mission to Spain: Jessup, I, 196. *Hay had recommended*: Dennett, *Hay*, 202.
"frank and murderous smile": Ibid, 340, quoting Hay to Henry Adams

6/15/00. *McKinley's satisfaction*: GBC 7/22/99. *Reid "simply frantic"*: Hay to McK 8/4/99, McK P, vol 35. See TR, *Letters*, II, #1320.

Later, however, the *Tribune* published enthusiastic reports of Reid's work from its Washington correspondent.

Platt's "indifference": Autobiography, cited, 405.

Platt's entire account is disingenuous. He actually went to Washington himself, arriving late on July 21, and conferred with the President the same night. The *New York Tribune* had the story on July 22 that Root was the subject of the discussion and that a good understanding was reached.

McKinley's comment on Reid: GBC 6/12/99. *The Reid peril, 1898*: Platt to McK 8/14,23/98, McK P, vol 17; Bliss to McK 9/30/98, ibid, vol 18; Reid to McK 11/15/98, ibid, vol 21. *Root's explanation of Platt's change*: Jessup, I, 202 (see 198-200). *Platt backed Choate*: TR, *Letters*, II, #1098. *Hay embarrassed*: Dennett, Hay, 209. *Roosevelt's first impression*: Letters, II, #1305.

384   THE CABINET: Long, *Navy*, II, 142, 144, 147. *Mr. Dooley*: Elmer Ellis, *Mr. Dooley's America: A Life of Finley Peter Dunne* (New York, 1941), 122; memo, GBC's hand 12/8/99, McK P, vol 43. Cf H. Adams, *Letters*, 368. *Bliss in office*: NY Eve Post 2/23/99. *H. Clay Evans*: See NY Trib 6/27,30/01; Nation 9/20/00.

Roosevelt removed Evans as pension commissioner. (See H. Adams, *Letters*, 383.)

McKinley intervened in War Department: GBC 1/31/01; *in Department of Justice*: Ibid, 1/10/01; information from Mr. Dawes. *Vetoes*:

McKinley vetoed six bills in all. The only one of importance was HR 4001 (5/4/00). The others were HR 2219 (5/16/98), Senate Bill 708 (1/20/99), HR 1454 (5/16/00), HR 3204 (3/1/01), and HR 321 (3/1/01).

384-385   MCKINLEY AND ROOT: *"a man of great power"*: Olcott, II, 346. *Root relieved McKinley*: Jessup, I, 238. *Platt stepped aside*:

Root had employed William Cary Sanger, the inspector-general of the New York National Guard, on special assignment for the War Department, and had him in mind for the position of Assistant Secretary on the retirement of Meiklejohn, who aspired to a Senate seat. Sanger's appointment was announced early in 1901, but it had apparently been made without consulting the New York senators. Tom Platt announced his implacable opposition, and that of his colleague, Chauncey Depew. The matter was held in abeyance until Platt saw the President. His opposition meantime tapered off. Root may have had a part in this, for Platt and Depew were acquiescent when they called at the White House on March 14 (Jessup, I, 265; Platt to McK 3/7/01, McK P, vol 77; NY Trib 3/7-10,13,14/01; GBC 3/14/01).

Rathbone brought to trial: Jessup, I, 290-92.

McKinley also supported Root and Wood in the case of the Dady sewerage contract for Havana, in which Congressman Quigg was involved (ibid, 292, 293).

385   ALGER'S CORDIALITY: Alger to Root 7/21/99, McK P, vol 34; NY Trib 7/26/99, 8/2/99. *Recommendations*: Alger to McK 7/31/99 (3 memos), McK P, vol 35.

385–387   THE LEGAL QUESTION: Report of the Secretary of War, *War Dept Reports*,
1899, vol 1, part 1, pp 24-25; Root to Lyman Abbott 12/13/99, Root Papers.
"I took the United States for my client": Jessup, I, 215. Root to Griggs
7/26/99, ibid, 219.

388–389   THE STAFF SYSTEM: Jessup, I, 240-42, 251-53; Report of Secretary of War,
1899, cited, pp 45-55. *Chicago speech*, October 7: *Nation* 10/12/99. *Senior
officers*: GBC 12/20/99, citing Root. *General Miles*: Jessup, I, 243-51. See
Root to McK 9/4/01, McK P, vol 85. *Corbin*:
> The Adjutant General was not immediately shaken in his loyalty
> to the system. (See *War Dept Reports*, 1899, vol 1, part 2, p 32; *Nation*
> 11/9/99.)

390–394   CUBA: Gen. J. R. Brooke, Report on Civil Affairs in Cuba, *War Dept Reports*, 1899, vol 1, part 6, pp 5-21; Brooke to McK 9/26/99, McK P, vol 39;
Charles E. Chapman, *A History of the Cuban Republic* (New York, 1927),
96-110; Russell H. Fitzgibbon, *Cuba and the United States* (Menasha, Wis,
1935), 28-35; dispatch signed W. L. McP, NY Trib 4/10/99; dispatch signed
Veritas, ibid, 6/27/99; Root to L. Wood 1/27/00, Root Papers. *Demobilization*: Brooke to Corbin 5/24/99, McK P, vol 31. *Skepticism of U.S. intentions*:
Jessup, I, 286, quoting Root. *American troops*: NY Eve Post 8/16,18/98;
NY Trib 2/16/99, 5/28/99, 6/27/99, 8/18/99, 9/17/99. *President's instructions to Brooke*: Olcott, II, 196-202. *Effect of Foraker resolution*: Jessup, I,
296-97; W. L. McP, NY Trib, cited. See Alger to McK 5/17/99, McK P,
vol 31. *Brooke and Wood*: Brooke to McK 4/3/99, McK P, vol 28; Root to
TR 9/11/99, Root Papers; Root to Wood 1/27/00, cited; Fitzgibbon, cited,
30. *Alger recommended relieving Brooke*: Alger to McK 7/31/99, McK P,
vol 35. *"All right, go ahead"*: Jessup, I, 287. *Wood expected annexation*:
See Wood to McK 4/27/99, McK P, vol 29; TR, Letters, II, #1305. *O. Platt
dreaded*: Coolidge, *Platt*, cited, 314.

394–397   PORTO RICO: Report of Secretary of War, 1899, cited, pp 25-31; Gen. G. W.
Davis, Report on Civil Affairs in Porto Rico, *War Dept Reports*, 1899, vol 1,
part 6, pp 483-558; Gen. Guy V. Henry to McK 4/8/99, McK P, vol 28; Davis
to Root 8/11/99, McK P, vol 36; Root to Davis 9/11/99, Root Papers; McK
to Root 8/10/99, Root to McK 8/15/99, McK P, vol 36; Root to McK
8/18/99, Root Papers. *"easier to enlarge"*: Hay to McK 11/27/99, quoting
McK, McK P, vol 42. *Root's views*: Jessup, I, 378-79.

397–407   THE PHILIPPINES: *Call for troops*: McK to Root 8/3/99, McK P, Letbk 90;
Corbin to Otis 8/12/99, Otis to Corbin 8/14, *Corres Rel*, II, 1051-53; Root
to McK 8/15, telegrams 8/15,17, McK P, vol 36; McK to Root 8/19 (first
draft, recalling previous conversation), ibid. See Dunn, *Harrison to Harding*,
I, 249-50. *Lawton's "wonderful vigor"*: GBC 12/20/99, quoting Root.
Experienced officers: Root to J. R. Hawley 9/13, to F. Bartlett 10/24, Root
Papers; GBC 7/13/99.
> The staff officers of the new volunteer regiments did not maintain the
> extremely high standard of honesty which had been set in the war with
> Spain. Some frauds, especially in the commissary corps, and some trading
> in hemp necessitated trials at a later date.
Otis: LeRoy, II, chap 14; Robinson, 353-54; Dunn, I, 260; John T. Mc-
Cutcheon, *Chi Record*, in NY Eve Post 10/2/99; TR, Letters, II, #1352;

R. M. Collins to C. S. Diehl 6/29/99 (copy), cited, C. S. Diehl to C. A. Boynton 7/21/99 (copy), McK P, vol 33; Corbin to Otis 6/30, Otis to Corbin (recd) 7/1, *Corres Rel*, II, 1023-25.

It must be suspected that the newspaper correspondents were sometimes too antagonistic to Otis to be entirely accurate in their statements. For example, charges that Otis had never even visited the trenches around Manila are contradicted by photographs which show Otis with the troops. Complaints that Otis favored the expansionist New York *Sun* must be viewed in the light of the fact that the two Manila correspondents of that newspaper signed the round robin of protest against the censorship.

McKinley's admiration: Dawes, 203.

In late January, 1900, when Denby and Worcester were with the President, Cortelyou took in the translation of a telegram from Archbishop Chapelle of Manila, urgently demanding Otis's removal. The President read the message, read it again when the two commissioners had taken their leave. He started to give Cortelyou some instruction, then said, "Well, never mind, I'll think about it." That was the end of the matter. (Cable and note by GBC, McK P, vol 44.)

Success of campaign: LeRoy, II, chap 19. *Otis satisfied: Independent* 6/14/00. *Lawton:* Franklin Matthews, "Henry W. Lawton," *Harper's Wkly* 1/6/00; William Dinwiddie, "General Lawton's Last Fight," ibid, 2/24/00; O. O. Howard, "General Henry W. Lawton," *Rev of Revs*, Feb/00; Dean C. Worcester, "General Lawton's Work in the Philippines," *McClure's*, May/00; editorial, *The Army and Navy Journal* 12/23/99. *Drinking:* Corbin to GBC 8/22/99, McK P, vol 36; Lawton to Corbin 7/12 (copy), vol 34; Charles King to Lawton 6/5 (copy), vol 32.

This correspondence explains a handwritten letter from McKinley to William M. Laffan on October 7, 1898, thanking his correspondent for having "saved a gallant officer from any public humiliation," and stating that General Wood was now in command (McK P, Letbk 90).

Disappointed in assignment: LeRoy, II, 30. *Operations in spring campaign:* Ibid, 34-38, 42-45, 47-48. *Indiscreet comment:* Ibid, 58.

The most startling interview with Lawton appeared in *The Congregationalist*, September 7, 1899, over the signature of Rev. Peter MacQueen, who had been serving as an army chaplain in the Philippines. He quoted Lawton as speaking of "this accursed war," and stating that "It is time for diplomacy. . . ." MacQueen, under questioning, made only one admission of error—that Lawton had actually said "damnable war," a phrase unsuitable for *The Congregationalist* (NY *Eve Post* 9/8,16/99, 10/6/99).

Interview with Otis: Worcester, I, 322-23. *"pull his beard":* Funston, above cited, 159. *MacArthur:* LeRoy, II, 200-2; Charles B. Elliott, *The Philippines; To the End of the Commission Government* (Indianapolis, 1917), 4; Robinson, 355-56; *War Dept Reports*, 1900, vol 1, part 1, pp 77-79, part 3, pp 59-72. See MacArthur's statement before Senate Committee on the Philippines, *Sen Doc* 331, 57/1, part 2, pp 862-70.

408-409 MCKINLEY AT PITTSBURGH: NY *Trib* 8/29/99. *"Lincoln to Torquemada": Nation* 9/7/99.

CHAPTER 18
THE HERO'S RETURN

410–412　GREETING OF WASHINGTON: *NY Trib*, Wash *Eve Star*, 10/3/99; Bingham Coll, Box 16. *President's trip disapproved*: Hay to McK 8/28/99, Long to GBC 8/29/99, McK P, vol 37.

It was finally decided that Secretary Porter, representing the President, should accompany the committee which went up to New York to escort Dewey to Washington (Bingham Coll, Box 16).

"You save yourself": *NY Trib* 10/4/99. *Army parade banned*: Wash *Eve Star* 9/20/99. *President advised red fire*: Ibid, 8/9/99.

413–416　POLITICAL ENIGMA: *Leslie's Wkly* 4/30/99, 9/30/99; *NY Trib* 9/26,28/99; London *Daily News* 8/21, quoted in *Nation* 8/31/99.

The remark "A sailor has no politics" was contained in the much-discussed interview with Dewey which appeared in *Leslie's* of April 30. It had been granted on February 20 to Edwin Wildman. This was the same Edwin Rounsevelle Wildman—sometimes called by his middle name—who had been engaged in negotiations with the Philippine insurgents while he was acting consul-general at Hong Kong. On the outbreak of rebellion against the United States, Wildman had gone to Manila, and soon resigned his consular post to act as special correspondent for *Leslie's* and the *New York Journal* (*Leslie's Wkly* 11/25/99). While again in Hong Kong in June, 1899, he privately wrote two letters to Secretary Porter, expressing his belief that Dewey aspired to be President. The second letter reported the concurrence of Dr. R. A. Moseley, who was on his way to replace E. Fletcher Pratt as consul-general at Singapore, and who saw Dewey at Hong Kong. After a long confidential chat with the Admiral, Moseley exclaimed to Wildman, "My God, Dewey is a presidential candidate. . . ." (Rounsevelle Wildman to JAP 6/10/99, McK P, vol 32).

Wildman was the author of a number of articles and a book about Aguinaldo. He was drowned in 1901 in the wreck of the *Rio de Janeiro* in San Francisco Bay (*NY Trib* 2/24/01).

Tension in Ohio: Walters, above cited, 175-78; *Nation* 9/7/99; Hay to Charles Dick 9/11/99, *NY Trib* 9/13/99. Cf Hanna to McK, Grosvenor to McK, 6/3/99, McK P, vol 32. For threat to McKinley, see *NY Trib* 9/14/99; Hay to McK 9/15/99, McK P, vol 38.

417　SOME REASSURANCES: *NY Eve Post* 9/26/99; Murat Halstead to McK 9/26/99, 10/1/99, McK P, vol 39; Dawes, 201.

418–421　PRESENTATION CEREMONIES: Wash *Eve Star*, *NY Eve Post*, 10/3/99; *NY Trib* 10/4/99; Bingham Coll, Box 16. *The protocol of the drive*: Memo from JAP 10/[1]/99, McK P, vol 41.

Although argumentative about the drive, Secretary Porter thought that the President should hand the sword to Dewey, and may have originated the idea.

Long's speech: Long, *Navy*, II, 211-16. *McKinley's speech*: *Speeches and Addresses* (1900), 225-26. *"protestations of regard"*: Dawes, 201. *President smiling*: Wash *Eve Star* 10/3/99. *Fancied his speech*:

When the question arose of publishing a new volume of his speeches, the President insisted on having this short speech included (GBC 4/5/00).

White House dinner:
The stag dinner of 80 guests in Dewey's honor was the largest to date in White House history (Bingham Coll, Box 16; NY Trib 10/4/99).

422-424   LIGHT ON THE PHILIPPINES: *Schurman:*
Schurman, returning home in August, had promptly accepted the President's request to call at the White House on the evening of September 2 (J. C. Schurman to McK 8/23/99, McK P, vol 36). The conference lasted for several hours (NY Trib 9/3/99) but evidently failed to clarify the question of action by Congress, which Schurman recommended in a a statement given out at Ithaca on September 13. This statement and Schurman's address on the opening of Cornell University on August 28 made a deep impression on the public because of their assertion that the question of Philippine annexation had been definitely settled, and that the mission of the United States was to educate the people and aid them in governing themselves (NY Eve Post 9/14,28/99; Nation 10/5/99; see Schurman to McK 10/20/99, McK P, vol 40).

Denby and Worcester recalled: NY Eve Post 9/14,15/99. *Dewey: Autobiography,* cited, 252; Olcott, II, 96.
The interview with Dewey was held on the morning of October 4. The date "October 3" on the President's notes—a photograph of which is reproduced in the Olcott book—evidently refers to the preparation of the questionnaire.

424-426   CAMPAIGN TOUR: *McKinley's oratory:* GBC 2/16/99, quoting Hay, "political classics."
Cortelyou noted that the most effective portions of the addresses were often last-minute additions.

The Chicago labor union: Dawes, 196, 201-2; NY Trib 10/10,11/99. See *Nation* 9/14/99. *Situation in Ohio:* NY Trib 10/17/99, 11/6/99. *McKinley in Ohio:* Ibid, 10/19/99. *Outside assistance:* Beer, 304-8, 311-25; Herrick to McK 11/10/99, McK P, vol 41. See Walters, 178-79.

427-428   MCKINLEY SATISFIED: *Talk with Dewey:* GBC 1/13/00. *Report of Philippine Commission:* Sen Doc 138, 56/1, pp 180-81.
This report was put together with remarkable celerity. Denby reached Washington the night of October 23, Worcester two days later. Schurman arrived in time for the first full meeting, at which Dewey also was present, on October 30. The President sent for the commission on November 1, and, according to the newspapers, then explained the points he wanted the report to cover (NY Eve Post 11/1/99). The report was submitted, and made public the next day. Dewey contributed a memorandum denying that he had formed any alliance with Aguinaldo, or ever made him a promise of independence. Otherwise, he had no share in preparing the report, and it was said by some that he had not read it (Nation 4/12/00). Otis's name was also signed to the report, both in its preliminary and final form. For the full report, see *Senate Document 138,* above cited.

428-431   EXIT THE HERO:
The familiar story of Dewey's loss of popular favor and subsequent an-

nouncement of his candidacy is well told by Mark Sullivan in *The Turn of the Century* (above cited, 331-43).

Contributors to the house:

A list of the names, with the amounts of their respective donations to the "Dewey home fund," was bound in a handsome album and presented to Dewey. This volume was in the rooms occupied by Dewey and his wife on their honeymoon at the Waldorf Astoria in New York. They forgot to take it when they left, and curious reporters discovered that Mrs. M. M. Hazen had been put down for $50 (*NY Trib* 11/10,15/99). Although the fact was not noted, the President had given twice as much, besides a contribution of $50 to the Washington reception committee (McK P, vols 31, 39).

McKinley on the candidacy: GBC 4/5,7/00; Dawes, 221.

CHAPTER 19
FIRST LADY

432–434   ILLNESS: *Not discussed:* Information from Mrs. Belden, Mrs. Hartzell. *Disregarded:* Olcott, II, 363, reporting a conversation with ex-President Taft. *Determination:* Kohlsaat, 156; H. O. S. Heistand to McK 7/6/01, McK P, Box 211. *Aware of seizures:* Mrs. Hobart, *Memories*, 29; Kohlsaat, 155.

435   INTIMACY WITH HOBARTS: Mrs. Hobart, 13-14, 28-31.

435–436   TEMPORARY COMPANIONS: *Aunt Maria:* Chi *Record* 1/4/97; information from Mrs. Esselburne.

Mrs. Maria S. Saxton was the widow of Thomas W. Saxton and the mother of Samuel who had worked in the office at the North Market Street house in 1896 (*Repos* 3/31/40).

Mrs. Heistand: NY *Journal* 3/7/97; *America of Yesterday*, 170-71. See Chi *Record* 3/4/97. *Washington friends:* Information from Mrs. Dawes.

436–438   YOUNG PEOPLE AT THE WHITE HOUSE: *Mary Barber:* Information from Mrs. Hartzell, Mrs. Belden, Mrs. Dawes, Mrs. Putnam. *Hard kiss:* Information from Mrs. Cross. *Children:* Information from Mrs. Stanley-Brown. See Bessie Ainsworth Safford in Wash *Post* 3/4/97. *The President with children:* Dr. Bristol, *Sunday School Times*, cited; information from Mr. G. B. Cortelyou, Jr. *"such a good heart":* Olcott, II, 348, quoting Taft.

438   FLOWERS: *Conservatories:* Walden Fawcett, "The Conservatory at the White House," *Woman's Home Companion* Oct/99. *Gardeners' room:* NY *Herald* 3/20/98, clipping in Bingham Coll, Box 18.

439–440   HOLIDAYS, 1897: Mrs. Hobart, 46; McK to Fanny Hayes 7/2/97, McK P, Letbk 90. *The Plunketts:* McK to W. M. Osborne 10/29/97, ibid; Mrs. Bessie D. Plunkett to Miss Irene Poirier 2/4/47, information from Miss Poirier. *The Sloanes' dinner:* James Barnes, *From Then Till Now* (New York and London, 1934), 218-19; information from Mr. Auguste Chollet.

Mr. Barnes was wrong in remembering that the eagle was mechanical. *"vastly better . . . almost walk alone":* GBC 6/17/98.

441–444   IMPROVEMENTS AND FAILURES: Bingham Coll, Boxes 15, 16, 18; Chi *Record* 1/31/98; Wash *Eve Star* 1/1,15/98, 2/1-3/98. *President gave left arm:* Bingham Coll, Box 18. *Performed introductions:* Ibid, Box 16.

444–449   WHITE HOUSE ENTERTAINMENT: Mrs. Hobart, 29-30, 34; notes and table diagrams, Bingham Coll, passim; *America of Yesterday*, 217. Cf Benjamin Harrison, *Ladies' Home Journal*, Apr/97, cited. *The Clevelands' innovation:* Chi Record 1/23/97. *"Bengal tigers":* NY *Herald* 3/20/98, above cited. *Mrs. McKinley a "sedative":* "Mrs. McKinley and Mrs. Bryan: A Comparison," *Harper's Bazar* 8/11/00. *Prince Albert:* Bingham Coll, Box 18; Mrs. Hobart, 53-54.

    Albert did not actually become heir presumptive until the death of his father in 1905, but it was understood that he would succeed to the throne.

450-451 MRS. MCKINLEY "BETTER": Wash *Eve Star* 3/15/98, 4/5,16/98; GBC 4/9/98; Dawes, 147-50, 152-55; McK P, Box 227; Dr. J. N. Bishop to McK 4/25/98, McK P, vol 13; McK to W. M. Osborne 7/29/98, Letbk 90. *Trip to Baltimore:* Wash *Times*, NY *Trib*, 3/25/98. *Showed concern:* GBC 4/9/98. *"so gracious":* C. Bawsel to his wife 9/24/98, Heald MS, above cited. *John Barber had typhoid:*

    A bill for John's care from Garfield Memorial Hospital was paid by the President (McK P, Box 211).

Reception for Episcopalians: Bingham Coll, Box 18; clipping, Wash *Post* 10/8/98, ibid. *McKinley to unveil Peace Cross:* Henry G. Satterlee to McK 10/22/99, McK P, vol 19.

451-454 GEORGE SAXTON'S MURDER: Wash *Eve Star*, Chi Record, 10/8/98; Spencer report, cited. See *Cld Plain Dealer* 1/24/43. *McKinley depressed:* Dawes, 172. *Traveling arrangements:* NY *Trib* 10/10/98. *Case not expedited:* Chi Record 10/11/98. *The trial:* NY *Journal* 4/6-29/99.

    An interesting, but undocumented account, "The Murder That Rocked the White House," by Frank H. Ward, was published in *True Detective Mysteries*, March 1934. A typewritten copy was obtained through the courtesy of the Canton Public Library.

Feeling in Canton: Information from Mrs. Esselburne, Mr. Frease, and Mrs. Putnam. *Pomerene's temptation:*

    Phillip Shriver's doctoral dissertation, "The Making of a Moderate Progressive: Atlee Pomerene" (Kent, Ohio, 1954), gives a good account of the political stresses (p 151).

"nasty things": James J. Grant to McK 3/17/99, McK P, vol 27. See same, 10/4/98, vol 18, 5/9/00, vol 48. *McKinley's friendship for Pomerene:* Information from Mrs. Putnam. *Verdict cheered:* NY *Trib* 4/29/99.

454-458 MRS. MCKINLEY'S REACTION: C. Bawsel to his wife 10/21/98, Heald MS; Beer, 211. See Julia Foraker, above cited, 246, 261-62. *Saxton's will:* McK P, vol 19. *Signs of strain:* Clark Howell to Kohlsaat 12/22/21, quoted in Kohlsaat, 24; H. Adams to E. Cameron 1/29/99, *Letters*, 211; information from Mrs. Hamlin, Miss Hegeman.

    The description of the Hamlins' call at the White House is taken from the notes which Mrs. Hamlin kindly supplied from her diary for 1899. Miss Annie Hegeman had been an eye witness of the scenes at Jekyll Island.

Apparently much benefited: Dawes, 185.

459-461 NERVOUS COLLAPSE: *Illness of four or five months:* McK to Hanna 9/18/99, McK P, Letbk 90. *"great strain":* McK to John Barber 4/13/99, ibid. *Seclusion in New York:* NY *Trib* 4/29/99.

    William S. Hawk, one of the proprietors of the Manhattan Hotel, was a former Cantonian, a friend of Abner McKinley and also of the President and his wife. He had been one of the little boys in Miss Saxton's class at the Presbyterian Sunday school (W. S. Hawk to I. S. McK 8/29/99, McK P, vol 37). In 1898, the Manhattan had fitted up a suite for the President on the parlor floor, overlooking 42nd Street. It was always reserved for his occupancy or that of Mrs. McKinley on her trips to New York.

Quiet at Hot Springs: Dawes, 192. See Alger to McK 5/17/99, McK P, vol 31. *Dr. Rixey:*

This connection, formed on the recommendation of Secretary Long, had begun on the trip to Atlanta the previous December. Surgeon General Sternberg obviously had not time to spare for the trips on which Mrs. McKinley required a physician's attendance (W. C. Braisted and William H. Bell, *The Life Story of Presley Marion Rixey*, Strasburg, Va, 1930, pp 30-33).

At the Plunketts': Adams *Freeman* 6/29/99. *Weakness and depression:* Dawes, 195, 197. *The house: America of Yesterday*, 216; GBC 7/5/99. *Bluff Point:* Wash *Eve Star* 8/12/99; *NY Trib* 7/29,30/99.

Typewritten notes made by the clerk, B. F. Barnes, attached to the Cortelyou diary for 1899, are the authority for the crowds at Bluff Point, the reception at East Liverpool, and McKinley's fervent response to the greetings of Canton.

Hobart exhausted: Magie, above cited, 204-8. *Mrs. McKinley upset by cannon: NY Trib* 9/2/99, quoting Dr. Rixey. *Did not see house:* Ibid.

CHAPTER 20
WINTER OF DECISION

462   MCKINLEY'S CREED: Signed statement, 5/26/99, McK P, Letbk 90.
462–465   SHRINKING FROM A SECOND TERM: GBC 9/17/99, 12/15/99. See *America of Yesterday*, 216; Dawes, 199, 214. *"a world power":* GBC 9/17/99. *Interview with Payne:* Ibid, 12/15/99. See H. C. Payne to McK 11/27/99, McK P, vol 42. *Mrs. McKinley:*

Although she seemed quite well on the President's arduous tour of the West, she was weak and ill after their return to Washington (Dawes, 202, 211; *NY Trib* 10/20/99; GBC 12/12,15,19/99).

466–467   SADNESS AT CHRISTMAS: GBC 12/20,23,31/99. *Hobart's message:* Frederick Evans to McK 11/1/99, McK P, vol 41.

Hobart died on November 23. The President and other dignitaries attended his funeral at Paterson, New Jersey, two days later. That evening, on the return journey to Washington, McKinley spoke with feeling of his regard for Hobart and the influence which the Vice President had attained with the Senate (Dawes, 207).

Osborne: GBC 12/12/99; Dawes, 209. *Mrs. McKinley's presents:* GBC 12/23/99. See McK P, Box 212. *At New Year reception:* Bingham Coll, Box 15; GBC 1/1/00.

468–469   NAVY VS WHITE HOUSE: *Origin of feud: America of Yesterday*, 158-60; clipping, *NY Press* 2/13/98, Bingham Coll, Box 18. *McCawley:* See TR to Richard Olney 6/9/97, *Letters*, I, #738 and footnote. *New Year's Day*, 1900: Bingham Coll, Box 15; GBC 12/28/99; *America of Yesterday*, 218-19. *Army and Navy reception:* Bingham Coll, Box 15.

469–473   SOCIAL WORRIES: *Crowded receptions*: Bingham Coll, Box 15. *Snobbish publicity*: "The World of Society," Wash *Eve Star* 1/23/00; GBC 1/23/00. *Seating at table*: Pruden to Adee, Adee to Pruden, 1/3,17/00, McK P, Box 232; Bingham Coll, Box 15; Wash *Eve Star* 1/27/00. Cf *America of Yesterday*, 159. *Miss Cassini*: Countess Marguerite Cassini, *Never a Dull Moment* (New York, 1956), 6, 10-11, 137-38. *Complained of by von Holleben*: Bingham Coll, Box 16. *Regretted next diplomatic dinner*: Count Cassini to JAP 1/15/00, McK P, Box 232. *Secretary Hay's arrangement*: Bingham Coll, Box 15; Wash *Eve Star* 1/27/00. *Diplomatic dinner, 1901*: Bingham Coll, Box 5.

473–474   MRS. MCKINLEY: Wash *Eve Star* 1/25/00, 2/1,15/00; Wash *Post* 2/22/00, clipping in Bingham Coll, Box 5.

> The President was worried by an unusually bad attack which Mrs. McKinley suffered in late February. Detained in his office, he repeatedly sent back to ask how she was. Cortelyou preserved the report which Captain Loeffler brought back after one of these inquiries, "Better, and going to sleep now." (GBC 2/24/00.)

"I will go out with my Dearest": Mrs. McK's diary, 4/15/01.

CHAPTER 21

THE REPUBLICAN LAWMAKERS

475–477   BEVERIDGE'S SPEECH: *Congr Rec*, vol 33, 704-12; Dawes, 213; NY *Trib* 1/10/00.

477–481   PARVENU IN THE SENATE: *Indiana candidacy*: Claude G. Bowers, *Beveridge and the Progressive Era* (Boston, 1932), 83-85. *Committee assignments*: TR-Lodge, *Corres*, I, 421, 426, 427, 430; Bowers, 115-16.

> An entry that Dawes was trying to help Beveridge get on the "Foreign Affairs" [sic] Committee of the Senate (Dawes MS 11/28/99) has been omitted from the published journal. The story about "eulogistic matter" was mentioned by Dawes in conversation with the President and Cortelyou (GBC 1/5/00).

Dissuaded from sending speech: Dawes, 206. *Solicited President's interest*: GBC 12/12/99.

> Beveridge's claim to friendship with the President was based on several recent conversations about the Philippines. Beveridge had called at the White House in March, 1899, before he made his trip, and reported his impressions, at the President's suggestion, in early September (Dawes, 184, 198).

Showed resolution to senators: GBC 1/4/00. *President's opinion*: GBC 12/23/99, 1/4,5/00. *Hoar's rebuke*: *Congr Rec*, vol 33, 712. *Wolcott's rebuke*: Ibid, 810-11. *Depew's comment*: GBC 1/14/00, citing McK's account of story told by Hitchcock. His *"desperate break"*: Mrs. Hobart, *Memories*, 10-11. *His speech on the Philippines 2/27*: *Congr Rec*, vol 33, 2307.

481   THE NEW CONGRESS: NY *Trib* 12/15/99. See the diagram of the seating in the *Congressional Directory*, 56/1, p 184.

482–485   POLICY ON THE PHILIPPINES: *Spooner Bill*: *Congr Rec*, vol 33, 763. See Walter Wellman, "Spooner of Wisconsin," *Rev of Revs*, Aug/02. *"too argumentative"*: GBC 1/30/01, cited. *Lodge's speech*: *Congr Rec*, vol 33, 4689 ff. *Taft persuaded to go*: Olcott, II, 174-78; Henry F. Pringle, *The Life and Times of William Howard Taft* (2 vols, New York, 1939), I, 159-62; speech of President-elect Taft 12/13/08, Boston *Herald* [12/13/08], quoted in Rhodes, above cited, 196-97; Jessup, I, 353-54; McK to Day 1/30/00, McK P, vol 45; Wash *Eve Star* 2/6/00; *NY Trib* 2/7/00. See GBC 1/23/00.

The meeting between McKinley and Taft at the Days' is attested by Olcott, who talked with both Taft and Day. Olcott is wrong in supposing that the President's telegram to Taft was sent a few days later. Taft also was in error in recalling—in 1908—that the date was in February. The telegram was sent before January 23, and the interview had already taken place when McKinley wrote Day on January 30. Day, incidentally, had suffered a nervous breakdown after his return from Paris. He was appointed to the circuit court in April, 1899, but did not enter on his duties until the fall term (Dawes, 181; Day to McK 2/13,14,16/99, McK P, vol 25; same, 4/19/99, vol 28; *NY Sun* 4/27/99).

486-487   IMPERIALISM DISOWNED: *McKinley's speech*, 3/3/00: *Speeches and Addresses* (1900), 361-66.

487-492   PORTO RICAN TARIFF: *Free trade projected:* Root to Clarence Kelsey 1/15/00, Root Papers; *NY Trib* 1/20/00.

Payne's free trade bill was introduced on his own motion, after he heard the testimony before the Committee on Insular Affairs, and especially the report of General Davis (*Congr Rec*, vol 33, 1942). The Chicago *Times-Herald* (Kohlsaat's newspaper) examined the testimony given before Foraker's committee by the representatives of the beet sugar industry and the League of Domestic Producers, and concluded that before January 20 no Republican leader in the Senate dreamed of treating Porto Rico differently from any other United States territory (*Times-Herald* [3/5/00], editorial quoted by Tillman of South Carolina in Senate, *Congr Rec*, vol 33, 3211).

Protests of sugar planters: The Beet Sugar Gazette, Feb/00, cited by Bromwell of Ohio, *Congr Rec*, vol 33, 2044. *Tax imposed: Congr Rec*, vol 33, 1940-47; *NY Trib* 1/28,31/00, 2/3/00; *Outlook* 2/17/00. *President's first reaction: NY World* 2/18/00. See Nelson to McK 2/17/00, McK P, vol 45. For Nelson's previous article, see *Harper's Wkly* 8/19/99.

Complaints of the President's indifference were emphasized in an unpublished interview given to the Chicago *Record* by Representative Lorimer of Illinois, on February 18. W. E. Curtis sent this interview to the President. He also forwarded on February 21 a statement made by Lorimer that he could muster 60 or 80 votes at once, if the President would authorize an intimation that the Payne Bill should fail (McK P, vol 45). The statement that the President would sign the bill if it passed had already been published (*NY Trib* 2/16/00).

Payne's speech 2/19/00: *Congr Rec*, vol 33, 1940-47. *President sent for House leaders:* GBC 2/20/00. *Pressure for his active help: Congr Rec*, vol 33, 2078-79 (Grosvenor 2/22/00); Payne to McK 2/26, typed memo, GBC 2/26, typed memo [Payne?] 2/27, typed memo, D. B. Henderson 2/27, McK P, vol 46. See *Nation* 3/8/00, citing Chi *Times-Herald* 3/5. *Interview with bolters: Nation* 3/15/00; GBC 2/27/00, 3/5/00.

McKinley's active support of the Payne Bill was caused by the switch in policy of the House Democrats (Dawes, 217). A number of other Republicans were similarly affected. The *New York Tribune*, which had warmly endorsed free trade for Porto Rico, became suddenly alarmed by the danger of a precedent for the Philippines. (See editorials, 1/20,21,27/00, 5/30/01.)

Amendments accepted: Typed memo [Payne?] 2/27/00, cited, McK P, vol 46; NY *Trib* 2/27/00. *"petit larceny"*: Berry of Kentucky, 2/28, *Congr Rec*, vol 33, 2406. *The outcome:* GBC 2/28/00; NY *Trib* 3/1/00; *Outlook* 3/3/00. *"party misfortune"*: *Outlook* 3/10/00. *Special message: Congr Rec*, vol 33, 2482.

492–498   FORAKER IN CHARGE: Walters, 163, 165-70; *Sen Reports* 249, 56/1, vol 2; *Outlook* 3/17/00. *Resentment: Congr Rec*, vol 33, 2651. *"did things"*: GBC 1/5/00. *Bluff: Congr Rec*, vol 33, 3165 ff. *"you do not dare"*: Ibid, 3171. *Allen mutely appealed:* NY *Trib* 3/23/00. *Republican disunity:* NY *Trib* 3/27/00. *Foraker drove on: Congr Rec*, vol 33, 3355 ff; NY *Trib* 3/28/00. *President "laid down the lines"*: Dawes, 219.

The first object of the President's final compromise was, according to Dawes, "to save the House from reversal and humiliation." (See GBC 3/20/00.)

"well-disciplined army": Congr Rec, vol 33, 3170. *Crowds in Senate:* NY *Trib* 4/3/00. *Foraker regretted citizenship:* Foraker, II, 84. For his statements about the bill, see his speech before the Union League of Philadelphia 4/21/00, quoted in Foraker, II, 70-82. For comment on the outcome, see *Outlook* 4/14, *Harper's Wkly* 4/28, *Nation* 5/3.

495–498   BEVERIDGE AND PORTO RICO: GBC 3/18/00. *Foraker's impatience: Congr Rec*, vol 33, 3466. *Speech:* Ibid, Appendix, 279-86; Bowers, cited, 128-29; Dawes, 219-20.

Dawes's entry of March 28 is incorrectly dated March 26 in the published *Journal.*

Press had speech: NY *Trib* 3/23/00; *Nation* 4/5/00. *Pettus: Congr Rec*, vol 33, 3509; NY *Trib* 3/31/00. *Davis: Congr Rec*, vol 33, 3425. *Proctor:* Ibid, 3509.

499   ALLEN APPOINTED: Henry MacFarland, "Charles H. Allen, The First Governor of Puerto Rico," *Rev of Revs*, May/00; Jessup, I, 376; NY *Trib* 4/13/00, 7/8/00. *Napoleon's letters:* Dawes, 223.

501   MCKINLEY'S EXPLANATION: Dawes, 217.

The Dawes MS mentions six conversations between the President and Dawes in March, in addition to those that appear in the published diary.

Kohlsaat: Information from Mr. Dawes.

This was the *Times-Herald* editorial of March 23, above cited. Kohlsaat's newspaper had previously antagonized the President by a series of savage attacks on Foraker. See Walters (pp 176-77). For Dawes's final appraisal of Kohlsaat and his relationship with McKinley, see Dawes (pp 367-68).

CHAPTER 22
AFFAIRS OF STATE

504–508   THE TREATY: NY *Trib* 2/6/00; "Diplomatic History of the Panama Canal," *Sen Doc* 474, 63/2, pp 1-2, quoting Hay to Henry White 12/7/98, pp 11-17, quoting Lansdowne to Pauncefote 2/22/01; Dennett, *Hay*, above cited, 248-53; John T. Morgan to McK 12/2/99, McK P, vol 43. *Alaskan boundary:* Allan

Nevins, *Henry White* (New York and London, 1930), 145-47. *McKinley and Panama route:* Croly, 378, 380. See Dawes, 265-66. *"complicity . . . abrogation":* Hay to Choate 1/15/00, quoted in Dennett, 252. *McKinley elated:* GBC 2/4/00.

508-510　THE SENATE: *Report of the Foreign Relations Committee* 3/9/00, *Sen Doc* 268, 56/1. *Hay worried:* Hay to Lodge 2/7/00, quoted in Thayer, above cited, II, 223. *His angry expressions:* Hay to Henry White 2/27/00, 3/18/00, quoted in Nevins, *White,* 150-52. *Failure to consult:* Henry White to Hay 5/16/00, ibid, 153. See Lodge to White 12/18/00, ibid, 154-55. *Treaty defended:* John Bassett Moore in *NY Times* 3/4/00. *Best naval opinion: Sen Doc* 268, above cited. *Roosevelt's objections: NY Sun* 2/8/00. See Hay to [?], 2/12/00, quoted in Thayer, II, 225; TR to Albert Shaw 2/15/00, TR, *Letters,* II, #1516.

510-511　THE RESIGNATION: GBC 3/13/00; Hay to McK, McK to Hay, 3/13, quoted in Thayer, II, 226-28; Hay to McK 3/14, letter in possession of Mr. George B. Cortelyou, Jr; Hay to Henry White 3/18, above cited; to Adelbert Hay 3/17, quoted in Thayer, II, 229.

511-512　MCKINLEY AND HAY: *"trained under Abraham Lincoln":* GBC 2/4/00. *"coolness and courage":* Hay to Choate 6/15/99, quoted in Thayer, II, 206. See also Hay to Choate 8/18/00, ibid, 219; Dennett, *Hay,* 208. *Conference with Senate committee:* Hay to Choate 12/21/00, quoted in Dennett, 258.

513　THE HAGUE CONVENTION:

Signed at The Hague July 29, 1899, this convention was transmitted to the Senate by the President on December 20 (*Sen Doc* 159, 56/1), and was ratified February 8, 1900. McKinley had earnestly recommended favorable action in his Annual Message of 1899 (*Congr Rec*, vol 33, 24-37). See Frederick W. Holls, *The Peace Conference at the Hague* (New York, 1900); Andrew D. White, *Autobiography,* above cited, II, 250-347, passim. Vol 32 of the McKinley Papers contains three telegrams from Andrew D. White, and a long report from Seth Low.

513-514　THE SECOND CANAL TREATY: *Amended treaty rejected by England:* Lansdowne to Pauncefote 2/22/01, above cited. *New draft prepared:* Cullom, 380-81; Pauncefote to Lansdowne 4/25/01, "Diplomatic History," *Sen Doc* 474, 63/2, p 19; Hay to Choate 4/27/01, ibid, pp 21-22. *Favorably received:* Lansdowne memo 8/3/01, ibid, pp 25-27. See Holt, *Treaties Defeated,* above cited, 194.

514-517　THE OPEN DOOR: *For Rels,* 1899, 128-42; Griswold, above cited, 65-75; Dennett, *Hay,* 289-95. *British overture,* 1898: A. L. P. Dennis, "John Hay," in S. F. Bemis, *The American Secretaries of State and Their Diplomacy,* IX (New York, 1929), 122. *Ambassador Hay's inquiry:* Dennett, *Hay,* 285-86. *Day's recommendation:*

A communication from Secretary Day to the Speaker of the House, June 14, 1898, was cited by the President in urging that action be taken in his Annual Message of 1898 (*Congr Rec*, vol 32, 2-13). Congress failed to respond, and the recommendation was repeated in the Annual Message of 1899.

The term "Open Door": NY Trib 11/26,28/98.

518-523　SIEGE OF THE LEGATIONS: Dennett, *Hay,* 297-307; Long, *Navy,* II, 126-38; Report of Secretary of War, China Relief Expedition, *War Dept Reports,*

1900, vol 1, part 1, pp 11-22, 61-71; President's Annual Message 1900, *Congr Rec*, vol 34, 2-13.

> Military correspondence relating to the China Relief Expedition is illogically included in vol. 1 of *Correspondence Relating to the War with Spain*.

Conger's views: Griswold, 59-60. For a somewhat more conservative statement, see Dennis, *Adventures in American Diplomacy*, above cited, 207-8, quoting Conger to Hay 3/1/99. *Hay's skepticism:* Hay to Conger 3/22/00, *For Rels*, 1900, 111-12. *"independent protection":* same, 3/15/00, *For Rels*, 110. *Rockhill's opinion:* Dennis, *American Secretaries of State*, IX, cited, 144. *Conger directed to report:* Hay to Conger 6/15/00, *For Rels*, 155. Cf Conger to Hay 6/11 (recd 9/25), *For Rels*, 144-46. *"drama of the legations":* Henry Adams, *The Education of Henry Adams* (New York, 1918), 392. *President edited Hay's telegram:* Olcott, II, 234-35. *Other examples of editing:* Ibid, 243-44. *Identification "Alta":* Sarah Pike Conger, *Letters from China* (Chicago, 1909), 153.

524   PRESIDENT'S RETURN TO WASHINGTON:

> President and Mrs. McKinley came back to the White House on August 17, and stayed until September 11 or 12, when they left for Somerset, Pennsylvania, to attend the wedding of Abner's daughter Mabel to Dr. Hermanus Baer. They then went to Canton, and the President remained there, except for a trip to Washington, September 18-21, until after the election on November 6 (*NY Trib*, Dawes, passim). Mrs. McKinley had been in very poor health during the long stay in Washington (GBC 8/29/00).

524-526   MCKINLEY-ROOT DIPLOMACY: *Appraisal of Root and Adee:* GBC 8/29/00. *"yell at Adee":* Jessup, I, 382-83. *Reply to Germany on supreme command:* Olcott, II, 246-50, quoting record of telephone conversation, McK and Montgomery, Root listening in, 8/10/00. *Reply to Russia:* For Rels, 1900, 20; GBC 8/29/00; NY Trib 8/30/00. See Dennett, *Hay*, 311-14.

526-527   PRESIDENT IN SOLE CHARGE: *Anxious to withdraw from China:* Dennett, 314-15; Dennis, *Adventures*, 231-33. For delay, see Adee to Hay 9/4/00, quoted in Dennis, 256. *Adee's advice:* Adee to McK 8/21/00, McK P, vol 59. *Fears for Conger:* Ibid.

> Two excited cables from Conger, both dated August 14, are in the McKinley Papers, vol. 58. One was received on the date of dispatch through the Chinese Minister at Washington. The other was received August 20.

German proposal refused: For Rels, 1900, 341-42. *Root's illness:* NY Trib 9/14/00.

528   CONCESSION ON THE FUKIEN COAST:

> Though this inquiry was a guarded secret until 1924 (Griswold, 83-84), the Navy Department had probably persuaded the President to take a realistic view of obtaining a naval station, in the event of the partition of China. John W. Foster heard from John Hay that he had been cautioned by the President against renouncing a desire for territory (Foster, *Diplomatic Memoirs*, II, 257). One result of the President's close involvement in the negotiations was to increase his admiration for Japan. He stated to Cortelyou that "the diplomacy of Japan was the greatest in the world,"

referring to a document on the question of the offenders in China as "one of the most remarkable international papers he had ever read, and, what was particularly gratifying to him, that it was in entire harmony with the American position" (GBC 11/17/00).

CHAPTER 23

THE RUNNING MATE AND THE ISSUES

529–531   ROOSEVELT'S TRIP: Dennett, *Hay*, 340, quoting Hay to Adams 6/15/00; Foraker, II, 91-92. *"true greatness"* of Vice-Presidency: *Congr Rec*, vol 33, 743-44. *Root staying in Cabinet*: TR-Lodge, *Corres*, I, 427-29, 433-34; Jessup, I, 230-32. *"a very frank talk"*: TR-Lodge, *Corres*, I, 439-41. *Butler's trip*: Butler, *Busy Years*, cited, I, 226. For the attitude of the New York machine, see Chauncey Depew, *My Memories of Eighty Years* (New York, 1924), 162-65.

531–532   THE OPEN FIELD: *NY Trib* 6/10/00. *White House conference*: Ibid. *Appeal to Allison*: Dawes, 231. *Foraker's story*: Foraker, II, 90-91. *"there is only one life"*: *NY Trib* 6/14/00, quoting Hanna. *Woodruff*: *NY Trib* 1/7/00; TR *Letters*, II, #1469; Dunn, *Harrison to Harding*, I, 331. *Hazel appointment*: See *Harper's Wkly* 6/16/00; *NY Trib* 6/1,2,3,4,11/00; *Nation* 5/24,31/00, 6/7,14/00.

533–534   HANNA IN SUSPENSE: Croly, 320-21; Dawes, 220, 229, 230. *Poor health*: *NY Trib* 6/18,19/00. *Little known to delegates*: *NY Trib* 6/20/00.

A phenomenon of the proceedings at Philadelphia in June was the ovation which greeted Hanna when he called the convention to order, and the cheers that broke out after his first remarks. Edward W. Townsend, writing in *Harper's Weekly* (6/30/00), stressed the element of surprise in the demonstration—the unexpectedness of Hanna's pleasant appearance and manner of speaking.

Cuban postal frauds: Joseph L. Bristow's report, *NY Trib* 7/26/00; *Annual Reports of the Post-Office Dept*, 1900, House Doc 4, 56/2, pp 17-21, 828-29, 848-49; La Follette, 131-33; *Republican Campaign Textbook* (Philadelphia, 1900), pp 51-52, 368-69; Coolidge, *Platt*, 320-22, 332-34.

After the scandals broke in May, 1900, the investigation was for many months a lively topic in the newspapers. Estes G. Rathbone, incidentally, had been on cordial terms with the President, and had seen him at least once during a trip to the United States in 1899 (Rathbone to GBC 11/20/99, McK P, vol 42).

For Rathbone's earlier experience, see *Leslie's Wkly* 8/5/99; Dunn, I, 92. For involvement of Washington officials, see TR, *Letters*, III, #2610, #2634, #2645, #2648, #2688, #2808, #2843.

Disclosures of corruption in the Post Office Department led President Roosevelt to make an investigation in 1903, and Bristow was again placed in charge. Although originally commending Bristow as "entirely fearless and honest" (TR, *Letters*, III, #2645), Roosevelt came to feel that he was overzealous (*Letters*, IV, #3590). For Bristow's side of it, see Dawes, 405-6.

"Anticipation . . . a good regulator": GBC 12/28/99.

534–537   CONFUSION AT PHILADELPHIA: *NY Trib* 6/15-19/00. *Platt's broken rib*: Ibid, 6/21. *"an acceptance hat"*: Olcott, II, 270-71. *Hanna sticking to Bliss*:

Croly, 309-10. *Appeal to President:* Transcription of telephone conversation, Charles Dick to GBC 6/17/oo, 10:30 pm, McK P, vol 51. *President's reply:* Ibid. *Hanna in a rage:* Dunn, I, 334-35.

> Dunn was obviously wrong in drawing the conclusion that Hanna had talked with McKinley on the telephone. It is not improbable that Dick had been unable to reach Hanna after midnight at Haverford, and did not transmit the President's reply until Hanna was in his office on Monday morning.

538-539   DAWES'S INTERVENTION: Information from Mr. Dawes; transcription of telephone conversations, Dawes to GBC, 6/19/oo, at 8:40 pm and 1 am [6/20], McK P, vol 51.

> The Dawes journal (pp 232-33) places the scene with Hanna and the subsequent telephone calls a day later, but the date given by the methodical Cortelyou conforms with newspaper and other reports from Philadelphia. The probability is that Dawes posted up his diary after the convention, and confused the sequence of events. His mediation was apparently unsuspected by the press, but some correspondents knew that the President disapproved of Hanna's conduct. Dunn said that Corbin was sent to Philadelphia to warn Hanna against opposing the will of the convention (Dunn, I, 336).

"*Roosevelt is out of it*": NY *Trib* 6/20/oo. See comment on New York caucus, Dunn, I, 338-39.

539-542   STAMPEDE TO ROOSEVELT: NY *Trib* 6/21/oo. *Indifference to platform:* Townsend, *Harper's Wkly*, cited. *Effect of Quay's resolution:* Ibid; Dunn, I, 341. *Hanna's surrender:* Croly, 317. *President's assurances:* Transcription of telephone conversation, G. W. Perkins to GBC, 6/21/oo, quoted in Olcott, II, 281–82.

> Meeting Roosevelt on June 30 in Chicago, Dawes found that his intermediacy between the President and Hanna was known to the candidate (Dawes, 235). Perkins, as it happened, had been with the President when Dawes's first telephone call came through on the night of June 19. He told Roosevelt that Dawes, rather than Hanna, had been McKinley's representative at Philadelphia (Information from Mr. Dawes).

Excitement on Thursday: Townsend, *Harper's Wkly*, cited. "*yelled like an Apache*": Ibid. *Closing scenes:* NY *Trib* 6/22/oo. *Platt's comment:* Ibid. *Lodge's emotion:* TR to Lodge 6/25/oo, *Corres*, I, 234. *The White House:* NY *Trib* 6/22; Dawes, 234; McK to Hanna 6/22, quoted in Croly, 319; Hanna to McK 6/25/oo, McK P, vol 52.

542-544   ISSUE OF IMPERIALISM: *Republican platform weakened:* NY *Trib* 6/24,26 /oo; Hanna to McK 6/26/oo, McK P, vol 52; C. H. Grosvenor to C. E. Smith 7/2 (copy), McK P, vol 53. See *Nation* 9/6/oo. *President's speech 7/12/oo:* Proceedings of the Twelfth Republican National Convention (Philadelphia, 1900), pp 146-51. *Scene at Canton:* NY *Trib* 7/12,13/oo. *Hanna's views:* Croly, 305; Schurman to McK 6/1/oo, McK P, vol 49.

> Schurman was referring to a conversation in late May, during which McKinley had given the opinion that the Philippines would be the dominating issue in the campaign, while Hanna had expected the trust question to be forced by the Democrats in an effort to exploit class antagonisms.

"who is going to contract?": McK at Iowa Falls, 10/16/00, *Republican Campaign Textbook,* 1900, 74.

545–548   THE TRUSTS: *Inquiry and recommendations: Preliminary Report of Industrial Commission* 3/1/00, House Doc 476, 56/1, part 1. See NY Trib 3/12/00. *Bills in House:*

> HJR 138, calling for a constitutional amendment, was rejected by united Democratic opposition. HR 10539, amending the Sherman Act, passed the House, but was referred to oblivion in the Senate.

McKinley's expressions: Dawes, 185-86; Annual Message of 1899; GBC 1/5/00; President's Letter of Acceptance 9/8/00, *Proceedings, Twelfth Republican Convention,* above cited. *Deaf to Cullom's appeals:* Cullom, above cited, 329.

> Cullom is wrong in implying that he was worsted in trying to get additional railroad legislation in 1899. This bill (Senate Bill 1439) was not introduced until December 12 of that year. His struggle with his committee occurred mainly in the early months of 1900.

Claims for trust plank: Croly, 306; Foraker, II, 88–89. *"Whose ittle boy is oo?"* NY Eve Journal 5/30/00.

CHAPTER 24

THE VERDICT OF THE PEOPLE

549–552   CHALLENGE AND REPLY: Bryan's Indianapolis speech 8/8/00, *Republican Campaign Textbook,* 1900, pp 441-52; President's Letter of Acceptance, above cited. *Instructions to Taft Philippine Commission* 4/7/00: Cited. *Made public 9/17:* NY Trib 9/18/00. See Rhodes, above cited, 197-98.

552–553   MCKINLEY IN DOUBT: GBC 9/7/00.

> The decision to make a pledge of self-government, instead of independence, was made on September 5.

553–556   HANNA DISPLEASED: Croly, 328-34; Dawes, 239-40, quoting Hanna's letter of 8/2.

> Heath resigned July 23 (P. S. Heath to McK 7/23/00, McK P, vol 55). A full summary of Bristow's report appeared in the newspapers on July 26. Rathbone was arrested on July 28 (NY Trib 7/29/00).

"a business proposition purely": NY Trib 9/26/00, quoting Hanna's address at Cooper Union 9/25.

> The Chicago meeting at which Hanna made his blunder about the trusts took place on September 18. Hanna lunched with McKinley on September 22. He issued a correction of his statement on the trusts September 23 (NY Trib 9/19,23,24/00).

557   ROOSEVELT'S CAMPAIGN: NY Trib 7/8,31/00; Pringle, *Roosevelt,* cited, 223, 226; Croly, 327-28. *Trust Proposals:* TR's Letter of Acceptance 9/15/00, *Proceedings, Twelfth Republican Convention,* pp 182-83. See NY Trib 9/8/00.

557–558   HANNA AND THE COAL STRIKE: Dawes, 249, 252; NY Trib 9/28,29/00.

559–562   FEARS FOR THE PRESIDENT: *Precautions relaxed:* Memo, W. Dubois to GBC 9/13/98, McK P, vol 18; Dawes, 241. *Rumors of assassination:* NY World 7/11/00, 8/18/00; NY Trib 7/11/00, 8/1,19,21/00. *Redfern's memo:* This report and the action taken on it may be found in Dawes, pp 239-42. *McKinley still casually guarded:* NY Eve Post 9/7/01, quoting Detective Samuel R. Ireland of the Secret Service; photograph of presidential carriage at Buffalo, 9/5/01, *Collier's* 9/21/01.

562   MCKINLEY DEEPLY SOBERED: Dawes, 253; NY *Trib* 11/25/00. *Asked Cabinet to stay:* Dennett, above cited, quoting Hay to Adelbert Hay, 11/14/00.

CHAPTER 25
THE SECOND ACT BEGINS

563–566   THE NEW CENTURY: "The Story of the Nineteenth Century," NY *Trib* 1/6/01. *Americans "not as other men":* NY *Trib* 12/24/00. *The automobile:* NY *Trib* 5/25/99, 6/30/99, 8/2/00, 9/30/00; *Harper's Wkly* 1/27/00, 4/27/00 (advt), 8/11/00 (advt). *General Miles:* NY *Trib* 9/30/00. *President declined for parade:* John B. Wright to GBC 12/1/00, marked "No," McK P, Box 234. *Took a spin:* I.R.T. Smith, above cited, 35. *His New Year's Eve:* NY *Trib* 1/1/01.

566–567   THE PRESIDENT'S RECEPTION: Bingham Coll, Box 5; NY *Trib* 1/2/01; Mrs. McK's diary 1/1/01.

567–568   ILLNESS AND RECOVERY: Mrs. McK's diary 1/5-18/01; GBC 1/7-20/01; Dawes, 260.

The President began to sit up for a short time on January 11, but it was January 19 when Mrs. McKinley elatedly wrote, "I slept in our room."

Death of the Queen: GBC 1/22/99; Bingham Coll, Box 5; NY *Trib* 1/23/01. Memorial services at St. John's on February 2 were attended by the President and Cabinet and other officials (NY *Trib* 2/3/01; *America of Yesterday*, above cited, 222).

McKinley still thinking of Knox: GBC 1/30/01. *Reading* Hugh Wynne: GBC 1/31/01. *Social adjustments:* Bingham Coll, Box 5.

568–570   THE STRUGGLE WITH CONGRESS: *Army reorganization:* Jessup, I, 254-57; NY *Trib* 12/23,24/00. *President's comment:* GBC 1/25/01. *"a whopper of a bill":* GBC 2/3/01. *Spooner Bill revived:* NY *Trib* 1/26/01; Jessup, I, 359-60.

The first Annual Report of the Taft Philippine Commission, dated November 30, 1900, had been received at the War Department shortly before it was transmitted to Congress (Reports of the Taft Phil Comm, Sen Doc 112, 56/2, pp 3-113).

Antagonism in Senate: GBC 2/27/01. *House advised to concur:* GBC 3/1/01. *Platt Amendment:* GBC 1/30/01; Coolidge, *Orville Platt*, above cited, 337-44; Dawes, 263. See GBC 2/24,25/01.

Fears of an extra session had been immediately stirred by the message transmitting the report of the Taft Philippine Commission (NY *Trib* 1/27/01). The President was soon pressing the subject very vigorously in conversation with senators and other callers (GBC 1/31/01). On February 22, only three days before the solution was reported, congressional leaders were apparently resigned to an extra session, and were mapping out the program (NY *Trib* 2/23/01). Note that Dawes in his entry of February 25 (p. 263) calls Orville Platt's widely vaunted solution "The President's plan." (See also NY *Trib* 2/2,27/01.)

570   BRYAN'S VAIN EFFORTS: NY *Trib* 3/1,2,5/01.

571–572   CIVIL GOVERNMENT IN PHILIPPINES: *Urged by Taft:* Taft to Root (recd) 8/17/00, McK P, vol 58; Preliminary Report from commissioners (cabled), 8/21/00, Appendix D, Report of Secretary of War, *War Dept Reports*, 1900, vol 1, part 1; Annual Report of the Taft Philippine Commission, 11/30/00, cited; Pringle, *Taft*, I, 174-75, 180, 193-94, 198. *Solidarity of Filipinos:*

MacArthur's Report, *War Dept Reports*, 1900, cited, p 62. *Plan announced:* *NY Trib* 2/13/01.

The announcement, made at Washington on February 12, stated that the President would appoint Taft as soon as the Army Appropriations Bill, carrying the Spooner Amendment, became law.

Difficulties with MacArthur: Pringle, *Taft*, I, 168-70, 185-86; Worcester, I, 331; Jessup, I, 358; Elliott, *Military Regime*, above cited, 488-89.

573–575   THE SECOND INAUGURATION: *NY Trib* 3/1,2,3,5/01; *NY Eve Post* 3/1,4/01. *Inaugural address: NY Trib* 3/5/01.

575–576   RECIPROCITY PROGRAM: Olcott, II, 299-300. *Antagonism in Senate:* Cullom, 368-70, 374. *Assurances given Cubans:* Coolidge, cited, 344; *NY Trib* 5/8/01.

575–579   THE PRESIDENT'S TOUR:

The incidents of the trip, from the departure of the presidential party from Washington on April 29 until their return on May 31, have been taken from the *New York Tribune*. Mrs. McKinley's illness began to receive extensive coverage on May 13. The statement that her finger was first lanced in Texas (*NY Trib* 5/13,17/00) is in contradiction with a later notation of the President, dating the appearance of the felon after the arrival at Los Angeles. The President would have wished to avoid any implied criticism of Dr. Rixey, and the statement of a correspondent on the train has been preferred. The speech at the launching of the *Ohio* was reported by the press on May 19, 1901.

Party and itinerary: McK P, Boxes 202, 203. *President's memoranda,* 5/14-28/01: McK P, Box 294. See also telegrams, Box 204. *Dr. Rixey's devotion:* Braisted and Bell, above cited, 43-45. *Sweet smiles: NY Trib* 5/28/07, quoting Rixey.

On the train journey back from California, the President told Dr. Rixey that he would make him Surgeon General of the Navy when a vacancy arose (Braisted and Bell, 45-46). Roosevelt fulfilled this promise early in 1902.

579–582   WASHINGTON CONVALESCENCE: *President's memoranda,* 5/31/01-6/12/01: Dawes, 269-71.

A typed paper, corrected and dated June 8 in the President's hand, embodied the diagnosis on which the doctors agreed, and which was given to the press. This paper contains the statement mentioned above that the bone felon began in Los Angeles.

Third term talk stopped: Dawes, 269; GBC 6/10/01; *NY Trib* 6/12/01. See *NY Trib* 6/6,11/01; *NY Eve Post* 6/10. *President relaxed:* GBC 6/15,22/01. *Del Hay:* John Hay to H. White 6/18,30/01, *Letters and Diary,* cited, III, 212-13; Dennett, *Hay,* 241-42, 336-37; *NY Trib* 6/24/01. *Cortelyou offered comptrollership:* Dawes, 271-72.

Theodore Roosevelt, who "inherited" Cortelyou from McKinley, successively appointed him to the posts of Secretary of Commerce and Labor, Postmaster General, and Secretary of the Treasury.

583–584   CANTON HOLIDAY: Wm. S. Hawk, *Leslie's Wkly* 10/31/01, cited; Dawes, 274-75; *NY Trib* 8/20,27/01; *Buffalo Express* 9/1/01. "*division superintendent*": TR, *Letters,* III, #2130. *Dr. Rixey's vacation:* Rixey to McK 8/5/01, McK P, Box 235.

584–585   PREPARATIONS FOR BUFFALO: Memos and correspondence, McK P, Box 205; *Buffalo Express* 10/4/01. *The public reception:* Olcott, II, 314; GBC to Louis L. Babcock, [?] 1902, Louis L. Babcock, "The Assassination of President William McKinley," in *Niagara Frontier Miscellany* (The Buffalo Historical Society, 1947), chap. 23. "*I wish we were not going*": Mrs. McK's diary 9/1/01

CHAPTER 26
APPOINTMENT AT BUFFALO

586–589   PRESIDENT'S DAY: Buffalo *Express*, NY *Trib*, 9/6/01.
The crowds, the McKinleys' arrival at the Esplanade, their later activities, and the illuminations in the evening are all admirably described by the Buffalo newspaper. Mrs. McKinley wrote in her diary on September 5, "We visited the sights of interest today. My dear seemed to enjoy visiting very much."
Speech: Olcott, II, 377-84. *Salute of cannon*: Buffalo *Express* 9/5/01; Babcock, *Niagara Frontier Miscellany*, above cited.

589–590   NIAGARA FALLS: Buffalo *Express*, NY *Trib*, 9/7/01. *McKinley's clothing and effects*: List signed Nelson W. Wilson, M.D., McK P, Box 215. "*the restful day*": Wm. S. Hawk, *Leslie's Wkly*, above cited. "*brush up a bit*": Ibid. "*Good afternoon, Mrs. McKinley*": Ibid.

590–596   THE TEMPLE OF MUSIC: Babcock, cited. *Secret Service men*: NY *Eve Post* 9/7/01. *Czolgosz*: Walter Channing, M.D., assisted by Dr. L. Vernon Briggs, "The Mental Status of Czolgosz, the Assassin of President McKinley," *The American Journal of Insanity*, Oct/02; L. Vernon Briggs, *The Manner of Man That Kills* (Boston, 1921), 242-47, 267; NY *Eve Post* 9/7/01; NY *Trib* 9/8/01. See Robert J. Donovan, *The Assassins* (New York, 1952), *chap* IV, "The Man Who Didn't Shake Hands." "*so much service*": This wording is taken from Babcock's article, which quotes a statement signed by Czolgosz on September 6 and later secured by Mr. Quackenbush. A slightly different form of the statement is quoted by Dr. Channing.
The shooting: Olcott, II, 315-17.
Since Cortelyou left no record of the assassination, I have followed the account of a man who interviewed him. There is also a good account in the *New York Tribune*, September 7, 1901.
McKinley's expression: Hanna, *National Magazine*, above cited.
Mr. Milburn told Hanna that he read in McKinley's eyes the words, "Why should you do this?"
The operation: Olcott, II, 317-19; Briggs, cited, 239; Buffalo *Express*, NY *Trib*, 9/7/01.

597–599   FALSE HOPES: *X-ray machine sent*: NY *Trib* 9/8,9/01. *Scoffed at*: Briggs, 240, quoting Dr. Mann; NY *Trib* 9/10, quoting Dr. McBurney. *GBC in sickroom*: Olcott, II, 320-21. "*highroad to recovery*": TR, *Letters*, III, #2126-#2128. *Hay's despondency*: Babcock, cited.

600–601   PRESIDENT DYING: Olcott, II, 323-26; NY *Trib* 9/14/01; NY *Eve Post* 9/14/01; Dawes, 280-81. "*Nearer, My God, to Thee*": Mrs. McK's diary 9/14/01.

601–602   THE NEW PRESIDENT: Pringle, *Roosevelt*, 232; NY *Eve Post* 9/13,14/01; NY *Trib* 9/15/01; Jessup, I, 237-38; Depew, above cited, 156.

603   THE INDIANS' FAREWELL: McK P, Box 215.

INDEX

380, 383, 386, 424, 428, 430, 439, 450, 459, 460, 462-63, 464 ff., 469; affection for McKinley, 189-90, 582; and death of McKinley, 595-96, 597 ff.; Secretary to President, 471, 478, 479, 495-96, 508, 510, 512, 524, 525, 536 ff., 540, 547, 552-53, 559, 561, 566, 568, 569, 571, 578, 580, 581, 584, 588, 590

Cortelyou, Mrs. George B., 438
Cortelyou, Win, 438
Courval, Vicomtesse de, 383
Coxey, Jacob Silica, 55
Crane, Stephen, 304-5
Cridler, Thomas, 205
Cristóbal Colón, 255-57
Croker, Richard, 322
Cromwell, William Nelson, 506
Crook, William Henry, 122, 125, 126, 178
Crowninshield, Arent S., 156, 160, 161, 192, 195, 219, 233, 468
Cuba, 360, 388, 490; constitution, 569-570, 581; independence of, 282-83, 286 ff., 339, 369, 393, 576; insurrection, 97-99, 102, 115-16, 119, 120, 137, 140, 143, 144, 147-51, 157, 159, 161-62; McKinley's message of intervention, 181-89; and Maine, 163-64, 166-72, 173, 175-80; occupation of, 390-94, 402, 416; post-office scandals, 385, 534, 554-55; and Spanish-American War, see Spanish-American War

Cullom, Shelby M., 40, 71, 73, 104, 105, 547, 575; and patronage, 135-36
Cullom Bill, 482
Cullom Commission, 386
Curaçao, 218
Curtis, W. E., 230, 435
Cuyahoga County, Ohio, 427
Czolgosz, Leon, 592-96, 597, 599

Daiquirí, Cuba, 243-44, 245, 296
Daly, W. H., 317
Dalzell, John, 213, 490, 491, 502
Dana, Charles A., 103
Daughters of the American Revolution, 301
Davenport, Homer, 76
Davis, Cushman K., 175, 179, 184, 187, 329, 330, 341, 355-56, 479, 493, 498; amendment to Hay-Pauncefote Treaty, 509, 510, 512, 514
Davis, George B., 321
Davis, George W., 321, 395, 487, 499
Davis, Richard Harding, 227, 281
Dawes, Carolyn, 74, 133, 438

Dawes, Charles G., 67, 68, 73-74, 79, 86, 87, 100, 104-5, 114, 133, 135, 139-40, 142-43, 144, 153, 171, 181, 215-16, 233, 234, 238, 286, 417, 430, 452, 458, 462-63, 477, 478, 496, 497, 499 ff., 535, 538, 540, 541, 547, 553 ff., 561, 562, 580, 598 ff.
Dawes, Rufus, 73, 74
Dawes, Rufus Fearing, 74
Day, Luther, 93
Day, William R., 59, 68, 76, 101, 132, 138, 152, 153, 155, 163-64, 165-66, 171, 173 ff., 178, 179, 183, 184, 484 ff., 598; and Peace Commission, 328-29, 331, 339, 341, 342-43; Secretary of State, 191, 192, 211, 282, 283, 285-86, 287 ff., 515
Day, Mrs. William R., 173
Debs, Eugene V., 558
Declaration of Independence, 354, 355
Del Monte, Calif., 577
Democratic party, 3, 37 ff., 43, 48, 58, 60, 62, 184, 185, 187, 229, 316, 333, 337, 387, 407, 408, 481, 490, 570; campaign of 1896, 84-85, 86, 95-96; campaign of 1899, 414-15, 425; campaign of 1900, 542-43, 544-45, 548-50, 552, 556; and Philippines, 482-83, 490; and Porto Rico, 490-91, 492, 494, 497, 498, 501
Denby, Charles, 363, 364, 422, 426
Depew, Chauncey M., 95, 109, 480-81, 497, 536, 580
Detroit, Mich., 367-69, 370
Dewey, Charles, 413
Dewey, George, 159-61, 162, 169, 191-92, 196, 210, 212, 214, 242, 243, 253, 260, 265, 290, 331, 334, 336, 339, 342, 346, 350, 363, 400, 408, 574; and Aguinaldo, 283-85, 325, 414, 416; hero worship of, 208-9; homecoming reception, 410-13; house in Washington, 429; and Manila Bay, 203-9, 259, 297; marriage, 428-29; and politics, 413-18, 427-28, 429-31, 463; presentation ceremonies, 418-21; talks with McKinley, 422-24, 427-28; and White House precedence, 468-69
Dewey, Mildred McLean Hazen, 428-29, 469
Dewey Arch, New York City, 413, 431
Diamond Match Company, 110
Dick, Charles, 57, 62, 68, 271, 272, 465, 532, 536-37, 554
Dingley, Nelson, Jr., 104, 140, 184, 487